# ART OF THE EVENT

# THE WILEY EVENT MANAGEMENT SERIES

## SERIES EDITOR: DR. JOE GOLDBLATT, CSEP

*Special Events: Event Leadership for a New World,* Fourth Edition
by Dr. Joe Goldblatt, CSEP

*International Dictionary of Event Management,* Second Edition
by Dr. Joe Goldblatt, CSEP, and Kathleen S. Nelson, CSEP

*Corporate Event Project Management*
by William O'Toole and Phyllis Mikolaitis

*Event Marketing: How to Successfully Promote Events, Festivals, Conventions, and Expositions*
by Leonard H. Hoyle, CAE, CMP

*Event Risk Management and Safety*
by Peter E. Tarlow, PhD

*Event Sponsorship*
by Bruce E. Skinner and Vladimir Rukavina

*Professional Event Coordination*
by Julia Rutherford Silvers, CSEP

*Event Entertainment and Production*
by Mark Sonder, MM, CSEP

*The Guide to Successful Destination Management*
by Pat Schaumann, CMP, CSEP

*The Sports Event Management and Marketing Playbook*
by Frank Supovitz

*Art of the Event: Complete Guide to Designing and Decorating Special Events*
by James C. Monroe, CMP, CSEP

# ART OF THE EVENT

## COMPLETE GUIDE TO DESIGNING AND DECORATING SPECIAL EVENTS

**JAMES C. MONROE, CMP, CSEP**

**with Illustrations by Robert A. Kates**

JOHN WILEY & SONS, INC.

This book is printed on acid-free paper. ♾



Published by John Wiley & Sons, Inc., Hoboken, New Jersey
Published simultaneously in Canada



For general information on our other products and services or for technical support, please contact our Customer Care Department within the United States at (800) 762-2974, outside the United States at (317) 572-3993 or fax (317) 572-4002.

Wiley also publishes its books in a variety of electronic formats. Some content that appears in print may not be available in electronic books. For more information about Wiley products, visit our web site at www.wiley.com.

***Library of Congress Cataloging-in-Publication Data:***

Monroe, James C.
Art of the event : complete guide to designing and decorating special events / by James C. Monroe ; with illustrations by Robert A. Kates.
p. cm. — (The Wiley event management series)
Includes index.
ISBN-13: 978-0-471-42686-8 (cloth)
ISBN-10: 0-471-42686-5 (cloth)
1. Special events—Planning. 2. Decoration and ornament. I. Title. II. Series.
GT3405.M66 2006
394.2—dc22

2005008668

Printed in the United States of America

11

# DEDICATION

This book is dedicated with love to Jayna Monroe, my life and business partner; my personal copy editor and writing coach. Her enthusiasm for the special event industry inspires our designs. I see life through her eyes. Her inquisitive intellect keeps life interesting and her talent and dedication guided the creation of this book.

# CONTENTS

PREFACE xvii

ACKNOWLEDGMENTS xxi

INTRODUCTION: EVENT DESIGN BECOMES A PROFESSION xxiii

## Part One PRINCIPLES, PROCESSES, AND PRACTICES 1

Chapter 1 **PRINCIPLES OF DESIGN 3**
Design and Decoration in Events 4
Basic Event Design 5
Basic Aesthetic Principles 9
Practical Aesthetic Principles 10
Design and Global Event Management 16
Finishing Touches 18
Design Vocabulary 18
Studio Work 19
Recommended Readings and Research Sites 19

Chapter 2 **DESIGN AND DECORATION PRACTICES 21**
Research 22
Creative Techniques 26
Developing the Design 29
Communicating the Design 31
Finishing Touches 36
Design Vocabulary 36
Studio Work 36
Recommended Readings and Research Sites 37

Chapter 3 **VENUE 39**
Types of Venues 40
Site Selection Guidelines 49

Physical Requirements 49
Budgetary Requirements 53
Aesthetic Requirements 54
Site Research 54
Conducting the Site Inspection 55
Finishing Touches 59
Design Vocabulary 59
Studio Work 60
Recommended Readings and Research Sites 60

Chapter 4 **RESOURCES 63**
Financial Resources 65
Human Resources and Stakeholders 68
Knowledge and Education Resources 73
Technical and Physical Resources 75
Finishing Touches 79
Design Vocabulary 79
Studio Work 79
Recommended Readings and Research Sites 80

Chapter 5 **PROFIT AND LOSS 81**
Profit 82
Pricing 85
Job Costs 90
Accounting and Bookkeeping 96
Finishing Touches 96
Design Vocabulary 97
Studio Work 97
Recommended Readings and Research Sites 98

**Part Two THE DECORATIVE ELEMENTS 99**

Chapter 6 **BACKDROPS AND PROPS 101**
Designing with Backdrops and Props 102
Decorating with Backdrops 107
Decorating with Props 112
Staging 117
Finishing Touches 118
Design Vocabulary 119
Studio Work 119
Recommended Readings and Research Sites 119

Chapter 7 **DECORATING WITH FLOWERS 121**
Basic Flower Décor 122

Architectural Flowers 137
Finishing Touches 141
Design Vocabulary 141
Studio Work 142
Recommended Readings and Research Sites 142

**Chapter 8 FABULOUS FABRIC DÉCOR 143**
Special Event Fabrics 145
Wall Treatment 150
Ceiling Treatment 155
Table Linens 161
Finishing Touches 167
Design Vocabulary 167
Studio Work 168
Recommended Readings and Research Sites 168

**Chapter 9 BALLOONS IN BLOOM 171**
Designing with Balloons 172
Decorating with Balloons 176
Ceilings and Walls 180
Advanced Balloon Design 185
Balloon-Related Products 185
Finishing Touches 187
Design Vocabulary 188
Studio Work 188
Recommended Readings and Research Sites 189

**Chapter 10 THE ART OF LIGHT 191**
Design and Direction 193
Lighting Events 195
Aesthetics 200
Lighting Equipment 206
Risk Management 208
Changing Technology 208
Finishing Touches 209
Design Vocabulary 209
Studio Work 210
Recommended Readings and Research Sites 210

**Chapter 11 UNIQUE DECORATIVE ELEMENTS 213**
Entertainment/Living Décor 214
Decorative Signage 221
Food for the Eye 224
Decorative Lighting Effects 227
Candles 231

The Magic of Ice 234
Pyrotechnics 235
Finishing Touches 237
Design Vocabulary 237
Studio Work 238
Recommended Readings and Research Sites 238

## Part Three THE UNIVERSE OF SPECIAL EVENTS 241

**Chapter 12 NONPROFIT AND CHARITY EVENTS 243**
Designing for Nonprofit Event Goals 244
Decorating Different Types of Nonprofit Events 252
Finishing Touches 266
Design Vocabulary 266
Studio Work 267
Recommended Readings and Research Sites 267

**Chapter 13 CORPORATE CELEBRATIONS AND CEREMONIES 269**
Designing External Events (Marketing) 270
Designing Internal Events (Operations) 276
Decorating Advertising Events 278
Receptions 281
Decorating Public Relations Events 285
Decorating Human Relations Events 292
Finishing Touches 296
Design Vocabulary 296
Studio Work 297
Recommended Readings and Research Sites 297

**Chapter 14 MILESTONE AND SOCIAL EVENTS 299**
Party Design 300
Life-Cycle Events 302
Personal Social Events 312
Finishing Touches 323
Design Vocabulary 324
Studio Work 324
Recommended Readings and Research Sites 324

**Chapter 15 WONDERFUL WEDDINGS 327**
Nuptial Goals and Objectives 328
Ceremony 330

Style 337
Themes 339
Receptions 346
Related Events 359
Finishing Touches 361
Design Vocabulary 361
Studio Work 362
Recommended Readings and Research Sites 362

**Chapter 16 FESTIVALS, FAIRS, PARADES, AND SPECTACLES 363**
Festivals 364
Fairs 368
Parades 371
Spectacles 373
Finishing Touches 374
Design Vocabulary 374
Studio Work 374
Recommended Readings and Research Sites 375

## Part Four APPENDIXES 377

**APPENDIX 1 TYPICAL REQUEST FOR PROPOSAL 378**
**APPENDIX 2 CONTACT SHEET 381**
**APPENDIX 3 EVENT THEMES 382**
**APPENDIX 4 TYPICAL EVENT PROPOSAL 384**
**APPENDIX 5 SPECIAL EVENT SITE INSPECTION CHECKLIST 388**
**APPENDIX 6 ELECTRICAL FORMULA 390**
**APPENDIX 7 BALLOON CHARTS 391**
**APPENDIX 8 LABOR RATE CALCULATION: CHARGE-OUT RATES FOR LABOR 396**
**APPENDIX 9 DISPLAYING THE UNITED STATES FLAG 397**
**APPENDIX 10 LIGHTING EQUIPMENT AND VOCABULARY 399**
**APPENDIX 11 WEDDING CHECKLIST 402**
**INDEX 407**

[illegible]
[illegible]
[illegible]
[illegible]
[illegible]
[illegible]
[illegible]
Recommended Readings and Resources [illegible]

CHAPTER [illegible] FESTIVALS, FAIRS, PARADES, AND SPECIAL [illegible]
[illegible]
[illegible]
[illegible]
[illegible]
[illegible]
[illegible]
[illegible]
Recommended Readings and Resources [illegible]

## PART [illegible] APPENDIXES 377

APPENDIX 1 [illegible]
APPENDIX 2 [illegible]
APPENDIX 3 [illegible]
APPENDIX 4 TYPICAL EVENT PROGRAM [illegible]
APPENDIX 5 SPECIAL EVENT SITE INSPECTION CHECKLIST [illegible]
APPENDIX 6 [illegible] FORMS [illegible]
APPENDIX 7 [illegible] CHARTS
APPENDIX 8 [illegible]
APPENDIX 9 [illegible] UNITED STATES [illegible]
APPENDIX 10 [illegible] VOCABULARY [illegible]
APPENDIX 11 WEDDING CHECKLIST 402
INDEX 407

# SERIES EDITOR FOREWORD

Dr. Richard Florida is professor of Regional Economic Development at Carnegie Mellon University and author of *The Creative Class* (2002). In his book, which has been hailed by business leaders as a major milestone in the business literature, Florida suggests that "With 38 million members, more than 30 percent of the nation's workforce, the Creative Class has shaped and will continue to shape deep and profound shifts in the ways we work, in our values and desires, and in the very fabric of our everyday lives." In this important new book entitled, *The Art of the Event,* James Monroe, CMP, CSEP, who is a leading member of the Creative Class, will help you design more profound and meaningful event experiences for your guests.

James Monroe has more than three decades' experience in the art of event design. From producing retail promotional displays to designing award winning corporate events, he is truly a renaissance man in the field of event design. Mr. Monroe has served as a contributing author for major industry publications and his advice and counsel is widely sought by event planners throughout the world.

In this, the first book in our series that examines the expanding role of event design, Mr. Monroe has opened his treasure chest of design secrets and generously shared them to promote more efficient, creative, and innovative design opportunities for event professionals worldwide.

From simple food and beverage designs to complex multiple theme party scenes, Monroe has provided you with a veritable treasure trove of ideas and proven techniques to help you better serve your clients. Any one of these ideas could help you win the next major industry award for event design.

Perhaps most importantly, James Monroe has provided you with a practical approach to event design that can be easily understood by both novices as well as experienced event professionals. He approaches design for events as an integral element in the overall experience. Therefore, this book will significantly help to not only meet but also exceed the expectations of your guests for every future event.

Finally, James Monroe is a gifted teacher and inspiring mentor. He has earned both the Certified Special Events Professional and Certified Meeting Professional certifications as well as led industry study groups to help his colleagues advance their education. Now, you may also become one of his many students and learn from the master how to use The *Art of the Event* to rapidly accelerate your career growth.

Florida concludes *The Creative Class* by asking, "What do we *really* want? What kind of life-and what kind of society-do we want to bequeath to coming generations?" He suggests that the Creative Class must address these questions by harnessing all of our intelligence, our energy and most importantly our awareness. In the soon to be classic text, *The Art of the Event,* James Monroe provides us with a magnificent blueprint for not only transforming our events but also through events improving the aesthetics of human society.

Dr. Joe Goldblatt, CSEP
Series Editor
Temple University
School of Tourism and Hospitality Management

# FOREWORD

This book will provide event planners with expert advice and practical guidance. It is an extremely readable text, which is useful and unique. Jim Monroe covers the best practices of event planning and décor. The text is peppered with war stories, which illustrate the points he is conveying to the student and practitioner alike. He ties theory to practice, complete with tools for implementation.

The reader will find, in this book, the essential ingredients for success needed in this dynamic, expanding and increasingly sophisticated event management niche. Readers will learn principles and techniques that will enable them to look forward to planning events creatively. His style is direct, concise and jargon-free.

He focuses on the importance of doing research and writing an effective RFP. The logistical information is invaluable, and this will be a valued reference book for industry professionals. Students: Don't sell this book at the end of the semester. You will want this in your permanent library.

Patti Shock
Professor and Chair
Tourism and Convention Administration Department
University of Nevada, Las Vegas

# PREFACE

## THE FUTURE LOOKS BETTER AND BETTER

Midnight at the mall 27 or 28 years ago, Bill Reed called me to his side. "You have to meet Tommy Hansen," he said. "He's the best display man and decorator in this part of the country." We were putting up seasonal decorations in what was the most successful mall in terms of dollars per square foot in the world at that time. Decorations go up when malls are closed, and I was just getting used to the fact that I would be working when other people are playing or sleeping for the rest of my life.

I was introduced to a friendly old codger in a porkpie hat and paint-spattered coveralls, tamping out his pipe on the side of a battered old pickup truck that was equally paint-spattered. He and Bill Reed started chatting, and I stood back and thought about whether I might be seeing myself in Tommy Hansen in another 30 years.

I was not far from wrong in my prognostication, but it turns out to be not so bad. Tommy was the best in his profession, and I found out later that he lived in a fine house in a nice neighborhood and his other car was a brand-new Cadillac DeVille. But there was no way for me to see a promising future at that time, no path for me to follow, and little direction other than the occasional mentor who would take a neophyte under his or her wing. Over the next decade I worked at Bill Reed Decorations, and we became more involved in decorating parties and events and less involved in display work. The times were changing.

The crew there worked hard at figuring out which designs worked and which did not work for events that had worked for display. There was a new component in event work: the human being. People did not just view our work at events; they lived within it. It was environmental design, in many ways similar to the work of Alan Kaprow and the "happening." It drew from the same creative forces as the work of Jim Dine and Claes Oldenburg. It was very exciting to work in that kind of dynamic atmosphere, and every job brought a new discovery. Of course, half of those discoveries were exciting because of the aesthetic parameters and half were exciting because we were flying by the seat of our pants and frequently did not know what we should be doing.

A lot of what we did in my first decade in the event design and decorating business (without knowing it because there was no recognized event business back then) was not very profitable or efficient. Sometimes we did not make the right decisions. There was no event management body of knowledge, no way to get training, or no books about it to read. Now, however, the profession has come into its own and there is a market that is crying out for trained event professionals. The hospitality and tourism industry has grown to be the second largest employment category in the United States, behind only the U.S. government.

Two- and four-year schools now offer degree and certificate programs. There are certification programs, seminars, and training programs in all aspects of events. Industry leaders such as Dr. Joe Goldblatt, CSEP, are creating career paths and encouraging other successful professionals to share their knowledge. Julia Rutherford Silvers, CSEP, the author of *Professional Event Coordination,* another text in the Wiley Event Series, has set about (with help from professional friends) attempting to create and codify an event management body of knowledge (EMBOK).

## A PATH TO THE FUTURE

*Art of the Event: Complete Guide to Designing and Decorating Special Events* is a serious and needed addition to that body of knowledge. Designed as the definitive textbook on designing and decorating events, it is organized for the student of event design but is also a reference for working event professionals, meeting professionals, leisure and recreation experts, and anybody who negotiates, hires, produces, or interacts with events in his or her business or personal life.

The book is divided into three main parts. The first, *Principles, Processes, and Practices,* discusses and explains the basic principles behind design and the processes and practices that work in applying those principles to the event business. This section is about the philosophy and the business of designing and decorating events. It falls under the administration competency as described by International Special Events Society (ISES).

The second part, *The Decorative Elements,* is the operational section. It describes the various decorative elements that are used in special events and discusses how to use them in practical and specific ways. Guidance is given for the aesthetic, fiscal, and safety aspects of each element. Practical tips are provided from the experience of the author and the over two centuries of experience represented by professional associates who agreed to share their expertise. This part falls under the coordination competency described by ISES.

The third part, *The Universe of Special Events,* describes and defines the various types of special events an event professional may be asked to design or decorate. Charity and nonprofit events, corporate events of different types, social events, weddings, fairs, festivals, and parades all employ professional designers and decorators. They are all events, and they are all different. The chapters in this part offer practical design advice and point out which practices work across the board and which are exclusive to a specific type of special event. Further details about the content in each chapter are provided in the Introduction.

## THE JOURNEY BEGINS

Students in a formal learning setting with an instructor or facilitator will find that this book provides proper guidance but must understand that the concepts written about here come to life only with practical experience. Exposure to these ideas under a proper mentor will make learning on the job much easier and faster. If the students are self-studying, I applaud their initiative and suggest that they find a mentor, or more than one, in the event business. It helps if you can bounce ideas off another person and if you have someone to evaluate your chapter exercises that appear at the end of each chapter under the title "Studio Work."

Working event professionals can put this book on the shelf with other references, or they may find it makes pleasant light reading. They will find many concepts they recognize and several areas where their knowledge exceeds the purview of this text. We all have areas of strength and areas that are not our specialty. This book will be helpful when you have to go outside your normal areas of responsibility. The potential event professional or volunteer who is thinking about making this a profession will find that reading this book will expand his or her understanding of the work of a professional event designer and/or decorator.

Finally, people who hire event designers and decorators, meeting planners, volunteers, and people who entertain should read this book to gain a greater understanding of the services they are hiring and the professionals with whom they are contracting. This book defines professional event designers and decorators and their responsibilities. It discusses ethical and risk management practices and provides basic knowledge that the client should have before spending money with an event professional.

The next event awaits your artistry. Pick up your palette and brush. Stretch the wings of your imagination. With the tools in this book, you can help reinvent the modern profession of event design.

# ACKNOWLEDGMENTS


Memorable special events result from the collaborative efforts of a well-managed team of professionals applying best practices on a foundation of knowledge and experience. This textbook is the result of a similar collaboration and the individuals who contributed to it have my lifelong respect and undying gratitude.

Phil Hendron, the late Bob McClure, and Jerry Hanson, each provided unique and valuable facets of my foundation in best practices and knowledge of craftsmanship and design. Gale Sliger and Bill Reed contributed notably to my professional experience as associates and mentors. Nancy Halbreich and Peggy Sewell stand out among the many clients whose personal high level of taste contributed to my understanding of style. Robert (Bobby) Kates illustrated this text with the inimitable talent that has been a signature part of so many years of our event design work together.

The following professionals directly contributed their valuable knowledge and experience to this text:

Leo Bary
Randy Beckham
Charles Belcher
Robert Bifulco
Michael Carroll
Robert Cherny
John J. Daly, Jr., CSEP
Jo C. Dermid, CPCE
Patricia Duffy
Steve Kemble
Robin King
Debbie Meyers, CSEP
Brian K. O'Connor
Colleen A. Rickenbacher, CMP, CSEP
Coy Sevier
Patti Shock, CPCE
Julia Rutherford Silvers, CSEP
James Skistimas
Howard Eckhart, CSEP
Joan Eisenstodt
Joy Johnson Floyd
David Gisler
Leslie Hearn
William Host, CMP
John Jakob
William H. Just, CAE, CMP
Robert Justice
Lianne Pereira, CMP, CMM
Gregory Pynes
Karen Ranker
Mike Miller
Sharon Miller
Neils Skolberg
Katie Steffes
Betsy Wiersma, CSEP
Deborah K. Williams

And for graciously allowing copyright persmissions:
The Balloon Council
Pioneer Balloons

Finally, this book would not have come into existence without the inspiration and guidance of Dr. Joe Goldblatt, CSEP, of Temple University, Joanna Turtletaub and Melissa Oliver along with the rest of the professional staff at John Wiley & Sons, Inc.

# INTRODUCTION: EVENT DESIGN BECOMES A PROFESSION

Thirty-one years ago the CEO's secretary in a large mechanical contracting firm called the display studio where I worked as a scenic artist and scheduled a party to celebrate the twenty-fifth anniversary of the founding of the company. Back then she was called a secretary, not an executive administrator, and she was, almost always, a she. She contacted a display company because her options were to call the florist, a display company, or to let that talented fellow in shipping decorate the event.

Back then, display companies existed to provide decorations for big city department store windows, dioramas for museums, and theme décor in the lobbies of first run motion picture theatres. They also occasionally provided props and decorations for elaborate society parties. Society parties and debutante balls typified the height of events and seasonally employed a few artisans and carpenters on the side. Over three decades later we have come a long way. Event design and decoration is a full-fledged profession within the expanding hospitality, meeting and convention industry.

Today there are hundreds of firms specializing in design and décor for corporate and private events, employing thousands of people worldwide and generating hundreds of millions of dollars of business. Many of today's established names in the event decorating business started as display artists, scenic designers, and florists. They rose to the top of their profession by applying effective design and business practices. These practices are being organized and codified by the professional associations and educational institutions that have developed with the profession. The International Special Events Society (ISES) and the other 29 associations within the Convention Industry Council (CIC) are developing common terminology and accepted practices within the related industries. These practices are becoming the basis for a series of curricula evolving in today's colleges and universities. Patti Shock of the University of Nevada Las Vegas tells us that there are over 150 four-year programs in hospitality and tourism in the United States and hundreds of two-year programs. Forty-four institutions have been identified worldwide that offer two- and four-year programs specializing in Convention and Event Management.

As a scenic and lighting designer with a master's degree in Theater Arts from the University of Cincinnati, I developed an interest in the possibilities of alternative design opportunities while hosting a United States Institute of Theatrical Technology (USITT) State of Texas meeting at Texas Christian University in 1972. Mr. George Petit, a scenic designer with Peter Wolf Associates at the time, gave a presentation on what professional scenic designers *really* do for a living if they are not designing for Broadway. The following year I left university theater and went to work designing displays, parties, boutiques and truck stops.

## THE HISTORY OF EVENTS

Special gatherings and celebrations predate recorded history. The detritus and art of these bacchanals show up in, and on the walls of, prehistoric caves. An interesting thesis would be to track the development of western civilization by examining revelries, celebrations and other special events through history. The public displays of the Roman Empire are legion and legend. Productions of events throughout the Italian Renaissance gave us forced perspective for scenery and theatrical design techniques that are in use today. Theatrical conventions and the social revelries surrounding the Jacobean and Elizabethan stage provided the concept of special effects. From the excesses of the Louis XVI court to a homespun weekend at the county fair, special events have been, and will continue to be, a part of the human experience.

There exists a universe of events consisting of celebrations, festivals, fairs, parades, conventions, and conferences. From our point of view as event designers, the entire world is a play and our job is to decorate the playground. As the hospitality, tourism, convention and events industries have developed into full-fledged professions, the position of the special event designer has become respected, achieving both recognition and decent compensation.

Over the past 32 years I have had many opportunities, to design, decorate and work on different events, first with Bill Reed, then owner of Bill Reed Decorations, Inc., then as an associate of Gale Sliger, the owner of Gale Sliger Productions I, LLC. For the past 22 years Robert A. (Bobby) Kates, the talented designer who illustrated this book, has been a regular associate. I currently design and produce special events under James C. Monroe & Associates with Jayna Monroe, my wife for the past 38 years. Over the decades I have designed and executed large corporate functions with thousands of attendees and dinner parties with as few as 12 guests. We have worked with teams of professional associates and partners on many different types of events including society and corporate celebrations, meetings, training sessions, product rollouts, and other marketing events. This book will deal with the entire scope of event design and decoration within that experience.

# ROADMAP TO FABULOUS EVENTS

The structure that follows is a roadmap to designing and decorating special events. Aesthetics, the design process, and professional practices will be discussed in the first part, entitled **Principles, Processes, and Practices.** The second part, **The Decorative Elements,** is a practical how-to discussion of each of the various types of physical decorations, lighting, and special effects. The last part, **A Universe of Special Events,** describes various types of events that the designer will be asked to create and discusses the different requirements of each type with specific recommendations and illustrations from my experience and that of the many colleagues I interviewed.

This book is designed as a text for serious students of event design and production. It is also a valuable reference for specific design challenges that the event professional may encounter. A brief description of each section and chapter follows.

# PRINCIPLES, PROCESSES, AND PRACTICES—PART ONE

Design principles have remained essentially the same since those first cave drawings were painted onto the walls to commemorate a great hunt: composition, color, balance, and texture. The focus of this book will be the process of converting these principles into effective and functional event design and décor.

Chapter 1, **Principles of Design,** discusses the basics of aesthetics and design. Design does not exist in a vacuum, but fits within, and is governed by, event management. Dr. Joe Goldblatt, CSEP, discusses event management in detail in *Special Events: Event Leadership for a New World,* 4th edition. The blueprint for event management from the International Special Event Society follows.

**THE BLUEPRINT FOR BEST PRACTICES IN EVENT MANAGEMENT**

1. ADMINISTRATION
2. COORDINATION
3. MARKETING
4. LEGAL, ETHICAL, RISK MANAGEMENT

**GUIDELINE FOR EFFECTIVE EVENT PRODUCTION**

1. RESEARCH
2. DESIGN
3. PLANNING
4. COORDINATION
5. EVALUATION

In Chapter 2, **Design and Decoration Practices,** we look at the event design and decoration process and practices that work. Design decisions begin with the basic objectives and goals for the event and must follow logically in order to be effective. When a logical process is employed, inspiration can transform effective design into fabulous décor! A guideline for this process will be discussed in detail.

Throughout this book tips and guidelines will appear in boxes like the one above and key terms will be highlighted in **boldface type.** Examples from practical experience will appear under the heading *Idea Portfolio.* These examples from practical experience are frequently referred to as war stories in the special event business. This is appropriate, as much of the event business appears to follow logistics similar to a battle plan.

Once the design process is engaged, the first defining element is dealt with in Chapter 3, **Venue.** The environment in which the event takes place controls the possibilities, imposes the limitations that must be dealt with, and can provide inspiration as well. Decorations for typical venues will be discussed with

Idea Portfolio

## TYPICAL WAR STORY

To create a Great State of Texas theme party for 8,000 guests, 80 carpenters and technicians started arriving at Market Hall at 5:30 A.M. They reported to a check-in desk where they were assigned to specific crews with a lieutenant in charge of decorating a specific area of the 214,000-square-foot venue. Each lieutenant had a map showing placement of the décor, a rendering of their specific area, and a timeline indicating a probable completion schedule.

At 6:00 A.M. a 40-foot tractor-trailer arrived followed by two 24-foot bobtail vans. Each driver was assigned an unloading crew and a map showing the path around the hall and an inventory of equipment to be dropped off at each location. The overhead doors opened and the troops entered, going directly to their assigned areas. By 3 P.M. that afternoon the décor was in place, the lights were focused, and we were ready for sound checks.

This represents a typical installation of a large-scale event.

practical examples. The importance of proper site selection cannot be emphasized enough. My wife once suggested, after six months spent searching for the appropriate location to hold a fund-raiser, that I should write a book about the sites where a certain intense client decided *not* to hold her event. However, when the event was finally executed, it was an experience that defined success in all measurable ways. This client is a cutting edge individual whose personal taste helps create next year's trends. Every event we have done with her is impeccable and appropriate.

A Site Inspection Form is included in Appendix 5. Each designer will, with time, develop his or her own procedures for site inspection, event production, and scripting. The Appendixes contain the author's forms, which are available for use, exclusive of copyright. Feel free to use these as is or modify them to fit your specific needs.

The other controlling element is dealt with in Chapter 4, **Resources.** Resources include first and foremost, budget. Volunteers, existing elements, sponsorship, and many other elements are potential resources, all of which are dealt with in detail in this chapter.

**Profit and Loss** is the title of Chapter 5, which deals with methods of buying, managing, and marking up materials and labor costs. Loss is part of the title because it is a part of the real life of the event designer. Professionals in nonprofits and volunteers committed to charity functions realize that these events have a profit function in real terms, usually described as Return on Investment (ROI).

## THE DECORATIVE ELEMENTS—PART TWO

Party props and backdrops, flowers, fabric, food, balloons, and lighting are each potential decorative elements available to the designer, and each is its own discipline, requiring different talents and technical knowledge. Material for this section comes from our personal experience and that of many of our expert associates who have willingly shared their decades of experience and expertise.

As discussed in Chapter 6, **Backdrops and Props** can be built and painted from scratch to fit a custom design, rented from a prop rental house, or be ordered from an online catalogue. This chapter discusses each approach and how to determine which is appropriate for specific requirements. It details common methods employed in design and construction of props and backdrops and describes procedures and rigging for dealing with rented goods. Rigging is the term for hanging, installing, propping up, or otherwise making useful application of decorative items.

For Chapter 7, **Decorating with Flowers,** I blatantly stole the title from Renaldo Maia's book by the same name. Many wonderful books have been written on this theme and this is one of my favorites. The rest of my favorite books on floral design for events are found in Recommended Reading, and the thoughts and ideas of the authors from many of these appear throughout this text. In this chapter I have dealt with specific requirements and limitations regarding floral design for special events.

Chapter 8, **Fabulous Fabric Decor,** deals with the many ways that fabric can be used to create or enhance the environment for a special event. It also discusses flame-retardant properties of various fabrics, makes suggestions for purchasing options, and details some specific techniques for installation and rigging.

Chapter 9, **Balloons in Bloom,** shows that they are more than just a child's toy. We have made them part of some of the most sophisticated events we have designed, discovered new and different ways to make them a critical part of an effective design, and found people who can create incredible artwork from this lowly, cost-effective party art element.

In Chapter 10, **The Art of Light,** we explore the entire rainbow palette with which an event designer can create an event. Lighting is critical to all events, for function, mood, and effects. Different events require different types of lighting expertise and different equipment. These approaches to different types of events and the equipment required for lighting them is discussed in practical detail.

Chapter 11, **Unique Decorative Elements,** discusses entertainment and signage as décor, food for the eye, decorative lighting effects, candles, the magic of ice, and pyrotechnics.

## THE UNIVERSE OF SPECIAL EVENTS—PART THREE

Humans celebrate occasions. This is what separates us homo sapiens from other living creatures. Corporations use events to recognize achievement and for marketing, sales, and motivation. Families celebrate weddings, anniversaries, graduations, birthdays, various religious and passage rituals; things that are going to happen and things that have passed. Holidays are reasons for celebration, and events are used both for purely social reasons and to raise money for various causes.

Each of these reasons to hold an event requires different decorations and each requires a design approach if it is to become the truly unique and outstanding experience it deserves to be. Part Three deals with each of these types of events, gives guidance, makes decorative suggestions, and gives tips on dealing with the client in each of these situations.

Chapter 12, **Nonprofit and Charity Events,** deals with the special challenges required for events with humanitarian goals. This chapter shows ways to achieve goals with limited resources, offers operational and procedural suggestions, and illustrates these suggestions with actual examples. Procedures for dealing with committees and volunteers are offered and the conflict between profit-oriented supplier vs. nonprofit client is considered in practical win-win terms.

Chapter 13, **Corporate Celebrations and Ceremonies,** describes the types of corporate events that the professional event designer will encounter, and the different design approaches that work for each. Specific examples from our experience are given and practical recommendations provided.

Chapter 14, **Milestone and Social Events,** deals with the varied types of social events that we have executed over the decades. It describes specific challenges that were posed and how these challenges were met. While solutions to the problems posed are given, the aim of this chapter is not to offer specific ideas, but to communicate a creative problem-solving attitude or process.

Chapter 15, **Wonderful Weddings,** deals with a topic about which, like floral design, much has been written. This chapter discusses designing and decorating the ceremony, the reception, and related events in several different religious and cultural traditions, styles, and themes.

Chapter 16, **Festivals, Fairs, Parades, and Spectacles,** discusses some basic design and decorative principles and offers some specific guidance and techniques that apply to the separate industries of producing festivals, fairs, parades, and large spectacular events.

After 30-plus years, we have only the highest expectations for the future. Technology, market forces, and human nature have combined to assure that there will continue to be bigger and more dramatic events. There is a need for trained professional event designers and this book provides the framework for that training. The principles and practices of event design and decoration that follow can help any theatrical, floral, or graphics designer become a professional special event designer and any talented individual to develop professional special events abilities.

# Part One

# PRINCIPLES, PROCESSES, AND PRACTICES

In this part you will learn about basic principles of design, best practices for event design and decoration, the venue and how to design to it for maximum effect, what resources are available and how to manage them, and profit and loss for the event designer and decorator.

The five chapters in this part deal with the research, design, and planning steps of the Guideline for Effective Event Production. These steps fall under the administration competency of the Blueprint for Events.

# Chapter 1

# PRINCIPLES OF DESIGN

*We don't do art; we just do as well as we can.*

**—anonymous sculptor, Bali**

---

## IN THIS CHAPTER

You will discover the basic principles for designing events and decorations for events.

**Basic Principles of Event Design**

- Focus
- Space
- Flow

**Practical Aesthetic Principles**

- Line
- Color
- Composition
- Texture

**Design and Global Event Management**

- Research
- Design
- Planning
- Coordination
- Evaluation

---

Traditionally, the art of design and decoration has been considered an intuitive activity, and in fact, there are people who seem to have an innate or "natural" talent for it. However, in the multi-billion-dollar business world of special events we can no longer, like the Balinese sculptor quoted at the beginning of the chapter, "just do it." In an increasingly competitive field, professional practices and a planned design approach give the working decorator an edge. Although designing and decorating may appear to be intuitive, they follow established principles that please the eye and achieve the desired effect. This chapter will present the elements of basic event design and basic aesthetic principles and show how they apply to special event production.

## DESIGN AND DECORATION IN EVENTS

In business and personal matters, for seasonal and marketing purposes, it appears that it is human nature to adorn and beautify our surroundings through art and design. Art in an event is achieved through design and decoration. **Event design** is the conception of a structure for an event, the expression of that concept verbally and visually, and, finally, the execution of the concept.

**Decoration** is the adornment and beautification of the event, the primary focus of this book. Decoration is a **multidisciplinary craft,** employing carpenters, artists, floral designers, seamstresses, lighting technicians, and many other craftpersons and specialists.

When the decoration and the design combine to advance the event, a form of synergy is achieved. **Synergy** happens when two or more elements combine to achieve an effect greater than the sum of their parts. In producing events, this will result in both art and measurable, practical success.

Idea Portfolio

### DESIGN, DECORATION, AND SYNERGY

A gas pump hardware manufacturer decided to have a presence at a conference in Texas to promote brand awareness among the attending operations managers and purchasing agents. The company determined that it would host an evening reception with food, beverage, and entertainment. The event planner hired our firm to decorate the event.

We designed a western theme concept that was consistent with the conference location, using western storefronts incorporating brand identification signage. This was **design.** We presented our ideas to the client via verbal description, floor plans, and sketches; that was also part of the design process, the subject of Chapter 2.

The decorations that had been presented then were produced and installed. The production and installation of the props and other decorative items was the actual **decoration.** The ultimate product was both decoration and the embodiment of the design concept, which is also called the design.

Incorporating the company logos into the props and decorations was more effective than just hanging banners. Attention was attracted to the logos, and we heard comments about them being made by the guests. Designing the brand identification into the decorations created a form of **synergy** between logo presence and decorations.

# BASIC EVENT DESIGN

Determining the **goals and objectives of the event** and researching the material requirements and the expectations and demographics of the attendees are the first steps in basic event management and are preliminary to beginning the event design. After that, basic event design begins with focus, space, and flow.

## FOCUS

Just as determining the goals and objectives of the event is the first step for the event manager, determining the focus of the event décor is the first goal of the event designer. The best way to research this is to ask the client directly what is important in this event. Preliminary or additional research on the company or family can yield helpful information as well.

Some events have a natural focus. With award ceremonies, the focus is usually the honorees, and the reception will focus on the nominees; however, the ceremony may have a split focus, recognizing the nominees but also advancing the brand recognition of the corporation or association. In product rollout events, the focus is usually on the product, brand, or corporate identity being promoted.

The event professional also needs to be on the lookout for hidden or secondary agendas that will not be spoken or be immediately evident. These agendas may be achieving personal goals for the vice president of marketing or advancing the stock price or reputation of the chief executive officer (CEO).

Having determined the focus of the event, the designer implements the design elements and aesthetic principles in a way that achieves that focus. When the guests enter the room, their eyes and attention are directed toward the desired object, logo, or person being featured. This can be achieved through line, composition, and color, directing and attracting attention to the focus. Notice in Figure 1-1 how the design focuses attention on center stage by framing the area and providing a predominant item dead center in that space.

Focus can be achieved with color by using bright primary and secondary colors at eye level around the focus object. Using pure color around the focus object or person and blending receding colors in the foreground and background will achieve the same effect in a more sophisticated way. The effect also can be achieved by means of repetition, putting the object of the desired focus in front of the attendees at numerous locations and places throughout the event.

Focus can be achieved in ways other than the purely visual. Audio design can create focus through **audioscaping:** the creation of an environment of sounds that enhance the visual décor and direct attention (focus) through the placement of speakers and careful manipulation of tone and volume controls. The environment can be designed to surround the guests with audio, tactile, taste, and olfactory elements with the same care that is used for the visual elements. All the senses fall within the design environment of the event

**Figure 1-1**

designer. We can, by design, direct the focus of the guests throughout the event.

## SPACE

Space is critical. From a practical point of view, the décor must fit within the physical confines of the space and its elements must fit through access doors and hallways.

Décor should not take up too much space when space is limited but can be used to cut down or fill up space when the hall is too large. Simply placing decorative items around the perimeter of the room a few feet from the walls can make a hall that otherwise would be too spacious nice and cozy.

Certain events require more space than others. People are comfortable in close proximity to one another when attending an event with theatrical or auditorium-style seating, but while eating, people need enough room to feel that they are not inconveniencing or encroaching on one another.

Too much space per person can ruin certain events. People naturally try to establish a certain comfort distance from strangers. If too much room is allowed, guests will achieve that distance and not have to interact with people they do not know. An example of this is a typical American Protestant wedding reception. Often seating is provided for everyone in a spacious environment. People separate into the family groups they know and sit down without interacting with other guests. Everybody eats, and after a while people get up and leave, with nobody having had a particularly good time.

Idea Portfolio

## HOW WILL WE GET IT INTO THE ROOM?

A number of years ago, Gale Sliger and I were asked to meet with an event manager who was designing the grand opening of a hotel. The centerpiece of the décor for the opening was to be a life-size ice carving of a stage-coach with galloping horses in the ballroom. He was going to sculpt it in the basement and wanted us to provide the base on which it would sit.

As we discussed fabric for skirting the base and the drip pans that would have to be fabricated, I perused the construction drawings of the hotel. I asked him what the dimensions of the sculpture were and noted that there were no elevators big enough to accommodate it and that the doors were too small to allow access out of the basement. He told us that that would be our problem. Not seeing a solution to this problem, we declined the project.

Several months later I watched a late-hour news program in which the humorous closing piece was about the grand opening of this hotel and the giant ice sculpture that no one could get out of the basement. The picture faded as the piece was being destroyed and tossed in the gutter to melt.

Remember to design with not only the end result in mind but the steps and spaces in between as well.

Let us consider simply the impact of space in this example; cultural and other elements are discussed in Chapter 15, *Wonderful Weddings.* A wedding is a celebration. The bride is the focus, and the intent is for the guests to have a good time and create a memorable experience of her day. Too much space can defeat this purpose by allowing people to stay too far apart. To correct this, one can design enough seating for half the people and provide standing tables for the rest. This will result in greater interaction. (This is the case when age demographics allow; a mature crowd requires a larger seating allowance of two-thirds or three-quarters of the total guests. A mature crowd will contain a larger number of people who cannot stand long because of physical impairments.) If the family insists on seating everyone, the reception needs to be a seated dinner with all the ritual and ceremony that a seated dinner entails (see Chapter 14).

If we put the reception in a space that is just big enough to house the number of people present, we are putting them in close proximity to one another and encouraging interaction. We can, by design, encourage people to interact with and get to know one another. This is an important element in the design of all events, social or corporate.

Space is a major aesthetic as well as practical influence on all other design elements (see "Event Space Requirements" later in this chapter). Space is important in composition and in balancing the overall picture within the environment. A decorative item or prop can look out of place if it is too small or too large for the event space. An 18-foot-tall tree, for example, may be in proportion in a ballroom with a 25-foot ceiling but can be cramped and look inappropriate when crammed into a room with a 16-foot ceiling. A prop that is too large can overwhelm the guests or obscure the view, whereas one that is too small for the space can look humorously out of place or simply not be noticed. In either case, it can be a waste of resources and a distraction from the purpose of the event.

The number of attendees must be known so that the appropriate space is available to accommodate them and the entertainment and activities desired within the floor plan. When one is planning a social function such as a wedding reception, the guest list needs to be made in advance of selecting a venue, or the venue will control the guest list. In doing a corporate reception as part of a conference or convention, it is often difficult to estimate the number of guests who will attend. It is important to make every effort to control attendance through invitations, tickets, or RSVs so that neither too many nor too few guests show up. Keeping an attendance history will be extremely valuable for future events.

## FLOW

Flow is the movement of the guests or attendees within the event environment. All events must allow entrance (ingress) and exit (egress) space. All events require enough space for efficient flow of the guests into the room and to and from the buffets, dance floor, rest rooms, and any other spaces for activities. The design of the flow can encourage or discourage access to each element, depending on the goals and objectives of the event and the needs and requirements of the guests.

**EVENT SPACE REQUIREMENTS**

Note: The dimensions given here are a rule of thumb for preliminary site selection. The dimensions shown do not allow for buffets, dance floor and bandstand, special audiovisual requirements, or other special activities. They also do not take into account local, state, or national ordinances or codes.

| | |
|---|---|
| Theatrical or auditorium-style seating | 7–10 sq. ft. per person |
| Schoolroom-style seating (at 18″ tables) | 7–10 sq. ft. per person |
| Banquet-style seating (at 60″ round tables) | 10–12½ sq. ft. per person |
| (at 72″ round tables) | 12–14½ sq. ft. per person |
| (at 8′ banquet tables) | 10 sq. ft. per person |
| Cocktail receptions | 10 sq. ft. per person |
| Trade shows and exhibit floors | 160–200 sq. ft. per booth |
| Exhibit floors | Double total booth footage for aisles |

Any event that includes an activity requires the design of traffic patterns that will enhance and encourage flow to and around that activity. For example, in a fund-raising event with a silent auction, the most effective place to put the display is in the paths between the tables to the bars and the tables to the rest rooms. This increases the exposure of the auction and encourages impulse bidding and buying.

Popular entertainment activities such as sketch artists and souvenir photo shoots require enough space for the activity, plus room to accommodate a line of people waiting to participate. Placement of the activity and identification (signs, props, a subfocus) will increase visibility and encourage participation. Also, there must be an exit route for people who have completed the activity.

Most people involved in events understand that it is a mistake to place the bars close to the entrance or the check-in tables, as that area becomes crowded and congested. If you want to move people into the room, place the bars or other attractive entertainment or giveaways far enough into the room to draw people in.

Flow is best planned through the use of scale floor plans or ground plans, which are discussed in detail in Chapter 2, *Design and Decoration Practices.* We can, by design, move people throughout an area for the duration of an event.

## BASIC AESTHETIC PRINCIPLES

We see a beautiful sunset or a majestic view of the Alps, and it pleases or awes us. A common and effective approach in designing events is to reproduce naturally pleasing scenes as either representational or abstract copies of the real world. Certain places, artifacts, and cultural icons can be replicated to inspire us, such as the Lincoln Memorial or a waving flag. Primal elements preceding civilized history may influence our aesthetics: fear of fire, survival, and sexual and emotional elements. Audio design can make use of rhythms ranging from the orgasmic pounding heartbeat to the soothing sounds of a sleeping baby's breathing.

Still, we largely learn our aesthetic values. In Western civilization these values are rooted in the Hellenic Greeks and the Italian Renaissance and flow from the great masters of painting and sculpture to the Impressionists and abstract expressionists. The masters and schools of fine arts provide inspiration and aesthetic direction for modern event decorators.

Current schools of design can provide aesthetic direction, inspiration, and contrainspiration. Popular styles of design spring from traditional schools or the current "in" designer of fashion, interiors, floral stylists, or architecture. It is common for a current fad to impact our sense of aesthetics in event design. All media relating to culture and lifestyle are a source for what is happening in design. Traditional or classical design elements are always in style, but

## INSPIRATION FROM MASTERS

Master artists can also provide direct ideas and concepts. Sally Dillon, the noted textile artist, designed a wonderful modern art theme party in the 1970s for Bill Reed Decorations.

Among many modern art takeoffs was a replica of Wyeth's "Christina," a wonderful magic realism painting of a young, fragile girl lying on the ground, staring at her house on the horizon, only the back of her head and body visible in the yellow grass. It was painted 14 feet tall by 24 feet wide. The only difference from the original (other than the monumental size) was that the subject, Chistina, was lying in the grass looking at a bottle of Coca-Cola rising on the horizon, thus combining Andrew Wyeth and Andy Warhol.

The classical and modern masters of fine art are a major resource for the event designer.

events are both current and transitory, and it may be appropriate to reflect a current trend or fad in event design.

# PRACTICAL AESTHETIC PRINCIPLES

The aesthetic practices that influence design have been developed from experience, study, and history. The following is a rudimentary discussion of principles that work.

## LINE

**Line** is a basic element that can be used to reinforce a message, feeling, or atmosphere in the décor on a stage or at any focal point of a room or venue. Line is a two-dimensional representation of composition that is created by the placement of identical elements or, more subtly, through arrangement of different but dominant elements so that one can draw a line straight through them and see a vertical, horizontal, or **diagonal movement** or direction (see Figure 1-2).

A **vertical line** can be elegant or dominant, while a **horizontal line** tends to be calming and peaceful. A **diagonal line** tends to express dynamics or tension.

In traditional Western art, a line from upper left to lower right expresses a tension but feels proper, whereas a diagonal line from upper right to lower left creates an irritating tension.

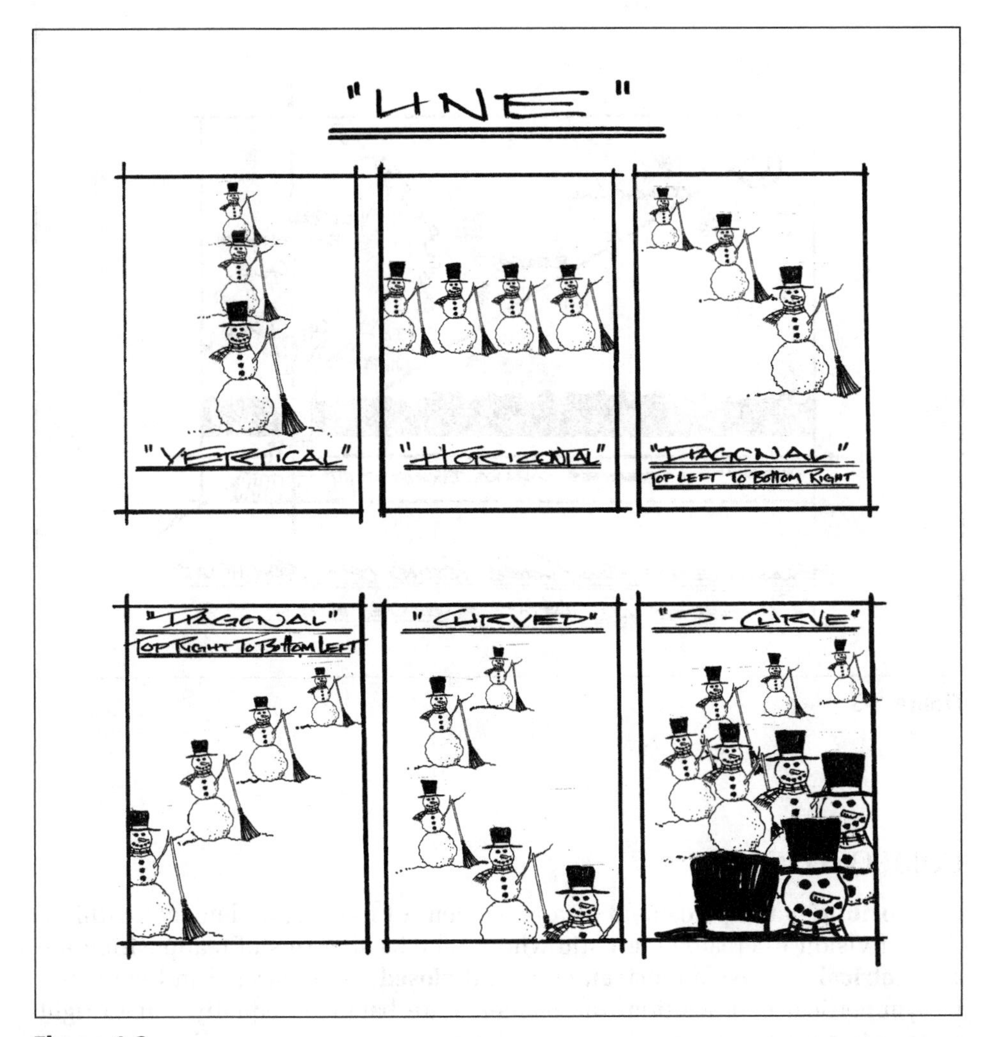


**Figure 1-2**

Curved lines can commonly be used to increase tension or interest or to diffuse tension, depending on whether they form a convex curve (crescent) or a concave curve. A crescent from upper left to lower right has a calming effect, whereas a reverse curve from upper right, over the center, to lower left can be very "in your face." An S curve generally softens the impact of the general line it follows but can add overall interest.

Any **visual picture**—of a stage, through a door or portal, or framed by architectural or natural boundaries—can be enhanced by attention to line (see Figure 1-3).

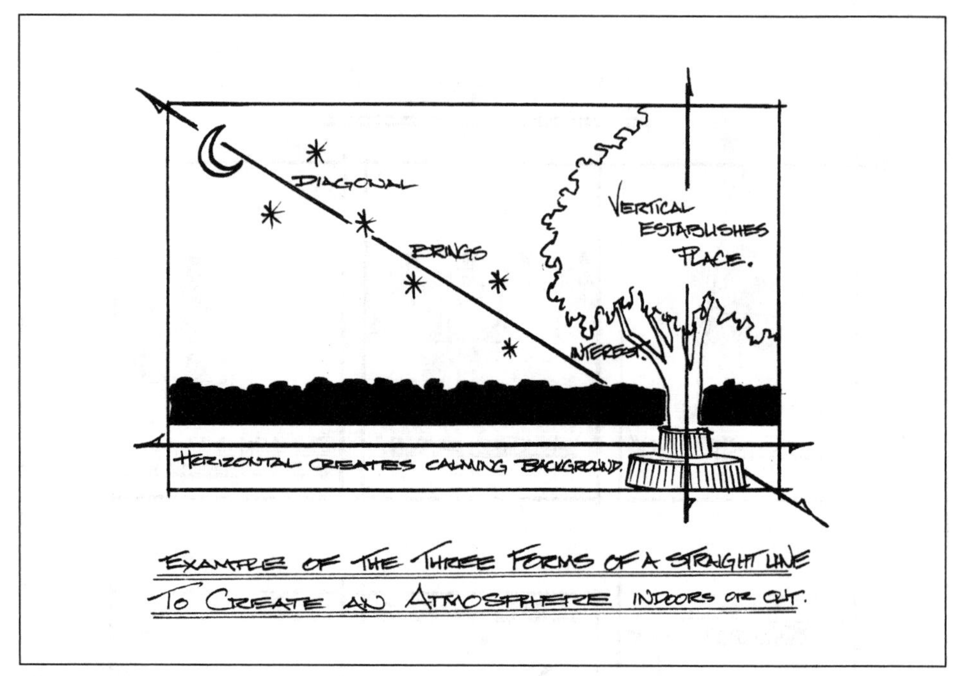


**Figure 1-3**

## COMPOSITION

**Composition** is the placement or arrangement of items and elements within a field of vision to create an artistic whole. The basic forms of composition are **symmetrical** and **asymmetrical, open** and **closed,** as illustrated in Figure 1-4. In symmetrical composition, the elements are balanced equally, left to right and top to bottom. This tends to evoke harmonious, relaxing feelings. In asymmetrical composition, one area is loaded with an impact element balancing against the rest of the entire visual picture. The image is off balance, and the result is dynamic, creating a tension between the elements. This generates interest and can be emotionally unsettling.

Whether a composition is symmetrical or asymmetrical, the eye is drawn to the top. In Western cultures, where reading is typically from left to right, the upper left corner is where the eye begins. (Asiatic cultures, where reading is from right to left, frequently start at the upper right.) Traditional composition in Western art is structured from the upper left and tends to incorporate horizontal rather than vertical separations. A horizon is a natural example.

*Closed composition* includes all the compositional elements within the framework of the picture, whereas in *open composition* the visual picture spills out of those boundaries. Open composition is the original "out of the

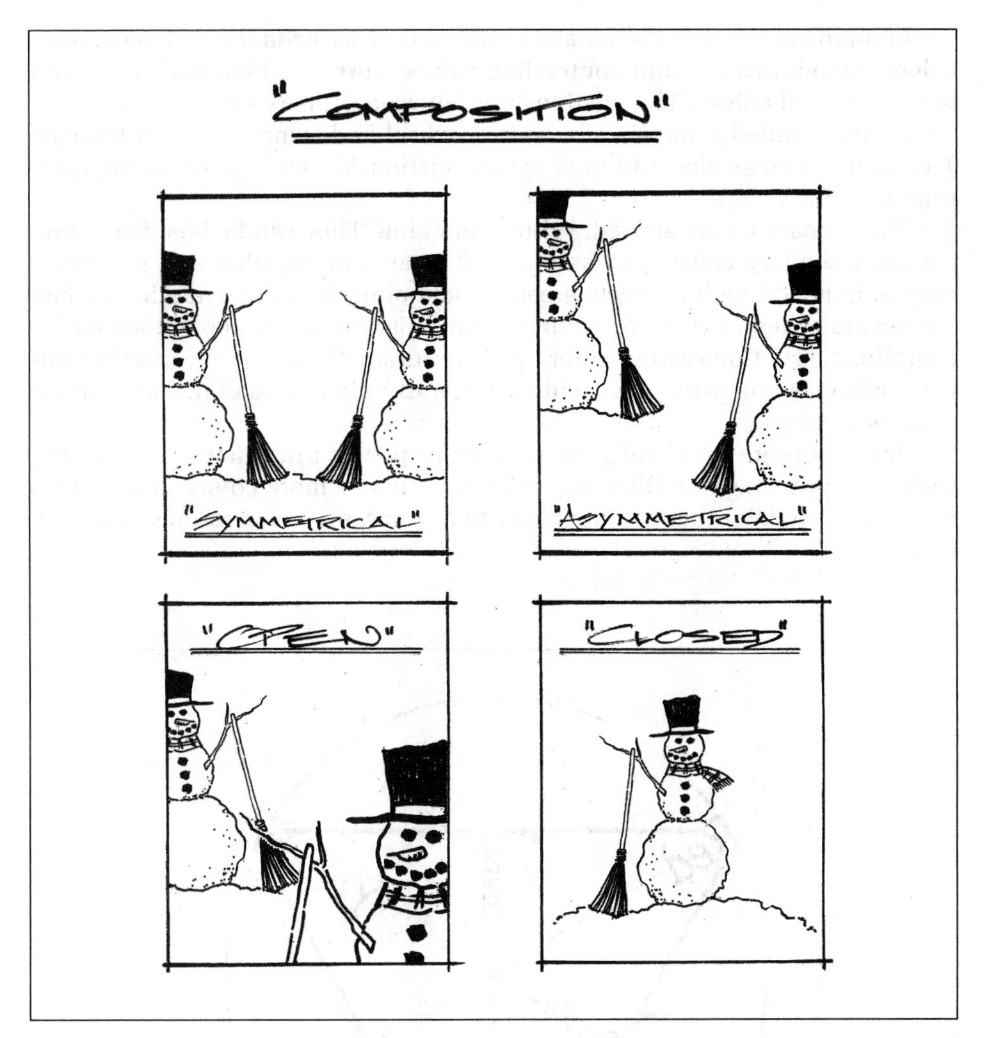


**Figure 1-4**

box" design element. Closed composition, like symmetrical composition, is settled and solid; open composition extends the viewers' imagination beyond the current moment.

## COLOR

Of all of the elements of design, the most has been written and discussed regarding color. The average human eye can discern the differences between 250,000 different hues, and some people with particularly good color definition can distinguish up to 600,000. This makes the verbal description of colors a daunting task.

In simplistic terms, colors are characterized as **primary** and **secondary colors, complimentary** and **contrasting colors, pure** and **blended colors,** and **warm** and **cool colors.** The relationships between primary and secondary colors are represented sometimes by a color wheel and sometimes by a triangle. The triangle comes closer to their actual relationship on a graph of the spectrum (see Figure 1-5).

The primary colors are red, yellow, and blue. They can be blended to create the secondary colors: red and yellow create orange, blue and red create purple, blue and yellow create green. Colors opposite to one another in Figure 1-5 are called contrasting colors; colors adjacent to one another are called complimentary. Contrasting colors provide dramatic attention, creating impact, whereas complimentary colors generally elicit peaceful, harmonious responses.

Pure colors are basic and generate basic responses from viewers and guests, such as happy laughter. Blended colors mix two or more colors to achieve a more subdued color that is more likely to be appropriate for serious corporate events.

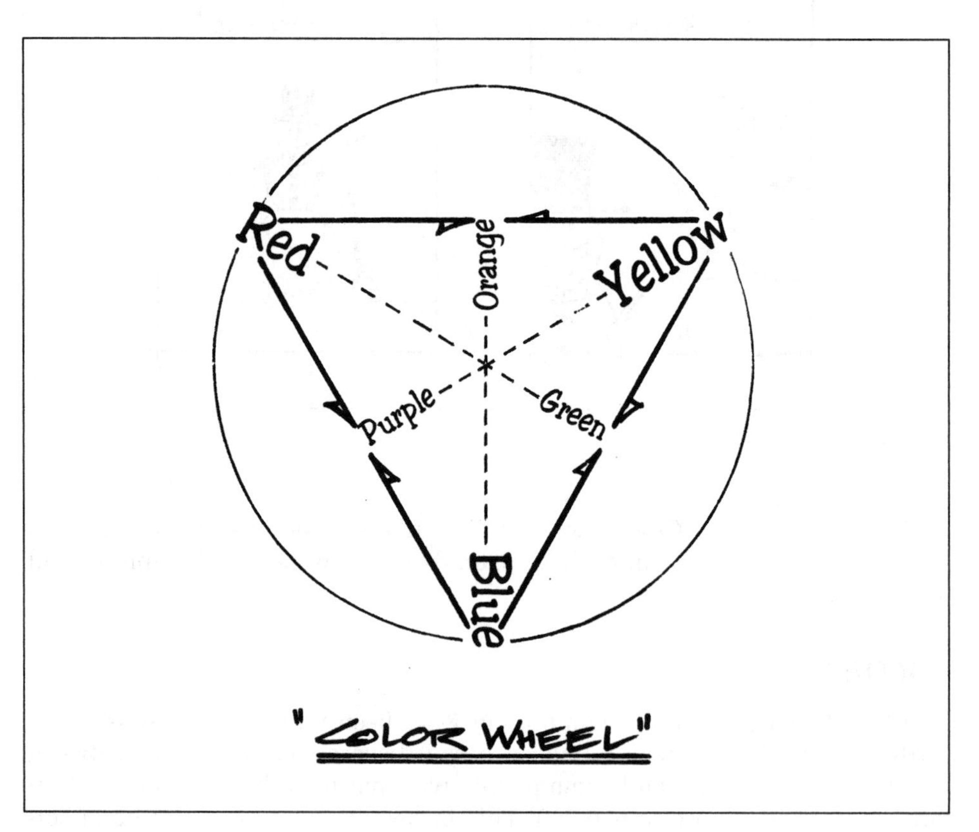


**Figure 1-5**

Warm and cool colors are so basic that everybody knows that the cools are the blues and greens and the warm colors are red, yellow, and orange. Their emotional impact is equally well understood, whether this is cultural or is created by species or environmental conditions. Different colors have a different emotional impact in different cultures: White, for example, is the color of funerals in India, and red is the color of Joy in China.

A poorly understood aspect of color differences is that the human eye is focused on the red end of the spectrum and has trouble focusing clearly on blue. Add to that the fact that blue pigments are more difficult to create and have lower light transmission and reflectance coefficients, and the cool end of the spectrum can be hard to achieve effectively.

## TEXTURE

In many cases, what separates professional design and decoration from amateur attempts is attention to **texture.** Viewed texture can produce a pleasing finished look by replicating surfaces found in the real world. Fabric texture can elicit feelings, such as the hard smooth texture of satin made rich by falling in folds or the inherently rich texture of velour giving a warm ambience to the environment.

Texture, or modeling the surface of decorations, can be "real" or "faux." Real texturing can be natural to the surface (wood grain) or added to the surface (plaster texture). Oblique lighting (from the side, bottom, or top) enhances the effects of real texture by casting shadows on the surface. Faux texturing uses any number of scene painter or mural artist techniques. These techniques include faux wood graining, sponge painting, spattering, and even texturing with a feather duster.

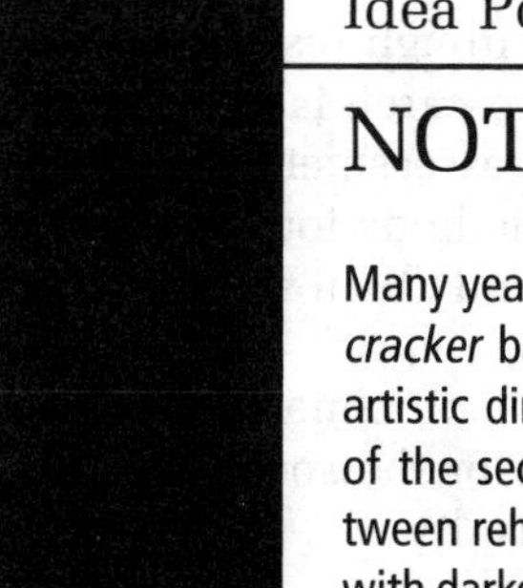

Idea Portfolio

### NOT BLUE ENOUGH!

Many years ago, when I was lighting the *Nutcracker* ballet for the Fort Worth Ballet, the artistic director complained that the opening of the second act was not blue enough. Between rehearsals, more, higher-wattage lights with darker blue gel were added, but he would not be pleased.

During the second rehearsal a miscue resulted in pink side lighting being added to the stage picture. "That's it!" the director shouted. "That's perfect!"

To achieve a feeling of cool blue, it was necessary to add a warm accent to relieve the eye and provide a counterpoint to the blue wash.

Idea Portfolio

## UP CLOSE AND PERSONAL

The texture of the linens, drapes, and other environmental elements that the guests touch and interact with has a big impact on their perception and experience of the event. Never order linens without sitting at a table and experiencing your bodily interaction with them.

Most tablecloths will profit from a table pad, and some absolutely require it.

Never order napkins without having one in hand and trying it out on the lips. Some visually beautiful napkins have an unappealing texture. White linen napkins are always acceptable.

Never order drapes, draping, or skirting material without having it in hand to see how it drapes and experience its visual and tactile texture. Look at it under the simulated lighting of the event.

The texture must be appropriate to the setting, season, and occasion.

# DESIGN AND GLOBAL EVENT MANAGEMENT

"All successful events have five critical stages in common to ensure their consistent effectiveness. These five phases or steps of successful event management are *research, design, planning, coordination* and *evaluation.*" This is stated in *Special Events: Event Leadership for a New World* by Dr. Joe Goldblatt. He calls this the Guideline for Effective Event Production. This guideline relates directly to the effective design and decoration of events. A brief discussion of these five steps as they relate to design and decoration follows.

## RESEARCH

The goals and objectives of the event are determined through research, as are the needs and expectations of the **stakeholders.** Major research is properly the realm of the event manager and often involves a needs assessment and an extensive analysis. The research required and the best methods for implementing it vary widely, depending on the event type, style, and client requirements (see Chapter 4, *Resources*).

For the design process, interviewing the client or event manager may provide enough information, but researching the company or the social status or cultural background of the client can yield valuable results.

## DESIGN

Design is the creation of the environment to satisfy the needs of the stakeholders and attendees, meeting the goals and achieving the objectives of the event. Design and decoration are the topic of this book, along with where the event designer fits most appropriately into the process of effective event production.

## PLANNING

The planning phase of event management follows design and deals with managing historically limited resources, including finances, time, and human resources (see Figure 1-6).

The design must fit within the budget that has been allotted, or the budget must be revised and additional finances secured. Time directly affects the design, as limited production and **I&D (installation and dismantle)** time will limit what can be done. Staff is ultimately the most important resource: the talents and abilities of the event management and design team.

## COORDINATION

Coordination is the execution of the event management plan. Interpreting the design through the decorations is properly a function of coordination. Design and decorations are closely related and rarely are developed totally separately.

**Figure 1-6**

True synergy is most often achieved as the design concept is executed in the physical manifestation of the decorations, including props, flowers, fabric, and lighting. These functional components are discussed in practical detail in Part Two, *The Decorative Elements.*

### EVALUATION

One of the primary resources the event designer and decorator have is history and experience. Post-cons (the after-event wrap-up meeting), surveys, and other evaluation tools that are critical to the success of the design and decoration of future special events will be discussed in Chapter 2, *Design and Decoration Practices.*

## FINISHING TOUCHES

The tips, aesthetic guidelines, and rules discussed in this chapter really work; their success is objective and measurable. However, in practice they can be successfully and effectively ignored or violated. That is one of the reasons designing events is so much fun.

I do not know a single professional designer who sits down when doing every event and follows the Guideline for Effective Event Production number by number. However, I know a couple who would do a better job for their clients if they did, and this is a reliable approach for the beginning or the volunteer event designer. As I studied event design as a discipline, years into a successful professional career, I discovered that our company usually follows this procedure. We evolved into following these steps naturally because it is the right way to manage an event.

## DESIGN VOCABULARY

Terms appear below in the order in which they first occur in this chapter.

Event design
Decoration
Multidisciplinary craft
Synergy
Goals and objectives of the event
Audioscaping
Line
Diagonal movement
Vertical line
Horizontal line
Diagonal line
Visual picture
Composition
Symmetrical composition
Asymmetrical composition
Open composition
Closed composition
Primary colors
Secondary colors
Complimentary colors
Contrasting colors
Pure colors

Blended colors
Warm colors
Cool colors
Texture
Stakeholders
I&D (installation and dismantle)

## STUDIO WORK

1. In an art book of your choosing, select reproductions of paintings or photos and with tracing paper draw the line you see in each image.
2. In an art book of your choosing, locate reproductions of paintings or photos and pick examples of open composition and closed composition.
3. In a short (one-page) essay, describe your understanding of how space and flow can effect focus in an event.

## RECOMMENDED READINGS AND RESEARCH SITES

Eiseman, Leatrice, PANTONE Guide to Communicating with Color, Design Books International, 2000.

Goldblatt, Joe, Special Events: Event Leadership for a New World, John Wiley & Sons, 2004.

Riley, Noel, ed., Elements of Design: A Practical Encyclopedia of the Decorative Renaissance to the Present, Simon & Schuster, 2003.

Tansey, Richard G., Fred S. Kleiner, and Christin J. Mamiya, Gardner's Art through the Ages, Harcourt, 2001.

Thomas, Mark A., Exploring the Elements of Design, Delmar Learning, 2003.

The Alphabet of Art: The Robert J. McKnight Memorial Web Site, by Robert J. McKnight and Jack Massa

www.guidancecom.com/alphabet/authors.htm

Composition and Design: Elements and Principles, by Marvin Bartel

www.goshen.edu/art/ed/Compose.htm

# Chapter 2

# DESIGN AND DECORATION PRACTICES

*There are two kinds of people in this world: hosts and guests.*

**—William G. Host, CMP**

## IN THIS CHAPTER

You will discover the best practices for creating and communicating event design and decoration concepts.

**Research Methods**

- The Interview
- The Five Ws
- Tips and Techniques
- Goals and Objectives

**Creative Techniques**

- Brainstorming
- Individual Brainstorming
- Free Association
- List Making
- Browsing
- Research
- Imitation and Variation
- Developing Ideas

**Design Development**

- Media
- Archives
- Internet
- History
- Themes

**Communicating the Design**

- The Proposal
- Sketches and Renderings
- Scale Floor Plans
- Samples

Defining one's professional position in the event world, as explained in the quote from meeting planner Bill Host that begins this chapter, is the first step in determining best practices. This chapter will explain the most effective practices for creating and communicating the design and decorations for special events, including research, creative techniques, and ways to develop and communicate the design.

In *Blueprint for Best Practices in Event Management* by the International Special Events Society (ISES) and as part of the Certified Special Events Professional (CSEP) program, design falls under the ADMINISTRATION competency and decoration falls under the COORDINATON competency.

An event professional may be called on to serve multiple functions, including those of event manager, designer, and/or decorator, with responsibilities ranging from partial to total design authority. However, it is important to recognize the difference between an event **designer** and an event **decorator.** The designer is the conceptualizing force, and the decorator is the artisan who executes the design concept in the form of physical elements. In many instances, there will be multiple designers, including the client, the **event manager,** and the **design director,** who has the ultimate responsibility for producing the design and decorations.

The process of designing an event begins with research to determine the goals and objectives of the event and the needs and expectations of the client. During the research process the resources available are determined as well (see Chapter 4, *Resources*). After research to determine the direction, creative techniques can be employed to determine an appropriate design concept. The next step is developing the design, which moves beyond concept into reality. This is the transition from designing to decorating and usually involves a collaboration between the designer, the decorator, and the client. The final stage is communicating the design through a written description in the form of a proposal, sketches and renderings, a scale floor plan, and samples.

## RESEARCH

The designer rarely initiates the event or the design process. There will be a phone call or an email, or someone will send a **Request for Proposal (RFP)** or walk in the door. Whether initiated by a professional event manager, a meeting planner, or the mother of the bride, the **first contact** is where the research begins. (See Appendix 1, *Typical Request for Proposal.*)

The professional designer/decorator starts by gathering basic information, including the client's name and address and the type of event. If known, the date and location are determined, and all this information is collected on a **contact sheet.** The information on this form must include all contact phone numbers, fax numbers, and email addresses; the name and position of the decision maker who is authorized to sign contracts and make legal agreements; and the name and address of the person or organization responsible for paying the bills. Additionally, the contact sheet should have space for the names, numbers, and email addresses of other "players," such as the venue contact, the event coordinator (if different from the designer/decorator), and audiovisual and other suppliers. See Appendix 2, *Contact Sheet.*

It is essential that the potential client not be allowed to hang up or leave the building before some basic information has been collected on a contact sheet, or critical information may be missed. This sheet can also be secured into the client file so that contact and billing information is available to whoever needs it, from the project manager to accounting.

The name, date, and time of the event should each have a separate line. All lines need to be filled in or labeled "tbd" (to be determined) in pencil if they are not yet known.

During the first conversation it is possible to gather information, but often a first-time client will be interviewing you to determine if you can meet his or her needs. Years of experience have proved that it is good practice to be honest with yourself about your ability to service clients' needs. Listening is the best way to gather information, but in a preliminary contact asking the right questions can prequalify a client while the client is trying to prequalify you.

If an elaborate event is being described that would obviously require extensive resources, it can be useful to find out what the budget is. Are you available on the date set for the event? Is the scope of the event within your experience and resources? Is the client shopping for ideas or looking to hire a professional? Sounding each other out in advance can save you both unnecessary time and effort. A face-to-face first contact can segue into an interview. All other first contacts that seem to prequalify as desirable projects within the capabilities of the company should lead directly to an interview.

## THE INTERVIEW

An effective interview during the first meeting should be conducted largely by listening. Asking leading questions will help the client tell you what he or she knows. The **Five Ws** describe the best practice for the goals of an effective first interview: *why, who, when, where,* and *what.*

Idea Portfolio

### SILLY, BUT TOO TRUE

You meet with Dave, a potential client, and you hit it off immediately. One of you mentions an idea, the other picks up on it right away, and the creative juices are flowing. An hour later the two of you have designed the entire event conceptually. The job is as good as sold; you two are the best of friends and are shaking hands and slapping backs as Dave leaves. You turn to your associate, who just showed up as you were waving good-bye to Dave as he pulled out of the parking lot. You say: "Did you get his last name and phone number?"

Salespeople and designers both tend to get deeply involved in the process when meeting with clients. The practice of using a contact sheet at all first meetings will assure that critical information is collected.

### Why

Why is the most important, because it asks the basic question about goals and objectives for the event. Goals and objectives, along with their companion needs and expectations, are the fundamental reasons for the event and should drive the event design.

Our most effective interviewing technique is simple and straightforward: We are having a pleasant conversation with a new acquaintance who we hope will become a friend. As previously mentioned, aside from gathering basic information, the primary technique is listening. Your client wants to talk about the event; let the client do so. A first-time client may want to hear about or see pictures of work you have done for others. Be prepared to roll out a small presentation (otherwise known as a **dog and pony show**), but be sensitive to the client's reception to it. Some people may want to see more of what you have done, but others may be intimidated by it or may not be interested.

### Who

Who are the primary stakeholders? In the case of a wedding, who is the bride? Who are her parents? Who is the groom? Traditionally, the bride's family pays the majority of the wedding and reception expenses. However, traditional arrangements both in family structure and in expense responsibilities do not necessarily apply any longer. Another very important issue is who is paying for the event. Finally, who will be attending?

Who are the primary stakeholders in the case of a corporate reception? Who is the client's agent, and with whom will you be dealing? Who will sign off on the design, and who will sign the contracts and agreements? Other nice things to know are who your contact reports to and who are the company's VIPs.

### When

When the event occurs is a critical factor in many elements, such as pricing of the venue, food and beverage, and entertainment. When in the year, when in the month, when in the week, and what time is the event? When is the venue available for moving in, and when must it be cleared out?

For the designer and decorator, when the event occurs affects floral availability and pricing. Many flowers are only seasonally available, and some are much more expensive at certain times of the year. The time and season in which an event takes place also affect the appropriateness of the design style or theme and, most important, labor costs.

Overtime for weekend or late-night installation and removal will have a major effect on the budget. Some times of the year are more expensive because everyone is busy and prices are not very negotiable. Other seasons may allow for off-season or **shoulder season** discounts.

### Where

Deciding where the event will take place can be one of the event designer's tasks; sites and site selection are covered at length in Chapter 3, *Venues*. The location is extremely important, as the physical environment will determine what can be done and what must be done. The venue can provide either a challenge or an inspiration, sometimes both.

Whether for a private social function or a corporate event, the location often is determined before the designer/decorator is brought into the process. ICW events are those which are held "in conjunction with" a convention or conference. This type of event will often have its location selection choices limited by or determined by the show's management.

One of the early actions in the design process should be a joint site visit by the designer and the client. This first site visit provides an opportunity to get a feel for the client's expectations or vision. As in the first contact meeting, listening is a good approach, perhaps tossing out a few ideas to confirm that you and the client are thinking along the same lines.

### What

What is the event? If it is a corporate reception, is it being held in conjunction with another occasion? Is it a repeat event that has previous history to be drawn on? If it is a product rollout, what is the product? If it is a wedding, is it a first wedding? Will it be a religious ceremony, and if so, what denomination? *What* can go beyond a simple description and become "what is the purpose of this event?"

The event must be designed to meet its goals and objectives, which we determined when we asked why it was going to be held. *Why* the event is being held always determines *what* the event will be.

## INTERVIEW TIPS AND TECHNIQUES

Before the interview it is a good idea to do some research on the company or family putting on the event. Family information may be available through the local social directory or contacts at a country club or another venue. Corporate information is commonly available on the Internet, especially for publicly traded companies. Effective events are not designed in a vacuum; the more familiar the designer is with the corporate culture or family, the more likely it is that an effective design will result. A good icebreaker at the beginning of a first meeting is to ask knowledgeable questions about the company.

Asking a social client about personal interests or asking a corporate client about company community activities can help determine a theme or design style. Once the client's personal expectations are stated, testing their importance to the client will give direction to the design. It is a good idea to have at least two pairs of ears in a meeting so that notes and understanding can be compared afterward. If there is a difference in understanding of what the client said about an important concept, it is important to contact the client to clarify that issue.

Finally, it is extremely important to get a budget out of the first meeting. Some clients are hesitant to give a figure for fear that the event designer will spend all of it. Sometimes the budget figure they have in mind is comprehensive and the portion available for design and décor depends on other expenses. In rare cases, usually in the case of first events, the client has not established a budget.

It is the job of the event professional to establish a relationship of trust, explaining that clients will get the most for their money if they share budget information up front. This means the event designer can concentrate his or her efforts on realistic designs and not waste time trying to arrive at a design that fits the unknown budget. In the other cases it may become part of the job of the event professional to help the client determine his or her budget and budget allocations.

### GOALS AND OBJECTIVES

The importance of determining the goals and objectives and the related needs and expectations was mentioned previously. When one is working with professional meeting or event planners, it is easy to determine the goals and objectives. The professional planner will have established clear and objective, measurable goals and will want to share them with you.

The planner will have determined the **needs and expectations** of the **stakeholders** before meeting with the designer. The goals and objectives of an event can be met only if the needs and expectations of the attendees and the client are satisfied.

Primary goals and objectives for the fund-raiser or social or life-cycle event are usually obvious. Secondary goals can require more research. When one is working with an established, recurring event, there will be a history. A first-time event without a history requires more research to determine goals and expectations.

## CREATIVE TECHNIQUES

Having accomplished a first contact interview and having determined the goals and objectives and the needs and expectations for the event, one may have discovered the design direction and decorative concept for the event as well. Sometimes the client has a vision he or she is able to communicate clearly, or the designer gets an inspiration, and the event seems to design itself. But most of the design inspiration comes from traditional perspiration. At these times there are several proven techniques that will result in an effective design concept.

**Brainstorming** is our favorite technique for coming up with design concepts. This term originally was described by Alex Osborn in his book *Applied Imagination.* One person selected as facilitator, who can also participate, will direct a group. This group can include designers, possibly the client, and other interested persons. It is helpful at this stage to have nonprofessionals in the group. The facilitator explains the rules, which are as follows: (1) There are no bad ideas; (2) unusual ideas are a good idea; (3) evaluation of ideas is not part of this process. The facilitator is responsible for keeping up enthusiasm, encouraging fun, and recording the ideas. After the brainstorming session, the recorded results are evaluated if necessary. Sometimes the design concept becomes evident during the process and the session is halted so that an evaluation session can be convened.

**Individual brainstorming** is a similar process but involves only one person. The technique here is to clear the desk and the mind. With only a pen and a fresh pad of paper, one leans back in a comfortable chair and starts to think of ideas, however off-the-wall. Write them down and move on to another idea; write it down and see if another idea spins off from the first one. It is necessary to achieve almost a state of meditation in order not to stop and consider the ideas as they flow. Setting an alarm is a good idea; when it goes off, it is time to move to the evaluation phase to see which ideas have merit.

**Free association** is closely related to and can be used with brainstorming in either of its versions. The mind is cleared, and the facilitator throws out a word or phrase related to the event. Participants start feeding back words, phrases, and feelings as they come to mind. After a short period, another word is thrown out for the group to respond to. The facilitator should keep things moving smartly so that the participants do not have time to think about their answers. The responses collected are then reviewed for ideas that will spring from free association and collected terms that may lead to a design concept or a solution to the problem. Free association can be used to jump-start a brainstorming session or at any point in the design or decoration process when inspiration is necessary to solve a design problem.

**List making** is a popular way to get creative juices flowing. On a chalkboard or flip chart create three columns: one for event elements, one for goals, and one for ideas (see Figure 2-1). Then the group is encouraged by the facilitator to add items to each of the first two columns. After the first two columns are filled in, the group is directed to switch to the ideas column and fill it in. A version of this uses three flip charts. After the session, rather than being evaluated, the lists are posted in a highly visible location so that the participants can see them daily. Design ideas can flow from this approach.

**Browsing** is another effective design technique. The designer may browse through an archive, past events, photos, slides, or magazines. Sometimes one can get an inspiration by browsing through *Architectural Digest* or through catalogues. One is not looking for an idea so much as looking for a stimulus to spark an idea in the left (creative) side of the brain.

The latest version of browsing is using the World Wide Web. One of the many Web search directories such as Google, AltaVista, and Dogpile or subject directories such as Yahoo! and LookSmart can be used by typing a one- to three-word phrase in the search window and left clicking the submit button. Techniques used to narrow the search vary from engine to engine. A recommended website on search engine techniques appears at the end of this chapter.

**Figure 2-1**

**Research,** like browsing, involves looking into existing sources. The difference is that rather than looking for inspiration, the designer is looking for historical bases for the design. Researching the company's history, the history of the times surrounding the company's history, or the time and place behind an event or celebration can lead to the design. A corporate client can provide the history and artwork for historical logos. When you are planning an anniversary celebration of any kind, research the history of the date of the occasion being celebrated. Design inspiration also can come from researching the geography and culture of related locations.

**Imitation** is the sincerest form of flattery and a great way to get design ideas, but borrowing can become theft of intellectual property. The upshot of browsing or research may be discovering an idea or picture that is perfect for your event. Copying that verbal or visual picture should be done only with the permission of the original creator, and in fact, copying without permission may lead to civil or criminal penalties. Still, borrowing ideas is one way to arrive at a design concept. The safest way is to use the discovered design as an inspiration and interpret it uniquely so that it becomes your design and your intellectual property.

**Variation** is a technique closely related to imitation and can spring from it. Imagine an idea or theme to be a variation of another theme or an addition to a theme. Imitate a concept seen in a magazine or an old standby, but add a twist that makes it special and original. Years ago a client challenged the design team I was with, asking for a French theme party, but she wanted it to be special. We developed the concept of a Matisse street festival featuring hand-dyed silk replicas of his famous collages hung across the streets of Paris. Another variation might be to take the standard cowboy theme and turn it into a "Tour of the Old West" featuring famous towns such as Amarillo, Tombstone, and Dodge City.

I have seen few truly original ideas in three decades of designing special events, but some great creativity has been displayed in variations. Like fine music, a well-composed party will exhibit multiple variations on its theme.

## DEVELOPING THE DESIGN

Developing the design concept into decorative details is where design and décor blend. This is the phase where transformation takes place: from design to décor, from concept to interpretation, from dream to reality. It can be the responsibility of one person but is usually the product of a team of professionals. Research and inspiration take over at this stage. The preliminary design research that has been done can be useful, but after there is a design concept, subsequent research becomes focused. "The devil is in the details," an old saying goes, and the details will make or break special event décor.

Historical designs may call for some standard props, such as hay bales and a split-rail fence for a western party or a speakeasy door for a Chicago flappers theme. To create a truly special event, the décor should capture a unique element, such as historical logos of the hosting corporation or a replica storefront from the founder's past. Events can use cultural or geographical details for authenticity or just for fun. A swamp party in Louisiana can make use of Spanish moss in bare branches, rolling fog, and swamp sound effects, and another area can feature "crawdad races."

**Media** is a great starting point for developing the design. There is an enormous amount of print and video media on almost any topic that can be turned into event decorations. The designer/decorator will have an active library card (or a design assistant with one) because the public libraries of large cities generally have great resources and a reference system to locate publications, books, and other information sources. Many city libraries have photo archives, and all of them have a reference librarian who wants to help you learn your way around the reference department.

**Archives** are the backbone of any design firm. They consist of clipping and photo files, flyers and brochures, samples and suppliers' catalogues. A typical professional event firm may have an entire room dedicated to files and samples. Individual designers and decorators will start their careers with a four-drawer file cabinet and rapidly develop an archive worthy of a second room. The trick is organizing and cross-referencing these items, because an item is useful only if you can find it easily and it contains up-to-date information.

Design and decoration firms I have worked with have kept a cross-reference file for the archives. The challenge is to keep it current.

**Internet** resources are rapidly replacing the public library due to the development of powerful user-friendly **search engines,** as discussed in the material on browsing in this chapter. There is minute detail available on your desktop if you can find it. The professional designer needs to become an expert on the popular search engines. Many times Internet research will lead you to the public library; at other times the inspiration you are looking for will appear on the screen before you.

A warning about the Internet is that it contains a universe of information and details. Some of it is accurate, some of it misguided, and some of it false. Cross-referencing, double-checking, and maybe a trip to the library are required when no confirmation is found online. A second warning involves copyright laws. Copyright laws apply to information on the Internet as well as to the books and periodicals in the public library.

The **history of an event,** as was mentioned before, is crucial. However, history from other events can provide reams of information and inspiration. One can reference either jobs with similar themes or jobs with similar goals or formats. Although a professional designer attempts to create a unique event each time, there are many similar events, and it is not necessary to redesign the same concept each time a similar version is being produced.

Like the archives, a well-organized file of past jobs is a necessity. One easy process is to use 14- by 18-inch manila envelopes in horizontal legal files, collected by year and alphabetized by job name. Use the generic name the job was known by, because that is the name it will be recalled by in the future. Keep only the crucial documents and design notes. If more than one envelope is required to keep the crucial data and notes, use two. If more than two envelopes are required, clean out the envelopes; you are keeping too many documents.

At the same time, of course, an archived and indexed file of past jobs and designs should be kept in your computer files, with reference to the hard-copy envelopes. Sometimes simply reviewing past job proposals and billing information can provide the inspiration needed. For jobs that repeat year after year in a similar fashion, each past year adds to the foundation of references for the next year's project.

Specific **themes** are inherent in certain events, such as Valentines or Christmas parties, and may provide a challenge to the decorator to come up with a new twist on an old theme. Other themes have been imposed on the event before the event decorator is called upon. Sometimes the theme can be the inspiration for design, or something about the event, the client, or the intent of the event inspires a specific theme.

The client occasionally will get theme-struck and become very excited over a theme or the concept of doing a theme party. This can be good, because an excited client can help inspire a successful party. However, the theme needs to be compatible with the goals and advance them. It must be chosen within the framework of the objectives and not detract from them. The responsibility of the event designer or decorator is to guide the party toward its objectives and goals. This can be done in the context of a theme, but the goals, not the theme, should drive the design.

It is critical in theme party design that *theme follow function.* A nautical theme may be appropriate for unveiling a new line of marine hardware but not the best choice for a new car show and may be totally inappropriate for introducing an incentive program to a mountain destination. A western theme would be appropriate for a national product unveiling in Tucson but a distracting choice in Boston unless it was for the opening of a cowboy-style restaurant or to unveil a new western-style pickup truck.

**Inspiration** can come from many places when one is considering a theme. Keeping a shelf of art books can provide inspiration. There are many good books on theme parties, such as *Themes, Dreams, and Schemes,* by Eugene Wigger. Local or nationally available party decorators and prop houses should be the primary source of inspiration when one is working with limited resources. Appendix 3, *Event Themes,* contains lists of possible themes.

## COMMUNICATING THE DESIGN

Designing and decorating events is a uniquely human endeavor and as such requires talented application of that uniquely challenging ability of human beings: communication. We have seen how communication can be involved in an exchange of ideas in developing the design. Once the design is developed, it must be communicated and/or sold to the stakeholders, such as the client, investors, or production partners, and to the potential stakeholders, such as the designer, the decorator, technicians, and artists.

The methods used to communicate the design are a **written description,** usually in the form of a proposal or contract; **scale drawings,** usually floor plans and elevations; and some type of conceptual or **artistic drawing,** a sketch, perspective drawing, or full-color rendering. Other assorted **communications/sales tools** include photos, models, swatches, and sample boards.

The methods selected to communicate the design on a project will follow from the talents and inclinations of the designer and/or decorator or from the requirements of the event or client. Different people have varying degrees of experience and conceptual abilities when looking at a drawing. Some people can look at a floor plan, read a description, and automatically conceive what the event will look like. Others will not have an idea of what it will look like unless you build a scale model.

Finding the most effective method of communication for your project and your stakeholders is crucial, because these tools all require resources. Resources should not be wasted on unnecessary or ineffective communications tools.

The written description will follow the style of the designer or writer, some being flowery and poetic and some being spare and technical. Appendix 4, *Typical Request for Proposal,* shows an example of one style of proposal. The proposal should not just follow the style of the individual writing it but should meet the needs of the client as well. It is not necessary to use the same style for all clients. Sometimes an itemized detailed proposal is required; at other times the client wants to see the concept and the bottom line and not be bothered with the details.

The concept of the scale drawing is essential for anyone involved in event design or decoration. The scale drawing is an **orthographic projection;** this simply means that it is a parallel line representation. The lines do not converge, as they appear to in a distance view, but stay in the same geometric relationship as they are in three-dimensional reality. This means that items can be measured on the drawing and constructed exactly to those measurements. The two most common orthographic projections are the floor plan and the elevation.

First, the concept of scale needs to be considered. A 6-foot-tall (6′) man can be drawn to scale as a 3-inch-tall (3″) figure. This figure would be drawn in 1/2 inch = 1 foot (1/2″ = 1′) scale. The same man could be sketched as a 3/4″-inch tall figure, because 3/4 inch equals 6 eighth-inches (6/8″ = 3/4″). That would be an eighth-inch = 1 foot (1/8″ = 1′) scale. See Figure 2-2.

Once we understand the concept of the scale drawing of a man, let us look at a representation of him standing in a doorway, next to a table, with chairs on one side and a potted tree on the other (Figure 2-3).

What we have in this sketch is a scale **elevation,** or upright drawing. If we turn our point of view 90 degrees to look directly down on him, we will have a scale floor plan that will show a scale representation of all the elements in the drawing and their exact (scale) size and relationship to one another (Figure 2-4).

The drawing of these scale sketches was done by hand; we refer to them as sketches because some of the elements were drawn freehand, without the use of tools. When tools are used to create the straight and curved lines, it is called drafting. Drafting traditionally was done by hand until the recent development of **CAD programs.** CAD stands for **computer aided/assisted drawing/drafting,** and there are numerous CAD programs in use in the hospitality and events industry. Currently, the best-known CAD program in the events industry is AutoCAD. A sample CAD drawing appears in Chapter 10 (see Figure 10-1).

Before we leave the discussion of scale drawings, there is one drafting tool that every event professional should own and know how to use. The **architect's scale rule** is usually three-sided and has 12 different scales on it, from 1/16 of an inch to 3 inches. The architect's scale is used to draw the plans and interpret the drawings. An event professional should be able to place various elements on a job site exactly where they are meant to go by reading the floor plan with a scale rule. It takes practice to become familiar with an architect's scale rule (Figure 2-5), but it is an essential tool. (There is also an **engineer's scale rule** with tenths and twentieths of an inch. This generally is not used in the event business.)

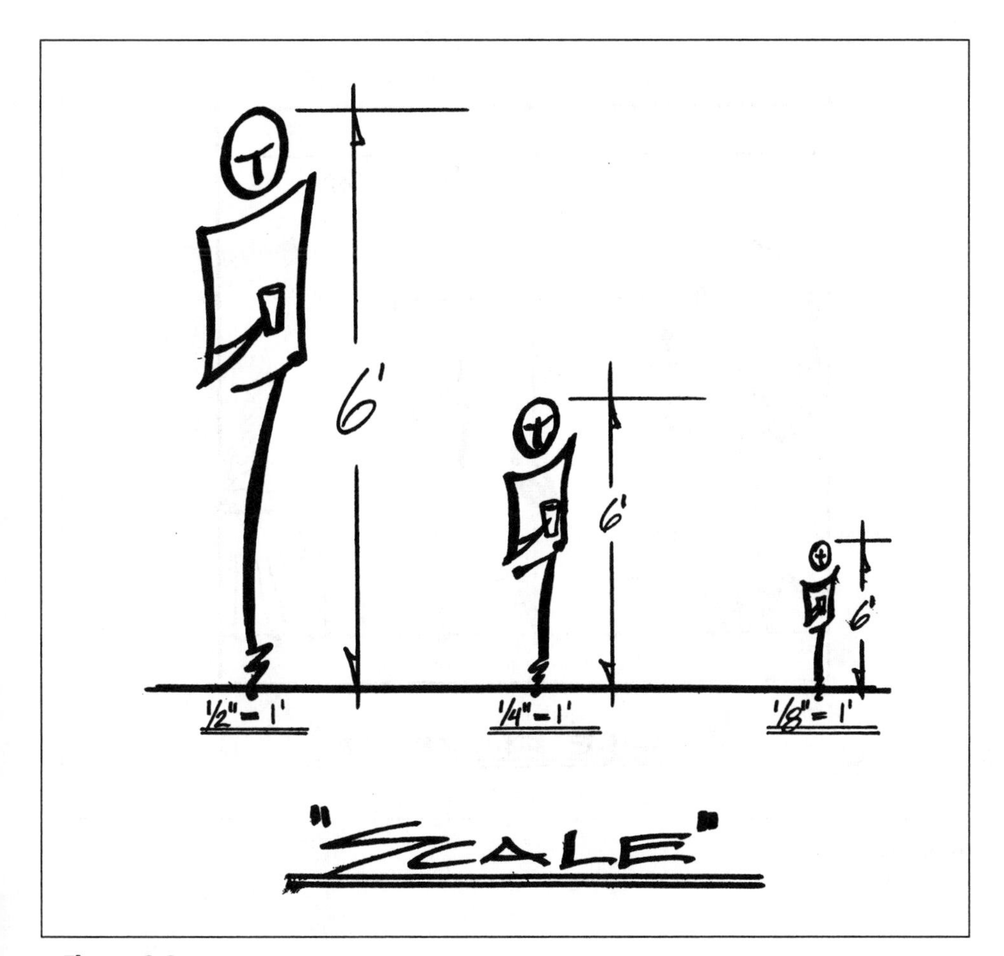


**Figure 2-2**

**Conceptual** or **artistic drawings** can vary from "not very artistic" sketches that succeed in communicating the concept to extremely precise full-color renderings that capture the entire concept in full perspective. A drawing of a design is called a rendering. A rendering with converging lines that capture the illusion of disappearing in the distance is called a perspective drawing. The quality of the artistic drawing depends on the talent of the artist and the commitment of resources to the rendering of the concept. Extremely complete designs in full color are called **architectural renderings.**

Other communications/sales tools include photos, models, swatches, and sample boards. When one is incorporating multiple elements into a design, a combination of the verbal description and **photos of props** and other individual elements that are being used can help communicate the concept. Photos of similar or identical decorations are helpful.

**Figure 2-3**

When the resources allow and the project requires it, nothing will communicate a concept the way a **full-scale model** will. Time-consuming, and therefore expensive, models communicate the idea and can have moving or changeable parts that will show the changes that take place through the duration of the event. A model is a strong selling tool.

**Swatches** of the fabrics being proposed—the paint colors, patterns, and texture—can be displayed separately or combined in a collage on a **sample board.** Swatches can sell the concept, but some colors and patterns can be misleading if only a small sample is shown. The designer or decorator should order or view samples large enough to get a feel for the full pattern, the effect of the color in large pieces, and the way fabric hangs or how it feels if it will be touched.

Swatches, drawings, floor plans, and sketches or elevations can be combined onto a board or a series of boards that become the **storyboard**(s) for the event.

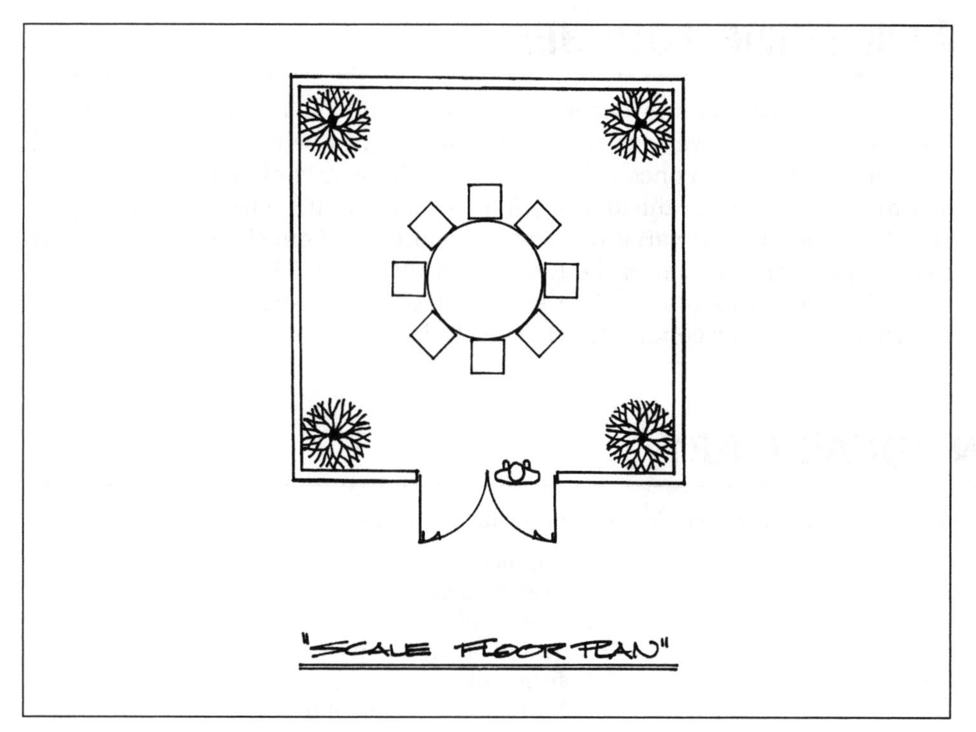


**Figure 2-4**

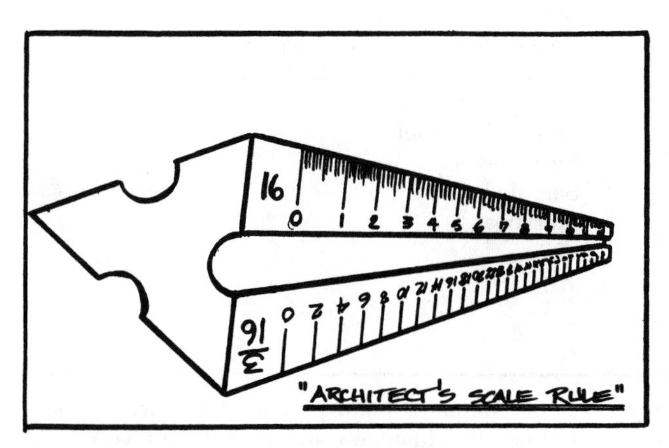


**Figure 2-5**

## FINISHING TOUCHES

The event designer and/or decorator interviews the client, paying attention to the critical Five Ws. Various creative techniques can be used to come up with ideas and develop a concept for the event. These techniques include brainstorming, individual brainstorming, free association, list making, browsing, research, imitation, and variation. The concept then is developed into a design that supports and promotes the function of the event. This design is communicated to the stakeholders via a written description, scale drawings, artistic drawings, and other communications techniques.

## DESIGN VOCABULARY

Terms appear below in the order in which they first occur in this chapter.

Designer
Decorator
Event manager
Design director
Request for Proposal (RFP)
First contact
Contact sheet
Five Ws
Dog and pony show
Shoulder season
Needs and expectations
Stakeholders
Brainstorming
Individual brainstorming
Free association
List making
Browsing
Research
Imitation
Variation
Media
Archives
Internet
Search engines
History of an event
Themes in an event
Inspiration
Written description of design
Scale drawings
Artistic drawing
Communication/sales tool
Orthographic projection
Elevation
Computer aided/assisted design drawing/drafting programs (CAD)
Architect's scale rule
Engineer's scale rule
Conceptual/artistic drawing
Architectural renderings
Prop photos
Full-scale model
Swatches
Sample board
Storyboard

## STUDIO WORK

1. Write a short RFP to send to a designer for an event, either real or imaginary.
2. A company is having its seventy-fifth anniversary and wants to combine a celebration of it with the rollout of a new product line. Have an imaginary first interview and answer the Five Ws.
3. Join with two other members of your class and brainstorm to come up with the most unique

theme design concept for a corporate reception. Describe it in one page.

4. Using Figure 2-3 and a scale rule, answer the following questions:

   How tall is the ficus tree?
   How high is the ceiling?
   What is the height and width of the entry arch?
   How big is the dance floor?

# RECOMMENDED READINGS AND RESEARCH SITES

Malouf, Lena, *Behind the Scenes at Special Events: Flowers, Props, and Design,* John Wiley & Sons, 1998.

Obsorn, Alex, *Applied Imagination: Principles and Procedures of Creative Problem Solving,* 1957, out of print.

Silvers, Julia Rutherford, *Exam Preparation Self-Study Guide,* 2nd ed., 2002, The Special Events Society.

Silvers, Julia Rutherford, *Professional Event Coordination,* John Wiley & Sons, 2004.

Tutera, David, *A Passion for Parties,* Simon & Schuster, 2001.

Wigger, G. Eugene, *Themes, Dreams, and Schemes: Banquet Menu Ideas, Concepts, and Thematic Experiences,* John Wiley & Sons, 1997.

Brainstorming.co.uk—a brainstorming techniques site
http://www.brainstorming.co.uk/

GoCreate.com®: Creative Center of the Universe—a creativity resource site
http://www.gocreate.com/HeadShed/tools.htm

Partypop.com—a resouce and research site
http://partypop.com/

Web Search Strategies by Debbie Flanagan
http://www.learnwebskills.com/search/main.html

# Chapter 3

# VENUE

*To serve the City of Los Angeles by enhancing its prominence as a primary destination for conventions, trade shows, and events that generate significant economic benefit. To provide a venue for the promotion of local business activities, community-based organizations, and regional events which attract and serve local residents.*

**—Mission Statement of the Los Angeles Convention Center**

## IN THIS CHAPTER

You will discover how important the venue is and learn ways to define and control its impact on the design and decoration of events.

**Types of Venues**

- Standard Venues
- Nonstandard Venues
- Off-Site Venues
- Unique Venues

**Site Selection Guidelines**

- Physical Requirements
- Budgetary Requirements
- Aesthetic Requirements

**Site Inspection**

- Conducting the Site Research
- Preselection Site Inspection
- Postselection Site Inspection

The **venue** in which an event takes place is the physical location, also known as the **site.** The quote that starts this chapter describes the purpose of the Los Angeles Convention Center; it clearly enumerates the reasons why most cities build a convention center. Venues that are built specifically to accommodate events have physical characteristics that allow ease of installation and removal of event décor. These characteristics include loading docks and large doors, rigging points from the ceiling, and heavy-duty electrical power.

The physical, financial, and aesthetic characteristics of the venue determine much of the design and what can be done in the way of decorations. Ceiling heights, for example, determine how tall the decorations can be, and door widths determine which decorations can fit into the room. After the goals and objectives, the venue is the next major element that defines the event. The selection of the appropriate venue is extremely important to the success of the event.

## TYPES OF VENUES

There are numerous types of venues, from hotel ballrooms to football stadiums; events can be held in country clubs or on streets. Some venues are designed to accommodate special events; others are designed for another purpose, such as a rodeo arena or an ice skating rink, but can be used for special events. **Standard venues** are sites that were designed for events; **nonstandard venues** were designed for another purpose and are not used primarily for events.

Almost any hotel ballroom is considered a standard venue, as ballrooms are designed to handle both corporate functions and social events. An example of a nonstandard venue would be the locker room of a National Football League team when it is used for a bar mitzvah celebration or a corporate team-building event.

Corporate events held in conjunction with a meeting, conference, or convention are referred to as **ICW** events (in conjunction with). These events are further classified as either **on-site events** or **off-site events** in relation to the **host site** for the meeting. If an event is to be held at the main or host hotel or at the convention or conference center where a tradeshow or the general session is being held, it is an on-site event. If it is held at any other location, it is an off-site event. An alternative hotel ballroom can be an off-site location, but a football stadium or a ranch might be considered more off-site (see the box "Types of Venues").

**Unique venues** are either those which normally are not used for events and are not equipped to service events of any kind or **stand-alone sites** that are not part of a hotel or another event complex. In corporate terms, these are the most off-site venues. Examples of unique venues include a pasture, an airplane hangar or empty warehouse, and an unfinished floor of an office building. Another common event venue that can be unique, depending on the type and scope of the event, is a residence.

A stand-alone site is usually a custom-built or renovated building that was designed with specific types of events in mind (see *Idea Portfolio:* The Ranch That Isn't a Ranch, later in this chapter).

**TYPES OF VENUES**

- Standard Venues
  - For Corporate Events
    - Conference centers
    - Convention centers
    - Hotels
  - For Life-Cycle Events
    - Community centers
    - Hotels/country clubs
    - Religious institutions
    - Restaurants/nightclubs
    - Stand-alone event venues
  - For Festivals and Fairs
    - Pastures, fields, barns, and other rural spaces
    - Stadiums and arenas
    - State and county fairgrounds, Renaissance fairs
    - Streets, parks, parking lots, and other urban spaces
- Nonstandard Venues
  - For Corporate Events
    - Country clubs
    - Museums, concert halls, and historical sites
    - Pastures, fields, barns, and other rural spaces
    - Residences
    - Restaurants/nightclubs
    - Stadiums and arenas
    - Stand-alone event venues
    - State and county fairgrounds, Renaissance fairs
    - Streets, parks, parking lots, and other urban spaces
    - University and corporate campuses
  - For Life-Cycle Events
    - Conference centers, convention centers, and other corporate venues
    - Pastures, fields, barns, and other rural venues
    - Stadiums and arenas
    - State and county fairs, Renaissance fairs
    - Streets, parks, parking lots, and other urban venues
  - For Festivals and Fairs
    - Airports
    - Racetracks
    - Other large appropriate spaces
- Unique Venues
  - Airports
  - Museums, concert halls, and historical sites
  - Pastures, fields, barns, and other rural spaces
  - Racetracks
  - Residences
  - Stadiums and arenas
  - Stand-alone event venues
  - State and county fairgrounds, Renaissance fairs
  - Streets, parks, parking lots, and other urban spaces

## STANDARD EVENT VENUES

Standard event sites such as hotels, country clubs, and conference centers are frequently the most cost-effective locations in which to hold an event. They come with the amenities required for producing events, including tables, chairs, china, linens, service staff, waste disposal, and rest rooms. Certain hotels are classified as convention hotels and are best suited to corporate events. Convention hotels may provide staging, hanging/rigging facilities, and large electrical power sources **(electrical disconnects)** for big stage shows or audiovisual presentations. Other hotels specialize in weddings and other life-cycle events and may have silver serving pieces and custom table skirting or offer **kosher** or other ethnic or cultural catering specialties.

In negotiating with hotels, it is important to remember that they receive 90 percent of their revenue from room nights, so events with room nights have priority over catering events. Meetings, conferences, and conventions at hotels are generally contracted through the sales staff, and events are handled by the convention services staff. The catering sales department handles stand-alone events with no appreciable number of room nights. Some hotels charge for using electrical power, water, storage, and other services. Make sure to get a list of all potential charges and be certain your contract states that no charges will be incurred that are not on that list. Also, remember that almost all charges are negotiable *before* the contract is signed and none are negotiable afterward.

Country clubs specialize in private life-cycle events. Having all the amenities for these events, they are easy to work in and are cost-effective. It used to be standard policy that only members could hold an event at a private country club. These days many clubs are opening their doors to nonmember events, both private and corporate. Putting on corporate events in a club may require bringing in audiovisual and/or production-staging companies as these production elements will not be found on site as they would in a hotel or conference center. When a private club is used for a corporate event, the image and reputation of the club must be compatible with the corporate image, goals, and objectives.

Convention centers and conference centers are specialty venues that also provide event space and services. Events at these sites are usually held in conjunction with a corporate or association meeting, conference, or convention. Most will accommodate stand-alone events if the conference or convention calendar allows. They may or may not provide the complete array of event services of a hotel or country club. Most convention centers are owned by a city, a county, or another public entity. They charge per square foot for exhibition space, and all other uses, services, and amenities are billed from a published price list.

Conference centers offer a Complete Meeting Package (CMP) that includes rooms, a standard menu of food and beverage, all standard audiovisual services, and meeting spaces with amenities such as **ergonomic seating.** Special events may or may not be included in the CMP. A typical CMP package is shown in *Idea Portfolio:* CMP Pricing.

## NONSTANDARD VENUES

Restaurants and nightclubs are frequently used for life-cycle and corporate events such as small wedding receptions, corporate awards presentations, and holiday parties. It is important to remember that such sites are most comfortable doing what they do daily and that asking them for services, room setups, or service styles different from what they normally provide can present a challenge to them. Changing tables and chairs can be next to impossible if they

Idea Portfolio

## CMP PRICING (TYPICAL)

Garrett Creek Ranch Conference Center

***PRICING (2004)***

**Our Complete Meeting Package**

Single occupancy: $220 per night per person
Double occupancy: $190 per night per person
Executive suite: $115 per night
Adjoining sitting room: $85 per night

**Included**

Overnight guest room
Continuous beverage service with AM and PM snacks
Meeting room, notepads, pens
Basic audiovisual equipment
Breakfast, lunch, and dinner
On-premise recreational activities
Professional conference planning

**Not Included**

Transportation to and from ranch *(arrangements can be made)*
Special decorations, entertainment, special menu selections
Alcoholic beverages
Special audiovisual needs
State and local taxes
Use of challenge (ropes) course

lack storage space. In considering a restaurant or club for an event, look at what it does best and design the event around that.

Religious institutions and community buildings frequently are used for private life-cycle events and social affairs for families, associations, and groups. They generally have limited equipment, services, and staff available for events. Churches, synagogues, temples, and mosques can come with restrictions for both sanctified and nonsanctified areas, such as synagogues that require kosher catering and prohibit certain activities on the Sabbath.

Community centers also may have restrictive use policies and, like religious buildings, may have limited custodial staff for setup, dismantle, and general housekeeping services throughout the event. Amenities such as tables, chairs, linens, and staging will be available, but with limited options. Many public museums, parks, garden centers, ranches, amusement parks, and sports and festival venues have special event departments or were designed with special events in mind. The amenities provided and the costs and service structure vary widely, but the event professional has a wide range of nonstandard venues to consider.

The growth in special events has been accompanied by the growth of commercially viable **stand-alone venues.** These are buildings or rooms that have been designed and equipped specifically to be rented out for and accommodate special events. They exist in desanctified churches, strip shopping centers, and freestanding warehouses or buildings erected for this purpose. They may provide exclusive catering or allow outside caterers. Some are built and decorated around themes, and some are neutral spaces. Some offer full-service event production, and some are rented out as empty halls. Each stand-alone event venue has its own character, policies, and procedures. As with restaurants, in considering a stand-alone venue for the first time, the best practice is to concentrate on what it does best. If it specializes in serving barbeque buffets, do not expect it to supply a four-course seated dinner equally well.

**Residential sites** commonly are used for small parties and occasional weddings or wedding receptions within the family. However, when used for large social affairs or corporate events such as a large reception or a holiday party, they can be challenging and costly. An event in an occupied house or yard poses special challenges for the professional decorator because of the lack of available services combined with the intrusion into people's daily lives.

Sometimes events are held at a particularly large estate through the corporate or political connections of the client with the owner. Some residences are volunteered by the owner for social, religious, or political causes or for the wedding or another life-cycle event of a relative or close friend. A residence can become a minefield of problems and relationships for event designers as

Idea Portfolio

## THE RANCH THAT ISN'T A RANCH

An example of a stand-alone event venue is Eddie Deen's Ranch in downtown Dallas. This facility has two rooms: one that can accommodate up to 350 and one for up to 1,500 people. The smaller room is an Old West saloon with rustic wooden paneling and western signage and décor. The larger one is decorated as an old-time western town. Both rooms come with a built-in stage, sound system and multiple table setups, linen, and food service options.

Located adjacent to the Dallas Convention Center in a renovated building that used to house an apparel manufacturer, this venue, like most stand-alone sites, was designed for a specific purpose. It exists to service the convention center business, providing the "western experience" that many conventioneers expect in Dallas.

Idea Portfolio

## A WEDDING AT HOME

The mother of the bride asked me to look over their backyard and discuss helping her with her daughter's wedding reception at home. She was a woman of taste and some social standing and was anticipating a very nice affair for 300 to 350 guests in a tent. We did a preliminary site inspection, at the end of which she confided that one of the reasons they were having the reception at home was to save money. I told her that there were a lot of good reasons to have the reception at home: It was personally meaningful for the bride, it was comfortable for the family, the event could be customized, and it would be much more intimate than a hotel. However, it would be two to three times more expensive than having it at a hotel or country club. She told me that I was wrong because they could save so much money on beverages.

We did not do the wedding reception, and the incident drifted from my memory. Several years later I was helping an associate give a presentation to the local garden club. Afterward, a charming lady approached me and reminded me of that incident; she was the mother of the bride. She said she had wanted to tell me that I was right; there were many good reasons to have a wedding at home. It had been lovely. She also wanted to tell me that her husband estimated that it would be another five years before their personal finances would recover from the wedding expenses!

Nonstandard venues can be the most expensive sites on which to hold an event. If your clients are considering a nonstandard venue, make sure they carefully balance the advantages of the venue with their available resources to assure an acceptable **ROI (return on investment).**

they attempt to execute essentially a commercial endeavor at somebody's house.

*Unique venues* are venues that were not designed for and cannot easily accommodate special events. Streets, parks, parking lots, and other **urban spaces** are common venues for fairs and festivals but become uniquely nonstandard venues for corporate or private events. The political, legal, operational, and environmental challenges of doing an event in the street or in another public space add to the usual event challenges. The corporate, social, or wedding planner will face a whole portfolio of problems not encountered in a hotel or country club.

Pastures, fields, barns, and other **rural venues** provide even more challenges to an event designer. They may not have the ordinances, licensing, and other governmental restrictions that have to be dealt with in urban event spaces. However, they may lack the amenities of urban civilization, such as water, sewers, paved roads, and a department of public safety. An on-duty ambulance with a team of paramedics is a standard requirement for a large event

Idea Portfolio

## AAA TAKES TO THE STREETS

At the annual presentation of the American Automobile Association's Five Diamond Awards, the Adolphus Hotel wanted to do something different for the welcoming reception. The following night the awards banquet would be held in the baroque splendor of the turn-of-the-century ballroom. It was decided to close an adjoining street and throw a western hoedown reception featuring the music of the Light Crust Doughboys, southwestern cuisine, and cowboy hats and bandannas for everyone. This required a street closing permit, rapid setup and dismantle to avoid causing traffic jams, and coordination with the police department for traffic and security coordination. For the hotel, this became an off-site catering job; for the decorators, it was as if we were working in a field or pasture, except we could not stake the decorations down; and for the entertainment, it was as if they were playing at a county fair. For the guests, it was indeed like being at a western country fair, but surrounded by high-rise buildings midway between the Adolphus and Neiman Marcus, a real Texas experience.

When looking to create a unique experience, you need to think creatively. A unique venue may be right there on the street in front of you.

in a pasture. Other challenges include fire ants, wild and domestic animal life, and poisonous foliage.

Museums, concert halls, and historical sites have a primary function that is inherently at odds with event production. When one is doing a wedding or corporate reception at a public museum, certain areas will be gallery spaces where no food or drink may be taken, and **installation and dismantle (I&D)** may be limited to times when the museum is closed to the public. The curators may place restrictions on where and what decorations may be used. However many of these institutions also obtain needed funding by renting out as an event venue. As a result, there are many facilities that have a special event director and differing event services available. As difficult as it may be to produce an event in a museum or another artistic or historic space, the cultural environment can enhance the experience and help achieve the goals and objectives of the event.

## TENTS

There are many tenting options available (see Figure 3-1), although the costs vary widely depending on proximity to the tenting companies and geographical practices and pricing. **Pole tents** or **guy tents** consist of a canvas held up by poles and stretched between ropes staked to the ground. This is what you probably think of when you think of tents, although the canvas is actually

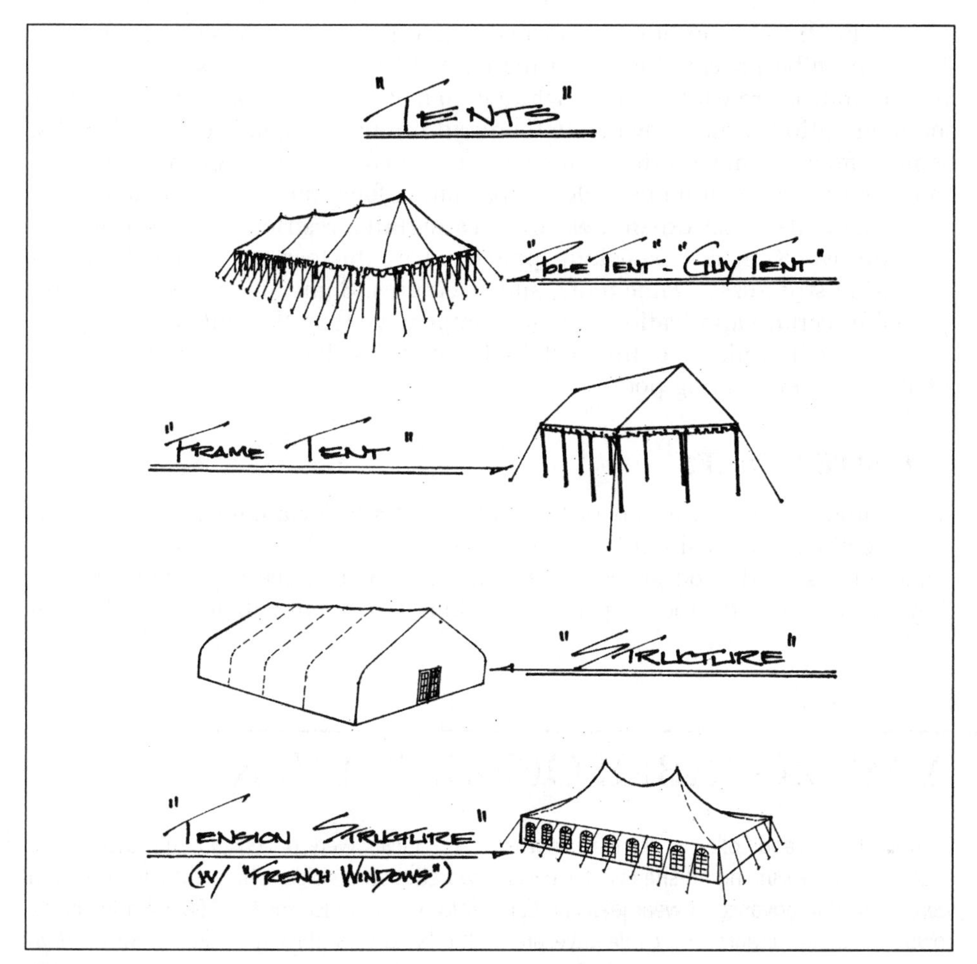


**Figure 3-1**

flame-retardant, reinforced vinyl these days. The other standard type of tent is a **frame tent,** called a **marquee** in the United Kingdom. On a frame tent the vinyl top is stretched over a metal frame, which is staked to the ground in a few places. **Structures** are very large frame tents that use I-beams as support frames. Like frame tents they do not have poles obstructing the interior. **Tension structures** are closely related to and look like pole tents but take advantage of modern fiber technology and computer aided designs.

The most common tops and sides available in rental tents and structures are white. Normal white vinyl tops and sidewalls are translucent and allow a certain amount of sunlight to come into the interior tent environment. Some companies have "blackout white" tops and sidewalls that are opaque white, keeping excessive light from the interior. This allows greater control of the interior lighting for audiovisual or decorative purposes. However, it requires that lighting be provided even during daylight hours. Clear walls are a common option, as are walls that are white with clear "French" windows. Another common option, usually available for an additional charge, is clear sidewalls. Some companies have solid color or white and color striped tops for their guy tents, and for enough money, clear tops can be fabricated for frame tents.

Using tents in an urban area involves permits, restrictions, and fire marshal approval. Generally speaking, pole tents are the least expensive, followed by tension structures, frame tents, and structures. Some amenities that are required for certain applications are more expensive than the tent, such as flooring. A typically unique tenting installation may involve decking and installing a tent over a swimming pool.

## OFF-SITE VENUES

Any venue that is not a part of the authorized site for a conference, convention, meeting, or exposition is an off-site venue. It can be another hotel, a dude ranch, or a secluded ocean beach. The thing they all have in common is that they require some degree of special attention. If an event is held at another ho-

Idea Portfolio

### A MEMORABLE OFF-SITE EVENT

Garrett Schwabb and Colleen Rickenbacher produced an award-winning off-site event. Guests were notified in advance to wear jeans and/or cowboy clothing suitable for a cattle drive, and upon their arrival they were given denim jackets to wear that evening. As they arrived at the sidewalk pickup area outside the hotel, there was a Hummer stretch limousine waiting. As they realized that they would not all fit in the Hummer, an announcement was heard: "Ladies and gentlemen, start your engines!"

Fifty Harley motorcycles, led by four motorcycle policemen, came around the corner and pulled up to the sidewalk to pick up the guests. Waivers were signed, and guests hopped on behind the members of a local Harley motorcycle club. People who were uncomfortable riding on a bike were delivered in the Hummer limo.

Guests were driven through town to the warehouse district, where they were driven into a warehouse for the 1960s Harley party. The band was playing "Ticket to Ride," *Born to Be Wild* was showing on a large movie screen, and the buffets and bars featured 1960s menus. During the evening guests could get fake tattoos and piercing or have souvenir photos taken while sitting on Harley-Davidson bikes. The centerpieces were made from Harley parts. The sponsors' names were on custom place mats, and the favors were Harley-Davidson-theme beanie babies and T-shirts.

This event would not have been nearly as effective in a hotel as it was in a warehouse, and motorcycles probably could not have been allowed to carry guests into the ballroom.

**MONROE'S RULE FOR OFF-SITE EVENTS**

The further off-site and the more unique a site is and the less commonly used for and prepared to service events a site is, the more expensive it is to produce an event there.

tel that is similar or identical to the host hotel, it still will require separate negotiation and transportation. If it is at a unique venue not designed for events, it may be necessary to build a ceiling and walls (a tent) and provide flooring or basic infrastructure such as electricity, toilets, water, and trash removal.

Off-site events are popular because they provide a break in the routine of a conference, which can become stultifying and lead to poor attendance at seminars and early departures. These events allow a vendor to focus on a specific demographic or customer list by controlling the invitation list. They are popular because they are fun for both guest and host.

Off-site events are not easy or inexpensive to design and produce, but they will always be in high demand and be highly demanding of the event designer and decorator.

# SITE SELECTION GUIDELINES

**Site selection** needs to be done early both because it will define the design and because there will be limited sites available. Even the largest urban areas have limited event sites, and if a date has been selected, options will be restricted further. The best practice for **site inspection** for the designer/decorator is to generate a **site inspection checklist** for each event. This begins with determining what is required for the event.

The following physical, budgetary, and aesthetic requirements should be considered and discussed by the key stakeholders in advance of the site inspection and should serve as a guide to generate a site inspection checklist.

## PHYSICAL REQUIREMENTS

The number of people who will attend and what they will be doing will determine the size of venue that an event requires. A stand-up cocktail reception requires less space than does a formal dinner-dance with a full orchestra and a dance floor. Associated activities such as auctions, displays, or entertainment will require additional space.

Trying to fit too many people into too small a space can result in uncomfortably close seating, poor service (because the service staff cannot get through the crowd), or an unexpected end to the event if the **fire marshal** shows up and closes the event down.

> **Fire Marshal:** the standard designation for a safety control officer, usually operating under the auspices of the local fire department. The fire marshal is the legal enforcement officer of public safety ordinances, which local ordinances are usually based on and which refer to the **National Fire Protection Association (NFPA) codes.**

When faced with too small a space for the event and no alternative location, seek creative ways to solve the problem. Some solutions include tenting a patio or terrace, tenting the loading dock area, expanding into (and decorating) an adjacent garage or cutting down the required internal space by hiring a disc jockey (DJ) or a small combo instead of a full orchestra. Creative solutions can make an event work in a space otherwise too small, but when looking for these solutions, work with the fire marshal and/or safety officer of the venue. *Do not risk the safety of the participants in trying to solve space problems; it is better to cancel the event.*

Ending up with much more space than the event requires can have a negative impact by allowing too much space between the guests, creating the appearance of poor attendance or requiring unnecessary resources. If networking or celebration is part of the event, people will relate best when forced to be close together to some degree.

More space than is necessary for the number of guests is an easier problem to deal with but can require additional resources. Simple solutions include spacing the tables a bit farther apart than usual. Mixing different size tables and using a minimum of chairs at each one can help fill up the room. Wider aisles and perimeter space can help, and if the budget can support it, additional perimeter décor moved in from the walls combined with well-controlled area lighting will solve the problem of having too much room.

Creative solutions can turn this problem into an asset. One idea is to move the prefunction reception into the ballroom from the foyer. Adding some trees, fencing, street lamps, a gate unit, or other theme décor to divide the room can have the advantage of adding décor that will be seen for the entire event, and the ballroom décor (and possibly music) can be used throughout the reception as well. The best solution, of course, is to find just the right size space for the event.

> **RULE OF THUMB FOR SPACING BETWEEN TABLES**
>
> Twelve inches is the minimum distance required from chair back to chair back for people (or servers) to pass comfortably between them. There must be one aisle for every four rows of tables so that servers do not have to go more than two tables deep. People average 24 inches when sitting in a chair at a table, so 12 inches between chairs equals 5 feet between tables. Many banquet setup crews use a special 5-foot spacing stick to place tables.

Idea Portfolio

## TAKEN FOR A SLEIGH RIDE

During the preselection site inspection of the thirty-fifth-floor high-rise restaurant and club, careful measurements were made of the remote loading dock, the half mile of hallways, and both freight elevators. This was necessary to make sure the sleigh for the photo shoot at the corporate holiday party would fit.

Upon arrival, the sleigh was hauled up to the thirty-fifth-floor kitchen, where it was discovered that it would fit nicely into the kitchen but would not fit through the doors leading into the rest of the club. The sleigh had to be hauled back down to the loading dock and another one procured that could be dismantled to fit through the doorway.

The photo shoot was very popular that evening but was not very profitable because of the additional costs incurred. This expense could have been avoided with a more careful and complete site inspection.

Additional physical elements need to be determined when one is doing a site inspection. The path from the loading dock to the venue must allow access for the equipment and decor. Cars, wagons, and large pieces of scenery must be able to be unloaded at the dock, and the ingress must be wide enough, straight enough, and high enough to allow passage into the room.

Often the structural capacity of the ceiling beams comes into play in hanging scenery, lighting, or speakers. The structural capacity of the floor is occasionally a factor, for example, if one wants to use a 15,000-gallon water effect such as a waterfall and a pond with live fish. One gallon of water weighs 8.1 pounds; 15,000 gallons weighs 61 tons.

**Sightlines** are the direct lines of sight from the guests' physical point of view to the featured object, stage, or video screen. They are determined and depicted as lines on a floor plan or vertical section. **Projection throw** is the distance between a screen and a projector and all the clear space needed between them. Any physical element that may interfere with sightlines or projection throw is important, such as chandeliers, columns, and centerpieces that are too high (see Figures 3-2 and 3-3).

Other, less visible physical elements that may be important to a specific event are the sources of power, water, and drainage; security; transportation; parking; and satellite and Internet issues.

Electrical power requirements vary widely depending on the stage show and/or audiovisual components of an event. Lighting is currently the largest power draw for a staged event. A moderate-size show that is part of an event in conjunction with a conference or convention can easily require a *600-amp 120/240-volt three-phase service,* which is equivalent to *200,000 watts* (see Appendix 6, *Electrical Formula*). Most venues charge for the use of power and have limited power at any specific location. Power requirements in excess of

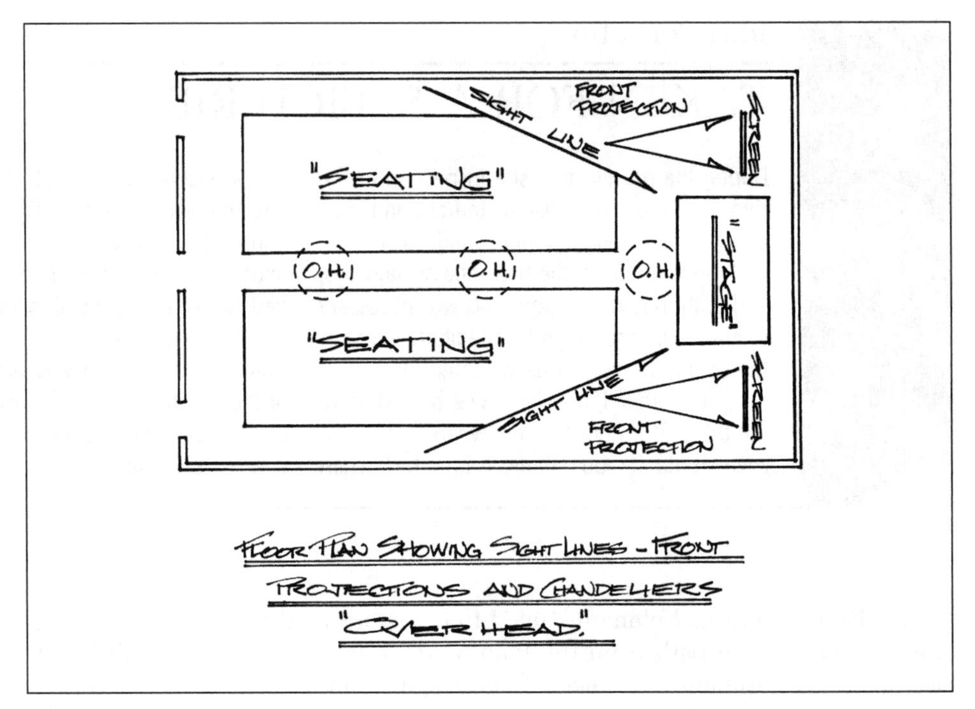


**Figure 3-2**

what is available at the site will require a generator or another temporary power source.

Water sources are necessary if there will be water effects such as fountains or waterfalls. Whatever water is brought into a venue also must be removed. Major laser shows use water-cooled lasers that require both a reliable water

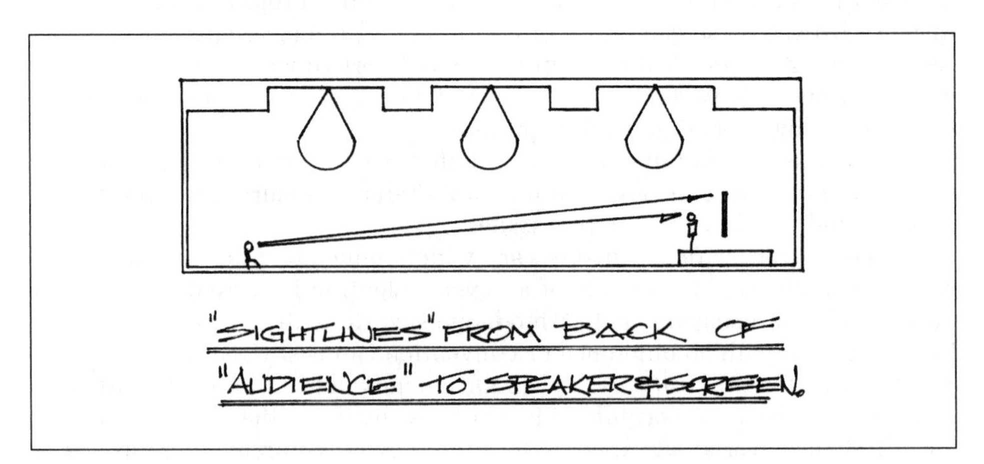


**Figure 3-3**

source and a continuous drainage system. Many types of floral arrangements that are popular for events, such as tall vases, certain oriental styles, and very large arrangements, are most easily assembled on site. This requires both water and work space reasonably close to the event space.

Security, transportation, parking, and satellite or Internet connection issues are all event-specific issues that can present special challenges or even keep a venue from qualifying for a given event. Developing relationships with qualified experts in each of these areas is one of the requirements for successful event design and decoration.

## BUDGETARY REQUIREMENTS

Venue costs can be direct or indirect. **Direct costs** are those paid directly to the venue, and **indirect costs** are those paid to another supplier but required by the venue or by a governing entity. Direct costs include space rental, food and beverage, and rental and service charges. Examples of indirect costs are requiring protective covering over a limestone floor and requiring the use of the in-house rigging or audiovisual company. Some municipalities require **special use permits** or the presence of a fire marshal if, for example, a smoke machine is being used.

These costs vary greatly between different types of venues such as a hotel versus a convention center and are relatively similar between similar venues. However, do not assume that because there was no charge for tables, chairs, or staging at one hotel, there will not be a charge at the next. Unexpected direct costs that might be incurred could be for the use of electrical power, water, or cleanup. It is not unusual for a venue to charge extra for cleanup of confetti or for removal of balloons or other decorations left on the ceiling. Some venues prohibit the use of these elements. This can become a major problem if the client and/or designer do not find out about restrictions until they are in the middle of the installation. No contract should be signed before one reads the restrictions and regulations regarding the use of the venue. Each cost should be negotiated and agreed on in writing, with a clause in the contract stating that all costs required by the venue be listed in the agreement.

It is not unusual for a venue to have preferred or exclusive agreements with audiovisual, rigging, or other suppliers. These exclusive agreements are ostensibly to assure a certain quality of service and safety and may indeed have that effect. However, there is almost certainly a percentage paid back to the hotel for the exclusive contract. This may raise the costs for these services above local market rates. Sometimes a contract can be "bought off" to allow a client to use his or her preferred vendor. It is important to remember that in principle, all costs are negotiable *before* the contract is signed.

Some venues may be under union contract. This may entail direct costs reflecting four-hour minimum calls and mandatory overtime rates. It also may require the use of unionized vendors, which may affect the cost of the service.

### AESTHETIC REQUIREMENTS

It is critical that the venue provide the appropriate look, feel, and image for the event. If the demographics of the attendees and the goals and objectives have been determined, as was discussed in previous chapters, the appropriate **ambience** (a French term used to describe the style, mood, and feel of an event) should be obvious.

Business receptions should reflect the corporate image the client wants to project. A **product rollout** (event jargon for the introduction of a product to the public) would require a different environment than would a team-building weekend. Social events need to be held at venues where the stakeholders will be comfortable. A fraternity party may work well in an empty warehouse in an urban industrial area, but that is an unlikely place for a wedding reception.

Intimate events that encourage close one-on-one conversations may take advantage of a venue with lots of small connecting rooms, but a major corporate announcement may need to be staged in a large single ballroom or even in a field. When Les Alberthal, then CEO of EDS, announced the company's breakaway from General Motors to the employees, he used a giant **Jumbotron** video screen with a major sound system in a circular lawn in the middle of the EDS corporate campus in Plano, Texas. This was an appropriately monumental presentation for a monumental announcement.

Many social or life-cycle events are held at a place reflecting the tastes or interests of the honoree. A bar mitzvah or bat mitzvah celebration may be held at a zoo for a child who loves animals, or a baseball fanatic may choose the local ballpark for his or her birthday celebration. There are many places that may serve for a wedding, depending on the family. Traditionally, the ceremony takes place in a house of worship, with the reception also held there, or at a local hotel or country club. It would be an unusual wedding that was held on an ice rink, in the stockyards, or underwater. (Of course, if one is a hockey player or the couple are cowboy and cowgirl or divers, one of these venues may be considered appropriate these days.)

## SITE RESEARCH

An **event-specific checklist** will help you match your requirements to the venue that can best accommodate them. During the design process other needs may arise that may require revisiting the site. The farther away the venue is from the designer, the more comprehensive the original site inspection checklist should be (see Appendix 5, *Special Event Site Inspection Checklist*). *When going on a site inspection, always take a checklist, a pad and pencil, a tape measure, and a camera.*

The checklist should be prepared in advance and should reflect everything that is known about the event so far, including any preliminary or tentative design concepts. A pad and pencil are necessary for taking notes and recording dimensions. Even if the event designer takes notes on his or her **PDA (personal digital assistant),** a pad will be necessary for sketching dimensions. The need for a tape measure is self-evident, but it should have a three-quarter-inch or 1-inch blade so that it will be stiff enough to run vertically for ceiling and other vertical measurements. For large spaces either the rolling measurement device that landscapers and tent installers use or a laser measurement device is helpful. A camera is most useful if it is digital, as it can be used immediately upon returning to the studio and images can be both printed and emailed as required.

# CONDUCTING THE SITE INSPECTION

There are two different conditions under which the designer will find himself or herself conducting a site inspection. The designer may be asked to accompany the client on a preselection inspection to determine which facility best meets the needs of the event, or the designer may be given a place, date, and theme in advance and then have to conduct a postselection inspection to determine which design concepts and decorations will work within the space selected. (Additionally, one **postevent inspection** should be scheduled to confirm the return of the site to its original condition.) *If distance, budget, or time considerations limit inspections to one preevent visit, that inspection must be comprehensive.*

## PRESELECTION SITE INSPECTION

In the best-case scenario, the decision makers and the event designer conduct the preselection site inspection jointly. Inspections of several properties may be required, and it can be cost- or time-prohibitive to involve every

**SERVICE STYLE AND INSTITUTIONAL PERSONALITY**

The questions that can determine this are as follows:

How was I greeted upon arrival?
What was my impression of the people who greeted me?
Is the driveway/portico clean?
How do the service personnel address me?
Is the foyer clean and organized?
How clean are the hallways?
How clean are the back hallways and staff-only areas?
How clean and organized is the dock area?
How does the staff act and interact in the back hallways?

stakeholder. Sometimes the designer or decorator will not be hired to accompany the client on a preselection site inspection. When a designer-client relationship is comfortable enough, the designer can prepare a preselection site inspection checklist for the client to take along (see Appendix 5, *Special Event Site Inspection Checklist*).

Different types of venues require attention to different details. Hotels, convention centers, and country clubs require attention to physical, aesthetic, and budgetary considerations, as was discussed earlier. Off-site and unusual venues require particular attention to infrastructure details that may be assumed to exist at standard event venues.

**MINIMAL PRESITE SELECTION INSPECTION GUIDELINES**

1. Delivery and access routes to site
2. Physical size and characteristics of site
3. Potential layouts and floor plans for site
4. Where to put band, buffet, auction, speaker, and other major elements
    - Sightlines, traffic patterns, audio
    - Move-in and access
    - Security
    - Power, lighting, Internet, water
5. Services available from venue
    - Electrical, lighting, audiovisual
    - Decorations
    - Entertainment
6. Catering styles, menus, and options
    - Styles of full-service seated dinners
    - Buffets and food stations
    - In-house and off-site
    - Themes
7. Infrastructure—available options
    - Tables, chairs, linens
    - China, silver, crystal
    - Staging, lights, sound, production
8. Staffing
    - Catering and banquet staff
    - Engineering
    - Busing and housekeeping
    - Reception, security, support
9. Restrictions
    - Physical—what is not allowed
    - Advertising and media
    - Vendors
    - Entertainment and activities
    - Food and beverage (F&B)

## POSTSELECTION SITE INSPECTIONS

As was mentioned in the previous section, the event designer or decorator may not be called in until after the event site has been selected. A professional designer will optimize the situation, understanding that the venue and its restrictions and characteristics will determine the design and decorations options.

Once the site has been selected, an inspection with the primary decision maker is desirable, but limiting the number of stakeholders involved at this time allows the designer to focus on the site. It is helpful if a representative from the venue is available who can answer questions and access engineering, the chef, and the general manager to get answers to questions that may arise.

Sometime during the site inspection process the event designer should plan on spending time alone in the venue to focus on design (focus, space, and flow) and aesthetic elements (line, color, composition, and texture), as was discussed in Chapter 1, *Principles of Design.*

Look at the space to determine if there is a natural focus, a place the eye travels to when one enters the room or environment. What is the first thing seen, opposite the entrance, upon walking into the room? Perhaps there is a long wall where a stage can be centered. If there is a natural focus, can it be used, or will attention have to be redirected to another focus that will be created for the event? Is there an element that will distract from the focus, such as a large window or, in an outdoor venue, a highway in the background?

How does the space feel? Is it big, maybe monumental, or does it have a cozy feel? Is it balanced, or is it long and narrow? Is the ceiling height appropriate for the size of the room, or does it feel too low? Does it feel right for the event? High ceilings and big rooms require a "big" design treatment, and small props, no matter how clever, may look out of scale or be lost in the grandeur of the space. Large rooms with low ceilings can sometimes be broken up aesthetically into many cozy sections through the use of draping, lights, and props or plants. Some spaces have elements such as chandeliers or mirrors that affect the space, focus, and flow even though they are not physical barriers.

Is the space open and unobstructed allowing a flexibly designed flow for the event? Or are there elements that require attention in designing the flow, such as a natural (or only) entrance, a built-in stage, or bars? The locations of the kitchen (for serving), the rest rooms and coat check, registration/check-in areas, valet parking, elevators, loading dock, and the electrical disconnect all may affect the flow of the event.

**MONROE'S LAW OF VENUE AND DESIGN**

The aesthetics and physical aspects of a venue and the event that takes place within the venue are totally interconnected, with one element influencing and inspiring the other.

The inherent aesthetics of the venue need to be considered, especially in regard to the way they may impact the design aesthetics of the event. Many modern meeting rooms, ballrooms, and exhibit spaces have been designed in neutral tones with soft colors, texture, and fabrics specifically to provide a neutral palette for the meeting planner and event manager to work with. Some older venues and some unique venues that were not designed with events as their primary function provide aesthetic challenges.

There may be a vertical line to the room created or emphasized by physical elements such as columns or pilasters, or if it is a symphony hall lobby or modern art museum, there may be a diagonal line in the architecture. Generally, if the space has a natural line, you will notice it as soon as you enter the room. You will find your attention drawn immediately to it or to the area.

Idea Portfolio

## DEALING WITH DIFFERENT AESTHETIC CHALLENGES

A hotel where we have done many events used to feature its Regency Ballroom entirely in red velvety wall covering, red ceiling and carpet with gold accents on the pilasters and capitals. You could not design an event in that room without considering the color. You could design something compatible with that red, or you could choose to pretend that it wasn't there, but as a designer you could not ignore it. Local clients still refer to it as the red room even though it has been beige for a decade.

The gallery of an art museum that had in it a 45-foot-tall Claes Oldenburg piece called "The Stake Hitch" used to be a very popular event space. The "Stake Hitch" is a diagonal rope 30 inches in diameter coiled around a giant stake on the floor and running diagonally to the ceiling. You could do a corporate reception, a wedding, or a bar mitzvah in that space, but as the designer, you could not ignore the stake hitch. Your options when facing a dramatic permanent aesthetic element like that are to incorporate the element into the design by reinforcing the line, design something in counterpoint to the line that creates aesthetic tension, or draw attention away from the element with an equally strong dramatic piece.

We once hung flowering vine in compatible line to the "Hitch." We once stretched blue lamé fabric across the space in counterpoint to it. One time I built a 16-foot-tall floral arrangement directly in front of it, and it became the background for a dramatic floral centerpiece at a wedding reception.

I have had several opportunities to experience the architecture of I. M. Pei up close and personal. Doing events within his very distinctive architecture always is a study in line. His line is so distinctive that rather than try to reinforce or counterpoint it, I use geometric shapes to be seen against it. He uses concrete, natural textures, and materials that create monumental neutral backgrounds. I use balls, squares, and triangles in bright, warm colors.

Dealing with the idiosycratic aesthetics of certain venues can challenge the designer to create new and unique decorations that achieve a very high level of art and effectiveness.

This architectural element will be strong enough that it will have to be incorporated into the design of the décor for the event, requiring designing to reinforce that line or in counterpoint with it.

Frequently a temporary stage will be built in a venue with a front lighting truss and a fabric backdrop, and it will look out of place, as though someone had dropped it into the room. When designed correctly, it will be fit into the existing space so well that it will appear to be a permanent part of the architecture.

The color decisions for an event need to be made within the context of the existing colors of the venue. As in line and composition, some people have a natural talent for color. For the rest of us, it is necessary to understand the basic principles of contrasting and complimentary colors discussed in Chapter 1. The color decisions made by the event designer are intended to move the message and achieve the goals for the event. A minor but important part of site selection is considering corporate colors and/or logos and how they work with the existing colors of the venue. Every event designer should own a **PMS color swatch book** (Pantone Matching System) for the purpose of communicating colors between designer, client, and vendors.

Composition follows naturally from consideration of these elements at the site. The designer will determine how best to direct the focus, control the flow, and reinforce or design in counterpoint to the existing spatial elements through the use of composition. Texture will come into play as a design element, and the designer must determine whether it is necessary to "soften" the feel of the room or add some hard-edged elements to reinforce the message and objectives of the event. Texture plays with color in the designer's mind, which means that they work together to achieve the same goals.

## FINISHING TOUCHES

In this chapter we have learned about the different types of venues and how to establish guidelines for effective site selection. We also have learned some of the pros and cons of various types of venues and ways to determine those pros and cons for a specific event. We have considered preselection and post-selection criteria and have learned how to create a site inspection checklist for an event.

## DESIGN VOCABULARY

Terms appear below in the order in which they first occur in this chapter.

Venue
Site
Standard venues
Nonstandard venues
ICW (in conjunction with)
On-site event

Off-site event
Host site
Unique venue
Stand-alone site
Electrical disconnect
Kosher
Ergonomic seating
Stand-alone venue
Residential sites
ROI (return on investment)
Urban spaces
Rural venues
Installation and dismantle (I&D)
Pole tents
Guy tents
Frame tents
Marquees
Structures
Tension structures
Site selection
Site inspection
Site inspection checklist
Fire marshal
National Fire Protection Association (NFPA) codes
Sightlines
Projection throw
Direct costs
Indirect costs
Special use permits
Ambience
Product rollout
Jumbotron
Event-specific checklist
PDA (personal digital assistant)
Postevent inspection
PMS color swatch book

## STUDIO WORK

1. A well-known firm is planning a product rollout for a new brand of inkjet cartridge. The firm is known for its expertise in consumer appliances but needs to establish itself as a brand for high-tech supplies. The rollout is to be combined with a celebration of the company's hundredth anniversary. Write the guidelines for a site selection checklist for the proposed event.
2. List the ways in which an off-site event may increase the costs of a reception for 250 guests.
3. Pick an actual event venue and write a critique of its pros and cons as an event site.
4. In 200 words or less, discuss how the goals and objectives of an event will affect the site selection for that event.
5. Create a site inspection checklist for the event described in item 1.

## RECOMMENDED READINGS AND RESEARCH SITES

Connell, Barbara, ed., *Professional Meeting Management, 4th ed.,* Professional Convention Management Association Education Foundation, 2002.

Goldblatt, Joe, *Special Events: Event Leadership for a New World,* John Wiley & Sons, 2004.

Krug, Susan, ed., *The Convention Industry Council Manual, 7th ed.,* Convention Industry Council, 2002.

BizBash—a regular e-mail event newsletter containing a lot of regional venue information; originally based and centered in New York

City; continues to expand and is now in Florida and Toronto
http://bizbash.com

*Event Solutions* magazine—one of the two top national trade publications for the event industry; contains much information on venues nationwide; Event Publishing LLC
http://www.event-solutions.com

Google Directory—Event Planning and Production—Venue Locating Services
http://directory.google.com/Top/Business/Business_Services/Event_Planning_and_Production/Venue_Locating_Services/

Open Directory Project—Top: Business: Business Services: Event Planning and Production: Venue Locating Services
http://dmoz.org/Business/Business_Services/Event_Planning_and_Production/Venue_Locating_Services/

Special Events Magazine—the original national trade publication for the event industry; contains much information on venues nationwide; Primedia Business Magazines and Media
http://specialevents.com

# Chapter 4

# RESOURCES

*It is not so much the depth of our knowledge as the breadth. We do not need to be experts in every area, but we need to know a little bit about a lot of areas.*
**—William H. Just, CAE, CMP**

## IN THIS CHAPTER

You will learn that the design of any project is achieved through the use of four classes of resources: financial, human, knowledge, and technical. In this chapter you will discover how to manage these resources.

**Financial Resources**

- Types and Sources
- Budgeting and Cash Flow

**Human Resources and Stakeholders**

- Client
- Staff
- Suppliers and Associates
- Strategic Partners
- Managing Professional Relationships

**Knowledge and Education**

- Liberal Arts and Industry
- Formal and Experience
- Library and References

**Technical and Physical Resources**

- Technology
- Space
- Time
- Tools and Equipment

Bill Just is a noted association manager and Convention Industry Council (CIC) Hall of Leaders inductee and one of the founders of the Certified Meeting Professional (CMP) designation. In the quote that starts this chapter he

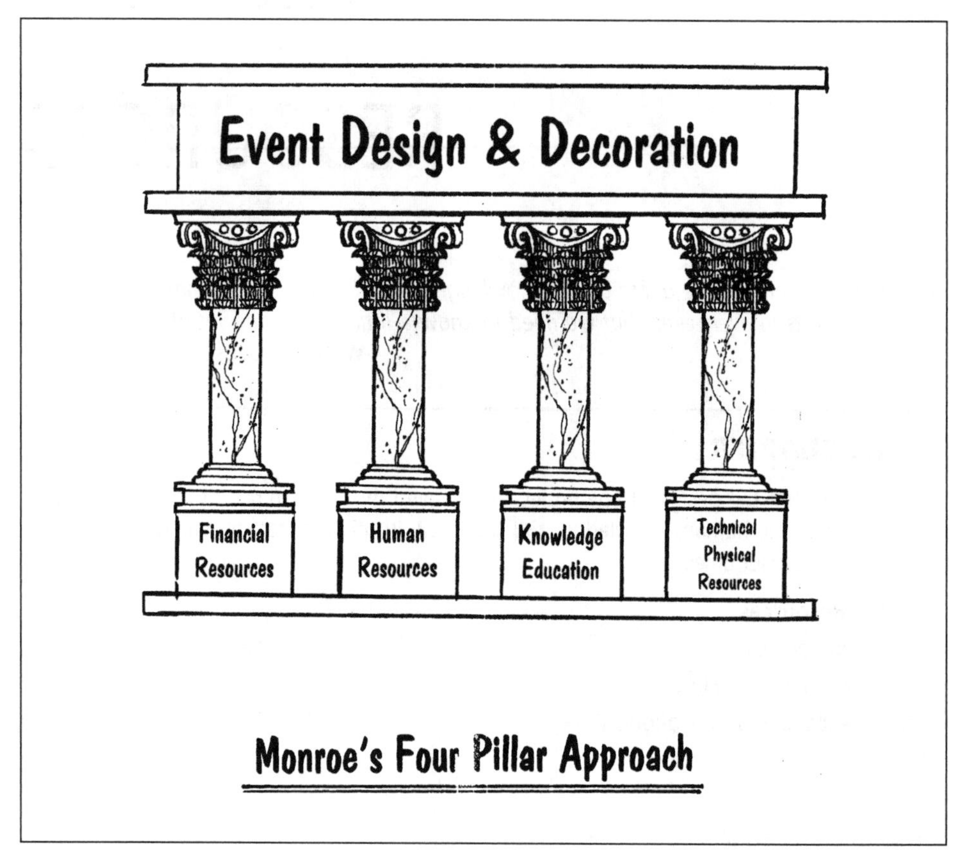


**Figure 4-1**

makes a succinct statement about one of the four basic resources available to the event designer or decorator. As a meeting planner with decades of experience, he figured out what he had to know to function effectively. As event designers and decorators, we need to figure out what resources we have, what resources we need, and how to manage them (as seen in Figure 4-1, which should be compared with Figure 1-5).

An event design is inherently limited to the resources available for that event, and *event resources are always in short supply.* Event design will translate at some point into real physical elements that will require financial, human, knowledge, and technical resources to produce. Every event designer wants to produce the best, most effective event with the finest decorations possible. This means that no matter what the budget is or how extensive the resources are, the event designer can conceive of more and finer elements than resources will allow. Successful event design and decoration will occur only with balanced management of the available resources.

# FINANCIAL RESOURCES

Financial resources are those at the disposal of the designer and decorator to decorate the event and otherwise execute the design. These resources are directly controlled or indirectly controlled. The event designer or decorator will have either complete or partial responsibility for the production and/or décor budget and for working within the cash flow of the project.

## TYPES AND SOURCES OF FINANCING

Corporations, individuals and associations, and nonprofit groups can make payments to a designer and/or decorator under a contractual agreement. The designer/decorator then will pay the invoices as they arrive. In this case, the designer or decorator has **direct financial control.** He or she is directly responsible for budgeting and paying the bills for the décor and production.

Idea Portfolio

### MHA USES MULTIPLE TYPES OF FINANCING FOR DECOR

At my first meeting with the primary contacts from the Mental Health Association (MHA) to consider decorating the Prism Luncheon, its upcoming fund-raiser, we discussed financing and the budget. MHA had set aside a certain amount of money from ticket sales and underwriting for centerpieces and head table décor. In addition to that amount, they had a special arrangement with a **decorating contractor** to supply the pipe and drape around the screens and stage and with BBJ Linen to supply tablecloths. Those items would be heavily discounted or supplied as an in-kind donation, depending on the amount needed and the specific items requested. The association would be billed for any costs incurred from those suppliers. I, as the designer, would have direct control over the floral décor and indirect control over the selection of linens and pipe and drape.

When financial resources come from several sources, they may come with restrictions and directions. Underwriters have the right to influence the design with their personal taste, donated or deeply discounted items generally come from the donor's existing inventory, and the items over which the designer has complete freedom of choice are limited by the limited resources.

To maximize limited resources we used an existing logo that had been created by one of the sponsors the previous year. We reproduced it as four supergraphics in front of compatibly colored pipe and drape and brought in a few striking neoclassical columns to provide drama and majesty to the head table stage. In this way we got the most impact using donations, which allowed us to direct the limited revenue assigned to décor into the floral centerpieces.

Sometimes the designer will be hired for a flat fee and given a set amount of money out of the overall **event budget,** or the decorator may be hired by the event manager, who will allot a portion of the overall funds for the **decorations budget** or **production budget.** When the client or the event manager is paying the bills for individual suppliers, the designer or decorator will have **indirect financial control** over the decorations budget. It is not unusual for the decoration budget to consist of both types of financing; this happens frequently when the event is a charity fund-raiser.

## BUDGETING AND CASH FLOW

Although the client or the event manager determines the types and sources of financing, the designer and/or decorator has responsibility for managing the design/decorations budget. When best practices are employed, that person also will have input in creating the budget for his or her areas of responsibility. The most common practice is for finances to be allotted and a design to be created that can be executed within that budget. A production schedule is then created that reflects the projected cash flow for the event. A typical budget for a small event is shown in "Typical Small Event." Larger and more complex events are proportionally more extensive and require more detailed and extensive budgets.

A normal contractual agreement between an association and an event designer may entail the payment of one-third upon approval of the event, one-third of the balance due midway to the event, and the balance due upon completion of the installation. Under these conditions it is necessary to confirm a compatible payment schedule with your suppliers. If the normal conditions of payment for one supplier require a 50 percent deposit with the order, the order must wait until the second payment from the client or new

**TYPICAL SMALL EVENT**

**CRYSTAL BALLROOM**
**NOVEMBER 15, 2005**
**BUDGET**

| Item | Description/Allowance per Item | Cost, $ |
|---|---|---|
| Entrance décor | Trusswork entrance with uplights and neon | 3,000.00 |
| Stage décor | Lamé backdrop and signs | 3,750.00 |
| 120 centerpieces | Abstract/oriental floral @ $85.50 each | 10,260.00 |
| 120 pinspots | To spot individual centerpieces @ $30.00 each | 3,600.00 |
| Delivery fees | | 250.00 |
| Design and coordination fee | | 2,000.00 |
| | Total: | 22,860.00 |
| | Sales tax: | Exempt |
| | Grand total: | $22,860.00 |

**CRYSTAL BALLROOM**
**NOVEMBER 15, 2005**

**INCOME AND EXPENSE (CASH FLOW) PROJECTION**

| Date | Action | Amount, $ |
|---|---|---|
| August 15 | Acceptance of agreement with one-third deposit | $7,620.00 |
| | Order props, drop, and floral containers | (3,600.00) |
| October 1 | Second one-third payment due | 7,620.00 |
| | Order and receive signage; receive drop, above; send deposit to lighting company | (3,750.00) |
| November 15 | Final contract balance due | 7,620.00 |
| | Lights and props, balance due upon completion | (3,300.00) |
| November 16 | Installation and dismantle labor | (1,500.00) |
| November 25 | Additions and adjustments due net 10 days | |
| December 1–15 | Pay balance of bills; floral and floral containers | (4,020.00) |

terms must be negotiated with the supplier. An **income and expense projection (cash flow projection)** for the small event budgeted above follows.

A **production schedule** will have to be generated concurrently with the projected cash flow, as they relate directly to each other. Compare the production schedule for the income and expense projection above with the production schedule that follows.

**TYPICAL SMALL EVENT**

**CRYSTAL BALLROOM**
**NOVEMBER 15, 2005**
**PRODUCTION SCHEDULE**

| Date | Action | Amount, $ |
|---|---|---|
| 8/18–9/15 | Order and send deposits for props; entrance | 1,500.00 |
| | Order and send deposit for backdrop | 300.00 |
| | Order containers for floral centerpieces. | 1,800.00 |
| 10/01–10/15 | Send 50% prepayment to lighting company | 1,800.00 |
| | Order custom signage; send 50% | 875.00 |
| 10/15–11/15 | Receive signage; balance due | 875.00 |
| | Receive floral containers, balance due 12/15 | |
| | Receive drop, balance due | 600.00 |
| 11/15 | Lighting company finishes install, balance due | 1,500.00 |
| | Flowers delivered, balance due 12/01 | |
| 11/16 | Delivery service | 150.00 |
| | Dismantle; contracted install and dismantle labor | 1,500.00 |
| 11/17 | Return ship drop, send thank you notes, schedule final payments and invoice for extras | |

The projected income and expenses in this example work well with the production schedule. However, the income flow is not always compatible with the payment outflow. It is a good practice to discuss the importance of the contracted payment schedule with your client contact, confirming that it is compatible with his or her organization's policies. Many large corporations and associations ignore the written agreement and simply inform you that company policy supersedes supplier payment agreements.

The best practice is to find out what the client organization's policies and payment history are in advance. Then you can arrange for the client to meet the agreed-on schedule or add charges to the contract to cover the cost of having the client hold your money. One way to do this is to add 10 percent to each cost in the contract and then give a 10 percent discount for payment on the stated terms. Solutions to this potential problem are most easily found in preventive actions.

### MANAGING FINANCIAL RESOURCES

Financial resources for the designer and decorator are always in short supply and will be controlled either directly or indirectly. Production expenses must be budgeted, and income and expenses then are planned with a cash flow projection. The production schedule that follows will guide the production through to completion, compatible with cash flow.

## HUMAN RESOURCES AND STAKEHOLDERS

It is hard to see how an event could be staged without contributions from each of the four classes of resources. However, if there is one class of resource that is more important than the other three, it is human resources. Consider the concept of the **stakeholder,** which was introduced in Chapter 1, *Principles of Design.* A stakeholder is anyone who invests time, money, or emotion in an event. There are different levels of stakeholder, depending on the amount of investment and commitment. **Key stakeholders** include the client, the event manager, the designer and decorator, and the major staff and suppliers. Registration, security and installation and dismantle (I&D) staff are also stakeholders, as are the attendees.

### THE CLIENT

The first and most underappreciated human resource is the client. Without the client to supply the reason and the financial resources, there would be no need for an event. But beyond that, the client or **client contact** is your original source for the goals and objectives of the event. Clients may or may not use those terms or that concept, but they are your best guides to a successful event. In addition, they are your prime source for research into the organization and into the past history of the event.

When a sense of respect and trust develops between you and the client, a partnerlike relationship occurs and a successful event should follow.

## STAFF

Whether between employees, volunteers, or peers, staff relationships need to be partnerships on one level and follow a structure of authority and responsibility on another level. A good event manager will spend time building a team and will establish clear responsibilities and a chain of authority. A good designer or decorator will follow these practices as well.

The key to effective staff management is communication. Communicating a sense of teamwork involves getting staff members to "buy in" to the concept, to take **ownership** of their responsibilities. This means that the staff members take personal responsibility for their assignments rather than just accept them. Staff members will do this more readily if an appropriate amount of authority accompanies those responsibilities.

## EMPLOYEES AND CONTRACTORS

Event design and decoration is always under a deadline and always short of resources and as a result is a stressful occupation by definition. Studies have shown that stress is highest in occupations, such as nursing, where there is significant responsibility but little authority. Most event design and decorations companies are small businesses, often of the "mom and pop" variety. Owners of small businesses tend to micromanage, taking personal responsibility for all operating details. Delegating authority is difficult for them.

Whether contract labor or employees, a distinction discussed in the next chapter, paid staff needs to be managed with care. Professional staff members must be compensated at least at market level according to their experience and talents. However, although compensation is important, it is not the only or even the most important motivating factor for professionals. Professionals need to be recognized by their supervisors and their peers to achieve job satisfaction.

The organizations that thrive and grow delegate authority with responsibility and establish a chain of command with reporting procedures and accountability. They publicly recognize and show appreciation to their staff and compensate for talent and experience at or above market level.

## VOLUNTEERS

Volunteers present a challenge to the professional designer or decorator. Proficiency in various areas and level of commitment must be determined for each individual. The successful management of volunteers lies in finding out

Idea Portfolio

## JEANNE JUST WANTED TO DO ART

Many of our artistically inclined clients have asked over the years if they could come to work with us. Jeanne was one of them, but she pursued her desire strongly. The wife of an extremely creative and successful businessman, she hired us occasionally to "help" with her events at home. Mostly, she designed and decorated them quite professionally.

One time she called us when we were shorthanded, and we hired her on the spot to sculpt and paint props and scenery. She was with us for a year, until her husband developed health problems that required her attention. During that time she produced professional props and decorations and took home a regular paycheck, making the transition from volunteer to event professional.

We found out later that she had sent her net pay to a local charity. She was not doing it for the money, but she was doing what she wanted. She was working as a professional artist. That was what was in it for her.

what each volunteer can do and what they want out of the experience. Volunteers come with different talents and motivations. Some need the recognition, and some need an artistic outlet; some are there for the social standing or approval, and some are following in their friends' or parents' footsteps. A key concept is **WIFM (what's in it for me?).**

Matching the needs and talents of each volunteer to the requirements of the event project is crucial to successful volunteer management.

Recognition is another key to the successful management of volunteer staff, as are clearly defined roles and authority. Delegation of authority to volunteers must come with clear limitations on that authority.

Professional associations with adequate financial resources usually have a volunteer manager on staff to maximize this human resource. The event designer/decorator will find this professional very helpful in maximizing the volunteer effort.

## DONATED STAFF

Community-oriented corporations are always looking for ways to give back through financial contributions and **in-kind donations.** One of the in-kind ways a corporation can contribute to community projects is to donate staff to charitable functions and events. A common situation is for an accounting firm to donate registration personnel, auction cashiers, or checkout staff members for an event. Sometimes a corporation will solicit volunteer staff from among its employees for setup or dismantle.

Another major contribution a corporation can make is to donate a professional event manager to chair or otherwise manage the production of an event. Whether the donated corporate personnel are volunteers or paid professionals, they can be a significant resource for the event designer or decorator. Either way, positive working relationships are required. An event professional working with a donated staff must strive to satisfy the needs of that staff, usually by making its members look good. Doing a good job and giving credit to the volunteer or loaned talent will create a **win-win situation** in which the donor and the donated person both receive kudos and personal satisfaction.

## SUPPLIERS AND ASSOCIATES

**Suppliers,** also known as vendors, are the people and companies that provide goods and services to the design or decoration of an event, for which they are compensated either financially or through advertising or public relations. **Associates** are peers who work in conjunction with the designer or decorator. If an event decorator provides the floral decorations for an event, the wholesale florist is his or her supplier. If the decorator is providing the stage decorations and another firm is supplying the flowers, that company is an associate firm.

The line between supplier or vendor and associate frequently blurs when firms work together closely, sometimes serving as suppliers to one another.

## STRATEGIC PARTNERS

Companies and individual talents can work so closely together on an event that they appear to be one company when seen from outside. When this happens, either by design or by good fortune, these companies have developed a **strategic partnership.**

**Strategic professional partner relationships** develop most often between suppliers and purchasers that strive for mutual profitability. These companies generally see themselves as professional partners and describe their working relationship as a team effort. These companies and individuals do not have a formal agreement promoting one another or one another's success. However, they have an ongoing relationship that depends on each one remaining healthy and profitable. As will be shown in the next chapter, a supplier who is not making money from a professional relationship with another firm will cut corners, cheat, or go out of business.

The strategic professional partner relationship is the most common and the easiest and safest version of strategic partnerships. There is no legal or contractual agreement concerning the partnering, and it is a situation that arises out of mutual respect and ethical business dealings. Frequently this type of relationship is a direct outgrowth of interpersonal relationships between individuals from the two companies. The danger is that the exchange of too much pricing information can make one company vulnerable to the other or lead to an anticompetitive situation or verge on price-fixing, which is both unethical and illegal.

Idea Portfolio

# HELPING A TEAM MEMBER AVOID A LOSS

In the rush to get a bid out under a deadline, Show Service International, a trusted supplier known for value, took the specifications for our job over the phone and faxed a proposal for draping the walls of a meeting room in a local hotel. Time did not allow a site inspection. Upon receiving and reviewing the bid, we recognized that it was well below what we had anticipated.

This company had a reputation for meeting its obligations, and we knew that if they said they would do it for this amount, they would. However, it did not seem like enough money, and we did not want to hurt a valued professional partner.

A phone call revealed that they had never worked in that particular room and had no idea how long and involved the load-in process would be. After a quick site visit to inspect the loading dock, the path to the elevator, the freight elevator, and the path from there to the venue, they faxed a revised bid that was considerably higher than the first one but still a very fair and competitive amount.

We passed up a chance to make a quick windfall profit on one job and now have an ongoing, mutually profitable relationship with a valued strategic professional partner.

## STRATEGIC PROJECT PARTNERS

When two companies do a joint venture for an event, they agree up front to form a strategic partnership on the project and split the profits. This can be an event management company and an event design firm, an event designer and a decorating firm, or any two or more companies that agree to work on the same project under one contract. There are several ways to structure this kind of agreement.

Strategic partnerships can be agreed on for a project in which the division of responsibilities is clear and both entities are of equal professional ability, reputation, and confidence. The agreement can be to split the investment in the project 50-50 and then share the profits or losses 50-50. The danger in this agreement is that different companies bring different talents and different internal investments and costs to each project, and so a 50-50 split may not be fair. Also, if the profits fall short of expectations or become losses, disagreement over responsibility can lead to an unsatisfactory business experience.

Another structure for a strategic project partnership is for one company to be the **managing partner** and agree to give percentage shares of the profit to another company or companies. The managing partner puts up the operating capital and contracts for the liability, for which it takes a percentage to cover overhead and profit on its investment. At the end of the project the profits are

Idea Portfolio

## A TYPICAL STRATEGIC PROJECT PARTNERSHIP

Over The Top Design has a long-standing relationship with Monroe and Associates, supplying artwork and creative design talent on a speculative basis and under a strategic partnership agreement.

A typical partnership agreement from a recent project called for Over The Top to supply floor plans, sketches, and a color rendering to sell the job and develop the production details. Monroe and Associates would order, manage, and pay for supplies, custom fabrication, all subcontractors, and transportation **per diem** (daily living expenses). Over The Top supplied on-site I&D supervision side by side with Monroe and Associates.

Monroe and Associates then shared the design and coordination fee from the contract 50-50 with Over The Top and additionally paid it 15 percent of the gross profits from the job.

divided according to the prearranged agreement. The danger under this arrangement is that the managing partner has control over the expenses, which directly affect profitability. Also, it has first and final accounting responsibility, so the other partner or partners must have faith in its management abilities, honesty, and fairness.

### MANAGING HUMAN RESOURCES

As has been shown above, managing relationships in the event design and decoration profession is largely a matter of communication and trust. Recognize, appreciate, and use the talents of the human resources around you, starting with the client. Develop a relationship of mutual respect and trust with people you work with, but establish clear definitions of responsibility and authority. Understand and employ the concepts of ownership, what's in it for me? and win-win. Develop strategic partner professional relationships with your regular suppliers.

# KNOWLEDGE AND EDUCATION RESOURCES

One of the four resources that can separate a design or decoration firm from its peers is the foundation of knowledge and education it offers its clients. When discussing a style of design, a historical period, or another theme or inspiration with the client, knowledge of that style, period, or theme gives the designer an advantage. Brainstorming potential themes with a client is more effective (and more fun) if all the participants have a lot of knowledge in a lot of different areas. Knowledge comes in different forms and from different sources. The types of knowledge and education available to the event designer and decorator are described in the next three sections.

## LIBERAL ARTS AND INDUSTRY KNOWLEDGE

**Liberal arts** is the study of general knowledge for the purposes of expanding the intellect or increasing one's intellectual skills. Industry knowledge is practical, utilitarian, vocational, or professional knowledge. The value of a liberal arts education and the development of a firm foundation of general knowledge cannot be underestimated. It also takes a long time to achieve and for many people is the subject of lifelong learning. The advantages of a liberal arts education are an extensive vocabulary, a comprehensive view of different cultures and history, and an understanding of beliefs and thought processes and the ways they have changed historically. Also, one will develop an understanding of the arts and art history and the ability to understand new abstract concepts as they emerge.

Industry education and knowledge have been growing exponentially with the advancement of the special event industry to a professional status. The event industry is a multicultural experience that consists of many disciplines and professions. Specialized knowledge and education are available in many different event design and decoration areas, including floral design, painting, lighting, fabric and draping treatments, food styling, and balloon decoration. The event designer and/or decorator has many areas in which he or she can pursue specialized knowledge and skills.

## FORMAL EDUCATION AND EXPERIENCE

There are many sources for a liberal arts education, traditional and nontraditional, formal and experiential. The concept comes from the university, and a baccalaureate degree with a major in history, political science, English, social studies, or psychology is considered a formal liberal arts education. Recognizing the value of a base of general knowledge, colleges require a liberal arts basis for BAs in the sciences and more vocationally oriented majors as well. Less formal ways to access a liberal arts education include reading, travel, and cultural exploration through seminars and study groups sponsored by museums, community groups, and community colleges.

## LIBRARY AND REFERENCES

Public libraries have always been a valuable source of knowledge. Many large public libraries have photo and/or clipping archives in addition to book stacks, reference department, and periodicals. Effective use of the public library system is facilitated by the assistance of a local librarian, and developing a relationship with the library staff can be immensely valuable.

The event professional also will develop a personal reference library consisting of books by other professionals from specific areas in the event field and from related fields such as theater, interior decorating, and seasonal décor. These books are useful from a "how to" standpoint and for inspiration and ideas. In addition to his or her personal library, an event professional also will develop a **morgue** and a **catalogue library.** The morgue consists of a set of files alphabetized by topic. This is where magazine articles, invitations, photographs, and other theme ideas and design concepts can be put when they are discovered. The catalogue library is where the plethora of catalogues an event firm receives are filed and cross-referenced for easy access.

A library of any size will require an index, which also is used as a place to sign out books if the staff uses it (and it will). The morgue is harder to keep cross-referenced, so the easiest way to do this is to have generic file names such as "Holiday—Christmas," "Holiday—Non-Christmas," "Entertainment—Musical," and "Entertainment—Nonmusical" and large files that will be perused when one is seeking inspiration. A catalogue file is best indexed in a card file that can be used as a general reference for vendors and sources.

Modern event professionals keep their card files and other cross-indexed resource files in the software format of their choice. This can be done in a data file such as MSAccess or contact files such as Lotus or MSOutlook. The author uses Cardscan by Corex, which is fast and will cross-reference by any word in the entry.

# TECHNICAL AND PHYSICAL RESOURCES

Contemporary research can be done through computer technology, which the author assumes is available to some degree for the reader. Although the library is likely to have more in-depth information on any topic, preliminary research, general directions for conducting research, and many sources and vendors can be located through the Internet. An event professional is likely to conduct research through the Internet before making a trip to the public library. Users of the World Wide Web will be familiar with the process of **bookmarking,** in which the user files a website address so that it will be available in the future.

## TECHNOLOGY

Internet resources have increased the speed of preliminary research and brought the entire world of vendors and sources into the event professional's office. Files that are discovered or recommended by other professionals can be filed away (bookmarked) for future use. Vendors can be located and contacted by email. Proposals and contracts are emailed along with images of samples, renderings, and floor plans. A fast Internet connection has become a necessary tool of the modern design office to transmit images quickly and easily.

Technical resources also include **computer aided design (CAD)** software, which is rapidly replacing drafting in creating floor plans and elevations. There are many CAD programs with varying degrees of sophistication and differing degrees of difficulty in terms of learning to master them. Four popular CAD programs among meeting and event planners are Meeting Matrix, Optimum Settings, Roomviewer, and ExpoCad. The leading program worldwide among technical draftsmen is AutoCad. An example of an AutoCad drawing of a two-story exhibit booth and the lighting plan for it is shown in Figure 4-2, courtesy of Art of Light, Inc.

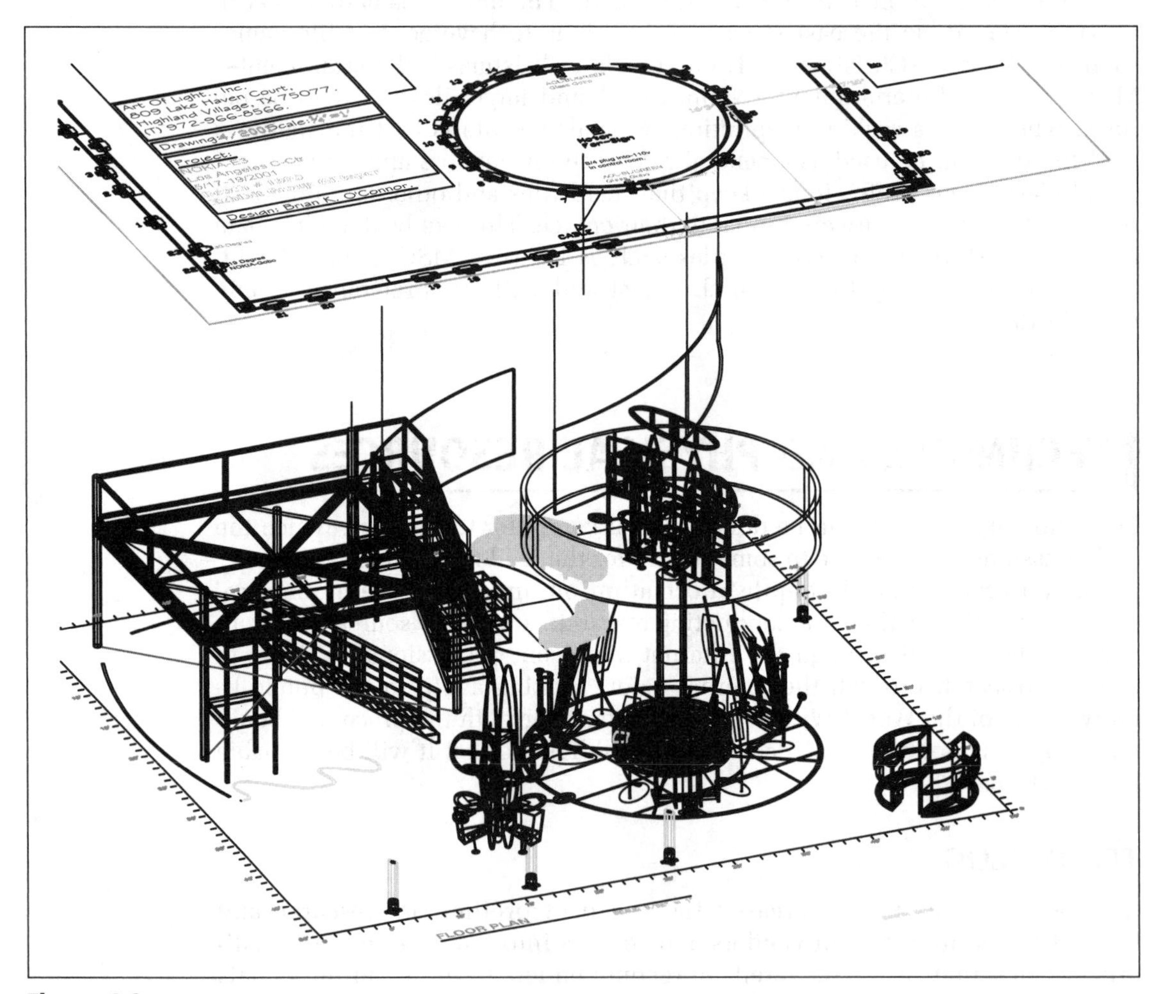


**Figure 4-2**

Accounting software is an important resource that will be discussed in the next chapter. Perhaps the most common and pervasive technical resource is email. Email serves two functions in that it allows us to communicate details at times when only one party is available, facilitating communication, and it is "in writing." Before email we would say that all orders, changes, and communications relating to a job should be in writing to protect all parties and assure mutual understanding. However, this was stated in principle more often than it was followed because it took time to communicate in writing even with facsimile (fax) communication. Email, however, can be written at the sender's convenience and read when the recipient has time. It still requires follow-up and a response to make sure the intended recipient received it.

## PHYSICAL RESOURCES

The physical resources that need to be considered are space, time, tools, and equipment.

### Space

Some space is always required to prepare for any event: office space, fabrication space, storage space, and warehousing space. If in-house fabrication is planned, there must be enough space to accommodate it. If acquisition of props and decorations is anticipated, storage space must be acquired.

For most event professionals, space translates into finances, as it must be rented or purchased. Space is a resource that needs to be managed carefully through efficient design of storage spaces and thoughtful layout of office and shop areas. When temporary space is needed for preliminary assembly or temporary storage, it can be rented or possibly bartered for. The application of creative techniques in dealing with space considerations can yield cost-saving results.

Idea Portfolio

## BRAINSTORMING PRODUCTION

In preparation to begin production of the decorations for the Rose Queen's Coronation Ball as part of the Tyler Rose Festival, we held a brainstorming session to deal with some production concerns, one of which was lack of storage space and lack of space for preliminary assembly.

Two of our strategic partners came to our rescue. One offered storage space in its warehouse, and the other offered its shop for preliminary assembly. Both were longtime professional associates with whom we had had mutually profitable experiences. Each was pleased to be able to help us and did not charge us for the use of its space.

### Time

Time is considered here as a resource although most professionals see it as a challenge. One way or the other it is a unique resource, as it is the only nonrenewable resource. There is only so much time, and once it has passed, it can never be recovered. Time management is an essential part of event design and decoration. An essential practice is to analyze each project and create a detailed production schedule. Then refer to it often, modifying it as the project progresses and changes to meet the reality of delivery times and material availability.

Implementation of a **SWOT analysis** and a **GAP analysis** can help avoid time crunch problems. SWOT stands for "strengths, weaknesses, opportunities, and threats." A SWOT analysis should be held in a meeting with key stakeholders to determine the strengths and weaknesses of the situation and to look for opportunities and threats. The designer may identify labor availability as a strength and the limited time the space is available for move-in as a weakness. If these items are identified far enough in advance, it may be possible to schedule the strength (labor) to cancel out the weakness (space and/or time shortage). A venue that was architecturally pleasant and required limited spending of resources for decorations would be an opportunity, whereas a budget that depended upon as-of-yet-unsold tickets would be a threat.

A GAP analysis is the process of reviewing the event plans and looking for an unplanned element, or a "gap" in the plans. An example might be discovering that another event being held at a neighboring facility on the same evening will create a difficult parking situation. Adding valet parking might bridge that gap. The point of these analyses is to identify potential problems and their solutions in advance, while there is time to do something about them.

### Tools and Equipment

Tools and equipment make up another aspect of the physical resources available to the event designer/decorator. The actual physical elements that the designer or design firm, decorator, or event-decorating firm executes in-house determine the tools that are required, although in many cases the reverse may be true. The tools that a design or decorating firm has in-house determine what elements of the design that firm can execute in-house.

Woodworking requires woodworking tools, and the more sophisticated the project is, the more and better tools must be acquired. Painting requires both space and equipment and possibly an ecologically sound, ventilated **Occupational Safety and Health Administration (OSHA)**-approved paint booth. Metalworking requires a different set of tools that need to be kept separate from the woodworking tools because the heavy use of petroleum products in metalworking can spill onto wood and prevent it from taking paint as expected.

## MANAGING TECHNICAL AND PHYSICAL RESOURCES

Computer-related resources include access to the Internet and CAD design programs in addition to the accounting and data management software programs mentioned earlier in this chapter. A major part of managing event design and decoration is determining and procuring the tools that are necessary and determining which elements should be farmed out to subcontractors. Space, time, and tools are critical elements that determine what design and décor elements can be executed in-house. SWOT and GAP analyses are important practices in event design and decoration.

## FINISHING TOUCHES

Acquiring tools is not sufficient but must accompany elements of the other three classes of resources. It takes substantial financial resources to acquire tools. It requires skilled human resources to work with those tools to fabricate and assemble quality decorations. It takes knowledge to design the event and plan the décor so that the available tool resources, space, time, and talent can produce them in a cost-effective manner. In other words, it takes all four types of resources to support a successfully designed and decorated special event.

## DESIGN VOCABLUARY

Terms appear below in the order in which they first occur in this chapter.

Direct financial control
Event budget
Decorations budget
Production budget
Indirect financial control
Decorating contractor
Income and expense projection
Cash flow projection
Production schedule
Stakeholder
Key stakeholder
Client contact
Ownership
WIFM (what's in it for me?)
In-kind donations
Win-win situation
Suppliers
Associates
Strategic partnership
Strategic professional partner relationship
Managing partner
Per diem
Liberal arts
Morgue
Catalogue library
Bookmarking
Computer aided design (CAD)
SWOT analysis
GAP analysis
Occupational Safety and Health Administration (OSHA)

## STUDIO WORK

1. Report on the financial resources required to produce a specific event that you know about by interviewing the event manager or designer, through direct knowledge and experience, or through research. Describe the types of financial resources used and the control the designer

and/or decorator had over their budget and do a cash flow projection or report. (*Note:* A cash flow report is identical to a cash flow projection except that it is produced during or after the event and reflects actual income and expenses.)

2. Make a list of different stakeholders that might be involved in an event and put it in descending order of investment, with the key stakeholders at the top.
3. In your own words (300 words or less) explain why a liberal arts education is valuable to an event decorator.
4. Do a Web search and see how many suppliers you can locate to produce the hypothetical small event described in the cash flow projection and production schedule in this chapter. (You will have to make design decisions.) List the URLs and your reasons for selecting them.

## RECOMMENDED READINGS AND RESEARCH SITES

Goldblatt, Joe and Frank Supovitz, *Dollars & Events: How to Succeed in the Special Events Business,* John Wiley & Sons, 1999.

Goldblatt, Joe, *Special Events: Event Leadership for a New World,* John Wiley & Sons, 2004.

Silvers, Julia Rutherford, *Professional Event Coordination,* John Wiley & Sons, 2004.

Bloodhound Network.com—Human Resources—an extensive listing of definitions and explanations of human resource management issues, including a list of selected resources under each issue

http://human-resources.bloodhoundnetwork.com/

Corbin Ball Associates website—home page for the leading technology expert in the meetings industry; includes many articles on current technology; under "Tips and Tools," offers many free software downloads of forms and tech tools

http://www.corbinball.com

Corporate Event Channel—a resource for event equipment and services nationwide

http://www.corporateeventchannel.com

International Special Events Society—a source for education and professional event resources; visitors can use the finder service under "Resources" to locate event professionals worldwide

http://www.ises.com

SpecialEventSite—a resource for special event equipment and services nationwide

http://www.specialeventsite.com/

# Chapter 5

# PROFIT AND LOSS

*He profits most who serves best.*

**—Arthur F. Sheldon**

## IN THIS CHAPTER

You will discover specific practices and decisions that will determine profit and loss in event design and decoration.

**Profit**

- Profit = Revenue − Expenses
- Gross Profit
- Overhead
- Net Profit
- ROI and ROE

**Net Profit**

- Overhead
- Project Profit
- Profit versus Nonprofit Events

**Pricing**

- Markup versus Profit Margin
- Materials
- Labor
- Subcontractors
- Flowers
- Entertainment
- Pricing for the Independent

**Job Cost**

- Proposal
- Estimating
- Purchasing
- Design and Coordination Fee

**Discounts, Commissions, and Ethics**

**Accounting and Bookkeeping**

**Profit and loss** is one of the more complex topics in this book but also should be one of the most interesting, especially to small business owners and entrepreneurs. This chapter contains real information on pricing accumulated by my associates and me over decades of experience in operations, estimating, and production in successful special event design and decorating firms.

Two warnings: First, this chapter contains pricing guidelines, but each owner and manager must develop his or her own methods and procedures that work for that particular company. Second, while concentrating on profit, do not lose sight of the fact that we are in a service industry. In the long run, as in the quote at the start of this chapter, the person who provides the best service will profit the most.

# PROFIT

**Profit = Revenue − Expenses**

Profit equals revenue minus expenses. When revenue is greater than expenses, a profit is achieved. A loss occurs when expenses exceed revenue. This is the most important of all business principles.

Profit is either **gross profit** or **net profit.**

## GROSS PROFIT

In evaluating the profitability of an event, gross profit = project revenue − job costs. Consider the following example of an event **profit and loss (P&L) statement** (see Chapter 4, *Resources*).

As is shown in the "Event Design Project Profit and Loss Statement" on the next page, gross profit equals event revenues minus job costs: gross profit = project revenue − job costs.

Net profit is determined by adding job costs and overhead and then subtracting that total from project revenue: net profit = project revenue − (job costs + overhead).

## OVERHEAD

The totals of all the expenses that are not incurred directly in producing a project are overhead. This includes rent, utilities, administrative salaries, office expenses, and anything that is not charged to a job.

The percentage of gross income that needs to be allotted to overhead is calculated by adding up all the expenses in running the business that are not related to a specific project **(operating expenses)** and dividing them by gross income. Gross income is all revenues before deducting expenses. All expenses not directly related to projects are operating expenses. This can be expressed in the formula and the "Typical Small Event" box that follows.

$$\textit{Overhead \%} = \frac{\textit{operating expenses}}{\textit{gross income}}$$

| EVENT DESIGN PROJECT PROFIT AND LOSS STATEMENT | | | |
|---|---|---|---|
| **Event project:** | Typical small event, Crystal Ballroom, 11/15/05 | | |
| **Start date:** | 8/01/05 | | |
| **End date:** | 11/16/05 | | |
| **Payments received:** | 8/15/05 | $7,620 | One-third deposit |
| | 10/01/05 | $7,620 | One-third payment |
| | 11/15/05 | $7,620 | Final balance |
| **Total project revenue:** | | **$22,860** | |
| **Job costs:** | 11/15/05 | $4,500 | Entrance and pin spots |
| | 11/05/05 | $650 | Lamé drop and hardware |
| | 11/30/05 | $750 | Signage for stage |
| | 11/16/05 | $920 | Stagehands |
| | 11/30/05 | $3,900 | Flowers, wholesale |
| | 11/14/03 | $750 | Freelance floral designers |
| | 11/17/05 | $150 | Delivery service |
| | 11/30/05 | $1,550 | Designer and coordinator |
| **Total event expenses:** | | **$13,170** | |
| **Gross event project profit:** | | **$9,600** | 42% |

An existing company should do this calculation over the last three-year period to get a meaningful and current figure. A new company will have to estimate expenses and revenues to achieve a forecast or projection. Overhead is the cost of doing business and needs to be accepted as such. The growth of a company usually comes with increased overhead. Controlling overhead costs, however, is one of the basic principles of managing a successful event business.

## NET PROFIT

Net profit is determined by multiplying the event revenue by an overhead percentage, adding the resulting cost figure to the job costs, and subtracting that total from gross revenue. Consider the example of the "Typical Small Event"

**TYPICAL SMALL COMPANY, INC.**

If a small company had $100,000 in total annual expenses for rent, utilities, salaries, taxes, insurance, office, and auto expenses and total gross revenues (income) of $350,000, overhead would be 28.6 percent of gross income.

$$\text{Overhead \%} = \frac{\text{operating expenses}}{\text{gross income}}$$

$$28.6\% = \frac{\$100{,}000}{\$350{,}000}$$

| GROSS PROFIT DETERMINATION | | |
|---|---|---|
| **Event project:** | Typical Small Event, Crystal Ballroom, 11/15/05 | |
| **Total project revenue:** | $22,860 | |
| **Overhead percentage:** | × 28.6% | |
| **Overhead (charged against project):** | $6,538 | |
| **Total event expenses:** | +$13,170 | |
| **Job costs + overhead:** | **$19,708** | |
| **Net profit:** | **$3,152** | **13.8%** |

produced by Typical Small Company, Inc. The revenue and cost figures come from the "Event Design Project Profit and Loss Statement" which was produced by Typical Small Company, Inc.

## ROI AND ROE

**ROI (return on investment)** is an important business concept for the key stakeholders who invest money in a company. **ROE (return on event)** is the concern of key stakeholders who invest money, time, and emotions in an event. The ROI on the investment in an event company is measured in net profit and growth that will lead to future increases in net profit. In the previous example, a 13.8 percent ROI would be considered a good return compared with the average return on the stock market over time of 10 percent.

ROE is measured in terms defined by the goals of the event. If the event is a fund-raiser, the dollar amount raised is judged against expectations. If the event is a public relations function, ROE is judged by the positive exposure in the media and the response of the participants.

## PROFIT VERSUS NONPROFIT EVENTS

Most events called "nonprofit" are events for nonprofit organizations, usually **fund-raisers.** Although called nonprofit events, fund-raisers are very much profit-oriented, with the profit being the net funds raised for the cause. Sometimes nonprofit organizations tend to focus on job costs such as production and decorating, concentrating on ways to save or cut expenditures to maximize net funds raised. They might be better served to focus on effective design, marketing, and promotion to increase income and maximize gross funds raised.

Truly nonprofit events have goals and objectives that are related to public relations, marketing, or human relations. Nonprofit event examples would be a **break-even event** designed to establish the presence and name identification of a new organization and an employee appreciation party designed to give employees recognition and a fun time, with the goal being to raise or maintain morale. Typical for-profit events would be a **retail sales event** such as a holiday promotion at a mall, a new car show at an automobile dealership, and an industry wholesale **tradeshow.**

An entirely sponsored fund-raiser is said to be 100 percent **underwritten,** and the corporation does it for the publicity and to build its image as a corporate citizen. A break-even event is designed to pay for itself, or "break even." Its purpose is usually to establish brand name or logo identification and to build association or corporate presence in a community. Retail events are self-explanatory in that they are designed to sell to the public, although they may have secondary public relations goals such as increasing brand awareness. Tradeshow events are typically wholesaler-to-retailer marketing events.

# PRICING

Pricing is one of the secrets in the event business because most companies consider it proprietary information; also, it is a violation of the Sherman Act and therefore a federal felony for companies to get together and discuss their pricing. This section supplies some guidelines and dispels some of the mystery, but pricing decisions and methods remain entirely at the discretion of the managers and owners of an event business.

## PROFIT AND MARKUP

Because this is one of the most commonly confused concepts, it is important to understand the difference between profit and markup. An item that is marked up 100 percent results in a 50 percent gross profit. If an item wholesales to you for $300 and you mark it up 100 percent, you are selling it for $600. Your profit on the item is 50 percent. The confusion arises not during the estimating process but after the sale, frequently misleading sales and production people and sometimes management into thinking the company is taking in more money than it actually is (see "Profit Percentage Table").

**PROFIT PERCENTAGE TABLE**

| Markup | (On $100) | Selling Price | Gross Profit |
|---|---|---|---|
| 10% | $10 | $110 | 9.1% |
| 20% | $20 | $120 | 16.7% |
| 30% | $30 | $130 | 23.1% |
| 40% | $40 | $140 | 28.6% |
| 50% | $50 | $150 | 33.3% |
| 100% | $100 | $200 | 50% |
| 200% | $200 | $300 | 67% |

## MATERIALS

Materials can be priced in different ways and are priced differently at the same event company depending on how they are purchased and how they are used or sold. Some items are purchased wholesale for resale as is, such as party favors, potted plants, and expendable decorative items such as ribbon. These items frequently have a **manufacturer's suggested retail price (MSRP),** and the designer or decorator can choose to sell it at that price, at a discounted price, or at a premium. Decorative materials that are purchased for one-time use and then are discarded are called **expendables** and typically are marked up 100 percent or more.

Some items are purchased as raw materials to fabricate props and decorative items. Raw materials usually are marked up between 50 and 100 percent. If the product being fabricated will become a reusable prop belonging to the decorating firm, materials may be marked up only 50 percent. If the product will belong to the client, a 100 percent markup is normal.

For example, a removable awning to convert a client's parking garage into a usable event space may require only a 50 percent markup on materials if it is going to remain the property of the design firm, which then will rent it to that client for future uses. If the client wants to own it, a 100 percent markup or more will be required.

Careful research and investigation can result in new sources of materials, sometimes allowing you to purchase materials from the manufacturer instead of from a distributor. If the materials are purchased for a lower cost than competitors are paying, it should be possible to take a larger markup and still sell the finished product at a lower price than before. Some materials, however, have to be purchased retail, and the markup will have to be much lower if these materials are available to the client at the same price.

Careful buying is critical to success and does not always mean buying the least expensive materials. In most design projects, the materials cost accounts for a third or less of the total budget. If inexpensive materials require more labor, they are not a good buy. Buy the best materials the project budget can afford, but buy them at the best price.

## LABOR

Pricing labor for profit is a complicated process in any industry and is made more complicated by the variety of talent and varying levels of skill and expertise required to design and decorate special events. The profession requires a lot of manual labor just in **drayage,** which is moving props and decorations from the shop or warehouse to the venue and back. Skilled carpenters fabricate décor that is designed by artists and painted by scenic artists; riggers, electricians, and different kinds of technicians all work for different pay scales.

Many companies follow the old rule of thumb that labor should be priced at three times cost to cover overhead, **downtime,** employer contributions to FICA and Medicare, and profit. *Downtime* is a term for time on the clock that is not productive, which means non-revenue-producing for calculation of profit and loss. Some companies have different labor rates for different tasks, and others average the costs and the resulting charges to establish a single labor rate for all tasks.

It is not unusual for a company to have two different rates: one for charging by the hour and one for estimating purposes. Charging by the hour sometimes is combined with a pre-agreed-upon markup for materials and called **cost plus.** Cost-plus billing carries little risk for the company, as delays and other unexpected expenses are borne by the client. **Estimating** involves the risk of guessing what labor will be required as well as the risk of incurring unexpected costs that are beyond the estimator's control, such as a flat tire or a jammed-up loading dock that requires unforeseen waiting time.

Modern accounting software can provide reports that list what hours were spent working on which projects for the purpose of analyzing the number of revenue-producing hours generated in a year. A **charge-out rate** for labor realized can be determined from this analysis and can be used to adjust and improve the overall profitability of a company. An average over three years will provide the most accurate picture of the charge-out rate realized. Any company can increase its percentage of profit from sales by increasing the markup on materials or by raising its labor rate. See Appendix 8, *Labor Rate Calculation Charge-Out Rates for Labor.*

Most new companies determine a charge-out rate by researching their competitors. However, an astute entrepreneur can estimate what the charge-out rate should be by plugging projected figures into the analysis in Appendix 8. A new company will achieve success through a combination of research, careful projected analysis, and luck.

## SUBCONTRACTORS

An event design and decorating firm is contracted to perform work and supply design and decorations. A **subcontractor** is another firm that is hired by the first firm (or the contractor) to provide some of the materials and services

**TYPICAL SMALL COMPANY, INC.**

**LABOR CHARGE-OUT RATE CALCULATION**

The average cost of labor paid is **$15.00 per hour.**
7.65% is added for employer contribution to FICA and Medicare.
28.6% is added for overhead.
25% is added for downtime (based on six chargeable hours out of eight).
12% is added for employer's contribution to health insurance.
6.75% is added for vacation and paid holidays.
100% is added for profit.
180% × 15.00 = **$42.00/hour charge-out rate**
Estimating rate: add 19% contingency = **$50.00 estimating rate**

required. Dealing with subcontractors profitably is both an art and a science. The easy aspect of using subcontractors is that the cost is controlled; the difficult aspect is that the product is not in the direct control of the hirer, so communications, mutual understanding, and a high level of trust are essential.

The contractor supplies the details in a request for proposal (RFP) or purchase order (PO). Costs quoted by subcontractors need to be in writing and either refer to the RFP or PO or contain enough detail that the contractor understands exactly what is being supplied. Subsequent changes in details and/or price need to be confirmed in writing. There should be no surprises in regard to what is expected or what is delivered.

An event designer typically subcontracts lighting, sound, and decorations. The decorating firm may subcontract some of the décor to a specialist such as a plant rental firm or a table-draping company. It also may contract with an associate firm that has existing props that can be integrated into the design. The costs of using such subcontracted props typically are marked up from 30 to 50 percent.

## Flower Pricing

A floral designer is one of the specialists that may be subcontracted by an event design or decorating firm. It is not unusual for an event firm to have an agreement with a florist to supply centerpieces and arrangements at a discounted price. When this is the case, a 20 percent discount combined with a 30 percent markup will result in a modest increase in the selling price of 4 percent over retail, or the event firm may choose to sell the flowers at retail. Retail would result in a 25 percent markup. (See the "Profit Percentage Table" earlier in this chapter.) A 50 percent markup will result in a 33.3 percent profit, which may be within the range of the perceived value of the end product.

It is not unusual for an event design firm to provide the flowers directly or for a florist to be a special event decorating firm. Costing for event flowers may be based on typical flower shop practices that use a ratio markup method

**RATIO METHOD OF FLORAL PRICING**

A 3 to 1 pricing ratio means that if the total materials cost is $20,

$$3 \times \$20 = \$60 \text{ selling}$$

If a ratio plus labor figure is employed, say, 3 to 1 plus 20 percent, for the same piece,

$$3 \times \$20 = \$60 + 20\% = \$72 \text{ selling}$$

Large special events can be priced at ratios as low as 2 to 1 because the flowers are a large special order with a limited risk of loss of this perishable product.

The larger ratios are used for arrangements using inexpensive materials because the same overhead and labor are involved, as well as for weddings, which tend to be labor-intensive.

to cover cost, overhead, and profit. These ratios may begin at 5 to 1 and go down to 2.5 to 1.

Many floral shops figure at 3 to 1 and add a 20 percent figure for labor. The floral designer must determine the actual cost of the materials and then calculate the perceived value of the finished product. The owner or manager must determine what ratio will cover the actual costs and overhead of its operation and result in an acceptable ROI.

A floral arrangement can be sold for the value perceived by the client, and this perceived value will be affected by the company's reputation, salesmanship, and marketing as well as the design talent of the artist (see Chapter 7, *Decorating with Flowers*).

## ENTERTAINMENT

**Incidental entertainment** frequently falls within the purview of the event designer or decorator. Called **sight acts,** this is entertainment that must be watched to be appreciated, such as juggling, mimes, and living statues. Sometimes this type of entertainment serves primarily a decorative purpose. Walking décor, such as costumed models greeting the guests or mimes incorporated into a buffet, provide a live component that adds interest to the décor (see Chapter 11, *Unique Decorative Elements*).

The markup used when one is employing entertainers is known as a **commission** in the entertainment industry. When you are talking to the talent or their agent, a price will be quoted either "net to you" or as "commissionable" at a particular percentage. For example, a walk-around magician who will be costumed in an outfit that matches the theme of the evening may quote $375 for two hours, net. The event designer then may incorporate this entertainer into a proposal at $450, which would be a 20 percent commission.

Alternatively, when one is speaking to a talent agency about a team of stilt walkers at the entrance to an event, the agency may quote $1,500 **commissionable** at 20 percent. In this case, the event designer will pass on the cost of stilt walkers at $1,500 and receive a check from the agency for $300.

When asking the talent to wear specialty costumes, be aware that there may be a charge for a **fitting session** at the costume shop. Also, speak with the talent or their agent about what breaks, food and beverage, and changing/break rooms are available or required. Commissions in the entertainment industry typically run from 10 to 50 percent.

## PRICING FOR THE INDEPENDENT

Independent event designers have the same problem all people starting their own independent businesses have: deciding what they can, should, and need to charge for their time. William G. Host, CMP, Host Meetings and Event Management, gave the following formula to me when I was starting my business. This formula works only if you are able to bill out the total number of hours per year that results.

**HOST INDEPENDENT BILLING FORMULA**

Begin with 365 days in a year and subtract the following:

| | |
|---|---|
| 15 | Personal days |
| 9 | Holidays |
| 5 | Illness allowance |
| 26 | Paperwork (45 minutes/day x 4 days per week) |
| 52 | Marketing |
| 12 | Training |
| 104 | Weekends |
| 223 | Nonrevenue days |

This means that 142 days remain to bill.

142 × 8 hours = 1,136 billable hours

Determine what salary you would like to make and add in all overhead. Then divide by 1,136.00.

For example, to make $40,000 per year plus estimated overhead of $26,000 = $66,000/1,136 = $56/hour:

$60,000 + $26,000 est. OH = $86,000/1,136 = $76/hour

This formula is only a guide, and correct estimating of overhead costs is as important as billing the 1,136 hours.

## JOB COSTS

In addition to understanding the importance of overhead and pricing to net profit it is necessary to understand and control job costs. This starts with the proposal, or contract offering. During the early design phase while you are developing the design concepts by employing brainstorming and free association, it is important that budget not interfere with creativity. However, soon afterward it is necessary to design to the budget. The design becomes finalized conceptually while one is writing the proposal.

### PROPOSAL

Some proposals are specific and itemized, and others are general descriptions of the decorated environment. It may be necessary to supply a general version to satisfy the needs of a specific client. However, the correct way to write a proposal is to break the design down into elements such as entry, stage, table treatment, delivery, and design fee. Then, for estimating purposes, these elements can be broken down to smaller units. The design firm must have all the elements broken out for pricing and production purposes. An example for our typical small event follows; also see Exhibit B in Appendix 4).

Each event professional has his or her own style that will determine the literary style of the descriptions, but it is necessary that the description provide a clear and accurate picture of the products and services being proposed. If done correctly, these descriptions not only will help sell the project but also will provide valuable assistance to the decorator or production staffs after the job has been sold.

**TYPICAL SMALL EVENT**

**CRYSTAL BALLROOM**
**NOVEMBER 15, 2005**
**PROPOSAL**

TYPICAL SMALL COMPANY, INC., herein called "Supplier," agrees to supply TRADEASSOC, INC., herein called "Client," the properties and services described in Exhibit A, for the cost shown below. Costs shown are for the use of supplier's properties and include installation and removal unless otherwise noted.

TOTAL COST: $22,860

**TERMS:** One-third ($7,620) due upon acceptance of contract
One-third ($7,620) due October 1, 2005
Balance due on or before November 15, 2005

**NOTE:** When signed by both parties below, this agreement becomes contractual in nature and shall consist of three (3) pages which contains conditions pertaining to this agreement.

**EXHIBIT A**

1. **Entrance Décor:** Guests receive an upbeat welcome with a high-tech trusswork arch with sequencing neon and a custom sign saying "TradeAssoc Everytime!" $3,000.00
2. **Stage Décor:** Opposite the entrance is a silver lamé backdrop, repeating the "TradeAssoc Everytime!" theme with sequencing neon showcasing the company logo. $3,750.00
3. **120 Centerpieces:** The sea of tables is an abstract design of bright colors with multicolored tablecloths and abstract/oriental floral centerpieces with neon glow necklaces entwined in sophisticated designs with unique and colorful tropical flowers, @ $85.50 (Tablecloths to be provided by hotel.) $10,260.00
4. **120 Pinspots:** To spot individual centerpieces, @ $30.00 $3,600.00
5. **Delivery Fees:** $250.00
6. **Design and Coordination Fee:** $2,000.00

| | |
|---|---|
| **TOTAL:** | $22,860.00 |
| **SALES TAX:** | Exempt |
| **GRAND TOTAL:** | **$22,860.00** |

**PRODUCTION TIP**

It is a good practice to lay out the proposal in such a way that the prices can be eliminated and a copy of the proposal can be given to the craftspeople and artists who are executing the design. They will both understand the "feel" that is being sought and occasionally catch a detail that was left off the work order or PO they are working from.

## ESTIMATING

Estimating for events, like many aspects of the event industry, requires both an analytical, scientific approach and a lot of original thought and creativity. Beginning with the proposal, the various elements are broken down to their individual pieces, priced out, and then reassembled conceptually. Some degree of experience in executing event design and decoration is helpful. At the very least, experience supervising or watching the fabrication, installation, and removal of decorations is necessary.

Although designers and decorators tend to develop their own forms and methods of estimating, standardization is desirable. Estimating should serve two purposes. The first is the obvious purpose: to determine the selling cost of an item. The second function is to track the costs and the items planned for use in the event. Short-term tracking comes into play when the job is sold and has to be built, assembled, and installed. Frequent references to clear and logical estimating forms are common when one is ordering materials and issuing work orders. Long-term tracking is handy both for repeating jobs and for similar jobs or jobs that use identical or similar elements. The **estimate sheets** then become research materials.

The estimate sheet has a place to record a brief description of labor, including the hours estimated and the hourly rate. There is a labor column that should include the total hours. Those hours should be multiplied by the rate in this column, and a total moved into the center (selling price) column. Opposite the labor half is a materials section with a space for the description. It is a good idea to include the name of the intended supplier. The cost of material per unit should be listed, and the total cost of the material should be listed in the materials column. Then you should insert a markup percentage and the resulting selling total in the center (selling price) column. The figures in the center column should be totaled and shown beneath a double line, which indicates the selling price for this item. Then a line should be drawn across the page, and the next item should be estimated.

Estimate sheets should be filed in the job envelope containing all the working files, documents, and purchasing history for a project. This becomes valuable if any disagreements arise at the conclusion of the project, and it serves as long-term research material for future jobs.

A section from the estimate sheet for the typical small event follows:

| Labor | Hours | Selling | Cost | Material |
|---|---|---|---|---|
| **1. Entrance décor: truss with neon and uplights** | | | 120<br>60<br>180<br>+ 50% | Truss rental: 2 × 20″ × 10′; 1 × 20″ × 8′ Robin's Rig Shop |
| | | 270 | 270 | |
| Pick up rentals, 1 hour | 1 | 50 | | Neon (from stock) 6 × $20 + $20 for |
| | | 140 | | transformer rental |
| Install: 2 men × 8 hours @ $50 | 16 | 800 | 650<br>+ 70% | Custom sign, Frank's sign shop |
| | | 1,105 | 1,105 | Quoted 8:30 a.m. 8/2/05 |
| Dismantle: 2 × 4 (OT) @ $75 | 8 | 600 | | |
| | | 35 | | Misc. electrical allowance |
| **Total selling entrance:** | | **$3,000** | | |

## PURCHASING

Purchasing can affect profit through the use of negotiated discounts, quantity pricing, and price research. It is responsible for loss through overordering, ordering the wrong item, or underordering and thus necessitating rush shipping charges. Both profit and loss in relation to purchasing are the direct responsibility of the individual who places the order. It is a bad practice and unfair to that person not to have a second pair of eyes review and approve the PO.

Establishing standard purchasing procedures is necessary even for a one-person operation to track expenditures as well as for accounting and production. These procedures should include a standard **purchase order (PO)** form, including description, quantity, price per unit, total, terms, and discounts. Other important information includes the name of the vendor, the vendor contact ordered from and the date and time the order was placed, and the date and place delivery is required. Purchase orders, like estimate sheets, will become important research sources in the future.

**PURCHASING TIP**

When you are ordering commodity materials (as opposed to services or custom items), discuss the details and ask for a quote. After receiving the quote, ask for a wholesale discount. It can't hurt, and every now and then somebody gives you one.

It should be clearly understood who has the authority to approve purchase orders and for up to how much. It is necessary that everyone know what the procedure is once a purchase order is started so that if one gets bogged down, it can be traced to the right in-box. Also, though this may seem silly, everybody needs to know what color copies go where.

## DESIGN AND COORDINATION FEE

Some design firms charge only a design and management fee, and the client contracts with and pays the decorator and the other vendors directly. This fee can be based on an hourly charge of $50 to $150, depending on the talent and reputation of the designer.

Most decorating firms cover the cost of designing and coordinating a project with a design fee that can vary from 5 to 15 percent of the total job cost. Some event decorating companies do not charge a design and coordination fee and include those costs in overhead. This is particularly true of some decoration companies that work primarily for event designers, as many designers do not want to see a design fee on the proposal. Rather than bury the cost in other items, it is a better practice to label it as a coordination and supervision fee.

The design and coordination will vary widely depending on the needs of the client. There will be some time involved in preparing the design even if it was conceived by the client. This may involve drafting, searching for materials, and liaison with other companies working on the project. Some coordination will be required with the venue, the entertainment, the caterers, the valet parking service, or several of the many other vendors that may be involved in the project.

This fee should be estimated as to hours and a suitable rate and included in the proposal as a line item. If it is divided and added to the other charges and does not show up as a line item, when the proposal goes through revisions, it can be reduced or lost entirely. In fact, as the job goes through revisions, the work of the designer and the coordinating manager usually increases rather than decreases.

## PRO BONO

The event world has borrowed this phrase from the legal profession, in which a lawyer may do a certain amount of work for free; the term comes from the Latin for "for the public good." However, in the event world, **pro bono** work is done largely for exposure, to please an existing client, or to try to get new clients. The WIFM principle comes into play when one is considering whether to donate design and/or decorations: What's in it for me?

The questions to consider are the following: What is the publicity value? What measurable return will we get from it? How much will it cost out of pocket? Will it help or hurt my market? Does the donation target my market?

A certain part of your marketing budget may be set aside for this type of work, which, if handled correctly by the client, can provide excellent publicity. When asked to donate, it is acceptable to ask back: What exactly will we get out of it? Our company name in the program? A table for ten? Mention in advance publicity and a listing in the invitation and program?

How much will it cost? Sometimes you will find the client will be able to cover some or all of your actual costs if you forgo your design fee and profit factor. Your talent and expertise is your most valuable commodity, and that is what they are looking for.

Make sure that the donation will help you, not hurt you. Donating too much and too often can establish your price list for the community to which you are donating. We have been known to donate to personal charities under the stipulation that they *not* publicize the fact.

Finally, if you decide to donate for the exposure, make sure that the organization's demographics fit your targeted market. As was discussed in Chapter 3, there are always limited resources; try not to waste them. Spend as much time analyzing the pro bono job as you would with a revenue-producing job. Also, plan in advance how you will evaluate the success of the donation.

## DISCOUNTS, COMMISSIONS, AND ETHICS

Commissions were mentioned earlier in this chapter, and they are a normal part of doing business for certain segments of the event industry. Discounts often are given for quantity or for early pay or as an incentive. Some vendors offer discounts that are paid in the form of credit against future work. **Kickbacks** are under-the-table payments from a vendor to a purchaser or a purchaser's agent. Kickbacks differ from commissions in that they are hidden and the client is misled (as is the boss sometimes).

Another variation on this is the **finder's fee.** A finder's fee is either a set amount of money or a percentage of the job that is paid to the person or company that brought the client or job to you. The fee may be justified if it brings a job that would not be available without help from the finder, if help is provided in selling the job, or if a valuable liaison with the client is provided. Finder's fees run the gamut from honest commission to kickback, depending on how they are handled and whether they are hidden from the client.

An ethical event manager never engages in practices he or she would be embarrassed to have the client discover. Commission rates do not have to be revealed, but the fact that a commission is being paid or received should not have to be concealed. The fact that discounts have been negotiated with certain suppliers can actually be a selling point from the point of view that the vendor is helping underwrite the design fee. Finder's fees need to be handled very carefully. Never pay a finder's fee to someone who asks you not to tell the client if asked or to anyone who has a business or employer-employee relationship with the client that may make it unethical or illegal.

Kickbacks are unethical and in many cases illegal.

## ACCOUNTING AND BOOKKEEPING

Accounting is a separate discipline with its own terminology and best practices. Several publications listed at the end of this chapter can help an event professional become familiar with the basic principles. Most designers and decorators do not find this discipline interesting and would be best off hiring a professional bookkeeper or accountant.

Most event design and decoration firms will need a bookkeeper full-time or on a monthly basis to keep the day-to-day books, balance the multiple accounts, and maintain accurate financial records. They will hire an accountant (usually a CPA) to structure the accounting system, audit financial records, give tax advice, and provide financial consulting.

It is important to match the bookkeeper to the business. A certified public accountant (CPA) is too expensive and has more talents than the average design or decorating firm needs on a full-time basis. A bookkeeper, in contrast, needs to have enough talent, training, and experience to meet the needs of the firm at its current stage of development. An experienced bookkeeper can help a start-up company set up the right procedures and practices.

Whether a bookkeeper should be hired to work in-house or the work should be contracted out is a matter for serious consideration. It is a good idea to seek advice from fellow event business owners and managers. Whether you are hiring an individual or an accounting or bookkeeping firm, interview them carefully, using a prepared list of questions.

Accounting software, like the accountant or bookkeeper, should be matched to the needs of the company. There are many versions of stock and customizable accounting software available to the event business world that can track expenses and labor costs in ways never before available to a small business owner. Evaluating accounting software requires knowledge of what the business requires and of what the software offers. This will require a team effort involving the manager of the event business and a trusted accounting professional.

## FINISHING TOUCHES

The basic principle of all business is profit equals revenue minus expenses. Learning how to calculate profit and understanding the difference between profit and markup are basic. There are many variations in pricing events, different markups, and a range of markups and procedures, depending on traditional pricing, how well the item is purchased, and what the perceived value of the finished product is. Each business needs to establish its own pricing structure on the basis of its overhead, market, and needs. Job costing is an art and a science that begins with the proposal and ends with tracking expenses.

## DESIGN VOCABULARY

Terms appear below in the order in which they first occur in this chapter.

Profit and loss
Gross profit
Net profit
Profit and loss (P&L) statement
Operating expenses
ROI (return on investment)
ROE (return on event)
Fund-raisers
Break-even event
Retail sales event
Tradeshow
Underwritten
Manufacturer's suggested retail price (MSRP)
Markup
Expendables
Drayage
Downtime
Cost plus
Estimating
Charge-out rate
Subcontractor
Incidental entertainment
Sight acts
Commission
Commissionable
Fitting session
Estimate sheets
Purchase order (PO)
Pro bono
Kickback
Finder's fee

## STUDIO WORK

1. An event decorating job brings in total net revenues of $26,000 and has job costs that total $14,000. The decorating firm has 26 percent overhead on average. What is the gross profit on the project? What is the net profit on the project?
2. If a service worth $5,000 is marked up 30 percent, what is the profit percentage? What is the profit? Is it net profit or gross? If materials sold for $7,500 with a 33.3 percent profit included, what was the markup?
3. For a client's outdoor holiday party, $2,000 worth of gifts and favors are purchased along with $5,000 of raw materials to fabricate a temporary patio enclosure. The labor involved in the patio enclosure is estimated to be 40 labor-hours at a charge-out rate of $60 per hour. The cover for the patio enclosure will be subcontracted to a tent company with a 30 percent markup. A 15 percent design and coordination fee will be added to the entire amount. What is the contract price to the client?
4. Three years after a product rollout in San Diego has been completed and paid for, the client calls up and wants you to design and decorate a similar product rollout in St. Louis. What information can you find in the job file that might help with this new project? What information will not be there?
5. An associate comes to you with a proposition. This associate has inside information on a major corporate anniversary celebration for a Fortune 100 company. The client can introduce you to the human resources director who is in charge of the project and make a strong recommendation for you. A 10 percent finder's fee is requested. Is this ethical?

## RECOMMENDED READINGS AND RESEARCH SITES

Allen, Judy, *The Business of Event Planning: Behind-the-Scenes Secrets of Successful Special Events,* John Wiley & Sons, 2002.

Allen, Judy, *Event Planning Ethics and Etiquette: A Principled Approach to the Business of Special Event Management,* John Wiley & Sons, 2003.

Goldblatt, Joe and Frank Supovitz, *Dollars & Events: How to Succeed in the Special Events Business,* John Wiley & Sons, 1999.

Pinson, Linda, *Keeping the Books: Basic Recordkeeping and Accounting for the Successful Small Business,* 5th ed., Dearborn, 2001.

Pottol, Harry, *Money Meter: Small Business Accounting with QuickBooks,* Money Meter Publishing, 1998.

U.S Internal Revenue Service
http://www.irs.gov

U.S. Small Business Administration
http://www.sba.gov

# Part Two

# THE DECORATIVE ELEMENTS

In this part you will learn specific methods, practices, and tips for decorating an event with backdrops and props, flowers, fabric, food, balloons, lighting, and other elements. This is a "hands-on" section that will tell you how to execute the design principles discussed in Part One by using the various elements available for decorations.

Hands-on experience is necessary for a complete understanding of some of what is covered in this part. However, special event students and practitioners can avoid learning through making mistakes and advance their careers more rapidly by studying this text.

Throughout this section on the decorative elements, in each chapter we consider the elements of design, budget, and resources that fall under the administration competency of the Blueprint for Special Events as defined by the International Special Events Society (ISES). Each chapter also discusses ways to execute the design; this falls under the coordination competency.

Risk management competency remains a consideration at all times and in all phases. It is a legal and ethical fact that all attendees at special events have an expectation of a safe and secure environment. It is the responsibility of the designer and decorator to assure that the environment is safe from harmful situations and secure from future dangers.

# Chapter 6

# BACKDROPS AND PROPS

*Props may be realistic, stylized, impressionistic, symbolic, abstractions or distortions. They may be functional, fanciful, or fragments of images. They may be used to create a cave or castle, urban jungle or enchanted garden, village or villa, ancient ruins or outer space, heaven or hell, under the circus big top or the ocean floor.*

**—Julia Rutherford Silvers, CSEP**

## IN THIS CHAPTER

You will discover how to decorate events by using backdrops and props.

**Designing with Backdrops and Props**

- Risk Management of Props and Drops
- Contracting Backdrops and Props

**Decorating with Backdrops**

- Rigging Backdrops
- Advanced Tips for Backdrops
- Alternative Backdrops

**Decorating with Props**

- Two-Dimensional Props
- Three-Dimensional Props
- Constructing and Painting Props
- Types of Props
- Sculpted Props
- Decorating with Staging

When you are considering the various props and drops that can be used to decorate an event, do not lose sight of the basic goals and objectives of the event. When successful design decisions are made, synergy is achieved. The assemblage of decorative items achieves a total impact that is greater than the individual items and that supports and enhances the goal of the event.

Julia Silvers, CSEP, a leading event manager, educator, and author, describes some of the many uses of props in the quote that begins this chapter. In my career, I have used props and backdrops in all the ways she describes. The quickest way to establish a theme is to paint a scene on a piece of canvas and hang it up against a wall. A few dimensional and semidimensional props are placed around the room. We lower the lights, and poof! We have created the illusion of another place and time.

## DESIGNING WITH BACKDROPS AND PROPS

The term *backdrop* is used generically to describe any decorative treatment at the back of a stage or behind an entertainment or presentation. In this chapter we consider **scenic backdrops** and **props.** Scenic backdrops are large fabric panels, usually sewn from unbleached muslin, with a decorative scene painted on them. Scenic backdrops create an illusion of place or a theme and can cover large areas. Their function can be purely decorative, or they can serve multiple purposes, such as hiding an unattractive or inappropriate architectural feature or reducing the size of a room that is too big for the event.

The term *props* is short for *properties.* In theater or films, props are dimensional items used to decorate the set or carried by the actors. In the event world, a prop is any hard scenic element used as décor, whether two-dimensional or three-dimensional. Two-dimensional props usually are constructed of flat stock such as plywood or foam core that has been cut out into a given shape, framed, and painted. Three-dimensional props are constructed, manufactured, or sculpted items.

Although not usually referred to as a prop, **staging** is an integral part of backdrops and props. Staging meets the practical requirement of providing height and visibility for the entertainment or presentation component of the event. Staging has the special challenge of having to support the weight of moving human beings.

Drops and props are selected or created based upon aesthetics, appropriateness, budget, and other criteria determined during the design and planning phases (administration) of the event. For example, it may be decided during the design and planning phases that the goals of promoting the Texas Department of Agriculture could be well served by having a Texas theme party. It then becomes the operational goal (coordination) of artistic design and scenic artistry to create or select decorations to support that goal.

In designing the décor package, theme props such as a giant Lone Star or a profile of the state could be chosen. Backdrops of an old western town or of the skyline of Houston could be used. Real props such as split-rail fences, western saddles, and tack also could be incorporated. Alternatively, more generic props and drops can be selected, such as a big sky drop on which a western sunset can be "painted" with light. In addition to the design and plan-

Idea Portfolio

# CREATING A BAYOU IN SAN ANTONIO

Coming into the courtyard of the old desanctified cloisters, guests entered a tent where moonlight filtered through hanging moss and spilled across the bayou, illuminating the cedar shack in the swamp. It really was an old convent, but where did the cedar swamp come from in San Antonio, Texas (see Figure 6-1)?

The illusion began with a scenic backdrop rented from a decorating firm in New Orleans. The stage, where a traditional Cajun band would play, was decorated as a boat dock in the swamp, with pier pilings, crates and barrels, and cotton bales. The dock appeared to project out from the swamp drop. Wild grapevine with lacy green southern smilax and droopy Spanish moss was wired across the top of the drop and extended randomly along the tent frame throughout, wrapping the guests in a bayou fantasy. Romantic moonlight from blue clip-on lights and projected gobos seemed to stream through the branches and spill across the entire area. (See Chapter 10, *The Art of Light,* to learn how to achieve this effect.)

**Figure 6-1**

ning considerations, operational concerns come into play, such as size, function, rigging, and handling issues, along with risk management.

Consider the size of decorative elements in relation to the venue and the places where you want to use them. They must fit within the space available, and they need to be in an appropriate scale. A backdrop larger than the space allows may be folded at the top and bottom to fit the space, but this might ruin the image you wanted on the decorative piece.

In the example of the swamp backdrop, we folded it at the top, carefully stapled the folded backdrop onto a wooden **batten,** and folded the excess at the bottom. (Wooden battens are one way to hang a backdrop. See "Rigging Backdrops" and Figure 6-3 in this chapter.) This was done with long staples by holding the staple gun at an angle to the surface to be stapled so that the staples did not penetrate deeply. The critical factor was extremely careful removal of the staples to minimize damage. If you are renting the backdrop, discuss this process in advance with the supplier to assure that it is acceptable to the rental company and what possible charges for damages might result.

Numerous questions need to be answered before you select props and drops. Will a low ceiling feature or chandelier hide the décor? If there is décor behind a band, will the drummer be sitting in front of the prettiest part? Will the speakers obscure the scene? Where will the sound technician and the large mixing board be placed?

One of the most common questions asked by designers is, Where did those ugly speakers come from? Those "ugly speakers" were a given from the time the client signed the contract with the band. Perhaps a pair of large flower arrangements should go in front of them.

## RISK MANAGEMENT OF PROPS AND DROPS

Risk management is a constant concern. If props are used as an entrance, can people walk under them? Does the access meet fire code and ADA (Americans with Disabilities Act) requirements? Are the backdrops and props either inherently or treated with flame retardant?

Can you install these elements with your crew and equipment? Will they fit through the doors? Is there a truck-height dock?

A professional special event designer has to research these questions of practicality and design and make a decision about the speakers, the chandeliers, accessibility, and all the other elements well in advance of the installation. Some décor items or equipment must be protected from unauthorized access because they can be potentially dangerous if mishandled or tampered with. It is surprising how many people will climb onto tables, chairs, or railings to retrieve small (or large) décor items to keep as event mementos.

## CONTRACTING BACKDROPS AND PROPS

The advantage of designing with painted backdrops is that they are easy to ship and store, folding into a small square pile and usually being stored in canvas bags with drawstrings. Because of these characteristics, there are international resources for renting backdrops. The talents of the finest scenic artists in the world are available to us via the Internet and modern shipping companies.

**JULIA RUTHERFORD SILVERS, CSEP, ON RISK MANAGEMENT FOR PROPS AND DROPS**

Every aspect of the event's design and décor should be examined from a risk management perspective. The equipment and materials used and their installation may present hazards but may also be used to prevent hazardous conditions and should be used to support any risk response plans.

People's movement in an emergency situation is based on their familiarity with the venue, the quality and clarity of exit routes, and the physical conditions facilitating or impeding that movement, such as crowd density, lighting, and obstacles.

Lighting, for example, may be used as a decorative component; its placement and intensity can attract or distract attention. The absence of sufficient illumination, however, can cause problems with crowd or individual mobility as well as lessening social control (in the dark you can be anonymous).

Props, décor items, or production equipment must be positioned and installed in such a way it does not create a fall (down, on, or over) or trip hazard, or cause obstructions to any *means of egress,* which includes the access to an exit, the exit itself, and the exit discharge. No décor should ever obstruct or detract attention from exit signs.

When selecting an event theme, decorators and their clients would do well to familiarize themselves with available props and backdrops, especially when working with a limited budget. The warehouse of a neighboring party prop rental house or the online catalogue of a backdrop rental company may provide inspiration for the next event.

Local event décor studios that rent props and drops are a great source. Not only are props and drops available, they frequently come with free advice on selection and installation. Local theaters and theater groups are a potential resource, as are nearby display and exhibit companies. However, the new paradigm is the universal availability of coast-to-coast resources through the World Wide Web and modern air express shipping companies.

Among the resources with catalogues on the Web are Dream World Backdrops at www.dreamworldbackdrops.com, Grosh Scenic Rentals at www.grosh.com, and Oliphant Studios at www.ostudio.com. Do your own research, as there are many other sources and the World Wide Web is constantly changing.

Consider the cross-country shipping and handling that may be required. Shipping times are critical, and the cost can be surprisingly high, especially for bulky items and when rush delivery is required. If you are renting from established event professionals, they can guide you to the best options.

Nonstandard sources for props include any company, individual, or association that has something you can use to decorate an event *if* you can talk them into allowing you to rent or borrow it for your purposes. For example, if you are doing a railroad theme party, see if there is a local train club. It may have sources for train-related props such as whistles and signs. If you are doing a 1920s or 1960s theme party, talk to local vintage auto, boat, or airplane clubs.

Once, while talking to a client about his parents' fiftieth wedding anniversary, we discovered that he was an antique auto collector and had several mint condition 1920s roadsters he would allow us to use as décor. Another time we were fortunate to find an enthusiast who was happy to park his shiny red 1960 Mustang convertible on the stage of the local high school for $100.

The first tricky aspect is getting these nonevent professionals interested in helping or renting you their prized collectibles. The next possible difficulty is that these people do not understand the event business. Their presentation and participation or interaction with the guests may be disappointing to you or to them. However, when carefully thought out and appropriate in all ways, these nonstandard sources can provide unique and effective props for an event.

Most props available from professionals are easy to assemble or come with instructions from the rental house. The challenge in renting props begins with hauling them. They may be bulky and fragile and may be susceptible to wind or weather damage, requiring a large closed truck. It may take two or more people to move them or, in some cases, a forklift. It is worth asking for an installed and removed price. Some rental houses will not allow the client to install their props or will have restrictions on the use of some of their more difficult, expensive, or delicate props.

It is your responsibility to confirm that the props and drops you rent will fit where you want to use them. Do not trust sales personnel or a brochure or catalogue entry about the actual sizes of either the space or the prop.

Idea Portfolio

## INCREDIBLE SHRINKING ELEVATOR

Billy Harper, an associate at Bill Reed Decorations, Inc., rented out that company's most popular gazebo for a wedding reception at a club in a downtown high-rise. The client told him that she had checked the dimensions of the freight elevator, but actually she had just called the catering manager, who had assured her that it was spacious. When delivery was attempted, the need to take actual measurements became obvious when the gazebo panels would not fit in the elevator.

Fortunately, Billy had enough time to bring the gazebo back to the shop, where the metal frame was cut and modified so that the panels would break apart and fit back together. Only Bill Reed Decorations' commitment to service and the client's willingness to pay the additional costs involved kept the bride from being disappointed at her reception.

# DECORATING WITH BACKDROPS

Backdrops cover a lot of wall space relatively inexpensively. The Cajun swamp backdrop in the tent that created the illusion described earlier in this chapter was 15 feet tall by 40 feet wide. The tent was on 10-foot poles, so the backdrop was carefully folded to allow the artwork to fit the available space.

This backdrop was painted in **perspective,** or **trompe l'oeil,** a style of painting that gives the illusion of photographic reality.

Constructing and painting backdrops is the discipline of the **scenic artist** and is beyond the scope of this chapter. However, event decorators need to understand the basics of their construction and painting.

Drops should be sewn from flame-retardant-treated unbleached muslin with horizontal **flat fell seams.** They usually have a reinforcement jute web at the top and a pipe pocket to accept weighting pipes at the bottom. Theatrical drops have grommets and ties at the top; some party drop systems use Velcro.

Before being painted, drops are stretched horizontally just off the floor or vertically on a paint frame and attached at all four edges. Then they are painted with a starch or glue to prepare the surface to accept paint. The design is then transferred to the drop in charcoal through the use of projection or a grid system. The scenic artist then lays in the color and texture, heightening the illusion through the use of highlight and shadow.

Chapter 10, "Scene Painting," in *Scenery for the Theatre* by Burris-Meyer and Cole provides the best explanation of various scene-painting techniques that I have read. *Scenery for the Theatre* is out of print but is available in bookstores specializing in collectibles and in libraries. There are other texts available for the aspiring scenic artist.

The impact of a scenic backdrop can be increased by using two- or three-dimensional props in conjunction with it. Dimensional representations of elements that appear in the backdrop can create the illusion that they are spilling out of it. For example, pairs of dimensional columns in front of a ballroom drop can match columns painted on the drop. Similarly, a three-dimensional working fountain in front of a drop can enhance the illusion of time and place (see Figure 6-2).

**Perspective:** The drawing or painting illusion in which objects recede or get smaller in the distance; a technique employing one or more theoretical vanishing points to achieve this effect.

**Trompe l'oeil:** A painting style that gives the illusion of photographic reality; this style employs perspective and other techniques, such as shading, modeling, and the use of receding colors, to enhance the illusion of reality. From the French for "to deceive the eye."

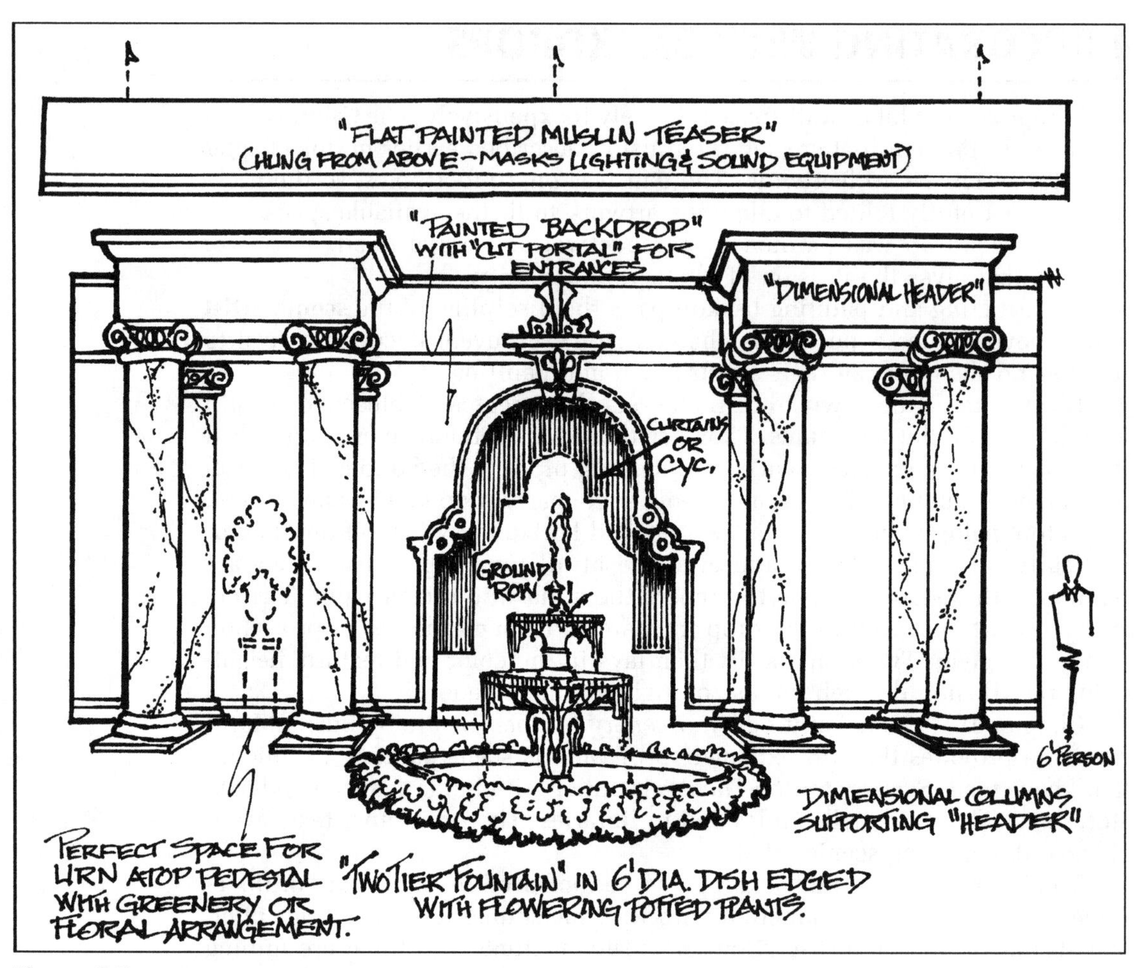


Figure 6-2

## RIGGING BACKDROPS

The installation of backdrops is called **rigging** them, and the two versions of rigging backdrops are either **flying** or **ground support.** In the theater and some event venues there are permanent pipes, called battens, to which scenic backdrops can be attached and flown. It is common these days to bring chain motors into ballrooms and exhibit halls to fly truss for lighting purposes. Backdrops can be flown from minitruss in this fashion. Flying generally is used for backdrops 20 feet high by 50 feet wide and larger.

The other way to rig backdrops is called ground support, and there are two versions of it. One way involves truss that is raised and supported on lifts that are raised manually or electrically through cables on winches. This is used in larger venues to rig drops up to 20 feet high by 40 feet wide.

The other common ground support method uses adjustable-height metal pipes called **stanchions.** The stanchions fit on metal bases that can be **sand-**

**MONROE'S RISK MANAGEMENT NOTE**

Drops over 12 feet high, or lower if they are in a windy or heavy draft environment, must be secured with tie lines or safety wires to a secure architectural feature. Many venues allow nails or screws to be placed in positions where visible surfaces will not be damaged if the screws or nails are removed after the event. Check with management for approval in advance and carry insurance to cover liability for unintended property damage as well as personal injury.

**bagged** for added stability and support a wooden batten held at the top by a hook (Figure 6-3). This method works well for drops from 12 to 16 feet high. The drop is stapled to the batten, which is inserted into the hooks at the top of the stanchions. The stanchions are then carefully raised to the height at which the drop will play (stay). Sandbags or heavy stage weights are placed on the bases for safety, and if the drop is over 12 feet high, it is a good idea to tie the stanchions off to something secure.

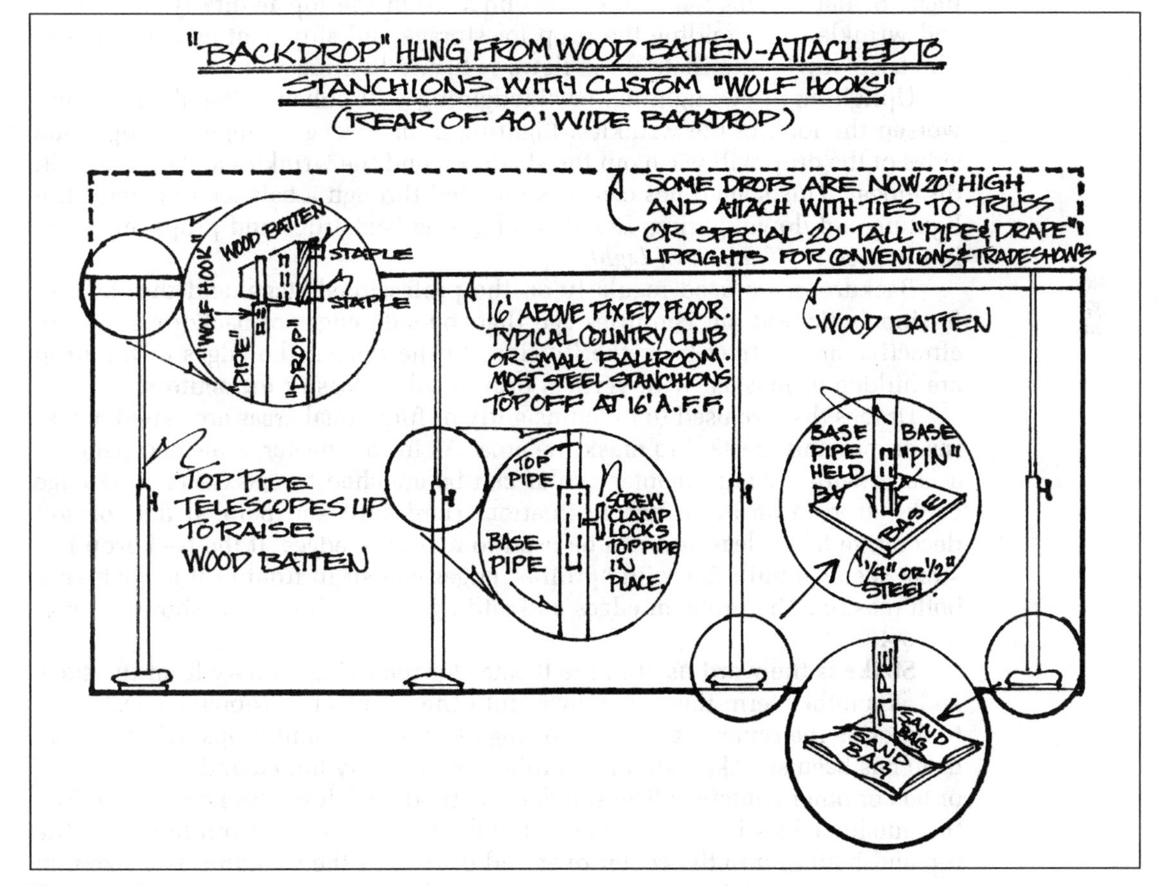


Figure 6-3

## ADVANCED TIPS FOR BACKDROPS

The visible edges of a backdrop—the top, bottom, and sides—can detract from the **illusion** painted on the drop as the sky comes to a sudden stop at the top edge and the hanging mechanism shows at the top. In the theater a horizontal curtain called a **teaser** hides the top edge of the drop, and this technique sometimes works for events as well. Other possible design solutions include controlling the lighting so that the top fades off in the dark, or vine, garland, or Spanish moss can be strung along the top edge to soften the visible edge and heighten the illusion.

The bottom of the drop usually does not present a design problem, as we are used to horizons in real life. However, using a scenic prop called a **ground row** can enhance the illusion. This is a low two-dimensional prop along the bottom edge of a drop that can consist of painted scenery or a black profile silhouette. Ground rows frequently are used to conceal lighting instruments employed to uplight the drops.

The bottom of the drop is both weighted by a pipe and hung off the floor, or it is rolled on boards to try to stretch out the horizontal wrinkles. A large piece of flat rectangular fabric suspended from the top naturally has waves and wrinkles, and folding the drop for storage and shipment creates creases. The best way to eliminate these flaws is to use lighting.

Uplighting, downlighting, or sidelighting will enhance the shadows and worsen the look of the wrinkles. Lighting from 45-degree angles on opposite sides of the drop will wash out the shadows, and the wrinkles and creases will disappear. This sometimes can be simulated through a balance of careful uplighting and downlighting. Details on lighting backdrops and props are given in Chapter 10, *The Art of Light.*

Backdrops are used regularly on the professional stage, and theater professionals figured out centuries ago that the side edges of backdrops are not attractive and detract from the illusion. In the theater the edges of the drop are hidden or masked with vertical drapes called **legs** or **tormentors.**

Drapes that are used to hide unsightly or functional areas are called **masking** drapes and are said to **mask** the area. As in the theater, a pleated panel of a fabric with a complimentary color can be attached to mask each side edge of the drop in an event décor situation. Hard-built and painted flats or soft decorative fabric legs also can be used to mask the edges. If the backdrop is a street scene, a built flat with "profile" edges can sit in front of it at each end, both masking the problem edges and adding to the illusion, as shown in Figure 6-4.

**Strike** is the word used in the theater for removing scenery from the stage and is another term that has moved into the event professional's vocabulary to describe the removing or dismantling of backdrops and props. After a backdrop has been struck, it should be rolled or carefully folded and put in its bag or box or other container. The standard method for folding backdrops is to fold the outside edges into the center of the drop over and over and then fold the top and bottom into the center over and over until the backdrop is a size that can be handled. This minimizes creases in the center of the drop.

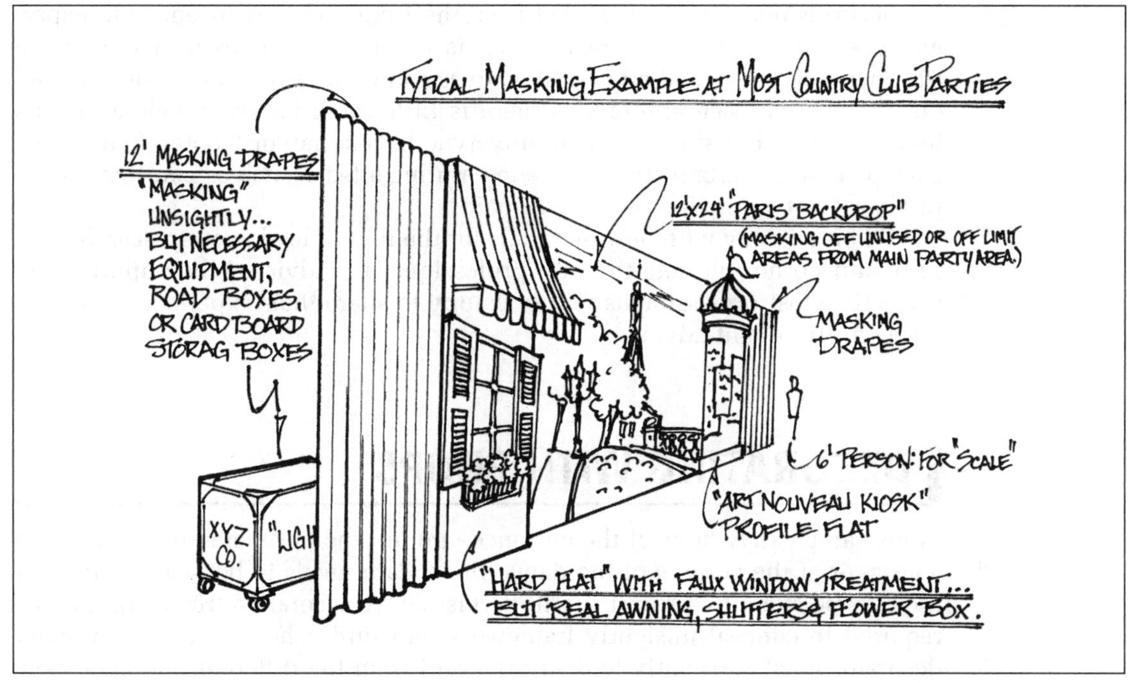


**Figure 6-4**

## ALTERNATIVE BACKDROPS

Other materials used for decorative scenic backdrops are up to the imagination of the designer, but unusual materials and techniques that are new should be experimented with in a small-scale sample. Some popular materials are sharkstooth scrim and duvetyne or velour, which are discussed in detail in Chapter 8, *Fabulous Fabric Décor.*

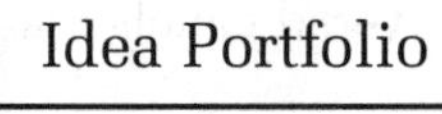

Idea Portfolio

## AN ORCHESTRA AS IF BY MAGIC

We once were asked by a client to make a 60-piece symphony orchestra appear magically in a country club ballroom. After careful experimentation, we painted a scrim with dye to look like the interior of a Baroque ballroom and installed it in front of the stage we built for the orchestra. When the guests arrived, there was a quartet in period costume and powdered wigs playing in front of the drop. Later in the evening the quartet left, and on cue the symphony started playing, the lights changed, and the symphony orchestra appeared magically in the middle of the ballroom. The scrim then opened, and the illusion of the orchestra playing became real.

**Scrim** is opaque when lighted from the front and translucent to transparent when lighted from the rear. Scrim is painted with dyes to maintain the transparency for special effects. Most dyes cannot be painted over or removed once they have been applied, so there is little room for error. Velour and its less expensive but similar cousin duvetyne have a nap or "tooth" that can be used to achieve certain stylized scene painting effects, such as painting scenes in black-light (ultraviolet)-sensitive paint.

When working with new materials for the first time, do your research carefully and do not hesitate to ask a professional for advice. When approached correctly, most professionals will be happy to share their experience and give respectfully sought advice.

# DECORATING WITH PROPS

Props can go anywhere: at the entrance, around the perimeter, out among the guests, or at the corners of the dance floor. Care needs to be taken to inspect the reverse side of a prop if it will be visible. A decorative treatment may be required to conceal unsightly framework and unfinished surfaces. An event decorator must constantly look at the event from the different points of view of all of the attendees. Many a stakeholder has gone to the mezzanine to see the event in all its glory only to see "THIS SIDE UP" stenciled on the tops of the props.

## TWO-DIMENSIONAL PROPS

**Flats** are rectangular two-dimensional props that are scenically or decoratively painted or covered with decorative fabric. Another standard two-dimensional prop is the cutout **profile piece.** This can consist of representational artwork that is "cut out" along its outline, such as a clown, cowboy, cactus, or cruise ship. Numerous decorative two-dimensional hard props are available, including lattice panels, folding screens, and fabric-covered panels that you can rent, buy, or build.

The advantages of two-dimensional props are that they generally store face to face and back to back, minimizing storage and transportation space. They are much more easily stored and transported than are the three-dimensional props described below. They also can be installed in levels, one in front of the other, in front of a backdrop, for example. This creates a nice illusion of depth and dimension.

The disadvantages are that small profile details such as the finger in "Uncle Sam Wants You" or the gun barrel of a cowboy cutout gunfighter are vulnerable to damage. While capable of adding depth and dimension, they do not approach the reality of a three-dimensional prop, and they take up more space and are more expensive to ship than a canvas backdrop (see Figure 6-5).

"3D & 2D Props" (Pros & Cons)
"2D Props" store easily and are cheaper to make....
However... They are better viewed from afar... and not from behind. (See Fig. 6-6)
"3D Props are more expensive & need more care... However they look good from all sides and can be "in" the party space ~ not on the outside.


Figure 6-5

## THREE-DIMENSIONAL PROPS

Three-dimensional props are either constructed or sculpted. Tall columns can be constructed from seamless paper tubing; doors, frames, pediments, pedestals, planters, and piles of other wonderful items are available, depending on your imagination, budget, and local prop rental warehouses. Props can be sculpted from high- or low-density styrene or urethane foam and coated with a protective finish that will take paint, or they can be molded out of light high-impact plastic or created from fiberglass. The wonderful signature props from Blaine

Kern's Mardi Gras Warehouse in New Orleans (http://mardigrasworld.com) are good examples of quality three-dimensional props.

The advantages of three-dimensional props are that they are self-standing, are usually easy to install, and look real. With careful placement and lighting they can have a wonderful design impact. The disadvantage is that they are expensive and bulky to handle, transport, and ship.

## CONSTRUCTING AND PAINTING PROPS

Today all materials are potentially useful in constructing props. In the scene shop of yesteryear, all two-dimensional scenery was muslin or canvas stretched over flat frames with fabric fir plywood added for profile effects. These days, there are different materials available and different skill levels in prop shops. Also, costs have escalated to a point where new more cost-effective techniques are welcome.

The distinctive grain of fir plywood is visible if the prop is painted directly without a muslin glue-down cover, but birch, maple, and lauan plywood are available in the same or better price range and do not have a grain problem. Designs can be projected or transferred onto the plywood directly, and it can be saber-sawed to the shape desired and then box-framed with lightweight dimensional stock (1-inch by 2-inch or 1-inch by 3-inch softwood lumber), as shown in Figure 6-6.

It is a good idea to treat this unit with a flame-retardant chemical before painting it, as this is much easier than dealing with it after the fact. Different areas and applications have different flame-retardant requirements; check with the local authorities in advance. The best practice is to exceed the National Fire Code requirements.

Another popular product is a plastic foam core sheet covered with a medium-density paper overlay. These products are manufactured by several companies and sold under the trade names Fomecore and Gatorfoam, among others. Experiment with these products the first time you use them. Characteristics you should investigate include possible warping when painted and difficulty of attaching to the framework without nails showing. I know one talented designer who made a good living with white Fomecore, an Exacto knife, a straightedge, and duct tape, creating decorations for chic department store fashion shows.

A necessary piece of equipment for this work is a projector, which is the easiest way to transfer the design when one is working on relatively small-scale two-dimensional props. An opaque projector or other form of **orthographic** projector is best. *Orthographic* is the technical term for two-dimensional (nonperspective) drawings.

## TYPES OF PROPS

Three-dimensional props can be found objects such as a 1954 Corvette parked outside the entrance to a 1950s party, built props like a speakeasy door entrance into a 1920s prohibition-era "flapper party," and sculpted objects such

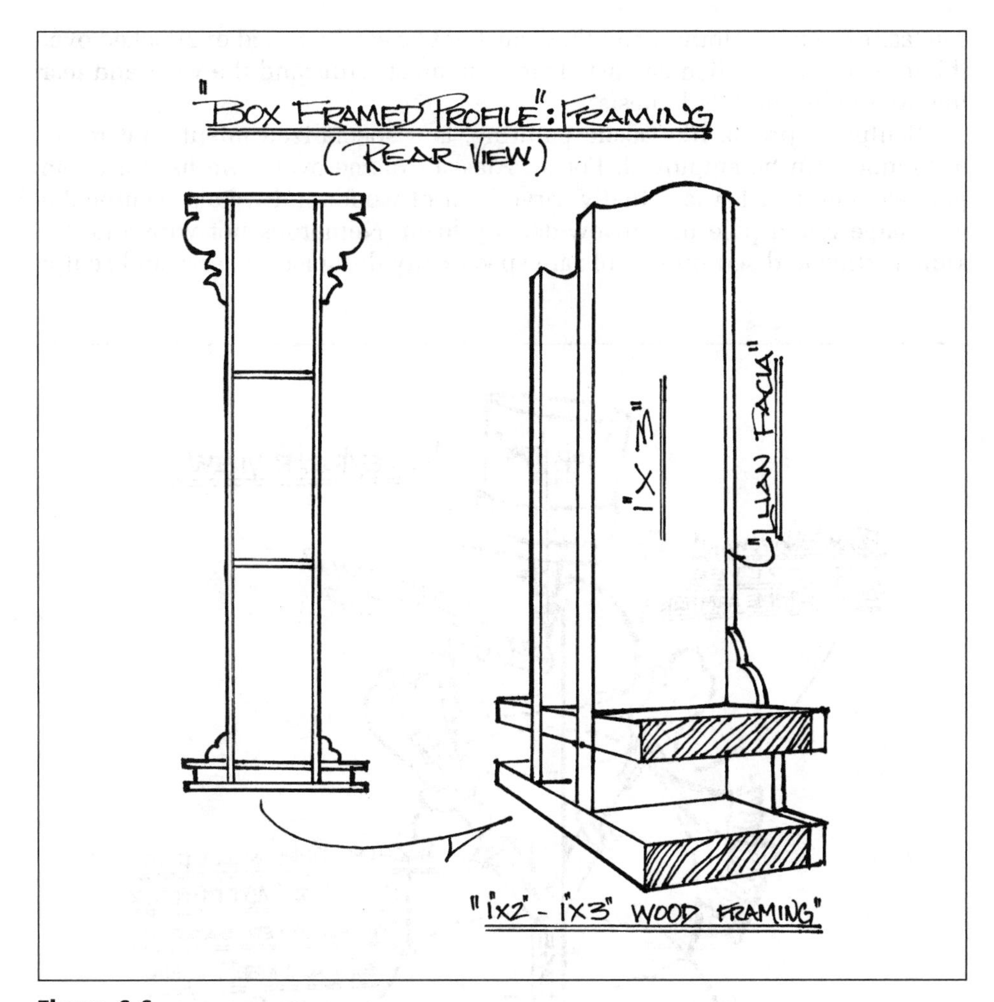


**Figure 6-6**

as a snowman for the souvenir photo shoot at a corporate holiday party. Each type and style has its own challenges and offers its own decorative impact.

Working with classic cars presents the challenge of dealing with an expensive collectible at a party and if it is indoors, the added challenge of meeting fire code requirements. Fire code requirements for the display of autos indoors generally require less than one gallon of fuel in the gas tank and mandate that the battery cable be disconnected. Check with the local authorities. Any found props that were not designed to be event décor can create these types of challenges.

Built props are more straightforward in their requirements. The primary caveat with them is that if the guests will touch, handle, use, or feel them, they must be safe and secure. They cannot have splinters or sharp edges that can tear expensive clothes, and they must not be easily pulled or knocked over if bumped into or fallen against. They also must withstand the wear and tear imposed by uninhibited guests.

Sculpting props, like scene painting, is a specialized talent, and many techniques can be employed. For an Alaskan theme event, we used a totem pole we found that was actually carved out of wood, and we also sculpted a very large totem pole out of low-density foam. Numerous hot wire and hot knife cutting and sculpting tools are specifically designed to carve and sculpt

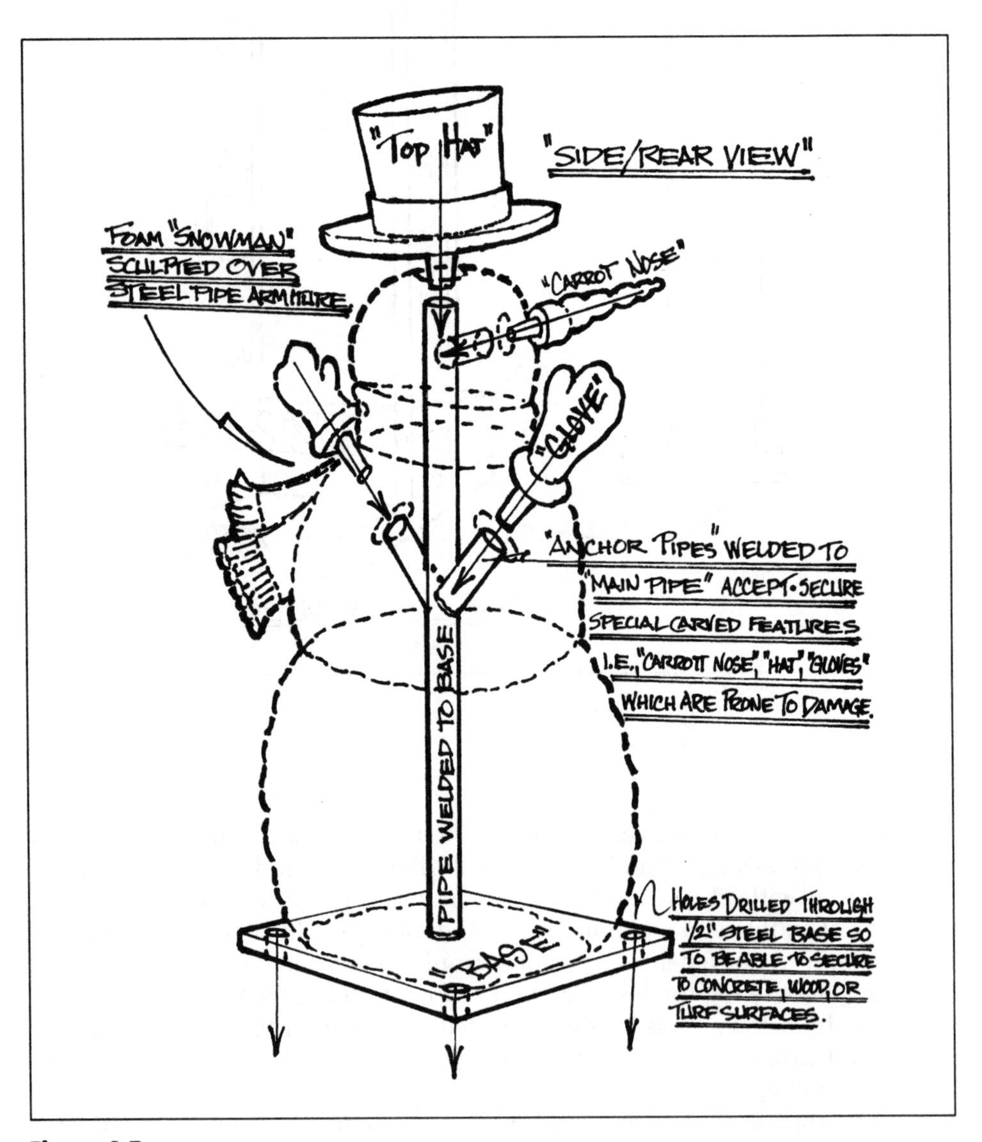


**Figure 6-7**

foam. Finishing low-density foam sculpture used to be a bit tricky, as it will melt if any petroleum product comes in contact with it. Today there are products specifically made for this purpose (Elasta-Shield and Styrothane, among others) that protect it from interaction with petroleum-based products and from the elements as well as providing protection against abrasions and puncturing wounds. These tools and materials can be found at various arts and crafts suppliers or ordered from arts and craft suppliers on the Web; search for "foam coating."

Foam sculptor and prop master Robert Justice prefers to use a double coating of low-cost latex stucco, as it is easy to use and nontoxic. He says: "You can add paint to the material for coloring, and it develops a tough skin that is resistant to puncturing and mechanical damage. Its shortcoming is that you have to stir it a lot to get something approaching a really smooth surface."

Often a wooden or metal armature must be constructed as the support for a foam sculpture. The foam can then be glued around it in pieces. The best way to glue pieces of foam together for sculpting purposes is to use two-part expandable urethane foam. This takes practice, but it results in a unit whose attachment points can be carved or sculpted like the snowman shown in Figure 6-7.

Very few of these foam products are inherently flame-retardant, so much research needs to be done before each application. If the unit is of major proportions, it may not satisfy the flame-retardant characteristics requirements. Consider safety first at all times; do the research. Also note that carving these materials with a hot wire cutter and using two-part foam during the sculpting process both can put out noxious and possibly toxic fumes. Always work in a well-ventilated area and wear approved ventilators.

## STAGING

We once designed and constructed a custom stage as a sunken ship lying canted on the "sea bottom" where the former *Tonight Show* bandleader Skitch Henderson provided dance music for a high-society party. There was also a more traditional stage where the Jackson Five provided late-night entertainment. The bandstand stage was a special construction that allowed the decorative shell to be canted, and the performance area was level and plumb to support the performers. The stage for the late-night entertainers was constructed out of traditional staging in accordance with the requirements of the **contract rider** for the band.

Strictly custom stages such as the sunken ship need to be designed and engineered on a job-by-job basis and are very expensive. Traditional staging that can be decorated with props and backdrops, such as the swamp dock stage described at the beginning of this chapter, are available for reasonable rental prices or come with the rental of the room from the venue. Standard hotel staging normally comes in 6-foot by 8-foot sections that fold up in the center and can be rolled into place on their wheels. No tools are required to assemble stages with this system, which generally comes in 16-, 24-, and 32-inch heights and has a carpetlike finish on the top surface. Steps are built with 8-inch rises, and three-step units have railings that may or may not be detachable.

Most other staging systems come in 4-foot by 4-foot or 4-foot by 8-foot modules, because the ¾-inch plywood used for their tops is manufactured 4 feet by 8 feet. Plywood is the most popular material for use as tops or decks because of its good ratio of strength to weight. The available theatrical systems feature wood frames with changeable legs or lightweight trusslike framing systems with removable tops or decks. This second system is called **parallels** because of the way the frames fold for transport and storage. There are also numerous commercially available systems that can be rented or purchased, each with its own pros and cons. Theatrical staging and step units generally come with 6-inch rises.

The legs and supporting structure usually need to be hidden with masking, either fabric **skirting** or hard **facing.** Hotel and venue staging comes with fabric that snaps on or attaches with Velcro. Theatrical staging has black skirting available to staple on, or you can have custom fabric skirting sewn to match the décor. Alternatively, you can construct and paint decorative facing for the stage and steps that matches the backdrop and props on top of the stage.

It is important to know the details of the staging system to integrate it into the décor package. It may have metal frames or decks that limit the ways you can attach scenery. Note that theatrical and event staging is usually fabricated in 6-inch-high increments, while typical hotel staging is fabricated in 8-inch heights. This means they are the same height only at 24 and 48 inches. Also, 48 inches is the maximum height for typical hotel staging.

If you have special needs, such as displaying a car or supporting the weight of a full-grown African elephant, you may need to double-top it or reinforce the legs and support framing. If there is to be a lot of activity on the stage, such as rock 'n' roll dancing, we sometimes separate the staging with the three-dimensional props from the performance staging by an inch or two to keep the props from rocking and rolling with the performers.

## FINISHING TOUCHES

Backdrops and props can be used in special events in many ways to create an illusion or theme or for decorative or functional purposes. When you are using backdrops, props, and staging, risk management concerns should always be a primary consideration. There are many tricks to the event decorating trade, and the best way to hone your skills in these areas is through practical, hands-on experience.

The event designer or manager does not need to be an expert in handling backdrops and props, but he or she needs to have a working knowledge of the principles involved. This is necessary so that he or she can hire and communicate effectively with the special event scenic experts.

## DESIGN VOCABULARY

Terms appear below in the order in which they first occur in this chapter.

Scenic backdrops
Props
Staging
Batten
Perspective
Trompe l'oeil
Scenic artist
Flat fell seams
Rigging
Flying
Ground support
Stanchions
Sandbagging
Illusion
Teaser
Ground row
Leg
Tormentor
Masking
Mask
Strike
Scrim
Flats
Profile piece
Orthographic
Contract rider
Parallels
Skirting
Facing

## STUDIO WORK

1. Connect to the Internet, do a search of available props and drops rental houses, and make a list of usable URLs.
2. Locate a scenic backdrop that could inspire an event and describe dimensional props that could be used with it to achieve synergy in the event décor.
3. Describe a decorative package around the band stage in a thematic design concept of your own.
4. Locate, sketch, or describe the backdrops and props you would use to execute your thematic design concept in item 3.

## RECOMMENDED READINGS AND RESEARCH SITES

Burris-Meyer, Harold, and Cole, Edward C. *Scenery for the Theatre: The Organization, Processes, Materials, & Techniques Used to Set the Stage,* Little, Brown, 1972.

Malouf, Lena, *Behind the Scenes at Special Events: Flowers, Props, and Design,* John Wiley & Sons, 1998.

Parker, W. Oren, Harvey Kennedy Smith, and R. Craig Wolf, *Scenic Design and Stage Lighting,* Thompson Learning, 1996.

Silvers, Julia Rutherford, *Professional Event Coordination,* John Wiley & Sons, 2004.

Creations Fantastic—scenic and event backdrop rental and purchase
http://www.backdropsfantastic.com

Dream World Backdrops—scenic and event backdrop rental and purchase
http://www.dreamworldevents.com

Ents Web Directory: Scenery, Sets & Props, Design & Supply—online directory of predominantly United Kingdom firms
http://www.entsweb.co.uk/theatre/scenery/

Google Directory: Business > Arts and Entertainment > Tools and Equipment > Props—online directory of event props manufacturers, sellers, and rental houses
http://directory.google.com/Top/Business/Arts_and_Entertainment/Tools_and_Equipment/Props

Grosh Scenic Rentals—scenic backdrop and curtain rental and purchase
http://www.grosh.com

Oliphant Studio—scenic backdrop and curtain rental and purchase
http://www.ostudio.com

PLSN Links: Scenic Design Manufacturers and Sales—online directory
http://www.plsn.com/linksp/Scenic_Design_Manufacturers_and_Sales

Scenic Backdrop Rentals, by Charles H. Stewart—complete online catalogue
http://charleshstewart.com

# Chapter 7

# DECORATING WITH FLOWERS

*Be sure you see the trees in the forest!*

—**John Daly**

---

**IN THIS CHAPTER**

You will discover how to effectively integrate flowers into successful event design and decoration.

**Basic Floral Décor**

- Table Centerpieces
  - Traditional
  - Nontraditional
- Garland
- Flowers for the Buffet
- Flowers on Stage

**Architectural Flowers**

- Flowering Vine Illusion
- Hanging Flower Baskets and Balls
- Floating Flowers

**Other Floral Décor**

**Growing and Blooming Décor**

- Potted Plants
- Trees and Foliage Plants

---

John Daly, one of the most respected event floral artists in the world and an award-winning event designer, says: "Don't get so overwhelmed that you do not see the details." His point in the quote that opens this chapter is to stress the importance of attention to details in event design. He says, "If you do the details correctly, the guests may not notice, but if you don't do them correctly, they certainly will notice. For example, if you hide the ugly black plastic containers that the trees come in, people may not notice, but if you don't hide them, people will notice that."

# BASIC FLOWER DÉCOR

Arranging flowers is an art that has been practiced for many centuries in many styles around the world. Traditional floral design in the West has emphasized the elements of shape, line, and focus. Color has been defined in monochromatic, contrasting, and compatible variations. Every culture, age, and fad has its own style and aesthetic interpretation in using flowers. Event designers must be knowledgeable about the styles and fads of their age and time whether they personally design flowers or hire someone to do it for them.

There are many talented floral designers practicing today who have little or no knowledge of the most basic requirements, limitations, or design parameters of special event floral work. A student of event design will study floral design, as a professional event designer needs to be conversant with the various flowers and design styles. In this chapter, information is supplied about the techniques and practices that allow floral design to be integrated effectively into successful event design. It is about the use of flowers as décor, not how to arrange flowers or create basic centerpieces or arrangements.

Many texts and numerous classes on floral design are available for the neophyte to the master floral designer. I have learned over the years that some people have a natural talent for floral design, color, and composition. My brother, John Monroe, runs the Four Seasons Flower Shop in Westfield, New York, and is a brilliant floral designer who has never taken a course in floral arrangement. The good news for the rest of us is that these talents can be studied and learned. I took a series of floral design courses before adding floral design to our services. Several books on basic floral arrangement are recommended at the end of the chapter.

Color, design style, and the actual flowers are selected on the basis of aesthetics, appropriateness, budget, and other criteria to support the goal of the event during the design and planning phases (administration). However, if pure floral design is implemented without considering seasonal availability, height, attachment points for hanging arrangements and garland, or other operational concerns (coordination), the goals of the event may not be achieved.

The perception of flowers as lovely, fragile creations belies the reality of heavy, dripping design creations, possibly including metal armatures, flaming candles, and electrical lights and cords. Risk management is also a concern with floral decorations, as it is with all decorative elements.

## TABLE CENTERPIECES

Centerpieces add a touch of elegance, welcome guests, and enhance the décor. In a home or a restaurant these are their main functions. Centerpieces for events, however, are called upon to serve other functions as well and do so within limitations and constraints. A centerpiece designed for an event can serve a stylish, welcoming, or decorative function, but its actual objective will be determined by the event. It may be used to enhance a theme, promote networking, or sell a product. The objective of the event will define the style of the centerpiece for the designer.

**Nonfloral centerpieces** will be covered in this chapter along with floral creations, as they follow the same rules, restrictions, and design and decoration practices as floral centerpieces.

If a theme has been selected for the event, there is an underlying purpose for that theme of which the event floral designer should be aware. For example, even if a Great Gatsby theme has been selected for a fund-raiser, the underlying objective is still to raise money. The Great Gatsby theme, from the novel by F. Scott Fitzgerald, is based on the excesses of a certain segment of high society during the 1920s. A thematically perfect centerpiece would be one that featured all white roses, expensive white lilies, and a lush overdone look. However, the designer needs to coordinate closely with his or her client, who may have to explain to the underwriters why such expensive centerpieces were incorporated into the fund-raiser. That centerpiece, while thematically appropriate, may not support the basic goal of the event.

One way fund-raisers can have fabulous centerpieces is to create centerpieces that are salable or create the centerpieces in a container that can be purchased at wholesale and sold for a price that will pay for the floral design. While it is a gamble that the centerpieces will sell, if successful, this approach can raise the quality of the centerpieces significantly. Silver-plated or crystal wine coolers as containers frequently are used to create salable centerpieces. When centerpieces are sold, arrangements must be made to collect the money and prevent departing guests from carrying them away without paying. It also may be necessary to box the container. Any time centerpieces are designed to be carried away, consideration must be given to water level, size, and stability in the recipient's auto.

If the event is primarily a networking function, the height of the centerpiece is crucial, as it must not interfere with communications across a table. However, a creative designer may go beyond this and design an interactive centerpiece that encourages discussion or even requires team-building interaction. Perhaps a "construct-it-yourself" centerpiece can be conceived, with a prize for the best one.

I attended an event where my place card was a piece of a child's puzzle. The instructions were to locate the other attendees who had the other parts to that puzzle and the table at which that puzzle was built into the centerpiece. In the process of finding my table, I interacted with many other attendees, which was, of course, the reason for the design. Other interactive possibilities involve creating underwater, robot, Tinker Toy, or Lego® centerpieces (see Figure 7-1).

For sales or marketing events the centerpiece is often an afterthought because without one the tables would look empty. A creative event floral designer will include some element in the design that will promote the product

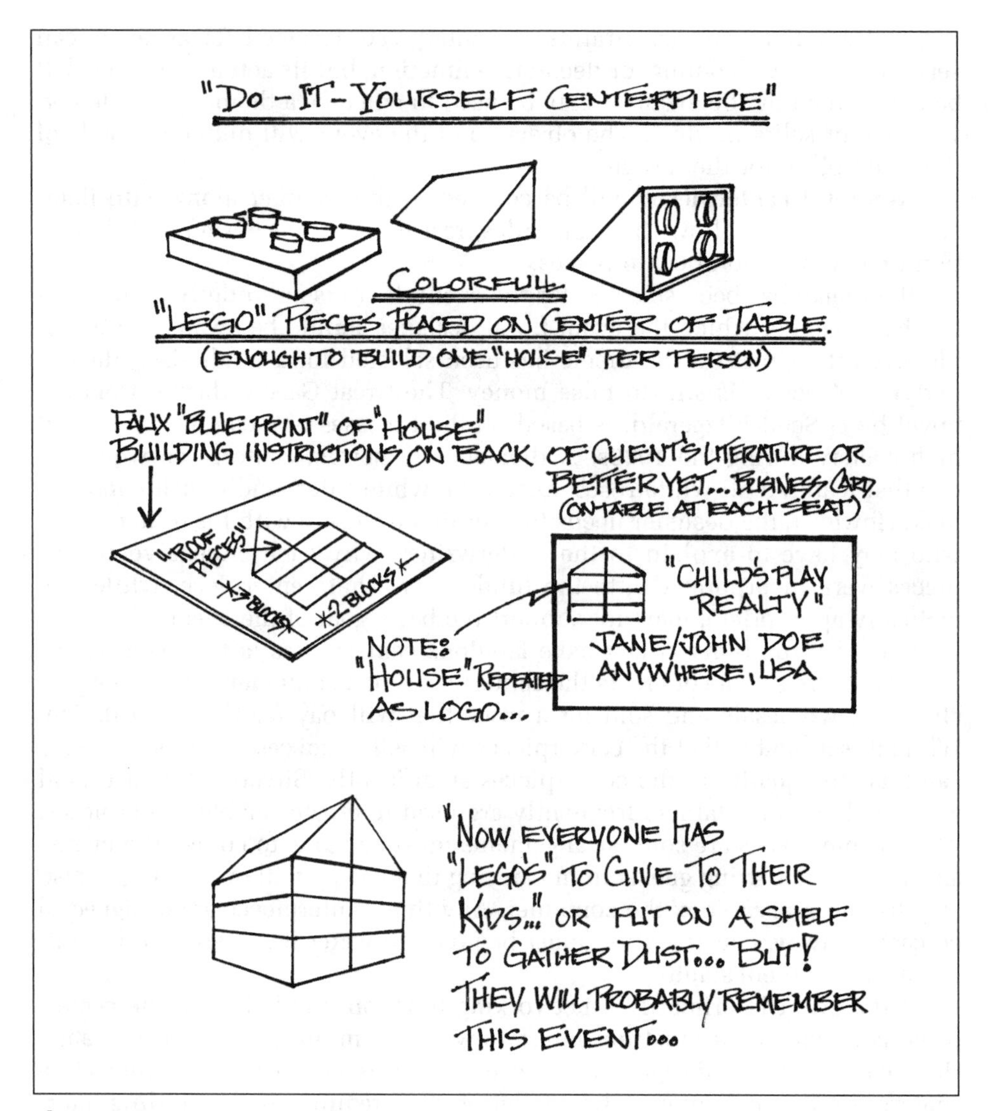


**Figure 7-1**

directly or perhaps subtly promote the corporate image by incorporating the corporate colors into the centerpiece and the table treatment.

## TRADITIONAL CENTERPIECES

Traditional floral centerpieces (as seen in Figure 7-2) come in many styles but always incorporate the basic principles of color, line, and composition into a 360-degree round centerpiece. Traditional concerns are height, space taken on

Idea Portfolio

# A THEMED INTERACTIVE CENTERPIECE

Our conference theme last year was "non-profit housing builds strong communities," and I used large Lego Duplo® blocks as centrepieces. Each round of 10 had about 20 to 30 of the colourful blocks on the table, and the guests could "play" with them, share them with neighbouring tables, and so on. Tables were encouraged to "build" houses and share them with the neighbouring tables to "build" communities. We ended up with some wonderful creations, which we moved to the stage area and enjoyed during the after-dinner entertainment. As we were doing live-to-screen video anyway, we had the video cameraman go around and focus on table creations during the eating part of the evening. It gave us a nice break from just having our logo on the screen.

PS—The Duplo was really inexpensive from Toys R Us (they had a one-day door crasher sale, and we went around to every store in Toronto to buy the maximum). The cost per table worked out to about $5 to $6.

Patsy Duffy, Conference Coordinator
Ontario Non-Profit Housing Association
Toronto, Ontario

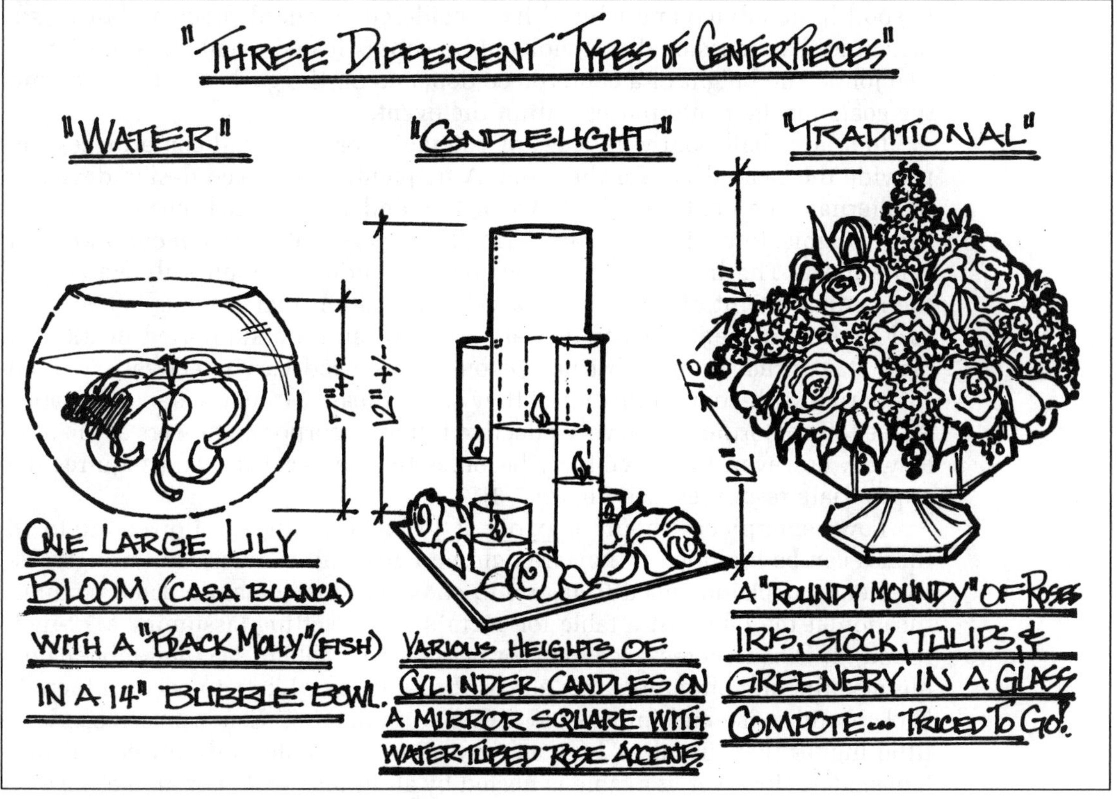


**Figure 7-2**

**SOME NONFLORAL ACCENTS**

**Pick.** The generic name for any small collection of decorative elements that are assembled around a pointed plastic, metal, or wire stem (pick) to allow it to be inserted into floral foam or wired into an arrangement.

**Ting ting.** A long thin dried wand that is available dyed and glittered in various colors; one of many types of dried flower material that can be purchased in colors or glitter finishes.

**Glitter garland.** Any of various springy wire garlands in glittery colors, frequently with foil stars, musical notes, or other specific theme elements attached along it.

the table, and compatibility with the room and/or event décor. Other traditional elements that may come into play are thematic elements incorporated into the design through containers, flower selection, and nonfloral accents such as **picks, ting ting,** and **glitter garland.**

Height is a frequently discussed design element. John Daly says that centerpieces should not exceed 14 inches in height or should start at 24 inches. His rule of thumb is that when he puts his elbow on the table with his arm straight up in the air, the centerpiece should be no higher than his wrist. This is good basic advice and should be considered standard practice, but it is a principle that occasionally is violated by sophisticated event floral designers like John. The height of a centerpiece depends on the goals for the event and the goals for the centerpieces within the event.

In a large ballroom with a sea of 100 tables or more, tall centerpieces can provide the basic décor for the room. A frequently employed design device is to alternate the centerpieces between low and high, sometimes even using three heights: low, high, and very high. The key is to not use a medium-height centerpiece. The height of 14 inches recommended by John Daly actually is the median height of a window for communication that extends between 12 and 24 inches. Centerpieces that are very tall and are supported on thin or clear stands that do not obstruct vision can be used very effectively without interfering with communication if they start at least 24 inches above the table. These tall centerpieces are very effective if they incorporate flowers at the base as well; however, this effectively becomes two centerpieces and requires the appropriate resources (see Figure 7-3).

Low centerpieces should max out at 14 inches, although flowers up to 18 inches can be included if they are light and airy and can be seen through easily. Height decisions need to take into consideration the anticipated communication at the table. At a table for 10 in a social setting (assuming a 72-inch round), it is considered necessary for people to be able to see their tablemates, but meaningful communication across the table is unlikely to occur if there is background noise and impossible if a band is playing. Centerpieces can be a little higher than usual as long as they allow a visible nod between distant tablemates. However, if a table is hosted by an industry CEO or marketing vice

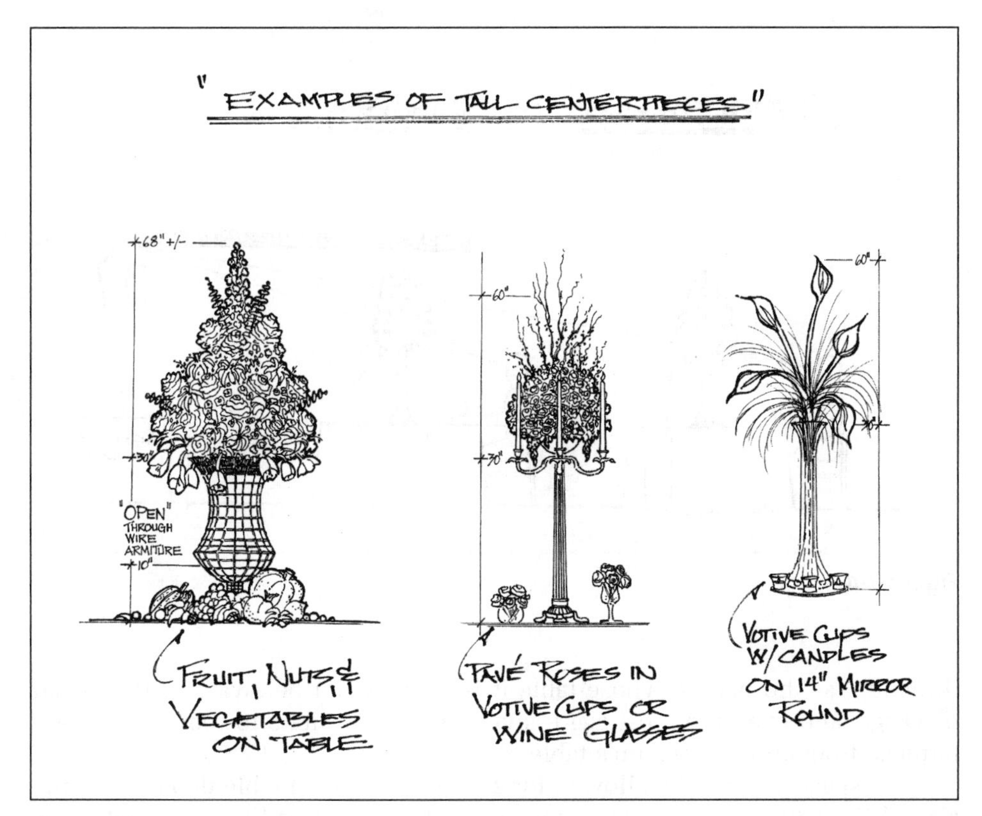


**Figure 7-3**

president, either of whom may be used to intense one-on-one eye contact with his or her associates, any centerpiece higher than 12 inches risks ending up on the floor. "Take-charge" **tablehosts** are likely to remove what they feel is a barrier to their communication needs.

Another crucial height concern that is violated frequently with disastrous results is the use of tall centerpieces when there is a stage show or an important presentation. This is when sightlines (discussed in Chapter 3, *Venue*) become extremely important, and the event floral designer needs to coordinate with the event designer or whoever is in charge of the **floor plan.** (**Table layout,** floor plan, **ground plan,** and **plan view** are all synonyms, although the table layout usually contains fewer details than does the floor plan or ground plan.) The floor plan will show the tables in relation to one another and can be used in combination with a **sectional view,** also called a **cross section** or **vertical section** (Figure 7-4), to determine whether tall centerpieces will create a problem.

As shown in Figure 7-4, the tall centerpiece does not create a problem for the table it is on but does for the table or tables behind it. This poses a major

**Figure 7-4**

difficulty, as the people whose table it is on may not be aware of the visual blockage, and even the most aggressive CEO will hesitate to remove the centerpiece from another person's table.

The space that can be allowed for a centerpiece on a table depends on the size of the table, the style of service (and the corresponding place settings), and the number of people to be accommodated at that table. Formal place settings with a base plate, a bread plate, two or more wineglasses, a water goblet, and multiple pieces of silverware will take up at least 24 inches of depth, allowing only 12 inches for a centerpiece on a 60-inch round table and 18 to 24 inches on a 72-inch round. The same is true of a luncheon with preset salad, desserts, and a breadbasket. In contrast, a 72-inch table at a buffet luncheon with no plates, crystal, or flatware can look like a vast wasteland until the guests sit down. In these cases, an ornate centerpiece used in conjunction with colorful napkins folded in a water goblet can improve the look of the table without cluttering the table space needed by the guests.

Traditional centerpieces can have added elements to enhance and support a theme, such as sports pennants for a sports theme bar mitzvah, star-glitter-wired garland or 35-millimeter film strip to support a Hollywood theme, or seasonal greenery picks to enhance a winter wonderland theme. Remarkably often one finds centerpieces that are not compatible with the theme, color palette, or room décor. This usually happens at nonprofit or fund-raising events when one element or another is donated or a committee assembles the event. There is no excuse for donating an inappropriate centerpiece. Since the primary reason for making donations is to get future work, it is important to

Idea Portfolio

## SOME FLOWERS FOR SPECIFIC THEMES

| Theme | Flower | Comment/Use |
|---|---|---|
| African | Protea (various) | Symbolic flower of Africa |
| Caribbean/tropical | Orchids, birds of paradise, ginger, and halyconia | Expensive but long-lived |
| | Banana leaves | Can be used on tabletops |
| English garden | Roses (various), lilies, delphinium | Many garden flowers |
| Western | Cactus, kalanchoes, Texas blue bonnets, sunflowers | Many desert-looking types of foliage and grasses are available |
| Underwater/lost city | Protea (various), lilies, spider mums, hanging amaranthus | Lacapodium and various types of eucalyptus can look like marine plants or seaweed |
| Chanukah | Various blue and white flowers (the colors of Israel's flag) | Holiday flowers are traditional and well known |
| Christmas | White hydrangea, red and white roses, ixia (berries), silver or iridescent accents | Holiday flowers are traditional and well known |

donate your best work and make sure it will fit in with the other plans for the event.

### NONTRADITIONAL CENTERPIECES

Centerpieces are limited only by the concerns expressed above and the imagination of the designer. Sometimes flowers are not a major component or are not used at all; we will still consider them in this chapter for convenience. Balloons as centerpieces will be discussed in Chapter 9, *Balloons in Bloom.* Pin-spotting centerpieces is extremely effective and is discussed in detail in Chapter 10, *The Art of Light.* Food centerpieces have become a trend in budget events, as a creative chef can design an edible centerpiece for dessert or carve "flowers" from fruits and vegetables. These "food for the eye" centerpieces are covered in detail in Chapter 11, *Unique Decorative Elements.*

Tropical paradise theme centerpieces can be created with exotic fruits and a few orchid blooms. Underwater theme centerpieces can feature fire under water by using submerged glass candles with the flame below the surface of the surrounding water or blooms floating in bubble bowls with live swimming fish. For a Moroccan theme event we used 5-foot palm fronds in 26-inch-tall palace vases on paisley tablecloths. Individual ice carvings can make very effective centerpieces. There is at least one company that will freeze decorative items or flowers into ice globes and supply a lighted base for them. Clear acrylic centerpieces uplighted or downlighted with or without flowers are another idea that can be quite effective.

One way to design original nontraditional centerpieces is to employ the creative techniques suggested in Chapter 2, *Design and Decorations Practices.* However, there are some specific concerns that need to be addressed in following the nontraditional approach. These concerns are reliability and repeatability, unpredicted or unexpected results, and, most important, safety and risk management.

Reliability and repeatability is a critical concern for an event professional floral designer. Once a preliminary sample centerpiece, called a **prototype,** has been shown to the client, it is imperative that it can be re-created for the actual event. The event professional will let the client know about the potential supply challenges inherent in the floral industry such as weather and shipping problems that are beyond local control.

The client may request a floral prototype, and the event professional should be prepared for this, usually charging a reduced price to cover costs. We charge for such a request at actual cost plus 30 percent to cover labor and handling, especially if we have priced our work with minimal profit to maximize minimal resources, as when we do a nonprofit or fund-raising event. Sometimes the prototype is included as part of our presentation to help us sell the event in which case it is figured into the overall cost of the event or absorbed as overhead if we do not get the event.

A prototype is required for nontraditional centerpieces to avoid unpredicted or unexpected results. Even if the client does not see it, a prototype is necessary for internal purposes. A unique and unusual centerpiece may come with unique and unexpected side effects. For example, many tall and elegant centerpieces have blown over when placed on tables in an open tent. The prototype not only should be identical to the final product but should be placed in an environment similar to the final event environment for a similar length

**MONROE'S RULE OF FLOWER ORDERING**

The event professional must investigate the probability of reliable delivery and not propose a flower, plant, or other design element that is unlikely or impossible to obtain on the date of the event. If availability is questionable, a backup must be chosen and the client must be notified of the potential change.

Idea Portfolio

## A NONTRADITIONAL CENTERPIECE FOR AN UNDERWATER PARTY

As part of a "Lost City of Atlantis" theme, Howard Eckhart of Party and Event Designers helped us create a centerpiece for a debutante party that started with rough lichen-covered branches plastered into a **maché** container. The branches were taken to our favorite Christmas tree supplier, who flocked them, making them resemble branching coral formations. We then hot-glued small bubble bowls into the crotches of the branches. Some of the bowls eventually held votive candles, and each of the rest held one Siamese fighting fish *(bettas).* These colorful little fish have the unique ability to breathe atmospheric oxygen and therefore can survive quite well in small bowls with little or none of the dissolved oxygen required by most fish. (They are known as fighting fish for a reason. Do not put more than one male in each bowl.)

Those armatures became the bases on and around which floral accents were attached, using lily and orchid blooms and underwater-looking greenery such as podacarpis to create romantic interpretations of sea anemones in an underwater garden (see Figure 7-5).

Nontraditional centerpieces can be very effective but can require copious development time to design and build trial prototypes. These costs must be included in the cost of the final product or be a line item in the proposal under design or prototype.

of time. Even in a ballroom, air-conditioning can create drafts that cause candles to blow out or burn irregularly, leading to dangerous wax buildup.

Centerpieces that incorporate nontraditional components require expertise beyond that of an event floral designer. When one is using live fish in a centerpiece, it is desirable to secure the help of an aquarium fish expert who can judge the amount of oxygen in the water and handle both the fish and the water to keep the fish alive. We heard about a tragic case in which live birds were used in centerpieces. The birds were in small cages, some of which were placed over candles. The heat from the candles proved fatal to the birds that were not rescued by the guests. Thoughtful experimentation with a prototype can avoid embarrassing unexpected results.

In dealing with all the elements of an event, the safety of the participants must be the primary consideration. One form of nontraditional centerpiece we have seen incorporates radio-ignited pyrotechnics into the centerpieces. Doing this with guests sitting at the tables is a bad safety decision and is illegal in most jurisdictions. More commonly, candles are used in and with centerpieces. Many jurisdictions prohibit the use of **tapers,** traditional tall thin candles, unless they are enclosed in glass. A safe solution for candelabra or candlesticks is to use **pegged candleholders,** glass candleholders that are designed with rubber-collared pegs that fit into the socket of the candlestick and

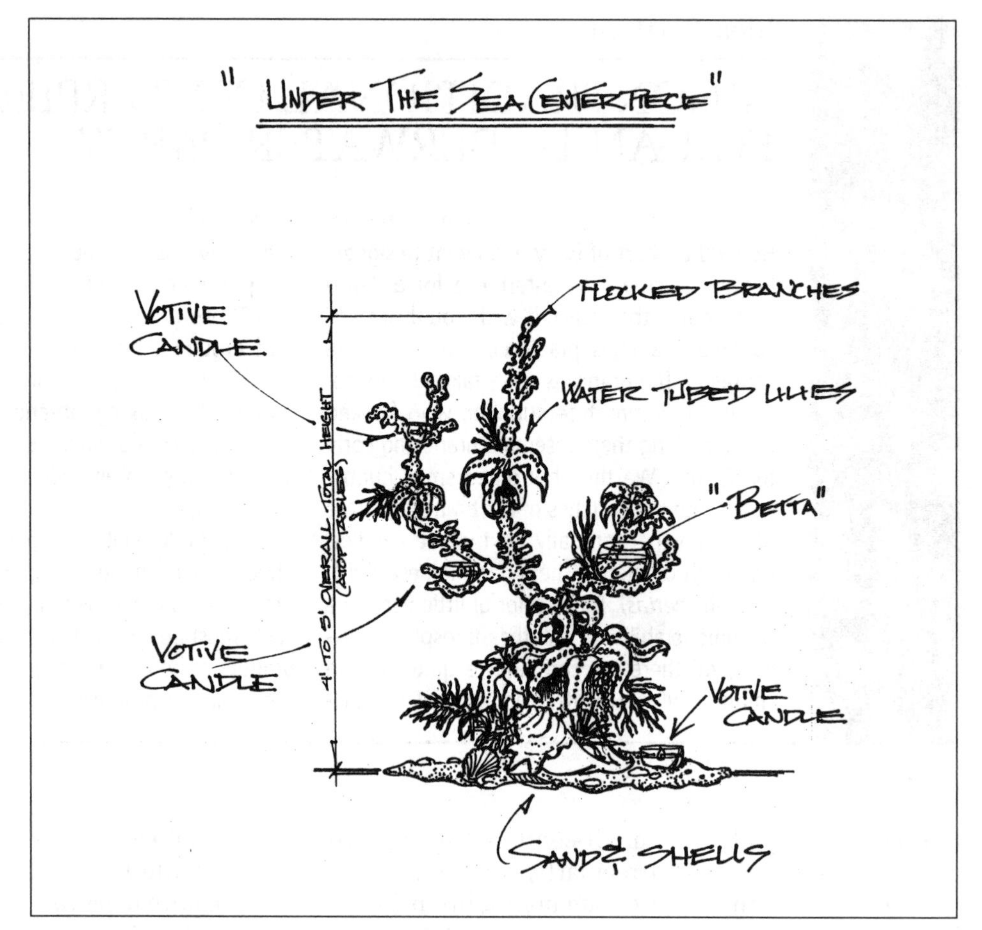


**Figure 7-5**

hold a **votive candle** or **tea light.** Another solution is to use glass chimneys that protect the candles. Any time candles of any sort are employed as or with table decorations, the wait staff should be instructed to observe them for safety, and one person should be assigned to do preevent inspection and ongoing observation throughout the event.

## FLOWERS FOR THE BUFFET

Buffet centerpieces are similar to table centerpieces except that they are larger and (usually) come with fewer restrictions. Centerpieces for the buffet and other floral treatments must be designed in consultation with the chef or **food stylist.** It is essential that the buffet have enough room for an attractive display, access by guests, and access for service. The centerpiece or other floral

Idea Portfolio

## RISK MANAGEMENT CENTERPIECES

- Many of the decorations, picks, and floral accent devices and garland sold by floral wholesalers are not flame-retardant and should be tested before use. The closest I have come to a disaster was when some plastic decorative materials that were clearly marked flame-retardant were used on candle sconces and caught fire in the middle of the event. Fortunately, our self-appointed **firewatch** spotted the problem before the guests did and before it became a potential disaster.
- Many municipalities do not allow candles unless they are enclosed in glass. If the venue and the local authority allow tapers, limit the height to 15 inches. We once allowed a client to persuade us to use 24-inch tapers, which were quite impressive and stylish. A draft from the air-conditioning created uneven melting, which built up a reservoir that collected melted wax. A guest's $3,000 gown was ruined by candle wax. The size of the flame from a 24-inch taper could have caused an even worse result.

treatment should enhance these aspects, not interfere with them. One way to do this is to use an urn or other tall container that raises the floral treatment and narrows at the base so that it does not take up too much space. Another way is to work with the chef, using low floral and greenery accents among the containers and chafing dishes.

John Daly always does flowers for the buffet so that the base of the arrangement begins at chest height. When people stand at the table, the centerpiece is not lost but is still visible across the room. Floral treatment for buffet tables needs to be carefully coordinated with the selection of tablecloths and skirting. Table linens are treated in detail in Chapter 8, *Fabulous Fabric Décor.*

## FLOWERS ON STAGE

Stage florals should, like all others, enhance and support the theme of the event and the purpose of the stage. A stage is included in an event for a reason, usually to provide a platform for the band or to provide focus for a presentation or show. On occasion I have designed an otherwise unnecessary stage into an evening and put a band or another activity on top of it because the design or the room needed a focal point. The floral treatments can accent the primary décor or be the primary décor and can serve practical as well as decorative functions.

All decorative elements on stage need to allow room for the function of the stage. If the band requires a 12-foot by 32-foot stage, it must be allowed that amount of space, and additional space needs to be provided for flowers and décor.

Idea Portfolio

## FLORAL DECORATIONS FOR A STAGE FOR ACTIVE ENTERTAINERS

Entertainers who incorporate dance or a lot of physical movement into their act can cause vibrations or outright movement of the stage, which can translate into unexpected and distracting movement of the floral arrangements. It is sometimes a good practice to separate the stage used by the performers from the staging used for the décor by 1 inch or 1½ inches to isolate undesirable movement from the decorative elements.

Staging frequently is provided by the venue at little or no additional cost, and that makes it an attractive option. However, it is often necessary or desirable to secure urns or pedestals that hold flower arrangements by screwing or nailing them to the stage. Hotel and institutional staging is not always suitable for this treatment, or such methods may be prohibited by the venue to protect its investment. Check with the venue in advance and inspect the staging. It may be necessary to bring in special staging for the décor.

If the stage is to be used for a **presentation,** either a floral arch or a pair of flanking floral arrangements can be used to direct the focus to the primary presentation area. Various forms of presentations include awards ceremonies, fashions shows, and society coming-out parties. If you use the basic design elements discussed in Chapter 1, *Principles of Design,* floral décor can be employed to focus the guests' attention center stage, downstage, left, or right (see Figures 1-1 through 1-3). Sometimes onstage floral décor can serve as the focus for the room décor. Figure 7-6 shows monumental columns leading toward a stage with a monumental floral arrangement. This design was used by Gale Sliger Productions to decorate a fund-raiser in the Chantilly Ballroom of the Wyndham Anatole Hotel. The floral arrangement was so tall that artificial "silk" flowers were used to save weight and because they were so far away from the audience that it was impossible to distinguish this silk from the real thing.

The practical applications of floral design, beyond the aesthetics and objectives, can be as simple as providing guidance for nonprofessionals on stage. A floral path can show them where to walk, and carefully designed floral hedges can show them where not to walk. One of the most frequently overlooked staging elements is the speaker stacks of the band, which usually are placed on the downstage right and left corners of the bandstand. Many a designer has complained bitterly after completing a beautiful stage design only to have the band show up and put big black speaker stacks on the downstage corners and a drum riser upstage center. The design professional will have

**Figure 7-6**

Idea Portfolio

# MONROE ON ARTIFICIAL FLOWERS

Artificial flowers are popular in many cultures and communities as well as many commercial applications because they are durable and cost-effective when reusable or used in permanent installations. These very characteristics keep them from being appropriate for special events. A special event is a unique happening in time with a beginning and an end, during which a magic and ephemeral ambience should be created that will leave a lasting memory or impression.

A live cut flower is a special creation with stages of its life from bud to full-blown bloom. It has a beginning and an end and leaves an impression or memory but does not last forever. Although repeated, it can never be duplicated. Artificial flowers can be reused and last a long time. They are not unique and last long enough to look really tacky if used over and over. The best artificial flowers look perfect but will not be special and will not look real.

I use them when they will not be seen closely and all I need is something that looks like a flower. They are much lighter than real flowers and do not need water or maintenance.

read the **contract rider** for the band, will have communicated with the band's technician, and will know that the speakers and the drum riser are coming. Event professional floral designers can use floral arrangements in urns or on specially designed pedestals to obscure the speakers without blocking the sound and will have designed the backdrop or upstage décor to accommodate the drummer and her or his equipment.

## GARLAND

Most commonly used as swags and spirals of seasonal greenery with ornaments and bows during the winter holidays, garland can be an effective decorating tool all year long.

Artificial seasonal greenery often is used for commercial decorating for Christmas and New Year's and occasionally at events because it is reusable and long-lasting. With repeated reuse, however, artificial greenery can look tired and worn. Generally it is best limited to commercial applications and places where it will be seen from a distance.

When one is working with artificial greenery, the most frequently forgotten item is the time it takes to **fluff** the greenery when it is removed from the original packing. Also, if you are planning on future reuse, it is necessary to strike, pack, and store the artificial décor carefully at the end of the season. It will still need to be fluffed.

Prefabricated garland made from cut seasonal greenery that has been wired together is available from most large Christmas tree suppliers, nurseries, and wholesale florists.

The types of greenery used depend on the supplier, but noble fir is a common garland and noble fir mixed with balsam and cedar is one of my favorites for event decorating. Freshly cut pine is flammable and becomes more so when it dries, so this garland should always be flame-retardant-treated when used inside. For the lush look that usually is desired, it may be necessary to double commercially available garland.

Floral garland and greenery garlands with floral accents commonly are used for weddings. Solid floral garland can be created by weaving certain types of flowers together around a rope or wire for mechanical strength or by using floral foam wrapped in chicken wire. Some of the books that are recommended at the end of this chapter have detailed suggestions for creating garland. Boxwood, huckleberry, magnolia leaves, and wild smilax are several of the types of greenery commonly used to create garlands. Floral accents can be added to these garlands by using individual blooms in **water picks** (small plastic tubes with a perforated rubber cap) or by wiring in small nosegays done in **floral foam** buttons.

Floral foam is manufactured by Oasis and others and normally comes in bricks that hold water and help provide structure for floral arrangements. It also is manufactured in many shapes and forms for specific applications such as the one described above.

Other garland applications include architectural accents and ceiling treatments. Architectural flowers are discussed below, and it is sufficient to point out here that garland frequently is employed on mantelpieces, around mirrors, and over pediments and door and window casements. For ceiling applications, there should be at least two attachment points for each swag or, if you are creating a canopy effect, an attachment point center to carry the weight of all the swags and one for each swag around the outside. Garland can be created around a strand of wire or cable for mechanical strength and can be made quite large (12 to 24 inches) as required by the space. Before it is hung, the garland can have miniature lights entwined in the greenery for a truly special romantic effect. The wiring can be hidden in the vine and run to a predetermined location at one end or the other.

## ARCHITECTURAL FLOWERS

An **architectural floral treatment** is created when floral design is employed to conceal, change, or accent the structure or architectural details of a venue. These are flowers in positions other than on tables, on buffets, or in urns on a stage. Sometimes architectural floral design enhances the existing architecture in a room, and sometimes it covers it up. It is used frequently to establish the primary composition of the event design, establishing focus and line, as discussed in Chapter 1, *Principles of Design* (see Figure 1-1).

Architectural floral treatments are specimen arrangements, garland, hanging baskets, or unique treatments that draw the eye and the attention of the guests to a designated focal point or establish the feel and style of the event. Several styles of floral treatment that can be used as architectural flowers are described below.

### FLOWERING VINE ILLUSION

To create the impact required to achieve the primary focus in a large room, the floral treatment must be large and strong. Flowering vine can do this, but it takes a lot of flowers and labor to achieve this visual impact. A design technique we first saw employed by Russell Glenn Studios in 1989 uses potted flowers and grapevine to achieve the illusion of a large flowering vine.

In this technique the grapevine is stripped of its leaves and installed as the base for the vine, allowing some really interesting lines and curves. Then pot-grown flowering plants (we prefer azaleas, caladium, and geraniums, but any flowering plant can be used) are removed from their pots and put in Baggies, which are wired shut around the stem(s) with paper- or plastic-covered wire twist ties. A relatively strong (18- or 20-gauge) green **floral wire** is passed through the root ball and used to wire the flowering plant onto the grapevine. Floral wire is a medium stiff iron wire manufactured for the floral industry and packaged and sold in 18-inch lengths. A second wire around the stems may be required to hold the exact position desired for each plant. The plants are arranged separately and in groups, facing in all the desired directions. After the potted plants have been placed, the visible Baggies and wire need to be covered up, or **greened,** with moss. Spanish moss or sheet moss can be purchased from a floral wholesaler. It can be pulled apart and pinned to the root ball with special stiff wire two-prong pins called **greening pins** that are manufactured for this purpose.

Potted ferns, ivy, and other potted foliage plants can be incorporated, or wild smilax vine, huckleberry, or boxwood garland can be added to soften the look. Other variations include adding clear miniature lights entwined in the vine, ribbons, individually water-picked blooms, and small nosegays (see Figure 7-7).

## HANGING FLOWER BASKETS AND BALLS

Another architectural floral treatment involves hanging flower baskets from the ceiling, creating a focus within the complete control of the designer as long as there are an unlimited or at least a large number of potential **rigging points** (hanging positions). Baskets can be created from traditional hanging basket forms by lining the forms with sheet moss and filling them with presoaked floral foam in Baggies or wrapped in self-clinging wrap. Presoaked floral foam is heavy (a gallon of water weighs 8.34 pounds), and it is necessary to do a prototype to assure that the mechanism and support wire or cable will hold together safely over the guests' heads. It is a best practice to weigh the basket and seek engineering help for the rigging point and hanging mechanism.

The problem with hanging baskets is that they are usually seen from below and the bottom of the container is the most visible part of the arrangement. Therefore, a flower ball becomes an attractive idea. Flower balls can be constructed, as described above, from a standard wire hanging basket from the nursery trade, sometimes wiring two together, one upside down on the other, with presoaked floral foam bricks stacked inside before they are assembled. Aside from the mechanical and rigging concerns, it is important to remember that when the flower stems are poked through the Baggies or the self-clinging wrap, water is going to seep out and drip down on whatever is below. Another reason for doing a prototype is to see how long it takes before the flower ball stops dripping and can be hung over tables, people, and a finished floor. It is a good idea to leave it hanging and see how long the flowers survive after the water has dripped out.

## FLOATING FLOWERS

Another architectural flower treatment for smaller ballrooms to define the dance floor or an area over the wedding cake, bridal canopy, or another special area to be set off involves the use of flowers strung on monofilament line.

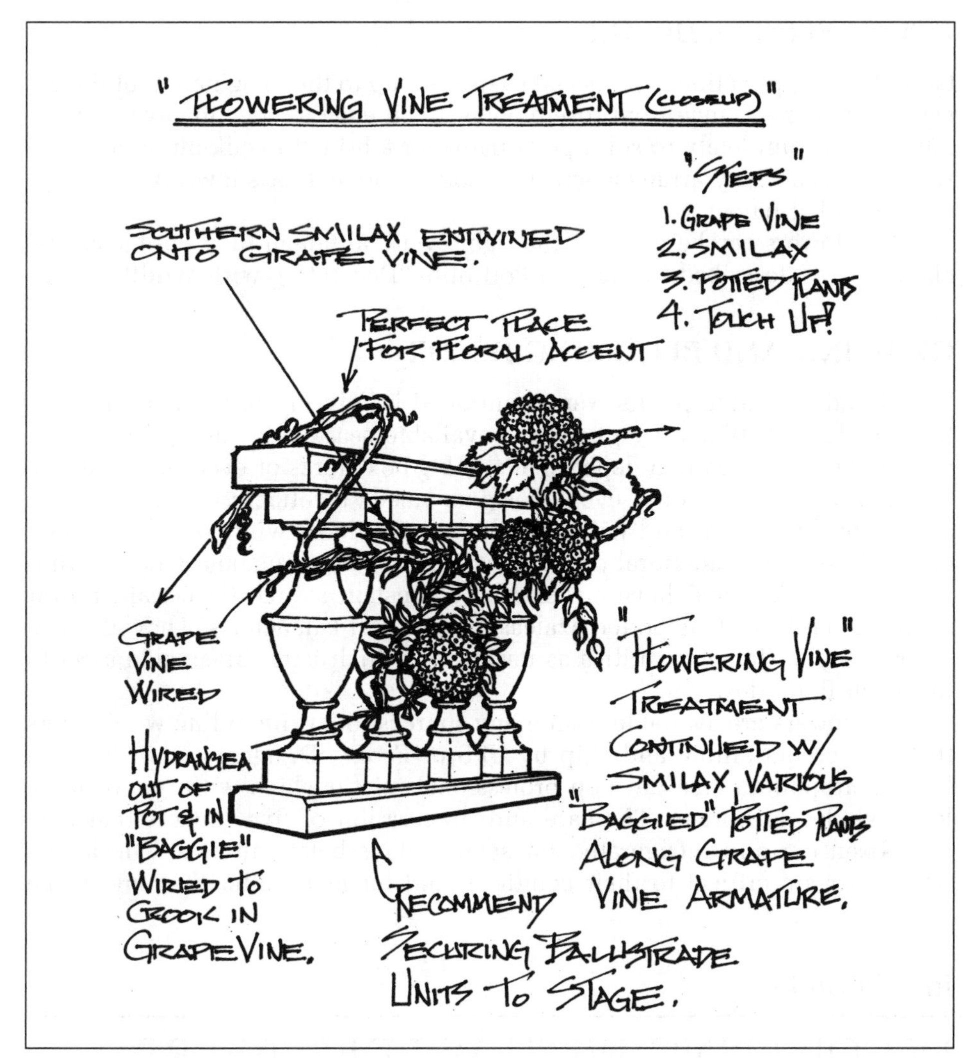
"FLOWERING VINE TREATMENT (CLOSEUP)"
"STEPS"
1. GRAPE VINE
2. SMILAX
3. POTTED PLANTS
4. TOUCH UP!
SOUTHERN SMILAX ENTWINED ONTO GRAPE VINE.
PERFECT PLACE FOR FLORAL ACCENT
GRAPE VINE WIRED
HYDRANGEA OUT OF POT & IN "BAGGIE" WIRED TO CROOK IN GRAPEVINE.
"FLOWERING VINE" TREATMENT CONTINUED W/ SMILAX, VARIOUS "BAGGIED" POTTED PLANTS ALONG GRAPE VINE ARMATURE.
RECOMMEND SECURING BALUSTRADE UNITS TO STAGE.

**Figure 7-7**

The blooms can be threaded on with a large needle and kept refrigerated until just before they are hung. They can also be hung with glass candles in between for a wonderful romantic effect. (The hanging glass candles can be candles in straight-sided votive or tea light holders that are put in rose bowls with a fluted lip and tied with three no. 5 ribbons to a point overhead. The ribbons should be wired for safety, and the candles can be hung easily from a hidden architectural feature such as a cove or from a tee track-ceiling grid.) The hanging flower blooms on monofilament can be hung from pins in an acoustical ceiling or from pins wedged under the trim of ceiling downlights.

## OTHER FLORAL DÉCOR

Other floral applications for special events are up to the imagination of the designer. They may range from rose blooms glued edge to edge to cover a decorative prop completely to solid petal paths for a bride to walk on or guests to walk between. (Any arrangement with solid blooms that show no surface or filler is called pavé.)

Wildflowers can be used for the right event, although they pose a special challenge, as described in the Idea Portfolio, "Decorating with Wildflowers."

## GROWING AND BLOOMING DÉCOR

Potted and blooming plants were mentioned briefly in the section on architectural flowers. Blooming plants are available seasonally through nurseries and the home and garden departments of big box stores or even the local grocery store. A professional event designer needs a reliable and predictable source for these items and will work with one or more wholesale floral nurseries. These wholesale floral professionals can advise you about what is available at what time and have a remarkably constant source for certain flower shop standards such as potted azaleas, mums, and kalanchoes. They also can bid reliably on large quantities as necessary, which is an invaluable asset to the event floral designer.

Cut flowers are available from many sources today, including wholesalers that take orders online and ship by UPS or FedEx. Designers who live in a large metropolitan area develop professional relationships with two or more local wholesale florists. The care and preparation of live flowers that may have been cut and refrigerated for several days before their arrival at the wholesaler are critical to their condition and longevity after they are in the

Idea Portfolio

# DECORATING WITH WILDFLOWERS

When given an opportunity to decorate a fund-raiser for the National Wildflower Foundation at the LBJ Ranch for Lady Bird Johnson, I was dispatched to the Hill Country of central Texas two weeks before the event to see what was available and how it would work for floral arrangements. The variety of wildflowers growing alongside the roads was amazing. Collecting a large assortment from several private lands as well as the LBJ Ranch, I carefully followed the advice given to me by the National Wildflower staff: to carry the bucket of water to the flower, not cut the flower and take it back to the car.

I cut a couple of buckets of wildflower specimens and drove them back to Dallas, where I arranged them the next day, and they stayed fresh for several more days. The key in working with wildflowers is to cut them and *immediately* immerse the stems in water.

hands of the designer. Also, it is generally desirable to have the blooms fully open for event floral design. This can take more than a week for some flowers, such as the Casa Blanca lily.

Flowers were one of the first global elements in the event profession. They come from around the world and are subject to global weather patterns as well as seasonal demand and availability. A knowledgeable and attentive salesperson with a reliable floral wholesale company can be invaluable as a reference and guide as well as a treasured supplier.

Trees and small shrubs also may be available through a wholesale floral nursery supplier. However, trees and shrubs generally can be rented from a local interior nurseryman who specializes in servicing the foyers and lobbies of large buildings and offices. Many urban areas have one or more plant rental services that specialize in renting for parties and special events. One generally pays about what these plants wholesale for to rent them, but they come with labor to install and remove them and do not have to be stored or maintained. An event professional plant rental service also has an assortment of containers and supplies a number of related services, such as miniature lights in the foliage of *Ficus benjaminus,* uplights in palms, and possibly the creation of custom ponds and waterfalls.

## FINISHING TOUCHES

The role of the centerpiece and other floral elements in the design of an event is to support and enhance the goal of the event. The goals and the resources will determine the style selected. The height of centerpieces and sightlines are critical. Garland, buffet, and stage floral treatments each have special applications, restraints, and considerations. Architectural floral treatment can be used to create line and focus as well as to enhance or conceal features of the venue.

Various floral and plant treatments are available to event designers. Each floral design treatment, as well as each flower, has its own characteristics and limitations that must be known to the designer. The care and preparation of the flowers are critical to the success of the design. Reliable and knowledgeable suppliers are essential to the professional event floral designer.

## DESIGN VOCABULARY

Terms appear below in the order in which they first occur in this chapter.

Nonfloral centerpieces
Picks
Ting ting
Glitter garland
Tablehost
Floor plan
Table layout
Ground plan

Plan view
Sectional view
Cross section
Vertical section
Prototype
Maché
Tapers
Pegged candleholders
Votive candle
Tea light
Firewatch
Food stylist
Presentation
Contract rider
Fluff
Water pick
Floral foam
Architectural floral treatment
Floral wire
Greened
Greening pins
Rigging points

## STUDIO WORK

1. You are designing a dinner for the board of directors of a Fortune 500 corporation. Would you use hybrid delphinium, which averages 17 to 24 inches tall, in the centerpieces? Why?
2. You are designing a dinner with a floor show featuring a nationally known entertainer. Your client wants you to emphasize the flowers, using 26-inch-tall palace vases with large arrangements on the 80 tables. What should you explain to your client?
3. Your client decides that he wants a heavy floral treatment onstage behind the performer, possibly with a specimen arrangement upstage center. What would you call the type of floral treatment you would design for this?
4. You want to design a floral treatment that includes heavy green garland with miniature lights entwined pulled up to a center point in the ceiling, where you will hang a flower basket. What must there be in the ceiling for you to do this?
5. Your client's favorite flowers are peonies. You are doing an event for her in November. Who would you call to see if peonies are available then? Are they likely to be?

## RECOMMENDED READINGS AND RESEARCH SITES

Blacklock, Judith, *Teach Yourself Flower Arranging,* McGraw-Hill, 1992.

Maia, Ronaldo, *Decorating with Flowers,* Harry N. Abrams, 1978.

Packer, Jane, *Complete Guide to Flower Arranging,* Dorling Kindersley, 1999.

Pryke, Paula, *Flowers, Flowers: Inspired Arrangements for All Occasions,* Rizzoli International, 1993.

Roehm, Carolyne, *A Passion for Flowers,* HarperCollins, 1997.

Rose, Jerry, Lisa Shelkin, Tim Lee, and Bruce McCandless, *A Year of Flowers: Fresh Flower Arranging: A Seasonal Guide to Selection, Design, and Arrangement,* Running Press, 1994.

Google Directory: Business > Wholesale Trade > Floral > Flowers—online directory of wholesale flower sellers
http://directory.google.com/Top/Business/Wholesale_Trade/Floral/Flowers

SpecialEventSite—a resource for special event floral services nationwide
http://www.specialeventsite.com/Portal/list.php3/c_Event+Services/categoryID_316/

Yahoo! Directory: Florists—an online directory containing extensive listings, including flower wholesalers
www.yahoo.com/Business_and_Economy/Companies/Flowers

# Chapter 8

# FABULOUS FABRIC DÉCOR

*You can cover more square footage with linen faster and cheaper than with any other decorative element.*

**—Jo Dermid**

## IN THIS CHAPTER

You will learn some of the many uses of fabric and best practices for using it to create event décor.

**Special Event Fabrics**

- Theatrical Fabrics
- Exposition Fabrics
- Display Fabrics

**Wall Treatment**

- Pipe and Drape
- Semicustom Drapes
- Custom Drapes

**Ceiling Treatment**

- Banner Style
- Valance Style
- Canopy Style
- Freestyle Ceilings

**Table Linens**

- Tablecloths
- Napkins and Chair Covers
- Table Skirting
- Other Custom Table Treatments

Fabrics are an incredible tool for the event designer. They can provide sweeping curves that lift the spirit and color the environment in a delightful palette of the designer's choosing. Fabrics can be hung, swagged, draped, gathered, pleated, scrunched, or puddled. They can be soft, velvety, tailored, sheer, filmy, shiny, fuzzy, rich, or glitzy. No single class of decorative element can serve so many functions or span so many styles. There are infinite possibilities for using fabric, limited only by the designer's creativity.

Fabrics are manufactured for many purposes and come in many colors, styles, and costs. Event designers are always looking for new materials and new ways to use material. Several years ago, for an elegant over-the-top wedding reception, we used a couple of upholstery brocades for table overlays and a custom portal that wholesaled for $50 and $75 per yard. However, there usually are more limited resources in the event business, and we are always looking for cost-effective ways to decorate large spaces. At the start of this chapter Jo Dermid, national director of sales at BBJ Linen, points out that there is no more cost-effective way to cover so much of a room as with (rental) tablecloths.

Idea Portfolio

## FABRIC IS THE SOLUTION

Certain design challenges can be met better with fabric than with any other material.

Gale Sliger Productions needed to achieve the goal of transforming the ballroom of the Brookhollow Golf Club into a rich, colonial American Williamsburg atmosphere for Janie McGarr, the chair of the Sweetheart Ball (a fund-raiser for cancer), and Nancy Halbreich, the decorations chair. A blue toile was selected that BBJ Linens agreed to add to its rental tablecloth stock. Gale Sliger Productions purchased a quantity of raw fabric that matched, sewed it into panels, and installed the panels inside the existing molding panels on the wall, converting the room into a period ballroom.

James C. Monroe & Associates (JCM) was faced with the fairly common problem of trying to stage an elegant event in a sterile 20,000-square-foot exhibit hall. A selection of fabrics for pipe and drape to cover the walls and custom valances to conceal the ceiling was an effective answer.

Shortly after that JCM was asked to provide stage scenery for a general session on one side of a ballroom and concurrently provide scenery for a luncheon on the other side of the ballroom, immediately followed by a gala in the combined space. An original design of **ground-supported** stretch fabric and a flexible lighting design combined to solve that design challenge.

Although built props and scenery, backdrops, flowers, or balloons could have been employed in each of these cases, the best and most cost-effective solution for each scenario was to use fabric.

# SPECIAL EVENT FABRICS

Any fabric can be used for decorating special events at any time, but certain fabrics meet specific criteria that make them particularly appropriate for special event applications. These criteria are *fire resistance, suitability, serviceability,* and *cost-effectiveness.*

A fabric can be **fire-resistant** either through **flame-retardant** treatment or because it is inherently flame-retardant as a result of the materials used or added during its manufacture. The flame-retardant characteristic, Julia R. Silvers, CSEP, reminds us, "rules out running to the fabric store for material to be used to drape or create swags for that stage back, wedding **chuppah,** or tent interior. Many theatrical fabrics are flame-resistant (and you should receive a fire resistance certificate with their purchase), but most clothing fabrics are not. They have to be treated with a commercial flame-retardant solution."

Suitability means that a fabric has the right look (color, texture, and surface) and feel (weight and opacity) for the event and the design application.

Serviceability for a drapery fabric means that the material drapes well, hangs evenly, and does not crush or show wrinkles or creases when folded. It

**MONROE'S GUIDE TO FLAME-RETARDANT AND FLAME-RESISTANT (FR) FABRICS**

Any material will burn if it gets hot enough, including steel and glass. In categorizing special event fabrics as flame-resistant or flame-retardant, the ultimate legal ruling comes from the local fire marshal. However, the National Fire Protection Association (NFPA) sets the standards. Generally, the test for acceptability in event draping is the NFPA 701 Small-Scale Vertical Flammability Test.

In this test a small flame, such as that from a match or lighter, is held to a vertical sample of the fabric for approximately 30 seconds. The fabric should either not develop a flame or self-extinguish immediately after the flame is removed.

Note that passing this test informally, as described here, may be acceptable to some officials and not to others, depending on local jurisdiction and ordinances. Many localities insist on a formal FR certificate from the manufacturer or the company that treated the fabric.

Although the NFPA sets the standards, they are interpreted by the local fire marshal, who is the final legal authority. It has been our experience that a local fire marshal, when confronted with a new material or a material used in a new and unexpected way, will always err on the side of caution.

The best practice is to introduce the design concept to the fire marshal in advance for preapproval. This will include providing floor plans, elevations or sketches of the concept, samples, and flame-retardant certificates in advance, along with an explanation.

Establishing a healthy professional relationship with the local fire marshals alleviates potential stress and confirms positive risk management practices.

also is convenient if the fabric can be laundered or cleaned without losing its flame-retardant characteristics. For tablecloths, the ability to be laundered and pressed easily and high resistance to staining are important. It is not commercially feasible to dry-clean tablecloths or napkins.

Cost is a self-evident factor, but the lowest-cost fabric is not always the best choice for event decorating and not always the most cost-effective. Rather, the long-term cost-per-use ratio will be one of the determining factors in the selection of fabrics for event décor.

Neils Skolberg of ScenicSource, LLC, a fabric supplier to theaters, scenic shops, and event decorating firms, says that the desirable characteristics for event fabrics generally are found in theatrical fabrics, exhibition fabrics, and visual merchandising (display) fabrics.

## THEATRICAL FABRIC

Theatrical fabric is fabric that traditionally is used in theaters, concert halls, and similar public access venues for draperies and **cycloramas** (see Figure 8-1). The traditional theatrical draperies are as follows:

- **Traveler curtains** open and close horizontally to reveal what is onstage.
- **Legs** or **tormentors** are vertical drapes that frame the sides of the stage.
- **Valances** or **teasers** are horizontal curtains that finish the top edge of the stage picture.

### MONROE'S GUIDE TO THEATRICAL FABRICS

**Velour:** a heavy, fairly permanent fabric lasting 15 to 20 years or more; the **nap** (fuzzy finish) is woven in; very expensive.

**Commando cloth:** a less expensive substitute for velour; similar to duvetyne, although the names sometimes are used interchangeably; tends to be heavier (16 ounces); the nap is created by roughing the surface after weaving.

**Duvetyne:** a less expensive substitute for velour; similar to commando cloth, although the names sometimes are used interchangeably; tends to be a lighter, finer weave (12 oz.); the nap is created by roughing the surface after weaving.

**Sharkstooth scrim:** a special effect fabric that is opaque when lighted from the front and transparent when lighted from the rear; sometimes used in front of cycs to eliminate wrinkles or seams and reduce **bounce** (reflected light); expensive and very wide (20 feet or 30 feet), scrim can be painted with dyes to become scenery (see Chapter 6, *Backdrops and Props*).

**Leno cloth:** a filled scrim; very good for cycloramas, as it absorbs light rather than bouncing it back.

**Muslin:** comes in natural or black in many widths, including very wide for seamless cycs and backdrops; commonly painted and used as scenic backdrop material (see Chapter 6, *Backdrops and Props*).

**Bobbinets and various nets:** various scenic applications, including cut and net drops; painted scenery contains cutouts, and net is used to hold the drop together.

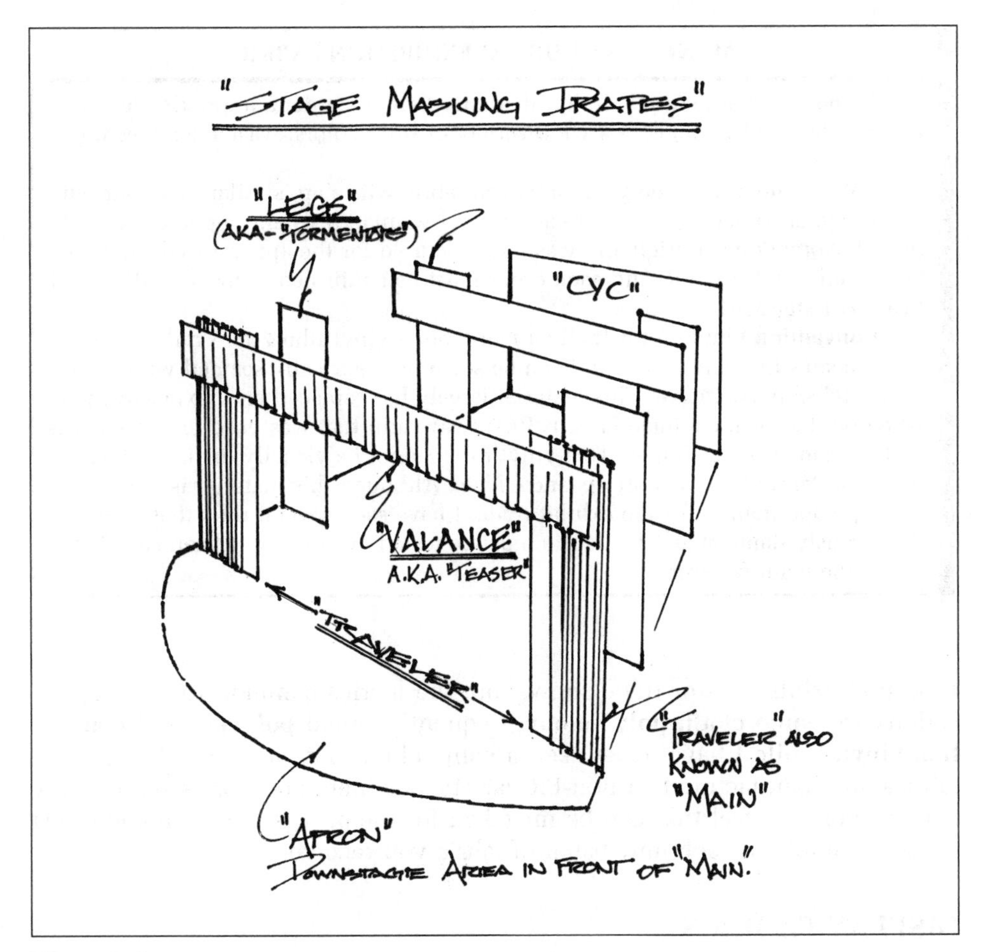


**Figure 8-1**

The cyc (cyclorama) is the stretched curtain at the very back of a stage and is sometimes called a **sky drop** because it frequently is lighted to look like the sky. Cycs get their name from Greek *kuklos* for "circle," and *orama,* meaning "sight or vista," as in *panorama.* These curtains sometimes are curved to enhance the illusion of an infinite sky.

The materials used for theatrical drapes and curtains are readily available for use in the special event industry. They are almost always flame-retardant and frequently are woven quite wide, but they come in a limited palette of solid colors.

## EXHIBITION FABRIC

Used primarily as divider draperies to create exhibit booths in North America, this fabric, like theatrical fabrics, must be flame-retardant as it is used in public access venues. Very occasionally velour, duvetyne, or commando cloth

**MONROE'S GUIDE TO EXHIBITION FABRIC**

**Banjo cloth:** a textured cloth, inherently flame-retardant, approximately 47 to 60 inches wide; comes in a wide variety of solid colors; washable; does not wrinkle; inexpensive.

**Poly velour/velvet (polyvel):** a woven fabric with nap; similar to velour but much lighter; inherently flame-retardant and wrinkle resistant; moderately priced. *Note:* Polyvel originally was manufactured for the apparel trade and still is. Not all polyvel is FR, and each order must be confirmed to meet NFPA Small Scale 701 standards.

**Convention vinyl:** not actually a fabric but a vinyl film 2 to 4 millimeters thick; comes in many colors and can be sewn or electrically seamed with a hot wire device; inexpensive. This material largely has replaced an inexpensive polished twill known commercially as Broadway satin that was used for table skirts and occasionally for drapes. This vinyl film cannot be visually distinguished from real fabric from a short distance. *Note:* Although this material is manufactured predominantly for the exhibit trade, I have seen several rolls that were dangerously flammable. This fabric *must* be tested even if it has been certified FR by the manufacturer.

is seen at exhibitions or trade shows, but the fabrics common to these applications are **banjo cloth, poly velour** (frequently called **polyvel**), and **convention vinyl.** While I have never seen a banjo cloth that was not FR, the other fabrics are manufactured in non-FR varieties or there are fabrics with a very similar look and feel that can be mistaken for them. It is always a good idea to test a sample of each new batch of fabric you receive.

## DISPLAY FABRICS

Display fabrics are visual merchandising or event fabrics that are used for display and temporary decorations. Many of these fabrics originally were intended for other uses, such as apparel or upholstery, although they may be manufactured for the display or event industry today. They are used for a creative, artistic purpose and are primarily visual rather than utilitarian. Their FR characteristics must be confirmed.

Like other fabrics, these can be made inherently flame-retardant during their manufacture or FR-treated after the fact. Because not all of these fabrics are intended for use in public access areas, some cannot be flame-retardant-treated. Some can be treated, but the treatment will ruin the fabric for future or extended use, as the salts in the FR chemicals may corrode or otherwise damage the fibers used in the manufacture of these fabrics.

Natural fabrics such as cotton, linen, and wool can and must be treated. This treatment will be removed by washing or cleaning and can lose its effectiveness over time from exposure to the humidity in air or mechanical abrasion. Painting also negatively affects it.

Artificial (man-made) fabrics can be FR treated after manufacture, or chemicals can be added to them in the liquid phase of manufacture that make them inherently flame-resistant. Some fabrics, such as nylon, are difficult to treat, and acrylic-based fabrics are impossible to treat. Polyester-based fabrics are particularly known for being manufactured with inherent FR characteristics, but not all polyester-based fabrics are FR.

Any fabric can be used in any special event as long as it is flame-resistant, suitable, serviceable, and cost-effective. The look of any fabric depends on the threads selected and the way they are woven into fabric. Woven fabric consists of continuous threads, called **warp,** running the length of the fabric as it comes off the loom that are intertwined over and under with horizontal threads called **weft** (or **woof**). The edges of the fabric, where the ends of the weft are rough, are finished by the **selvedge.**

### MONROE'S GUIDE TO DISPLAY FABRICS

**Lamé:** there are several variations on these fabrics, from heavy glitter fabric to filmy tissue lamé, but they are all shiny metallic and come in many different solid colors and several iridescent versions; moderate to very expensive.

**Faille:** a variety of fine textured fabrics, including Bengaline, a popular display fabric that usually is acrylic-based and therefore is not FR-treatable; moderate to expensive.

**Print:** a fabric with an image or series of images printed on it; currently popular styles are Tuscany, Country French, and English toile; usually have a **repeat.**

**Imprinted:** fabrics with a pattern that was pressed into the material; common with some inexpensive moirés.

**Moiré:** an irregular wavy finish on a fabric.

**Damask:** a satin-look pattern is woven into the fabric using a **Jacquard** loom; tends to be expensive because of the way it is woven.

**Brocade:** a pattern or design that is woven or embroidered so that it is raised above the base fabric; although it is thought of as an expensive fabric, there are broad cost ranges.

**Sheers:** many variations from silk organza to polyester bridal illusion (tulle); these fabrics are so thin that they need to be manufactured FR, as there is no body to the fabric to absorb and hold the flame-retardant chemicals; available in many materials and many costs; frequently inexpensive.

**Stretch:** fabric that can be cut and sewn and then pulled into various shapes and forms because of its elastic properties; can be used to make fabulous abstract settings and provides a great "canvas" for a lighting design; the best known brands are Spandex and Lycra; FR versions are pricey.

**Toile:** a plain woven fabric or twill; originally linen, now with a linen look.

**Felt:** a nonwoven fabric available in FR and in many brilliant colors; lacks mechanical strength and stability; tends to be a "craft" fabric and usually is inexpensive, although cost depends on composition (50/50, which is 50 percent wool and 50 percent cotton rag, is expensive; 70/30 is inexpensive).

# WALL TREATMENT

Among the many uses fabric is put to, covering, accenting, and creating walls are among the most common. **Pipe and drape** is the standard for the exhibit, or exposition, industry in North America; it is used to create booths and walls in the vast exhibit halls of convention centers (Figure 8-2). (In Europe, hard surfaces are used to create exhibition booths at an exposition or **congress.** These booths are called **stands.**)

## PIPE AND DRAPE

Pipe and drape uses sewn fabric panels, usually banjo cloth or polyvel, with pockets in one or both ends that are large enough to accept a horizontal pipe called a **top rod** (also called a **crossbar**). The fabric is gathered on the top rod,

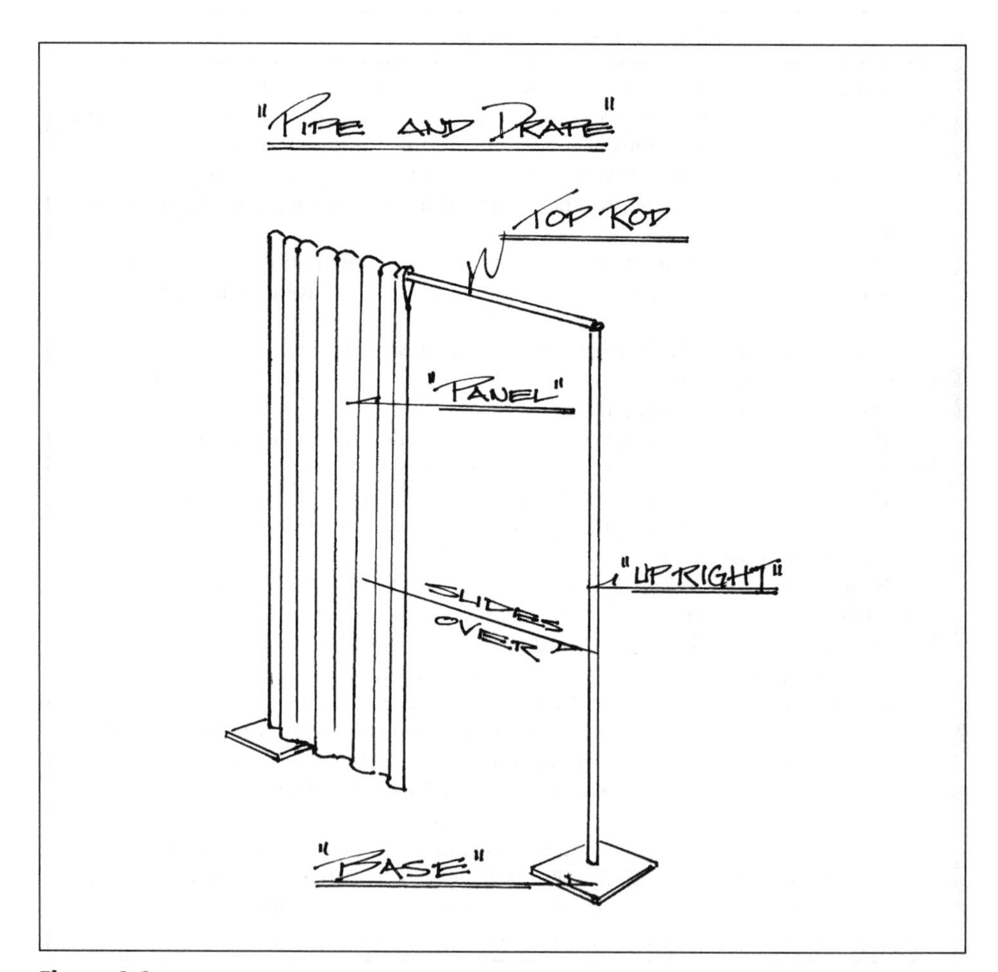


**Figure 8-2**

which then hooks into the slots at the top of two **uprights (posts)**, which in turn fit onto metal bases **(feet)** that hold them up. The fabric panels then are manually adjusted to approximately the same amount of **gather**, or **fullness.** The top rods and uprights come in stock sizes, with the top rods being either 10 feet long or adjustable and the uprights being 8 feet tall. Standard uprights and fabric panels are also available up to 16 feet; these sizes are commonly the most useful to an event designer.

Adjustable uprights, or posts, are used to create inexpensive dividers, backdrops, and wall coverings. Polyvel is a good pipe and drape fabric for the event decorator because it is an inherently flame-retardant fabric that drapes well, comes in many colors, and has a nice texture.

The event designer usually gathers fabric on the top rod to between 50 and 100 percent fullness; that is, 2 feet of gathered material contains between 36 inches and 48 inches of material. Another way to consider this is that a 10-foot top rod will need between 15 feet and 20 feet of material (four to five panels of polyvel) gathered on it to make it look full and finished.

## SEMICUSTOM DRAPES

Another way to put up drape to create a wall (or backdrop) is to use a wooden batten held up by metal stanchions, as was explained in Chapter 6, *Backdrops and Props.* This allows the designer to employ **neoclassical swags** (Figure 8-3) by stapling or pinning the fabric to the wooden horizontal batten. Stock exhibit fabric panels can be used, or any flame-resistant fabric the designer chooses can be sewn into panels.

First, a piece of fabric is run horizontally on the batten. This piece can be half the width of the fabric that is being used for the vertical panels. Then the batten is marked where the fabric will be attached at two places per panel, allowing the rest of the fabric to drape into a swag. The key is to remember that the swags look best at 20 percent of the width of the panel. For example, a 45-inch-wide panel would best be draped at 36-inch intervals, and a 48-inch

Idea Portfolio

### FULLNESS IN PIPE AND DRAPE

David Gisler, national sales manager of Freeman Decorating, tells us that the taller the drape is, the fuller it needs to be. It is standard practice at 8 feet high to use as few as three panels of banjo cloth doing standard 8-foot-high pipe and drape for convention booths. At 10 feet to 12 feet, standard practice is to use four panels, and up to 16 feet requires as many as five panels. The event designer generally will be more demanding when using drape as décor rather than for trade show functions and will require more fullness for a better look.

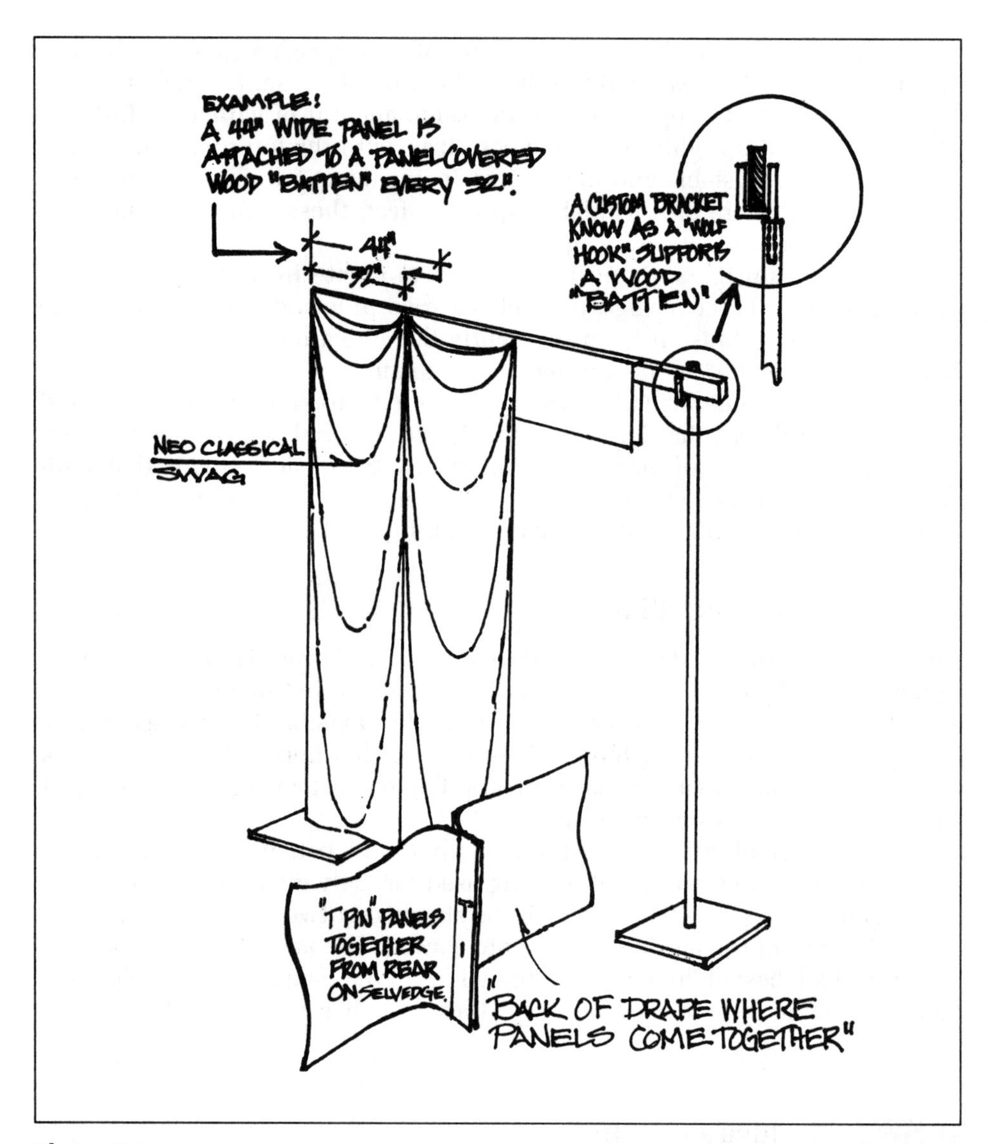
EXAMPLE:
A 44" WIDE PANEL IS
ATTACHED TO A PANEL COVERED
WOOD "BATTEN" EVERY 32".
44"
32"
A CUSTOM BRACKET
KNOW AS A "WOLF
HOOK" SUPPORTS
A WOOD
"BATTEN"
NEO CLASSICAL
SWAG
"T PIN" PANELS
TOGETHER
FROM REAR
ON SELVEDGE.
"BACK OF DRAPE WHERE
PANELS COME TOGETHER"

**Figure 8-3**

panel would be draped at 38½-inch intervals. The 20 percent figure is a benchmark, not an absolute.

**Valances** need to be cut and sewn so that the pattern or nap runs the same way as it does on the full panels. Then the same technique and the 20 percent rule can be applied. When ordering fabric, remember to allow for the straight run of fabric that goes below the swag fabric.

## CUSTOM WALL DRAPING

Custom wall draperies can be sewn from any fabric that can be flame-retardant-treated. Organza sheers and films can be sewn and either swagged or gathered, but the structure that is supporting them will show through the fabric. We frequently employ this type of fabric to create a mood effect, allowing the guests to see into the next room before they get there. When you are using standard pipe and drape hardware to support these fabrics, paint the steel to match the color of the fabric; for example, paint the uprights and top rods gold to match gold sheer fabric.

Some venues, frequently hotels and country clubs, have a molding trim high on the wall or another concealing architectural feature that allows the decorator to hang fabric by stapling into it in places where the damage will not show. Always check with the management before doing this. Many unprofessional or thoughtless decorators leave staples and nails and are careless about their attachment procedures, doing damage to the wall surface and to the reputation of decorators in general (see Figure 8-4).

Another way to use fabric as wall treatment is to stretch it flat and hang it like a tapestry. This is done with attractive prints or solid-color panels, and it can be an effective design element. However, the designer needs to understand the nature and characteristics of the fabric that will be used. For example, all large rectangular pieces of fabric, when hung from the top, tend to pull inward toward the bottom under their own weight. This creates wrinkles at the edges on the left and right. This is a traditional problem with painted backdrops; that is why we always either design an element to hide or obscure the edges or find a way to stretch them. (In the old days of fine craftsmanship,

Idea Portfolio

### A WEDDING ILLUSION

Ann was planning a wedding reception in the Dallas Museum of Art and wanted to add a warm but modern feel to the long sterile hall between the cocktail reception and the formal seated dinner. Cynthia Ray, a designer for Gale Sliger Productions at that time, found a beautiful gold metallic sheer organza that was available in iridescent colors. With a gold woof and colored weft threads, it achieved a wonderful iridescence.

She designed a series of freestanding panels of this material alternating down the terraced hall. At each terrace there was a panel: one to the left, the next one center, and the next to the right. This created a series of alternating transparent portals through which the guests would weave their way to dinner.

The uprights were painted gold, and the panels created see-through walls and a wonderful inside-out illusion. To carry the look into dinner, she had overlays for the tables sewn from the same fabric.

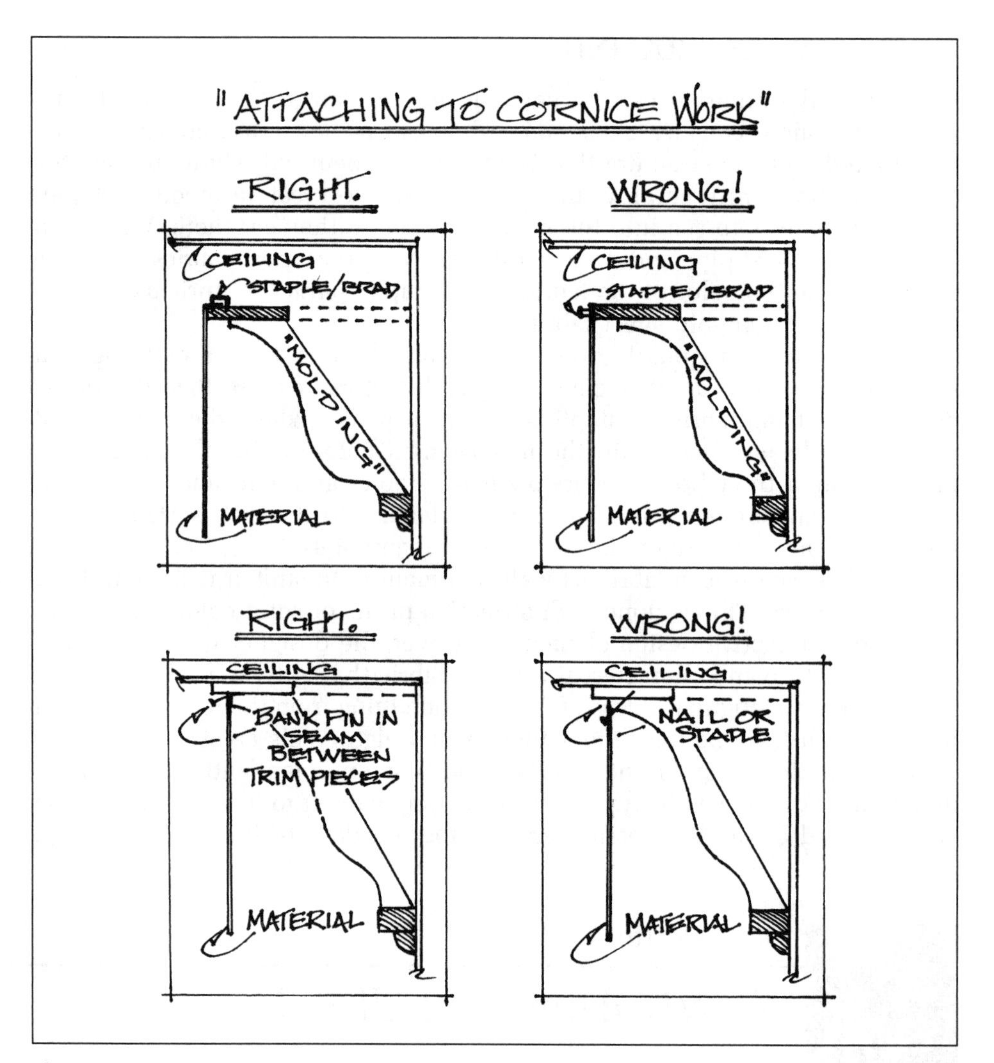


**Figure 8-4**

large flat backdrops were cut and sewn as trapezoids, getting narrower from top to bottom, which eliminated the wrinkles.)

Other custom wall draperies are sewn from theatrical, display, or event decorating fabrics. In manufacturing draperies, the panels are sewn with a predetermined percentage of fullness: flat, gathered, or pleated. They traditionally are sewn to a tape or reinforcement fabric at the top edge that also is used as the place from which to hang them. If you need short heights and widths, there are numerous sewing houses and individuals with many patterns to choose from. A theatrical scenic house will be best suited in terms of equipment, space, and experience to deal with very large draperies or very heavy material such as velour (see Figure 8-5).

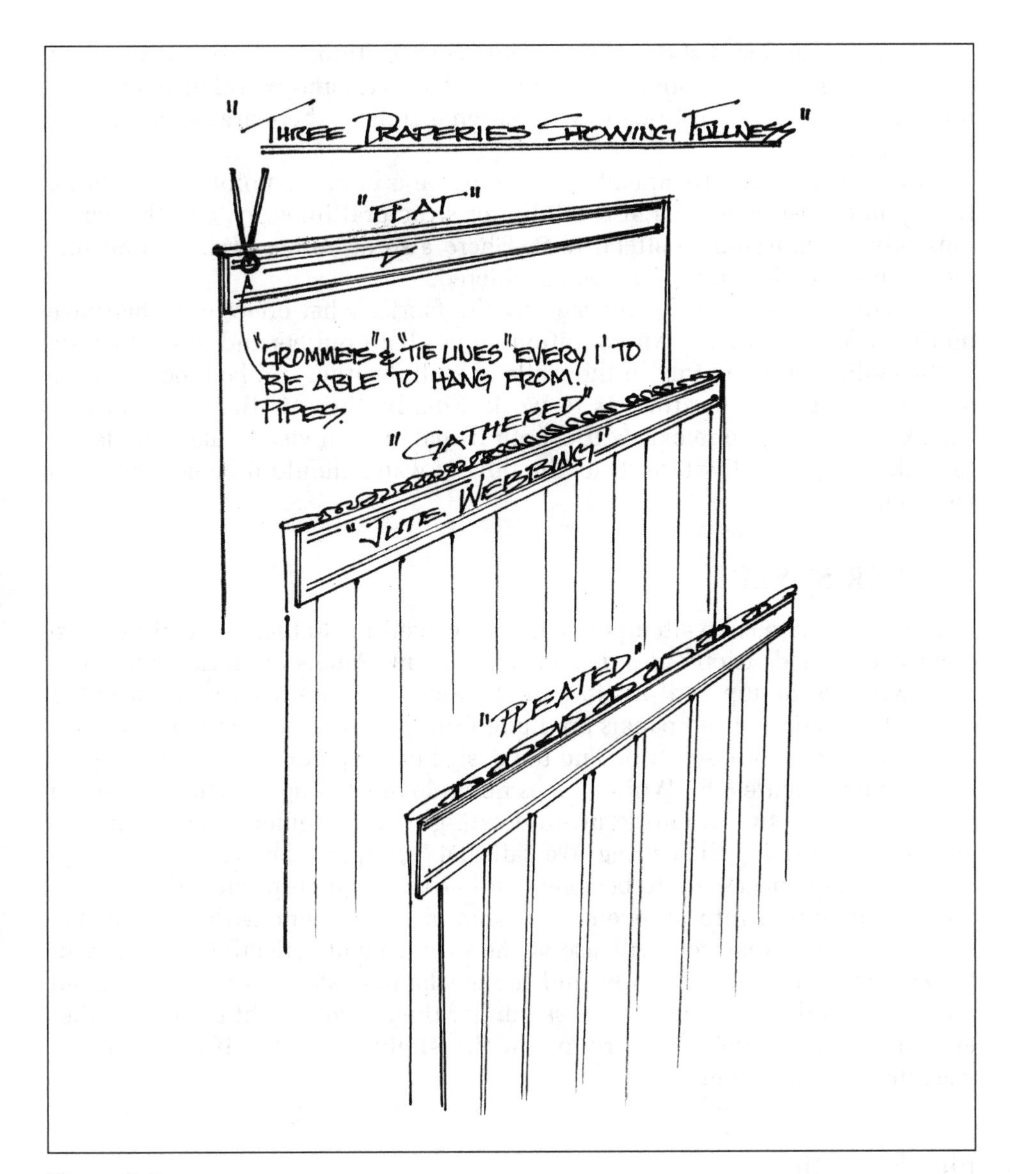


**Figure 8-5**

## CEILING TREATMENT

One of the most effective ways fabric can be used is to conceal or change the look of a ceiling. A basic event design fact is that after a large space fills with guests, especially at a reception at which many people stand and mix, any decor below 6 feet is visually lost. Overhead décor has an impact throughout the entire event.

There are different styles of overhead décor to stimulate the creative juices of each designer. The options available are **banner, canopy,** valance, and any number of custom styles. Before you design a ceiling, there are several points to consider.

To hang a ceiling treatment, there must be a point or points to attach to. Each point must be looked at carefully for structural integrity, and the venue must give permission to attach to it. There also are other architectural elements in the ceiling that must be considered.

If lights are going to be blocked by the fabric, what effect will that have on the look of the room? Air-conditioning has both outlets and inlets that are in the ceiling and possibly in the walls as well. Neither can be blocked if the air-conditioning (or heating) is to work. Finally, there is the question of a sprinkler system. If one exists, it is both illegal and unwise to hang the fabric in such a way that it will obstruct the flow of water should it be needed in an emergency.

## BANNER STYLE

In this style, there is no attempt to conceal the ceiling. Rather, the ceiling treatment is designed strictly as a decorative element. Panels of fabric have pockets sewn into the top and possibly the bottom. Rods are inserted to keep the fabric stretched, and the panels are hung from points in the ceiling. The look comes from the fabric selection and the design of the pattern in which the panels are hung (Figure 8-6). While it does not hide the ceiling, this technique can distract from it by providing an interesting visual element that keeps the guests from noticing the ceiling. We call that "stopping the eye."

It is always necessary to become familiar with the properties of the fabric you are designing into an event. You should experiment with it under the same conditions that you will use at the event. Light reflectivity, opacity or transparency, the natural drape, and the mechanical stability of the fabric all must be considered. Some fabrics sag under their own weight or, at the other end of the spectrum, blow around in the slightest breeze if they are not weighted at the bottom.

Idea Portfolio

## AN UNDERSEA CEILING

For an underwater theme event Gale Sliger conceived of a series of lamé panels in shades of blue that were gathered and pinned to the ceiling in widening circles around three chandeliers in a ballroom. All the walls were draped in matching fabric. Each chandelier was hung out from an air-conditioning outlet, and as the unit pumped in air, the ceiling rippled outward as if each chandelier had been dropped into the water.

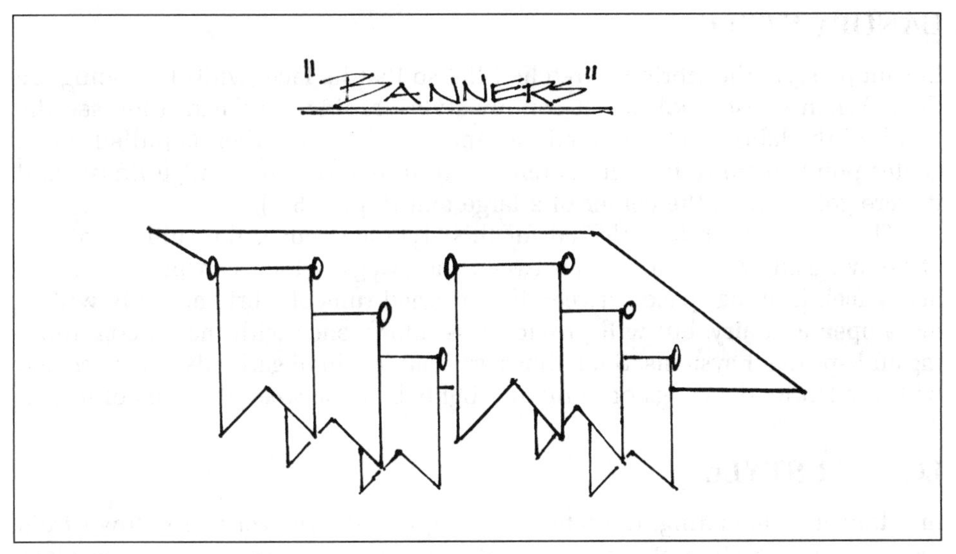


**Figure 8-6**

Idea Portfolio

## INCREDIBLE STRETCH

Many years ago, the display house I worked for devised a clever and cost-effective design concept for a spring promotional event at a shopping mall. We designed a series of colorful felt panels in shades of different colors in different "stretch" areas between the anchor stores. We measured carefully to achieve maximum color exposure while keeping the material beyond the reach of the public.

The material was installed, and the upbeat colors were a positive and successful addition to the promotion. At the end of the week, however, we received a phone call telling us to come out quickly: We had hung the banners too low, and people were jumping up and playing with them.

The banners had all stretched 12 inches under their own weight over the period of a week, and they all had to be trimmed. Felt, not being a woven fabric but manufactured from textile or animal hair fibers that are compressed and held together with a binder, has little mechanical stability or strength.

Before hanging a fabric for an extended period of time you need to consider what it will look like after it has been up for a while. Will it stretch? Will it fade or collect dust?

## CANOPY STYLE

In canopy style the fabric is stretched flat so that its face (width) is facing the floor. When guests look up at canopy-style draping overhead, they see the width of the fabric: flat, gathered, or tapered. The fabric then is pulled into a center point like a round circus tent or up to one or more "ridge lines" as if it were going down the center of a large tent (Figure 8-7).

The fabric or fabrics selected for this style may cover the ceiling entirely or be swagged with space left between the swags, which can provide a less heavy feel. Leaving space between the swagged runs of fabric not only will be more open and airy, but will provide less interference with the air-conditioning and sprinkler systems. Sometimes greenery or floral garlands are alternated with the fabric, or strings of miniature lights hang between the runs of fabric.

## LOUVER STYLE

In a louver-style ceiling, the fabric is hung in valances vertically down from the ceiling in a straight line across it. Successive valances are hung close enough together that they hide the ceiling unless one looks straight up. The

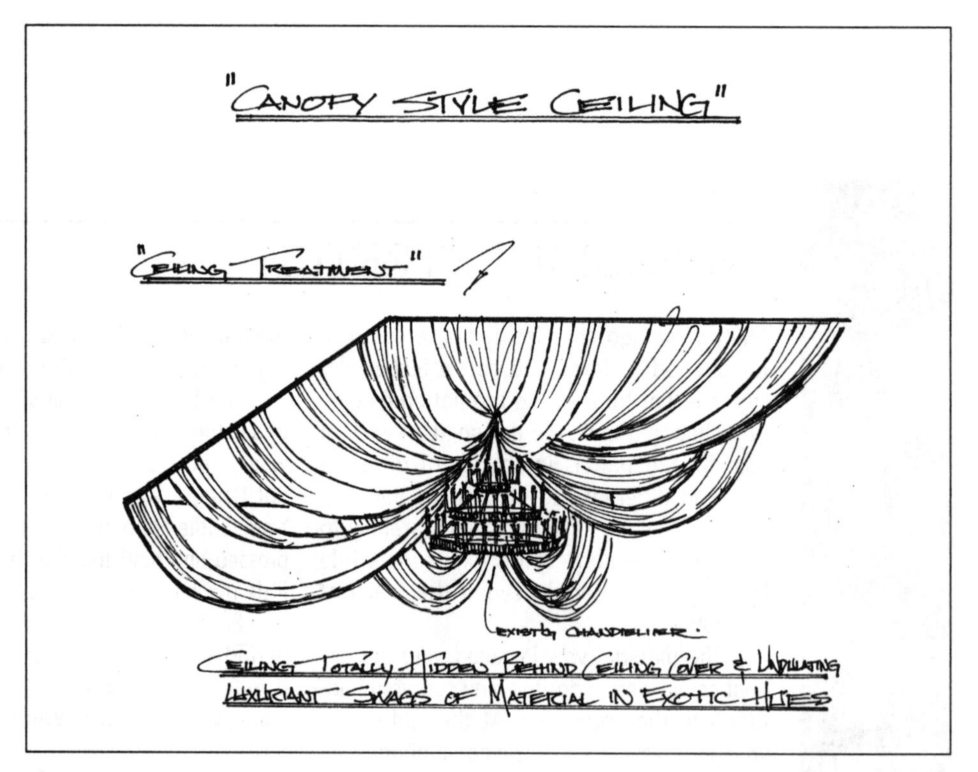


**Figure 8-7**

distance between the valances depends on the width (or depth) of the valance and the height of the ceiling. This distance can be determined by doing a vertical section of the room and establishing the vertical sightlines, as can be seen in Figure 8-8.

This style has the advantage of not blocking heat and air registers or air return vents. It usually can be designed around a sprinkler system and allows lighting to be hung between the valances. The disadvantage is that it does not conceal the ceiling fully.

Valences (Figure 8-9) can be straight runs of fabric that are hung flat, creating a very "hard" contemporary look. They also can be gathered or pleated, creating fullness. In a pleated drape, anywhere from 50 to 100 percent fullness is desired. Another look can be achieved by swagging the valance. If you tie swags into a draped piece of flat-hung fabric, you also need some fullness or it will stretch flat after the first couple of swags. As little as a 3-inch pleat every 18 inches usually is adequate, but it is a very good practice to do a prototype in advance of the installation.

## FREESTYLE CEILINGS

Freestyle ceilings are unusual treatments that do not fit into the definitions given above. These treatments include stretched fabric abstract shapes and forms, asymmetrical ribbons of fabric stretched across the ceiling or between the walls, ribbon ceilings, and a host of nonfabric or hybrid ceiling treatments. Some nonfabric ceiling treatments are done with miniature lights, vine, or foliage garland. Garland can be suspended in swags, for example, or grapevine can be hung "naturally" from the ceiling and accented with foliage or flowers.

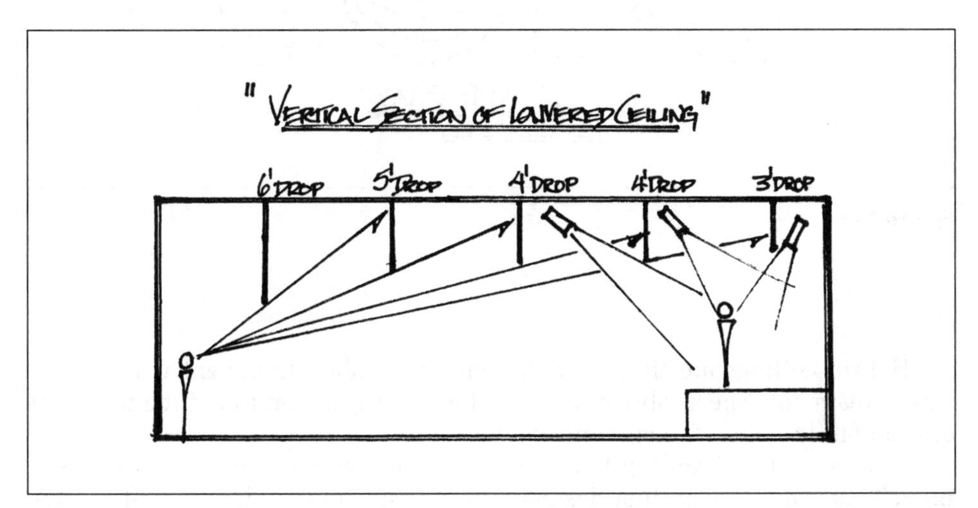


**Figure 8-8**

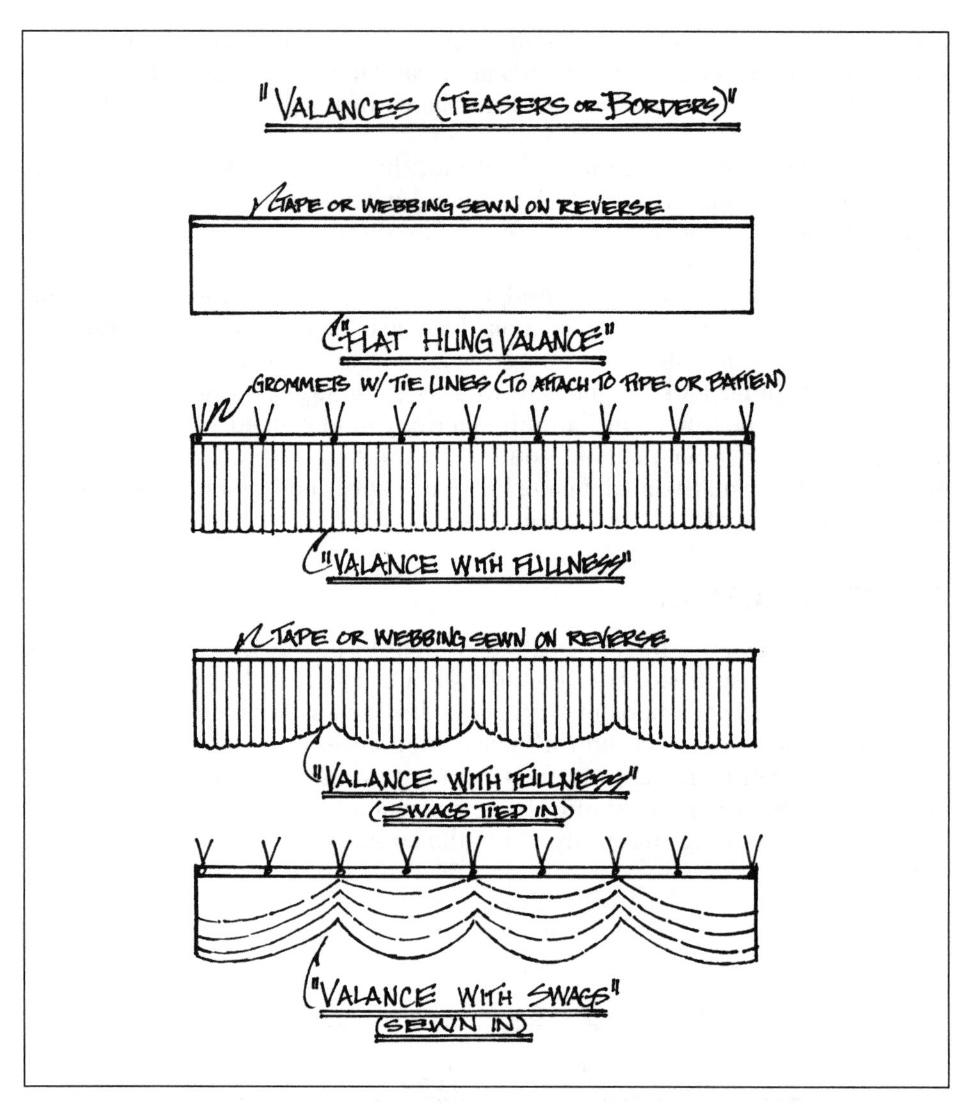


**Figure 8-9**

Hybrid ceilings are those which combine a fabric treatment with a non-fabric treatment. Sheer fabrics can have lights swagged on top of the fabric, or opaque fabrics can alternate with light swags.

Another type of ceiling that we include under this category is the **tent liner.** This is a presewn liner designed to fit inside and under the tent canopy to finish it off. Tent liners are popular for weddings or any other particularly elegant or gracious event held in a tent.

# TABLE LINENS

Linens can make or break an event. They can have a huge impact, and nothing is more elegant than tablecloths to the floor. The term *table linens* traditionally refers to tablecloths and napkins. We also will discuss chair covers in this section, as they are part of the decorative fabric table treatment.

## TABLECLOTHS

Jo Dermid states: "Most people enter the event design process with two things: a vision and a budget. Our job is to bring the two things together. There is a balance between the vision and the reality of execution—the design needs to match the resources available."

Serviceability is critical in commercial rental tablecloths. They must be launderable, stain-resistant, and durable. **Polyester** is the fabric of choice for meeting these requirements, and recent technical developments in fabrics have created polyesters that look and feel like cotton, linen, or silk. With the advent of the Internet and the development of reliable and quick commercial air shipping such as FedEx and UPS, a wide variety of reasonably priced linens have become available throughout the United States and many other countries. Poly cloths in a huge palette of solid colors, satins, damasks, brocades, and an unlimited selection of theme prints and textures are available to event designers.

Still, there is a finite limit to the sizes and individual cloths available on any given day. Early planning and designing to available rental stock will give a designer the most satisfactory results.

Joy Johnson Floyd, national sales support, BBJ Linen, offers the following pointers for working with rental linens:

- Order extra.
- The more organized and detailed you are, the more creative you can be.
- When possible, dress the whole room wall to wall. Dress the buffets and the DJs (disc jockey's) table—anything that shows.
- Know about the resources that may be available at little or no charge.
- Have a realistic time line and know what will happen when. Do not dress the room with tablecloths and chair covers and then have the lighting crew come in and move all the tables and chairs around to focus the lights.
- Linens are best placed after everything else has been done.

Tablecloths are a reasonably priced option for covering a vast amount of ballroom space with color, texture, pattern, and/or theme. If your budget does not permit linen rentals, the venue, if it is a hotel, restaurant, or country club, usually will supply square white linens for the tables. If two square cloths are used, one on top of the other, with the points alternating, they will provide a fair approximation of "cloths to the floor." Overlays of 72 inches or 90-inch squares are very inexpensive to rent and can be placed over a square cloth

**JO DERMID'S DESIGN ADVICE**

A vision can be interpreted at several budget levels. You may be able to achieve your vision at several different price points. For budget events, mixed palettes of solid color poly overlays can add depth and texture to the event design.

My best single bit of advice is to plan the details and supply a floor plan for the event. With a plan we (linen professionals) can help determine what linens you need and make sure that you order correctly. Be prepared with a floor plan.

A common mistake people make with fabric is not taking the advice of the linen professionals they are dealing with. They will walk into a ballroom and match a swatch of fabric to the carpet, determining that everything has to match that color. They are looking at an empty room, not one filled with tables, chairs, and people. They would not match their sofas, pillows, chairs, and drapes to the carpet at home. Look for complimentary colors.

A lot of people do not realize what linens look like under event lighting. The lighting affects the color of the linens. Linens are only one element in a design. In a good design all the elements balance.

You want to see it and feel it. This is a very tactile element. You want to see the way it drapes and reflects light.

Timing is critical for linens. Fabric can be produced in one country, dyed in another, and finished in a third, and then it arrives in the United States. Long shipping times, short lead times for events, and the fact that many prints and woven fabrics are one-off production items lead to limited resource availability for any single tablecloth. As a result, you see many large events with different tablecloths designed. This ends up adding texture and visual interest when designed correctly and has started a trend in event design.

Along with the trend of mixing different tablecloths is the **retro** trend of mixing different sizes and shapes of tables, as if there were not enough of the same shape and size available. This can be lovely, but it also can strain limited resources, as there are only basic sizes of rental tablecloths available. Unusual sizes of tables or sizes that do not match rental stock can limit a designer's choices unless there is a budget for custom cloths or creative overlays and/or pinning up can be employed.

The designer on a budget who wants to mix sizes of tables should do so with the rental inventory in mind so that he or she can select tables for which cloths are available.

supplied by the venue to add color and texture to the room. When the budget permits, cloths to the floor are very elegant and can be layered or have a square complimentary overlay.

## NAPKINS AND CHAIR COVERS

If the tactile character of tablecloths is important, you can multiply that by 10 when it comes to napkins. Napkins are a very personal item because you put them to your lips. Some people prefer to have white napkins every time.

**MONROE'S GUIDE TO TABLE CAPACITY AND TABLECLOTHS**

| Table size, inches | Tablecloth | Seating, persons |
|---|---|---|
| 18 | 78″ round floor length | 2 |
| 30 | 60″ round lap length | 2–4 |
| | 90″ round floor length | 2–4 |
| 30 (standing) | 108″ round (puddles 6″) | 4–6 |
| | 60″ square (double cloth = lap length) | |
| 36 | 96″ round floor length (rare) | 4–5 |
| 36 (standing) | 120″ round floor length | 4–6 |
| | 90″ square overlay brushes floor 3″ | |
| 48 | 108″ round floor length | 6 |
| | 60″ square (double cloth = lap length) | |
| | 60″ square overlay drops 12–36″ | |
| 60 | 108″ round lap length | 8–10 |
| | 120″ round floor length | 8–10 |
| | 90″ square overlay drops 15″—brushes floor 3″ | |
| 72 | 132″ round floor length | 10–12 |
| | 90 square overlay drops 9–27″ | |

Other people hate white napkins because they tend to leave lint on black dresses and tuxedos. I do not like satin napkins because they are not absorbent. From a design standpoint, they can add to or detract from the look or ambience of the event, and nobody ever stayed home because he or she was afraid of the napkins.

A word about **napkin folds** (Figure 8-10): There are many artistic napkin folds, and some venues and caterers specialize in one fold or several folds. They can add to the look of the table décor or detract from it. This is an item that needs to be considered and not left up to the banquet manager after the event designer has left. There are tall folds that can be quite attractive but may hide the centerpiece. Some tall folds are difficult or impossible to do without heavily starched napkins. There are flat folds that can add style to the table setting, such as a **tuxedo fold** on a plate with a single flower tucked into it.

Chair covers (Figure 8-11) are an effective way to change the character of an entire room, but they are not an inexpensive proposition. If you are doing a seated event for 1,200 people and the chair covers cost $7 per chair, that comes to $8,400. You also must consider the labor needed to install and remove them. Depending on your locale and local labor costs, a $5 chair cover could cost twice that once it has been packed, shipped, installed, removed, packed, and shipped back. Still, if tablecloths can impact the design of a room, chair covers can vastly increase that effect.

There are several different variations of chair covers, and not all of them fit all banquet chairs equally well; thus, it is a good practice to order a sample and try it on the chair that will be used at the event. Some chair

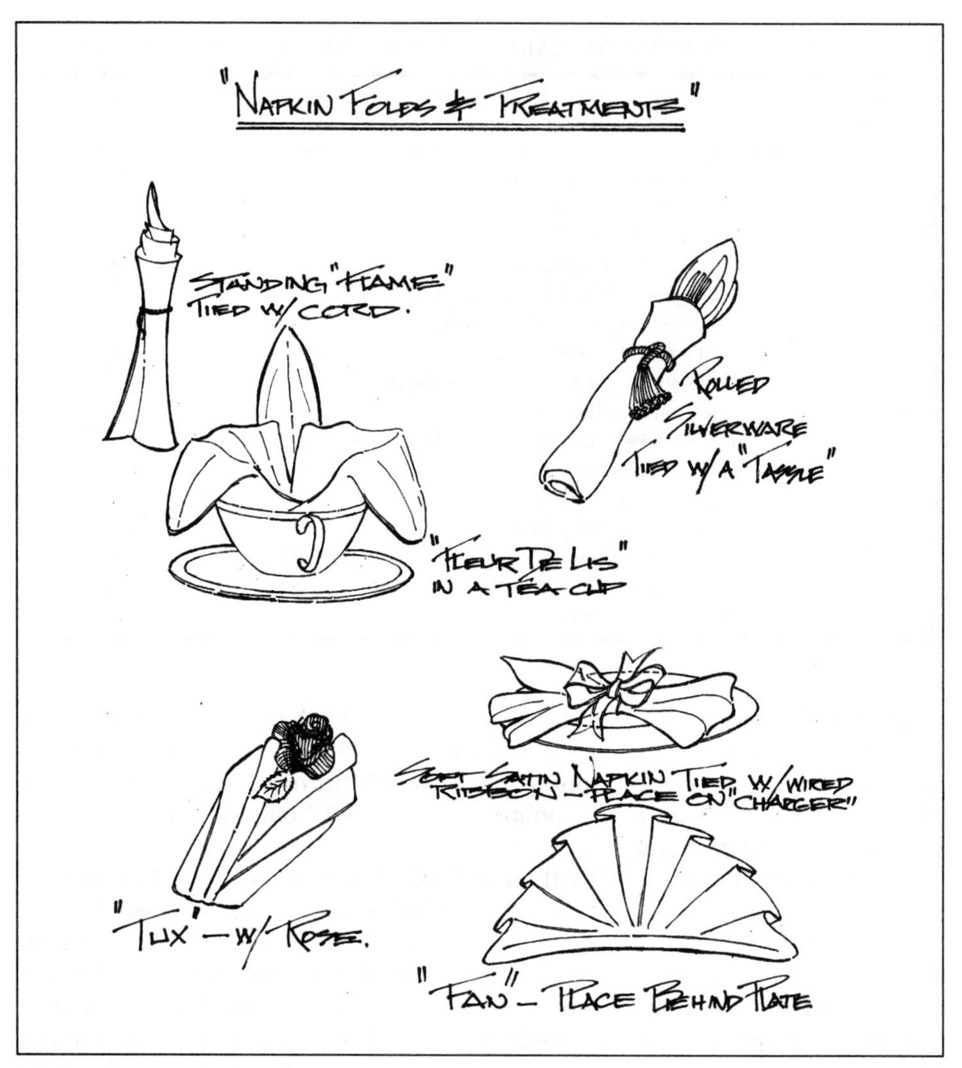


**Figure 8-10**

covers are sewn as slipcovers that slip over the chair and cover it completely. They come with rectangular sashes that can add color, texture, or elegance. Chair ties can be tied many different ways, such as into a bow or a knot.

Other chair covers include self-tied covers and stretch fabric covers. A self-tied cover is essentially a large fabric square that can be tied around the chair. Stretch fabric chair and table covers are stretched over the chair (or table in the case of stretch tablecloths) and hooked onto the legs. A unique approach to decorating tables and chairs, they come in many colors. The chair covers often have color band stretch ties that match, contrast with, or complement the base cover.

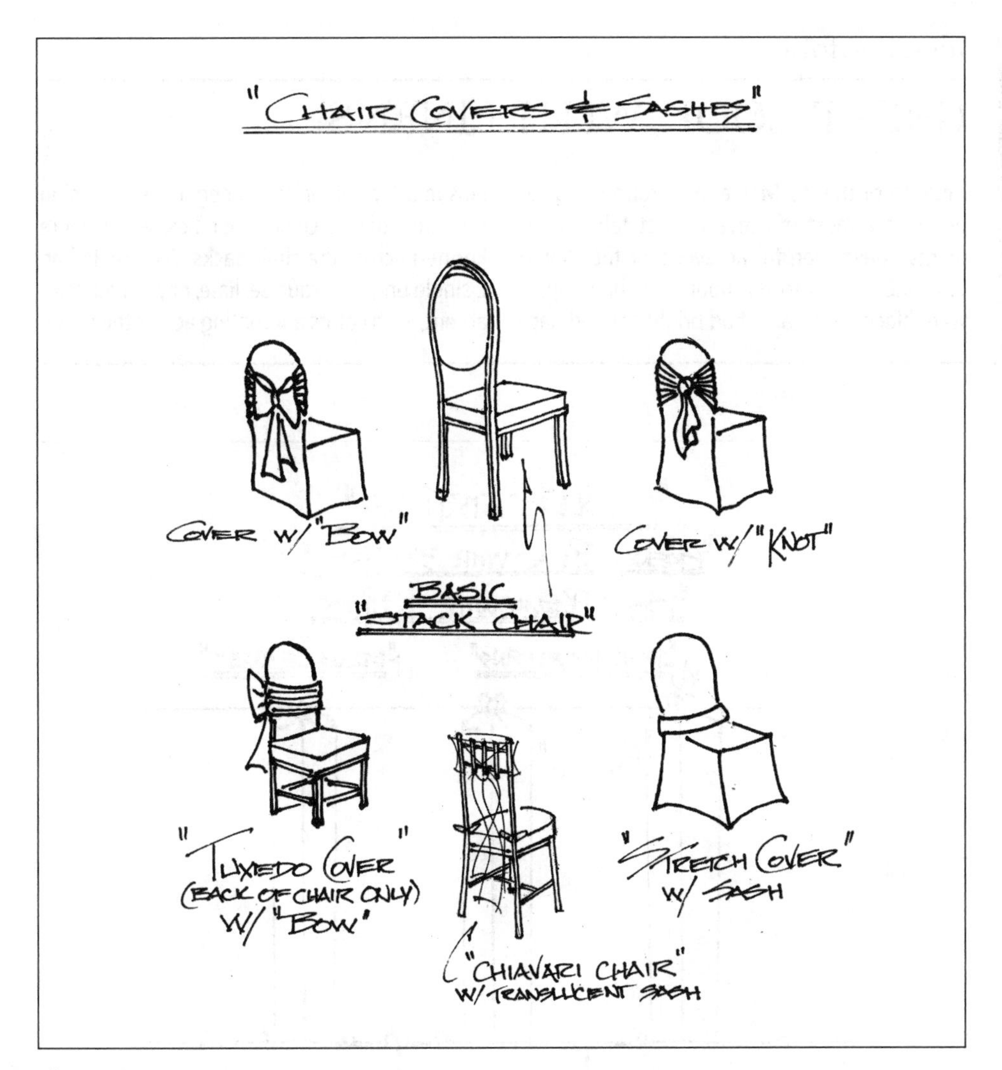


**Figure 8-11**

Chair covers and ties are available in many colors and fabrics to fit any chair you are likely to use in an event. They add immensely to the overall design.

## TABLE SKIRTING

Buffets, registration tables, and cake and gift tables for social and corporate events all require special attention. The standard skirting for these tables at hotels is prefabricated pleated skirting that Velcros onto the table with plastic clips over standard white linens. It looks and is very commercial and cost-effective. For a more custom look, tablecloths can be selected and overlaid,

Idea Portfolio

# GREAT LOOK WITH LINENS

Jane Ito of the Ito Marketing Group designed one of the most effective budget table treatments I have seen for an event for the United Way. Tablecloths to the floor and chair covers were black. Each table had bright colored napkins in a fan fold in the wineglasses, matching the color of the chair cover ties, which were knotted across the chair backs. Each table had a single bright (turquoise, lime, or orange) color accent, with colors alternating across the room.

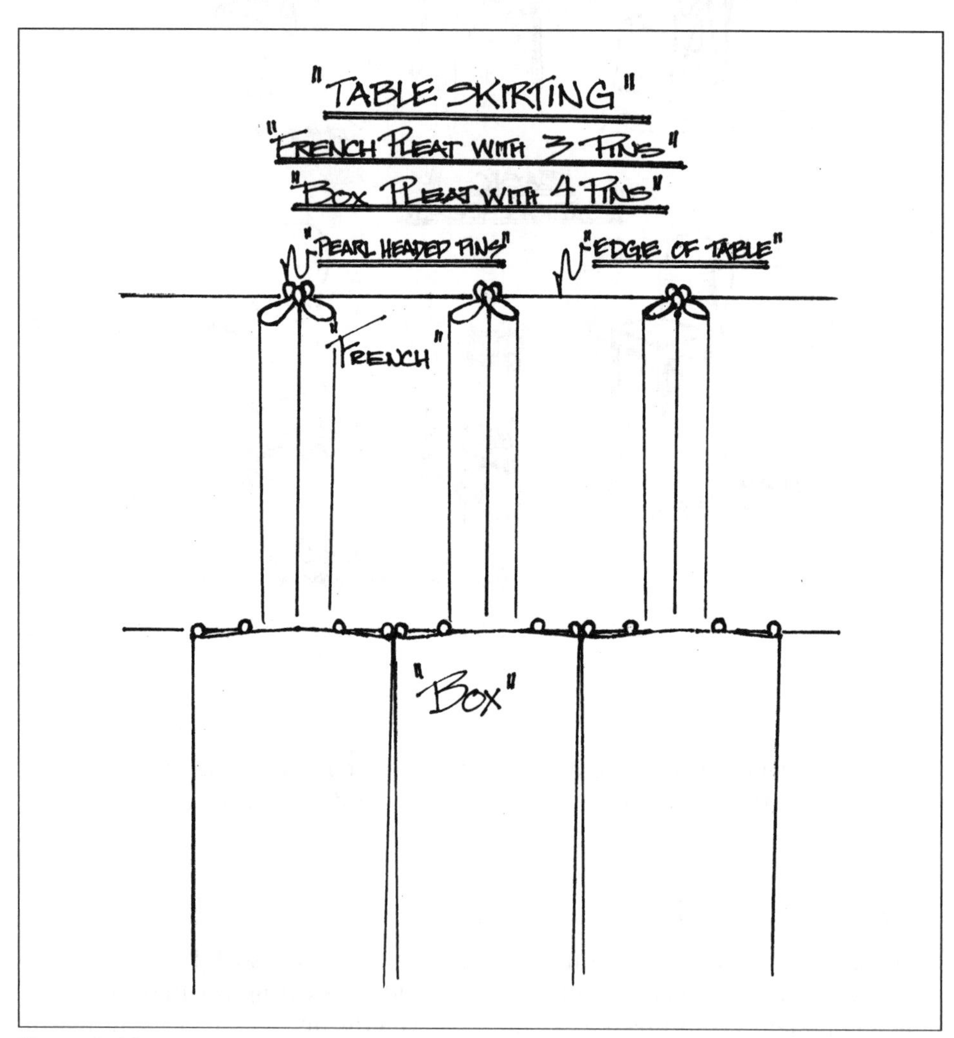


**Figure 8-12**

**MONROE'S POINT OF VIEW ON RISK MANAGEMENT FOR TABLE LINENS**

Risk management for table linens seems to be limited to the tripping potential of to-the-floor or puddled tablecloths, as fire codes and local ordinances appear to overlook them. This is the case because much of the exposed fabric is horizontal, which limits combustibility, and people tend to be close enough to be aware of potential burning conditions.

Most tablecloth material meets or exceeds the requirements for adult clothing, with cotton-polyester blends taking about 9 seconds to catch fire when exposed to flame and most 100 percent polyester taking 10 seconds.

Always test any unusual materials before using them as table covers and avoid any acetate or man-made fibers of unknown origin.

sometimes pinning up the overlays into graceful swags. For the most custom look, skirting can be hand pleated with pins, sometimes adding swags, rosettes, and/or ribbon accents.

Hand-pinned skirting can be box pleated or French pleated, as illustrated in Figure 8-12.

## FINISHING TOUCHES

Special event fabrics can come from several different specialty areas but need to meet the specific requirements of *fire resistance, suitability, serviceability,* and *cost-effectiveness.* The way these fabrics are used is entirely up to the creativity of the designer and decorator, but knowing the characteristics of the fabric is essential to good design. Always order a sample big enough to determine the draping, feel, light reflectance, and character of the fabric before including it in the design. Risk management, always a factor in the execution of the design, is critical when it comes to hanging fabric around and over the heads of attendees.

## DESIGN VOCABULARY

Terms appear below in the order in which they first occur in this chapter.

Ground-supported fabric
Fire-resistant
Flame-retardant
Chuppah
Cycloramas (cyc)
Traveler curtain
Legs
Tormentors
Valances
Teasers
Cyc (cyclorama)
Sky drop
Velour
Nap

Commando cloth
Duvetyne
Sharkstooth scrim
Bounce
Leno cloth
Muslin
Bobbinet
Banjo cloth
Poly velour
Polyvel
Convention vinyl
Lamé
Faille
Print
Repeat
Imprinted
Moiré
Damask
Jacquard
Brocade
Sheers
Stretch
Toile
Felt
Warp
Weft
Woof
Selvedge
Pipe and drape
Congress
Stands
Top rod
Crossbar
Uprights (posts)
Feet
Gather
Fullness
Neoclassical swags
Valances
Banner
Canopy
Tent liner
Polyester
Retro
Napkin folds
Tuxedo fold
Fan fold

# STUDIO WORK

1. Research potential suppliers of theatrical, exposition, and display fabrics and order swatch cards and catalogues from them for your reference library.
2. Design a wall and ceiling treatment for an event of your choosing. Describe and sketch it and write a two- to three-page essay justifying your design decisions as being appropriate for the event.
3. You are designing an event that requires hanging a ceiling treatment, draping the walls, and providing table linens. Pull together a set of swatches of the fabrics you would like to use and the table linens to go with them.
4. Describe in words and sketches, with swatches, the buffet table treatment you would like to use for your next birthday party.

# RECOMMENDED READINGS AND RESEARCH SITES

Holloway, John, *Illustrated Theatre Production Guide,* Focal Press, 2002.

Ionazzi, Daniel A., *The Stagecraft Handbook,* Betterway Books, 1996.

Lang, Donna, and Judy Petersen, *Draperies & Swags (Make It with Style),* Crown, 1997.

Miller, Judith, and James Merrill, *Judith Miller's Guide to Period-Curtains and Soft Furnishings,* Overlook Press, 2000.

Randel, Charles T., and Patricia M. Howard, *The Encyclopedia of Window Fashions,* 5th ed., Randall International, 2002.

Debbie's Book—entertainment industry resource guide; has 18 listings under Theatrical Draperies, Hardware & Rigging

http://www.debbiesbook.com/catalog/T/B1160.html

Grosh Scenic Rentals—a theatrical backdrop and theater drapery rental house with an extensive inventory

http://www.grosh.com/subsection.asp?secid=342

Hoffend & Sons, Inc.—a major theatrical rigging company; this site has its Theatre Drapery Guide, which contains some nice drawings and explanations of various styles

http://www.hoffend.net/theaterdraperyguide.htm

J & C Joel, Ltd.—manufacturers of theatrical drapery in the United Kingdom; some nice photos and drawings; interesting comparison with Hoffend & Sons for terms for styles of curtains

http://www.jcjoel.co.uk/contents.html

NY411—New York Production Guide—18 listings under Draperies and Window Treatments

http://www.newyork411.com

Sew What?, Inc.—manufacturers of all kinds of theatrical drapery; extensive and inspiring drawing and photo portfolios defining all types of draperies

http://sewwhatinc.com/

Showbiz Enterprises, Inc.—manufacturers of all kinds of theatrical drapery; extensive rental inventory

http://www.theatricaldraperies.com/

# Chapter 9

# BALLOONS IN BLOOM

*Balloons elevate expectations.*

**—Jim Skistimas, Balloon House Design Studio**

## IN THIS CHAPTER

You will discover how to decorate events by using balloons.

**Designing with Balloons**

- Why Use Balloons?
- When to Use Balloons
- How to Use Balloons
- Risk Management
- Hiring a Balloon Professional

**Decorating with Balloons**

- Helium-Filled versus Air-Filled Balloon Decor
- Columns and Arches
- Clusters and Centerpieces
- Ceilings and Walls
- Special Balloon Effects

**Advanced Balloon Design**

**Balloon-Related Products**

Balloons make us smile. According to the Balloon Council, an association of balloon manufacturers, distributors, and retailers, the modern **latex balloon** was invented during the Depression by a chemical engineer named Neil Tillotson who was trying to make inner tubes. Since that time they have become the endemic happy devices. With over a billion being produced worldwide every year, they transcend language and culture. Because they are in such common use and are seen as an inexpensive item, balloons frequently are overlooked as a serious professional design element. In fact, balloons are an extraordinarily flexible decorating tool with limitless possibilities in the hands of a creative balloon professional.

Certified Balloon Artist Jim Skistimas, innovator, inventor, and, with his spouse, Pat, award-winning balloon designer and artist, provided the opening quote for this chapter. Jim goes on to say: "Balloons are an aphrodisiac for creative design solutions. More important, they are an untapped opportunity for the planner to make an event unique. With the availability of so many shapes and balloon materials, décor possibilities are endless."

# DESIGNING WITH BALLOONS

Balloons provide a magnificent palette with which the designer can paint the walls, stage, and ceiling. With the methods described in this chapter, balloons can be used as color accents or complete environmental conversions for entrances and stages, dance floors, and dining rooms. They can reach great heights without the need for a ladder or lift. They can be used to "paint" a room with solid, multiple, and contrasting or complementary colors.

Balloons not only come in many colors but also can be stuffed inside one another to create more custom colors. They come in many sizes and, although the balloon we all think of when we hear the word is the latex balloon, several different materials. Even latex balloons come in different "finishes" or looks. The number of ways balloons can be designed into décor has not been determined, as each new creative balloon professional can come up with new designs.

## WHY DECORATE WITH BALLOONS

Probably the best reason to use balloons is expressed in the opening statement of this chapter: Balloons make us smile. An old saying is that you only have one chance to make a first impression. Certain design elements, such as balloons, tents, and music, have an inherent effect on people. They put people in the mood to have a good time.

One of the reasons professional event designers think about using balloons is, in the words of Leo Bary, international balloon decorator, "You get the most bang for your buck!" They are extremely effective in projecting color and shape and creating a mood through the use of color. You can get a lot of look for the decorating dollar.

Another reason to use balloons is that they are light and, when filled with helium, lift themselves up. They are valuable in venues with minimal or expensive rigging capabilities and allow the designer to create large decorative pieces that require little or no rigging. This characteristic of balloons can also solve the problems of having a short installation time, working in a venue with structural restrictions, or working with limited floor space.

In the hands of a creative balloon professional, the new shapes and forms in which balloons are available allow endless possibilities. Latex balloons

Idea Portfolio

## SKISTIMAS BALLOON IDEAS

Lighter means safer and with less rigging. It opens up possibilities to create sculptures of objects in scales that would be prohibitive in other medias. One time we constructed a 45-foot-long parade float on a golf cart.

As an example, an event with a construction theme could have a bulldozer created on a platform and some means of motivation that could carry in the keynote speaker or chairman. The scale is limitless. Can you imagine the excitement of a 10- or 15-foot-tall monster machine entering the event, being "operated" by the speaker, raising and lowering the blade, and mixing in audio of the engine and tracks of the machine with the engine lit up by strobes and billowing smoke?

This could be constructed out of golden balloons to cover a wire frame shaped like a tractor, using silver balloons as tread, black balloons as gears, and silver foil balloons for the dozer blade that raised and lowered with a wooden lever.

How about a gigantic suitcase or package opening up for a parcel delivery show, or a plane, or a gigantic swan bringing in the queen, a parrot soaring overhead at a pet show, or gigantic gears spinning overhead at an auto show? The list goes on.

come in 5-, 7-, 9-, 11-, 14-, 18-, 24-, 30-, and 48-inch as well as 5-foot round shapes. They also come in heart, blossom, doughnut, and tube shapes of various sizes. The most common tube shape is the Q260 (2 inches by 60 inches), which is used to make balloon animals. **Foil balloons** come in 18-inch and 36-inch rounds and various sizes of hearts, stars, and the letters of the alphabet. In addition, numerous theme shapes and prints are available.

## WHEN TO USE BALLOONS

Balloons are best used when the designer is looking for a big effect with lots of color impact. Do not skimp on balloons; they are most effective when there are a lot of them together. A pair of solid spiral columns is more effective than the same number of balloons loosely gathered in clusters and spread about. Balloons can enhance the effectiveness of the props with which they are used.

The entrance to an event is an effective place to employ balloons. Whether in the form of a few simple columns or a complicated series of arches, balloons can give a wonderful first impression.

Helium-filled balloons can be used as centerpieces when a lot of height is desired. Also, centerpieces can be created out of small shaped balloons for an unusual treatment, as shown later in this chapter.

Balloons can be used effectively at many places and times. However, although often used for races and marketing events, they can be a problematic outdoors. Wind and rain can twist them or blow them sideways, and latex balloons take on a frosted look when exposed to sunlight. Heat has a negative effect on balloons, shortening their flying time or bursting them.

## HOW TO USE BALLOONS

As a design element balloons are best used in ways that take advantage of their unique characteristics. They provide a great choice of color for the designer, are light and can be self-supporting, and can be used to maximize limited resources. Columns can be done in alternating colors or can be constructed with multiple colors. They can color or cover ceilings without complicated or expensive rigging, and they can be installed reasonably quickly.

Balloons can be used to magnify the effect of other props or as a unique material to build signature props or a visual centerpiece. If a large room needs to be decorated with limited resources, balloons may be the answer. There is no better way to color a room quickly or add geometric structure to a room. Balloons can divide or shrink a room with much more style than pipe and drape. All this will be treated later in this chapter.

Balloons have a reputation of being inexpensive décor, which can work to the detriment of the event designer at times, making them hard to sell as a quality design element. Actually, when a designer uses large quantities of balloons to cover a wall or constructs a major balloon sculpture, balloons can be quite pricey. The most expensive aspect of balloon decorating is the labor, and there can be an immense amount of labor in some balloon projects.

## RISK MANAGEMENT

Balloons frequently are misunderstood in regard to ethical and risk management issues. A popular special effect is the balloon release, when hundreds or thousands of balloons are released to signify the start of an event. This raises environmental concerns. However, an ethical balloon professional will release only latex balloons with no ribbons attached. The Balloon Council says that most balloons rise to approximately 5 miles, where they freeze and burst into nontoxic strips. The few latex balloons that remain on the ground appear to have no ill effects on the livestock or wild animals that may consume their remnants.

A latex balloon exposed to air and sunlight has approximately the same decomposition rate as an oak leaf. Latex is produced from the sap of the rubber tree, which also serves the rain forest functions of cleansing the air, removing carbon dioxide, and generating oxygen through its leaves. The inadvertent release of foil balloons or balloons with ribbons attached, such as those sold for personal amusement, *can* become an environmental hazard or a danger to wildlife.

Foil balloons sometimes are mistakenly referred to as Mylar balloons; actually, they are constructed from metalized nylon and polyethylene. Mylar is

**GOOD BALLOON PRACTICES FROM THE BALLOON COUNCIL**

- Follow the professional guidelines for balloon release. Use only hand-tied latex balloons with no plastic attachments. Never release foil balloons.
- Never attach metallic ribbon to helium-filled balloons. If the balloons are released accidentally, the ribbon can become tangled in power lines and cause a line fault.
- Supervise young children with balloons. Adults should supervise children under age six playing with balloons. Never allow children to play with uninflated balloons or broken balloon pieces, as these could cause choking or suffocation.
- Attach weights to helium-filled balloons to prevent accidental release. Balloons not intended for release should be attached to a plastic weight, mug, vase, or any object heavy enough to counter a balloon's lift.
- Don't tie helium-filled foil balloons together. Each balloon should be attached individually to a weight. This will prevent the balloons from rising as a cluster that can catch on power lines should they become untied from the weight.
- Dispose of balloons properly. Cut balloons with scissors directly above the knot or sealing point and then dispose of them.

a trade name for certain polyester materials that are not used in the construction of balloons. Foil balloons have to be used carefully, as they can conduct electricity, are flammable, and will pose environmental problems if they are not disposed of properly.

For safety purposes, all balloon clusters should be tied on individual ribbons and masses of helium-filled balloons, as in columns, arches, or walls, should be removed at the end of the event and never be released.

Check with your venue before decorating with helium-filled balloons. Many venues have restrictions on their use because they can get caught up in the rafters or in an open ceiling structure.

## HIRING A BALLOON PROFESSIONAL

We all grew up with balloons and feel that we "know" them. Like the perception of balloons as cheap décor, this is a simplification, if not a total misconception. If you are contemplating a major animated piece or decorating a tradeshow with 30,000 balloons, you need a balloon professional.

Balloon professionals, like any other special event professional, can best be located by means of recommendations, interviews, and examination of their portfolios. The Qualatex Balloon Network (QBN) has a Certified Balloon Artist (CBA) program. Professionals with this certification have at least a minimum of knowledge and have gone to the trouble to get certified.

There are two specialties that balloon decorating companies tend to lean toward. Some emphasize the artistic and creative aspects and will take the time and effort to create a unique sculpture for the client. Others tend to be commercially oriented and can produce copious numbers of columns, arches, walls, and centerpieces, each an exact copy of the others, quickly and efficiently. Different projects may require different balloon designers.

# DECORATING WITH BALLOONS

## HELIUM-FILLED VERSUS AIR-FILLED BALLOON DÉCOR

Events are temporary occasions with a beginning and an end. Balloon decorations, especially helium-filled balloons, have a limited life. Helium is the smallest molecule and is capable of escaping through the latex wall of a balloon over time. An 11-inch standard latex balloon filled with helium should be considered to have an average flying time of 12 to 18 hours.

If 11-inch standard latex balloons are installed 36 hours before the projected end of an event, some action has to be taken to extend their life. Some suggestions are attaching other balloons with enough lift and a long enough life to hold them up or by using a product such as **Ultra Hi-Float.** Ultra Hi-Float can be sprayed into latex balloons to greatly extend their flying time.

Helium-filled foil balloons have a flying time of several days and will stay inflated for extended periods. Because the material is heavier than latex, they have a lighter lift capability, with an 18-inch foil balloon averaging 1 ounce of lift as opposed to 1.8 ounces for an 18-inch latex balloon. Average flying times and lift capabilities for various balloons can be found in Appendix 7, *Balloon Charts.*

Air-filled latex balloons will last several days, and air-filled foil balloons will last for months. However, they must have some form of structural support or be rigged from overhead. They are still light and easy to fly with nylon twine or heavy-duty monofilament. **Balloon swags** hung from a central point in a ceiling can be very effective (Figure 9-1), and complex constructions using lightweight frames called **armatures** are very easy to hang.

## BALLOON COLUMNS AND ARCHES

Balloon columns are created by tying helium-filled balloons on 40-pound or 50-pound monofilament line and anchoring them to the floor. (The pound figure refers to the manufacturer's rating of the line's breaking strength.) They can be loose columns with space between the balloons or can be pushed up tight to create a solid column. The solid columns become spiral columns if the balloon colors are alternated sequentially as they are tied to the line. They can be anchored with small sandbags, held down to hard floor surfaces with 2-inch clear tape, or hooked into a carpeted surface with standard drapery hooks. A 12-foot column of 11-inch balloons will have approximately 16.8 ounces of lift. If it is going to be up for more than 18 hours, a 3-foot balloon can be added to the top of the column or Ultra Hi-Float can be used.

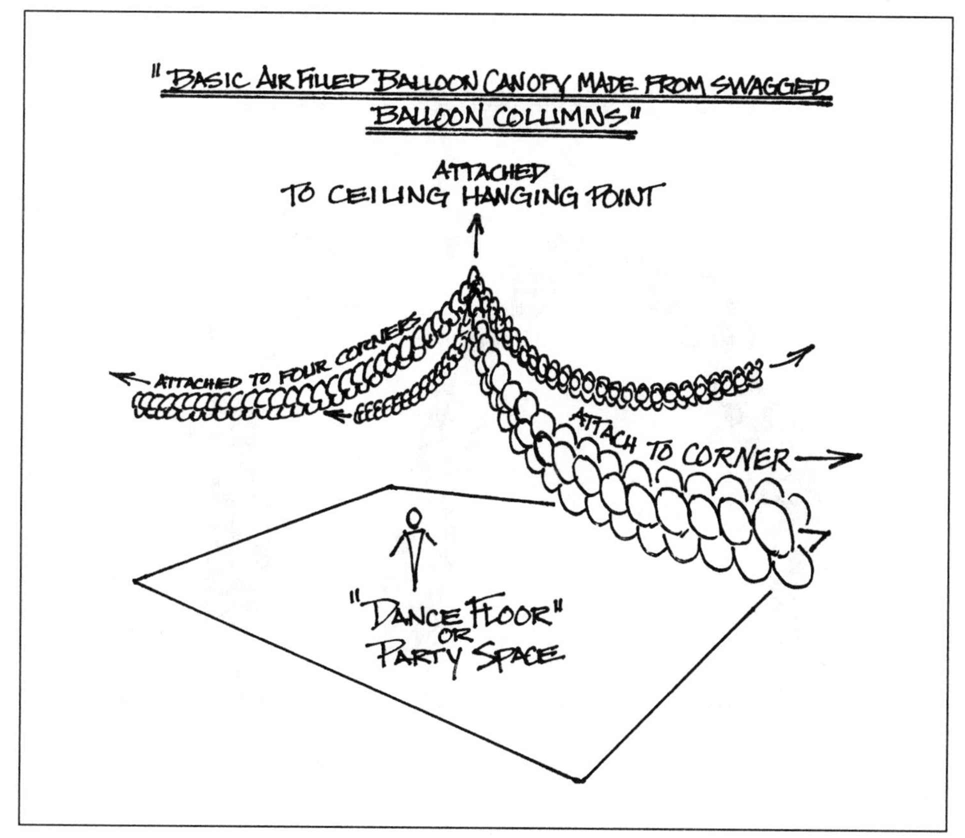


Figure 9-1

If columns need to be up for several days, air-filled balloons should be used, which can be supported by an upright post on a base. Miniature lights can be added for more visual impact or a romantic look. We have rotated columns of balloons with miniature lights, using small rotators with an electrical outlet built in.

**Balloon arches** are created by tying helium-filled balloons equidistantly on a monofilament line and attaching both ends of the line to the floor or other surface. The natural tendency of the line of balloons is to rise into a natural and attractive **parabolic curve.** A spiral column can be made very long and attached at both ends to become a spiral arch. Multiple arches can be used to create an entrance or a ceiling. Miniature lights can be added to arches to increase the visual impact, but this will shorten the flying time. If they are going to be up for 12 hours or more, Ultra Hi-Float can be sprayed into each balloon or 30-inch or 36-inch balloons can be added at regular intervals to extend their flying time (see Figure 9-2).

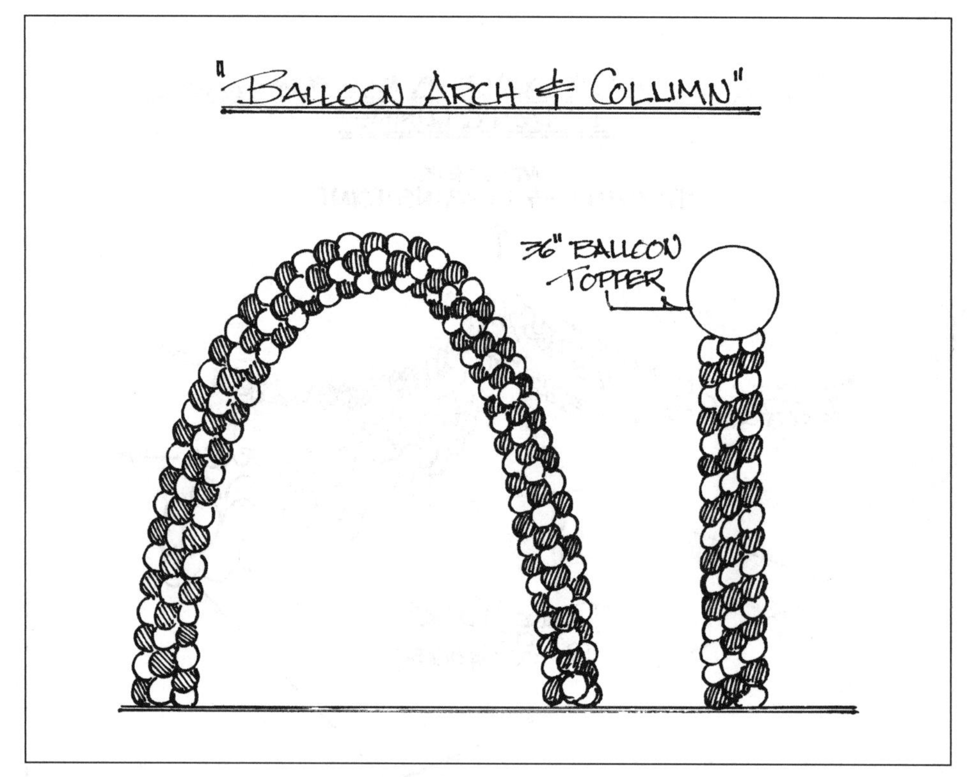


**Figure 9-2**

## CLUSTERS AND CENTERPIECES

Balloons frequently are clustered into bouquets and used as gifts; the clusters also can make an effective centerpiece. You can select the colors of balloons and use either matching or contrasting ribbons to make the clusters round and fat or tall and skinny, depending on how many balloons are used and the relative lengths of the individual ribbons.

In creating centerpieces, sizes and styles of balloons can be mixed, or they can be used with small theme props. Mixed foil balloons, balloons mixed with flowers, and latex balloons of different sizes tied with Q260 balloons are all effective variations.

Generally, bouquets are most attractive if tied on individual strings that are tied to a sandbag wrapped in tissue paper or a concealed weight. Air-filled balloons can be added to helium-filled balloons, and props or flowers can be incorporated. Sometimes the centerpiece is a floral or prop centerpiece, and the balloons are added to enhance it.

Another centerpiece effect that is used occasionally employs the balloon-stuffing device sold to create unique gift wraps. Using this mechanism, it is possible to put a teddy bear, a bottle of wine, or another item into an air-filled

Idea Portfolio

# BALLOONS IN HIGH-TECH CENTERPIECES

For an unusual party for Middle Eastern royalty we created a high-tech look by using clear air tube and intelligent lighting. Air tube is a balloon-related product that consists of a continuous tube filled with air from a concealed fan. Tied to the architectural fixtures in the wall or ceiling, it can be angled and bent into interesting shapes, dynamic lines, and curves. For the centerpieces we used battery-operated abstract neon shapes and added Q260 balloons in abstract shapes that matched the air tube, as illustrated in Figure 9-3.

The intelligent lights were programmed to trace the clear air tube in slowly changing colors and patterns, enhancing the cutting-edge high-tech illusion. Balloons may not be considered a high-tech design element, but as was stated before, in the hands of a creative designer their uses are limitless.

**Figure 9-3**

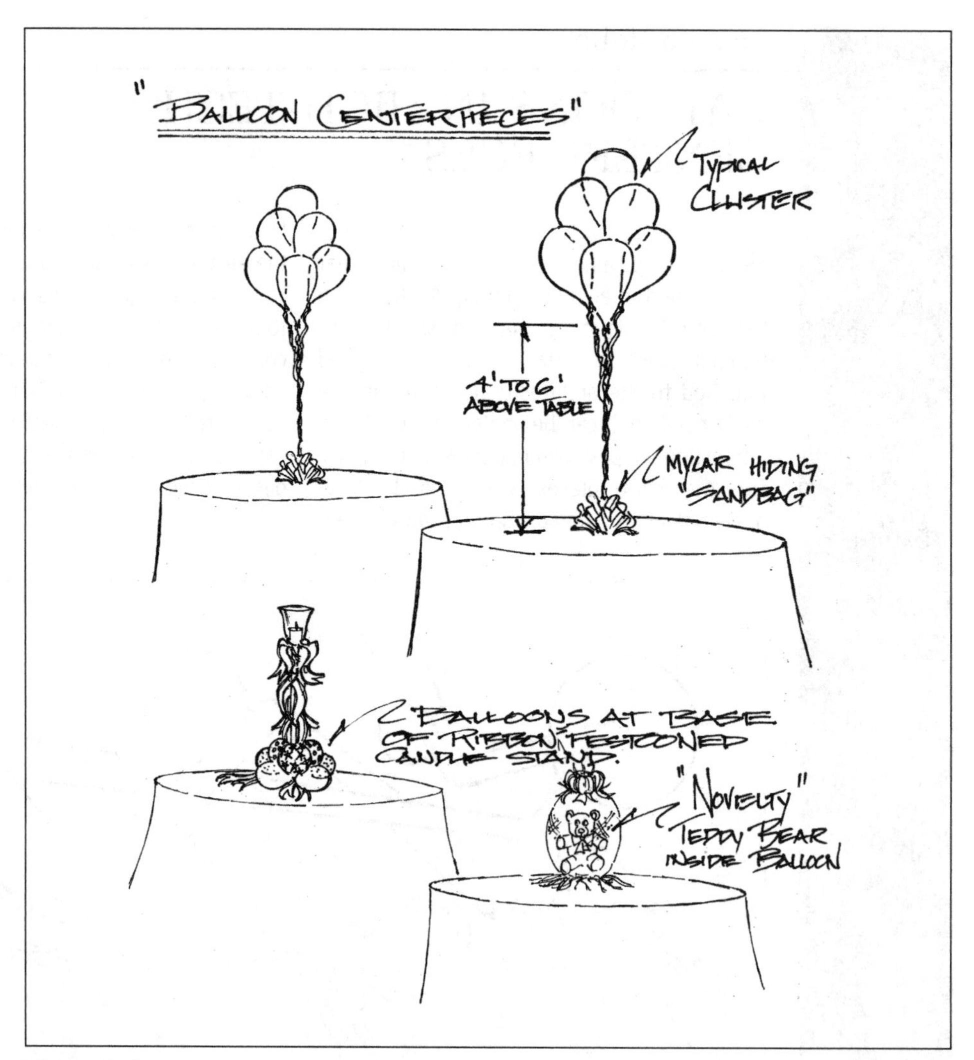


**Figure 9-4**

balloon, which then can be incorporated into a centerpiece by nesting it in foil tissue paper or a floral ring (see Figure 9-4).

## CEILINGS AND WALLS

**Ceiling treatments** using balloons may use arches, swags, or helium fills, or a designer may create a unique treatment for a special use. One can make a single balloon arch, called a **string of pearls,** that is created tying single balloons

Idea Portfolio

## AN UNDERWATER CEILING

At the entrance to a delightful underwater fantasy party, a painted backdrop established the portal and a costumed King Neptune merman, perched on a reef, greeted the guests. Over the entrance a rustic antique "stone" sign welcomed them to the Lost City of Atlantis. The effect was finished by the use of clear balloons in different sizes to create a bubbles and foam effect as seen from below. In the entrance and throughout the underwater party we used small clusters of 5-inch and 7-inch clear air-filled balloons suspended from the ceiling to give the effect of bubbles rising from the sea floor.

onto a continuous nylon line, or one can create spiral arches. If the arches are carefully designed with multiple colors or different hues of the same color and placed in precisely the right position from one arch to the other, a wonderful pattern can be created.

**Arch ceilings** have balloon arches butted up so that they touch one another and appear as a solid ceiling. This architectural creation has a major aesthetic impact and an interesting effect on people's perceptions. Even though they *know* these are just helium-filled balloons, people feel that there is a monolithic construction floating over their heads.

Arches also can be used aesthetically to lower or conceal architectural features without being solid. Balloon arches spaced apart still "stop the eye," giving attendees the feeling that whatever is past or behind them is not important and therefore is out of their perception. The attendees' memories of the event stops at the colors and patterns created, and they rarely remember what was beyond the décor.

When you are heavily decorating or fully covering a ceiling, remember that the existing lighting will pass through colored latex balloons. This will reduce the light level and tint it with the color of the balloons.

**Swag ceilings** are air-filled streamers of balloons that are tied to the ceiling and swag downward and outward. These swags have the same effect in covering the ceiling or distracting the eye that arches have and can have the same effect on the lighting. The differences are twofold, one practical and one aesthetic. Practically speaking, balloon arch ceilings have a flying time of 18 to 24 hours, while swags will last a week or longer.

Aesthetically, a different feeling can be engendered through the use of swags. Whereas arches sweep overhead and can give one the feeling of being beneath a vast vaulted sky, swags sweep upward in an elevating curve. This can cause an inspiring, almost spiritual feeling.

**Balloon fill ceilings** take advantage of existing ceiling configurations, coffers, and other structures. If the ceiling of a room is structured so that it can contain helium-filled balloons in a controlled way, the balloons can be released onto the ceiling to stay there. This has a very festive effect, provides great color to the space, and is a very effective design. It is customary to tie ribbons onto each balloon to provide even more color.

An additional effect can be created by tying reflective ribbons onto each balloon and then shining a tight beam of light through the field. This creates the effect of thousands of tiny strobe lights as the ribbons move in the air currents. This technique is particularly effective over dance floors.

Several things have to be considered before one designs a balloon fill (Figure 9-5). Air-conditioning systems will be working at full intensity during an event, and the air registers in the ceiling may have a negative effect on the balloons, blowing all of them into a corner. If there are chandeliers in the ceiling, ribbons can become entangled in them, causing the need for additional labor to remove them and possible damage. Some ceilings have invisible sharp components in their finish; these are what we call balloon-eating ceilings. Finally, it is important to remember that tying ribbons, especially foil ribbons, onto helium-filled balloons requires proper care and disposal after the event.

## WALLS

Designing a wall treatment is similar to designing a ceiling treatment in that it can be a complete environmental makeover or can employ carefully placed elements such as columns and clusters to achieve an aesthetic effect and stop the eye. Using regularly placed spiral balloon columns is one of the two most cost-effective ways to design color into an entire room, the other being lighting.

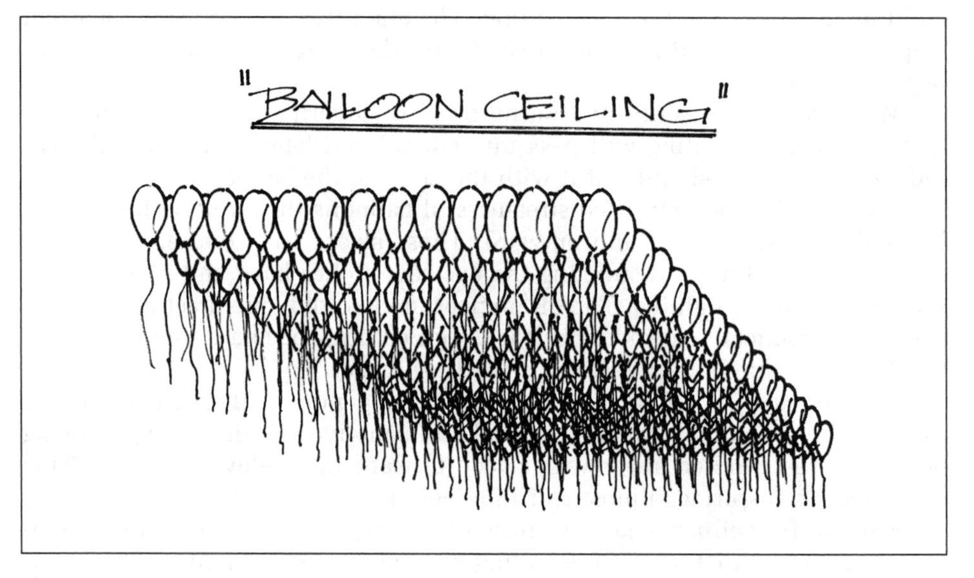


**Figure 9-5**

Unique walls that create an entrance or are used as a stage backdrop can be built by using helium-filled columns and attaching them together. They also can be constructed on frames to achieve patterns of color to re-create a flag or some other recognizable decorative element. Pioneer Balloons sells the SDS system of metal frames, which designers can use to create outstanding balloon wall effects. For larger applications, custom units can be designed and engineered to create support structures for walls, portals, and tunnels.

## SPECIAL BALLOON EFFECTS

The **balloon release,** which was discussed in the risk management section earlier in this chapter, is one of the best-known popular effects. Helium-filled latex balloons are placed in a net, a polyethylene tube, or specially constructed boxes and then released on cue to rise in a swarm over the heads of the attendees.

Another popular effect is the **balloon drop,** in which air-filled balloons are collected in a plastic bag or net over the heads of the guests and then released to drop down on them at the appropriate moment. Some of the most memorable balloon drops have occurred at political conventions to announce the candidate for president of the United States.

**Confetti drops** are an effect in which balloons are burst on cue to shower confetti down on the attendees. To achieve this effect, air-filled balloons with confetti inside are tethered or suspended overhead. On cue they are remotely burst, usually through the use of electrically ignited **squibs.** Consult a licensed pyrotechnic professional about this effect. *Never use confetti without permission from the venue, as it is prohibited in many places because of the difficulty of cleaning it up.*

Idea Portfolio

### BALLOON CURTAIN DROP

A client of Gale Sliger Productions planned a fashion show that would be followed immediately by dancing. Our client was worried that people would go home after the fashion show, thinking it was the end of the event. To facilitate the transition between the show and the dancing, we designed the following effect.

The fashion show was in the center of one end of the ballroom. The bandstand was concealed behind a thin silver curtain at the other end of the room, held up with 36-inch silver latex helium-filled balloons.

At the finale of the fashion show, sparkle fountains were ignited around the fashion show stage. As they were about to fade, whistle-bang sparkle fountains at the other end of the room drew everybody's attention in that direction. Then the 36-inch balloons were burst, the curtain dropped, and the Bill Tillman Band hit the downbeat on "Give Me That Old Time Rock 'n' Roll." The dance floor filled in the first two minutes.

Idea Portfolio

## GALE SLIGER BALLOON REVEAL

Thousands of helium-filled balloons are tied to long individual ribbons that are held down under 2-inch Velcro. The bottom half of the Velcro, either loop or hook, is attached to a hard-surfaced floor or a board that is weighted down. The top half is split in the center where the opening will begin and has a lightweight control cord running offstage in both directions. The hook and loop tape holds the balloons down, and enough balloons are used to create a wall that hides whatever is to be revealed. On cue, the control lines are pulled at a steady pace, firmly and not too quickly. The balloons rise in a natural arch that looks like an opera curtain until they are all against the ceiling, creating a festive picture with all the long ribbon tails hanging down.

One of the most original balloon effects I know was invented by my associate Gale Sliger and executed by Leo Bary of Balloons To You. They created a balloon wall release that originally was used for the unveiling of the McKinney Avenue Transit Authority's first renovated trolley car. I have been using it ever since for band curtains, fashion shows, and product reveals.

## ADVANCED BALLOON DESIGN

Balloons can be used to create eagles, octopuses, and airplanes. Their uses are limited only by the creativity of the designer, the capabilities of the balloon professionals, and the resources available for design and execution. Jim Skiskimas, as was mentioned earlier in this chapter, is one of the most award-winning designers in balloon decorating. See "Jim Skistimas Interview" on the next page for some of his thoughts on advanced balloon design.

## BALLOON-RELATED PRODUCTS

Several design elements are in the balloon realm even though they are not traditional balloons, specifically **air tube** and various **inflatables.** Both of these products were developed for and are used primarily in the advertising industry. Air tube was referred to earlier in this chapter in the *Idea Portfolio* "Balloons in High-Tech Centerpieces." It consists of continuous polyvinyl tube that comes in a broad selection of colors and several different sizes and is inflated with fans.

**JIM SKISTIMAS INTERVIEW**

- A passion for possibilities has driven me in this industry, but everything boils down to education.
- Balloons can be lighted in front, backlighted and lighted from within, up-lighted, or downlighted. They can really glow!
- Balloons can be used as projection screens.
- Air-filled latex balloons in a structure last about two weeks.
- Balloons are not just ephemeral. We built a logo for Southwest Airlines out of air-filled foil balloons for their twenty-fifth anniversary that lasted until their twenty-sixth. All they had to do was clean it.
- Balloons are very compatible with Lycra or Spandex. You can work balloons with Lycra inside it to create unusual spatial design components.
- The reflective properties of foil balloons make them work well with neon and other lighting effects. Also, clear Mylar (polyester) balloons work well with changing lighting.
- There are some exciting new developments in balloons. Look at the new balloon shapes that use the alphabet. L and S have some exciting possibilities as design elements rather than just letters. Balloons with form change shape as you twist and turn them.
- The more you can look at a form in different ways, the more you can create with it.

Air tube is lightweight and flexible and easily can be hung overhead in random or carefully designed patterns to create ceilings, entrances, tunnels, walls, abstract air sculptures, and color accents. It can be suspended, curved, and angled and can be used to wrap buildings and decorate tents, fences, scaffolding, ballrooms, or lobbies. It can be used effectively in conjunction with **intelligent lighting,** which can be programmed to track the geometric structure of the air tube. One of our favorite design approaches is to use clear air tube in a ballroom or over a dance floor and then color it with moving beams of changing colored light (Figure 9-6). See Chapter 10, *The Art of Light* for more details on intelligent lighting.

There are several manufacturers of air tube products, and numerous balloon professionals and professional decorating companies are competent in this specialty. Most air tube meets or exceeds National Fire Protection Association (NFPA) 701 flame-retardant standards, but as is the case with all special event materials, this should be confirmed in writing before ordering, be accompanied by a flame-retardant certificate, and be field-tested by the purchaser and designer. *Keep the flame-retardant certificate and a sample with you in case either is required by the fire marshal.* Designers are warned to be especially careful of any shiny metallic finished air tube.

**Helium inflatables** and **cold air inflatables** are available for rental or purchase or can be custom designed. The name *helium inflatable* generally describes a self-contained balloon envelope that can be filled with helium,

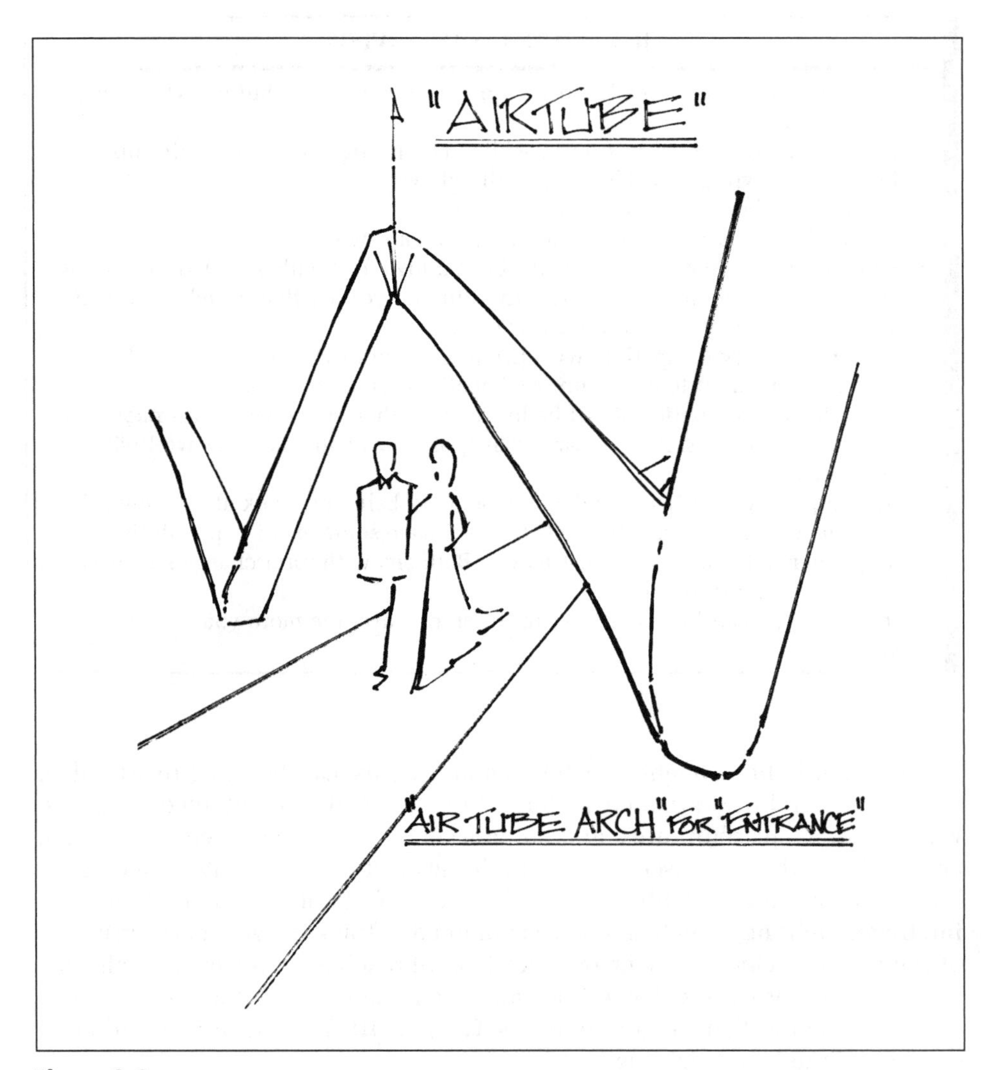


**Figure 9-6**

air, or another gas and can be sealed and remain inflated. A cold air inflatable is an envelope with an opening at one end; it is kept inflated with an electric fan. The most familiar helium inflatables are the giant characters seen annually in the Macy's Thanksgiving Day parade. There are many unique and creative variations on cold air inflatables, although the most common ones are the large hot air balloon reproductions one sees as advertising gimmicks on gas station canopies, stores, and shopping malls.

Helium inflatables are readily available in several forms as advertising specialties; the hot air balloon reproduction and large blimp forms as well as traditional balloon shapes and spheres. For indoor use there are remote con-

Idea Portfolio

## CONTROLLING A GIANT FOOTBALL

For a luncheon for the Cotton Bowl Association we had a giant football inflatable created with the Cotton Bowl logo to suspend behind the head table, flanked by giant foamcore logos of the competing teams hanging from the ceiling. Because there was a quick turnover of the room, we decided to fill the inflatable with helium in advance and move it into the space.

Our balloon professionals at Balloons To You were experienced with giant inflatables. They provided a blend of helium and air so that the lift produced by the balloon was not too strong. Without their professional knowledge and experience we would have filled it with helium, making it hard to control, or let some of the gas out, making it sag and look soft.

trol helium blimps 6 feet and larger that have the capability of dropping prizes or literature over the heads of guests or attendees. Inflatables also are available as theme characters such as giant gorillas and dinosaurs that can represent King Kong and Godzilla. It is still a memorable experience to see a high-rise building sporting a giant gorilla inflatable between the seventh and ninth floors or a 40-foot spider on Halloween. Although they are very specific elements, helium inflatables can have a place in certain special events other than parades.

Cold air inflatables are either stock rental or sales items that hold advertising banners or can be custom made to represent a product or character or reproduce a three-dimensional logo. Some other cold air inflatables have been designed specifically for or are particularly suited for event decorating. These include the dancing vinyl air characters seen at Super Bowl halftime shows and a host of other holiday, theme, and abstract creations, such as those available through Air Dimensional Design, Inc., www.airdd.com.

In addition, there are inflatable children's attractions such as **bounce houses** and **inflatable slides.** These inflatables are more closely related to the amusement industry than to the balloon industry but are popular for children's parties and large corporate events with a family component.

# FINISHING TOUCHES

Balloon decorations are one of the most popular and underappreciated design elements available to event professionals. Their cost-effectiveness belies their unique properties and limitless flexibility as a useful design tool. Balloons put the attendees in the mood to have a good time; they have a big impact and provide a wide palette of colors in a lightweight and easy to use form. Latex balloons are environmentally friendly, but all balloon decor needs to be designed and used according to professional guidelines and best practices. There are many ways to use both helium-filled and air-filled balloons with props and other décor, as props and décor, and as special effects. Air tube and helium and cold air inflatables are other balloon-related tools that are available to the event designer.

## DESIGN VOCABLUARY

Terms appear below in the order in which they first occur in this chapter.

Latex balloon
Foil balloon
Ultra Hi-Float
Balloon swag
Armatures
Balloon arch
Parabolic curve
Ceiling treatment
String of pearls
Arch ceiling
Swag ceiling
Balloon fill ceiling
Balloon release
Balloon drop
Confetti drop
Squib
Air tube
Inflatable
Intelligent lighting
Helium inflatable
Cold air inflatable
Bounce house
Inflatable slide

## STUDIO WORK

1. Describe the characteristics of balloons that make them desirable decorative elements. Also explain any downside or negative aspects there might be to employing balloons in an event design.
2. A carpet distributor is celebrating its fiftieth anniversary and wants to give a party for its employees and best customers. The clients decided to have the party in their warehouse, bringing in catering and entertainment. They want to use the occasion to build employee morale and as a marketing event. In four pages or less, propose a design concept employing balloons and balloon-related elements.
3. Design and describe a unique theme balloon centerpiece for a theme party of your choosing. Explain the theme and describe the components to be used and the way they are assembled. Include a sketch of the centerpiece.
4. Design and describe a unique balloon environment you would like to use at an event. Explain what you find particularly effective about it.

# RECOMMENDED READINGS AND RESEARCH SITES

Air Dimensional Design—suppliers of air animated inflatables such as FlyGuys, AirTicklers, AirFlames, and other dancers and puppets
http://www.airdd.com

Balloon Council—a research, education, and promotional organization for balloon manufacturers, distributors, and retailers
http://www.balloonhq.com/BalloonCouncil

Balloon Headquarters—an online network of balloon professionals; includes an e-mail idea exchange and discussion list, a finder service, and advertising opportunities
http://www.balloonhq.com

Balloon Headquarters Classic Balloon Décor 101 & 102—practical how-to descriptions of ways to design and construct specific classic balloon décor elements
http://www.balloonhq.com/faq/deco_decor_101.html
http://www.balloonhq.com/faq/deco_decor_102.html

Betallic, L.L.C.—balloon manufacturer
www.betallic.com

Big Events, Inc.—a commercial advertising supplier with a broad variety of helium and cold air inflatables available for rent
http://www.surfernet.com/big-events/

Inspireworks—offers step-by-step instructional videos for balloon decorating and sculpting
http://www.inspireworks.com

Macy's Parade official website—includes, among many interesting elements, a virtual parade and the steps in constructing large helium inflatables
http://www.macysparade.com

Qualatex website—the comprehensive website for Pioneer Balloons, a manufacturer of balloons for 80 years; includes information and application forms for the Qualatex Balloon Network (QBN) and the Certified Balloon Artist (CBN) designation
http://www.qualatex.com

T.K.Innovations, Inc.—a balloon manufacturer
http://www.tkinnovationsinc.com

# Chapter 10

# ART OF LIGHT

*Good relationships between professionals are how the best lighting gets done.*
**—Charles Belcher, President, Onstage Systems**

## IN THIS CHAPTER

You will discover how to light events and how to decorate events with light.

**Design and Direction**
**Lighting Events**
- Small Events
- Stage Productions
- Large Events
- Tented Events
- Production Companies

**Aesthetics**
- Principles of Color
- Angle of Incidence
- Light Levels
- Intelligent Light

**Lighting Equipment**
**Risk Management**
**Changing Technology**

Lighting can be a difficult thing to sell to clients because they turn lights on and off all the time and know how to change a lightbulb. They think, therefore, that they understand lighting. Lighting is actually a very sophisticated design element and an extremely technical discipline. This chapter shares a few of the design concepts and a minuscule amount of the technical aspects. Students of event design are well advised to learn this much and make friends with a lighting designer who will continue to teach them.

Lighting may be the key to the success or failure of an event. If the lighting design is done well, it transforms a nice event into a great event by creating a mood, enhancing the décor, and focusing the guests' attention on the right place at the right time. If it is done badly, it can interfere with the desired mood, hide the décor, and distract the guests. Attendees may not know what is wrong, but they definitely know that something is. An event manager does not need to know the color temperature of a particular tungsten-halogen lamp. He or she does need to know enough of the lighting vocabulary and have some understanding of what light can and cannot do to talk to a lighting designer.

The quote that began this chapter is Charles Belcher's best advice for an event planner, and it goes beyond lighting. Good relationships between professionals are how the best work gets done. Charles is president of Onstage Systems, a 26-year-old production company that provides technical support for national touring shows, concerts, symphonies, fairs, festivals, and special events of all types, and has been nominated twice for Country Music Association awards. He goes on to advise that "the event designer or planner who needs lighting for his or her events should become moderately familiar with the instruments and what they can do, enough to understand the key vocabulary terms of the lighting designer. Lighting professionals can help you learn the vocabulary and, more important, what the instruments can do. Event designers and decorators need to establish a rapport with one or two good lighting designers."

Idea Portfolio

## AN UNSUCCESSFUL AUCTION

We once attended a fund-raiser that was not as successful as the producers desired but provided a lesson in how to light and how *not* to light a silent auction. The gala had a Hollywood theme, and the primary décor in the ballroom was replicas of scenes from four classic films in the four corners of the room. The four settings had been lighted dramatically and were very well done.

One of the major fund-raising elements was a large silent auction that had been set up in each of the four corners, but nobody had gone to the trouble of lighting the auction tables. When the lights were turned down to party level, the auction tables were in the dark except in the areas where the dramatic lighting on the décor spilled across them.

My wife and associate, Jayna Monroe, noticed the difference in the bids between the items that were lighted by accident and the items that were adjacent to them that were in the dark. We walked around the room during the evening, cataloging price differences between the lighted items and the unlighted items. The lighted items sold for 75 to 110 percent of their retail value, while the unlighted items sold for 10 to 20 percent of their retail value.

Lighting is crucial to the success of the auctioning or sale of items at a fund-raising gala. We can extrapolate this result to assume that lighting is critical in marketing events as well.

# DESIGN AND DIRECTION

The terms **lighting designer** and **lighting director** appear at first to be interchangeable, and in many circumstances they are. The difference is that the lighting designer plans the **lighting design,** does the **light plot,** and provides the preliminary **light cues.** The lighting director is the on-site lighting expert who supervises the installation, runs the crew, makes on-site adjustments to the plot, and **programs** the final **cues.** In theater this is usually the same person, but in touring shows and in most audiovisual (AV) and many **production companies** and *probably at your next event,* the lighting director and the lighting designer may be different professionals.

A production company is one that supplies the lights and sound for a show or event. A large production or AV company may have several productions running concurrently but only one lighting designer.

The lighting design is both the original aesthetic phase and the functionally necessary phase of lighting. This is where the aesthetic decisions that create the final mood and focus are made and where the inventory that will be required to achieve those effects is compiled. The designer creates the light plot, which is the plan that shows where each instrument is hung, what color or colors it will have in it, and how it will be circuited, or patched. This plan is drawn as a **reflected ceiling,** which is essentially a floor plan with the light rigging and instruments overlaid on it. There also will be a **sectional view** illustrating a cross section of the room and the angle at which the light will be illuminating the stage, décor, and performers.

Light plots can be drafted by hand, but most designers work in a **CADD (computer aided design and drafting)** format. A typical CAD-generated light plot is shown in Figure 10-1. Note that the designer, Brian O'Connor, has included a thumbnail **elevation** above the **plate** with his company name (Art of Light) and address and the scale of the drawing shown. The drawing originally was planned to be (¼″ = 1′) scale, but has been reduced for reproduction.

The drawing also contains a thumbnail sectional elevation showing typical room décor below the plate. It is convenient but not essential that the event designer be able to read a light plot, but he or she should at least understand the principles of scale drawing and representative symbols, such as those explained in the key in this drawing.

Frequently an event designer or decorator is hired after the production company is in place or has to hire a production company in another town. In these cases, it is valuable to have an event professional who is knowledgeable about lighting and other aspects of production such as sound and staging to call on to serve as the **production manager.**

Bob Cherny is a seasoned professional who has been a hotel production manager, worked for production companies, and managed a meeting and entertainment facility. Bob gives the following advice on hiring a production manager and a production company.

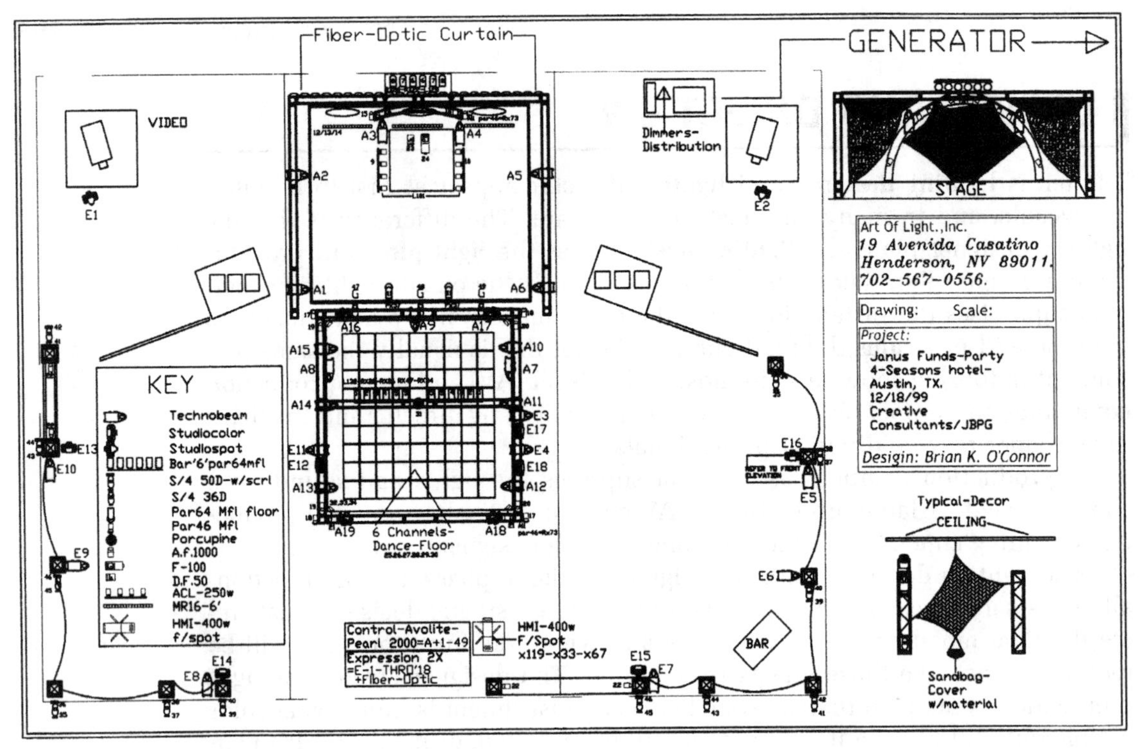


**Figure 10-1**

## CHERNY'S ADVICE ON HIRING A PRODUCTION COMPANY

- Hire a local production manager.
- Go to your local Meeting Professionals International (MPI), International Special Events Society (ISES), or other professional organization meetings and ask who has worked with a production manager local to your base (not the city where the event is to be held), and find three or four likely candidates. Interview them. Give them the scope of the meeting and ask for bids. Remember that the quality of the chemistry between you and your production manager is more important than the raw price.
- *Give your production manager a budget. Make him or her stick to it.*
- Your production manager will research the vendors in the area of your meeting and decide which vendors to use locally and which to bring in from out of town. You will need to meet frequently with your production manager to be sure the meeting is properly planned. These meetings should be at your convenience in your location.
- The differences between production companies are as vast as the continent is wide. Remember that production managers who are employed by a production company have no more incentive to shop around than does a site selection company that gets a commission only from one hotel chain. However, a production manager who always works with the same crew knows its strengths and weaknesses.
- There are companies that do it all, but remember, the company is only as good as the tech who sits behind the **control console.**

# LIGHTING EVENTS

Event lighting is a cross between theater, concert, residential, and decorative lighting, each of which is a separate discipline and has had volumes written about it. There is no specific event lighting discipline, and the experts in the field have created their own competency. Las Vegas based–lighting designer Brian O'Connor, with whom we have worked on some memorable events, offers the following ideas:

> *The lighting designer needs to be on the same wavelength as the event designer. The theme is very important to the lighting designer. I like working with designers who know material and its properties when lighted. We use different lenses for different material selections to be lighted. I am a big fan of* ***backlighting*** *material, which gives a great illusion and conceals a multitude of sins. It also means the cable is already concealed behind the material.*
>
> *Event lighting involves a lot of compromises. You cannot always put instruments where you want to, especially in tents. Designing in advance, preplanning, and coordinating execution with all the other elements are crucial. The designer needs to be choosy about which instruments to use. The power source can be a challenge. I prefer working with generators. Coordinate all the technical people for* ***dark time, sound checks, focus,*** *and power so that they all get what they need when they need it—the production time line is so important!*

## SMALL EVENTS

Lighting is as important for small events as it is for large ones. The ambience, or atmosphere, is created by and can be destroyed by the lighting. Think of being at a dance with dim, romantic lighting and what happens when it is over and the lights are turned on full.

Many times lighting a small event is simply a matter of dimming the existing lights. However, this dims *all* the lights, including those on the flowers, food, and guest tables, and does not add any enhancements to the décor. With some readily available equipment it is possible to add atmosphere by washing the walls with color, accent the décor with spotlights, or pin-spot the centerpieces.

**Dimmer** control over existing lights either exists or it does not. If it does not, consider adding dimmers to the existing circuitry. However, lights also can be dimmed by unscrewing selected lightbulbs or replacing them with lower-watt bulbs.

Color can be added either by exchanging the existing **lamps** (lightbulbs) for colored lamps or by putting **gel** (heat-resistant plastic film color media) over them. Existing light fixtures can be gelled by securing color media in

**MONROE'S GENERAL RULES FOR LIGHTING EVENTS**

Warm white or light pink is a flattering color for people.
Blue is romantic but not flattering.
Dim is romantic but hard to eat or talk by.
Backlighting is always romantic.
A blend of pink and blue generally works well for events.
Too much light is as bad as too little.
Only white light should be used on food or flowers.
White is an excellent accent color when surrounded by colored light.
Spots draw attention.
Green light makes greenery look artificial.
Green light makes people look dead.
When you are lighting flowers or other décor, sit in the chair or stand where the guests will be standing and make sure the light will not be in their eyes.
Everything you do with lighting, every decision you make, should have a reason or it will look inappropriate or out of place.

front of the lamp, taping or pinning it to the trim, fixture, or ceiling. Plan this in advance and try it in the darkened room to make sure it works and does what you want it to do.

Backlight—light coming from an instrument behind rather than in front of fabric—is especially effective and can be done in colors. **Uplight** on foliage plants, trees, and many other decorations can be dramatic, but do not uplight people. The same aesthetics discussed later in this chapter apply to small event lighting as well as to lighting large events.

Adding light to draw attention to a specific item or area or removing or dimming existing lighting around that item is called **accent lighting.** Accent lighting also can involve adding color. This can entail lighting (accenting) floral arrangements or décor, lighting a musical combo, or lighting the area where the best man will make a toast. **Extension sockets, goosenecks** or **clip-on lights** with **spots,** and **floodlights** (Figure 10-2) work for accent lighting. Color can be created by using colored lamps or by putting gel over them.

The lamps commonly used with these fixtures include **PAR lamps** and **R-type** lamps, which come in various sizes and wattages, as do **MR-16 lamps.** Clear PAR 38 lamps come in spot and flood. They are available in colors, including several shades of pink and blue and a cool blue-white color, usually only in 100 watts. These different lamps come from different manufacturers, and finding a useful blend of colors is a matter of trial and error (see Figure 10-3).

If you are accenting with swivel extension sockets or goosenecks in existing ceiling lights, remember that they will be dimmed when the lights are lowered. Use higher-wattage lights in this case so that they will be brighter than the surrounding dim light.

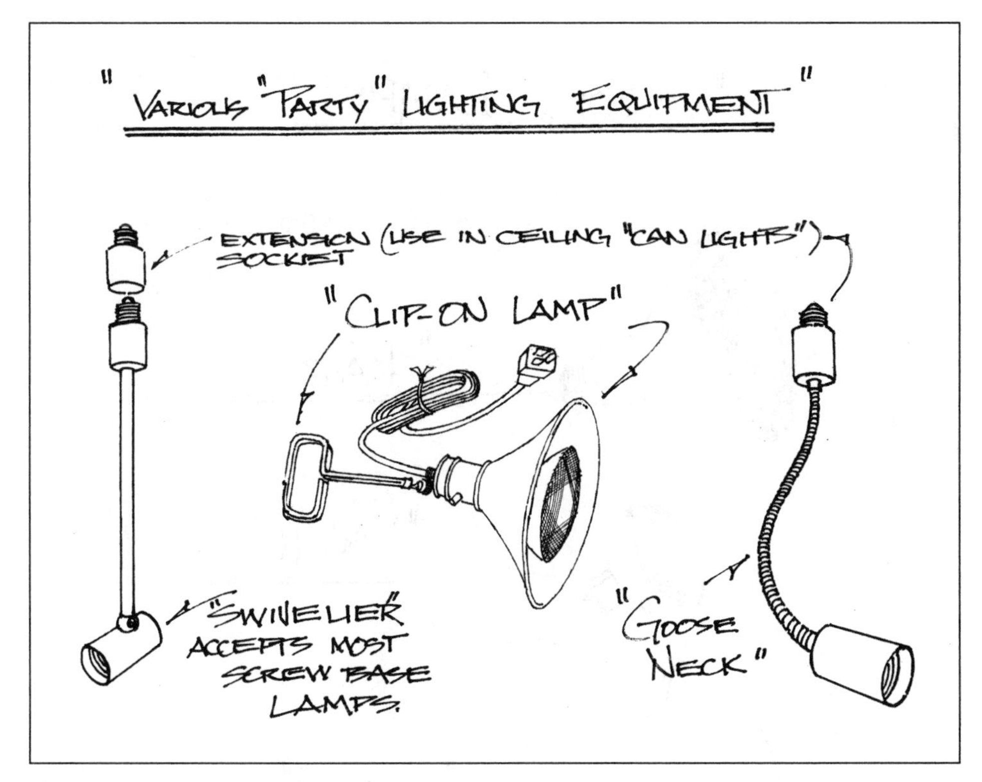


Figure 10-2

## STAGE PRODUCTIONS

Any event that has a live stage production to be lighted, even if it is only a dance band or a speaker, needs to have the required lighting (and sound) integrated into the event design and décor. If it is not, the band equipment will not fit or will hide the pretty stuff or add an unplanned technical look. *A best practice for the professional event designer and decorator is to find out what is going to be on the stage for entertainment or production before the stage is designed or the décor is planned.*

Many bands and all name entertainment acts include a **rider** or **technical rider** as part of the contract. This document legally obligates the signer to provide very specific sound, light, and other production equipment for the performance. Most productions today require a front and a rear truss with **PAR cans** and a number of **intelligent lights.** In addition, there may be several **lekos** for "specials" and for projecting **gobos** on the stage, walls, or dance floor and one or two **follow spots.** All operators will have to be connected via a **Clear Com** or another communications setup to the lighting director (LD), the **stage manager,** or whoever is the **cue caller.**

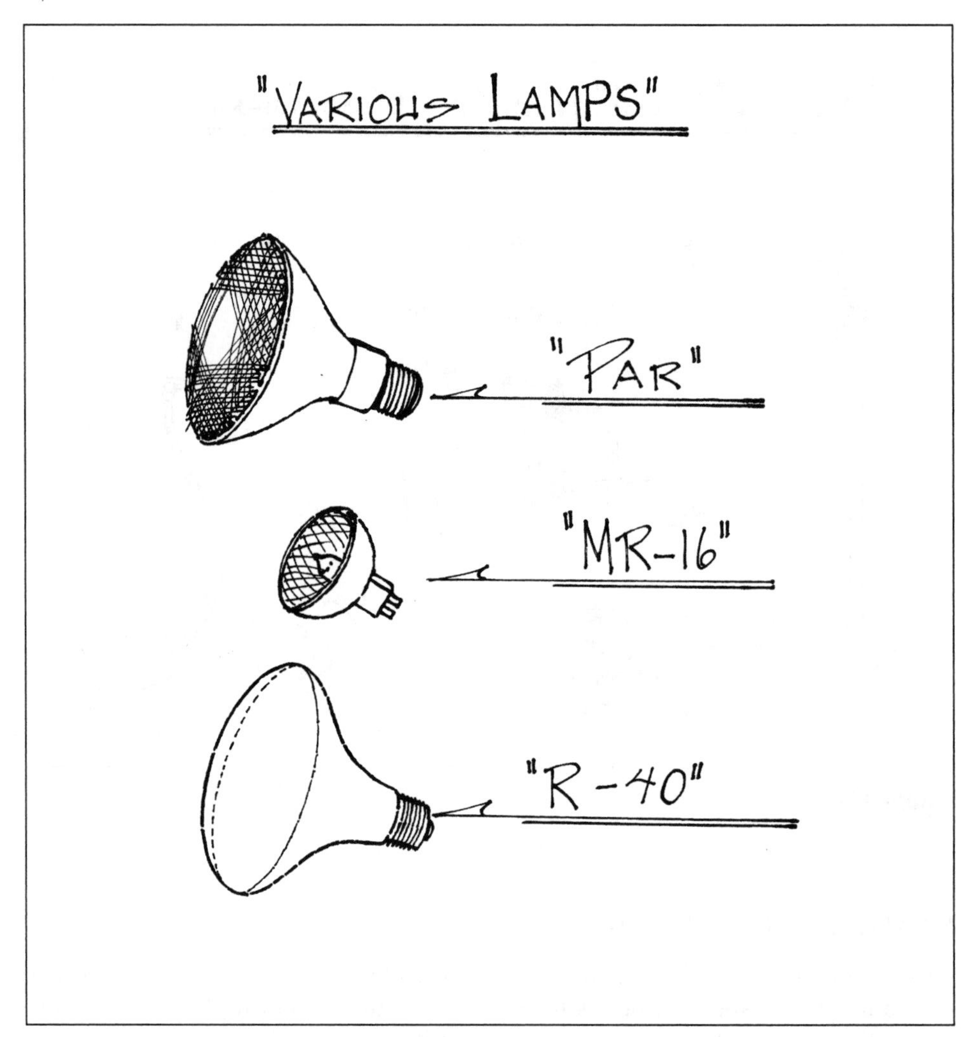


**Figure 10-3**

Typical lighting for a show band (Figure 10-4) includes a **three-color wash** from a **front truss** along with several **specials** to light the stars or highlight the main performance area, a **rear truss** in several colors, a **follow spot,** and several intelligent lights. The color wash typically is supplied by **1-kilowatt PAR cans** or the equivalent; lekos are used for specials and gobo projections. The follow spot will be set up at the rear of the room on a tower to raise it and the operator above the crowd.

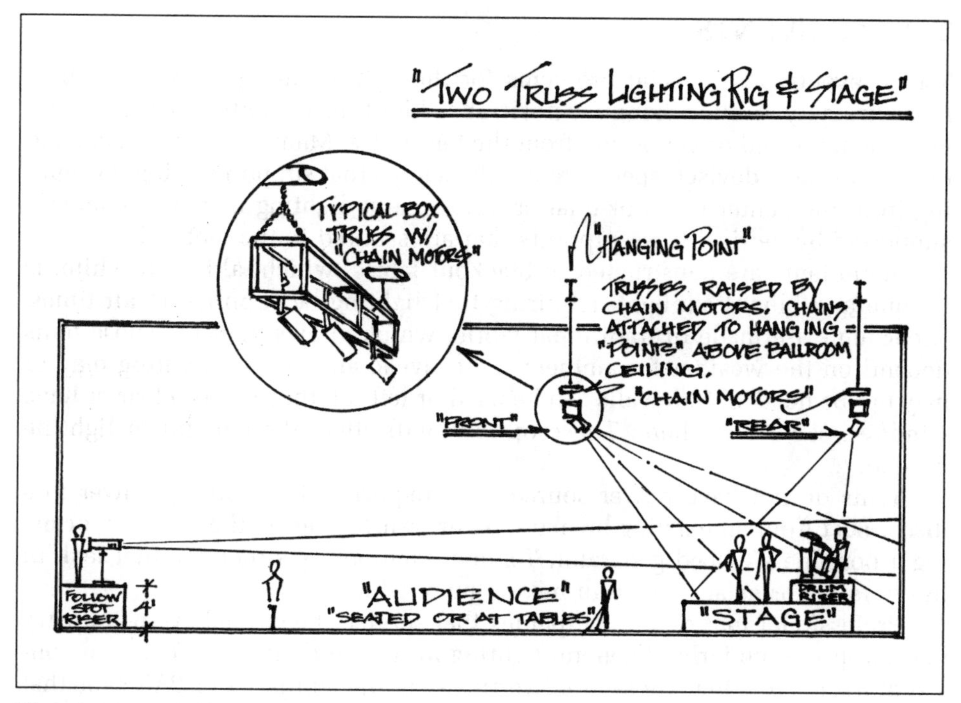


**Figure 10-4**

## LARGE EVENTS

Large events typically include a stage show plus additional **general lighting** and/or effect lighting. General lighting in large events can require a lot of electricity and a lot of rigging to hang it from many different positions. Monroe's General Rules for Lighting Events, shown in a box earlier in this chapter, apply for large events as well as small ones. Power requirements can be reduced through the careful selection of lighting instruments. Uplighting the perimeter walls or the décor can alleviate the need for some rigging but puts power cable on the floor, where it must be dealt with at doorways.

General lighting washes can be done with PAR cans with **color changers,** which can scroll through selected colors by means of remote programming. Projected gobos in what are called **breakup patterns** (small irregular patches of light) provide reduced light with a texture rather than just flooding an area with light. Accent lighting large events is easier because we use theatrical instruments, which are designed with controls for the shape, size, and color of the light.

### TENTED EVENTS

Tented events pose special problems for the lighting designer because there are extremely limited hanging positions. Lighting in tents must be either ground-supported or supported from the tent poles. Many event designers and decorators have devised special tent pole clamps that support rigging for lighting from the center poles or quarter poles. Large lighting rigs are frequently supported by vertical truss supports that are secured to the tent poles.

Some tents are constructed of blackout fabric, which, although white, is opaque and blocks sunlight, requiring that lighting be supplied at all times. Other tents are made of traditional fabric, which allows light in. These tents depend on the weather for ambient light levels, and general lighting may or may not be needed. Sidewalls can be used or left off; they can be clear or have windows sewn into them. These options will affect the amount of lighting needed.

Tents do not have power sources and require either running power to a **disconnect** from an existing breaker box or transformer on the property or using a portable silenced generator. Tents are temporary structures that leak in heavy rain storms and move in heavy, gusty winds.

Professional tent rental companies that service the special event industry may supply some form of general lighting for use in their tents. This can consist of track lights that are secured vertically to the tent poles or PAR cans that are clamped to the perimeter poles and shine up to reflect off the white tent canvas top. Most of these companies have in-line dimmers available. Beyond this minimal lighting, a professional lighting designer with experience in tented events should be employed for aesthetic, functional, and risk management reasons.

## AESTHETICS

Good lighting designers must be competent in three areas. First, they must be technically competent with the equipment. Second, they must be operationally competent, organized, and capable of handling resources and risk management. Third, they need to understand the aesthetic principles of good lighting design. Unfortunately, many have considerably more training in the technical and operational aspects of lighting than in the aesthetic principles. It is important that the event designer know what lights can do and be able to communicate clearly what he or she wants to the lighting designer.

### PRINCIPLES OF COLOR

White light is a combination of all other colors of light. Blending combinations of primary red, primary blue, and primary green light in different proportions creates all the colors in the visible light spectrum. Black is the absence of light. Light is invisible and is revealed when it falls on an object that is being viewed.

These basic concepts can be confusing because we are more used to talking about color as paints or pigments. If you mix many different colors of light together, you get white light. As a result of the impurities in pigment, if you mix many colors of paint together, you get gray or brown, colors that cannot be achieved in light.

Color is achieved either by using colored lamps (light bulbs) or by putting color filters, called gels, in front of the **instrument** (light fixture). **Reflected light** also will pick up the color of whatever it bounces off.

Some basic practical results of these principles of color that the event designer will discover include the following:

- Bright colors are not achieved by putting a lot of colors together but by keeping them separated. A bright, multicolored look is achieved by lighting in different colors that do *not* overlap. When they overlap, they blend and become white.
- Pure white light looks unnatural to the spectator or audience because most natural and artificial light is a combination of white light and the reflected light from the surfaces from which it bounces.
- "Natural" light on stage generally is achieved by using a **warm color** (light pink or light amber) on one side, a **cool color** (light blue) on the other, and a **neutral color** (light lavender) from the front to create a blended white light. These colors should be spectrum-balanced to achieve a white when mixed together. This is a variation of the **McCandless system,** which was described in the 1930s by Stanley McCandless of Yale University, one of the first professors of lighting.
- Lighting on a brightly colored floor will reflect that color on the décor, the scenery, and the people who walk on it.
- Because light tends to blend to white in nature, any **saturated color** will seem unnatural and/or have a dramatic effect. Some examples are "moonlight" blue, which has a dramatic romantic effect; red "flames," which have a dramatic "hot" impact; and green light, which looks unnatural, especially on greenery and people.
- Because light is invisible and a mirror reflects light, you cannot "light" a mirror. In the case of mirrors or reflective glass, such as windows at night, the way to light them is to light what will be reflected in them.

## ANGLE OF INCIDENCE

The **angle of incidence** is the angle at which light beams strike the object being lighted. The optimal natural lighting would have the cool and warm lights striking the object at 45 degrees off center and the neutral light dead center, all mounted above the object or person being lighted at a 45-degree angle from vertical, as illustrated in Figure 10-5. The addition of a backlight puts an attractive halo around the speaker or performer.

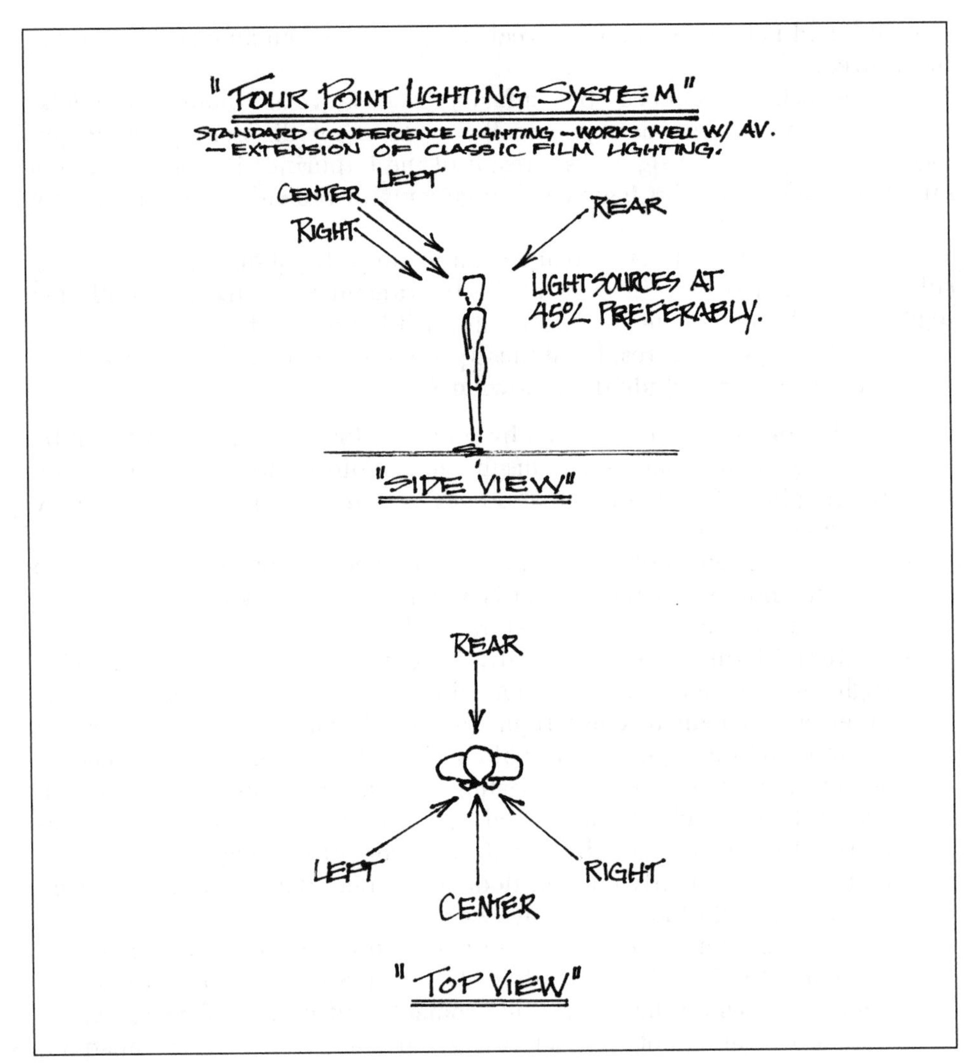


**Figure 10-5**

The **three-point system** (from film studio lighting; see Figure 10-6 and check out http://www.3drender.com/light/3point.html for inspiration) starts with a primary light source at 45 degrees, called the **key light,** and adds **fill light** at a lower angle and from the opposite side to light the environment and fill in the shadows; then **backlight** is added.

Other lighting practices that are used today were developed for rock concerts. The basic light plot is typically a three-color wash so that colors can be alternated to match the music or blended to achieve different stage pictures and a reasonably attractive and natural-looking front light. This typically is

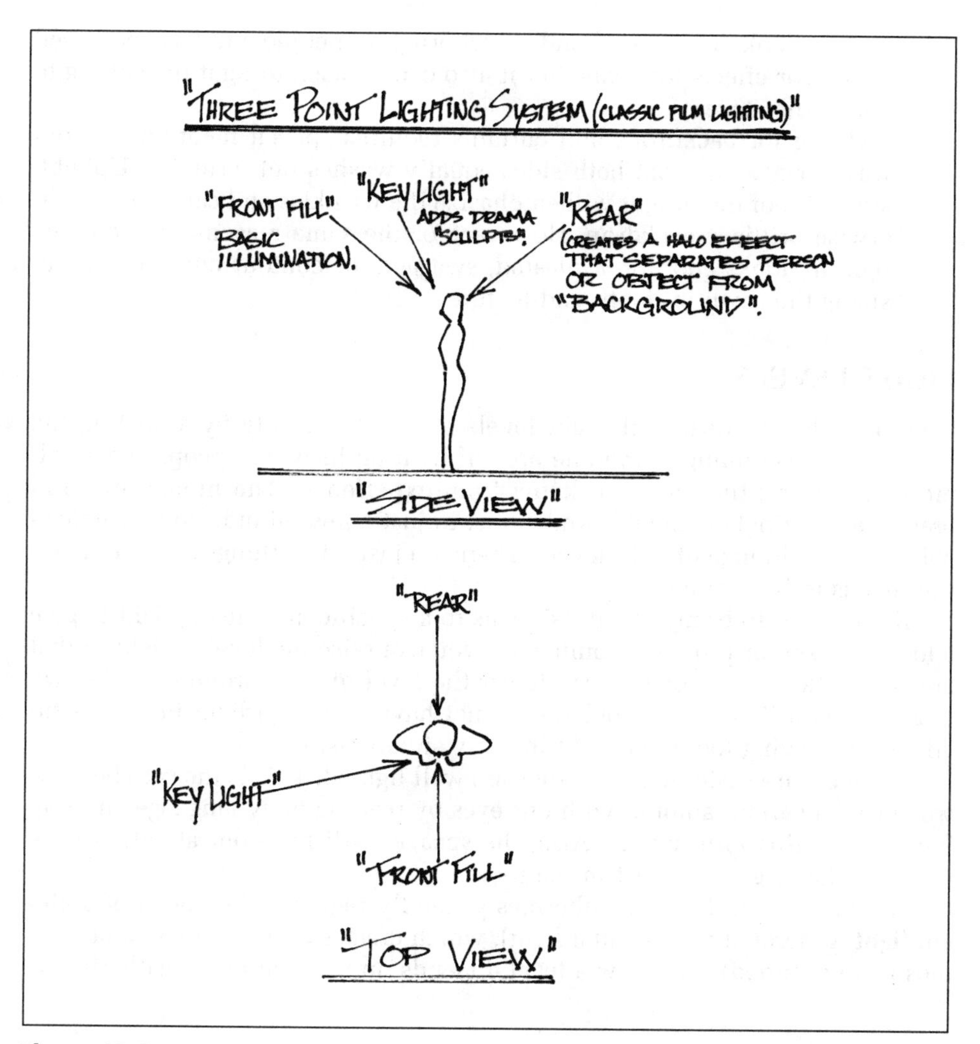
"THREE POINT LIGHTING SYSTEM (CLASSIC FILM LIGHTING)"
"FRONT FILL" BASIC ILLUMINATION.
"KEY LIGHT" ADDS DRAMA "SCULPTS"
"REAR" (CREATES A HALO EFFECT THAT SEPARATES PERSON OR OBJECT FROM "BACKGROUND".
"SIDE VIEW"
"REAR"
"KEY LIGHT"
"FRONT FILL"
"TOP VIEW"

**Figure 10-6**

achieved by circuiting and coloring every third PAR can separately and using them to flood the stage evenly in one of the three colors selected or in a blend of those colors.

Other angles of interest to the event designer include the following:

- **Sidelight** emphasizes contours and profiles of scenery and people and enhances movement.
- Very steep angles or overhead lights throw dramatic shadows. These dramatic angles are not always flattering and most often are used as backlight. Steep sidelight can be very effective at creating sunrise and sunset atmospheres.

- Uplight looks very weird and unflattering on people and has been used for horror effects for years, but it also can be used to light the ceiling to match the stage.
- Lighting for backdrops and curtains requires special mention. A front wash or a wash from both sides equally washes out wrinkles. Uplight, sidelight, or downlight will emphasize the wrinkles and can ruin an otherwise brilliant backdrop. However, for the same reasons, this oblique lighting looks good on a pleated, swagged, or contour curtain, emphasizing the sewn-in depth and texture.

## LIGHT LEVELS

Everybody has to deal with light levels at events, if only by adjusting the house lights. Dimming is the one area of lighting in which people know almost everything they need to know from experience. The human eye and brain are amazingly adaptable and adjust in just a few minutes to be comfortable in a broad range of light levels. There are just a few things an event manager needs to be aware of.

If you want to bring attendees' focus to a specific area, using light to give a logo, speaker, or product prominence, you can raise the level of light in that area or on that object or you can lower the level of light around it. The two most common light level problems are not having enough light in work situations and having too much light in party situations.

Speakers are easier to hear if they are well lighted. This is the case because we "hear" a certain amount with our eyes by reading body language and seeing the way lips form words. Also, the speaker will have our attention if he or she is the brightest object in the room.

Celebrations and social gatherings generally require a low level of **ambient light** (general environmental light), which creates a relaxing **ambience** (atmosphere or mood). How low a level depends on the goal of the gathering. A

Idea Portfolio

## LIGHT MOVES A CROWD

At a debutante party we watched from the light booth as the first guests gathered at the entrance to the ballroom, blocking the way into the event for the other 1,500 guests. As a couple of our associates tried to herd the guests, we had the idea of dimming the lights at the entrance and raising the lights at the bars on the far side of the room. Shortly after we did that, the crowd thinned, and for the remainder of the evening we kept the room balanced by raising and lowering the lights to move the crowd.

An event designer absolutely must consider the effects of light in designing the event.

bride needs to be seen when she arrives at the reception, and the family and friends need enough light to recognize one another easily. As dinner is served, the light level can go down a bit more but should remain high enough that people can see to enjoy the meal. Late in the evening the festivities will be enhanced by still a lower level for dancing. Corporate celebrations are very similar, except for sales and marketing events, or networking events, where the light levels should remain higher longer. Also, participant demographics affect the amount of light for an event. Older people need more light to see by, and younger crowds like it dark.

Pin-spotting flower arrangements on guest tables has become very popular. One or more extremely narrow beam instruments are used to illuminate individual centerpieces from overhead. Expensive flowers do not have to become invisible when the light level is lowered; instead, they seem to glow from within. Another benefit of pin-spotting arrangements is that the pin spots frequently throw a small area of ambient light onto the table, creating low-level party ambience throughout the room while giving the guests enough light to see the food and one another.

When using pin spots or other accent lighting that is plugged into the same sockets as the general lighting for the room, remember that those lights will be dimmed when the rest of the lights are dimmed. To work around this, unplug or unscrew the balance of the lights in the dimmable circuit or use brighter lights in the accent lights than in the rest of the fixtures.

Tents, especially open tents or tents with clear sidewall, pose another challenge at sunset. The human eye can be fooled as the sun goes down, and people perceive the twilight as darkness. It is desirable to raise the light level at that time. When darkness is achieved, it can be lowered to a level appropriate for the activity or goal of the evening.

## INTELLIGENT LIGHTING

Computer-controlled moving lights are referred to generically as intelligent lighting, **robotic lights,** or moving lights. These lights vary in their capabilities, depending on the manufacturer and the model, but they all feature a computer programmed to control a moving light beam that changes color and may also change shape or be used to project patterns called gobos. To show the moving beams, it is standard practice to **haze** the room with a nontoxic mineral oil fog from a **fogger** or **hazer.**

The Vari-Lite Company of Dallas, Texas (www.varilite.com), developed the first intelligent lights, patenting them in 1983. They featured moving beams of light and **dichroic** lens color changing, which allowed almost instantaneous color changes with up to 60 colors. They were first used in rock concerts and tours. They brought a new dimension to lighting, and many other companies developed different intelligent lighting instruments. With the explosion of intelligent lighting, it did not take people long to get tired of moving lights. The challenge for the event designer is to use intelligent lighting intelligently.

## LIGHTING THE PRINCESS BRIDE

A wise bride hired a fabulous dance band but insisted that she did not want a bunch of flashing and moving lights at her wedding reception. A spectacular tented affair, the event was the height of elegance, and she did not want anything to distract attention from her and her bridal party.

Moving lights are effective because they attract the eye, but without an appropriate reason this attraction becomes a distraction. Instead of the usual lighting for this band, we created a romantic starry sky environment that framed the evening in romance.

A bank of bright white moving lights can move together from upstage to downstage and then break into individual moving lights rotating around the stage and room in changing colors and patterns. This is a very effective light cue the first time. If it is used over and over, it becomes tiresome, then annoying. Effects add impact to an event when they are unexpected. Constantly or too frequently moving lights lose their effect.

## LIGHTING EQUIPMENT

Robin King of Creative Productions, Inc., who has lighted award-winning stage sets for my event company, says, "A good lighting guy can tell you what your best options are in any given situation. If you need to know what instrument you need to project a gobo from 40 feet, you should be able to call up your lighting guy and ask him." However, when the lighting person answers that you need a medium-throw leko, you need to have some idea of what she or he is talking about.

Events in small ballrooms, country clubs, and residences require fewer and smaller lighting instruments and equipment. Lower ceilings mean a shorter **throw** (the distance between the light fixture and the object being lighted). Bulky and expensive theatrical lighting equipment may be inappropriate when residential or industrial equipment can be used or modified to provide lighting for small venues. An inventory of small-venue lighting equipment useful to the event designer and decorator can be found in Appendix 10, *Lighting Equipment and Vocabulary.*

Different theatrical lighting instruments put out light with a different character because of the differences in **lenses, reflectors,** and light sources (lamps). The white light in the beam varies widely depending on the light source. (The colors in the white beam are described by its color temperature, which is gen-

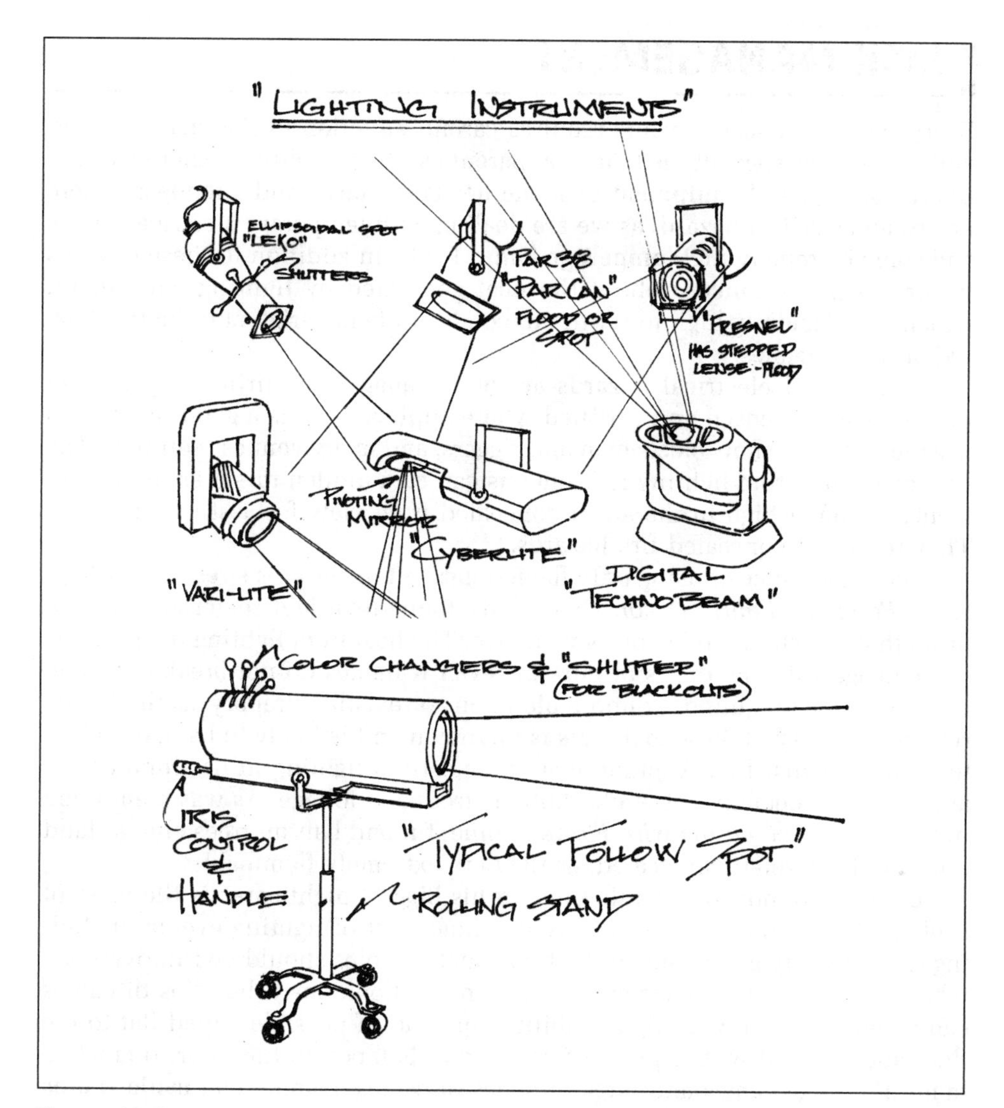


**Figure 10-7**

erally a measure of the amount of blue in the light.) These details are beyond the need to know of an event designer, but some degree of understanding and familiarity is required (see Figure 10-7). An inventory of theatrical lighting equipment terms that are likely to be of use to an event designer can be found in Appendix 10, *Lighting Equipment and Vocabulary.* Appendix 10 contains other terms and a description of their applications to lighting that are essential to event designers and decorators.

# RISK MANAGEMENT

Every aspect of special events requires careful attention to risk management, and in no other specialty is that as apparent as it is in lighting, where we routinely hang tons of equipment over the heads of guests and attendees. There is also an electrical hazard, as we are dealing with temporary electrical cables and some extremely high-**amperage** (amp) loads. In addition to these obvious factors, there is concern about the heat generated by lighting equipment, which is sufficiently high to set fire to combustible material, and the trip hazard of power cables.

Rigging and electrical hazards are best managed by hiring only trained professionals, licensed and certified where applicable. It is a good practice to use the in-house show electrician and riggers, and many venues require it. The heat generated from lighting instruments can be a hidden threat as the instruments are often high in the air or concealed from view for aesthetic reasons. They represent concealed fire hazards.

The importance of using only flame-retardant material is stressed in Chapter 8, *Fabulous Fabric Décor.* Using only flame-retardant material does not mean that one should relax one's vigilance. The heat from lighting instruments can damage valuable drops or curtains even if flames do not break out. Special care is also required around table linens or existing drapery, as the flame-retardant quality of these materials is unknown and is likely to be insufficient to protect against fire. Another area of concern is lighting in or around trees and foliage, especially cut winter holiday trees and foliage. As was mentioned in Chapter 7, *Decorating with Flowers,* pine, fir, and balsam trees and garland must be flame-retardant-treated, as they are extremely flammable.

Brian O'Connor told me that one of his biggest nightmares is the mass of cable and how to conceal it. Safety is a huge part of lighting events, including rigging safety and cable on the floor safety. Cables should be run overhead whenever possible, and when they are on the floor, small bundles of cables can be taped down with high-visibility tape and, if possible, taped flat to the floor and covered with a piece of carpet that is taped to the floor to create a ramp. For large cables and large bunches of cables, commercial **cable ramps** are available that provide a visible ramp for people and protection to the cables in vehicular situations, such as running cables across a driveway.

# CHANGING TECHNOLOGY

Every book that mentions any form of electronic, digital, or computer technology runs the risk of being outdated by the time it is published. This is especially true in the lighting industry, in which, after a century of strictly physical refinements to basic lighting equipment, intelligent lighting was developed. In the relatively near future, the entire incandescent technology behind the lightbulb may be replaced by **LED (light-emitting diode)** technology.

Currently the cutting-edge technological developments are in lighting control, which is 90 percent computer-controlled in theater and special event applications.

Charles Belcher tells us: "The biggest trend in lighting right now is in the control systems, as the manufacturers are refining **WYSIWYG** (pronounced "wizzy-wig"), a software acronym that stands for 'what you see is what you get.' In functional terms, this means that there are two monitor screens in the studio. One shows the three-dimensional image of the actual stage set to be lighted, and the other shows the lighting rig. The designer can then write the cues for the show in advance and see them represented on the replica stage, including light beams in colors. This is potentially a tremendous saving in time.

"If you had an infallible Internet connection and a camera showing a real-time image of the stage, you could actually run the show from the studio."

## FINISHING TOUCHES

Whatever the trends are when and where you are at any point in time, it is imperative that you strive to keep up with them. An event is a unique occurrence over a finite stretch of time, and the successful event designer will create timely and appropriate experiences for the client and the guests.

An event designer needs to have some familiarity with the capabilities and vocabulary of lighting to communicate with lighting professionals. Different events and different venues have different requirements for lighting and may require different lighting professionals. Hiring the appropriate professional, providing a budget, and coordinating the production time line are all critical responsibilities of the event designer, as is risk management at all times.

## DESIGN VOCABULARY

Terms appear below in the order in which they first occur in this chapter.

Lighting designer
Lighting director
Lighting design
Light plot
Light cues
Programs
Cues
Production companies
Reflected ceiling
Sectional view
CAD (computer aided design and drafting)
Elevation
Plate
Production manager
Control console
Backlighting
Dark time
Sound check
Focus
Dimmer
Lamps
Gel

Uplight
Accent lighting
Extension sockets
Goosenecks
Clip-on lights
Spot
Floodlight
PAR lamps
R-type lamps
MR-16 lamps
Rider
Technical rider
PAR can
Intelligent lights
Lekos
Gobos
Follow spots
Clear Com
Stage manager
Cue caller
Three-color wash
Front truss
Specials
Rear truss
Follow spot
1-kilowatt PAR cans
General lighting
Color changers
Breakup patterns
Disconnect
Instrument
Reflected light
Warm color
Cool color
Neutral color
McCandless system
Saturated color
Angle of incidence
Three-point lighting
Key light
Fill light
Backlight
Sidelight
Ambient light
Ambience
Robotic lights
Haze
Fogger
Hazer
Dichroic
Throw
Lenses
Reflectors
Amperage
Cable ramps
LED (light-emitting diode)
WYSIWYG (what you see is what you get)

# STUDIO WORK

1. Explain Monroe's General Rules for Lighting in your own words. Discuss and agree or disagree with these principles.
2. List several uses of intelligent lighting. Be specific and discuss ways to maximize its effectiveness in these situations.
3. Do some research and make a list of short-throw and long-throw instruments. Which are the longest-throw instruments you found?
4. Define the following terms: *boom, gobos, throw, wattage,* and *amperage.*
5. Write a short paragraph on risk management as it relates to lighting.

# RECOMMENDED READING AND RESEARCH SITES

Carlson, Verne, and Sylvia E. Carlson, *Professional Lighting Handbook,* Focal Press, 1991.
Miller, James Hull, *Stage Lighting in the Boondocks: A Stage Lighting Manual for Simplified Stagecraft Systems,* 4th rev. ed., Meriwether Publishing, 1995.
Moody, James L., *Concert Lighting: Techniques, Art and Business,* Focal Press, 2nd ed., 1997.

Parker, Oren, *Scene Design and Stage Lighting,* 8th ed., Wadsworth, 2002.

Rosenthal, Jean, *Magic of Light: The Craft and Career of Jean Rosenthal, Pioneer in Lighting for the Modern Stage,* Little, Brown, 1972.

Sammler, Ben, and Don Harvey, *Technical Design Solutions for Theatre,* The Technical Brief Collection, vol. 1, Focal Press, 2002.

Altman Lighting—home page for a longtime manufacturer of lighting equipment
http://www.altmanltg.com/

High End Systems—cutting-edge manufacturer of intelligent lighting and state-of-the-art lighting control systems; also developers of the Catalyst, the first intelligent projector
http://www.highend.com/

Kinetic Lighting, Inc.—a production and rental company specializing in events and large-format projection
http://www.kineticlighting.com

Levitron, Colotran Division—home page for a major manufacturer of lighting and lighting control equipment
http://www.colortran.com/

Stage Lighting Design 101, Edition 2.d, Copyright 1997–1999, by Bill Williams—an online course in basic stage lighting
http://www.mts.net/~william5/sld.htm

Vari-Lite—home page for the original manufacturers of the first intelligent light system and leading suppliers of intelligent technology
http://www.vari-lite.com

# Chapter 11

# UNIQUE DECORATIVE ELEMENTS

*KISS = Keep it simple, sweetie!*

**—Debbie Meyers, CSEP, attributed to Julia Rutherford Silvers, CSEP, attributed to anon.**

---

## IN THIS CHAPTER

You will discover other elements not covered elsewhere in this book that can be integrated into the design and décor of an event.

**Entertainment/Living Décor**
- Best Practices in Planning Entertainment
- Living Décor
- Living Buffets
- Living Statues
- New Looks for Old Acts
- Children and Animals

**Decorative Signage**
- Risk Management Signs
- Informational Signs
- Decorative Signs

**Food for the Eye**
- Decorative Buffets
- Other Custom Table Treatments
- Food Centerpieces
- Beverages as Décor

**Decorative Lighting Effects**
- Miniature lights
- Fiber-Optic Light Effects
- Rope Lights
- Centerpiece Lights
- Neon Light
- Black Light
- Lighted Dance Floors
- Lasers

**Candles**

**The Magic of Ice**
- Thoughts from a Master Sculptor
- Ice Centerpieces

**Pyrotechnics**
- Thoughts from a Master Pyrotechnician
- Types of Pyro for Events

---

This chapter contains sections on entertainment, signage, food, decorative lighting effects, ice carving, and fireworks. Each of these elements is potentially a component of a special event. If any one of them is used in an event, it will interact with the décor and must be designed into the event. Any one of these elements can be a major design or decorative element in any specific event.

Events are complex structures with many parts that interact with one another, and the event designer must create a cohesive event from these many separate elements. Because of this inherent complexity, all event designers and decorators employ the KISS principle whenever possible. As explained in the quote that opened this chapter, KISS stands for "keep it simple, sweetie." Do not make any element more complicated than it has to be; keep each part as simple and straightforward as possible.

## ENTERTAINMENT/LIVING DÉCOR

Event entertainment includes two categories: **main entertainment** and **incidental entertainment.** The main entertainment consists of the band, a dance troupe, a speaker, or other focal performances that command the attention of the entire audience. There are two types of incidental entertainment; musical incidental entertainment, which is called **background music,** and nonmusical entertainment, which is called **sight acts.**

Incidental entertainment is secondary entertainment and can serve as a décor element that enhances the theme, mood, or atmosphere, or it can be used to attract and direct traffic. Background music, sometimes called **wallpaper music,** is designed into the event to provide atmosphere or mood music rather than serving a primary function as a dance band does. Sight acts,

Idea Portfolio

### CARIBBEAN PARTY TAKES ON A NEW DIMENSION

At a summer party for employees and their families, guests were to be directed to a secondary entrance at the hotel that had an elevator leading directly to the swimming pool terrace level where the party was being held. Most of the guests did not have to be directed there, as there were two 16-foot-tall Caribbean characters on stilts called mocko jumbies in the Virgin Islands. People ran to see them, with some parents being dragged across the crosswalks by their children. The unusual sight excited everybody.

Later in the evening the mocko jumbies reappeared to lead a parade that ran throughout the event from the young children's playroom, past the pool where the teenagers were "hanging out," across the dance floor, and past the tables to the place where the CEO made a short speech.

The stilt walkers added a new dimension to an ordinary summer employee picnic.

such as clowns, jugglers, mimes, acrobats, and stilt walkers, can be used in their traditional garb or can be costumed and given direction to become an integral part of the design for the particular event.

The event designer will be able to plan the décor around the entertainer or book entertainment to suit the design. The event decorator most often will need to make sure that the décor accommodates the entertainment.

**BEST PRACTICES IN PLANNING ENTERTAINMENT**

Various types of events, including corporate, association, social, and not-for-profit, have different needs regarding entertainment and production, but the same principles and practices apply in planning the entertainment and designing the production for each event. The process begins with research to determine the goals and objectives of the event and the needs and expectations of the guests. The production then is designed to meet those needs and objectives. During this phase, the script for the event is conceptualized and the appropriate entertainment is selected.

The planning phase follows as the script and the timeline are developed and production elements are arranged for, always with the goals and objectives of the event kept in mind. Each production detail is carefully tailored to support the design concept. This assures an effective production and a successful event. After the event, the final essential step is evaluation. The history of each event will provide the foundation for future successful events.

The research phase can be as simple as interviewing the client, but preliminary investigation of the corporate entity or the family can be valuable. If the event is a repeated affair, history becomes invaluable. For associations and corporate functions, several different tools can be applied to research the needs and expectations of the attendees, including questionnaires, surveys, and focus groups. In addition to this motivational research, functional questions regarding space, attendance, site limitations, access, and power are determined at this time.

Creative concepts are developed during the design phase. A good way to begin this phase is to brainstorm with the client, using free association to list all the elements and all the entertainment that might be desirable. At this time there are no bad ideas. Once this list of wild ideas is made, they can be analyzed in light of practical considerations. Now a timeline, a financial structure, and a budget are applied to refine the design concept. The design phase is where the critical decisions are made, goals meet budgets, and the production is given direction.

The coordination phase is the actual production. Entertainment is booked, production support services are hired, and the timeline and production bible are refined and detailed. The most common mistake made in entertainment and production is to start this process out of order, becoming committed to certain entertainers or other production details before determining the goals and objectives, developing an event design or analyzing the resources. A corporate event, for example, may be a product rollout in which the main goal is product exposure or name identification. An outstanding **name performer** may be selected

*(continued)*

**BEST PRACTICES IN PLANNING ENTERTAINMENT *(continued)***

with the intention of creating a memorable event. If this is done before the event design is developed, the event may be remembered but nobody will remember the product.

A similar problem can happen at social events. A wedding, for example, should focus on the bride, the bridal party, and the life celebration that is taking place. The bride or her family might get the idea to really celebrate by booking name entertainment. This can become a major attraction for the guests, detracting attention from the bride unless she is also a celebrity. Name entertainment can be used at a wedding if the bride and her parents determine that they want it, but it needs to be carefully integrated into the celebration, and the family needs to be aware of the effect it is likely to have.

The most overlooked and underappreciated element in event production is the postevent evaluation. Once the party is over, production crews pack up their gear and go home, the guests go to bed, and it is all over except for counting the money. The professional event manager will have scheduled a wrap-up session, or postcon, to do an objective analysis of the event. This history becomes extremely valuable in doing repeat events or similar events in the future. Associations and corporations can get valuable feedback from their attendees through postevent surveys or questionnaires gathered on-site at the end of the event. The basic questions at the evaluation session should determine whether the goals and objectives of the event were achieved and the needs and expectations of the attendees were fulfilled.

Whether main or incidental entertainment, booking, production, and the care and feeding of performers constitute a special competency with its own disciplines and practices. *Event Entertainment and Production* by Mark Sonder, Wiley Events Series 2004, treats this discipline very well.

## LIVING DÉCOR

Certain sight acts are a natural for theme parties. Cowboys and saloon girls greeting the guests at an Old West reception, mermaids and mermen at an under the sea dinner, or **living statues** in classical togas at a Roman Empire party come immediately to mind as possibilities. These examples can add another dimension to an event under the direction of a creative event designer. The cowboys can stage a shootout on the dance floor later in the evening, and the saloon girls can be dancers who perform the cancan. The underwater merfolk can be designed into a seafood buffet, making it a **living buffet,** and the classical statues may be holding trays of food or drinks for the guests.

Debbie Meyers, CSEP, of BRAVO! Entertainment, an award-winning entertainment producer and a major contributor to this chapter, says, "Entertainment can become part of the décor; it can provide continuity, conforming with it. Entertainment can be an afterthought, or it can be part of the plan.

"Typically, entertainment is the focal point, but living décor attracts the attention without demanding the full attention of the guests. In living décor the performer can become part of the event, adding movement, style, and grace in an unexpected way. It adds subtle dynamics to an otherwise static display."

## LIVING BUFFETS

The living buffet can be handled in many ways. A performer in an oversized antebellum gown can appear, to support chafing dishes on her giant hoop skirt. A talking cabbage head can interact with the guests in the buffet line. Then there is the extreme body buffet, where the food appears to be served right off the body of the performer. Each method requires different technical skills and knowledge to execute effectively and safely in accordance with health and food service guidelines. More important, each needs to be appropriate for the event, the expectations of the attendees, and the goals of the event. The effectiveness of any live interactive performer depends on the talent and personality of the performer and the instructions and direction given to him or her (see Figure 11-1).

## LIVING STATUES

While it is part of the scenery, the living statue becomes a focal point. It is more than a prop and less than a show. It can be a subplot, a secondary focus to add a dynamic component to the scenery, enhancing it rather than drawing attention away from it.

Idea Portfolio

### ENTERTAINING BUFFETS THAT WORKED

We did a Don Rickles–style cabbage head that spoke to the guests in the middle of a buffet at a ranch and conference center that was an entertaining addition to the evening's celebration. It left a memorable impression on the guests, who were still talking about it 10 years later at another event at the same location.

We enjoyed a fabulous reception at a fine arts museum in Washington, D.C., where each course was a spotlighted "artwork" on a pedestal, including a liveried waiter silently offering martinis from a silver tray. It was so successful that we used the same idea in our own city several months later, only to find out that another associate, who also had been in attendance at the Washington reception, had been inspired to replicate it two weeks earlier.

Debbie Meyers, who contributed to this chapter, tells of a chocolate fondue body buffet where the reclining beauty offered comestibles that appeared to be dipped in chocolate off her body. This was obviously a cutting-edge idea that required a receptive audience.

All these ideas worked because they were designed specifically for the setting and the particular attendees.

**Figure 11-1**

The most common living statues are dressed as classical Greek or Roman statues and painted with body makeup to a uniform white or gray color. Debbie Meyers' advice to planners who want to incorporate living décor into an event is to spend time and money on lighting. The classical living statue is attractive and entertaining, "but uplighting it with a single PAR light from below shows each fold of the material and enhances the physique of the model."

## NEW LOOK FOR OLD ACTS

Stilt walkers are achieving new popularity with the advent of new stilt-walking technology, such as that used in the stage performance of *The Lion King*. Debbie tells us, "Stilt walkers bring a larger-than-life concept to the party, and it is human nature to be attracted to them." Traditionally costumed as clown jugglers, the new stilt walkers can be four-legged animals, robots,

Idea Portfolio

## THE BRAVO! ELECTRIC STATUE

The electric statue is as old as early experiments with static electricity but is still effective for the right event. A costumed model stands on a pedestal that contains a Tesla coil that generates a static electric field around the model's body. The model's hair stands out from his or her head, and when the model handles a lightbulb or a neon tube, it lights up and the glow moves along the tube with his/her finger.

Although the performer does not feel a thing, attendees must be kept away from this "statue" or they can receive minor static electric shocks.

dancers, or abstract alien characters. "In Texas the 'Long Tall Cowboy' is a popular greeter at Old West parties."

Many traditional mimes, jugglers, clowns, and acrobats are finding new interpretations of their talents. "The Le Cirque shows have added a new dimension to the way certain entertainers are perceived and the way they perceive themselves. Many of the entertainment styles, the juggling, contortionism, and acrobatics that are employed have been around for many years, but the costuming, story lines, and choreography have a slightly twisted attitude that gives a new perception of the old talents."

## CHILDREN AND ANIMALS

There is an adage among theater professionals: "Never work with children or animals." There are two reasons for this, and both apply directly to special events, though with somewhat different results. An actor does not want to work with animals or children because they command so much attention from the audience. However, in special events this is a good reason to use them. The other thought behind the adage is that they are unpredictable and not totally controllable. This is as true for special events as it is for theater and is a factor of which the event designer needs to be aware.

Children are not used in events very often. We have used all-boy and all-girl choirs at holiday parties with great success, and at weddings we deal with the ring bearer and flower girl, sometimes with less than resounding success. Wedding parties that insist on using children under six years of age are taking a chance that the bride will be upstaged on her wedding day or delayed as the four-year-old gets distracted or sits down and cries during the wedding procession.

We have used animals, mostly as décor, quite successfully over the years, but we have declined to use animals at certain times and have had second thoughts about a couple of experiences.

For tropical and jungle theme parties a trained macaw or a small pet monkey can be a delightful addition, providing interactive décor. However, when

Idea Portfolio

## A CIRCUS THEME CELEBRATION

At a circus party a number of years ago to celebrate the twenty-fifth anniversary of the Fairmont Hotel in Dallas, we re-created the grand opening festivities, matching circus acts to dinner courses and including a trained animal act that featured performing dogs. For the finale, with dessert, there was a circus parade, bringing all the performers to circle the ring and concluding by bringing the 80-year-old owner of the chain, Mr. Zwieg, in on the back of an elephant.

Standing backstage with the elephant and his handler, separated from the guests by the thickness of a velour curtain, I saw the elephant begin to sway from side to side. I asked the handler why he was doing that and was informed that he was getting bored and I should feed him some hay and pet him. That elephant got a lot of hay and much petting for the next 30 minutes before the courageous Mr. Zweig was ushered backstage to clamber onto the elephant's back for the best entrance a hotelier ever had.

I have never booked another elephant.

Idea Portfolio

## A FISHY PROBLEM

Many years ago, I was a young scenic artist working in the not-yet-professional world of events for a talented designer, Bill Reed. He designed a fabulous underwater party that wrapped the guests in an entire environment of underwater fantasy, including the profiles of live swimming fish projected onto the cyc around the room.

I was in charge of the fish projections and had experimented carefully with clear glass dishes and overhead projectors that were to be concealed in "coral formations" and a "sunken ship" bandstand in the middle of the floor. When the projectors were delivered, I noticed that a few of them were a different model from the ones I had experimented with. They fit the space allowed, though, so I did not worry.

Midparty I noticed from their 12-foot profiles on the wall that a couple of the fish were swimming sluggishly, and then one went belly-up. A giant "hand of God" plucked the unfortunate creature from the universe. It turned out that our new model projectors ran hotter than the prototype. Fortunately, it was late in the evening and we had more fish. We did add the element of iceberg-sized ice cubes to some of the walls.

Always check all your equipment in advance and never assume that similar equipment is identical equipment.

a client requested that a trained tiger be walked through the room, we declined because of safety and liability concerns.

We once brought an 18-foot-long, 85-pound albino boa constrictor into a teenage Halloween party. It was a huge success, at least as much because of the 6-foot 2-inch owner-handler and the way he interacted with the guests.

However, a goldfish going belly-up in the centerpiece can take away the fun at a party. The success of an animal component in a party is based largely on the abilities, personality, and knowledge of the trainer or handler. Always work with experts. Some booking agents specialize in animal acts.

Adding living décor to an event adds an interactive dimension that can carry the event to a new level and create truly memorable experiences for the guests and the event producer.

# DECORATIVE SIGNAGE

Every event needs some signage, if only to indicate the location of the rest rooms and exits. No single element is so often ignored, not to mention being distracting from a design standpoint, as the signs at a corporate function. Signs should exist in a symbiotic relationship with the décor, with each supporting and enhancing the function of the other.

Unfortunately, many decorators ignore the necessary signage or are not informed about it until it shows up at the site, totally lacking in style or, worse, done in a style or color that clashes with the décor. Corporate events that are held in conjunction with a conference, convention, or tradeshow usually have a conference logo that is designed by the graphics department, which guards its work jealously.

It is the responsibility of the event designer and a concern of the decorator to adapt the design and decorations to the existing signs and/or conference graphics.

## RISK MANAGEMENT SIGNS

These are necessary signs, and the designer or decorator who does not recognize this is inept and incompetent. Fire exit, fire extinguisher, and Americans with Disabilities Act (ADA) compliance signs are required by law and just make sense. Any event professional who covers, removes, or in any way obscures these signs is in violation of the law and can be punished to the fullest extent of criminal and civil liability.

Now that we have stated the importance of not blocking fire exits, note that exceptions to this rule can be granted by the fire marshal. There are times when there are more fire exits than necessary for the size of the group in the venue. In this case, the fire inspector will tell you which exits can be blocked safely and legally. Sometimes an exit may be obstructed by equipment or construction, and the fire marshal may insist that the fire exit sign be covered.

It is also possible, and sometimes desirable, to redirect the path to the fire exit. In this case temporary lighted exit signs may be installed, and the existing permanent signs covered.

In designing around permanent exit signs, fabric around doorways and exit signs can be cut and secured back to the wall around the sign, or new signs can be hung in front. The shiny lighted exit sign may not fit into your color scheme, but remember that these are everyday, everyplace occurrences and the average guest will tune them out. However, if a sign is going to end up in a location where it will be a distraction, work out a plan with the fire marshal to redirect potential exit traffic or redesign the floor plan and event design so that the signs are no longer offensive.

## INFORMATIONAL SIGNS

A certain number of signs, while not legally required, are desirable or necessary for operational purposes. These are various directional signs such as rest room location signs, registration signs, directions to the event or to an event within the event (e.g., VIP Reception →), silent auction signs, and so on.

Two things about these functional signs are very important: They must be in a style and color palette that is compatible with the décor, and they need to be in a **font** that is readable. The font, or **typestyle,** can be one of the thousands available, or the signs can be hand-lettered. This book is printed in Melior. It could have been printed in Arial Bold. Both Melior and Arial Bold are very easily read fonts, while Marlett and Tahoma are not.

The font or style selected for informational signs has to be readable, and the words need to be large enough to be seen from the distance at which the guests will be expected to view them. The best way to determine the right size is by experimenting at various distances.

The signs must be placed high enough to be read and should be placed where people will naturally look for or expect to find them (see Figure 11-2). *Remember that when a room fills up with people, most décor and all signs below 6 feet will become invisible.*

## DECORATIVE SIGNS

Decorative signs serve a purpose beyond the communication of information: They also add to the atmosphere, support the theme, or promote the brand. Sometimes they advance the goal of the event directly by advertising the logo for a marketing event, identifying the honoree, or reminding people of the charity they are there to support.

Decorative signs do not have to be easily and immediately readable, but they must be readily identifiable. They need to be large and be repeated in key locations. If they represent the company or display the conference logo, they should be large in high-visibility locations and should be repeated as a header on each of the smaller informational signs. If they represent the honoree or the

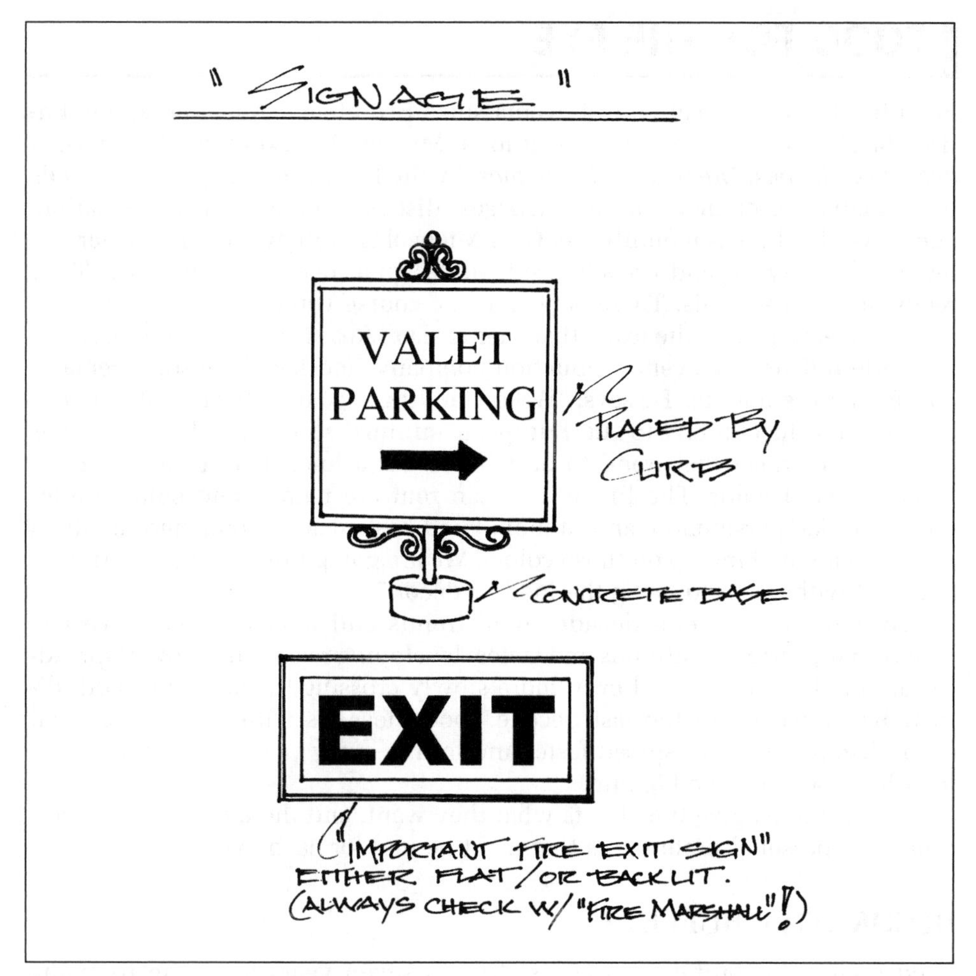


**Figure 11-2**

cause for the celebration, the graphics on the signs should have appeared on the invitation. If the invitations were done first or the graphics for the conference were finished before the design of the event, every effort should be made to incorporate them into the decorative signage.

Risk management takes priority over all other considerations. Informational signage should be in a style and a color that are compatible with the décor but should be clearly visible and in a readable font. Decorative signage should promote the goals of the event, be fully integrated into the décor, and provide a memorable brand identity that fully supports and advances the goals for the event.

# FOOD FOR THE EYE

Food has been a critical part of events since Eve offered Adam an apple. Entire libraries have been written about food. My favorite text on food for special events is *Themes, Dreams, and Schemes,* by the late Eugene Wigger. Hundreds of magazines, seemingly in all languages, discuss menus, food presentation, and clever food ideas monthly. Yet Chef Michael Carroll, when asked where he learned food styling and ways to use food design as decoration, told us: "They really do not teach this. There is no specific course you can take."

Michael Carroll is the executive chef for Don Ross Nabb Productions, a nationwide full-service event production company, and has done some remarkable food presentations. He says: "We are tending to go from the overabundance of food and decorations to the European minimalist style. A lot of color is back, and I expect that trend to be with us for a long time. Everything has turned toward color. The linens you can rent are named and colored after food: paprika, persimmon, and salmon. Food has so much color, and the linen suppliers are picking up on those colors. We are going from trying to surround our food with décor to using the food as décor."

Over the last several decades food trends and food fads have evolved slowly, with various traditions and tastes developing regionally, slowly spreading across the country, and even more slowly crossing the oceans in both directions. However, in the last decade, food ideas, as with all other special event disciplines, have spread faster and farther every year until the trends in food have become one big blur.

We still must give the clients what they want, and there are regional, cultural, and personal preferences that must be met for each event.

## DECORATIVE BUFFETS

Food styling for buffets in the last five to seven years has gone from the **chatchke** fill-in stuff overflowing and spilling out onto the table to the trend of a crisp, clean, tailored look with smaller portions geometrically presented. Look at Michael Carroll's experiences.

**CHEF MICHAEL CARROLL'S RULES FOR CREATIVE FOOD DÉCOR**

- Rules? There are no rules when it comes to food and décor.
- You just need knowledge of colors.
- Use your creativity.
- Most of the time it is a matter of common sense. You would not surround your beef entrée with a lot of green stuff because you don't want the beef to look green.
- Let your imagination run wild.
- Always allow your chef to have input.

## CHEF MICHAEL CARROLL'S BUFFET DÉCOR IDEAS

- Crisp clean acrylic and glass containers filled with fruit that match the linens: orange, gold, and yellow, matching the floral designs. Yellow, orange, and gold flowers in clear acrylic containers. Match the food to the flowers and the linens. In this case, use tuna and lamb. Beef would be the wrong color.
- Do a chocolate volcano on the dessert table, which can actually be mashed potatoes encased in chocolate with a Raspberry Suzette sauce coming out of it like lava.
- An underwater theme party with live fish in 14-foot-long aquariums—a lot of whole fish displays and actors and actresses costumed as mermaids and mermen. Use lots of shrimp, crabs, mussels, and oysters.

In the spare, geometric presentation described in the first example of this Idea Portfolio, the colors of the food were critical to the success of the design. The second provides an example of an old-school decorative food piece from the styles of overflowing largesse that Chef Michael commented on earlier. The underwater design idea incorporates live décor and multiple components.

### OTHER CUSTOM TABLE TREATMENTS

Table treatments can range from crude but effective rustic planks on whiskey barrels to antique lace swagged over custom Dupioni silk cloths over multiple tulle petticoats. Ice Magic, Inc., offers clear Plexiglas tables that can be lighted from within. Edwin Lashley III, at his company Metallic Design Studio, fabricates stainless steel tables and anodized aluminum table covers. Plexiglas or glass containers can be filled with fruit, colored water, or blossoms to create

Idea Portfolio

## A TRULY GREEN BUFFET

A number of years ago a cutting-edge client proposed a buffet concept that consisted of using fresh green sheet moss and potted plants as a tabletop. We sculpted a tabletop of foam designed to receive clear glass platters and blooming potted plants. Chef Dave of Brook Hollow Golf and Country Club then arranged colorful food pieces on clear, seamless glass serving platters that fit into the specially sculpted positions on the table. At first glance the fresh clean food appeared to be sitting au naturel on a mossy berm.

a bed to support the food offerings. Numerous companies supply custom buffets constructed out of trusswork, glass blocks, polyvinyl chloride (PVC), or other materials.

Gale Sliger once designed a carousel buffet on a turntable with miniature horses and a colorful base and canopy on a slowly revolving platform that allowed the guests to come to the buffet and be served by chefs. Rather than moving through a buffet line, the guests stood and the buffet moved past them.

## FOOD CENTERPIECES

Another good idea is to ask the chef to prepare an edible centerpiece that can be used for dessert. This is particularly useful when one is working with limited resources, as the chef may not charge extra or the charge may be minimal for this type of centerpiece. Edible centerpieces include pretty decorated cakes, bonbons on silver tiered trays, and a fruit tray around a "floral arrangement" carved entirely out of fruit and vegetables. Ice carving centerpieces are frequently the responsibility of the chef; they are discussed later in this chapter.

## BEVERAGES AS DÉCOR

For some themes decorative beverages are a tradition, such as luau or Caribbean paradise themes with colorful drinks with little parasols or served in coconut shells. A contemporary version is a frozen drink that can be customized to

Idea Portfolio

## DESSERTS AS PART OF THE THEME

At the very successful fund-raising luncheon for the University of Texas M.D. Anderson Cancer Center, "A Conversation with a Living Legend," a "living legend" celebrity is interviewed live in front of the audience. Sound and audiovisual are extremely important so that the audience can see and hear the entire conversation, and the theme décor has always centered on the career of the legend celebrity. It has been traditional to decorate the tables in the theme of the luncheon, including supplying wonderful desserts with a signature theme chocolate piece.

Chef Henri Mahler of the Wyndham Anatole creates a magical dessert around a chocolate piece supplied by Chocolates a La Carte. Over the years guests watched the forty-first president of the United States, George Bush, being interviewed in a replica of the Oval Office and ate chocolate mousse out of a white chocolate White House. They saw Lady Margaret Thatcher, the first woman prime minister of the United Kingdom, interviewed in a replica of Number 10 Downing Street and had dessert out of a chocolate teacup. And they enjoyed macadamia mousse out of a hollow white chocolate baseball for which Chef Henri supplied 24-karat gold trim on the threads while watching Paula Zahn interview baseball legend Cal Ripken, Jr., in a replica batting cage.

## FANTASTIC DECORATIVE DRINKS

Mike and Sharon Miller of Drinks Fantastic suggest some successful decorative drinks they have created.

"We had a request to do a nonalcoholic drink to complement a patriotic theme. In a pilsner glass we stacked Blue Horizon, Pina-Coladas, and strawberry. The wait staff passed drinks, and we successfully turned out 400 red, white, and blue layered drinks in 90 minutes.

"A frozen white chocolate macadamia with a garnish of shaved Ghirardelli chocolate and macadamia nuts enhances an elegant wedding reception. For those who prefer champagne drinks, the Champagne Blush is a soft rosy delight. When hard liquor is preferred, go for a Bellini. It is offered in different flavors: peach, raspberry, and strawberry. For a taste of the Southwest and if tequila is your favorite liquor, imagine a fusion of a Bellini and a margarita. It's awesome and is called the Blushing Bride.

"We can make drinks with or without alcohol and often get requests for both types. We'll assist in selecting two flavors of drinks made with alcohol and one flavor that is nonalcoholic for youngsters, nondrinkers, and designated drivers."

match the décor: Bellinis for a Party in Pink, drinks in red for the Hot! Hot! Hot! Party, and of course traditional frozen Margaritas for a South of the Border Party.

These decorative drinks do not have to be alcoholic but can add a refreshing detail to the finest party.

Carefully planned menus support a theme or the goal of the meeting or event, but food can go beyond mere support and become décor, as when the buffet becomes a major decorative piece or artfully presented desserts serve as centerpieces. Food also can be a component in a living buffet, as mentioned earlier, and in certain multicomponent ice sculptures, as is discussed later in this chapter.

# DECORATIVE LIGHTING EFFECTS

Various lighting effects, some common and some rare, are discussed in this section. Each type can have a unique effect on the design and décor of any special event. Some require the experience and knowledge of a lighting professional, and some can be executed by people with little or no technical skill.

## MINIATURE LIGHTS

Currently manufactured almost exclusively in Asia, **miniature lights** sometimes are called Italian lights (they used to be made predominantly in Italy) or B lights, the low-voltage precursor to today's miniature lights. In the United

Idea Portfolio

## ANIMATED DECORATIVE LUMINAIRES

We have designed city skylines with a moving traffic illusion and twinkling lights overhead, 12-foot-tall animated clown faces, and the Eiffel Tower with fireworks going off in the sky, all using miniature lights. Design a plan for creating the outline and windows, features, and so on. Drill holes in quarter-inch plywood flats, insert the individual miniature lights through the holes, and hot-glue each one in place. Household extension cords and simple sign sequencers will finish this sophisticated-looking but technologically simple **luminaire.**

Animated effects such as moving traffic can be done with three circuit sequencers, where each string (and therefore each individual lamp) flashes in order: one-two-three, one-two-three, and so on. The lights will appear to move away from or toward the viewer depending on the direction: one-two-three or three-two-one. Use red lights for taillights going away from and white lights for headlights coming toward the guests.

Kingdom, they are called **fairy lights.** These are the standard miniature Christmas tree lights, and they come in 35-light, 50-light, and 100-light sets with green or white wire and in a selection of colors or clear. The plugs can be stacked, and some will plug end to end. (Do *not* plug more than three strings of end-to-end lights together.)

These are used in many ways in event décor: to outline props, to create temporary lighted signs, and to decorate trees (other than Christmas trees) and foliage.

One of the most common and most charming uses of miniature lights is to entwine them in the foliage of rental trees such as *Ficus benjaminus.* This can be delightful if the lights are installed so that they appear random in the foliage. The cord should be tucked into the foliage and not be hanging out in the air or stretched between branches.

## FIBER-OPTIC LIGHT EFFECTS

**Fiber-optic light effects** are created by using a flexible plastic fiber that transmits light from one end to the other. A panel or a curtain will have many of these tiny fibers attached to it with the ends sticking out so that they are visible from the front. The tiny cables are bundled together and run to a light source. A random placement of the fibers creates a starry sky effect. The light source can have a color changer in front of it so that the color of the "starry" effect can be changed. Fiber-optic curtains are available through a number of theatrical scenic and light rental companies. These are delicate curtains and should be handled only by professionals.

The panels or curtain can be custom made to represent an image, or an image can be superimposed on the random "starry" effect, which then, through the use of two light sources, can be made to appear or disappear by dimming one of the light sources.

The development of LEDs (light-emitting diodes) commercially is likely to signal the end of fiber optics as a decorative lighting effect, as LEDs are more controllable.

## ROPE LIGHTS

A number of inexpensive **rope lights** can be used as décor. Some are solid plastic with the lights embedded in them. Since they can be walked on, these lights can be used to outline steps or dance floors. Rope lights come clear and in colors, have clear lights in colored tubes or colored lights in clear tubes, and can be purchased static or sequencing (called chasing).

Rope lights can be used to make signs, although not all types bend easily or into the tight curves that are necessary. They can be used to outline props and scenery or spiraled or entwined in truss or around columns or poles. They also can be swagged overhead. Some versions come with a hub that allows them to be plugged into a center fitting, over a dance floor, for example, then sequenced in time to the music.

Rope lights come directly from the disco craze of the 1970s and need to be used carefully. They can be fun and effective in the right place and time.

## CENTERPIECE LIGHTS

A number of new decorative light devices have been designed specifically for use in and with centerpieces. Although pin-spotting centerpieces as described in Chapter 10, *Art of Light,* is definitely the best way to illuminate most floral centerpieces, it is not always available, is expensive, and is not the only way to incorporate light into centerpieces.

The oldest form of electrical centerpiece light is the battery-operated miniature light string, which has 10 lights and a two D-cell-battery light source that must be concealed. The lights last barely four hours, and the light strings tend to be cheaply made and fragile. Newer forms of centerpiece lights employ LEDs and miniature batteries, so they are small. They last 8 to 12 hours and are inexpensive and disposable. Some can be concealed in a base to uplight the centerpiece, and some, activated by water, actually go into the water in a vase arrangement and light the vase itself. Some battery-operated neon light bases uplight the arrangement through a frosted plate. None of them puts light down on the blooms of a floral centerpiece, but they all have their effects and potential for the designer.

## NEON LIGHT

Neon light has a presence that most light does not have. This is partly the case because the viewer looks directly at the source and partly because neon comes in so many saturated colors.

A neon sign with an honoree's name makes a statement that cannot be equaled by any other sign technology. No other light can be formed the way a neon tube can be formed to accent a prop or a decorative item. Neon is a bit of a mystery to many people who are comfortable with normal lighting and electricity, and it has the reputation of being expensive.

Neon tubes vary in price depending on the color, but the tubes themselves are not the expensive part. Because they have to be bent by hand to the desired shape over a flame table, simple designs are inexpensive and complex designs are pricey. The transformers are expensive but last a long time and are reusable. New ground fault digital transformers have solved the problem of having high voltages near the guests. The tubes are still fragile and need to be protected, kept away from areas where they could be bumped or touched. Some event houses specialize in neon, keeping a stock of prebent tubes, transformers, and supplies to keep the pricing competitive.

Low-voltage battery-operated neon is employed in centerpieces either as uplights or as visible tubes. These neon centerpieces on black plastic bases can be abstract or representational: a neon guitar for a rock 'n' roll party or an inclined circle to wrap around a vase of flowers. Battery-operated neon can be expensive but is available for rental from a number of special event decorators.

## BLACK LIGHT

Most people are familiar with ultraviolet light, commonly known as black light because it is not visible to the human eye. The traditional black light tube looks like a black fluorescent tube, and the light from it causes phosphors to glow. Natural phosphors occur in teeth and fingernails. Phosphors are also found in some man-made fabric, plastics, and paints.

Black light fabrics and paints can be used in decorations. When the lights are turned out in the presence of a black light source, these painted or manufactured items glow in black light colors. Black light tunnels, entrances, and effects rooms are fun for the appropriate theme events, and modern black light generators, which are available through most theatrical light rental companies, are easier to work with than are the old black light tubes.

Some scenic houses specialize in black light effect scenery, such as UV/FX/LA, http://www.uvfx.com. Many entertainers use black light in their performances, and a few, such as the inspirational theater group Famous People Players from Toronto, Canada, depend on black light throughout their performances.

Ultraviolet (UV) light comes in three spectrums: UV-A, UV-B, and UV-C. Commercial black light tubes and generators for display and entertainment filter out all but the harmless UV-A spectrum.

### LIGHTED DANCE FLOORS

The movie *Saturday Night Fever* popularized the concept of a lighted dance floor. Some raised, lighted dance floors are available through event decorating firms, disco supply companies, and a few theatrical lighting rental houses. The first lighted dance floor I designed was installed over a swimming pool in a west Texas oil town back in the 1970s. It is still available for rental from Dallas Stage Lighting, a top-flight theatrical lighting supply company in Dallas, Texas. There are now several companies that sell or rent acrylic dance floors for installation over swimming pools. These floors can be modified to become lighted dance floors in a ballroom. Look for new lighted dance floors that will employ LED technology.

### LASERS

Entertainment lasers have moved from being a simple beam flashing over the heads of teenagers at a rock show or bouncing off mirrors in the Museé de Cluny on the Left Bank of Paris to being a full-fledged industry that is developing its own technology. Today's lasers can create **tunnels,** overhead **sheet effects** and **cone effects, colored fans,** and **animated images** that can be programmed to tell a story or designed to animate the client's logo or product. As is true of other technical elements in event design, they are only as good as the technicians who program them.

Ion lasers amplify and concentrate light into coherent beams that can be manipulated via a system of mirrors. High-power white lasers combine krypton and argon gases in a **plasma generator** to create pure white light that can be broken down into primary colors.

Most states issue permits for each job, as lasers are potentially harmful if misused or handled carelessly. Laser operators must be licensed. High-power lasers require not only electrical power but also a water source and drain to provide cooling for the plasma generator.

## CANDLES

Candles have been around parties for centuries longer than any other forms of light still in use today. They are traditional fixtures at parties and have been since time immemorial. But why were they not included in Chapter 10, *Art of Light,* and what is unique about them?

In spite of their venerable history, candles are no longer needed for light. In fact, their use is actually restricted or prohibited by many venues and municipalities. Yet they remain one of the most distinctive decorative elements a designer will ever deal with. Where else, except in a fireplace or in some pyro effects, does the designer have the opportunity to work with living flame?

Nothing captures a romantic mood like the flickering glow of candlelight. No other fixture expresses elegance like an elegant **candelabrum** with slim tapers slowly burning down.

The candles most in use are glass-enclosed candles, most commonly those referred to as votive candles. Most municipalities prohibit the public use of candles that are not glass-enclosed **(tapers, column,** or **pillar candles),** and some prohibit them outside places of worship (for which the votive candle was invented). For use in candlesticks or candelabra, where tapers are prohibited, there are various designs of **pegged votive** holders; glass candle holders with "pegs" on the bottom to fit into candle receptacles or sockets on candlesticks or candelabra.

Another form of candle, also originally designed for religious worship, is the spring-loaded **faux taper,** which holds a narrow candle inside that is raised by the spring as it "burns down." The actual flame is shown, but there is no wax, and the taper never gets any shorter. The Chace Candle Company popularized these candles, and they are sometimes generically referred to as **Chace candles;** the actual name for the product is Chace Never-Burn-Down Candles.

Candlesticks and candelabra frequently have a wide fitting below the candle socket called a **bobeche** that is designed to catch wax but also is ornamental. On many chandeliers, they are used to hang prisms around the light. Specially designed bobeches also accommodate glass chimneys on some candelabra; this meets the fire code in some jurisdictions, allowing tapers to be used in them. Many chimneys are available to accommodate columns and pillar candles of various sizes (see Figure 11-3).

There are several important functional practices when one is dealing with candles:

- Remember that the flame is actually fire and is capable of burning the building down or doing serious bodily damage if mishandled.
- Check the rules of the venue and local ordinances before designing candles into an event.
- If you have any doubt that the candle you are thinking about using will work, try it ahead of time in the same circumstance; in fact, try it even if you do not have any doubt.
- Candles do strange things in the wind, and sometimes they just blow out.
- Tapers require special planning, including spares to get through the evening and a pair of trained service staff members to change them out as they burn down without disturbing the guests.
- Air-conditioning and heating drafts cause tapers to behave badly, making them burn quickly, burn crookedly, or occasionally dump quantities of hot wax on the guests.
- The taller the taper, the greater the potential problem. Tapers taller than 15 inches should be considered dangerous novelties and reserved for residential use, where they should be used only with great care.
- Candles are not generally appropriate for luncheons or other daytime events.

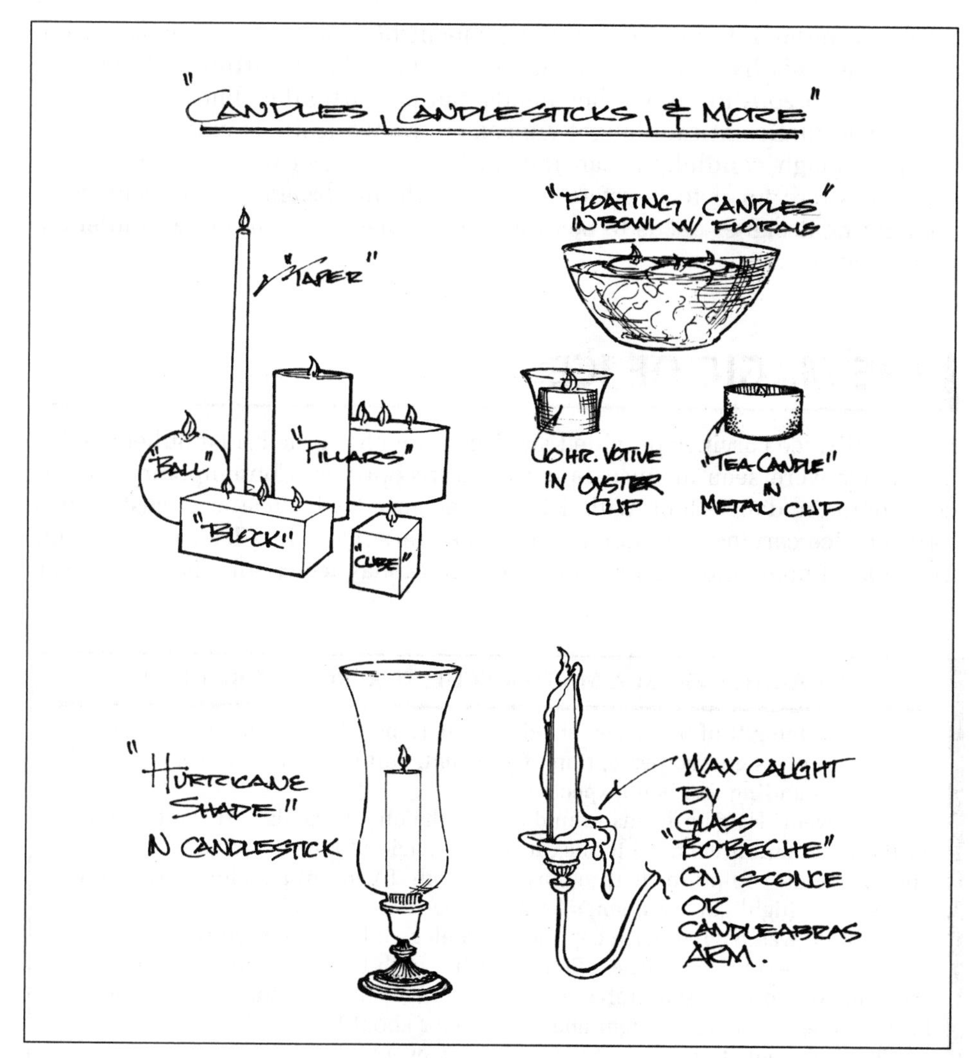


**Figure 11-3**

There are three common forms of candles. The most common are the modern **paraffin** candles; paraffin is a petroleum-based material with various additives to improve the quality or allow coloring of the wax. The most admired are **beeswax** candles, either hand-rolled from sheets of beeswax or melted and cast into solid candles. Beeswax candles are slightly honey-scented and last longer than do paraffin candles. They are also much more expensive. The third fairly common form of candle is a vegetable wax candle, mostly **soy wax,** which burns cooler than paraffin and generally is considered to be a little safer.

Scented candles are popular but should be used rarely in events and almost never used around food. Some people find the scent offensive or may be allergic to it. Because the sense of smell is a critical part of tasting food, scented candles interfere with the enjoyment of a meal. The notable exceptions where we have used scented candles have been parties and galas on ranches or in zoos to mask other smells that permeate the atmosphere.

The aesthetics of candlelight are something we learn as children, and although enough candlelight can indeed have an effect on the general light level, it is rare for it to interfere with the lighting design for an event. Still, the lighting designer needs to be aware of the plan to incorporate candlelight into an event.

## THE MAGIC OF ICE

Historically, ice carvings provided an elegant touch on the bridal buffet and occasionally were seen at upscale corporate receptions. Contemporary ice has come onto the dance floor, with acts such as Fear No Ice featuring custom performance ice carving as entertainment. There are many fine ice carvers among the ranks of hotel and country club chefs. But today ice carving has become an

**THOUGHTS FROM A MASTER SCULPTOR: ROBERT BIFULCO**

Ice has the gift of being perceived as something very elegant and sophisticated. It elevates guests' perception of an event. Unlike food or flowers, which can be outstanding, ice is unexpected.

The event designer needs to understand the client's goals and can bring us all the information we need to maximize the magic of the ice. What is the purpose of the ice sculpture? Is it to create a mood? To accent a table? To wow the guests, or to highlight the client's brand or logo?

A bride was having her reception in an elegant but very narrow ballroom. She wanted two ice sculptures. Being familiar with the space, I asked her why she wanted two large sculptures in such a small space. Did she want her guests looking at and talking all night about the ice or about her?

The ice needs to enhance the goals of the event.

Trends in ice are transmitted over the Internet seemingly instantaneously. A successful designer needs to be comfortable with the rapidly changing demands of the marketplace. Today's attendees want to participate in the party experience. They want to entertain themselves, and they love décor with which they can interact. The martini loupe, where the bartender mixes the drink and the guests serve themselves from the ice, is very popular.

A major ice piece will create discussion among the guests. Multicomponent pieces can be memorable, using the "boat-in-the-bottle" effect, where items are, or appear to be, frozen in the ice. Sometimes they are suspended in hollow ice. We have put violins, lighted street lamps, and a full-size rocking chair with a country music guitar and a cowboy hat inside ice. Take the inherent magic in ice and add to it something that is totally unexpected and an effect is created that will last in the attendee's memories long after the event.

event specialty, and today's ice carvings are used in all kinds of events in all locations. They have flowers, decorations, and even live dancers "frozen inside."

Robert Bifulco, executive chef and master sculptor, is one of those specialists. I have worked with his company, Bifulco's Vanishing Sculptures, and watched him create a 12-foot-tall classical pergola on Ionic columns, a 1-ton "underwater" seafood buffet, and, recently, a two-thirds-size replica longhorn steer that was used as a martini bar.

A source for crystal-clear ice is crucial for a master ice sculptor. Although some flowers and objects can actually be frozen in clear ice, the great illusion is to create an apparently solid chamber and suspend or install objects or entertainers in it.

### ICE CENTERPIECES

Individually carved ice centerpieces have always been very special, but until now they were priced beyond the budgets of most events. A company called Ice Magic, Inc., has developed a process for creating frozen ice crystal balls into which almost anything that does not dissolve in water can be frozen. You can ship them the item or items you want inside, and they will ship the ice back to you with lighted pedestals that will hold and illuminate the crystal ball.

## PYROTECHNICS

Fireworks! Nothing is more exciting than fireworks—explosions splashing color across the sky! They are wonderful on the Fourth of July, but they have their place in special event design as well.

Randy Beckham is a master **pyrotechnician** and the owner of Pyrotex, Inc., a fireworks display company that produces custom-designed shows; strictly

Idea Portfolio

### A WONDERFUL WEDDING DEPARTURE

At the end of a fantasy wedding reception in a huge tent on the front lawn of an estate, the bride and groom start off in an open-air limousine. As the car proceeds down the long driveway, it is preceded by a series of **sparkle fountains** going off just in front of it, while overhead 1,400 aerial bursts paint the sky over a two-minute period. The magnificent experience is etched in the memory of all who have attended, especially the bride and the groom, who did not know it was coming.

It was beautifully executed and carefully designed and planned. The departure took place at approximately 1:30 A.M., so the display was designed to be not only spectacular but quiet. Only an experienced special event pyrotechnic designer could have executed it with such perfection.

### THOUGHTS FROM A MASTER PYROTECHNICIAN: RANDY BECKHAM

When you are working with a fireworks display company, the first thing they will need is a room plan and stage plan (if it is indoor **pyro**) and a site visit if it is an outdoor display. We need the plan, a schedule of events, a theme for the event, and a clue as to why we are doing pyro in the first place. What is the goal? What are we trying to accomplish? As artists, we need to know the status of the pyro. Is it to be the big and splashy finale, or will it be just part of the show?

Pyro is either an accent to other things that are happening or it is The Event at the time. If you want a 10-minute fireworks show for everyone to enjoy, things are pretty easy for everyone involved. If the pyro is to be used in conjunction with other elements and people, we need a production meeting with everybody involved in a round table discussion. We all need to talk about what is taking place moment by moment two hours before the display and what will happen after it. People need to understand that things will be blowing up around them.

The trend in pyro post September 11, 2001, has been toward sweet and safe-looking displays. Lots of **salutes** (loud explosive sounds) and noise are frowned upon by some who fear causing crowd panic among guests and other people in the venue not associated with the event. Today's pyro runs more toward celebration as opposed to "flash and trash" destructiveness. Also, there is a lot of new product available as the Chinese, who manufacture most fireworks, realize that they cannot keep selling the same shells year after year.

Three factories in China build product for us to our specifications. I have one college that I do year after year and have different **shells** made up every year in the school colors. I have to work a year in advance for that kind of product.

When hiring pyro, make sure that all the operators are licensed by local, state and/or federal officials. All of our technicians are licensed operators. **Pyrotechnic** companies are licensed and permitted by the ATF (U.S. Alcohol, Tobbaco, and Firearms Department), the DOT (U.S. Department of Transportation), and the state. There are some differences in liability insurance. If the pyro company tells you that you need to carry the insurance on the event, find another company. Make certain the Pyro company names you and your client as additional assured on their insurance policy.

My recommendation for the most important practice is to never scrimp on safety. Too many event planners fail to understand that pyro also means explosives, and nothing can be too safe when one is handling hundreds of pounds of explosives in loading and firing a display. The pyrotechnics company will stress or demand that certain safety issues be met or it will refuse to load or fire the show. Cutting corners is not permitted. If they say it has to be flame-retardant, they mean it. It's the law.

A true pyrotechnic artist can design the perfect effect for any event, given time to prepare and the right venue.

art—in a safe and secure environment. He also designed the display described in the Idea Portfolio "A Wonderful Wedding Departure."

### TYPES OF PYRO FOR EVENTS

Indoor, **close-proximity displays** must use devices and effects designed specifically for indoor use. There is a vast array of **flash pots, flame projectors, flares,** sparkle fountains, **pinwheels,** and other flash/sparkle-related devices.

**Low-level displays** typically use preloaded boxes with multiple **mortars** per box to fire **comets, candles, mines, pinwheels, whistles, hummers,** salutes, and **aerial shells.**

**Aerial displays** use hundreds of mortars mounted in racks or sandboxes to fire full-size aerial shells for a traditional fireworks experience.

## FINISHING TOUCHES

There are numerous ways to incorporate living décor into an event, but the décor needs to be lighted and must be appropriate for the event. Signage should be compatible with the décor, but the required information signs need to be readable. Food and the way it is displayed can be more than just a meal and become a major decorative element. Numerous decorative lighting effects can be worked into the design, but they must be executed correctly to maximize their effect and must be integrated with the lighting design. Ice sculpture and pyrotechnics can both raise the level of perception of an event and can be exciting additions to the design. Incorporating any of these elements into an event should be done only when there is a reason and should support and advance the goals of the event.

## DESIGN VOCABULARY

Terms appear below in the order in which they first occur in this chapter.

Main entertainment
Incidental entertainment
Background music
Sight acts
Wallpaper music
Timeline
Name performer
Living statues
Living buffet
Font
Typestyle
Chatchske
Miniature lights
Fairy lights
Luminaire
Fiber-optic light effects
Rope lights
Tunnels
Sheet effect
Cone effect
Colored fans
Animated images

Plasma generator
Candelabrum
Tapers
Column candle
Pillar candle
Pegged votive
Faux taper
Chace candle
Bobeche
Paraffin
Beeswax
Soy wax
Sparkle fountains
Pyrotechnician
Pyro
Salutes
Shells
Pyrotechnic
Close-proximity displays
Flash pots
Flame projectors
Flares
Pinwheels
Low-level displays
Mortars
Comets
Candles
Mines
Whistles
Hummers
Aerial shells
Aerial displays

## STUDIO WORK

1. You have to decorate the hallway entrance leading to a circus theme reception in conjunction with a trade show in a venue that will be hosting several other events that night. You have been told that you cannot have the hallway until 20 minutes before the guests arrive. Describe your solution to this challenge.
2. You have been told that the client, a food company, wants a unique and memorable buffet display at a corporate reception featuring its new snack food item. Design and describe that buffet concept and the signage that will lead the guests to it.
3. You are designing an event to introduce the new logo for an old established company. What are some ways to make this logo memorable for the guests that you can design into this event?
4. The driveway leading to the venue where you are decorating a tropical theme fiftieth birthday party is curved and has several forks in the road. What will you do for the signage leading to the party?
5. You are designing a traditional wedding and reception, and the groom is a big rock 'n' roll fan and wants name entertainment with lots of flashing lights. What should you do?

## RECOMMENDED READINGS AND RESEARCH SITES

Bayley, Julian, ed., *Ice Culture: Ideas That Work(ed)*, IceCulture, Inc.

Garlough, Robert, Randy Finch, and Derek Maxfield, *Ice Sculpting the Modern Way*, Delmar Learning, 2003.

Lynch, Francis Talyn, *Garnishing: A Feast for Your Eyes*, HP Books, 1987.

Sonder, Mark, *Event Entertainment and Production*, John Wiley & Sons, 2004.

Wigger, G. Eugene, *Themes, Dreams, and Schemes: Banquet Menu Ideas, Concepts, and Thematic Experiences*, John Wiley & Sons, 1997.

IceMagic—a company specializing in ice and acrylic centerpieces and tables
http://www.icemagic.biz/

Mark Sonder Entertainment—the website for Mark Sonder, author of *Event Entertainment and Production*, the most comprehensive text on producing entertainment for events
http://www.marksonderproductions.com

Pyrotex, Inc.—a full-service fireworks display company specializing in events; the site contains a lot of vocabulary, explanations, and technical information
http://www.pyrotex.com

Sidney's Music and Entertainment—a typical entertainment booking agency in Washington, D.C., with a special category for living decor
http://www.sidneysmusic.com/variety/magicians.htm

UV/FX Scenic Productions of Los Angeles—a leader in the design, development, and painting of custom UV (ultraviolet or black light)-based scenery, murals, and scenic effects
http://www.uvfx.com

# Part Three

# THE UNIVERSE OF SPECIAL EVENTS

In this part you will learn tips and practices that work in designing and decorating specific types of events. However, all events are similar in many ways, and many of the tips and practices recommended in one chapter have applications to other types of events covered in other chapters. Despite the possible redundancy, it is recommended that serious students of event design and décor read all the chapters.

All four competencies in the Blueprint for The Certified Special Events Professional (CSEP)—administration, coordination, marketing and legal-ethical, risk management—are incorporated in this part. All the previously discussed elements are assembled into a final event experience.

# Chapter 12

# NONPROFIT AND CHARITY EVENTS

*The designer needs to know not to take it personally when they try to push you down in price. The bottom line is that all decisions are based on ROI.*

**—Leslie Hearn, executive director, American Heart Association, Dallas Division**

---

**IN THIS CHAPTER**

You will discover how to design and decorate for nonprofit and charity events.

**Designing for Nonprofit Goals**

- Fund-raising Events
- Education Events
- Marketing Events

**Decorating Different Types of Nonprofit Events**

- Galas
- Receptions
- Luncheons
- Auctions
- Awards Presentations
- Exhibitions, Tradeshows, and Expositions
- Conferences and Conventions

---

**Nonprofit,** an adjective used to describe many different types of trade associations, educational and fraternal organizations, and foundations, has become jargon for the very organizations it used to modify. They are now simply referred to as nonprofits. Charities, on the other hand, are institutions inspired by the love of humanity and dedicated to relief of the needy.

The goal of a nonprofit organization depends on the purpose for which it was founded. Leslie Hearn, who was quoted at the beginning of this chapter, works for the American Heart Association, whose mission is to raise funds for research and education. Other organizations may be founded to promote a sporting activity, such as a golf tournament or a sailboat regatta, and certainly are nonprofit but are not charitable in nature. In other words, all charities are nonprofit, but not all nonprofits are charitable.

This chapter deals specifically with designing and decorating events for charitable, educational, and promotional nonprofit organizations. The activities of other nonprofits are covered in Chapter 14, *Milestones and Social Events,* and Chapter 16, *Festivals, Fairs, and Spectacles.*

## DESIGNING FOR NONPROFIT EVENT GOALS

Fund-raising, education, and marketing are specific event goals. Many events include all three of these and more. Lianne Pereira, CMP, CMM, conference manager for the Susan G. Komen Breast Cancer Foundation, says: "Everybody in the meetings and event business talks about goals and objectives. Remember that the stated or printed goals may be very different from the reality of the underlying goals. The savvy meeting planner will understand both, as will the successful event designer. This is where many decorating firms fall short. They think they understand the agenda, but there will be multiple and secondary agendas working at the same time."

### FUND-RAISING EVENTS

Leslie Hearn says: "The two things I look for in a designer are compatibility with the volunteers and that he or she understands the nature of **fund-raising events.** Every charity tries to get the most for the least from every vendor. We try to be the best possible stewards of the donated dollars. Also, working with charities means working with committees, which can be a challenge."

**LIANNE PEREIRA'S MULTIPLE AGENDA OUTLINE**

The various functions of the sponsoring corporation have secondary objectives that the designer needs to watch for and incorporate into the overall design.

| DEPARTMENT | AGENDA |
|---|---|
| ■ Development | Impressing potential donors |
| ■ Education | Distributing educational content |
| ■ Legal | Limited liability exposure |
| ■ Marketing | Brand exposure |
| ■ Meeting | Cost and effectiveness |
| ■ Upper management | Corporate image |

The question, then, is why an event professional would want to work on fund-raising events. The answer is multilevel. When professional designers or decorators work for a charitable endeavor, they are contributing valuable knowledge and talent to the community as well as being paid for their professional services. This is both professionally and personally satisfying. Decorating on a budget requires great creativity and can be both a challenging and a rewarding experience. If the appropriate policies and practices are in place, it can be profitable as well.

A professional designer needs to establish an understanding of where fund-raising events fit into his or her business plan and develop a policy regarding them. Policies and practices for designing fund-raising events need to be in place before one meets with the chairperson, committee, or agency representative. It is standard practice to lower one's markup or reduce the design and coordination fee for charities. However, there should be a quid pro quo in terms of marketing for that donation. For example, if a professional lowers the markup from 50 percent to 30 percent and/or lowers or eliminates the design and coordination fee, there should be contractually agreed on exposure at an appropriate sponsorship level, including media exposure, recognition in the program, and mention from the podium during official thank-you speeches. With the exception of private donations to personal charities, the professional needs to recover donated costs from in-kind publicity.

Fund-raising events come in many varieties, including galas, auctions, luncheons, golf tournaments, **heart walks,** and **cancer runs.** Sporting-type events use banners, balloons, and possibly a decorated awards stage, but they are largely logistical in nature, whereas galas and luncheons usually require extensive decorating. Leslie Hearn says that her division of the American Heart Association does both large metropolitan galas and large metropolitan heart walks, both of which net over $1 million. However, the heart walk "is a matter of logistics, crowd control for 20,000 people, operational matters, and media orientation." Galas require design and decorating to create what she calls the buzz. The buzz is the image and the anticipation that cause people to talk about the event and to want to go there to see and be seen. "Gala decisions can be difficult. What is necessary to improve the bottom line? It becomes all about creativity and image. Ultimately, all decisions are based upon **ROI (return on investment).**"

Fund-raising design needs to optimize minimal resources. If there are very limited resources, do not spread them too thin; concentrate the effect to maximize the impact. For example, a $5,000 budget will not go far in a 20,000-square-foot ballroom (100 feet by 200 feet). If there are 150 tables, that would leave only $33 each for centerpieces and nothing for the entrance or stage. Rather than trying to fill the ballroom with decorations, design a smashing entrance treatment to create an impression and set the tone as guests arrive and also do a memorable stage treatment. Then see if the pastry chef can come up with a dessert that also will serve as a centerpiece, as discussed in the "Food for the Eye" in Chapter 11, *Unique Decorative Elements.*

Idea Portfolio

## WINNING WINE AUCTION

The annual Cotes de Coeur wine auction had set the goal of attracting more upscale participants, and it had been determined that that would mean elevated expectations, but still on a limited budget. The original design concept was to use the 24-inch-tall wineglasses that were available (Figure 12-1). As the designer for the event, we added interest by arranging burgundy lily blooms in gold metallic shred and alternating the glasses right side up and upside down. From a functional standpoint, we determined that the right-side-up glasses had to be raised on wine crates to increase the guests' visibility across the table. While brainstorming with the client and the volunteer chair, we developed the concept that raised the sophistication of the design.

Meeting on-site in the room, we were looking at linen, china, and flatware selections as well as prototype centerpieces. (This is a very good practice for developing an appropriate look for a room.) My associate and life partner, Jayna, was playing with various napkin folds and did a tuxedo fold on a plate. Mrs. John Watson, the volunteer chair, suggested that we put a single lily bloom in the folded gold satin napkin. That added another layer of detail to the table design, which was just the level of elegance required.

Brainstorming with the client and volunteers can help create the appropriate design for an event because it makes it easier to reach the client's expectation level. Also, by participating in the design process, the client takes immediate ownership of the design concept, which makes it an easy sell.

Where the resources need to be concentrated depends on the focus of the specific fund-raising event. Designing an auction means decorating to sell the auction items; designing for a luncheon with a program means decorating to lead the guests' focus to the stage. Decorations for a dinner dance may center on the dance floor as well as the stage.

Event design for fund-raising is all about optimizing value and return on investment or more correctly, **ROE (return on event).** If an event does not achieve the desired fund-raising success, it does not matter how inexpensive it was. Creative design can maximize value. Using existing or donated items and volunteer labor can also maximize value. Creative design can entail finding a way to use one gorgeous expensive flower to create an upscale ambience or can entail directing attention to a dramatic focal point that captures the message or expresses the mission statement.

## EDUCATION EVENTS

**Education events** are all about effectiveness in communicating content. Joan Eisenstodt, an association meeting planner, has been recognized as one of the leading meeting industry experts and is in the Convention Industry Council

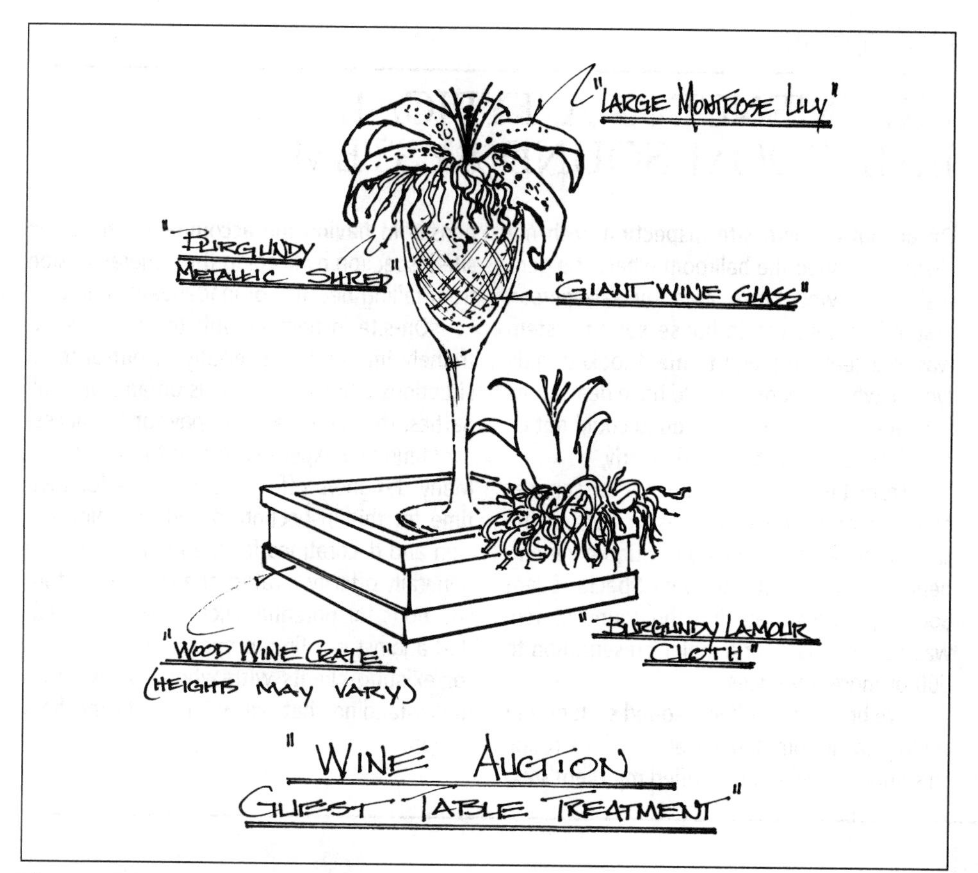


**Figure 12-1**

Hall of Fame. She says: "Any organization with a limited budget has to decide whether to spend it on table decorations or spend it on production values that can improve the educational content. The [association and nonprofit] trend appears to be moving toward production rather than décor. A lot of organizations are not going as far as they used to because of image." In these circumstances, the decorator needs to be fully aware of the mission of the nonprofit and target the limited décor budget to express the personality of that organization.

The designer must be concerned with production values even if he or she is not directly in charge of them. The event experience of the attendees is the sum of all the elements. If the audience cannot hear the speaker, the décor will not matter.

The single most important element for a presentation is the sound system. In my experience, the majority of ballrooms with built-in sound systems have systems that are inadequate for important presentations. It is essential for any educational effort to confirm that the quality of the sound system is suitable for the purposes and the number of people to be accommodated.

Idea Portfolio

## EXPERIENCING A TYPICAL BALLROOM SOUND SYSTEM

On an out-of-town site inspection with my client, we visited the ballroom where the general session would take place. The salesperson assured us that the in-house sound system was excellent, although to me it looked fairly typical, which meant it would have dead spots and weak spots where the sound could not be heard or could not be heard clearly.

From talking to the convention services manager and professional associates in the same town whom I located through my membership in ISES (International Special Event Society), I discovered that the sound system was not adequate for a major presentation to 600 or more attendees.

We brought in a flown sound system that could provide complete coverage of the room. This information alone justified my client's expenses in having me accompany her to the site inspection by keeping the general session from failing because of inadequate sound.

On-site inspection with the client is extremely important, especially in out-of-town situations where the venue is unfamiliar to all parties. The client needs to pay for the necessary time and expenses so that this can occur. Many designers offer reduced rates for their time for this inspection, based on doing design and decorations for the final project. We generally offer two rates: one for preevent inspections for potential clients, which is credited against our final proposal, and a second for existing clients with whom we have an understanding that we will execute the final design.

The educational event design needs to direct the focus and attention of the attendees toward the source of information delivery. This will be the speaker and/or data projection screen(s). As was mentioned in Chapter 10, *Art of Light*, a speaker must be well lighted because it is easier to hear and understand a speaker who is visible. A certain percentage of what we "hear" comes from our interpretation of body language and facial expression. In large venues, it is desirable to incorporate **I-mag,** which is shorthand for "image magnification." This procedure employs a camera or multiple cameras to project the image of the speaker on large projection screens so that the attendees can see the speaker's facial expressions clearly.

A major design consideration is to eliminate barriers between the presenter and the audience. Having the general session in the same space as a gala requiring a dance floor is a bad idea, as it creates an undesirable distance between the speaker and the audience. Speakers, facilitators, and presenters work best when they can see the audience and feel the feedback from their presentation. Putting a presenter on a stage that is decorated with a monumental setting that dwarfs him or her lessens the impact of the presentation.

If a huge stage is required, raise the speaker or set the speaker off to the side on a separate **podium.** (Podium is the correct term for a stage on which a speaker or speakers stand or sit. It frequently is confused with **lectern,** which is a structure behind which a speaker stands.)

In traditional Western aesthetics, the focus runs left to right (the way we read) and up to down. This means that the strongest position for a presenter is downstage left. This is only a rule of thumb and has little real effect on a presentation. Still, all other things being equal, put the lectern there, but not so close to the edge that it looks like it will fall off. Or you can create a counterpoint focus and put it downstage right. The other option is to put it downstage center, which also works. The point is that each of these three positions works for a different reason. Pick one position and put the speaker there. Do not place the lectern upstage, or in some nebulous location midway between left and right.

Decorations can be used to create or enhance focus through line and composition, as was discussed in Chapter 1, *Principles of Design.* An attractive flower arrangement at the base of the lectern can help achieve focus. Framing the lectern, stage, or screens with attractive, nonobtrusive décor such as a pair of attractive columns can enhance focus, but nothing should interfere with the view of the speaker or the screen or screens. For example, a pair of trees could frame a screen attractively, but care must be taken that the foliage or branches not interfere with the sightlines from all seating positions.

The placement of screens is critical to the effective communication of content. They should be in the same general location as the speaker. Ideally, they should be placed so that the audience can watch both the speaker and his or her enlarged image without moving. The sound should emanate from the stage, and the speaker and screens should be close to or on the stage.

Seating also controls the attendees' focus, with theater seating providing the most intimate communication distance. When workspace is required for the participants, schoolroom seating is best, and for workshops that include small group interaction, half-moon or crescent seating works well (see Figure 12-2).

The focus needs to be on one place, concentrated on communicating the intellectual content in the message. Note that this is not always the case in entertainment, where a split focus or a melange of media bombardment can be an effective method for the communication of emotional (rather than intellectual) content.

## MARKETING EVENTS

In the nonprofit world, most marketing events are largely **public relations events.** When advertising and promotional events are designed for nonprofit organizations, they follow the same principles used for corporate advertising events. The differences between **advertising events** and public relations events are explored in Chapter 13, *Corporate Celebrations and Ceremonies.*

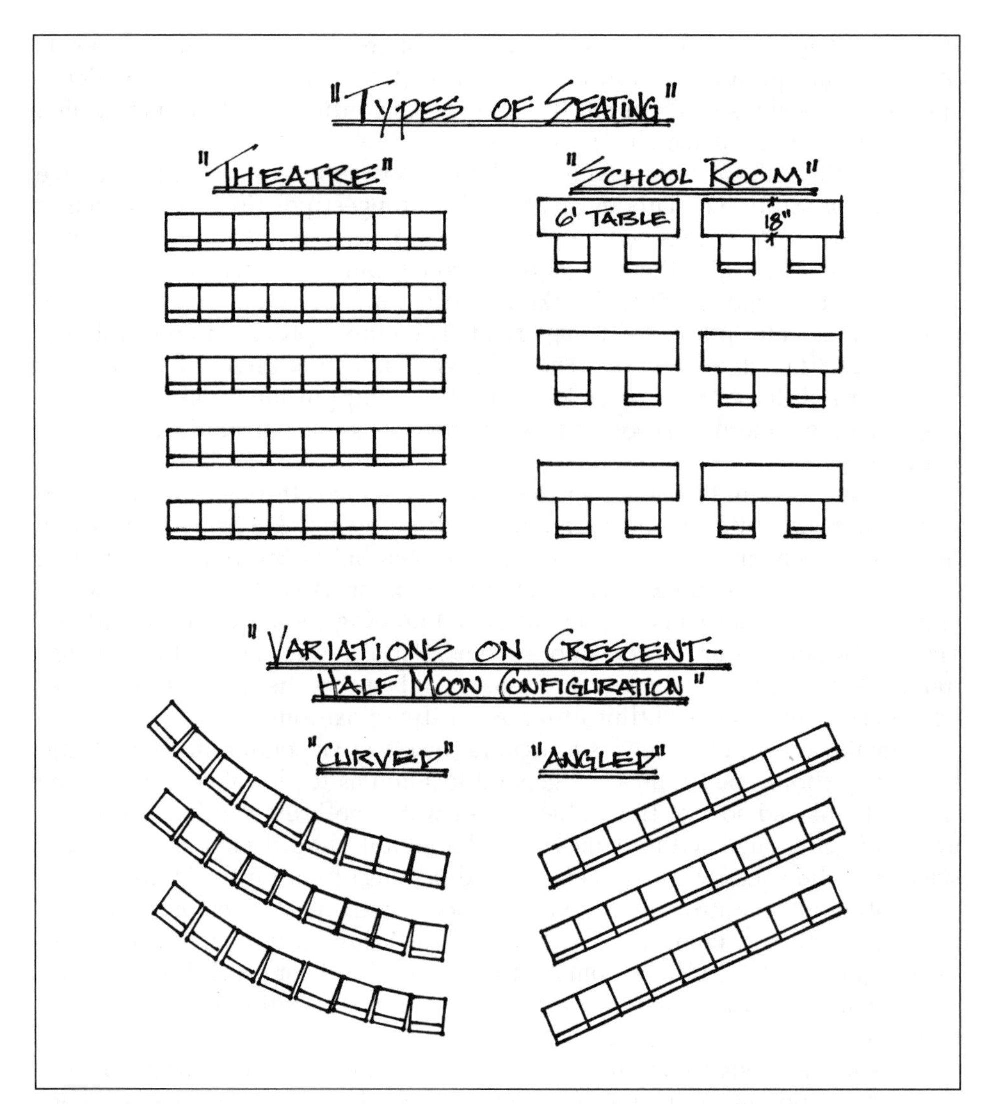


**Figure 12-2**

Public relations events promote awareness of the organization and its message. **Sponsorship events** promote and recognize sponsorship. It is possible for an event to have more than one goal, and sponsorship events can be closely allied with public relations or fund-raising events. A common marketing event is an **announcement party** for a major gala or a sports or other event. Similar to the announcement party are the **underwriter reception,** which is thrown specifically to recognize the sponsors, and the **thank-you party** or **wrap-up party** thrown after the event.

All these events are by invitation only. Local media are invited and encouraged to attend, write about, and promote the event, the organization, and the cause. Frequently these events are held in a sponsoring retail space, such as a department store or jewelry store, after hours. These high-profile events can be very effective, because both the organization giving the event and the sponsoring venue throw their weight behind the promotional and public relations effort.

Designers find this environment difficult to work in, as the sponsoring venue wants an opportunity to show off its wares, not have them covered by decorations. Since the space was designed for retail sales, not to accommodate events, decorations usually are limited to select floral designs and table treatments. However, this is a perfect place for living décor at the entrance for the arrival of the guests. Later, the entertainers may move through the aisles. If the main event will feature an auction, raffle prizes, or celebrity entertainment, one of these elements may be the focal point of the decorations at an announcement or sponsor appreciation party.

Other locations for these events include restaurants, private residences, and the venue at which the main event will take place. Each of these locations poses unique design challenges. Restaurants are designed to accommodate people at tables but may not accommodate the guest flow, display, or the speech and presentation that may be required. A solution may be to arrange for a moving company to remove, store, and later reinstall some of the existing furniture. Restaurants provide easy access to food service, plenty of seating, and the opportunity to use table centerpieces.

Private residences have the added difficulty of working in people's homes. The disruption to their personal lives should be kept to a minimum; also, they will have preferences and requirements that need to be met. Do not plan anything without the homeowner's input, and use a high-quality furniture moving company for moving and storing furniture as necessary. No subcontractor should be allowed on property without direct supervision by an event planner or decorator.

Decorating one of the public relations events in the venue where the main event will take place is the easiest from a functional point of view but may not be sponsored. This leaves the designer or decorator with limited resources.

**Fashion shows** are marketing events that can be fund-raisers and/or sponsor events, and many high-fashion boutiques will jump at the opportunity to expose their products to your guests. Designing fashion shows is a specialty, requiring knowledge of appropriate lighting, runways, and the use of neutral backgrounds to show off the merchandise. A fashion show can be a component of a gala or a stand-alone event.

The basic rule of thumb is that all fashion shows must be about the apparel. Runway lighting tends to be bright and either white or with slight color-enhancing media, such as special lavender or surprise pink. Backdrops and stage and runway coverings should be white or slightly off white.

**First-time events** are the hardest to manage because there is no history. They are also the hardest to sell, as potential sponsors, attendees, and volunteers may not know about the cause. As a result, a first-time event often has the primary goal of promoting awareness of the organization and the cause.

Idea Portfolio

## DEVELOPING THE FIRST-TIME EVENT

Representatives from the M. D. Anderson Cancer Center Development Office in Houston, Texas, met with Gale Sliger Productions to discuss a fund-raising luncheon to be held in Dallas–Fort Worth. Gale is a cancer survivor who was treated at M.D. Anderson, so she and I were very familiar with the hospital. However, most people in north Texas at that time considered it a Houston, not a Texas, hospital, even though it is ranked as one of the top two cancer research hospitals in the country.

Our goal was to assist them in developing brand awareness. The idea was to have a "Conversation with a Living Legend Luncheon" in which a celebrity would be interviewed live in front of the luncheon audience. (This brilliant concept, supported by numerous high-profile cancer survivors from the north Texas area, has become one of the most successful fund-raising luncheons in existence.)

We met the design challenges with heavy use of the M. D. Anderson logo, short tapes of the history and success of the institution, I-mag for the "conversation," and décor themed around the celebrity's life and career. For the first luncheon Nolan Ryan, the Hall of Fame baseball pitcher, was interviewed in a replica baseball stadium. The centerpieces were buckets of popcorn with baseball pennants surrounded by peanuts and Cracker-Jacks. The dessert was a chocolate baseball filled with vanilla mousse, which started a tradition of themed chocolate desserts that continues today.

Twelve years later and with over $5 million raised, I am proud to still be professionally associated with this luncheon.

Designers may find that they are challenged with establishing brand awareness and creating the foundation for all future versions of the event.

# DECORATING DIFFERENT TYPES OF NONPROFIT EVENTS

Aesthetics stay the same, and once established, goals usually remain constant. However, style and focus often change. The difference between designing for a **gala dinner** and decorating a sports awards luncheon is a matter of style and focus. In the first part of this chapter we discussed the different goals that one might have to design for in doing nonprofit events. In this part we will discuss different tips and practices unique to different types of events.

## GALAS

A **gala** is either a stand-alone social event or the primary social function of a conference or convention. It usually is held in the evening and includes entertainment and/or speeches after a formal meal. Decorations for a gala dinner should capture a sense of elegance and express the importance of the occasion. If resources allow it, decorations at the entrance will heighten expectations for the evening. Everyone who walks in the door should immediately embrace the vision of the designer.

One of the most successful decorating techniques is to create an entrance through which one sees a vista, as shown in Figure 12-3. This can simply be a field of decorated tables leading to a visual centerpiece behind the band but can be layered with a secondary decorative focus at the midpoint of the vista. For example, in Figure 12-3 an entrance gate frames the door, through which one sees a three-tier fountain in the middle of the dance floor leading to a decorated stage and a decorative backdrop.

Adding layers of décor adds sophistication and visual interest, but is more costly than a more uncluttered design. The decision about which way to design an event is a matter of ROI. Is it necessary to spend the money on a more sophisticated design to keep or attract the desired guests and/or donors? The event manager, in conjunction with the designer, must make this decision early and consider the expectations of the prospective donors.

**Figure 12-3**

Tablecloths to the floor on tables seating 8 at a 60-inch round table or 10 at a 72-inch round are the most appropriate for a gala. If resources are truly limited, seat 10 at a 60-inch round table or 12 at a 72-inch round. Most hotels have square tablecloths. Ask them to use double cloths at each table, alternating their points. Employing the cozy seating suggested here will obscure the fact that the cloths do not reach the floor. Also, more people will be seated at fewer tables, which will lower the number and therefore the cost of the centerpieces. If more expensive rental linens are used, fewer will be needed. The most cost-effective and physically efficient way to seat people per square foot is to seat 10 people at a 60-inch round table.

If there is to be a major presentation or name entertainment, it will be necessary to keep the centerpieces well within the 14-inch maximum height recommendation given in Chapter 7, *Decorating with Flowers.* Remember, tall centerpieces that allow the guests to see across the table will interfere with the sightlines to the stage from the tables behind them. Candles add an elegant touch to a gala evening, and when resources are limited, an arrangement of different size glass candles on a mirror round can be effective in terms of both cost and style (see Figure 7-2 in Chapter 7).

The stage height depends on the activities that will take place (Figure 12-4), the number of guests, the size of the room, and the resources available. A band looks best on a low stage (close to the dance floor) with multiple level risers. A 12- to 24-inch first level with a 24- to 32-inch second level, even rising to a third level if possible, is the most attractive. Check with the bandleader and her or his manager or agent for their requirements and note that each level needs to be at least 6 feet deep and that the top level should have a rail or chair guard to keep musicians from falling off.

If there are to be major speeches or name entertainment in a large ballroom (500 or more guests), a 48-inch-high stage will allow the majority of the seated guests to see the speaker or performer. Many name entertainers have performance riders requiring a 5-foot-tall stage. This causes an unnecessary barrier between the audience and the performer and is uncomfortably high for people at the front tables, where VIP underwriters and sponsors are seated. Discuss the rider with the performer's agent. Remind him or her that the space is a ballroom, not a large venue such as a stadium. It is likely that they will allow a 48-inch high stage. Dance productions, however, require a stage at least 60 inches high to allow people in the back to see the feet and legs of the performers.

If resources allow, additional layers of sophisticated décor, such as perimeter accent lighting on the walls, tall trees with miniature lights, or custom décor around the walls, are desirable, although they are rare in nonprofit events. The designer must be aware of the image the nonprofit wants to exhibit. There may be adequate resources for extensive décor, but the image the nonprofit or charity wants to project may require that the decorator stay away from anything that looks extravagant. If this is the case, avoid large floral displays, since people perceive them as expensive. However, most people do not think

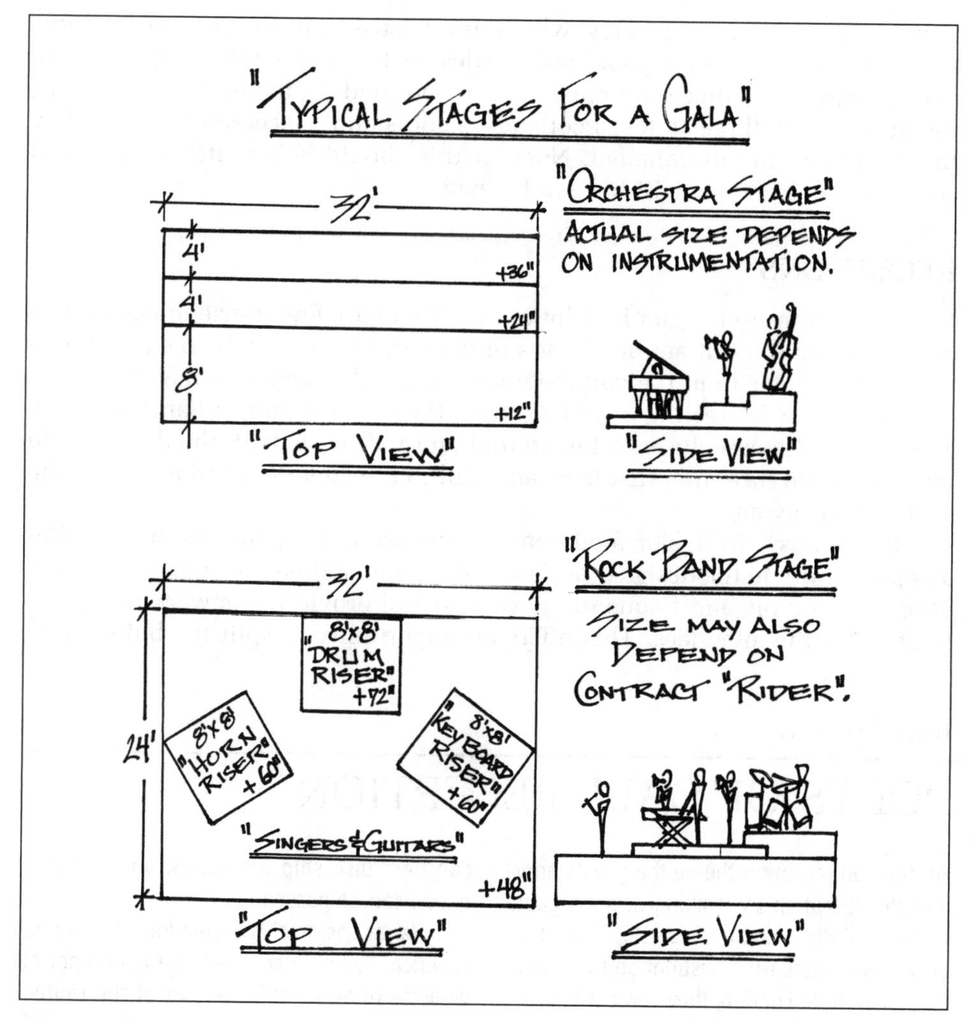


**Figure 12-4**

of linens as expensive, so it may be acceptable to use custom cloths to the floor with overlays and color-coordinated napkins. This can provide a rich look without giving the impression of extravagance.

In addition to the elements discussed so far, a gala dinner may include a live auction, a silent auction, casino gambling, raffles, sales booths, or informational exhibits. These elements pose specific challenges but add levels to both entertainment and visual interest. Gambling requires a clear space and bright light over the tables, and the decorator needs to work closely with the gambling supplier, because each game takes a certain amount of space and placement can attract players. Auctions, live and silent, and gambling prizes require high-visibility displays, which are discussed in the section on decorating auctions in this chapter. Raffles, sales booths, and exhibits require space and lighting and suffer from music that is too loud. In the best of all worlds, the decorator will create these collateral booths and concessions so that they fit into the event environment. None of this should be an afterthought, and compromise decisions will have to be made.

## RECEPTIONS

Decorating a reception can be a lot of fun. There are few restrictions, and one often is asked to decorate in all sorts of themes. Unfortunately, the event decorator may be far from the corporate decision maker and may never find out why he or she is creating a New Orleans theme reception in San Francisco. Most nonprofits are closer to the ground and will work with the decorator to create a theme reception that is meaningful to the attendees and advances the goals for the event.

Receptions with major food components are usually buffets, which offer an opportunity to the designer or decorator to add another level of décor. They encourage mixing and frequently have a goal of providing networking opportunities for the attendees. This offers an opportunity to split the buffets into

Idea Portfolio

### PORTS OF CALL RECEPTION

For this fun reception theme the guests arrive into the reception by walking down a gangplank, as if departing a cruise ship. Then they walk along paths from destination to destination. Arriving in London, they can eat fish and chips beneath a street lamp by the Tower Bridge. They can move on to Paris, where they are entertained by cancan dancers in the shadow of the Eiffel Tower and served crêpes suzette. Moving along, they come to Rome, where there is a pasta station next to the Coliseum and a street musician. Guests can visit Athens, St. Petersburg, or Hong Kong. The destinations can be selected according to what props and décor are available, making use of existing items. If multiple restaurants are donating food, this can be a theme that ties them together. The destinations can be anywhere in this fantasy cruise. The invitations can be cruise ship itineraries, and the programs can be passports.

Variations on this theme include "Across America," where each area is a geographical vignette of an identifiable part of the United States. Guests can visit the sunny beaches of the Southeast or the rocky shores of Maine. Or it can be done city by city, featuring New York to New Orleans to San Francisco. This can be done as a road trip or a train trip. Another variation is regional, such as the regions of Texas, from the Gulf coast, to the east Texas oil fields, to west Texas ranches and the San Antonio Mission Trail.

Each of these multicomponent themes allows the use of available props and décor and provides an opportunity to layer entertainment and leverage available cuisine.

food stations and divide the entertainment into different locations within the space, providing many places to create vignettes. The decorator, working closely with the food and beverage department of the venue, can build an entire environment, wrapping the guests in the total experience of the event. In this type of multicomponent event, timing is critical, and the event must be scripted carefully to keep the many different elements from interfering with one another (see Figure 12-5).

## LUNCHEONS

Luncheons tend to be less extensively decorated than gala dinners, with the notable exception of a few **gala luncheons,** such as the M.D. Anderson Cancer Center luncheon described earlier in this chapter. The typical nonprofit or

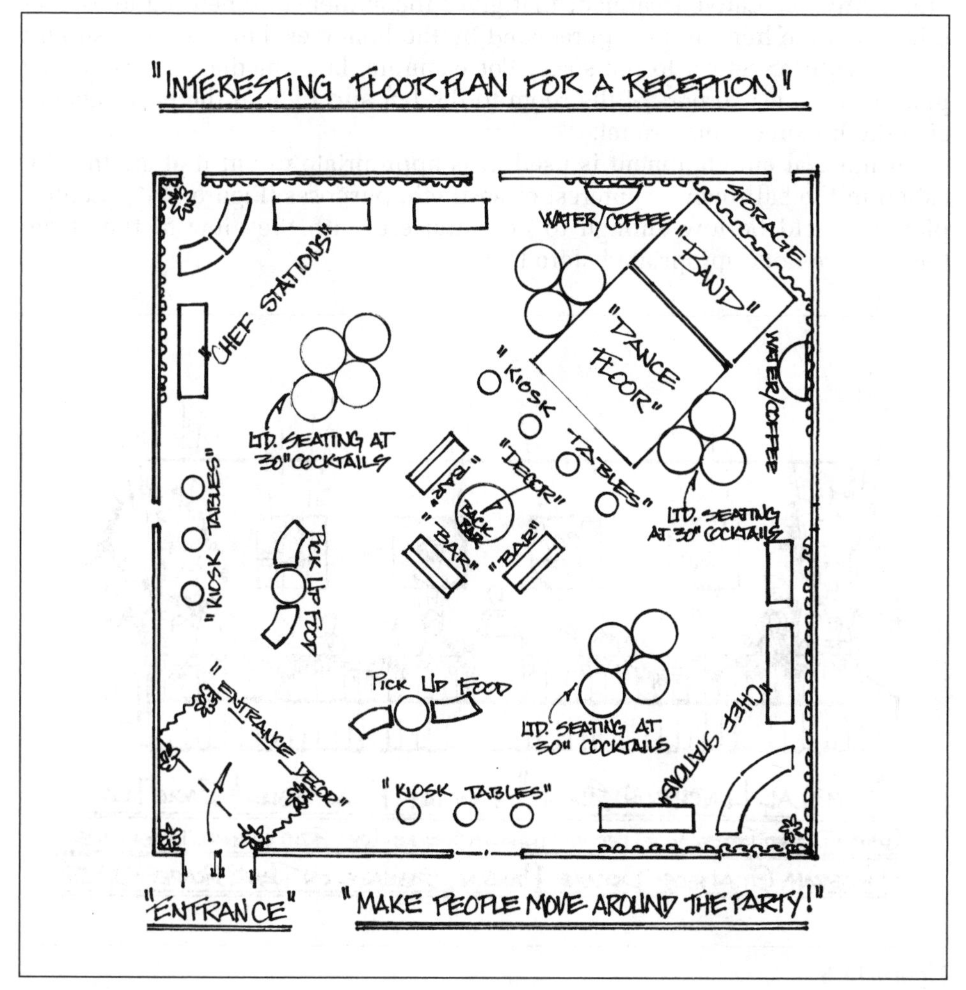


**Figure 12-5**

charity luncheon recognizes a person or persons who have contributed to the cause and/or community and requires attractive table treatments and a moderate-size stage for awards presentations and speeches.

The sound system is always of primary importance, and if the attendance and the room are large enough, I-mag must be included. The stage needs an elegant architectural and floral treatment appropriate to the importance of the event and the honors being given. A typical decorative treatment for a luncheon stage with a head table is shown in Figure 12-6.

Head tables come and go in acceptability, and I expect that they will keep doing so. In decorating a stage with a head table, the designer or decorator should understand that while ostensibly it is an honor, nobody enjoys sitting in front of everybody else and eating. The head table is placed up there so that the audience can see the VIPs and celebrities. Any decorative treatment or flowers should be low and unobtrusive to avoid obscuring the view of the honorees. Any decorative treatment that gives the audience something to look at other than the honorees is appreciated by the honorees, but the focus should remain with or return to the stage. For example, large media screens can be placed in the far corners of the room to the left and right of the head table to give the honorees some relief.

If musical entertainment is used, it is appropriate to put it at another location in the ballroom for interest or aesthetic purposes (Figure 12-7). Centerpieces should be low enough to not interfere with the view of the stage. Candles are not appropriate before 6 PM.

Figure 12-6

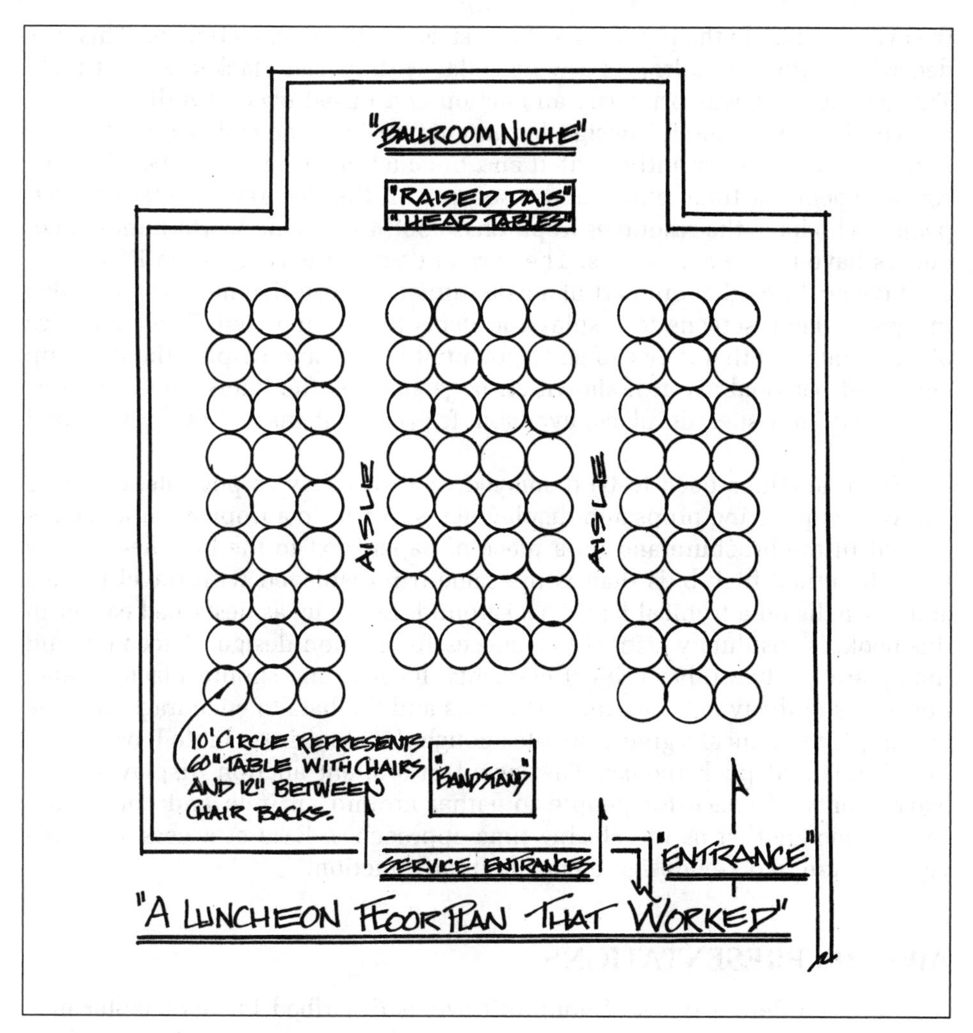


**Figure 12-7**

## AUCTIONS

**Live auctions** can be part of a gala evening or be the primary reason for one. The Idea Portfolio "Winning Wine Auction" and Figure 12-1 showed the table treatment used and discussed the creative process that accomplished it. What was not mentioned was the comprehensive decorative theme that was used throughout the event.

The entrance to the venue was decorated as the entry gate to a French or Californian vineyard. Inside the gate was a vast expanse of tables of wine displayed in crates and cases. This was an ongoing **silent auction** with areas that closed at preset times (posted in the program and on easel signs) throughout the evening. Inside the room was a focal stage for the live auctioneer. This was decorated with a backdrop of a wine cellar with barrels stacked 20 feet high. The gala evening was primarily an auction and raised over $1 million.

The key to successful design for an auction is to remember that the auction items must be brightly lighted and the auctioneer must not be. The reason for spending time, effort, and resources on the decorative details is that people who have the resources to purchase bottles of wine worth hundreds of dollars have high expectations. The correct decision was based on ROI.

Live auctions that are part of a gala dinner can use live models and video images on large screens to display the items to be auctioned. The advantage of live models is that they can go to potential buyers and display the items up close and personal. Even if shown on large screens, the items should still be on display in a specific place, available for personal inspection by potential bidders.

Silent auctions need to be displayed as attractively as possible, on risers and with supporting props and display items. A trip to a tropical paradise described in the brochure and on a piece of paper next to the bid sheet is less likely to attract high bids than is the same trip displayed with travel posters and seashells on a tropical fabric background. Lighting, as described earlier in this book, is absolutely critical to a successful auction design. Placement and timing are the two other critical elements. Ideally, one should place all auction items midway between the rest rooms and the bars to encourage impulse bidding. Timing means giving people enough time to drink a bit to loosen their inhibitions and pocketbooks. The layout of a silent auction display should leave plenty of space for people to gather around an item and counterbid against one another as the closing time approaches. Ease of access and high visibility are two key design elements in any auction.

## AWARDS PRESENTATIONS

Any of the different types of nonprofit events described in this chapter may have an awards presentation component, or the awards presentation can be the ostensible reason for the event. A number of charities use an annual awards luncheon as a primary fund-raiser for their causes.

The stage for an awards presentation (see Figure 12-8) should show off the honorees. The honorees, if they are known in advance, can come to the stage from backstage, accept their awards, and exit facing the audience down center steps. If the honorees are to be called to the stage from the audience, the steps should be to the left and the right so that they come to the stage with their profiles to the audience. If the stage is very large, making offstage left and offstage right steps inconveniently far, front steps can be used that turn left and right, minimizing the need for the honorees to turn their backs to the audience.

The décor should focus on the honorees as well. If the awards are for community or humanitarian achievement, the décor should be gracious and ele-

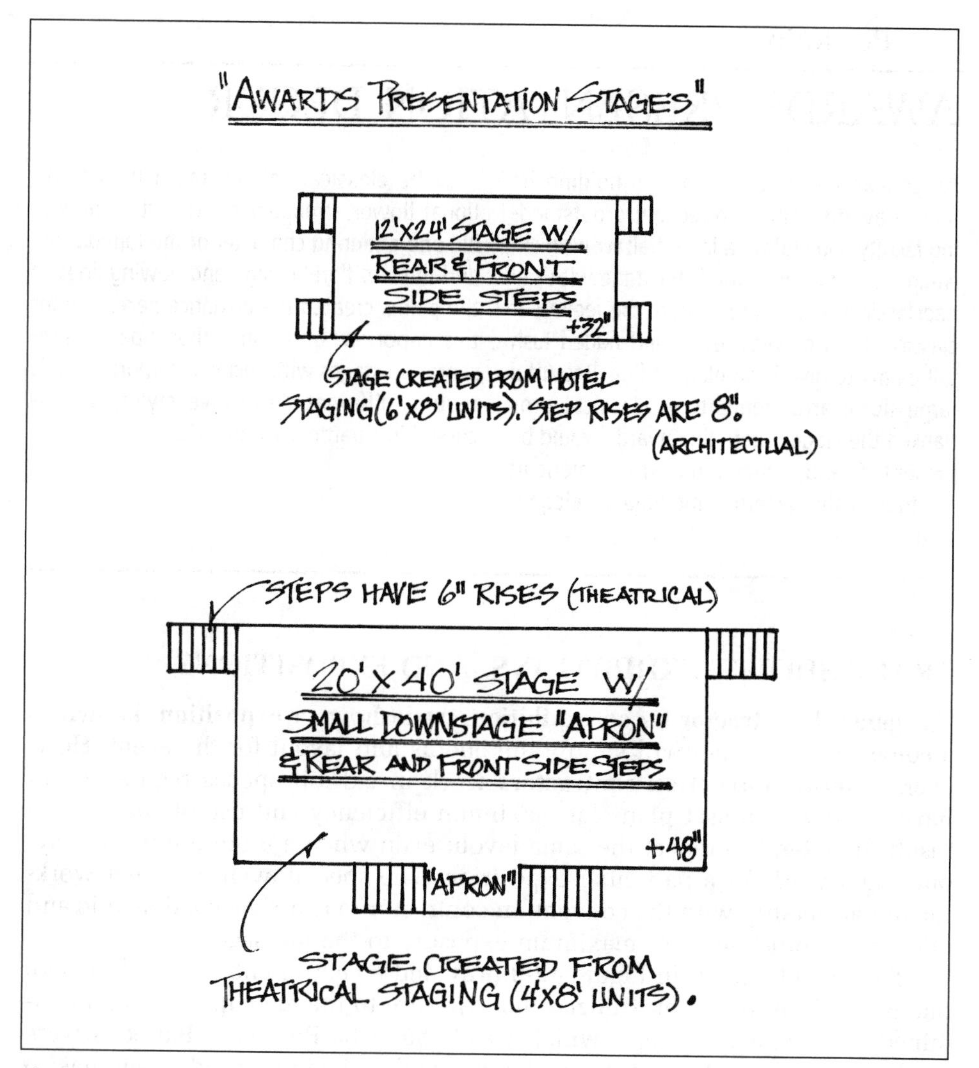


**Figure 12-8**

gant, reflecting the importance of the evening. If they are for sales or incentive achievement, the décor should be dynamic and exciting. In both cases, the awards should frame or draw attention to the awardees as they are presented. Backdrops, architectural pieces, flowers, and the corporate or association logo all can be used, but the setting should be designed to enhance the presentation and the experience of the evening. The décor should not overwhelm or distract from the honoree and must be appropriate for the association or organization's corporate image.

Idea Portfolio

## AWARDS PRESENTATION DÉCOR

An educational foundation was holding its annual awards dinner to recognize outstanding faculty and staff in a large hall with an existing stage. We decorated the stage with tall neoclassical columns to capture the feeling of classical halls of knowledge and added lush tall palms to give it an elegant line. Beautiful large floral arrangements in classical urns flanked the stage where the awards would be presented, and a matching arrangement at the foot of the lectern completed an elegant stage picture.

The classical column motif with traditional flower arrangements reflected the stable and enduring character of the foundation, and the rich floral design and flowing lines of the palms created the elegance necessary for this important occasion. Other types of presentation stages with social or corporate goals require different decorative styles, as discussed in Chapters 14 and 15.

## TRADE SHOWS, EXHIBITIONS, AND EXPOSITIONS

The **general contractor** for an **exhibition, tradeshow,** or **exposition** (known as a **congress** in Europe) will supply the booths and layout for the event. However, **general convention contractors** work in exhibit spaces regularly and have a series of preset plans for maximum efficiency and use of space. As a result, they tend to repeat the same layout even when a more interesting layout might work for a particular exposition. The special event designer working in partnership with the convention contractor may arrive at a dynamic and effective layout that gives maximum exposure to the message.

The layout shown in Figure 12-9 provided a central entrance aisle where one is rarely used and maximized the exposure to the **endcap** décor that contained the primary message, which was "Share the Promise." Balloons were used in the color palette of the conference and arched overhead to emphasize the main aisle and attract people down it. Balloons are a commonly used decorative element in expositions, but only resources limit creativity when it comes to decorating expositions.

Individual exhibits can be designed in any way that promotes and "exhibits" the product or brand as long as the exhibit fits within the guidelines of the exposition. Mostly this means fitting within a 10-foot by 10-foot module (10 by 10, 10 by 20, 20 by 30, etc.). Various expositions and tradeshows may have height limitations. Individual tradeshow exhibits can be simple 10-foot by 10-foot modular constructions with custom graphics or dynamic complex multilevel designs taking up huge chunks of exhibit floor real estate. Students interested in exhibit design will find several references at the end of the chapter, including *Designing the World's Best Exhibits* by Martin M. Pegler.

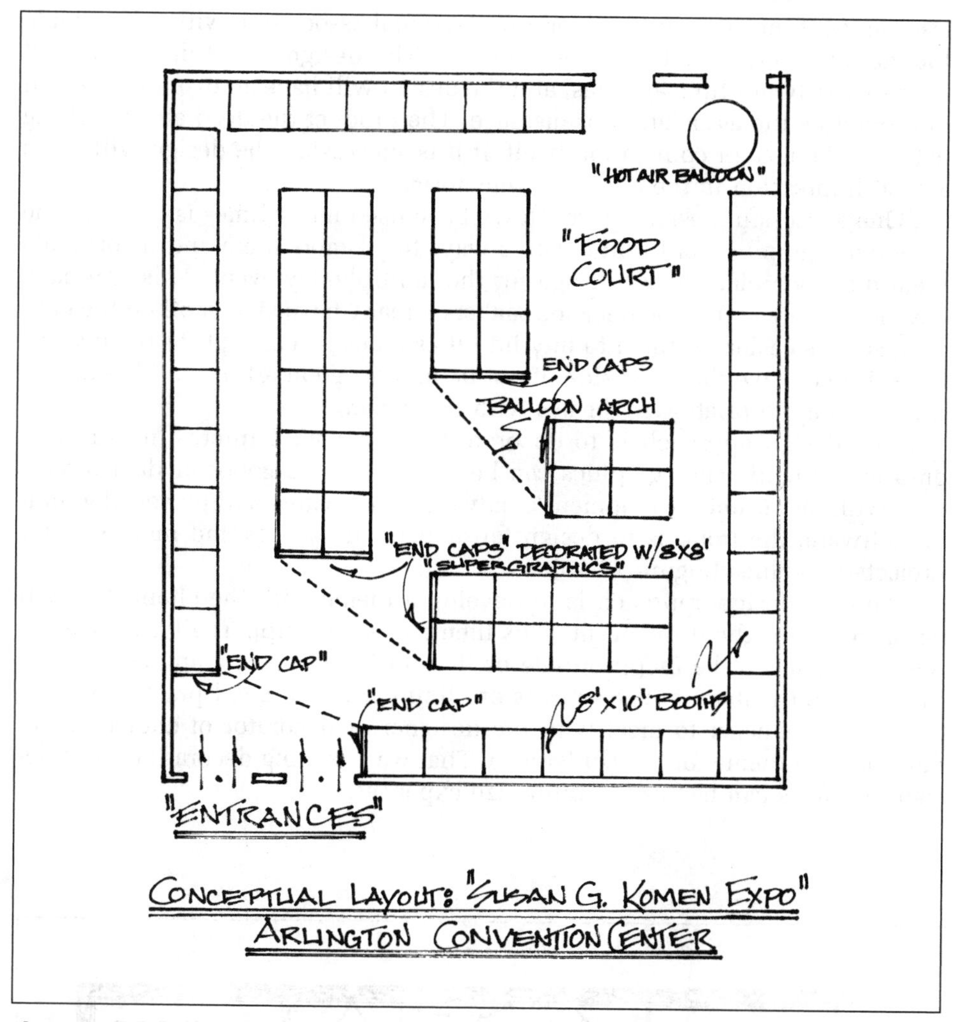


**Figure 12-9**

## CONFERENCES, CONVENTIONS, AND CONGRESSES

Conferences, conventions, and congresses are gatherings of groups of people for information, education, and meetings to discuss and exchange views, do business, network, and socialize. Tradeshows are a part of many conventions and congresses and some conferences. Conferences tend to be smaller and of shorter duration than conventions and congresses.

Designing and decorating for conferences and congresses for nonprofit associations or organizations involves designing for everything we have discussed in this chapter under one tent. There will be educational meetings, networking social events, awards presentations, luncheons, and probably a tradeshow. If the conference is for a professional association with a charitable foundation, there may be a silent auction. The designer and decorator will have to satisfy multiple agendas, and the design will have an overarching goal of promoting the association or message. The product the decorator is selling is the conference or convention itself. If it is successful, the design will leave a great impression in the attendees' memories.

One successful design approach we have used many times is to adopt the conference graphics and find creative ways to promote them and incorporate them into each element we design for the multiple-day event. This approach has the advantage that the decision makers already have signed off on the concept, so it is easier for them to buy into it as a design concept for the decorations. It may have the downside of not being very good art or not blowing up well to an appropriate size for use with the decor.

One design approach is to decorate the event with interesting surfaces onto which conference graphics can be projected with gobos or data projectors. With the recent development of advanced projectors and powerful graphics software, the trend is to design fewer painted settings and more sets for projected graphics (Figure 12-10).

Another design approach is to develop a theme with the client that will be carried throughout the event. This theme needs to support all the goals for the event and not be inappropriate or in conflict with the graphics used on the collateral materials. If resources are limited, it is a good practice for the conference manager to meet with the designer or decorator of choice before developing a theme for the conference. That way existing decorations and design resources can be used to minimize expenses.

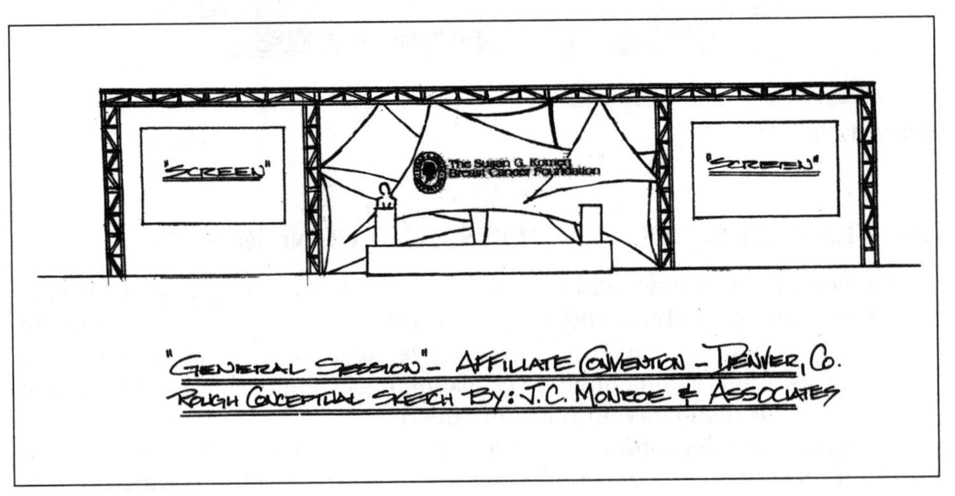


**Figure 12-10**

Lianne Pereira, CMP, CMM, conference manager for the Susan G. Komen Breast Cancer Foundation, says: "Creativity, uniqueness, cutting-edge design, pizzazz are *not* what a nonprofit is looking for. The three things I look for in a design are effectiveness, cost, and creativity. Effectiveness is number one. I need to get my message across above all things. Cost is number two, and it is the restrictive factor. If I do not have enough money, I cannot go all the way with my effectiveness, and I will have to compromise on it. Creativity and originality are last on the list and the first to be cut. Rather than look for creativity, we like to leverage existing décor and existing décor packages that were designed for someone else in order to avoid the costs of creating a brand-new look. For nonprofits, originality is not always a selling point; we are looking for middle-of-the-road rather than cutting-edge.

"Corporate work is frequently the opposite. The company I used to work for was a consulting firm, and the primary thing we had to sell was our image. It was extremely important to appear cutting-edge, 'out there,' unique, and forward-thinking. Creativity was the most important factor, followed by effectiveness, and cost was the least important consideration."

Idea Portfolio

## DESIGN CONCEPT FOR A CONFERENCE

In designing our fourth annual affiliate conference for the Susan G. Komen Breast Cancer Foundation, we were looking for a creative way to tie the dynamic graphics to the décor for the general session, the awards luncheon, and the other events held in conjunction with the conference. The conference planner had seen and been impressed with a stretch fabric look we had used earlier that year in another event.

The stretch fabric and visible truss high-tech motif had been around a long time, but I was reminded by the planner that only people who go to a lot of events or meetings are familiar with that look. Our affiliate attendees were largely a cross section of modern women, not a concentration of sales or meeting professionals who might be overexposed to that style.

Studying the abstract graphics for that year's conference, I began to see how we could enhance the graphics by projecting them on the abstract shapes and forms of the Spandex fabric stretched between pieces of aluminum truss. We designed several variations of that look for different events at the conference, combining the projections with color washes, and the result was dramatic. In addition to being effective, all the elements were in stock and had been designed for other events. By not designing and fabricating original decor, we achieved a great look for a reasonable price.

## FINISHING TOUCHES

Joan Eisenstodt says: "More and more associations are finding value in hiring professional event firms. If I am hiring a firm to design and produce an event for an association, I need to give that company background information and explain issues that are important to the group and the image the association wishes to project. The designer needs to know what the association is about. What it is about needs to be expressed in the design of the event and the décor."

Successful design for events is often a matter of meeting multiple goals and agendas. The main goals of most nonprofit events are fund-raising, education, and marketing, and the focus of the design and decorations will change depending on which goal is primary for a given event. Design aesthetics and organization goals remain constant, but style and focus vary with the type of event being designed.

Gala dinners for nonprofits have to balance the elegant image required with the need to avoid the appearance of extravagance. Decorating receptions usually is done with a lot of freedom in theme choice and allows easy layering of entertainment and décor. There are traditional décor approaches that work for luncheons, auctions, and awards presentations.

The general contractor for expositions and tradeshows usually designs the floor plan, but a partnership with an event designer can create unique layouts. Designing and decorating conferences, conventions, and congresses involve all other types of events and require meeting multiple goals and agendas.

## DESIGN VOCABULARY

Terms appear below in the order in which they first occur in this chapter.

Nonprofit
Fund-raising events
Heart walks
Cancer runs
ROI (return on investment)
ROE (return on event)
Education event
I-mag (image magnification)
Podium
Lectern
Public relations event
Advertising event
Sponsorship event
Announcement party
Underwriter reception
Thank-you party
Wrap-up party
Fashion shows
First-time events
Gala dinner
Gala
Reception
Gala luncheons
Live auctions
Silent auction
General contractor
Exhibition
Tradeshow
Exposition
Congress
General convention contractor
Endcap

# STUDIO WORK

1. Write a short description of a design concept, listing a few specific decorations that would be used at a celebrity chef auction. The celebrity chefs will provide dinner for 10 in the residence of the winning bidder. This is a fund-raiser for a child protection charity.
2. You have a budget of $5,000 to decorate a fund-raising awards luncheon for a local mental health association. There will be a head table and 50 tables of 10 for the guests. Be creative. Be specific.
3. Sketch a floor plan for item 1.
4. Sketch a floor plan for item 2.
5. Create a design concept, including possible decorative ideas, for a three-day conference for an association of emergency room nurses. There will be a general session, a luncheon, a tradeshow, and a gala dinner with an annual awards presentation.

# RECOMMENDED READINGS AND RESEARCH SITES

Andreasen, Alan, and Philip Kotler, *Strategic Marketing for NonProfit Organizations,* 6th ed., Prentice-Hall, 2002.

Drucker, Peter F., *Managing the Non-Profit Organization: Principles and Practices,* reprint ed., HarperBusiness, 1992.

Goldblatt, Joe, *Special Events: Event Leadership for a New World,* John Wiley & Sons, 2004.

Horton, Tony, and Martin M. Pegler, *The Power of Visual Presentation: Retail Stores/Kiosks/Exhibits/Environmental Design,* Watson-Guptill, 2001.

Miller, Steve, and Robert Sjoquist, *How to Design a "Wow!" Trade Show Booth without Spending a Fortune,* Hikelly Productions, 2002.

Pegler, Martin M., *Designing the World's Best Exhibits,* Visual Reference Publications, 2003.

*Event Solutions* magazine—a great resource for designers; one of the top two magazines in the special event field
http://www.event-solutions.com

International Special Events Society (ISES)—leading international organization for professionalism and education within the special event industry; ISES Finder Service is a great resource for suppliers in various cities and countries represented by members of ISES
http://www.ises.com

*Special Events* magazine—a great resource for designers; one of the top two magazines in the special event field
http://specialevents.com

# Chapter 13

# CORPORATE CELEBRATIONS AND CEREMONIES

*It's not about how much stuff you can fit into the ballroom. It's about research and orchestrated detail.*

**—Steve Kemble, event planner and Past President, International Special Events Society**

## IN THIS CHAPTER

You will discover the correct design approach and specific practices for decorating events for businesses.

**Designing External Events (Marketing)**

- Designing to Advertising and/or Promotional Goals
- Designing to Public Relations Goals

**Designing Internal Events (Operations)**

- Human Resources (HR) Events
- Structural Events

**Decorating Advertising Events**

- Retail Events
- Receptions
- Product Rollouts

**Decorating Public Relations Events**

- Charity Sponsorships
- Community Events
- Stand-Alone Charity Tie-Ins

**Decorating Human Relations Events**

- Appreciation Events
- Team Building
- Employee Parties

Corporate celebrations and ceremonies separate the unique from the mundane. We are called on as designers and decorators to create a unique environment and experience. However, corporate celebrations never take place without a reason. Steve Kemble, an internationally recognized event planner and past president of the International Special Events Society, says: "The days of having a party just to throw a party are over. Every event is done for a reason, either marketing, public relations, sales . . . something. The clients expect operational competence and professional execution." Regarding current trends in style, he states: "Ten years ago décor for an event meant a lot of flat props in a room; then we started lighting the props and put a few plants around them. We then added fancy linens and gorgeous florals. While all this still plays a part in events, what is important to the client beyond this is that the brand be seen, heard, and felt by those in attendance."

In the corporate world there are **internal events** and **external events.** External events are marketing events. **Marketing events** are **advertising events** or **public relations (PR) events:** public events that are held for the expected and measurable effects of sales or exposure. Internal events are either **human relations events** or **operations events.** These internal events serve the goals of motivation and announcement, respectively.

## DESIGNING EXTERNAL EVENTS (MARKETING)

There are two types of external event or marketing event that an event professional is asked to design and decorate. One type is an advertising event that has the goal of selling a product or brand. A successful advertising event gives the attendees a positive experience, which they associate with that product or brand. The second type of marketing event is the public relations event. Public relations events wrap a cause, positive message, or public service in the environment of the product or brand so that the public will associate the cause or message of the event with the product or brand. A successful public relations activity associates good works and goodwill with the brand or product in the minds of future purchasers and makes them predisposed to buy it in the future. Advertising is when you promote a product; public relations activities are when an uninterested third party promotes that product.

### DESIGNING TO ADVERTISING AND/OR PROMOTIONAL GOALS

**Retail events, seasonal events, tradeshows,** and **wholesale markets** are all examples of events with advertising and promotional goals. A shopping mall or stand-alone store may hold a retail event to attract customers to that mall or store. This event will be part of an advertising campaign planned locally or

**STEVE KEMBLE ON DESIGNING MARKETING EVENTS**

**On advertising events:** You are not just selling décor; you are selling a marketing concept. Do your preliminary research on the client; study marketing and study branding.
**On public relations events:** You have to add the Wow, the Buzz, the Pizzazz! The media will take every little thing and hype it, hype it, hype it!

by a national corporate office. Retail events include fashion shows, special sales, live events, and celebrity appearances. The key to designing for each of these events is return on investment (ROI). Just as in the nonprofit and charity fields, the return is measured in terms of revenue: sales and profit.

Retail events should last for a limited time, with lots of repetitions to cover and attract a lot of people and still leave them time to shop. Dr. Joe Goldblatt, in his book *Special Events—Twenty-First Century Global Event Management,* states that "the live event should be brief in duration (under 20 minutes) and offered frequently throughout the day to allow a variety of customers to experience the event activity."

Seasonal events frequently require extensive decorations. In decorating shopping malls, the designer usually will be working for the merchants' association. The director of the merchants' association will likely be a savvy

Idea Portfolio

## DESIGNING FOR A LIVE EVENT

Approaching the winter holiday season, Bill Reed, the owner of a successful display studio that would later grow into one of the premier special event prop houses in the Midwest, came up with the idea for a puppet. He had been decorating NorthPark Shopping Center, one of the most successful shopping centers in the United States, for several years and was looking for a new concept. During the summer of that year, he had designed a circus wagon puppet theater for John Hardman, who performed with a Don Rickles–style snake puppet. Bill Reed's idea was to reincarnate the insulting puppet into a Scrooge puppet inspired by Charles Dickens's *A Christmas Carol.*

The concept sold, and a young designer who had been with the company just a couple of years (the author) was given the job of designing a two-story Victorian house puppet theater. This was where I discovered the trials and tribulations of designing props for retail events. They must either be designed to withstand the assault of human hands and small children or they must be designed to keep small children and their parents away.

A friend who worked in amusement parks gave me the secret of using Chinese holly as a hedge around areas that are unsafe or undesirable for public access. Its needle-pointed leaves keep people away without doing serious damage to them.

advertising and public relations expert, working for management and trying to satisfy all the tenants.

Seasonal decorations must be designed to the **cultural demographics** of the buying public. The designer and decorator working in a retail environment should work closely with the advertising agency that surveyed the customer demographics. If the décor is religious, it will most likely offend and turn away shoppers of a different religion and those offended by religion in public spaces. When designing winter season décor in a large metropolitan area, one can choose to stay secular (avoiding angels and emphasizing snowflakes) or use a multicultural approach (combining décor for Christmas, Kwanzaa, Chanukah, and Chinese New Year, for example). In a smaller-market advertising campaign, however, it may be important to include the religious symbols of the people who shop in that store.

Tradeshows and consumer shows are exhibits for related products, with the trade show open only to members of a common industry and the consumer show open to the public. There are opportunities for the event designer in designing the layout, signage, and décor for the show and in designing for individual exhibitors. In designing for individual exhibitors, it is essential that the designer have a copy of the exhibitors' handbook, which contains the rules and regulations for exhibitors in that show as well as rates and charges for services.

Tradeshows can be extremely restrictive in regard to height and size, live entertainment, and what can and cannot be done to draw customers into each booth. In designing décor for the exhibition, clarity, simplicity, and visibility are critical, as the primary goal is to create an environment conducive to sales and allow the customers to find their way to exhibitors easily (see Figure 13-1).

Wholesale markets are generally regional in large metropolitan areas and hold seasonal sales events designed to attract retailers and resellers into a building or an area specializing in wholesale distributors and manufacturers. An event designer can find many design opportunities in showroom design, decorating both permanent and temporary showrooms for each market. These designs vary from simple window dressing to complete environmental makeovers to draw customers in and focus attention on the product.

**STEVE KEMBLE'S TIPS ON DESIGNING EVENTS**

- Watch major sports-related events such as the Super Bowl halftime and the Olympic ceremonies. There are spin-offs from them. What will they be this year?
- Look for technical shifts and new ways to use existing technology. I found fragmented lasers that way.
- Today's events should not be lavish and in your face. They should be elegant, understated, and detailed.
- Many of our clients are inexperienced but professional, and they want to be educated. In style.

**Figure 13-1**

## DESIGNING TO PUBLIC RELATIONS GOALS

Public relations events are events that get the media writing and talking about the event **(the buzz)** and include sponsoring existing charity events or stand-alone events such as grand openings, **product rollouts,** and sales events that can be tied into a charity or community event. The key to public relations events is ROE (return on event). How many media spots resulted? Was brand

Idea Portfolio

## DESIGN WORK IN A WHOLESALE MARKET

For several years a couple of decades ago, a craze for western fashion was sweeping the country. Bill Reed Decorations was hired by the local Apparel Mart to design and construct something to attract western wear wholesalers, and subsequently their clients, into an unused portion of the building on the upper floors. Bill Reed conceived of the Territory, which would be an old-time western town that would house the showrooms.

We (I was on staff there at that time) designed and constructed a reduced-scale town, including a town square with a hanging tree, a newspaper printer, a boardinghouse, and a saloon. All the western wear showrooms had to have stylistically similar exteriors with rustic siding and western gingerbread trim, second-floor balustrades, and the like. It was a hit. We and many other designers had a lot of fun for the next couple of decades designing western wear showrooms as the Territory expanded onto another floor. The western wear specialty wholesale market on the fifth and sixth floors long outlasted the nationwide craze.

or product awareness increased? When sponsoring charity events, the corporation usually contracts for a specific amount of brand or logo exposure for an agreed-on donation of cash or in-kind product. An example of how this works is shown in the Idea Portfolio that follows, along with the effect such sponsorship may have on the event designer.

To produce a stand-alone PR event, the client (or the client's public relations agency or event designer) asks a charity or community organization to be associated with a grand opening or other event. The charity receives all ticket revenues and possibly an additional contribution from the retailer. The retailer gets to associate his or her store name or brand with the charity and promote the event as a community service through local media outlets whose regular columnists and personalities will write and talk about it and promote it through **PSAs (public service announcements).** The charity will contribute its name and possibly its mailing list, and the retailer will underwrite the event in conjunction with the activity or product being promoted. The event may feature food and beverage and entertainment, possibly taking place at the retail location, and may be by invitation only.

These events provide an opportunity for a special event designer or decorator who is connected to the charity, the retailer, or the public relations agency. Designers who work on this type of event find themselves designing to multiple goals. The charity has a primary goal of raising funds and awareness. The sponsor wants to promote the charity's goal, but its primary goal is to associate its product with that charity. A secondary goal of the charity is to keep the sponsors happy.

Idea Portfolio

## EVENT SPONSORSHIP AS PUBLIC RELATIONS AND THE DESIGNER

A high-profile local charity throws an annual gala dinner as its major fund-raising event. Traditionally, they approach an automobile dealership to underwrite the cost of the valet parking. The dealership pays for the parking attendants and the parking lot, for which it receives exposure in the press as an underwriter of the charity. It is guaranteed exposure in the invitation and program as well as all other collateral printed materials, logo exposure on the large-screen videos during the event, verbal thanks from the podium, and the opportunity to park two of its cars with appropriate signage at the entrance to the event.

The effect of such sponsorship is the purview of the event designer and/or decorator, as they are required to accommodate the contractual exposure agreements within the design and décor of the event. It is incumbent on them not just to allow space for these agreements but to actively promote them within the design and décor. The designer can promote the sponsor's product in the following way:

- Placement of the product, which is usually up to the designer
- Lighting the product
- Designing surrounding decorations to focus on, set off, and flatter the client's product
- *Not* designing décor that hides, obscures, or detracts from it

Just as the sponsorship of a charitable event is a commercial endeavor, so is event design. Do not fall in love with your own design so much that you forget the goals of the event.

Idea Portfolio

## A GIANT OPENING CELEBRATION

When a well-known East Coast department store wanted to open its first Texas store, its PR director approached the local film council about being the recipient of the funds raised from a celebration of the twenty-fifth anniversary of the release of the film *Giant.* When the dust settled, a high-profile stand-alone charity tie-in event took place in a tent on the parking lot outside the store, with a reception in the store afterward featuring a celebrity appearance by Rock Hudson, one of the stars of the movie.

The inside was dressed in Texas and featured dancers, singers, Donnie Osmond, and the Marfa, Texas, high school marching band, which had been bused in from the west Texas town where the movie had been filmed. The tent had been "dressed" by Gale Sliger Productions and featured a Lone Star motif and an oil well entrance.

Stand-alone charity tie-ins are a win-win-win situation for the retailer, the charity, and the event professionals.

# DESIGNING INTERNAL EVENTS (OPERATIONS)

Operations entails performing the practical work of running a company, and internal events take place within a company to advance operational goals. Internal events generally fall directly under operations or the HR (human relations) department and serve motivational and morale purposes or structural purposes. HR events can be employee parties or recognition events, whereas structural events celebrate mergers, major management changes, or corporate restructuring. These events involve employees and possibly vendors and special clients, and their goals are always to advance internal company goals.

Human resources events deal with employee relations, motivation, enhancing morale, and team building. Holiday parties or employee picnics can serve to boost morale. Everybody likes a good party, and the décor, entertainment, and food and beverage need to live up to the expectations of the guests. When you are designing one of these events, the HR department can help you with demographics, which will define the attendees' expectations. Holiday parties are a minefield in large, diverse organizations, and the designer needs to be sensitive to multicultural issues and determine the client company's attitude in this area. Company picnics are usually family affairs, and demographics will play a huge role in determining what needs to be offered.

**Appreciation events** honoring individual and team achievements motivate employees, and incentive events are used to reward sales achievements. The designer needs to understand the purpose behind these events so that the décor focuses on the appropriate persons or activity. It will be necessary to display the names and images of honorees, possibly in more than one location. An effective design concept can be to display portraits of the nominees or honorees during a reception and use a large video screen during the main event to display their images and names as they are recognized.

**Team-building events** are used to develop team spirit and improve communications and interaction skills within a department or between departments or divisions that operate independently but need to interact. Team building is a specialty and requires a trained facilitator or staff. Event designers can work with team-building experts to create a memorable experience customized to the needs of the group.

**Structural events** are events that provide punctuation for a company. These events announce changes, establish new conditions, help form new relationships, and signify changes in corporate direction or management. Events that celebrate mergers of brands or new professional associations between companies can be used as media events as well as events to describe changes in corporate structure. These events can define new corporate relationships for the understanding of the employees in each company.

We have discussed design for several pages without talking about the design elements. We have done this because awareness of the goals and business

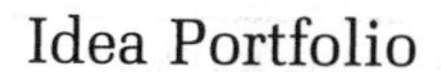


## ANNOUNCING A COMPANY'S INDEPENDENCE

Electronic Data Systems (EDS) was splitting off from its parent company, General Motors. On the morning of the official separation the CEO, Les Alberthal, wanted to speak to the entire company about the future. I was asked if it was possible to put up a large video screen and sound system outdoors that would work during the daylight hours so that the entire company at the headquarters campus could participate.

We arranged to fly in a 16- by 20-foot **Jumbotron** screen, which was shipped to the campus from the airport on a 40-foot flatbed truck and assembled on scaffolding at a predetermined location with the use of a forklift and a 100-foot boom crane.

At the appointed time 95 percent of the employees gathered on the lawn to hear the CEO announce the company's promising future and enlist their help in building a new EDS. This achieved esprit de corps and punctuated the end of the old era and the beginning of the new. It served the multiple purposes of an internal structural event, a motivating event, and a media event, creating a lot of buzz. It was both an internal event and a public relations event.

purposes of the event is critical to successful design. Steve Kemble says that when he is looking for a designer, "As much as I am looking for creative abilities, equally important is that the designer or decorator demonstrate exceptional business skills and a strong sense of professionalism. To be successful as an event professional today, you have to have a vast knowledge of marketing. You need to show the clients how the event is going to help them achieve their marketing goals and what their return on investment (ROI) will be. The design concept you pitch is important, but it is more important to be able to show them how it will achieve their marketing goals and support their overall business plan."

The style of the design for an event depends on the needs of the client, the creativity of the designer, current fashions, and the economy. John Jakob has 30 years of experience in the party rental business, including party décor, and is an award-winning event designer. He has this to say about style: "Styles of design seem to be cyclical. The changes in the last 15 years have been absolutely phenomenal. We went from a beginning of mediocre décor and budget, to a period of elegance in the 1980s, to a strong period of over-the-top awesome, bigger is better in the late 1990s, with huge budgets. The current period, starting about 2001, is one of smaller, less flashy décor and a return to understated elegance.

"We have gone from western décor to space age, through New Age, to behemoth settings, and to the current in look, which says we didn't really spend

**JOHN JAKOB'S TIPS ON DESIGNING EVENTS**

- Use fewer props and hard décor and a more refined, softer look. Décor is tending to be less representational and more abstract, more interpretational and less figural.
- Good décor sets the mood but does not draw the attention of the attendees.
- Any company that does décor or props is not complete without lighting.
- Anything can be a prop. A prop is nothing until it is put in the proper place and lighted.
- Juxtaposition can be a great tool in décor. That involves putting things side by side, next to one another. This can be compatible juxtaposition to reinforce a design or ironic juxtaposition to create a conflict, such as between trash and elegance.

too much on this. These cycles obviously are affected by financial conditions and political conditions, but other factors affect style, such as movies, television, sports, and fashion."

## DECORATING ADVERTISING EVENTS

The corporate logo or product should be reproduced often in highly visible places in the décor. The **PMS (Pantone Matching System)** color standard of the printing industry is used throughout event decorating and allows accurate reproduction of logos and communication of colors between clients and suppliers. Every event designer and decorator needs a current PMS swatch book. (It has to be kept current not because the PMS system changes but because pure colors tend to fade with time and accuracy is required to match colors.)

The actual decorative elements to be used depend on the location and duration of the event. Here are some advertising event ideas:

- A cute fantasy backdrop painted cartoon style, featuring characters from the line of juvenile products that is being sold
- Tropical plants and jungle props for a four-wheel-drive vehicle sale in an "It's a Jungle Out There!" sales promotion
- A beach party theme with ocean sound effects, trucked-in sand, a lifeguard, and beach umbrellas to sell vacation packages

The product being advertised or promoted should be the focal point of the décor (see Figure 13-2). The decorations should help the attendees remember the event, but the product should be foremost in their memory.

These are special sales or seasonal events and usually take place in a store or shopping center. The decorator is hired to create an environment that will support an advertising program and a sales promotion. This event may take place in a store, shopping center, or mall, or occasionally in an off-site location.

Retail event décor in a store coexists with **visual merchandising,** a display specialty, for exhibiting merchandise in the most attractive way. Many event decorators also specialize in display, and many display artists find part-time work with event decorators. In a retail store, the positions where décor can be installed are limited to window displays, center sales kiosks, any columns or uprights that may exist, and possibly display areas around elevators or escalators. Spatial limitation leads to the use of "flown" merchandise, in which apparel or other items are suspended overhead in an attractive arrangement to achieve high visibility in a crowded retail environment.

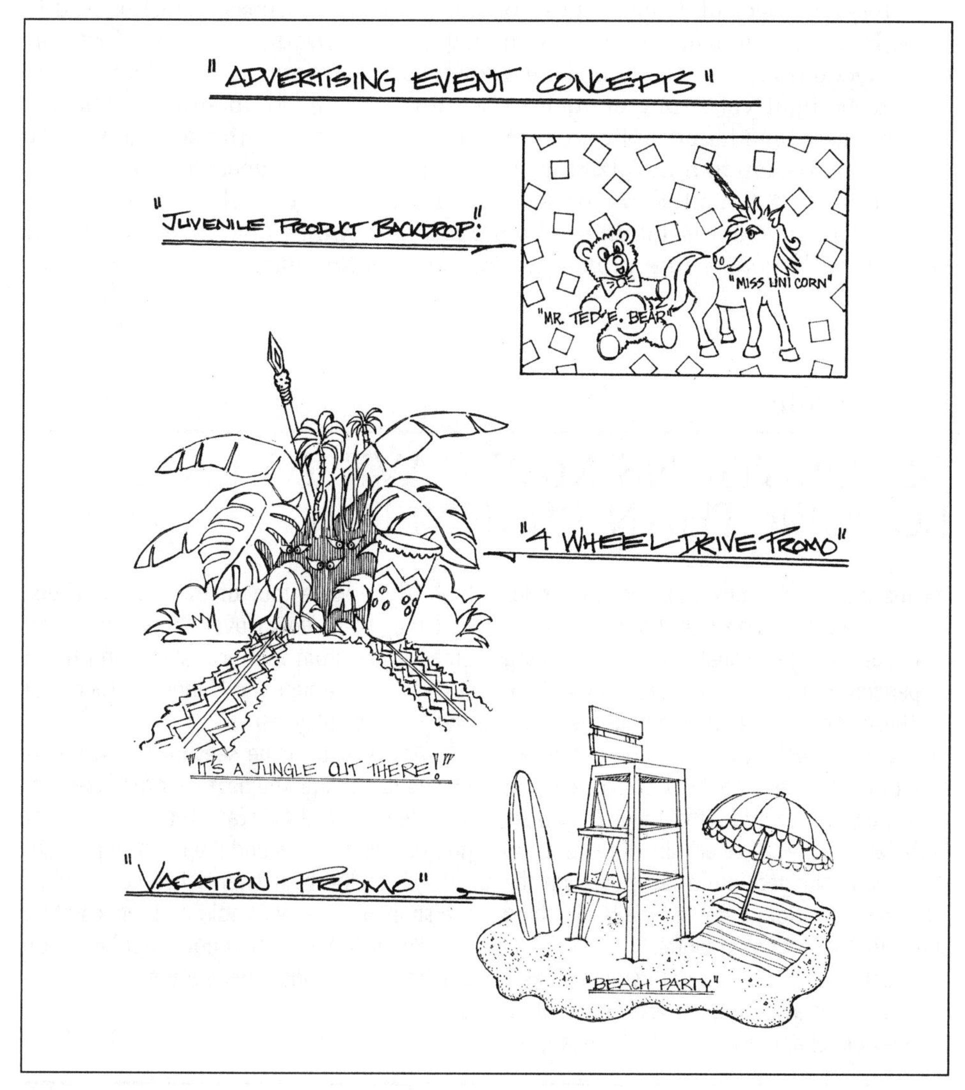


**Figure 13-2**

Good retail décor incorporates merchandising elements so that the décor serves two purposes: to advance the promotional or seasonal theme and to increase the number of ways and places to display merchandise. It must be lightweight and either self-supporting or easily attached to the existing architecture without damaging it.

Decorating events at shopping centers and malls is another specialty and is done on a larger scale than decorating retail stores. Decorations can be designed for entrances; the long passages, lined with stores, called **stretch areas;** and at or between various **courts,** which usually are at the junction of entrances or stretch areas.

The challenges of designing seasonal events were discussed earlier in this book. However there are practical considerations beyond durability. Most seasonal decorations have been designed for reuse over a set period. Decorations need to be light yet strong enough to be moved to and from storage. The designer must consider access doors into the venue and into the storage facility and should design to minimize the space required for storage. Crating or other protection for 11 months of storage, as well as the cost for the storage space, becomes a budgetary issue. *In the final analysis, composition, style, color, and creativity all must be interpreted in terms of functionality.*

Idea Portfolio

## DECORATIONS MAY HAVE TO LAST LONGER THAN PLANNED

For the first year's Christmas decorations for a brand-new shopping mall I was given the task of designing seasonal chandeliers to hang suspended over the ice in a five-story atrium. As these were seasonal decorations, I designed a relatively low-cost and lightweight structure of three-ring tiers constructed of white polyvinyl chloride (PVC) plumbing pipe. Each held a series of clear miniature lights on white wire, plugged into a receptacle on the PVC and held straight down by a lead fishing sinker that was painted white.

Each ring was rigged with stainless steel airplane cable at a different level to create a tiered-look chandelier about three stories high. There were four of those chandeliers, and they were flown over the ice by a talented rigger from the local stagehand union (IATSE, the International Alliance of Theatrical and Stage Employees).

At the end of the season they were removed to storage. The next year they were reinstalled, and they stayed up, except for annual maintenance and the replacing of light strings, for the next twenty-five years, when the shopping mall was sold and redecorated.

You just never know how popular a prop will be or how long a decoration will actually be used.

# RECEPTIONS

Receptions can be held for a multitude of reasons: to honor someone, recognize an occasion, announce a new product (a product rollout), or simply to assemble a group of customers or potential clients. The reason for the reception will determine the décor approach. For a mixing opportunity such as introducing the sales or service staff to clients, the décor should be similar to that of the networking reception described in the section on receptions in Chapter 12, *Nonprofit and Charity Events.* For a reception honoring a person or announcing a new product, the décor should provide a focal point at which a ceremony can take place in full view and hearing of the assembled crowd.

Among the themes that work are "a place in time" themes. For example, if an employee is being honored for 50 years of service, the event can be decorated either in the style of the time when he or she came to work for the organization, or a timeline or time tunnel theme can be used. If the person or occasion being celebrated is related to particular geographic areas, a variation on the ports of call theme can be used, perhaps by decorating sections of the room as different locations where the honored has worked for the company. A company that has locations or clients in different countries can use this theme as well. Another approach when decorating for an honoree is to base the décor on his or her special interests or life experiences.

The style of décor should fit the personality of the honoree and be compatible with the goals of the company. If it is an ad agency recognizing a

Idea Portfolio

## A FORTIETH-ANNIVERSARY SURPRISE PARTY

To celebrate the professional accomplishments of a lifetime in the advertising business, his colleagues put together a surprise fortieth-anniversary party for advertising legend Liener Temerlin, chairman emeritus of the Temerlin McClain advertising agency.

The décor featured giant photo blowups of Mr. Temerlin, and the room was decorated in icons from the early 1950s, when he began his advertising career as a copywriter. There was a soda fountain and a drive-in (with waitresses on roller skates), both serving food from the 1950s. There were 1950s automobiles and a giant 1950s-style television that was a rear projection screen showing mute versions of *I Love Lucy* episodes.

Tables in the soda fountain and drive-in areas were covered with oilcloth tablecloths and had bent metal chairs, napkin dispensers, and ice cream soda floral centerpieces. By the television there was an arrangement of 1950s-style couches and end tables.

This decorative style turned out to be extremely effective, as people from throughout his life were there and it became a nostalgic reunion of old associates.

dynamic executive, cutting-edge, dynamic décor featuring the latest technology may be appropriate. If it honors a retiring accountant or banker, a more solid and traditional décor in a style with understated elegance will be more appropriate. However, listen to the clients and do not approach them with preconceived notions. A nontraditional or outrageous décor approach may achieve their goals for the event.

Food service at receptions is either buffet or passed on trays: **butler service.** Chapter 11, *Unique Decorative Elements,* in the "Food for the Eye" section, has some interesting ideas that can create memorable receptions. Make sure there is light on the food service areas. People like to know what they are eating, and an especially beautiful display should be well lighted.

Lighting is an area that often is overlooked by decorators. Never do décor without lighting it unless it is outside in the daylight. Lighting can add tremendous impact to décor and can even replace décor in some instances (refer to Chapter 10, *Art of Light*).

Steve Kemble says this about lighting: "The use of lighting and technology is very effective in today's marketplace. You can overlay both of them virtually on any event surface. In a tight-budget economy you have to pitch the client a concept that can be used in various ways. For example, you may propose a sleek lounge look for the client's event. But by adding in lighting and technology at different levels, you can use the lounge concept for more than one event. Simply by changing the lighting and technology aspects (projections, neon accents, etc.) of the event, you can have a whole new look each time."

## PRODUCT ROLLOUTS

Product announcement parties are a common and effective way to expose a new product to a targeted audience and achieve media coverage at the same time. These events can take place as receptions and galas and in conjunction with tradeshows or national advertising programs. It is the decorator's challenge to make each new rollout unique and memorable. This can be achieved by using unique and memorable décor that emphasizes aspects of the product that make it outstanding or by surrounding the product in a counterpoint environment that makes it stand out.

Examples of emphasizing the attractive features of the product include an airline announcing a new luxurious class of seating at a reception where the guests actually sit in the luxurious new seats and taking attractive design features, blowing them up, and displaying them as **supergraphics.** Putting product in a counterpoint environment would involve showing a new model luxury car on the theater stage where the musical *Cats!* was playing, showing a fabulous new luxury automobile in a theatrical junkyard (Figure 13-3).

The major challenge at many product rollouts is the **reveal** (Figure 13-4), the moment at which the product is unveiled. A traditional unveiling involves pulling fabric off the product, or the product may be revealed from behind a

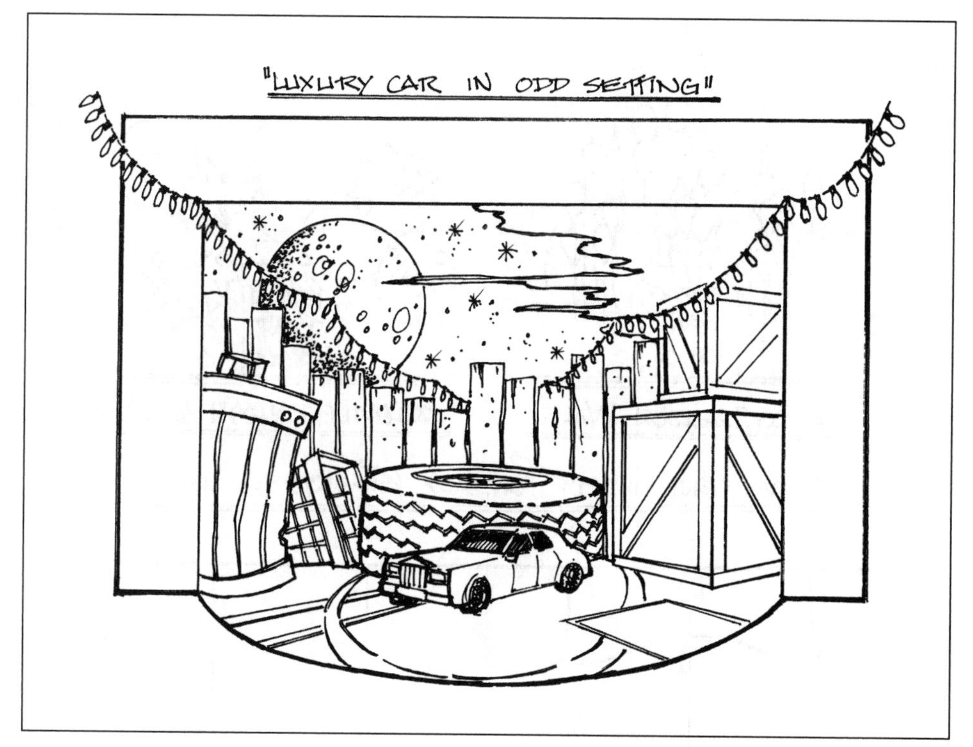


**Figure 13-3**

traveler curtain (traveler curtains are discussed in Chapter 8, *Fabulous Fabric Décor*). The traveler hardware and curtains are heavy, and if the space is not designed for rigging, this becomes a complicated installation. Another common fabric reveal is the **drop curtain,** sometimes referred to as a **kabuki curtain.** A lightweight fabric drops on cue to reveal what is behind it. Drop curtains can be rigged through a system of electrical **solenoids** and fall at the touch of a button or can be rigged inexpensively with **tie line** running through **grommets** and some type of ceiling eyes.

There are several forms of balloon reveals, in which the product is hidden from view by a wall of balloons that are exploded or released on cue to reveal the product. Some complicated reveals involve theatrical fog thick enough to hide what is happening on stage as the product is driven on, lowered from above, or raised on an elevator. These reveals can be particularly dramatic when combined with pyrotechnics, lasers, programmed moving colored light beams, and projections. Another form of reveal uses audiovisual, showing videos and/or computer animation on the screens. The design of the stage then becomes similar to the design of a **general session stage** for a conference or

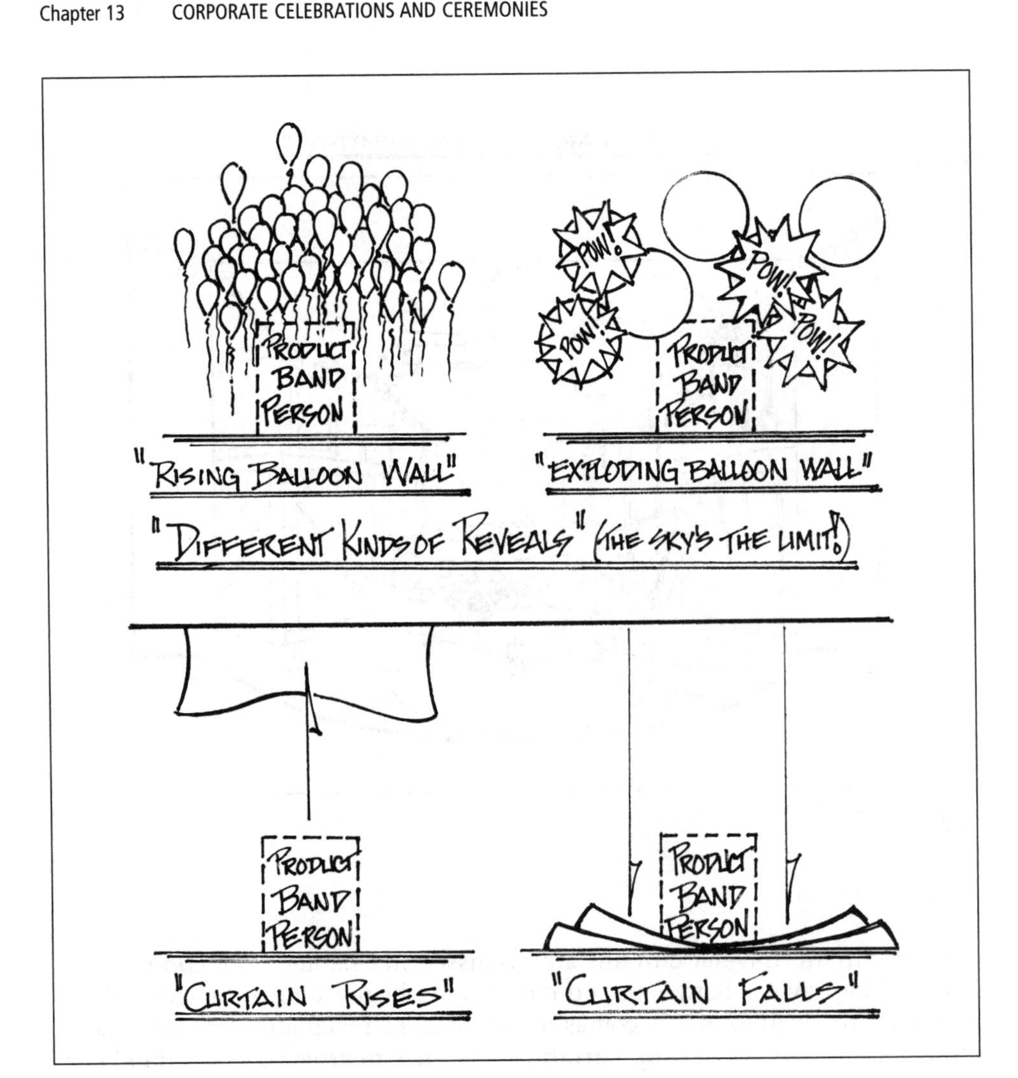


**Figure 13-4**

convention. The designer and decorator plan the environment to communicate the message. Which form of reveal to select is a decision that is based on the budget and appropriateness for the image of the company and its product.

There are many other types of advertising and sales-related events that a decorator may be asked to assist with, from sidewalk fairs to horse auctions. Although the design principles remain the same from event to event, decorations are practical and real with physical characteristics that make some appropriate for one event and inappropriate for another. **Foamcore** decorations trimmed with feathers, for example, may be effective in a retail store but may not survive the fresh spring breezes passing through a tent sale in the parking lot. If it is the designer's responsibility to make sure the style is appropriate for the event, it is the decorator's responsibility to make sure the decorations will survive the conditions in which the event is being held. The decorator must make sure the air-conditioning vents are not covered, the lighting system works, and all best practices regarding safety are followed. Decorating is the operational part of event design, and the decorator is responsible for the success of the practical parts of an event.

## DECORATING PUBLIC RELATIONS EVENTS

For advertising events, the corporate logo or product should be reproduced often in highly visible places in the décor. In public relations events, placement of the corporate logo is more sophisticated, as the idea is to associate the logo with the cause or community event, not dominate it. What is important is that the logo be seen and experienced up close and personal by the targeted market. This is why Tiffany wants its signature blue boxes at the place setting of each underwriter and Neiman Marcus wants its logo on the gifts to the guests at a high-profile society function. An event decorator needs to remember this when doing public relations events. Maybe embroidering the client's logo into the napkins would make a more lasting statement than would putting it 4 feet high behind the band stage, and there is no reason why you can't do both (except budget).

### CHARITY SPONSORSHIPS

In an example given earlier in this chapter, a car dealership underwrote the valet parking and received permission to display two vehicles as well as brand exposure at several locations as a sponsor. The decorator may be called on to spotlight the vehicles for high visibility without interfering with parking operations and to light the vehicles as well. The demands on the decorator can be much more challenging than this if, for example, the sponsorship agreement is to display the sponsor's logo over the stage and the headliner band requires a plain black background behind it when it performs. Another problem may be that the sponsor's logo colors clash with the designer's color palette for the event.

These problems and challenges arise as the decorator arrives on the scene to find that most of the critical decisions have been made but still accepts responsibility for making it all work. The decorator for an event is charged with seamlessly integrating the sponsor's logos and contracted signage into the décor for the nonprofit or charity. His or her primary responsibility is to the nonprofit, as was described in Chapter 12. The agreement between the charity and the sponsor should be a written legal contract that defines what is expected of both sides. This document details the decorator's responsibilities but may miss nuances that were agreed on between the sponsorship chair and the

Idea Portfolio

# A CLEVER AND MEMORABLE PLACE SETTING

For dinner in a ranch house during a **fam trip** to the Garret Creek Ranch and Conference Center, we selected bright chili pepper cloths with a black background, and at each place setting we tied a fan fold napkin with raffia, including a Garrett Creek Ranch key chain (Figure 13-5). It was a classy look for a barbecue, and the guests were noticed commenting on it as they slipped the key chains into their pockets.

*Note: fam trip* is short for **familiarization trip,** which is a hospitality event offered to possible clients by venues and **Convention and Visitors Bureaus (CVBs),** which may book the venue or city at a later date.

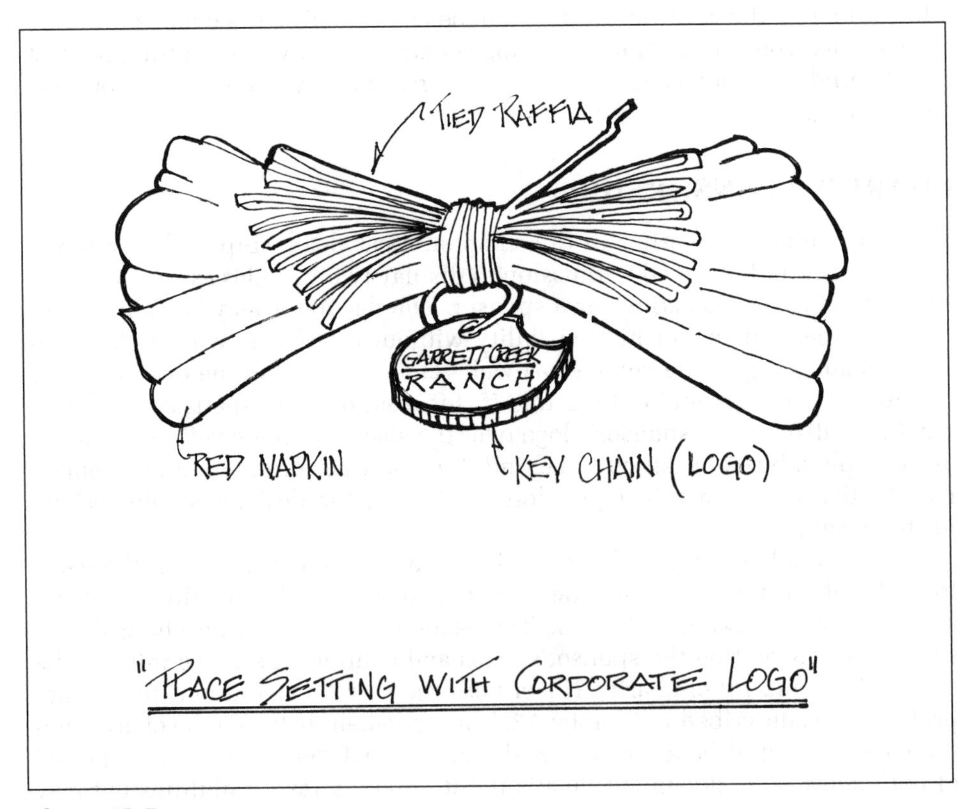


**Figure 13-5**

sponsor. The decorator must rely upon his or her contact with the organization that is producing the event.

## COMMUNITY EVENTS

**Community events** are events that either supply a lifestyle benefit to members of the community, such as a July Fourth fair and fireworks display, or make the community more attractive to visitors and conventions. Music festivals, arts fairs, and weeklong social events fall into this category. An event decorator may be asked to supply décor for any of these events, and the type of event, its goals, and its production conditions will determine the appropriate decorations. A local artist fair inside a community building will require a different design approach than will one held outside in a public park. The design and décor of community events such as fairs and festivals are discussed in Chapter 16; here we will just consider decorations from the sponsor's point of view.

These events are less targeted than are charity or arts foundation fundraisers and require a broader approach to spreading the logo and brand awareness. The decorator should treat these events like advertising events and incorporate the brand or logo often in high-visibility locations. In heavily attended events with large crowds of people, the logo should be high, as people in crowds tend to look up. Giant helium-filled balloons with the sponsor's logo can be used to identify key locations. If the event is at night, Air Stars, a nylon-reinforced balloonlike lighting device, can be used, and the sponsor's

Idea Portfolio

### CHAMPS AND CHALLENGES

A particular design challenge was to hang banners over the boxing ring per the agreement with the underwriters for Fight Night, a fine, if unusual, charity. At this particular Fight Night, people (mostly men) pay $500 each or more for a black tie dinner in a fancy ballroom, and the main entertainment is a fully sanctioned evening of professional boxing, including at least one title fight.

Lighting a boxing ring requires bright, even light with no shadows. Hanging banners over the ring creates shadows, but we had to have the banners to meet the agreement with the sponsors. The challenge was solved through careful design employing cross-sectional views of the lights and the ring, including the lighting truss (Figure 13-6). It was discovered that the height of the lighting truss would be determined by the crystal chandelier hanging over the center of the ring and that the banners, if hung right on the chandelier, would be above the light beams into the ring. This meant that extra lights would have to be hung to light the banners themselves.

This was an easy solution when solved ahead of time but could have been a disaster if discovered on-site just before the show. It is the decorator's responsibility to discover possible problems like this and resolve them as painlessly as possible in advance.

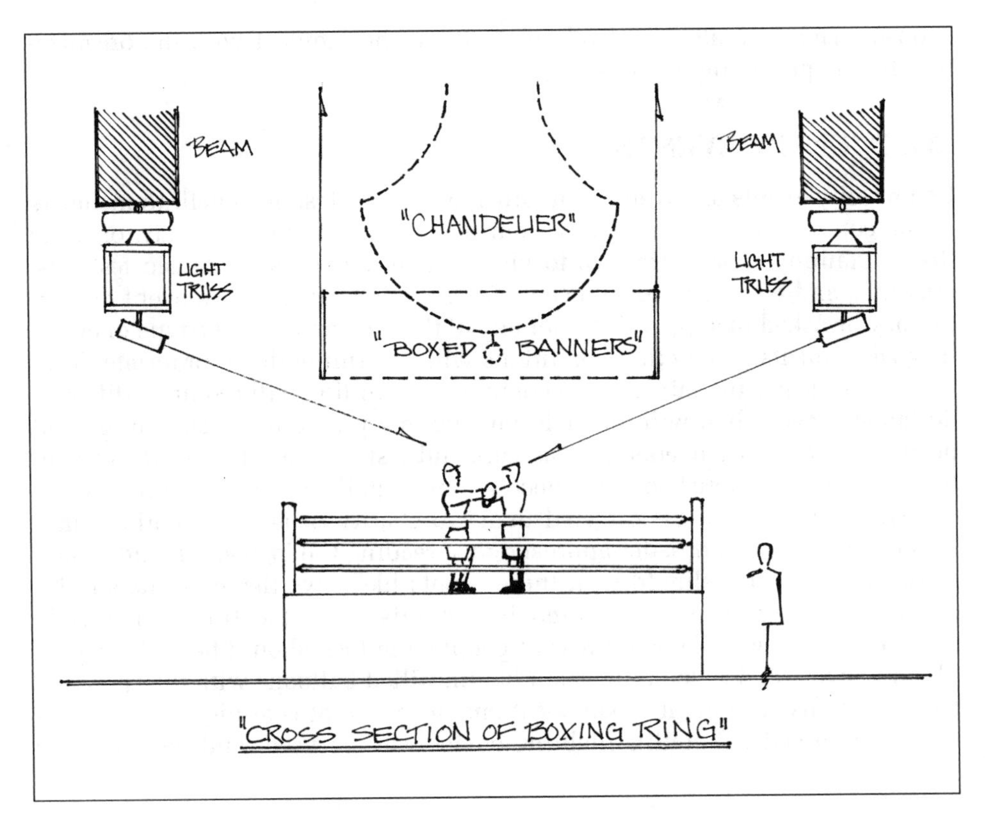


**Figure 13-6**

logo can be imprinted on them. Another popular way to display the sponsor is on large banners behind the main entertainment stage. One of the most important aspects of these large public events is signage, and a savvy sponsoring corporation will donate the signage, with the stipulation that the corporate logo appear on each sign.

Smaller community events, such as the opening of a new library or recreation center, may happily accept the donation of appropriate décor, and a decorator can provide props and décor for a ribbon-cutting ceremony that incorporate a company logo. For this type of event, colorful helium-filled balloons can be very effective. It does not cost much to print the logo of the city or community institution on the balloons and only a little more to print the corporate logo on the other side, thereby tying the corporate logo to the community institution.

## STAND-ALONE CHARITY TIE-INS

In spite of their connection to a charity, **stand-alone charity tie-ins** are commercial endeavors, and the corporation will hire a decorator to provide an environment that showcases the venue, product, or brand being promoted.

Frequently these events are held in a store, dealership, or warehouse of the company. The decorator's task for these events is to enhance and showcase the showroom or store. Decorations may add to the environment but should not conceal it. A red carpet, possibly lined with velvet ropes, is always appropriate to welcome special guests, and the decorator may add a special decorative entrance. Perhaps a lighted portal featuring the logo of the charity or, if it is a daytime event, a glitter entrance to pick up the sunlight will add to the guests' anticipation as they arrive (see Figure 13-7).

Inside the store, floral accents and an attractive table treatment at special guest tables brought in for the occasion can create a festive party space. If there will be entertainment or speeches, the decorator will create a stage and a decorative treatment for that area might feature the charity or the company logo along with the charity. Part of the decorator's task in bringing in staging and tables may be moving out some of the existing furniture and storing it until after the event. Another challenge for the decorator is that the store is open for business during regular hours, which can limit the setup time and require a late-night strike.

The charity is important because it is what draws the attendees and the media, but the company logo should appear wherever the charity appears. What the decorator should *not* do is bring in a bunch of props or hang yards of fabric that obscure the space that is being shown off. It may be appropriate to bring in rental trees and plants to soften the architecture and add a special festive touch or special accent lighting to create a party ambience. In a store or showroom, one rarely will theme the reception or event, as the venue is the

**Figure 13-7**

theme, unless the charity event being tied in has a theme it is promoting. A charity ball, for example, may have a theme, and the tie-in event is promoting that ball.

If the event is being held in a company warehouse, the decorator generally has more freedom to bring in props and hang décor, as most warehouses are not designed to impress. Some events may be themed to attract more attendees, such as a beach party theme in a carpet warehouse, a western party in a T-shirt warehouse, or a Parisian theme in a gourmet food warehouse. Warehouses are convenient as they have loading docks and facilities, space (which is always lacking in a store), and places from which to hang things. Some events in warehouse spaces are given to show off the space and require limiting the décor to accents as though in a store. This may be the case in showing off warehouse space to rent or in showcasing a high-tech automated warehouse facility.

Some stand-alone charity tie-ins are held in a country club or warehouse when the product being promoted is not tied into a given location. These can be automobile promotions (by the manufacturer rather than a single dealership), new beverage introductions, or maybe the promotion of a new scent by a major perfume manufacturer. Generally, the "theme" at these events is the product or brand, and all décor needs to enhance the image of that item or brand. Flowers, lighting, and logo reproduction are effective, and the decorator also may be asked to create a special environment for the presentation of the product, using any combination of decorative elements.

Beautiful flower arrangements atop custom pedestals featuring the company logo can flank the product. The flowers should be lighted, but the product should be lighted more brightly. This vignette enhances the product and should be planned so that it is the focus of the guests as they enter the room. To finish the vista, the company logo can be carved out of ice above and behind the product. For an example, see how the Lexus is enhanced in Figure 13-8. The ice logo also would be lighted, and the general lighting in the room would be dimmed to make the logos and the featured product glitter in the eyes and memories of the guests. When working in a ballroom space, a decorator is limited only by the goals of the event and the expectations of the client.

Doing a stand-alone charity tie-in to promote a new store, product, or brand is a win-win situation, and the decorator has the advantage of needing to satisfy limited goals and agendas. Other types of public relations events the decorator will be called in for include recognition events, in which a member of the company or a community member is being recognized for a special achievement such as winning an Olympic medal or flying a helicopter around the world. When this type of event occurs, there is little advance notice, and the decorator will be required to "jump through hoops" to make it happen.

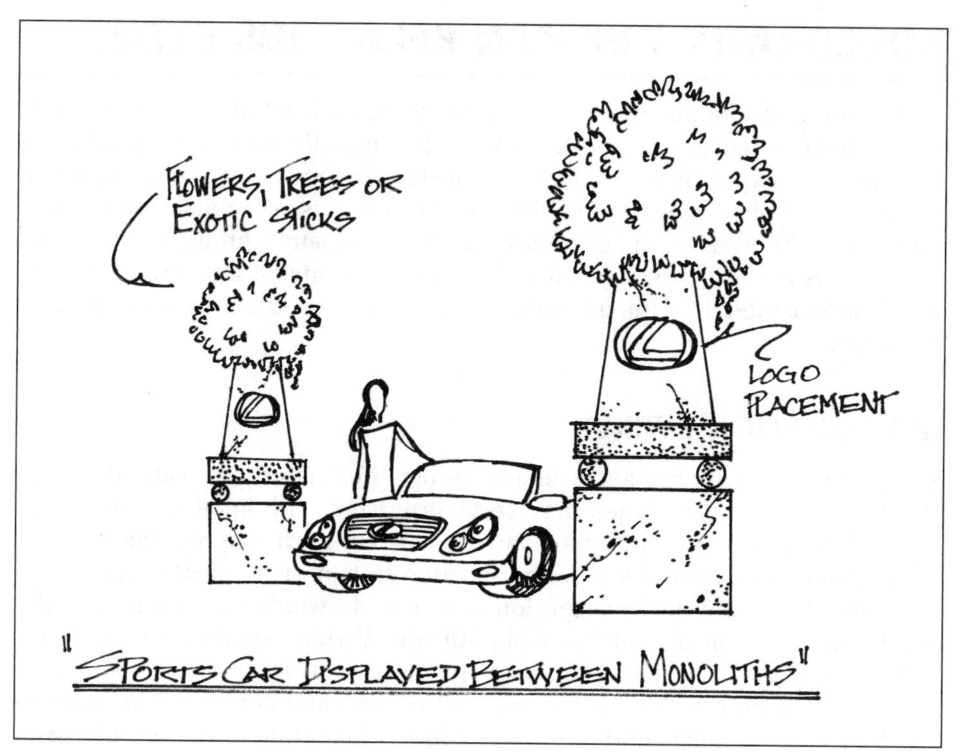


**Figure 13-8**

Idea Portfolio

## CELEBRATING A CIRCUMNAVIGATION

On September 30, 1982, H. Ross Perot, Jr., and J. W. Coburn completed the first around-the-world helicopter flight in a Bell Model 206L LongRanger II. Named "The Spirit of Texas," it covered a distance of 41,850 kilometers (26,000 miles). Bill Reed Decorations received notice on Friday that the pilots would be honored at a ceremony in front of city hall the following Monday, and could they please have a 30- by 30-foot banner recognizing the flight hanging from the front of the building by then.

Watching then general manager Gale Sliger deal with various subcontractors, each of whom would have to jump through hoops for this to occur, I learned how important trust and relationships between event professionals are. The banner was hanging on time for the ceremonies, and I learned the valuable lesson that an event firm is only as good as its suppliers and its relationship with those suppliers.

# DECORATING HUMAN RELATIONS EVENTS

Motivation and morale are the underlying forces behind all human relations events, but the decorator needs to look for the immediate goals or agendas that may drive any specific occasion. One constant in any human relations event is that it is all about people. The decorator is being asked to make people feel good about themselves, the company, and the company's future. Human relations events are as close to social and **life-cycle events** as any corporate function, but remember that the underlying goal is to do good for the company and its future.

## APPRECIATION EVENTS

Recognition of employee achievement, either lifetime or goal, can take place at a luncheon or gala dinner, may be incorporated with another event (such as a holiday party), or may be a stand-alone event such as a retirement party. These events can take place in any location but most frequently occur in a ballroom. Team and goal recognition events and awards ceremonies usually are decorated in an upbeat "winners" theme. Various sports stars, trophies, and academy awards themes are all popular, as well as ascending and high-flying themes such as hot air balloons, jet planes, and climbing Mount Everest. A local or regional sports team or an individual athlete who recently won a championship or gold medal can become the focus for an awards or achievement recognition event.

A decorative entrance should be used to establish the theme, and the view upon entering the room should be across a field of beautifully decorated tables. Centerpieces need to be low enough not to interfere with the view to the stage, which should be the focus of the décor. Any perimeter or peripheral décor should not detract from that focus. Living décor is very useful in this situation because it can add layers to help tell the story of the event but can go away before the ceremonies begin so that it does not detract from the recognition.

Telling a story is a way to describe a sophisticated design with complex décor and entertainment that combines to create an experience for the attendees. The following remarks are by Steve Kemble, talking about John Daly, who is quoted extensively in Chapter 7, *Decorating with Flowers:* "John Daly is so good at telling a story. Events should tell a story. Events with all the right elements layered over one another can tell a story. The décor needs to be detailed and layered to tell a story."

Other awards banquets and gala dinners featuring employee recognition can be themed for other purposes, including entertainment. As was discussed earlier in this chapter, the decorator needs to create an internal focus in the event so that the honorees are given appropriate recognition.

Idea Portfolio

# ANNUAL SALES AWARDS GALA

Approached by Tracey Smith, CMP, to decorate the annual award banquet for Thomson RIA, an accounting software company, we were told that they had decided on a Casablanca theme. The event was part of an intensive annual multiple-day sales conference. One of the main goals was for the employee attendees to relax and have fun, but there also would be an awards presentation to the leading salespeople.

We designed the entrance to make people smile and put them in the mood to party. As they turned the hall corner leading to the entrance, they were greeted by a 50 percent scale three-dimensional camel prop in the shade of a funky faux palm tree next to an Ali Baba jar. The entrance was draped in a colorful striped fabric, simulating the entrance to a tent.

The tables, draped with gold satin Bichon cloths to the floor, had two types of centerpieces. The outer tables had 5-foot-tall arica palm fronds rising from 26-inch-tall palace vases surrounded by candles. The inner tables had low "fire-under-water" centerpieces of cylinder candles with the flame under the water level of a clear bubble bowl on a palmetto frond surrounded by candles. The gold banquet chairs at the tables had chair ties, gold rope, and tassels to finish the elegant look of the room. Arica palms around the perimeter of the room created a feel of a lush tropical environment. The focus was drawn to the presentation stage with the placement of 10- and 12-foot-tall lush queen palms.

However, the most memorable part of the décor was the living décor. Upon entering the room, guests were greeted by "Rick" and the "French police lieutenant" and heard the sounds of "Sam" at the piano. These characters from the movie *Casablanca* added layers of interest to the event and heightened the anticipation of the attendees.

## TEAM BUILDING

Team building is a specific discipline related to the study of group dynamics and is an important part of human resources management. From a decorator's viewpoint, team-building events are similar to networking events. The design and décor need to provide opportunities for the guests to interact with one another. Themes can vary widely, as can the team-building exercises, which vary from outdoor ropes courses or similarly demanding physical adventures to facilitated intellectual team challenges.

Décor ideas that work for team-building events are living buffets and interactive bars, such as those described in Chapter 11 under "Entertainment/ Living Décor" and "The Magic of Ice." The kinds of themes that work are the same dynamic themes that were discussed in the material on appreciation events earlier in this chapter. Most team-building exercises require a lot of space, and décor is not a major requirement.

Imagine a fun Olympics weekend for the anniversary of an international company that has a major team-building component. The décor creates the framework for the conference, and all the events are hung on that theme. The team-building events can be exercises that vary from a taffy pull to a pool tournament, facilitated by trained team builders. We have implemented and decorated a fun team-building event like this. For a successful outcome, one must involve a trained and experienced master facilitator from the beginning.

## EMPLOYEE PARTIES

Fun! From start to finish, fun! That's what employee parties are supposed to be about. The décor should heighten the anticipation from the arrival of the guests and add to their experience throughout. The party must be designed for the demographics of the attendees. John Jakob says: "The design is keyed to the goal of the event when there is a stated goal, which quite often there is not. When this is the case, the elements the decorator needs to focus on are the professions of the attendees, the age of the attendees, the ratio of men to women, whether spouses are involved, whether alcohol will be served, and the location of the function." What will give this group a good time? What décor will they relate to? What will make them feel good? For a truly successful fun event, the food, décor, and entertainment need to be integrated so that the guests will be wrapped in an event experience.

Employee parties are holiday-related, specifically non-holiday-related, summer picnics, or incentives, and each one requires different décor. Holiday parties and the multicultural challenge already have been discussed. The decorator needs to know what decisions have been made in this regard. If the winter holiday party is to be a secular Christmas party, decorative elements that work include glass ball ornaments, candles, seasonal greenery and evergreen trees with Christmas lights, poinsettias, sleighs, snow and winter backdrops and props, and Santa and all his reindeer and elves. Fabrics that work with this theme include velvets, tartan plaids, certain heavy brocades, and tapestry fabrics.

If the event is to be entirely secular, drop the specifically Christmas-related Santa elements and the glass balls and do not decorate the trees except with clear miniature lights, creating a winter wonderland theme that can be successful throughout the winter season. If it is to be specifically Christian, angels, nativity scenes, and crosses can be added.

Some holiday parties are themed to tell a traditional story, such as Victorian Christmas, Old World Christmas (usually generically German, Dutch, or English), and the Williamsburg Christmas from Colonial America. These themes add an element of history and hearken back to traditional values of fellowship, hearth, and home. Another variation is Christmas around the world, which can easily become holidays around the world, allowing the addition of Chanukah, Kwanzaa, and Chinese New Year. Sources for Christmas and secular winter holiday decorations are numerous; all prop rental houses, craft stores and many online and mail order suppliers have a vast preseason inventory. However, once into the season, sources become slim and strictly retail, so most event decorators try to tie down their holiday parties in late summer or early fall.

Specifically non-holiday-related parties are typical of many large corporations, especially in the high-tech computer and Internet fields, where there are many non-Christian employees. Some companies have had to deal with legal issues over religious discrimination, and most are sensitive to their non-Christian employees. These companies might have an employee party early in the fall or late in the winter after the first of the year. These events can be almost any theme and usually involve several types of entertainment and activities for different groups, ages, and preferences. The décor runs the gamut, depending on the current style and employees' desires and expectations.

**Employee picnics** are mostly family affairs with something to do for everybody. This makes circus, carnival, rodeo, state fair, and similar themes popular. Other popular decorative themes are the traditional summer themes: Americana, Independence Day, county fair, and beach party. It is also popular to theme the event after a local popular region, because there are many decorations available locally on these themes to service out-of-town conventioneers.

Location is a key to which decorations work, as outdoor locations limit the types of decorations that can be used. In an outdoor picnic, flags, banners, and flowing streamers work well, as do built props, three-dimensional props, and other structurally sound décor. Flats, lightweight décor, and fabric décor must be planned carefully and secured in the event of wind or a storm. Feathers, flowers, and lightly constructed display materials and foamcore décor do not work well outdoors. Décor that will be damaged or ruined by rain or wind should be used only after careful thought and planning.

Picnic décor should be planned along with logistics and operational concerns. Tents may be required for shade and protection from bad weather. Rest rooms, first aid facilities, security, food and beverage service, and the intended flow and crowd movement all have to be considered in planning the decorations. Décor can be used to attract people to entertainments or activities but must not obscure vision and/or traffic patterns. Balloons can be and frequently are used as décor in picnics, but as was mentioned in Chapter 9, *Balloons in Bloom,* they can be a problem outdoors. Wind can turn them from decorative assets into annoyances, and they become frosted-looking as the latex starts to break down upon exposure to sunlight.

**Incentive parties** can be thrown when a goal is reached, when profits soar, or to kick off or celebrate the end of a sales or production incentive program. These parties tend to be dynamic, similarly to appreciation and team-building events, but they must have some really fun components to achieve their goal. Interactive décor works here, as do activities and top-flight entertainment. Decorating the space into separate areas allows mixing and mingling. Spaces should be allowed for both hearty partying areas and quiet areas to accommodate all personality types and moods. Multiple-room venues are excellent for this type of event. If the demographics recommend it, a dance floor with a good band or DJ should be included.

**MONROE'S DANCE FLOOR RULE OF THUMB**

Only 45 percent of the people dance at any time, and each couple takes up 9 square feet.

In a party with 250 guests, only 100 people will dance, which equals 50 couples who will require 450 square feet to dance. A dance floor of either 15 by 30 feet or 21 by 24 feet will be sufficient. These sizes are based on 3-foot by 3-foot square dance floor sections.

This is a rule of thumb and does not apply to crowds with a lot of dancers, dance bands that are so good that everybody dances, and ethnic celebrations with circle or group dancing.

If the event is held in a multiple-room venue, different decorative treatments with themed food and beverage in each area can make for a great party.

The incentive parties and employee parties discussed in the previous section are closely related to those in this one, and the elements used in one can be used in the other. The only differences are in the motivation behind the event and the tendency of incentive events to be more dynamic.

## FINISHING TOUCHES

Corporate events are done for a reason, and the designer and decorator need to know that reason and understand the basic principles of marketing, advertising, public relations, and human resources management. The key to advertising events is ROI (return on investment). The key to public relations events is ROE (return on event), an event-specific, sophisticated version of ROI.

For advertising events, the corporate logo or product should be reproduced often in highly visible places in the décor. In many public relations events, placement of the corporate logo is more sophisticated, as it appears in association with a cause or charity.

Motivation and morale are the underlying forces behind all human relations events: They are all about people. As Steve Kemble says, "The event professional must be able to show the client through marketing expertise how the event will achieve a return on investment."

## DESIGN VOCABULARY

Terms appear below in the order in which they first occur in this chapter.

Internal event
External event
Marketing event
Advertising event

Public relations (PR) event
Human relations event
HR (Human Resources)
Operations event
Retail event
Seasonal event
Tradeshow
Wholesale market
Cultural demographics
The Buzz
Product rollout
PSA (public service announcement)
Appreciation event
Team-building event
Structural event
Jumbotron
PMS (Pantone Matching System)
Visual merchandising
Stretch areas
Courts
Butler service
Supergraphics
Reveal
Drop curtain
Kabuki curtain
Solenoids
Tie line
Grommets
General session stage
Foam core
Fam trip
Familiarization trip
Convention and Visitors Bureau (CVB)
Community event
Stand-alone charity tie-in
Life-cycle event
Employee picnics
Incentive parties

# STUDIO WORK

1. List several possible measurable and objective goals for each of the two types of external events; put each list opposite an event that might have it as a goal. Do the same for several internal events.
2. Write an essay describing a hypothetical product rollout. Describe the goals for the event and explain how the design and decorations that you describe meet them.
3. List 10 operational elements that might fall within the responsibility of the event decorator at any specific event.
4. Write an essay describing a hypothetical public relations event. Describe the goals for the event and explain how the design and decorations that you describe meet them.

# RECOMMENDED READINGS AND RESEARCH SITES

Goldblatt, Joe, *Special Events: Event Leadership for a New World,* John Wiley & Sons, 2004.

Hoyle, Leonard H., *Event Marketing: How to Successfully Promote Events, Festivals, Conventions, and Expositions,* John Wiley & Sons, 2002.

Yaverbaum, Eric, and Robert Bly, *Public Relations Kit for Dummies,* For Dummies, Book and CD-ROM edition, 2000.

ACCEL-TEAM.com—a commercial site offering a lot of basic knowledge on team building and human resources management; a knowledge-based organization based on the west coast of Cumbria, United Kingdom; contains copyrighted information

http://www.accel-team.com

*Advertising Age* (print edition)—the weekly newspaper about advertising generally regarded as the bible of advertising industry; probably of value only to event professionals who specialize in advertising events

AdAge.com (online version)—the electronic version of *Advertising Age;* the two publications do not just duplicate information; worth a casual visit by the event professional on a regular basis to see trends in the advertising industry

http://www.adage.com

BusinessRanks.com—an online business directory; useful for basic research into some businesses, including ad agencies and public relations agencies

http://www.businessranks.com/advertising.htm

http://www.businessranks.com/publicrelations.htm

*Event Solutions* magazine—a great resource for designers and decorators; one of the top two magazines in the special event field

http://www.event-solutions.com

*Special Events* magazine—a great resource for designers and decorators; one of the top two magazines in the special event field

http://specialevents.com

# Chapter 14

# MILESTONE AND SOCIAL EVENTS

*The goal is to allow the client to enjoy the event as if he or she were a guest.*

**—Howard Eckhart, CSEP, TMF**

## IN THIS CHAPTER

You will discover how to design and decorate the many different and varied life cycle and social events.

**Party Design and Decoration**

**Life-Cycle Events**

- Coming of Age
  - Bar and Bat Mitzvahs
  - Debutante and Coming-Out Parties
- Anniversaries
  - Birthday Anniversaries
  - Wedding Anniversaries

**Personal Social Events**

- Holiday Parties
- Social Parties

Many events are held to celebrate a milestone, such as a **bar mitzvah** or coming-out party, or a **life-cycle event,** such as a wedding or the anniversary of a wedding or birthday. Other events are held simply because people are social animals and enjoy the company of others. We call these **personal social events** or **private special events (PSEs)** or simply parties. Parties are unique gatherings that last a brief period of time, held for pleasure and human interrelationship in a leisure environment. In the business world, we call this interrelationship networking; in the PSE world, we call it socializing or fellowship.

Whatever the reason or the apparent lack of one for a party, all parties have goals and objectives. Some may not be stated or even recognized by the host. An event designer or decorator working on a life-cycle event or PSE needs to know the reason the client is giving a party, just as he or she does in working on corporate and association events. Sometimes there is an obvious reason, such as a wedding party thrown after an out-of-town wedding to introduce the new spouse to friends and family who could not attend the ceremony. Sometimes it is a social obligation that is expected of the family by friends in its social circle. Sometimes it is just for fun. Whatever the reason for throwing a party, an event professional who allows clients "to enjoy the party as if they were a guest" will work often.

Howard Eckhart, who supplied the quote that opened this chapter, has over 50 years of experience in floral and event design and is the owner of The Party and Event Designers in Dallas, Texas. He has been an associate of and mentor to the author for over 30 years.

## PARTY DESIGN

Howard says that party design begins when you get to know the client. Interview clients at their homes. Even if the party is going to be held elsewhere, you need to see how they live. "Review the home, the size and style, color palettes, floral preferences, and then develop a folder for them which becomes the history of that client. Today we do it with digital photography and keep the client history files in the computer. Get to know the client and keep records. Social or corporate, they are still the client, and you need to know their lifestyle and characteristics. The addresses where they have flowers delivered can tell you about them. What clubs do they belong to? Where do they like to do big events?"

Private special events are very personal; they reflect the personality and taste of the individuals hosting them. You need to know the host well. While interviewing hosts, Howard says, "Listen to what they say. They know that they are having a celebration. But they may not know yet what they want. Interviewing first-time clients, I tell them that we will have a learning experience together. I learn about you, and you learn about how we work and what we can do for you." Frequently the designer needs to spend as much time getting to know the client as designing the concept for the event.

It is hard to decorate in a vacuum. When the other elements of the party are in place, the decorations follow naturally. If the design has been well conceived, the other elements follow naturally. We discussed in previous chapters how the food and beverage, entertainment, and décor must be compatible. When all the elements interrelate, synergy occurs and the party develops a life of its own. From Howard's point of view: "The designer's vision has to have two levels: the design and the total picture. What is the total picture that will please the client? You need to be a watchdog on all the other elements. Don't interrupt their flow, but communicate with all the other elements so that everybody is on the same page."

The designer also needs to determine the style preferred by the clients or help them develop a preference. "We deal within acceptable lifestyles of the times. Times change. Lifestyles change; you go with the flow, but always in good taste. Styles are not followed as stringently as they used to be. Styles are followed now for the comfort level they give and to meet expectations for an event. The designer's job is to keep the event flowing in good taste," Howard explains.

Designing and decorating social events requires a very broad knowledge of the history of style as well as current trends, because event professionals will be called on to meet many different tastes and preferences. Many times clients will have just returned from a trip abroad and be enthralled with some thing or place they have experienced and want to share it with friends. I have designed settings and decorations based on the Schönbrunn Palace in Vienna; the Hermitage Museum in St. Petersburg (Figure 14-1), Russia; and the Hall of Mirrors in Versailles, France, although I have never visited those places. Knowledge of those locations, the styles in which they were designed, and some of their history was absolutely essential. The research for these jobs is much easier today with the Internet, though, a tax-deductible visit to the location will add depth to the designer's experience and be more fun.

**Figure 14-1**

Cutting-edge, current, and extreme styles may require more research and a suspension of personal preferences. The event designer needs to know something about minimalism, modernism, and past and current cutting-edge design styles. Websites such as the Interior Design Start page (http://go.to/Startpage-Interior-Design) and the Yahoo Business to Business Directory for Interior Design (http://dir.yahoo.com/Business_and_Economy/Business_to_Business/Design/Interior_Design/) are directories that send you to other websites. This offers an incredible amount of exposure to event designers who want to learn about cutting-edge design styles around the world.

## LIFE-CYCLE EVENTS

Most life-cycle events have the advantage that they are already scripted. There are certain things that must take place in order and other things that can or cannot take place at a bar mitzvah in accordance with the traditions of the particular synagogue and rabbi. Certain scripted procedures and practices are followed in any debutante presentation that have been established by the organization that sponsors the event. These policies and procedures remain constant at a specific location or for a particular event but vary widely between similar events. It is absolutely essential that event designers or decora-

Idea Portfolio

### DISASTER AT THE SHUL

A crew from a local balloon company showed up at the Conservative synagogue (the **Shul**) on Saturday morning and began to unload the helium tanks to decorate a bar mitzvah luncheon to be held after the morning service. They were stopped and told that they could not load into the synagogue between sundown on Friday and sundown on Saturday (the Sabbath). The luncheon was without balloons, and the balloon company never had to worry about working in that synagogue again. The company had worked in other synagogues and had not run into that problem, so they assumed that they would be okay this time at this location.

Some synagogues have restrictions about what can be done and who can do it. For example, in the same synagogue a Jewish crew could not work there on the Sabbath, but a non-Jewish crew could as long as they did not plug in anything electrical.

Do not assume anything. Event professionals must learn about the people they are serving and the venue in which they are working. Most venues have a printed list of restrictions, policies, and procedures specifically to avoid this type of embarrassment.

tors become intimately familiar with acceptable practices and standard procedures in every venue and for every society event for which they design or provide decorations.

## BAR AND BAT MITZVAH

A Jewish boy becomes bar mitzvah at the age of 13; this requires him to observe the commandments, qualifies him to participate in religious activities as an adult, and recognizes his beginning adulthood. Most American synagogues (except Orthodox and Chassidic ones) also celebrate the **bat mitzvah** for girls who reach 12 years of age. It has become traditional to celebrate this occasion with a special service in the synagogue, followed by a party. The bar mitzvah party frequently matches or surpasses a wedding reception as an event and is uniquely multigenerational.

Different families have different visions, but each holds it closely, based upon family values and tradition. It is a very important event for the entire family, with a large Sabbath dinner the night before, including all the out-of-town guests. The bar mitzvah boy or bat mitzvah girl will invite school friends, and all family and friends will attend as well as the parents' friends, the grandparents, and older relatives who are able to travel. Different families accommodate the multigenerational aspect differently, from having the honoree and his friends in a separate part of the room to having them in a room totally separate from the adults. During the bar or bat mitzvah year all the Jewish boys and girls from the school and synagogue communities will be bar or bat mitzvah. A yearlong social season for 12- to 13-year-olds ensues.

When designing a bar or bat mitzvah, the professional will work very closely with the family to strive to achieve its personal vision of this once-in-a-lifetime event. There are probably more themed bar mitzvahs than any other single type of themed party. A hobby or interest of the honoree often inspires a bar mitzvah or bat mitzvah celebration theme. I designed a bar mitzvah that was a sports theme seated dinner at which the seating chart was a team roster and each table had linens in the colors of the team, whose name appeared on a pennant rising from a white floral arrangement. I also helped design a Venetian carnival bat mitzvah, complete with gondolier, overlaid with the annual historical fair to create a richly textured fantasy environment for the guests and the honoree. These events give designers and decorators great opportunities to stretch their creative talent at all budgetary levels.

The décor for a bar mitzvah party can be extensive or moderate but should be tasteful, meet the standards of the particular synagogue or congregation, and celebrate the stage in life the bar or bat mitzvah youth has reached. As with many other events, the entrance is extremely important and should set the feel of the theme. The view upon entering the room should enhance the theme of the entrance. As has been described for other events in this text, using layers of décor will create a sophisticated and complex vista with a view to the stage across the room, where the theme is anchored. In bar mitzvahs the stage decor frequently highlights a decorative sign featuring the honoree's name. Detailed table treatment, including themed centerpieces, tablecloths, and linens, shows respect for and will please the guests. This starts with theme **table cards** in the foyer (cards with guests' names and their table assignments) and the way they are displayed and presented to the arriving guests.

In a complex event, living décor is frequently employed. At a baseball bar mitzvah, for example, a talented juggler, acrobat, or magician may be costumed as a professional baseball player and interact with the guests, entertaining both children and adults. Often a DJ is employed to provide music, and a bar/bat mitzvah professional DJ may also serve as the emcee and event coordinator for the evening.

There are many possible elements that may be included at a bar mitzvah: incidental entertainment such as souvenir photos, caricaturists, and tattoo (temporary) artists. A video of the honoree's life may be part of the evening, and a candle-lighting service honoring special people in the young person's life may be included. Dancers may be brought in to entertain and teach current dance steps to the guests. Activities and entertainment must be keyed to the mix of adults, teens, and preteens in attendance, with something for everybody. Professional bar mitzvah designers and decorators need to keep current with "in" bar mitzvah entertainment, and cutting-edge designers need to stay ahead of the party curve (see Figure 14-2).

## DEBUTANTE AND COMING-OUT PRESENTATIONS

**Debutante presentations** and **coming-out presentations** represent the ultimate society party but also recognize a milestone in a young woman's life cycle. Originating in the court of Louis XIV along with the concept of etiquette, the debut party was then and remains today a way to arrange relationships (hopefully leading to marriage) between people of "acceptable" lineage and social connections. Seemingly a relic of bygone days and in America deriving di-

Idea Portfolio

### THE KEYS TO THE PARTY

Guests arrived at the high-tech trusswork entrance featuring photo blowups of exotic race cars for a sports car theme bar mitzvah. Inside the party there were plasma screens showing exotic cars and performance vehicles in action and a dessert buffet with a custom Porsche displayed on a ramp. To put everyone in the mood, guests arrived at the entrance to a valet parking kiosk, where uniformed valets handed each couple a key ring with their name and table number. This was the key to starting a great evening!

**Figure 14-2**

rectly from English aristocratic practices, the coming-out party remains a major social function in many communities and societies around the world, from the Philippines to Bourbon Street.

Debutante parties are usually sponsored by a **social fraternity** or society and increasingly by community organizations, such as the local symphony, as fund-raisers. Other coming-out parties, such as **quincineras** and **sweet sixteen parties,** follow less rigid social structures and are based on common practices among a local cultural group.

The key to designing a debutante presentation is to focus on "the girls." The stage and runway, if they are used, need to be framed in an elegant style that enhances the beautiful young ladies in their gowns. A typical presentation includes the entry, upon being announced, of the debutante onto the stage. In most presentations, she bows or curtsies to the crowd, after which her escort is announced and joins her on stage to escort her to the dance floor.

The easiest design may be the most flattering as the debutante walks onstage in profile and turns to bow facing the audience. Other design approaches have her enter center stage through doors that are paged open for her or arrive down a grand staircase, and in one case we brought her up through the center of the stage in an elevator. One of the challenges to a designer or decorator working on a yearly presentation is the fact that many of the guests attend every year. The challenge here is to keep the presentation fresh with new looks or a new approach to the presentation itself. Sometimes, however, in striving for a unique event, things can get a little silly and one may lose track of the goal. (At one presentation the girls were brought in on a camel.)

Most often the designer is asked to create a wonderful setting to frame the debutantes, and practical considerations such as budget, space, and functionality are the biggest challenges (Figure 14-3 illustrates one way decorators create the illusion of reality and achieve a beautiful effect on a budget.) Stairs, for example, create a wonderfully graceful entrance as long as no one trips and

**Figure 14-3**

falls. One should use visible steps on stage only when the participants are experienced with presentations or have had significant rehearsal time on stage. Otherwise it is best to hold off on employing grand staircase designs until after the deb is safely ensconced on the arm of an escort. Stairs should have railings and be stout enough to be safe if people misstep and need to catch themselves.

Bob Dole, as candidate for president of the United States, once fell after leaning against a decorative railing. Embarrassment could be the least of a decorator's worries. A decorative railing can be legally defined as an attractive nuisance or worse. If a participant suffered permanent physical damage from a fall, significant professional and financial loss could result.

The design principles, processes, and practices discussed in the first part of this book can be applied directly to the design of a presentation stage. In the best of all worlds, the debs would enter from **stage right,** because in Western composition the eye travels from left to right. (Stage directions take the view of a person standing on stage and facing the audience.) Traditionally, the stage picture was a closed composition with all focus downstage center. That is, if one drew a line connecting the points of visual interest from the audience's point of view, they would intersect downstage center (Figure 14-4).

Themed sets usually are created through the use of theatrical settings, as was discussed in Chapter 6, *Backdrops and Props.* They are enhanced with

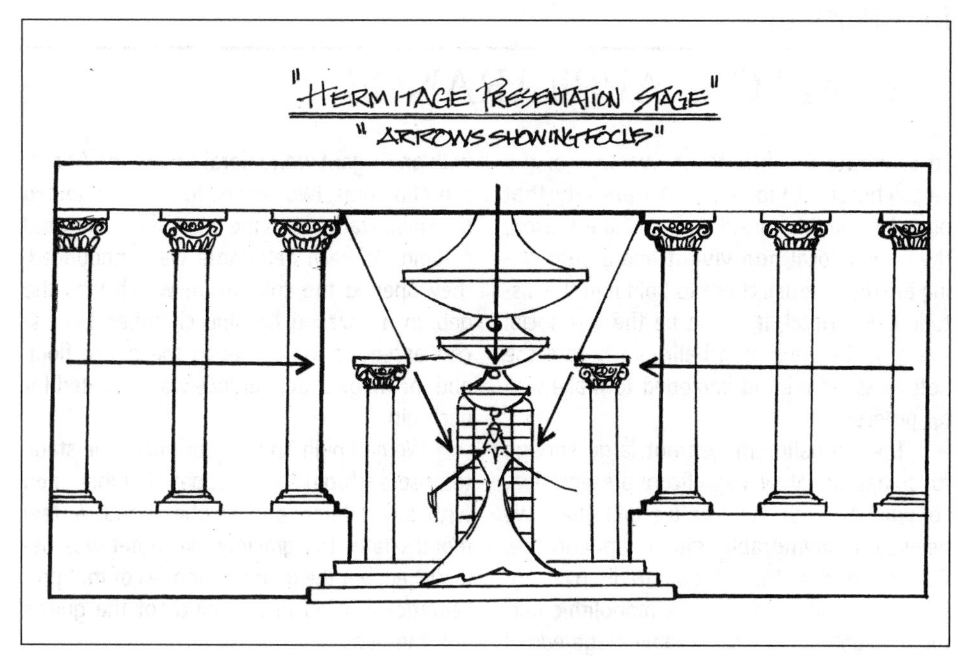


**Figure 14-4**

flowers, lighting, and other exciting decorative elements. However, it is possible to create a dynamic setting without a theme through the use of fabric, flowers, and geometric shapes and forms. The designer must analyze the expectations of the attendees and match the style to those expectations.

Sometimes the designer is faced with the challenge of breaking with tradition. The chairperson or board of directors of an annual social event may want to do an unusual presentation. This can become a business challenge if the designer or decorator chooses to skip that year and risk having someone else take the job in the future or chooses to do what is asked and risk offending future organization leaders. The designer should be the guardian of good taste; beyond that, such decisions become very subjective.

Other coming-out parties include sweet sixteen parties and quincineras. These parties celebrate a young girl's passage from childhood to womanhood. Sweet sixteen practices vary widely according to local social customs, and an event professional may be called on to create a fashionable environment for the event. Teas are popular for sweet sixteen celebrations, along with limousine rides, hair and makeup experiences, and any other "mature" experiences. One lady held her daughter's sweet sixteen party in a popular nightclub early in the day, before it opened. These parties can involve DJs, bands, flowers, and all other forms of entertainment. They also can be a day at the spa for the girl and her friends. There are no rules for a sweet sixteen party except common

Idea Portfolio

## THE MAGIC APPEARANCE

To celebrate the fiftieth anniversary of the Terpsichorean Club, a social fraternity that provided the final presentation of the season, the chair, a local **bon vivant** and a burgeoning **entrepreneur**), chose to hold it in the historic Baker Hotel. It would be the last social event in the venerated ballroom before the hotel was closed and imploded to make way for progress.

The old ballroom was not large enough for an appropriately magnificent presentation, so, working with the creative ball chair, we devised a memorable magic appearance. Guests arrived at the ballroom to discover, under the crystal chandeliers, a monolithic mirrored column atop a silver lamé stage edged with an elegant white floral treatment. At presentation time, two liveried footmen ascended the silver staircase to the base of the mirrored column. As each debutante was announced, they opened the column, in which was the deb, in a dazzling flashing chamber. Her escort ascended to see her to the dance floor, and the magical appearance was repeated for each girl.

We had built an elevator under the stage to raise each girl to the upper chamber lined with silver lamé and strobe lights. A few months later the gracious old hotel was demolished, but the magic memories of that presentation live on in the minds of the guests and the debs.

practice in some communities. The important thing is that the party be appropriate for the personality of the young woman being honored.

The quincinera celebrates the fifteenth birthday of a young girl in Hispanic society. It includes a Mass and a huge reception with a court of honor consisting of 14 couples and the honoree and her **chambelane de honor.** The details are lovely, and the decorations may be extensive. The dresses are always very important, and the party features food and dancing. Decorations can be extensive or moderate, depending on the expectations of the family and their friends and social circle. Although debutante parties have been declining in popularity in recent decades, the Hispanic population of the United States is growing rapidly. Demographics indicate that decorating quincineras is a growth industry.

## ANNIVERSARIES

The dictionary defines an anniversary as the annual recurrence of a date marking a notable event. Celebrations of notable events in life can be some of the most pleasant events to work on. Birthdays, wedding anniversaries, and other such celebrations are a time for reminiscing, joy, and fellowship. Some anniversaries, such as those connected to war, are more somber and must be celebrated with dignity and respect.

## BIRTHDAY ANNIVERSARIES

The celebration of the anniversary of a birthday is one of the first parties people experience as children, and there are many books and resources available for those who are planning birthday parties for children. As event professionals are rarely hired to design or decorate young children's birthday parties, we will spend little time on them except to make a couple of important suggestions. The first is about entertainment. It is extremely important to key the entertainment to the age of the participants. Ask entertainment professionals for guidance and listen to them. Two- to five-year-olds will not appreciate a magician, but they may like petting a bunny. The second suggestion is in regard to safety. Balloons that break can become a choking hazard for infants, along with anything else small enough to go in the mouth.

Birthday parties that employ professional designers and decorators usually start with teenage parties, sometimes related to sweet sixteen celebrations, as was discussed above. If a designer or decorator is employed, the client or honoree is looking for a party that will be unique and memorable.

We once were asked to decorate a birthday party that took place right around Halloween. We employed the usual pumpkins, cornstalks, and tasteful arrangements of gourds with a smattering of rubber bats and spiders, but the party did not get exciting until the living décor arrived: A tall thin man dressed in black walked into the backyard where the party was taking place with an 85-pound, 12-foot-long albino boa constrictor around his shoulders.

Idea Portfolio

## PRETTY IN CAMOUFLAGE

The mother of a 15-year-old girl wanted to give her daughter the party she wanted, and Gale Sliger was asked to help produce it. This was not the usual pretty in pink with feminine ruffles party. This girl was a big fan of the television series *M.A.S.H.*, and the décor was 1950s camouflage. The height of the party was when a Korean War–era U.S. Army tank (with rubber treads) came across the parking lot.

Sometimes unique and memorable events can be achieved through the use of an unexpected theme.

Successful decorating of teenage parties requires knowledge of two things: what's in with current teenagers and the expectations of the honoree and his or her friends. Unless you are a parent of teens, the first is the most difficult. Use friends or colleagues with teenage children for research.

After the teenage years and specifically after the twenty-first-birthday celebration, people tend to celebrate the round numbers: 30, 40, 50, and so on. There is something magical about achieving each of these milestones. Decorating these parties tends to get easier with the passing years, as there is more that can be included that is meaningful to the honorees and their close friends and family. One highly successful decoration is a large **dimensional** carved "30," "40," or whichever decade. They can be carved out of Styrofoam to give them dimension (depth) and mounted on a plywood base. Then they can be finished in glitter, which comes in many sizes and colors. For a nighttime party, they can be outlined with lights or spotlighted.

Many 40- and some 30-year-old birthday celebrations use the over-the-hill theme, which has become a cliché. The professional decorator may supply a coffin that can be used for this type of party, but a good decorator will find a less overused theme to capture the essence of the experience for the celebrants. One option that still has the effect of good-natured ribbing, but with many more opportunities for meaningful personal experiences, is the **roast.** In this type of event, the honoree is given a prominent position in the room where everyone can see him or her, and various people from his or her past are given time to tell moderately embarrassing stories.

Decorating a roast requires a riser or position of prominence for both the honoree and the roasters. A sound system may be required, as hearing the roasting remarks is critical to enjoying the experience. If balloons or other tall decorations are used, attention must be paid to the sightlines. Decorations for a personal party such as a birthday or anniversary should be compatible with the preferences of the honoree, expressing his or her personality and personal taste. For example, a sports theme or even a specific team theme may be right for a "superfan," whereas blooming potted flower decorations could be used for a gardener. This may seem elementary, but usually the planning of the party is done by friends or relatives who are not professionals. It may be the task of the designer or decorator to keep the theme on track with something that will please the honoree. Asking questions and listening helps you achieve this best. The right questions can lead the client to the correct decisions. For example, if the discussion tends to be leaning toward balloon décor, the decorator may ask, "Did you say that she grows a lot of flowers in her garden? Do you think we should consider using live flowers somewhere?"

## WEDDING ANNIVERSARIES

The celebration of wedding anniversaries is a celebration of love and fidelity in which two people reaffirm their commitment to join their lives together. Love is always a relevant theme, and like birthdays, the anniversaries become easier to decorate as the couple celebrate more years and life experiences together. A very popular decorative theme for anniversaries (it also works for birthdays) is the photo album display, in which photos from family albums are selected and inexpensively blown up and mounted on tall display boards so that the guests can peruse them at their leisure. A variation on this that is particularly effective is a walk through the ages, in which guests enter a hall (this is often used as an entrance treatment) that contains photo blowups of images from the couple's life and growing family. If this is used as an entrance, the hall should be quite wide so that people can stop and enjoy the photos without clogging the entrance. Many people will come back to this area later in the party (Figure 14-5).

Another decorating idea is to pick the decade in which the honored couple were married and decorate the event as a 1940s, 1950s, or 1960s party. There are many props and backdrops available from rental houses in large metropolitan areas, and many of them can be shipped or delivered to distant points. Photo blowups of celebrities and reproductions of movie posters from specific eras are available on the Internet. These are great resources, and the current freight infrastructure in most of the modern world brings many sources for decorations within reach, as was discussed in Chapter 6, *Backdrops and Props.*

Other themes are inspired by the couple's mutual interests. If they celebrate their Scottish heritage, a Highlands theme can create a fascinating and exciting event. Divers may like an underwater party, skiers a winter wonderland, and horse enthusiasts might like to recreate a Derby Day. The designer or decorator must research what is meaningful to the honored couple.

Buffets work best for this type of celebration because they encourage people to mix and mingle, sharing nostalgic thoughts and memories. As the crowds become older, more seating must be provided, but conversation areas and groups of small, intimate tables close together encourage fellowship. The entertainment for this type of event should be **wallpaper music.** It should be of the right period and feature the couple's favorite tunes, but mostly it should be unobtrusive.

**Figure 14-5**

In decorating all parties, a good practice is to stick to a theme, color palette, or style of dĕcor throughout the event. Do your research into the people attending the event and the reasons for it and find exactly the right theme, style, and colors. Use them consistently and often throughout the event. Show them in big effective ways at the entrance, throughout the room, and on the stage and then repeat them in the small details that will be seen and touched by the individual guests. Repeating the right motif with variations is like scoring a musical experience. It will create a symphony of memories.

## PERSONAL SOCIAL EVENTS

There are many types of private special events, and they take place in many venues. Residences, country clubs, hotels, restaurants, parks, buses, and airplanes have been used for personal events. As was discussed in Chapter 3, *Venue,* the location determines the design challenges and decoration options. The events discussed previously in this chapter fall into the PSE category, as do weddings. Weddings are such a huge industry that they are covered separately in Chapter 15. The balance of this chapter discusses other types of personal social events more or less in their order of commercial importance to the event designer.

## HOLIDAY PARTIES

Decorating holiday parties is a lot of fun. People celebrate holidays that make them happy, that mean something to them. It is important that the designer understand their expectations and desires and be helpful if he or she shares in the fun of the occasion. Unlike corporate holiday parties that accommodate many beliefs and cultures, social holiday parties should express the feelings and beliefs of the host or the hosting family.

People celebrate the Christmas holiday for its Christian significance and its peace on earth sentiments or for nostalgia, fellowship, and secular goodwill. Decorations can vary from richly detailed Nativity scenes to Santa and his reindeer. Local prop houses have a lot of Christmas props, and many backdrops are available from rental houses around the world. However, do not call up on November 1 expecting to reserve a sleigh and a snowy mountain backdrop for the weekend before Christmas. The reason there are so many decorative items available for rent is that there is a huge demand, which grows as Christmas approaches. Many professional decorating firms start signing Christmas contracts in June and are fully booked by the end of September.

Like all other party decorations, Christmas décor must fit the scale of the venue and the party. A popular decorative item that comes in all sizes is evergreen trees. A full-service Christmas tree yard can supply trees for a reasonable price in any size and species, although trees 12 to 14 feet tall are few and anything taller requires a special order. This type of yard will allow you to pick the trees and then treat them with flame retardant or flock them. It can deliver trees with lights on them and set them up on your schedule in a

Idea Portfolio

### CHRISTMAS COMING WAY TOO EARLY

Many people bemoan the sight of Christmas decorations going up just after Halloween in stores and malls. The fact is, many of the shopping centers that are putting up decorations way too early were the last ones to sign a contract. Although commercial Christmas decorating is a major industry it is seasonal, and there are only a few top-flight firms with proven reputations. Also, many of the decorations that are rigged over people's heads require major construction or assembly and have to be installed when the mall is closed. There are simply not enough days to do everybody's decorations. Everybody wants them up right after Thanksgiving, but only one or two clients can have that date. Many firms base the installation dates on when the signed contracts come in.

water stand or, for one-night parties, a wooden stand if you schedule it far enough in advance.

A simple vignette featuring a sleigh against a cluster of flocked trees with a snowy mountain backdrop is a lovely decorative element in a party. If a photographer is added, it becomes a photo opportunity, and adding a Santa and a couple of juggling elves will make people smile. If the sleigh is large enough for three, an adult couple will want to have a souvenir photo of themselves with Santa in his sleigh. All that is needed is a snowbank for the vignette to sit in (see Figure 14-6).

One way to create a snowbank is to fluff out upholstery Dacron or a similar product made for the display industry. Many decorators use this trick and stop there even though the illusion can be made much more effective. Fluff the snow so that seams do not show and the edges are rounded, then add some **scatter snow (shredded polyethylene).** Finally, lightly scatter **iridescent glitter** on top of the illusion for a complete (and messy) snow fantasy. The flammability of the upholstery material is suitable for the furniture industry but may not be for certain decorations or display applications.

Non-flame-supporting **faux snow** is available from decorator supply houses. The ultimate in snow possibilities may be seen at the website of a

**Figure 14-6**

company called Snow Business (http://www.snowbusiness.com). For faux snow flurries I prefer evaporative snow that leaves no residue, does not stain clothes, and is nonallergenic, nonflammable, and biodegradable. Snowmasters is one supplier of these machines (http://www.snowmasters.com).

Snow and trees remain a standard of decorating for Christmas and other winter celebrations. Artificial trees have the advantage of being made of non-flame-supporting materials and not needing water or shedding needles. (They do not smell as good, but a scent machine can be added for a piney woods ambience.) Adding some living décor such as a tame reindeer, costumed performers, or a living nativity scene can create a memorable event. For outside events in the southern latitudes, there are companies that will supply a snowy entrance for your guests by using manufactured frozen snow.

Decorative themes for Christmas stretch the imagination. They include a Victorian holiday; a Renaissance Christmas; Christmas on the ranch, farm, or boat; and extreme snow sports. Instead of using the traditional decorations such as Victorian shops and vignettes, anything can be made into Christmas with the addition of some pine garland and faux snow. Think about a Caribbean Christmas, Hawiian Christmas, or Australian Christmas. In addition to the many traditional representational and abstract backdrops that are Christmastime standards, we have used tropical sunset drops with snowbanks and snow attached to the drop with a Post-it type of adhesive.

An event professional also may be called on to design and decorate parties for the following holidays in the United States: New Year's Eve, Valentine's Day, Mardi Gras, Saint Patrick's Day, Easter, Independence Day, Halloween, and Election Day. There are also a number of minor holidays that occasionally inspire parties that need decorations, such as Mother's Day, Memorial Day, Flag Day, and Father's Day. Finally, there are local and regional holidays, many of which entail a lot of parties and collateral events, such as Derby Day in Louisville, Kentucky (when the Kentucky Derby is run), and Cinco de Mayo. Cinco de Mayo celebrates the freedom of Mexico and is celebrated both in Mexico, especially in the state of Puebla, and in the United States in the border states. Chinese New Year is a 15-day celebration that generates festivals and parades in communities with large Asian populations.

Jewish holidays rarely require professional design or decoration, being centered on the home or the synagogue. The only Jewish holidays I have decorated have been **incidental theme events.** One was for a bat mitzvah that occurred during Chanukah. Our balloon artist created a giant balloon menorah out of blue and white balloons over the buffet table, using gold foil balloons for the flames. We had the right number of candles "lighted."

In addition to private parties there is a lot of commercial work for event professionals on December 31. The nature of a New Year's Eve celebration traditionally borders on extravagant behavior and allows some extreme decorative treatments that would be considered gaudy, over-the-top, or tasteless at another time of the year.

Lighting and special effects are standards for New Year's parties, with flashing, moving lights changing colors (sometimes called the flash and trash),

Idea Portfolio

## NEW YEAR'S EVE REHEARSAL DINNER

The grandparents of the bride threw a fabulous New Year's Eve party. During the reception a tuxedoed pianist played tunes atop a 4-foot riser surrounded by an hors d'oeuvres buffet under a canopy of gathered bridal illusion with miniature lights. The ballroom was a sea of black and white taffeta plaid that was accented with hundreds of long-stemmed red roses, and a black and white taffeta backdrop behind the band showed "1999" in white neon glowing through silver tissue lamé. Silver latex balloons with long metallic silver streamers filled the ceiling coffers over the dance floor, and slowly moving intelligent lighting scanned through the files of streamers, setting off color-changing sparkles and glittery flashes.

Dinner was served, and the orchestra played until just before midnight, when neon numerals appeared around the "1999." As the bandleader counted down to midnight, the numerals disappeared. When the clock struck midnight, the neon behind the curtain changed to "2000" and was surrounded by flashing and sequencing neon lightning bolts as the robotic lights that had been lazily washing the room with color took off on a ballyhoo of flashing, moving color.

We had done work for these grandparents before, and they had an extremely high level of taste. They were fun people, but they never would have allowed us to supply that much **flash and trash** if it had not been New Year's Eve, a fun night to decorate a party.

sequencing neon, and other animated light source effects being popular. Use props and décor that reflect or enhance glitter and flash from these lighting effects. Mirrors and Mylar-covered and glittered props work particularly well for this type of party. Decorative themes tend toward sophisticated elegance, including elements such as a top hat and gloves, martinis and champagne, New York City, and Times Square.

Valentine's Day (February 14) is a minor holiday, and many Valentine's parties are incidental theme events. They are themed to the holiday because the party incidentally falls close to Valentine's Day. Decorations tend to consist of a lot of hearts and red roses. The decorator needs to let the client know that flower costs soar close to this holiday, doubling and sometimes (red roses) tripling. When hired to decorate a Valentine's Day party, the professional is usually expected to put a new twist on the theme. Hearts and Cupids are still the rage, but now they can fly across the room as gobos in an intelligent light fixture, be spelled out in laser light, or be carved in ice and blown up as part of a pyrotechnic set piece.

Saint Patrick's Day (March 17) is a fun time when everybody in the United States is Irish for a day. Parties with this holiday theme require decorations with the icons associated with the day: leprechauns, rainbows with pots of

Idea Portfolio

## A CELTIC NATURE WALK

While I was designing a weekendlong business-related social event at the Garret Creek Ranch and Conference Center, it occurred to my client that Sunday would be Saint Patrick's Day, and she thought it would be fun to do something for it. We planned and talked up a Sunday morning nature walk after breakfast. The entire group of guests followed me down a path into the woods, where I began what seemed like a real nature walk, describing the flora and fauna of the region. Before we went very far, glittery giant shamrocks started appearing along the pathway and the strains of what sounded like harp music began to be heard.

A little farther along the path we came to a clearing in the woods where a campfire burned, a lovely Irish miss played a Celtic harp, and a leprechaun danced around the fire. Cowboy waiters served Irish coffee and other beverages off the back of a chuck wagon, and the leprechaun kept the guests entertained with magic tricks and juggling feats.

This is an example of an incidental themed event.

gold, and shamrocks. Raising the party above the level of these commercially clichés can be done by adding authentic elements such as **Celtic knotwork, runes** (Celtic symbols and letters), dragons, and lettering styles. Also, using living décor adds texture and layers to the event experience. Like Valentine's Day, many Saint Patrick's Day parties are themed that way because the party incidentally falls on or close to the holiday.

Easter is perhaps the most serious Christian holiday, signifying rebirth, renewal, and salvation. It is a hopeful and uplifting holiday. Few private affairs are held on or immediately around Easter, but many social events are held by churches and social groups and clubs. Easter social events are family affairs involving the usual suspects: an Easter Bunny, Easter eggs, and baby chicks. Easter egg hunts are a common component, and other decorative elements include iconic spring items such as spring flowers, kites, and birds. Hot air balloons work as Easter-related event décor, as do boats and planes and almost anything pretty, uplifting, and outdoorsy. Color palettes are bright pastels with a lot of pink, yellow, lavender, and green against sky blue.

Independence Day parties are not common because this is seen as a family holiday during which many people leave town. However, there are enough of them that a professional decorator will hang many yards of red, white, and blue bunting over the years. Presewn **bunting swags** have a slick, finished look, but if many yards need to be hung, it will be cost-effective to use **tricolor bunting yardage.** If you employ the 20 percent swag rule, an attractive swagged skirt will result. For example, measure out 48 inches of fabric and bring it back 9 inches (20 percent) and staple or pin it. Attachment points can be measured and marked in advance, and a "thinking stick" can be used to measure each length of fabric. That is a stick cut to length, in this case, 39 inches (see Figure 14-7).

The United States flag is a major centerpiece for decorating July Fourth parties as well as for Election Day, Flag Day, and Memorial Day events. It is essential that a professional decorator know the correct ways to display the flag. See Appendix 9, *Displaying the Flag*.

Halloween is a major holiday commercially in the United States, and is growing in popularity in other countries. In recent years Halloween parties have grown in popularity as trick-or-treating has lost favor in major metropolitan areas. Halloween is now the second largest producer of retail sales after Christmas. Some parties are Halloween alternative parties given by people who find the holiday spiritually offensive. These alternative parties tend to be decorated as harvest celebrations with lots of cornstalks, pumpkins, gourds, and autumn leaves.

Halloween (October 31) party decorations can start with a graveyard as an entrance, featuring humorous tombstones and "scary" props and lighting. If you are using gravestones with funny inscriptions, make sure there is enough light

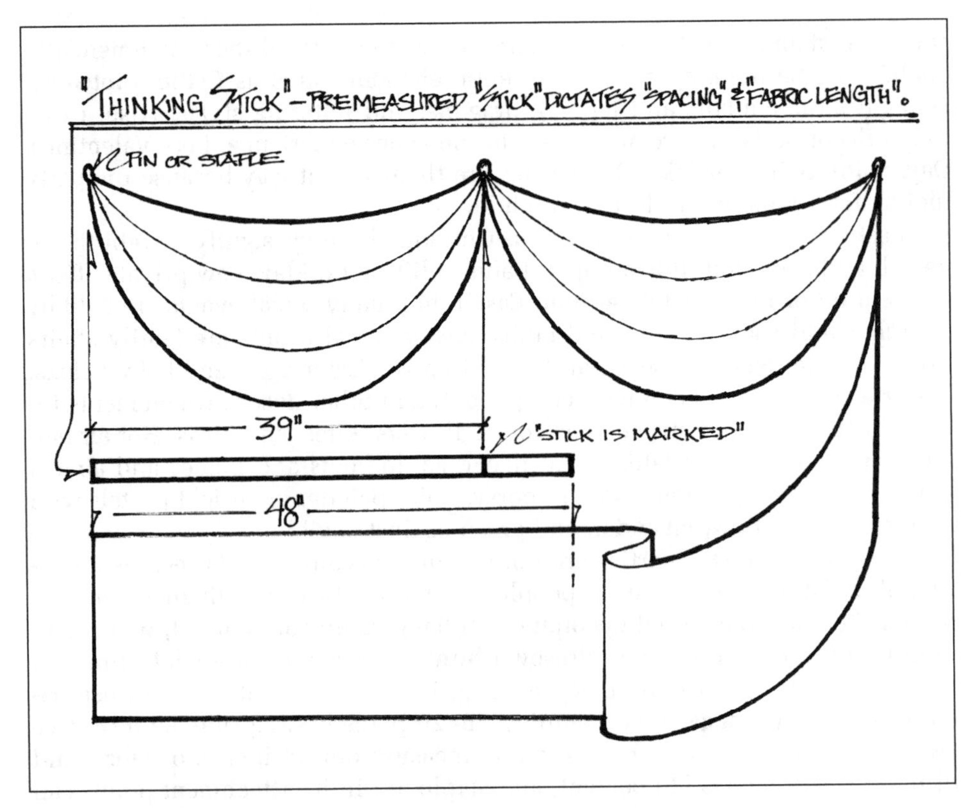


**Figure 14-7**

(usually in blue or green) to read them. This is a good place to employ **fog** and spooky sound effects too. Hands and arms placed as if coming out of the ground, hanging bats, and animated skeletons can add to the spooky ambience.

Cobwebs are the stock in trade of professional Halloween decorators. They can make any normal room or prop into Halloween. Cobwebs that can be stretched manually over furniture, branches, and architecture can be purchased in bags, and there are manufactured webs with spiders in the center that can be hung in corners. There are also very good **cobweb spinners** and **cobweb shooters** that can fill a room with webs in a short time. For an up close and personal effect, secure black threads at head level and let people walk through them in low light, feeling as though they were walking through real cobwebs.

Fill a room with cobwebs, add some sound effects and low-level lighting, and then add fog and you have created a Halloween environment. Most fog machines work on hot oil, and the fog rises as it dissipates. Fog coolers are available that will keep it low to the ground, and there are **ground foggers** with a heavier mist that tends to stay low. The product of **dry ice foggers** most closely resembles outdoor fog and stays low to the floor naturally, but these foggers require more work and attention.

Small decorative props include spiders and bats, black crows, skeletons, and various body parts. Larger props, such as coffins that open, electric chairs, zombies that pop out from behind doors, ghouls that rise from tombs, and skeletons that drop down, are manufactured by several décor studios and are available for purchase or rental. Living décor such as costumed performers and actors can be extremely effective. (They need to be trained and choreographed.) Large props such as those described above, the limited Halloween backdrops available, and the best costumes and actors are all booked early, well before October 31. Halloween is a holiday whose events need to be designed and decorations arranged for early, as there is much demand and limited availability.

Lighting is critical for Halloween parties, and the light effects employed include strobe lights, flickering bulbs, blacklight effects, projected images (using gobos or image projectors), and lightning effects. Colored PAR 38s in blue, green, red, or amber can be used to flood specific areas, and white PAR 38 spots with gel color media can be used to spot certain effects. Green uplighting and blue or red backlighting can enhance a ghoul or vampire (see Figure 14-8).

Hanging fabrics should all be made of flameproof material and be at a low level; flashing lights can blind guests, so the pathways and floors need to be clear to avoid trip hazards. All décor has to be securely rigged or installed so that it cannot be accidentally pulled over on the guests, and exits must be lighted and not blocked or obscured by the décor.

Election Day parties frequently feature the flag and lots of red, white, and blue bunting, as was discussed in the material on Independence Day parties. These parties need large-screen television or video screens where attendees

**Figure 14-8**

can watch the incoming results, and those featuring candidates need a speaking podium and sound system from which speeches can be made. A frequently overlooked item that can become an emergency at the last minute is the television feed. Do not assume that there is a cable, a satellite television, or even an antenna connection available at the venue without confirming it.

Big Election Day parties such as presidential watch parties can be large-scale spectacles that require big floodlights and speakers hung from cranes or boom trucks outside or convention center rigging points. These events, like the fairs and festivals discussed in Chapter 16, become logistical challenges in crowd control more than decorating jobs. Smaller watch parties for statewide candidates or local political parties and internal VIP parties for national candidates can be nice jobs involving table treatment, stages, and room décor. If not blatantly nationalistic, these parties tend to be understated elegance, rich but not extravagant and expressive of the candidate's personality.

Political events such as fund-raisers and campaign events follow the practices for nonprofit fund-raisers discussed in Chapter 12, *Nonprofit and Charity Events,* and in the material on advertising events and public relations events in Chapter 13, *Corporate Celebrations and Ceremonies.* They are not nonprofit as defined by the Internal Revenue Service, nor are they corporate events, but the elements covered in these two chapters apply to political events as well. A few points that are specific to political events will be mentioned here.

The event professional is well advised to keep politics separate from the business and his or her face and identity from being associated with any political affiliation. The exception to this is the niche firm or individual that serves one party or ideology exclusively. For most event professionals the best advice is to keep your political preferences to yourself in business. Another important point needs to be restated: When doing work for political organizations, religious organizations, or any group whose ideology transcends money, get your money up front, before the event.

Local holidays can provide great decorating opportunities. Many parties surround the Kentucky Derby, the Super Bowl, local and regional holidays, and sports events. As with any party, find out why it is being given, who will attend, what the clients expect and learn about any culture with which you are unfamiliar before proceeding and you will produce successful decorations.

## SOCIAL PARTIES

Social events include reunions, Super Bowl Sunday (and other sports celebrations), and milestone events not discussed above, such as graduation. People will find a reason to gather for a period of time in a leisure environment for amusement and interrelationship. In other words, people will party.

Some social parties are given as part of a social season, and some are given for no apparent reason other than that the client feels like having a party. Whether there is a stated reason or not, the basic goal is for the attendees to look forward to coming, have a good time, and leave with pleasant feelings and memories. As a designer and decorator, that should be your primary goal for the event. The party also must meet or exceed the taste level and expectations of the client.

Social seasons vary from country to country and from region to region within the United States. The United Kingdom has its social season from April to August, and although the original debutante season with its presentation to the king or queen was discontinued in the 1950s, the season still exists from

Idea Portfolio

## JUST A COUPLE OF SPEAKERS ON STICKS

As a young designer working on the decorations for a wedding reception, I called Mr. Lester Lanin, whose world-renowned orchestra was flying into Dallas to play for the wedding. Knowing that his orchestra was internationally known and quite expensive, I was concerned that he have a first-class sound system so that everyone could hear him throughout the tent where the reception would take place.

He was very nice and told me exactly what he needed for a stage. When he got to the sound system, he told me he just needed a couple of speakers on sticks aimed at the dance floor: "These people are coming to see and enjoy the bride and her family, not to hear a concert. I don't want the music to interfere with their conversation."

I learned a valuable lesson that night. The music was wonderful, and the orchestra played continuously all night long from memory. But I decided that what had made Lester Lanin really great was that he understood the goals of the party

Royal Ascot to Wimbledon. Throughout the American South it seems that the social season runs from some time after Labor Day until some time just after the first of the year, but this varies from community to community. There are summer social seasons in some communities as well.

Social seasons regularly include the presentation balls discussed earlier in this chapter but more often center on charity and community cause events. There are also private parties given to honor debutantes or recognize other persons or given simply to "see and be seen."

Because most society parties are given for people to "socialize," the goal of the decorations should be to enhance and flatter people. Color palettes should be neutral, running to soft pastels. An accent can introduce color, such as a blue toile fabric employed for texture, but the overall look should be ivory or soft pink, which flatters most skin tones. Vignettes and vistas should be elegant and traditional, not cutting-edge or over the top, unless the host is trying to make a statement. Flowers are always appropriate, as people look good next to flowers. The most flattering palettes for flowers are soft pinks, peaches, and ivories, but extreme colors are more acceptable in flowers than in any other decorative element, so flowers are the safest way to make an extreme aesthetic statement.

Orchestras and bands generally should be on a low stage or on the floor to avoid distracting attention from the guests, and the sound should be directed at and limited to the dance floor.

Decorations should be significant enough to be admired but not so wonderful that they demand attention. Themes can be used for social parties, but subtle underlying themes are more appropriate than are blatant in-your-face themes.

Idea Portfolio

## GYPSY TEA DANCE

I was asked by a very classy society lady to do decorations with a Middle Eastern theme for a tea dance. Upon getting to know her, I could tell she did not want a camel outside and belly dancers. We provided very tasteful floral centerpieces on custom paisley tablecloths and a fortune-teller in a side room draped in similar material. The floral arrangement on the mantelpiece behind the band was a traditional arrangement in Middle Eastern brass containers built around an antique hookah.

She wanted a theme, but it had to be at a level of understated elegance that expressed her personality and taste.

Parties given for no apparent reason usually have a reason, although the client may not have thought about it. In this case, the designer or decorator should find out what the clients want and try to give it to them at the highest possible level of execution. Whether it is a high society black tie function or a backyard barbecue, it should be the best it can be with the resources available. This goes back to a concept that was discussed in the first part of this text: There are always limited resources. This is the case because no matter how many resources have been allotted, the designer and decorator always try to maximize their contribution to the event. Therefore, they can always use more resources, more money, and more time.

These guidelines for social parties are just guidelines. Different cities and social groups within those cities have different tastes and expectations. If we as designers want to see that good taste is maintained, we need to become familiar with the expectations of the social group with which we are working. The best way to do this is to find a trusted mentor within that social group who can guide you until you learn those expectations. Also, as has been stated over and over in this text, the best guidelines come from getting to know the client. Howard Eckhart says we should "spend the time to get to know the clients, their taste, color preferences, and personality, before we ever start designing their events."

# FINISHING TOUCHES

Parties are unique gatherings that last for a brief period of time, held for pleasure and human interrelationship in a leisure environment. Personal social events (PSE) and life-cycle or milestone celebrations are given for a reason, just as corporate celebrations are, and the event professional needs to know the reason. In all social and life-cycle parties, the hosts should be able to enjoy themselves without worrying. Each type of social party requires that the event designer or decorator have knowledge about the society and/or culture, the venue, and the client's practices and preferences.

## DESIGN VOCABULARY

Terms appear below in the order in which they first occur in this chapter.

Bar mitzvah
Life-cycle event
Personal social event (PSE)
Private special event (PSE)
Schul
Bat mitzvah
Table cards
Debutante presentation
Coming-out presentation
Social fraternity
Quincineras
Sweet sixteen party
Stage right
Bon vivant
Entrepreneur
Chambelane de honor
Dimensional
Roast
Wallpaper music
Scatter snow
Shredded polyethylene
Iridescent glitter
Faux snow
Incidental theme event
Flash and trash
Celtic knotwork
Runes
Bunting swags
Tricolor bunting
Fog
Cobweb spinners
Cobweb shooters
Ground fogger
Dry ice fogger

## STUDIO WORK

1. Do research and design a bar or bat mitzvah party to be held in the ballroom of a local hotel. Design a theme party based upon the interests of a hypothetical honoree. Describe the entrance, the stage and table treatments, and the activities as they take place. You have a budget of $12,000 for décor and entertainment.
2. After doing research on the Internet, outline the social season of Atlanta, Georgia, for the coming year. Describe any possible design and decoration opportunities for the event professional.
3. Make a list of Western cities that are likely to have celebrations of Chinese New Year.
4. Design a hypothetical society event, first describing the event and its goals and objectives and then coming up with a short description of the decorations. Include at least the entrance, the stage treatment and décor, and the table treatment.
5. Design a fortieth-birthday party for 200 guests in a local country club. The honoree is a lawyer whose hobby is deep-sea fishing. You have a budget of $8,500.

## RECOMMENDED READINGS AND RESEARCH SITES

Malouf, Lena, *Behind the Scenes at Special Events: Flowers, Props, and Design*, John Wiley & Sons, 1998.

Malouf, Lena, *Parties and Special Events: Planning and Design*, CHIPS Books, 2002.

Reynolds, Renny, Elaine Louie, and Edward Addeo, *The Art of the Party*, Gibbs Smith, 2003.

Tutera, David, and Laura Morton, *A Passion for Parties: Your Guide to Elegant Entertaining*, Simon & Schuster, 2001.

Witkowski, Dan, *How to Haunt a House,* Random House.

AnniversaryIdeas: wedding anniversary information and gifts—a commercial gifts directory that has a lot of detailed information on historical and modern wedding anniversary traditions; has both U.S. and United Kingdom websites
http://www.anniversaryideas.com

Flag of the United States of America—a privately maintained website dedicated to the American flag; has much information regarding tradition and acceptable uses of the flag, including links to other pages offering more details
http://www.usflag.org

Judaism 101: Bar Mitzvah, Bat Mitzvah & Confirmation—a basic primer on bar and bat mitzvahs:
http://www.jewfaq.org/barmitz.htm;
the Judaism 101 website has basic information on all aspects of Judaism:
http://www.jewfaq.org

Mardi Gras New Orleans—contains parade schedules, general information, history and traditions, commercial links, and links to the leading Krewe websites;
http://www.mardigrasneworleans.com

Yard Haunter—contains many Halloween decorations ideas as well as advice and guidance on producing Halloween events; offers various Halloween decorations and effects for sale
http://www.yardhaunter.com

# Chapter 15

# WONDERFUL WEDDINGS

*The most successful weddings leave the bride and her guests feeling as though they have just stepped into another world.*

**—Katy Steffes, Director of Catering and Wedding Coordinator, Four Seasons Resort and Conference Center, Las Colinas**

## IN THIS CHAPTER

You will discover various practices for designing and decorating different types and styles of weddings, ceremonies, receptions, and related events.

**Nuptial Goals and Objectives**

**Ceremony**

Religious Tradition

- Christian
- Jewish
- Secular
- Other Religious, Ethnic, Cultural, and Multicultural Weddings and Unions

**Styles**

- Ultraformal
- Formal
- Semiformal
- Informal

**Themes**

- Traditional
- Nontraditional

**Receptions**

- Seated Dinners
- Buffet Receptions
- Hors D'Oeuvres and Dessert Receptions
- Tented Receptions

**Related Events**

Every little girl dreams of being a princess bride. An event designer and decorator who does weddings and wedding receptions should capture each bride's fantasy and for a magical moment allow her, as recommended by Katy Steffes in the quote that opened this chapter, to feel like she has stepped into another world.

It appears that there are 2.2 to 2.5 million weddings a year in the United States, costing between $40 and $50 billion, excluding honeymoons. Most industry sources agree that the average wedding costs about $20,000, and the statistics provided by Chris Jaeger at Sell More Weddings indicate that 40 percent of this is spent on the wedding reception. It seems that a coordinator is hired for about one-half of all weddings.

From experience we can estimate that most people who hire a decorator spend a minimum of $10,000 to $15,000 on the reception. Extrapolating, this means that a family that hires a decorator will have a reception budget of at least $25,000 to $37,500. We also know that a small percentage of people spend considerably more than this. A small percentage of 2.2 to 2.5 billion still represents significant business.

With the challenge of creating a fantasy world for the bride and the reality of the available resources, it makes sense that wedding design and decoration are an important part of an event professional's services.

## NUPTIAL GOALS AND OBJECTIVES

The goals of a wedding ceremony and celebration are to witness the serious lifetime commitment of two people within a community and then to experience joy and enjoy human interrelationships in a pleasant environment. However, there may be secondary goals and other agendas that need to be met and satisfied by the designer or decorator. These goals and agendas can involve satisfying the conflicting desires of the two families, meeting social expectations, and satisfying the separate needs of the bride and her parents.

### WHOSE WEDDING IS IT, ANYWAY?

Many decisions need to be made concerning the design and theme of the ceremony and reception. One of the first is the bride's palette, or the colors around which all else, including flowers, fabrics, and décor, will be selected. Jo Dermid, national director of sales at BBJ Linen, who contributed valuable information to Chapter 8, *Fabulous Fabric Décor,* has the following design advice regarding the palette: "Sometimes wedding planners bring in a swatch of the bridesmaids' gown fabric and try to match it. You would not walk into your living room with a color swatch and match the drapes, sofa, and pillow fabric to it. Use complementary colors such as slate and navy or silver and platinum."

Deborah K. Williams of Designs Behind the Scenes, Inc., has been an event decorator for over 20 years and has specialized in weddings for the last

Idea Portfolio

## A CHUPPAH OR NOT A CHUPPAH

A charming young couple was getting married in an art museum, with the wedding to be followed by a large reception on the grounds. We were told that there was a minor conflict between the desires of the two families. One family was from a Reform Jewish congregation and did not want a traditional **chuppah,** or wedding canopy, in the artistic environment, and the other was from the Conservative tradition and expected one.

The location allowed us to use several rigging points over the area where the ceremony was to take place, and we solved the problem by flying a floral canopy that looked very much like a chuppah. However, technically it was not a chuppah because the flowering vine that reached toward the earth at the four corners never quite touched it.

It was enough like a chuppah for the groom's family and the rabbi, who used it as a metaphor in the wedding sermon, yet it was sufficiently artistic to satisfy the taste of the bride's family, see Figure 15-3 on page 334.

A wedding designer or decorator will be called on to meet these types of multiple agendas.

5 years. She believes in letting the bride have the colors and flowers she wants and likes. "Let the bride have what she wants," she says, "Whose wedding is it, anyway? The designer's? The coordinator's?"

Deborah is correct that an event professional should not allow his or her aesthetic preferences to take precedence over the bride's. However, although the bride and her mother usually work together on these decisions, there are times when the bride does not get to make them. Sometimes the mother of the bride, a valued friend of the family, or even the father of the bride has the final responsibility for the aesthetic decisions. This can be due to family dynamics, because the bride is away at school, or because the bride is not interested in making them. It is important that the event professional determine early on who has aesthetic influence or will make the final aesthetic decisions as well as the budget decisions.

Many of today's brides are older and have professional careers and strong opinions about what they want. Deborah Williams says of today's brides: "They are more educated, in their midtwenties to midthirties, and the groom is often involved as well. Then there is the Internet. More girls are going there every year to find vendors. Many of these are girls who want to do the wedding themselves. They may be looking for arches or columns to rent."

## SECOND WEDDINGS

Second weddings tend to be smaller affairs, sophisticated but not lavish. It is common for the older children to serve as attendants at the ceremony. Although smaller than a first wedding, this is still a serious commitment

## DECIDING WHO IS IN CHARGE

During our first meeting with a bride and her mother, we could not fail to notice some tense moments between them. The mother would say something about fabric, and the daughter would disagree with her. The bride would say something about flowers, and the mother would disagree with her. They obviously had issues about who was going to make those decisions. After 20 or 30 minutes of this, the mother of the bride took a deep breath and turned to her daughter.

"Let's get something straight," she said. "This is going to be my wedding. When you have a daughter getting married, you can have your wedding."

Everyone relaxed after that, and we finished the meeting. The bride appeared to be happy throughout the remainder of the experience, and we produced a stunning wedding and reception several months later.

The event designer or decorator needs to understand that relationships and people do not always behave the way we think they should. But then, whose wedding is it, anyway?

between two adults. The reception that follows is usually a relaxed party involving friends, most of whom know one another. The decorations should express the couple's wishes, as they usually host the wedding jointly and make both the aesthetic and the financial decisions.

## CEREMONY

The wedding ceremony varies widely from one religion to another, and some couples may choose to be united in a secular service, especially if they come from different religions or cultures. In some religions the ceremony requires attention from the event professional, while in others the ceremony is strictly a family affair that is conducted in private. Couples who choose secular services can select from whatever traditions they want and frequently borrow practices from various religions and cultures.

Traditional elements of the ceremony supplied by the decorator or florist are **personal flowers,** including bouquets, boutonnieres, and corsages; hairpieces; and possibly a **flower halo** and basket for the flower girl and a ring pillow for the ring bearer. Church flowers and decorative elements may include a garland or ribbon across the main aisle, with guests being seated from the side aisles. There may be pew bows or floral pew markers either on the back two pews and the family pews or extending down the entire aisle, along with an aisle cloth, which is discussed later in this chapter. On the altar or flanking it there can be large floral arrangements, banks of flowers and trees, or a floral or foliage vine.

In many churches a large floral arrangement may be used on the altar, or there may be a pair of arrangements flanking the **ark** in a synagogue. (The ark is a cabinet that holds the **Torah,** the first five books of the Hebrew Bible.) Sometimes columns, balustrades, and urns are brought in, although many churches restrict floral arrangements to containers provided by the church. Candle arches and spirals are also popular with or without floral accents, but arrangements must be made to put plastic below them to protect the carpet from dripping wax, and some churches restrict candles to permanent candles that do not drip (see Figure 15-1).

Most churches, temples, and synagogues have a published list of dos and don'ts and a wedding coordinator who can tell the designer or decorator what is allowed and what is common practice for that congregation.

## CHRISTIAN

Protestant services vary among denominations, but most consist of a procession, a prayer, a sermon and/or ceremony, an exchange of vows, a **benediction,** and the exit. Most ceremonies feature music throughout and possibly readings by friends or family members, and many now include a **Unity candle**

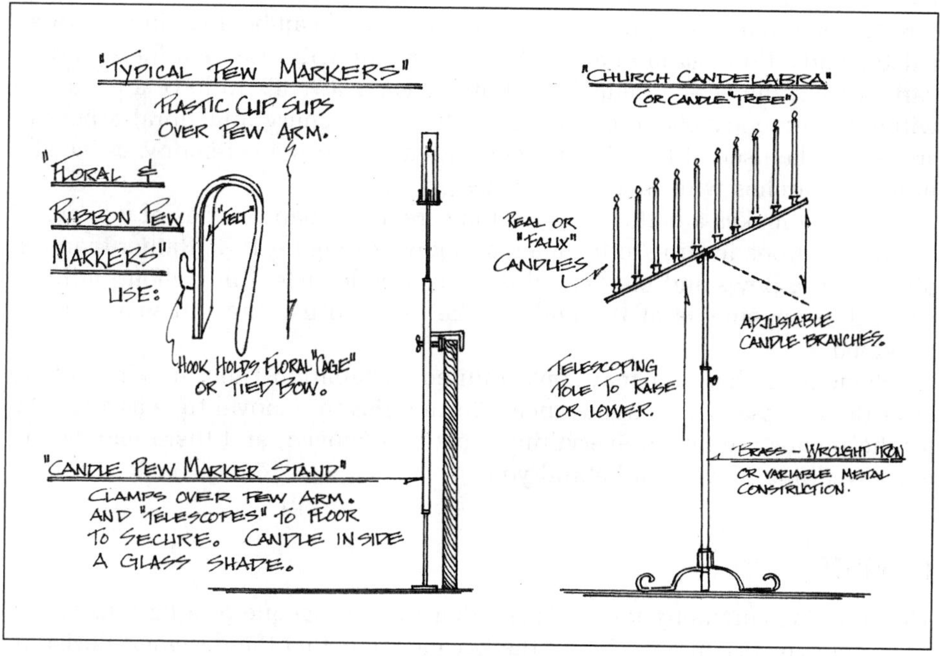


Figure 15-1

ceremony. Catholic services follow the **liturgy** (religious rites) more closely but are otherwise similar to Protestant ones, with a processional, a prayer, readings, a sermon, the blessing of the rings, and vows, followed by the recessional or a Mass and then a recessional. A Mass consists of the service followed by Communion, which will add 15 to 20 minutes to the service.

Decoration options vary depending on the practices of the denomination and the individual church. In some denominations, notably Catholic and Episcopalian, and in some individual churches, the decorator will be limited in the **narthex** (vestibule) to an arrangement on the book-signing table. In the sanctuary, the decorator will be allowed a pair of arrangements on either side of the altar in the containers provided and a limited number of **pew markers.** Most churches require padded attachments for pew bows and markers so that the finish in the pews will not be damaged. It is extremely important that altar floral arrangements not obscure the view of the cross.

Another element that is the responsibility of the florist or decorator is the **aisle cloth.** Although popular with many brides, the aisle cloth is a bone of contention with many decorators. It can pose a trip hazard, and the liability will fall on the installer. Some churches have wood or stone floors in the aisles and will not allow the aisle cloth to be taped down. We choose not to provide one in these cases and prefer not to use one in most cases. If the grandmother falls and breaks her hip, it will ruin the whole wedding.

Many Protestant churches are not restrictive regarding flowers and decorations and have even developed a tradition of using incidental decorations in window ledges, along choir lofts, on doors, and around the alter railing. Wreaths on the doors signify a special occasion and can be done in the bride's palette, and a floral garland across the center aisle will reserve it for the bridal party. (It has the added benefit of allowing early arrivals to have a good seat without everybody else crawling over them.) Greenery and floral arbors or arches can be used at the altar to focus attention on the ceremony, especially in large churches with huge altar stages.

Nothing makes a better vista for the ceremony than a series of wonderful pew decorations leading to the altar, as shown in Figure 15-2. Rather than traditional pew bows and markers, if there is a wide aisle, think about building vertical arrangements at the ends of the pews to use the full visual space provided.

Remember that you may have limited installation time or will have to clear the necessary time in advance. This applies to removal time as well. After the photos are taken, everything must be removed, and there may be another wedding moving in behind you.

## JEWISH

The wedding ceremony takes place either in a synagogue or a hall, usually a club, hotel, or restaurant. One of the key elements that the designer, florist, or decorator can provide is the chuppah, a fabric or floral canopy held up by four

**Figure 15-2**

poles under which the ceremony takes place (see Figure 15-3). Chuppahs can be made of any four posts and a piece of fabric. They can be as simple as four poles holding up a prayer shawl (or **tallit**) or as complex as a flown trusswork canopy covered in wild green vine and potted azaleas, with geraniums and caladium appearing to touch down at the four corners where the airy vine cascades to the floor.

The size of a chuppah is determined by how many people will be under it during the ceremony. The rabbi and the couple must fit beneath it, along with a small table to hold a glass of wine for the ceremony and a wrapped glass for the traditional breaking of the glass by the groom (who steps on it). This service can fit in an 8-foot-wide by 6-foot-deep chuppah. In some services, the parents of both the bride and the groom join the rabbi and the wedding couple under the chuppah; this will require a 12-foot-wide by 9-foot-deep chuppah. Sightlines and the scale of the venue need to be considered in designing the chuppah. The chuppah in a synagogue or temple sits on the **bima,** a riser in the front of the sanctuary. The stage or bima holding the chuppah can be decorated as lavishly or as simply as the family chooses. Flowers, candles, ribbons, and fabric are popular decorative elements and can be used on

**Figure 15-3**

the bima and the chuppah. Floral décor on a fabric-covered chuppah is popular and establishes the bride's palette, which will be carried through the reception.

## SECULAR

Wedding ceremonies that are not in a specific religious tradition are referred to as secular. They vary from nonreligious to generically religious, and the décor needs to reflect the desires of the bridal couple or the family. Sometimes a civil celebrant will perform a wedding between two people from different religious backgrounds and incorporate elements from both religions. At other times the couple are only mildly religious and want to celebrate their love and union in a generically spiritual way. From a design standpoint, these ceremonies are a clean slate and can be created in whatever style and theme pleases the couple.

## OTHER RELIGIOUS, ETHNIC, AND CULTURAL WEDDINGS AND UNIONS

Volumes have been written about different wedding ceremonies, and the reader will find some suggestions in the Recommended Readings and Research Sites section at the end of the chapter. A few words follow on some other types of ceremonies an event professional is likely to encounter.

### Hindu

There is a **mendhi** the night before at which the women in the bridal party decorate the hands and feet of the bride and themselves in ornate patterns with henna dye tattoos. The wedding takes place outside under a canopy and is an ornate and tradition-filled ceremony. Flowers are a very important element in a Hindu ceremony. The popular film *Monsoon Wedding* provides an accurate portrayal of the Hindu wedding ceremony experience.

### Islam

Muslim weddings vary widely from country to country. One Muslim wedding that I worked on was in the Pakistani tradition. The ceremony was a private affair with the immediate family only. There was a mendhi the night before, and decorating it was an interesting and delightful experience. We hung dozens of glass-enclosed candles from the ceiling (see Figure 15-4), on the stage, and on the tables. There was a stage for dancing and lots of pillows on the floor and traditional fabrics draped around the stage. The wedding reception was a seated dinner and featured a raised dais with a decorative fabric

## WHY NOT WHITE?

When I started working with a Pakistani-American family on their daughter's wedding, I was trying to convince the bride and her family that the white fabric canopy we already owned would be ideal for her wedding reception in a local hotel. They were interested because it would be cost-effective, but I could not persuade them to make a commitment to it, which I did not understand.

On the outside chance that I might pick up some ideas, I went to see the newly released movie *Monsoon Wedding*. In that film the father of the bride walks in on the installation of a canopy that the wedding planner is doing in white fabric because he has it and it would be relatively cheap. The father has a fit because white is the color of funerals in that culture. Although that movie was about a Hindu wedding and I was working on a Muslim wedding, the cultures are close enough that I understood the family's reluctance to use that color.

After I had done my research, I stopped pushing white and we provided a lovely lavender lace canopy for the reception.

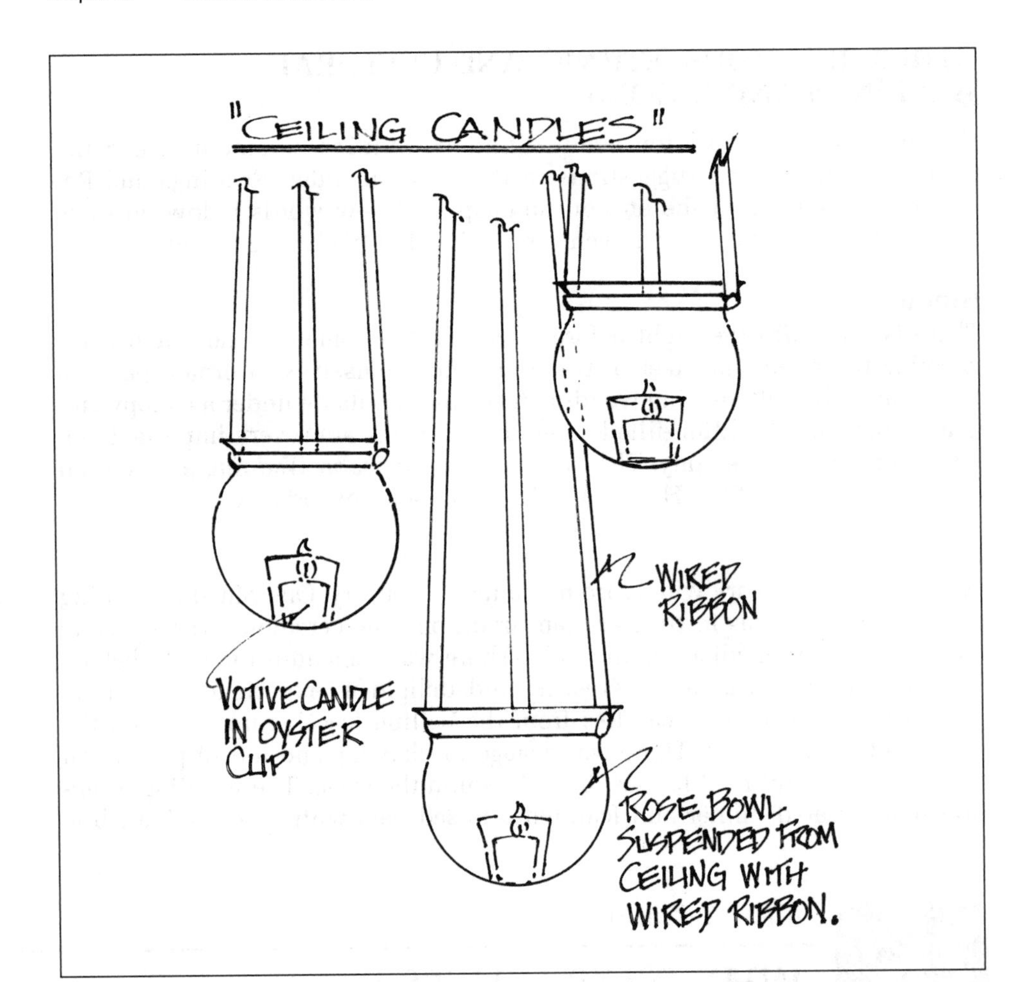


**Figure 15-4**

canopy (referred to in the Idea Portfolio "Why Not White?). There was also a bridal throne for the bridal couple and a pair of chairs for people to visit them, which is the custom.

### Other

There are many other cultures that practice weddings, holy unions, and commitment services, many of which may use the services of a designer or decorator. Buddhist wedding practices vary widely, but some weddings have extensive decorations for the ceremony or the reception that follows. Quaker ceremonies are religious but do not require decorations. Before working on a wedding in any culture you are not familiar with, do the research. If they have decided to use you even though you are unfamiliar with their culture, the clients will help you.

# STYLE

The style of the wedding the bride has selected determines the type of environment the designer or decorator will create for the ceremony and the reception. Traditional Western styles are **ultraformal, formal, semiformal,** and **informal.** The style determines the attire of the wedding party. For example, for full formal the groom and his attendants will sport a morning suit with a cutaway jacket before 6 P.M. or black tails and white tie after 6 P.M. For an informal wedding the groom and his attendants can wear dark suits. The style also determines the type of décor, with lavish classical arrangements appropriate for a formal affair and the option of going more free-form and modern as the level of formality lessens.

## ULTRAFORMAL

Brides who select an ultraformal ceremony expect elegance, tradition, and grandeur. The wedding parties are large, including 10 to 14 bridesmaids who are thoroughly decked out in formal gowns. Guests are expected to arrive in black tie. A fully formal wedding is lush and classical, featuring lots of flowers composed in traditional arrangements, as described in Chapter 7, *Decorating with Flowers.* A fully formal wedding and reception in a modern design style that was minimalist and cutting-edge would draw remarks from purists and traditionalists. (This may suit certain brides.) However, generally one can expect classically arranged flowers in urns, floral garlands, hanging baskets, rich linens, and carefully detailed treatments such as precise napkin folds tied with a flower of the bride's choosing by ribbons in her palette and engraved menu cards at each place setting.

The bridal gown will have a **cathedral train,** which requires a large aisle and will affect the design of the decorations. Pew markers will have to be above floor level or they may catch in the train, petals cannot be strewn on the floor because the train will sweep them up, and there has to be room to reposition the train before the recessional. Fully formal ceremonies are usually large events with at least 200 guests. A fully formal reception includes a dinner and a full orchestra in the evening. Space needs to be allowed for a receiving line. Fully formal weddings earlier in the daytime are followed by a luncheon, which is sometimes, in the European tradition, followed by a dinner that evening. Elegant linens and table décor are appropriate for early or late receptions but should reflect the time of day, with floral prints being appropriate for a luncheon and damasks or brocades for a dinner.

## FORMAL

Elegance and tradition are expected at a formal wedding on a slightly less grand scale than at an ultraformal level; usually there are six to eight bridesmaids. The bridal gown will have a **chapel-length train,** which needs to be taken into consideration by the wedding designer or decorator. As with ultra-formal weddings, the designer should approach this style of wedding with traditional elegance, using symmetrical floral designs, elegant linens, and up close personal details. Any number of themes can work, but they must be executed in a formal style. When the ceremony takes place outside a traditional house of worship, formal ceremonies require traditional designs and décor to re-create the formal feel of the church, synagogue, or chapel.

## SEMIFORMAL

Semiformal weddings usually have small bridal parties (three or four bridesmaids), and the bridal gown is usually street-length. Receptions can feature hors d'oeuvres, champagne, and cake or can be as lavish as the bride and/or the family desire. Semiformal weddings vary from almost formal to almost informal, with most following the pattern of a formal wedding. Decorations and flowers will be elegant but less lavish and may be less traditional. The typical semiformal wedding ceremony includes the traditional elements described at the beginning of this section, and the reception includes the elements described in the beginning of the section on receptions.

Semiformal ceremonies can use more innovative design and décor if that approach suits the bride's personality and wishes. Because there are fewer tra-

Idea Portfolio

### A SUNSET COWBOY WEDDING

The bride wanted to have her second wedding on the site of the house she had grown up in on her late father's ranch. It was decided to place the wedding ceremony on a bluff overlooking rolling hills falling away to a lake in the distance. We built a small stage and backed it with a floral entwined wrought iron arbor, and the ceremony was timed so that the sun set slowly behind the arbor as the couple were wed.

Guests arrived and made their way to the knoll, where we had set out some white wood chairs, and at the appointed time the bride was escorted to the stage by her two adult sons. She was wearing a dressy cowgirl outfit, and the groom was wearing a western-style suit. After the ceremony, the guests went into a red and white striped tent, where they enjoyed barbecue and danced country swing to the sounds of the Levee Singers. The bride's cake was chocolate frosted and decorated with cowboy icons.

The experience of being married on the site of her family's homestead was a meaningful one, and it was enhanced by the design decision to incorporate the sunset and the natural vista into the ceremony. The theme was one that could have been executed at a semiformal wedding by adding some additional flowers, using a white tent, and creating more of an altarlike environment. However, the couple's relaxed but devoted attitude toward one another was reflected in the design of the occasion.

ditional expectations than at formal weddings, there is more freedom for design and creativity.

## INFORMAL

This style has always been popular for second weddings and has grown in popularity in recent years with the relaxing of apparel styles and the increased average age of today's bride, who frequently has a professional career. This style lacks the pomp and circumstance of other wedding styles and is sometimes referred to as casual style. The ceremony can take place anywhere and is as likely to be secular as religious. Only the maid of honor and the best man usually attend the bride and groom.

Most of these are relaxed, modest affairs that do not require heavy decorations. However, the designer may be called on to create a wedding environment in a nonstandard location such as a beach, a yacht, or the top of a mountain. Conversely, the designer may be called on to create an unusual environment in a hotel or club, such as a jungle, unicorn, or underwater theme wedding and reception.

# THEMES

Katy Steffes gives the following advice: "Any party should have a continuing theme, whether it is obvious to the guests or not. Many brides flip through bridal magazines and pick a cake photograph they like or a dress or flowers. There is nothing to tie all the elements together. A successful party is one that is seamless. The food, beverage, location, lighting, flowers, cake, etc., all tie together, creating a memorable moment or experience for the guest." Weddings that have a theme have continuity and harmony and provide a better experience for the bride, her family, and the guests.

## TRADITIONAL

Themes can be obvious, or they can be subtle; in fact, many times the guests do not realize there is a theme. However, the use of a theme provides the glue that holds the event experience together. Traditional themes include historical, romance, the princess bride, a flower theme, a garden wedding, holiday and seasonal themes, and cultural heritage themes.

### Historical Themes

Favorite historical themes, especially for a formal wedding, are classical Roman and ancient Greek, allowing the introduction of statues that can hold real flower baskets and classical columns that can be entwined with flowers or support a heavy floral garland overhead. These props and floral treatments can be used in both the ceremony and the reception. Being classical in more ways than one, this can be subtle enough that no one thinks of it as a theme.

## Romantic Themes

Considered a common and very generic theme, this is actually a subjective theme that changes with each bride and her perception of what is romantic. One bride may think that moonlight and roses are romantic (Figure 15-5), and another that Fred Astaire and Ginger Rogers dancing is the most romantic thing in the world. For a first-time bride, the ideal wedding may feature moon-

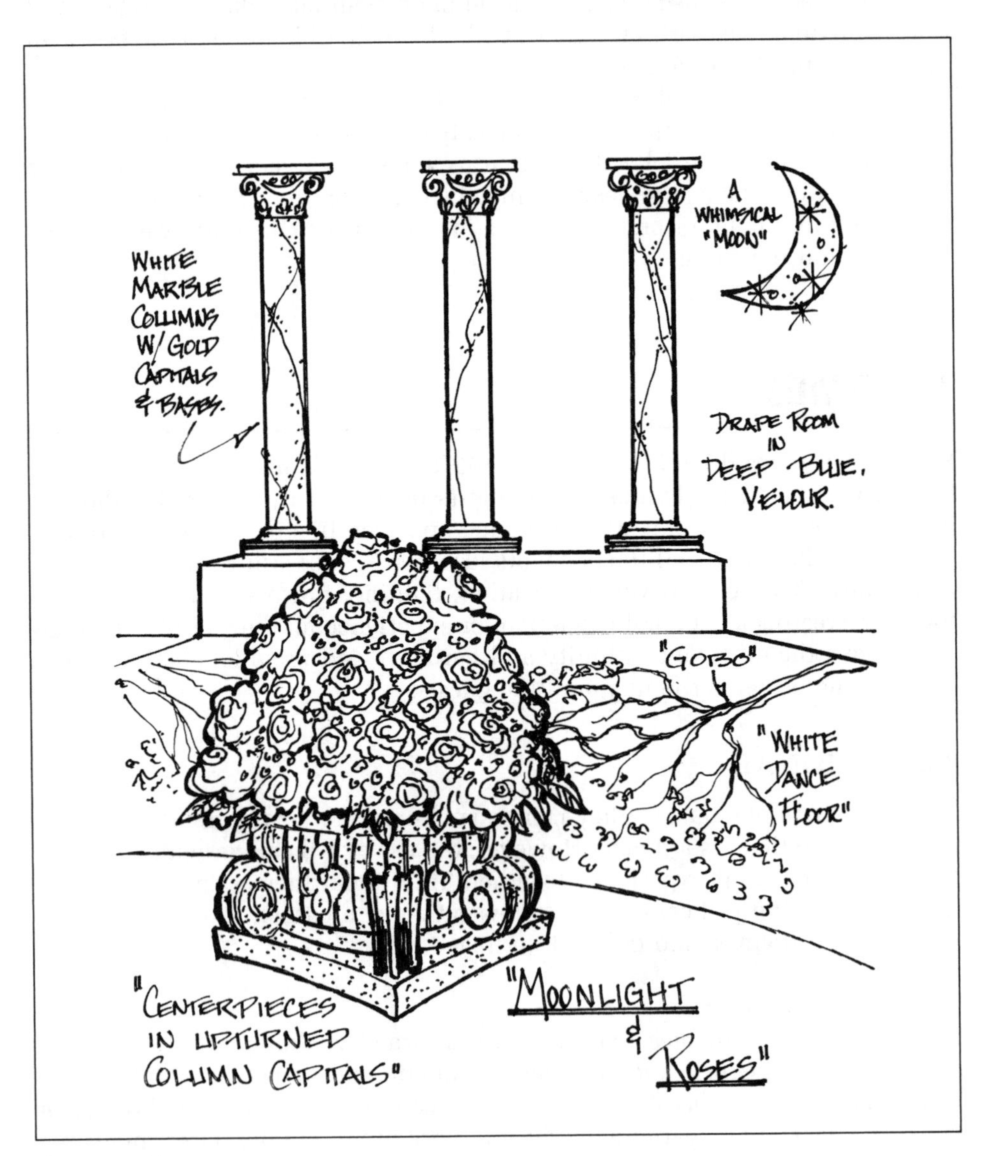


**Figure 15-5**

light streaming through the branches into a blooming rose garden. This effect can be achieved at the reception with gobos projected onto the dance floor and rose arrangements with garden prop accents on the stage and tables. A romantic theme wedding ceremony uses traditional arrangements, and in these examples it features roses for a first-time bride and white lilies for a second-time bride.

A second bride will want 1930s or 1940s dance band music and a formal feeling even if it is not a formal wedding (Figure 15-6). This feeling can be achieved through period floral designs, possibly featuring calla lilies, and by

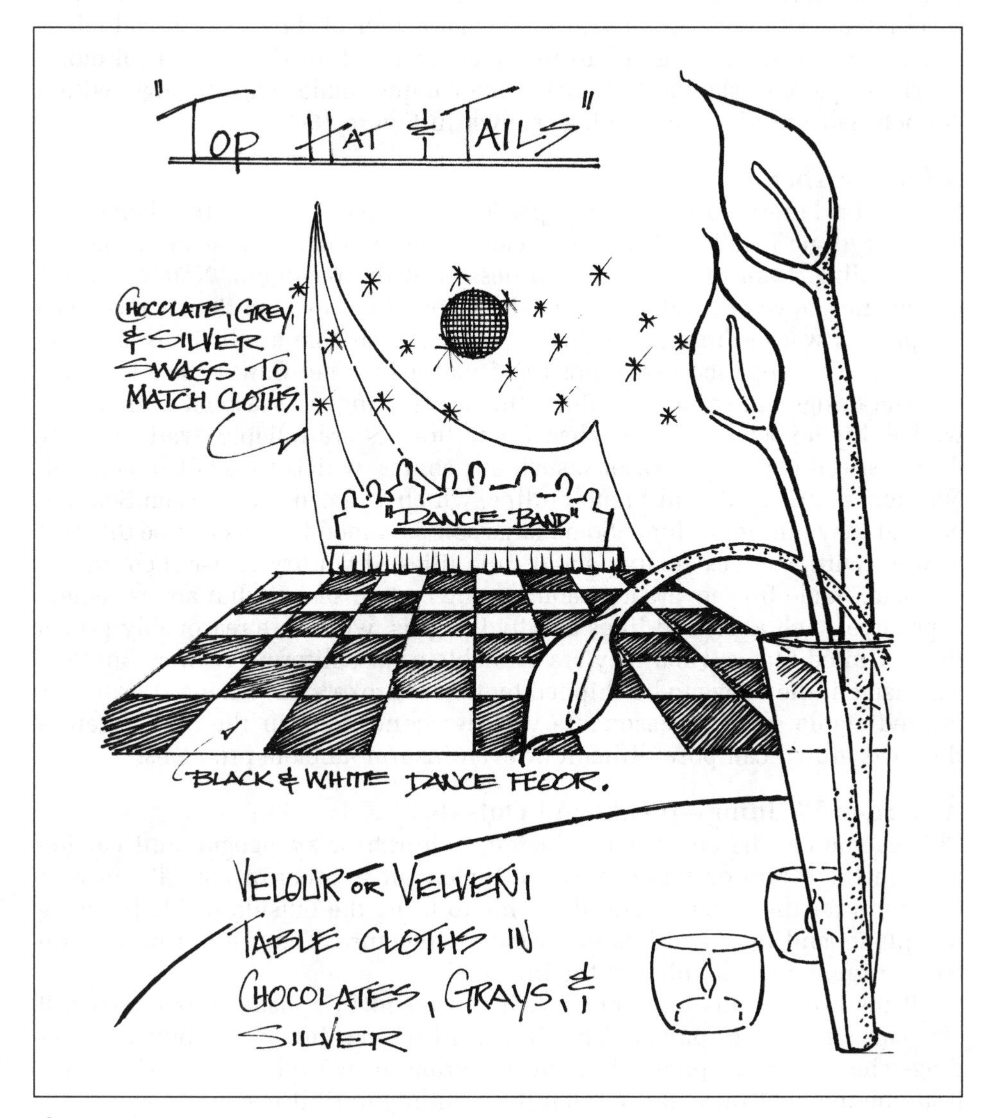


**Figure 15-6**

using silk- and satin-feel linens. A black-and-white ball captures the sophisticated 1930s Art Moderne style and probably would please this bride. If it is an evening affair, she will want a mirror ball over the dance floor. It is the designer's responsibility to get to know the bride well and find out which concept will realize her personal fantasy.

### The Princess Bride Theme

This theme is closely related to the romantic theme, except it is more egocentric. In this theme the bride is the center of all attention. This theme is also subjective, and the designer needs to find out what this particular princess feels is suitably regal. Table layouts for the reception probably will feature a royal table for the bridal party in the visual center of the room. (Royal tables are rectangular tables with a half round at each end. Bridal party royal tables consist of pairs of standard 30-inch-wide banquet tables edge to edge, with a 60-inch half round at each end, as shown in Figure 15-7.)

### A Flower Theme

When a bride falls in love with a particular flower, it can be the theme that ties everything together. The flower can be incorporated into every aspect of the wedding, from the invitation to dessert at the reception. Notable flower themes that have worked well are calla lilies, lilacs or a particular rose. The designer is warned that some flowers are not available at all times, and the bride must be apprised of the practicality of using "her flower" as a theme.

The design concerns for a floral theme wedding are seasonal availability, workability, expense, and weather. Some flowers are reliably available only during specific growing seasons, such as peonies, which are available only in November and April, and French tulips, which you can get between September and May but not in June. Some large soft-stemmed flowers can be difficult to work with, such as amaryllis and calla lilies, if you try to use them in floral foam. Some flowers are available during certain seasons but are extremely expensive, such as hybrid lilies and hydrangeas, which are reasonably priced in the United States when they are available from California growers but very expensive if they have to be shipped by flower brokers in Holland. Weather is unpredictable, and unseasonable weather conditions in the area where a flower is grown can pose difficult or even insurmountable problems.

### A Garden Wedding—Inside and Outside

This theme can be constructed inside a church or synagogue and carried through the reception without fear of inclement weather or ants. It can be a lot of fun for the designer and the bride to bring the outside inside by using live plants and trees and lots of garden architecture. The use of running water or a fountain will enhance the illusion.

If the bride wants to go outside, it can result in a magical experience. It also can rain on her parade. The first word of warning is that outside weddings should not be planned for brides prone to worrying; they will worry from the moment they start to plan the wedding until it is over.

**Figure 15-7**

The designer needs to deal with both the aesthetics and the logistics of decorating outdoor events. A natural-looking altar can be built for a ceremony against a beautiful natural setting, but make sure the distant vista of the background does not include a well-traveled highway or an afternoon softball game. Decorations that are perfectly safe and secure in an indoor setting may be subject to blowing over if a breeze comes up. Tall floral arrangements are especially subject to this problem. Outside weddings need to contain a backup plan, which can consist of reserving a ballroom close by or designing a tent into the event.

Idea Portfolio

## OUTDOORS INDOORS

In the ballroom where the reception was being held there were several steps down to the ballroom level at the entrance. Taking advantage of this, we constructed a series of different level stages that appeared to be built right into the steps and covered the steps with canvas that was faux painted flagstones.

The levels had been planned carefully so that we could fit three different small self-contained waterfalls and a small pond on each one. With the addition of a small Japanese-style bridge, it appeared as though the three waterfalls and pond were one meandering brook.

We added large stones, some faux and some real, to the different levels and then covered the visible staging with a combination of faux and real turf. Arranging some blooming potted plants, covering their pots with green sheet moss, and adding a street lamp and a park bench were the finishing touches. The guests seemed to be entering the reception down a garden path.

The effect would have been very nice even without the running water, but the appearance of a running brook beside the garden steps took the illusion to a higher level.

Despite all these warnings about these events, the most memorable wedding receptions I have done have been outdoors.

### Holiday and Seasonal Themes

Seasonal themes are popular, and we have worked on many Christmas and winter wonderland weddings through the years. Spring themes lend themselves to bright floral prints and spring flowers, of course. Summer wedding theme designs usually invoke cool green and blue places such as the beach and the mountains. Fall calls for leaves, and autumnal colors and harvest vegetables can be incorporated into the floral design and décor. Winter themes call for heavy velvets and rich brocades and can use all white flowers or feature deep hues of floral color.

One of the best holiday themes is Valentine's Day, which lends itself to a Victorian treatment with lots of hearts and lace. One can even use Victorian Valentine's Day cards for inspiration or re-create one behind the cake. Midsummer's Eve and May Day naturally lend themselves to lush floral treatments and allow the introduction of certain props that can be woven discreetly into a formal bridal fantasy. A maypole may be centered in front of the bandstand and have spiraling floral garlands leading out to the tables on the perimeter of the dance floor. When subtly designed, the wedding does not have to fall on the holiday to use a holiday theme.

Valentine's Day and Christmas are both romantic and expensive days to hold a wedding. Flowers become extremely expensive around these two holidays. New Year's Eve is surprisingly popular. These are the most traditional and popular wedding holidays as well as the most likely days on which to host a formal wedding.

### Cultural Heritage Themes

A Scottish theme formal wedding is both elegant and fun for a family of Scottish descent. This theme allows—actually requires—introducing the family tartan, which can be a delightful fabric accent. Various Scottish props and prints can be employed as well, many of which are similar to English hunt theme props: knights in armor, large crossed swords, and a blowup of the clan badge. The best part is all the living décor, with the male members of the bridal party in dress kilts with full formal regalia.

When the bridal party dresses in traditional costume, they actually become living décor and add another layer to the visual experience. Such living décor can occur with several Asian-American cultures and with an African-American theme if the bridal couple decide to do a "Roots" theme wedding. African-American theme weddings are gaining in popularity. Other traditional cultural heritage themes are Irish, Chinese, and Polynesian. Heritage themes offer the designer or decorator an opportunity to make the celebratory event particularly meaningful for the participants. However, the designer is challenged by a heritage theme wedding in terms of research and balance: the research to determine what is appropriate for that culture and the balance to avoid clichés and distractions. The theme, however obvious, should not distract from the bride, the ceremony, and the celebration of the commitment.

## NONTRADITIONAL

Nontraditional wedding themes are more obvious and visible to the guests just because they are unusual. They seem to be growing in popularity but still account for only a small percentage of all weddings. They offer business and creative opportunities for an event professional.

Certain fantasy themes can work for a wedding reception if they are executed with sophistication and taste. An angel theme allows the introduction of **putti,** small Cupidlike figures from Renaissance painting and sculptures. A well-designed castle in the sky can float over a dance floor covered with fluffy clouds. A unicorn sculpted from flowers could be the buffet centerpiece. Distinctive themes, however, run the risk of being over the top or too "cutesy" and should be used only when they are the bride's passion.

Renaissance and medieval are among the most popular nontraditional wedding themes. These idealized romantic versions are well removed from authentic ceremonies and celebrations of their times. The designer can use a rich tapestry of fabrics, flowers, and props to weave a twelfth- or fifteenth-century fantasy, creating a romantic vision of King Arthur's court or Romeo and Juliet's Verona.

A beach theme or seaside fantasy can use a dolphin or mermaid motif to capture the feel of the ocean for landlocked lovers. An otherwise traditional wedding can add seashell touches in a palette of cool blues and aqua with a sunshine yellow accent in silver containers. Live fish can be built into the centerpieces, which, using branches and protea blooms, can appear to be constructed from coral and sea anemones (see Figure 7-5).

Fall season weddings have become as nontraditional as a Halloween theme wedding. The designer will be challenged to keep this one tasteful and elegant but can end up with a truly memorable event. In an upscale vein, we once worked on an elegant hunt theme autumn wedding reception. The floral designer created rich hanging baskets, and we filled each door of the country club with velvet drapes of burgundy and hunter green. The tablecloths repeated the velvet motif with tapestry fabric overlays. A large (taxidermy) stuffed wild turkey and a couple of matching pheasants stalked the buffet on a hillock of dried wheat and leaves.

Other themes have included NASCAR themes for racing enthusiasts, nautical themes, and airplane theme weddings for two pilots getting married. Almost any theme can be appropriate for the right couple and their friends and family. We once decorated a friend's yacht for a second wedding. The couple were married by a uniformed chaplain on the upper deck in full-dress U.S. Navy uniforms. It is the responsibility of the designer and decorator to make sure the theme enhances the experience and does not distract from it.

## RECEPTIONS

Receptions are not unlike any other milestone social event except that they have a script and certain decorative elements that usually occur, some of which are unique to wedding receptions. The minimal script includes toasts, first dances, the cutting of the cake, the throwing of a bouquet, and the exit of the bride and groom, with other optional actions and happenings.

Traditional decorative elements include a table for the sign-in book or the sign-in pages if they are presented loose. This table should be raised to bar height if possible for comfort when guests are signing. It also sometimes displays a photo of the bride or the couple and displays the bridal bouquet on a stand or has a small floral arrangement on it. At a seated dinner there will be a display table for **table cards.** There is a bridal cake display, which in recent years often has a groom's cake next to it.

Other typical elements requiring decoration include the bandstand or DJ's stage, which can have an attractive thematic or fabric backdrop and flanking floral arrangements, and the guest tables, which call for nice linens, centerpieces, and decent chairs. A bridal party table, family tables, and/or a sweetheart table (just the bride and groom) usually get special decorative treatment. If it is a buffet reception, the buffet will need a decorative treatment.

The reception should continue the flow of the wedding style and theme. Frequently the ceremony follows traditional patterns established by the church, synagogue, or community, and the theme does not become visible until the re-

Idea Portfolio

## I'LL HAVE A PIECE OF THE ELEPHANT

The most interesting groom's cake we have seen was a standing chocolate elephant with a red, white, and blue blanket at an elegant fully formal wedding reception. The bride and groom had met at a republican national convention. The mother of the bride wanted to surprise the groom with this cake, but it had to be special if it was going to fit into the grandeur of a fully formal wedding on this scale (750 guests).

Gale Sliger hired a sculptor to create the armature, which was a sculpted foam elephant about 30 inches high with a fiberglass platform on its back to accept the actual cake. The chocolate cake would be carved to fit, and the entire creature finished by the pastry chef of the hotel.

The bride's cake was the focus, a 6-foot-high seven-tier confection with three separations, beautifully and tastefully decorated. A handsome chocolate elephant, in scale to the cake and the entire event, stood on guard until it was consumed.

The wedding decorator needs to design a display for the cakes and sometimes even assist the chef with the creation of the cakes.

ception. Some subtle themes never rise to visible recognition by the guests, but they remain to provide continuity. This section discusses how to incorporate the theme and style of the wedding into different types of receptions. Wedding receptions generally are seated dinners, buffet dinners, hors d'oeuvres and dessert receptions, and tented receptions.

Weddings are cultural phenomena and as such change with time. These changes in practices show up first and most often in the reception. Katy Steffes notes about the current trends: "Décor and food have been gaining importance at receptions over the last ten years. Cake and punch receptions are a rare thing. Brides are now budgeting differently than they used to and spending quite a bit more on the reception.

"As for décor, color has been a trend. Very rarely do you see an all-white wedding. Brides are using color in more than just flowers to create a mood. From specialty linens to lighting to food, brides are setting the mood with color.

"As for food, clients are looking for the 'wow' factor. They want things that nobody else has offered. They want to make a statement with the food and beverage. Even the way the food is presented has changed. Décor companies are getting involved in the display of the food items, even working with the chefs to create a tablescape that incorporates the style and theme of the event."

## SEATED DINNERS

Traditional at formal receptions, a seated dinner wedding reception can be held after any style of wedding. Components of the seated dinner that require attention from the designer or decorator are the bandstand or DJ stage, the

**KATY STEFFES'S WEDDING RECEPTION TRENDS**

**CURRENT TRENDS**

1. **Color:** chocolate brown and pink, chocolate brown and blue, shades of white, one signature color and white
2. **Buffet décor:** incorporates interesting chaffers, trays, passing trays, and displayers
3. **Tableware:** china, flatware, and stemware that continue the style and theme
4. **Flowers:** monochromatic arrangements
5. **Food bars:** raw bar, chocolate bar, and candy bar
6. **Interactive food stations:** attendants on hand to educate the guests about the food or beverage being served
7. **Creative containers for food items:** cigar boxes for duck flautas, coconut halves for coconut shrimp, edamame served in Chinese food "to go" cartons
8. **Comfort food**
9. **Clever beverages:** incorporating the bride and groom's favorite drinks or for color or to create a signature drink for the reception
10. **Tapas-style, family-style, and station-style receptions**

**LONG-TERM TRENDS**

1. **Lighting:** nothing changes or creates a mood of a room more than lighting; it is an element of décor that has gained a following and will continue to do so
2. **Live music**
3. **Specialty linens**
4. **Table draping**
5. **Food and beverage importance**

tables, and the cake. Optional decorating opportunities include the entrance, the ceiling, the dance floor, the perimeter, and any patios or outdoor amenities the venue offers.

## Stage

The bandstand or DJ stage and the sound system require access from the floor for the speeches that will be given throughout the evening. It is usually a focus for the room and should be treated as such with props, fabric, flowers, and lighting in the style and theme of the wedding. The technical rider of the band or entertainer will state the size of stage needed. If you are planning decorations for that stage, allow additional space for the decorations. (As an example, the band needs a 12-foot-deep by 24-foot-wide stage, and the decorations will take up 4 feet of depth at the rear of the stage and 3 feet of additional width at both sides of the front of the stage. The actual stage size required will be 16 by 30 feet.) Many decorators ignore the fact that a band needs to fit on the stage and then get upset when the presence of the band obscures their decorations. For essential details on planning functional staging, see the section on staging in Chapter 6, *Backdrops and Props*.

Fully formal dinners usually require a stage for a full dance band or a string orchestra. Formal floral arrangements in the appropriate scale can enhance the lavish mood of an ultraformal wedding. An attractive layout for a full formal dinner in the princess bride theme will feature with a large dance band with the cake display opposite and a royal table for the bridal party centered in the vista between them (see Figure 15-8). Large formal floral arrangements in urns, silver candelabras on the royal table, and a complementary fabric draped behind the band and the cake will create a delightful formal setting.

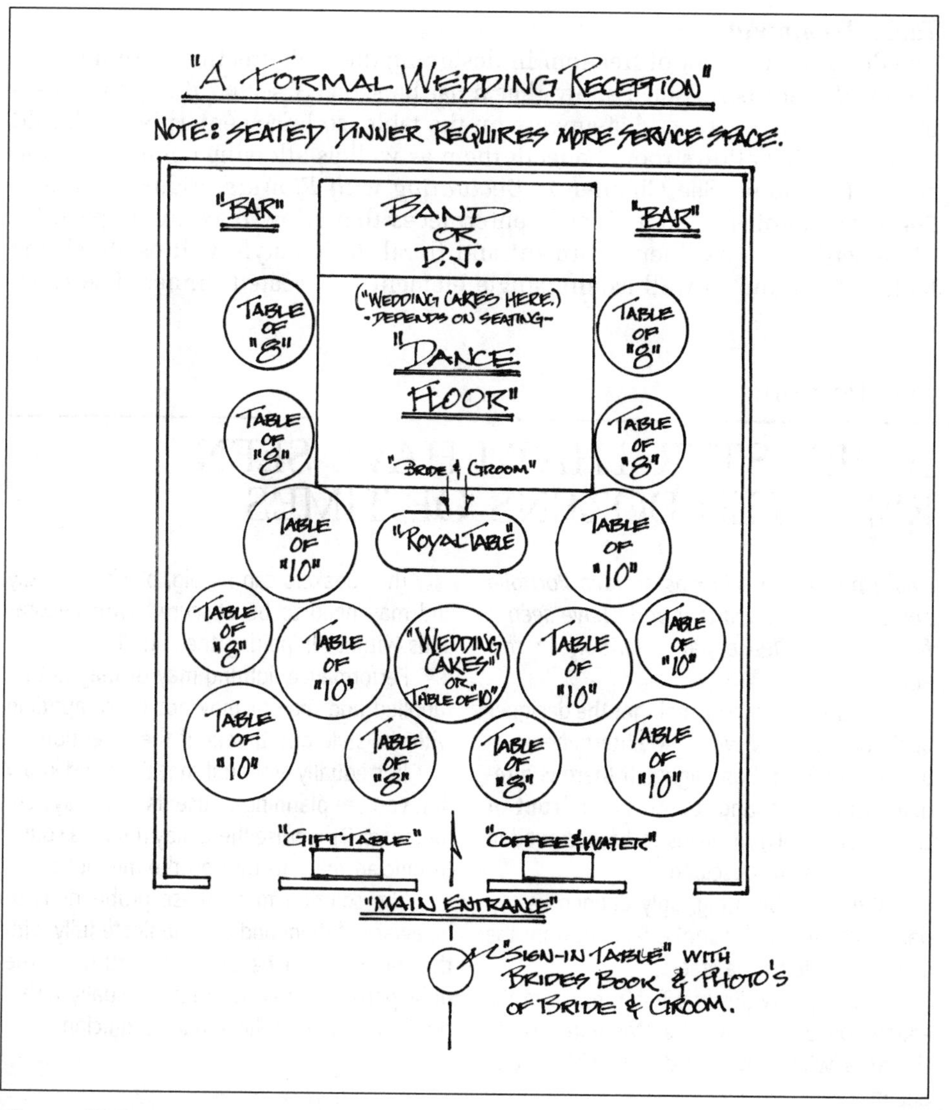


**Figure 15-8**

The designer sometimes will crowd the band in venues where space is tight, and some bands ask for more space than they need. However, an event professional needs to be aware that violin and other string players require enough space to stroke the bow across the instrument without poking one another or the decorations.

At a semiformal or informal wedding a DJ may be employed. The designer may find it desirable to extend the stage size or at least the stage décor beyond what is strictly required by the entertainer to fill up space to the appropriate scale for the venue and reception.

### Table Treatment

The designer has a lot of freedom in designing the table treatment for a seated dinner if there is no stage show that must be seen. A seated dinner means a lot of china, flatware, and stemware on the table, so large centerpieces should be raised. This allows room beneath them as well as allowing communication across the table. (See Chapter 7, *Decorating with Flowers,* Figures 7-3 and 7-4, for examples of large raised centerpieces that allow maximum space for place settings.) The linen treatment and floral design style will establish the look of the room as well as any single element in a seated dinner. The room

Idea Portfolio

## A DISASTER THAT I HAVE SEEN REPEATED DOZENS OF TIMES

*I have put this in a box as an Idea Portfolio because it is so important and I have seen it for decades. Please pay attention to this advice.*

It is absolutely essential that the designer or decorator know what the entertainers are bringing for sound and lights. If there is a requirement for a sound console in the **front of the house (FOH),** it needs to be designed in and concealed or obscured.

There will be a big, ugly dangerous trip hazard cable called a **snake** leading from the sound console to the stage.

A big sweaty guy in a T-shirt may run the sound console. He may be standing next to the area where the guests are sitting and eating.

The speakers can be big, black, and ugly and may need to be obscured with decorations without impairing the sound.

Performance lighting may or may not be supplied and may or may not be compatible with the style and theme of the reception.

It is equally essential that the band know that you are planning to use its sound system for toasts. Otherwise there may not be a sound technician there to turn on the microphone.

The solution to all these problems is to be aware of them and communicate fully with the band. It can be difficult getting to the right person to talk to; that is usually either the bandleader or the sound technician.

in a large dinner becomes a sea of tables, so the first impression one has upon entering is of the tables. Floral arrangements should be pin-spotted if at all possible

It is hard to ignore the chairs because there are so many of them. If a dinner has 30 tables, there will be between 240 and 300 chairs. If they are ugly or incompatible with the style or theme, something needs to be done with them. Sometimes it is easiest and least expensive to replace them with rental chairs. At other times chair covers appear to be the best design decision. I use chair covers for the right event and the right client. Gale Sliger, my mentor and associate of many years, finds them a waste of money. Katy Steffes agrees with Gale. She says, "They are a waste of money. By the time the guest sits on the chair, the cover will shift and the chair ties will come undone. By the end of the night, the room will look disheveled. When you select your reception location, ask to see a sample of the chairs the company provides. If you don't like it, rent a chair, but do not rent a chair cover."

My advice is to use them carefully and only after trying them out with the actual cover on the real chair, sitting in it, sliding around on it, and standing up and sitting down repeatedly. I also suggest that you have them installed by linen professionals, not by the hotel banquet staff or your own crew of carpenters, stagehands, or floral designers. I use chair covers successfully, and when they work, they are a valuable addition to the look of the room. There is a Spandex chair cover available for rent that looks very modern and comes in many colors and more than a few prints. It does not slide around or come loose, and for the right event it is an excellent choice.

## Cakes

The cake is a reflection of the bride on her wedding day and should express her fantasy for the day. It should be placed in a highly visible location (second only to the bride), lighted, and enhanced by its surroundings and presentation. The cake table should sport special linens to set it off, and one way to enhance the presentation is to display it with a groom's cake on one side and an attractive punch or coffee service on the other. Other decorating practices can be used to provide an attractive backdrop or to flank it with beautiful flower arrangements (see Figure 15-9).

Some cakes are decorated with icing alone, and others are decorated with live flowers. Many times I have seen a beautiful cake delivered into a beautiful reception environment, and it just did not look right. If the bride wants a cake decorated with live flowers, it should be done by the designer who is decorating the reception. If you are asked to decorate a cake with live flowers, be aware that several commonly used flowers are poisonous: poinsettias, alstroemeria, anthurium, caladium, and lily of the valley, among others.

An interesting groom's cake is described in the Idea Portfolio "I'll Have a Piece of the Elephant" in this chapter. The advent of the groom's cake has added interest to the cake display and, frankly, to dessert at the reception. Chocolate cakes covered with strawberries or giant chocolate shavings are

GRAPEVINE
&
SMILAX
"8' STEP"
"A CAKE DISPLAY"
A VINE COVERED ARBOR WAS CREATED ON AN
EXISTING STAGE WITH THE ADDITION OF AN 8' WIDE STEP.


**Figure 15-9**

popular. A themed groom's cake reflecting one of the groom's interests, such as fishing, hunting, or flying, is also popular.

A backdrop for the cake should be part of the overall environment. If the setting is a garden wedding, a vine-entwined lattice may be the right backdrop, or the cake can be put in a gazebo. Sometimes a simple fabric backdrop repeating the treatment behind the band, elsewhere in the room, is the right design decision. For a Jewish wedding we once put the cake inside the chuppah while the guests were in a reception in the hotel ballroom foyer. They returned to the ballroom where the ceremony had been held after it had been **turned** for the seated dinner.

Wherever the cake is located and however it is displayed, it must be lighted unless it is outside in the sunlight. Frontlight the cake in white or special lavender to enhance the true colors and then backlight it from two positions 90 degrees apart in blue and pink to create a romantic halo around it.

## Entrance

As in any other special event, you only have one time to make a first impression. If resources allow and the venue is designed for it, create at least a hint of what lies inside to whet the guests' appetite. This can be a floral arbor, a fabric arch, or an architectural structure. If the venue is not laid out in such a way that this works, consider putting it right inside the door to frame the view into the room.

### Ceiling

Ceiling treatments are labor-intensive and therefore expensive, but no other treatment is as visible throughout the event. It is a decorator's cliché that all decorations below 6 feet disappear when the room fills up. This is not entirely true, but it points out the fact that most decorations suffer reduced visibility after the guests arrive, especially at a standing reception. Ceiling treatments do not disappear but remain visible for the whole event.

Hanging floral baskets or flower balls are attractive if they fit the scale of the room and are placed in an attractive composition. Draped fabric and fabric canopies are another treatment that works. A canopy of miniature lights is extremely romantic, but arrangements should be made to put it under dimmer control so that the overall lighting can be adjusted to an appropriately romantic level. It may be most effective to use a ceiling treatment to highlight a single area or a few areas. Using a treatment over the bridal party highlights the bride, and it can be repeated over the bride's cake. We often do a ceiling treatment over the dance floor, which makes it the most romantic place in the room. Another treatment that we originally used for a mendhi and now use for many wedding receptions is to hang dozens of glass-enclosed candles from wire-edged ribbons.

### Dance Floor

Making the dance floor an especially romantic place, as was mentioned earlier in this chapter, enhances the wedding fantasy. In addition to a hanging ceiling treatment, other decorations that work include setting it off with balustrades and urns (Figure 15-10) with floral arrangements and putting a large fountain in the center and letting guests dance around it as if dancing in a European town square. Any appropriate architecture or props can create a special dance floor by edging it or building a centerpiece on it. Some examples are a giant ice carving for an Ice Castle Fantasy wedding, an open gazebo that can be danced through for a Garden or Vienna Waltz themed reception, and tall columns at the corners and center of the dance floor with fabric swagged between them.

### Perimeter

The perimeter of a ballroom generally does not have to be decorated, but the addition of some uplighting, palms with or without uplights, or ficus trees with or without miniature lights softens the room. If resources allow, various architectural pieces can be used with or without flowers and foliage plants. For example, pairs of columns can flank urns on pedestals with floral arrangements at selected locations around the room. This would work for a neoclassical fantasy, a Princess Bride reception, or any number of generic romantic themes. Columns around the room alternating with trees could work for a garden theme reception or a Renaissance or medieval reception, or they could be

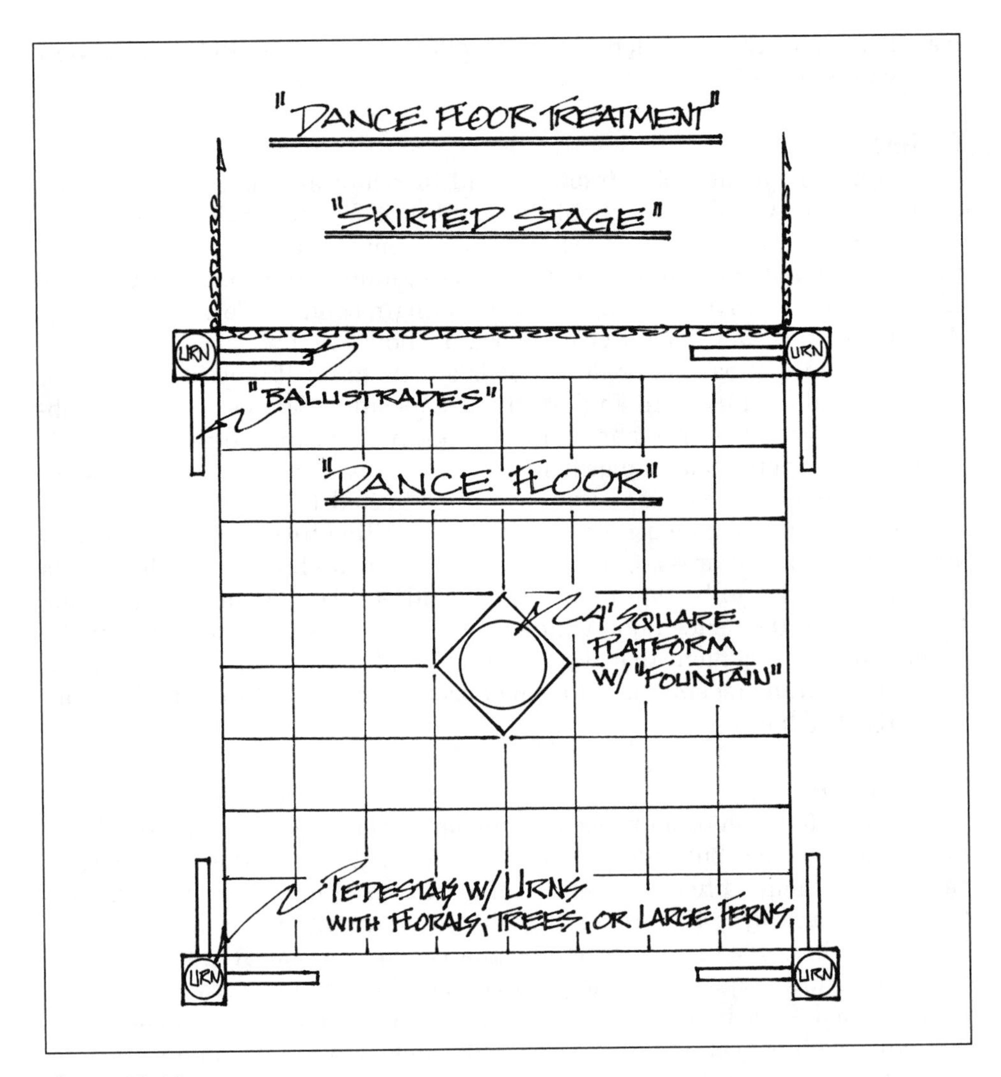


**Figure 15-10**

covered in fabric that matches the draping behind the band to enhance any other style and theme. Another treatment for the perimeter is to use projected gobos, either generic breakups to replicate moonlight through the trees or representational images such as wedding bells, angels, stained glass windows, or the couple's monogram, which also can be projected onto the dance floor.

## Patios

If the venue comes with an outside amenity such as a patio or terrace, some decorative lighting, candles, or even floral arrangements can add to or intensify the romance of the location. Adding a gazebo with miniature lights entwined or a floral arbor that replicates one inside can make an outdoor location part of an indoor event. If there is a romantic view from the patio or terrace, do not do anything to obscure it. Romantic lighting can be added if required, but do not do anything that blinds people temporarily. Also, if a garden path or another irregular walkway is part of the area, make sure it is well lighted for safety.

## BUFFET RECEPTIONS

Although purists expect a seated dinner at a formal reception, buffet dinners are acceptable in most social groups and are preferred for most other styles of wedding. Buffet service is preferred particularly when the couple's families do not know each other, as it encourages interaction between the guests so that the families and friends begin to know one another. All the design practices that apply to seated dinners work for buffet receptions except that there is the added element of the buffet. The buffet has three aspects that concern the designer: the layout, buffet decorations, and lighting.

### Layout

The placement of food and beverage service affects traffic patterns and the flow of the guests, which directly affects the success of the event. Arriving at a party and not being able to get in because somebody put a bar right inside the door and the crowd of guests has backed up to the door creates a terrible first impression. Place the bars deep inside the room and make sure they are lighted and visible. They will draw the crowd into the space where you want them to go. Portable bars in hotels and country clubs can be moved if plans have been made in advance for **back bar** service tables in order to move the crowds.

Back bars hold the glasses that will be used at a bar and possibly some other accoutrements that will not fit on the bar. Portable bars roll and can be moved midevent. Back bars do not move and need to be set up at both locations where they are likely to be used. We do this in large corporate receptions to move the crowd from the foyer into the ballroom on cue.

The placement of buffets involves two considerations: convenience of access for the guests and access to service them from the kitchen. Buffet space required for servicing guests varies depending on the menu and the way it is to be served. Usually a 16-foot buffet is considered adequate for up to 100 guests, or for 200 guests if it is double-sided. However, interactive stations such as pasta bars, carving stations, and omelet or crepe stations, require more room. The designer should work closely with the chef and the catering manager to create a functional and serviceable layout.

The trend away from buffet tables to individual food stations continues and requires very careful planning. People will still gravitate to the shrimp and the meat, so the tables have to be planned carefully or crowds will gather around one or two stations, ignoring the fruit and cheese. Work with the chef in planning food service layouts (see Figure 15-11).

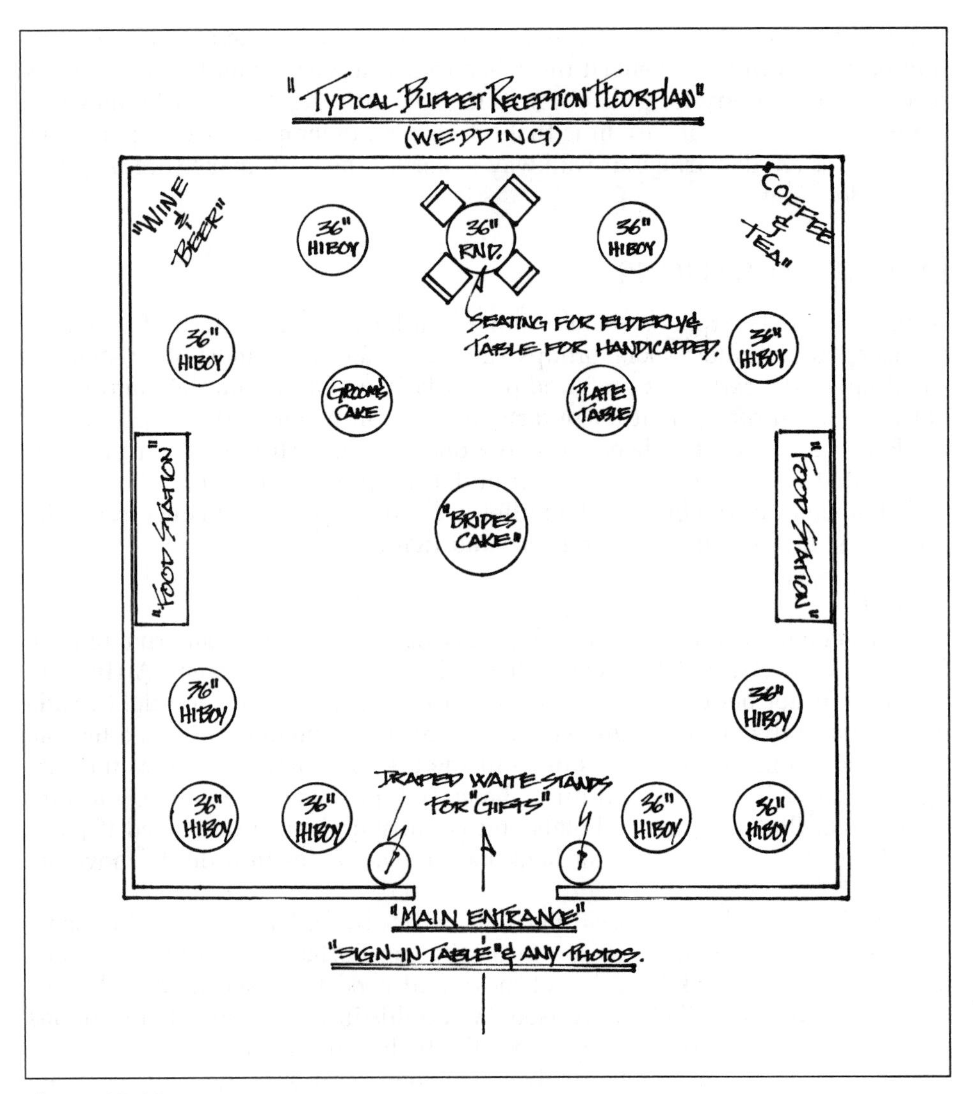


**Figure 15-11**

## Buffet Decorations

Unusual buffet presentations and décor often are requested, as was mentioned by Katy Steffes at the beginning of this section. They require a close partnership between the designer and the chef and his or her catering staff. Contemporary design treatments include monochromatic floral tablescapes, unusual and themed display and serving pieces, unusual table configurations, and specialty linens. Chapter 11, *Unique Decorative Elements,* contains a section on buffet decorations.

### Lighting

Placement of the buffets and/or food stations should be done with lighting in mind. Track lighting may be available and, extension sockets, and small theatrical lighting instruments can be brought in to light the buffet and the buffet décor. Several companies make lighted buffets: plastic tables with lighting beneath them. These lighted buffets are very "hip" for the right event but may still require overhead lighting to light the food and décor unless the food is displayed entirely on and in clear glass or plastic containers.

## HORS D'OEUVRES AND DESSERT RECEPTIONS

These receptions tend to be smaller affairs and are not as popular as they once were, but they can be delightful celebrations for weddings at the right time of the day, which is between mealtimes or late in the evening. Decoratively, the same practices apply as apply for dinner receptions, but with fewer components. Light and airy elegance is appropriate for these receptions, with linens selected for the time of day. One would be less likely, for example, to use big heavy architectural columns entwined with garland and more likely to use open wrought iron pieces entwined with airy foliage and just add floral accents.

Garden theme décor works, as well as foliage plants and trees. Candles and miniature lights add ambience for dessert receptions in the evening. Floral designs should be smaller than they would be for a dinner reception, but no less elegant. Smaller and fewer seating tables and standing cocktail tables should be designed to accommodate two-thirds to three-quarters of the guests. This encourages then to move, mix, and mingle and to accommodate one another. This is a trick used to increase networking in corporate events and works well for increasing socializing and interaction at wedding receptions.

## TENTED RECEPTIONS

Any event that can take place in a ballroom can take place in a tent, and all the design and decorative practices described in this chapter apply. However, there are special considerations, some of which are mentioned above in the section "A Garden Wedding—Inside and Outside." Weather is the most important element; wind, rain, and extreme temperatures must be prepared for in designing and decorating a reception or other tented event. Drainage must be considered, as during a heavy rain a tent will shed an immense amount of water, which must go somewhere. We once arrived at a job site after a heavy rain to discover that the runoff from the 100- by 200-foot **structure** (a very large beam- and rafter-supported canvas tent) had collapsed the 40- by 80-foot frame tent we were planning to use as an entry tent.

Even without rain, a natural grass surface can pose problems at a wedding reception where ladies wear heels and gentlemen show up in leather shoes. I recommend flooring tents for wedding receptions or, alternatively, letting all

Idea Portfolio

## A RIVER RUNS THROUGH IT

The florist had hired me to install some decorations and lighting in a tent for a wedding reception at an out-of-town residence. During the site inspection I noted that the plan was to install the tent against the house and that if there was a heavy rain, there would be no place for the water to go except onto the lawn.

It rained heavily the day before the event, and we arrived at the site to discover that the tent was keeping out the rain from above but the new lawn where the guests were expected to sit was a swamp. The forecast was for continued rain. The father of the bride was distraught and asked if I had any suggestions.

I asked him if he could get a landscaping crew, which he did quickly. I had them trench the lawn along the length of the tent and across the lawn under the tent to drain the water downhill. The family owned a distributing company, and there was a stack of exterior plywood in the warehouse, which he had trucked to the house and laid across the trenches.

I took my **bobtail van** and a helper to the local Home Depot and bought all the green patio floor covering it had. We stapled the green faux turf down over the plywood and set up the tables and chairs. The wedding reception was a huge success, but when the band stopped playing, if you listened closely, you could hear the river running beneath the floor.

Event decorators solve problems.

Idea Portfolio

## GETTING THE LADY'S ATTENTION

Before meeting with a demanding client to finalize the plans for a tented event in her yard, we had worked out all the details, and she was happy with our proposal. However, she informed us that before she signed it, she wanted a guarantee that the tent would not leak if it rained. After exchanging looks with my associate (and boss) to make sure it was all right for me to say what she knew I would say in this circumstance, I replied that we could give her one guarantee: We would happily give her a money-back guarantee that if it rained hard enough, long enough, the tent *would* leak. Not only that, I continued, if the wind blew strongly enough, the tent would blow down.

I went on to explain that we used the best tent installers and the best available rental equipment. We also used tents that were rated to withstand 70-mile-per-hour winds. However, they were not new tents and might have tiny holes in unfortunate locations, and the wind does blow harder than 70 miles per hour in a hurricane or tornado. We did the job, and the client went in with realistic expectations and an understanding that if it rained, there might be problems.

When you are doing outdoor events, make sure your client has realistic expectations and an understanding of the potential hazards.

the guests know that they will be attending a garden reception. Flooring a tent usually costs more than renting the tent.

Tents can be a lovely addition to the decorative environment. They provide places to hang things from and a canvas on which light effects can be projected to add to the decorative ambience and provide romantic indirect lighting. They also add that magic feeling that something special is happening in this place. However, tents leak.

## RELATED EVENTS

In addition to the ceremony and reception, there are other wedding-related events that an event designer or decorator may be called on for, such as showers, gift displays and teas, rehearsal dinners, and bachelor and bachelorette parties.

### SHOWERS

Close personal friends give wedding showers, and in some social groups family friends give prewedding parties to honor the couple. Bridal showers traditionally are given by the maid of honor and also may be given by other family friends and business associates. Rarely are designers or decorators called in unless it is a themed party that requires amenities such as tables and chairs, linens, and flowers. Showers can be held in a home, restaurant, or club and can be themed as a tea, a garden party, or these days a couples shower.

Prewedding parties can be significant affairs whether given as a luncheon, tea dance, or dinner dance and require the services of event professionals. If you are involved in a significant prewedding party, see Chapter 14, *Milestone and Social Parties*.

### GIFT DISPLAYS AND TEAS

A charming practice from the eighteenth century that is waning is the tea party shower held at home by the mother of the bride for gift viewing. Upon receiving a formal invitation, it is appropriate to buy a wedding gift and have it delivered to the home of the parents of the bride. Two weeks before the wedding, guests are invited to a tea to view the gifts that have been received. A decorator may be called in to set up an attractive gift display in a room in the house. Flowers and other amenities also may be required for the tea.

Displaying gifts is very similar to retail visual marketing. Individual items should be shown off at their best, sometimes using various gifts to assemble a place setting or displaying one piece from a set of crystal. For a large wedding with lots of gifts, it is common to bring in tables and risers and custom skirt them. Certain items may need individual pedestals for proper display, and depending on the location, special lighting may be required. A few floral accents properly placed among the gifts enhance the display.

## REHEARSAL DINNERS

Rehearsal dinners can be especially important if there is a large contingent of out-of-town guests. These should be relaxed affairs at which the families and friends get to know one another and enjoy themselves. The family of the groom usually throws the rehearsal dinner, and if they live out of town, the designer may be asked to assist with many of the details, including locating a site and negotiating a menu.

This dinner should be fun and, if it is a themed event, can require fairly extensive decorations. One approach is to decorate it with the theme of the honeymoon destination. The decorations for the rehearsal dinner should not overwhelm the decorations for the wedding and reception the following day, although many rehearsal dinners provide the best memories for visiting guests.

## BACHELOR AND BACHELORETTE PARTIES

Traditionally, designers and decorators are not involved in these parties. With changing times, however, fewer formal weddings, and a more free-form approach to the wedding experience, these parties are growing in size and scope.

Idea Portfolio

## MOST MEMORABLE REHEARSAL DINNER

For one of the most sophisticated and memorable weddings I have worked on, the bride and groom spent several months deciding whether to hold it in Dallas or New York City. They were from New York, and the groom's family and friends were in Germany. They decided on Dallas because all their friends had been to New York and Dallas would be different.

A full formal ceremony was held at 11 A.M., followed by a luncheon at a high society private club. Later that evening cocktails were served under a clear tent in the sculpture garden of the art museum, followed by a seated dinner inside with a string orchestra, after which everybody came back to the tent for dancing to an R&B band until 2 A.M.

It was a fabulous affair, and after it was over, the jet-setters agreed that the most memorable part had been the rehearsal dinner. We had bused them all to Billy Bob's in Fort Worth, the largest honky-tonk in Texas.

What makes an event successful is putting the right people in the right environment at the right time. As sophisticated as the rest of the weekend was, it was nothing special to this group. Honky-tonking was.

Possibly because wedding couples are frequently older and both partners have professions, the lengthy process of showers and teas is giving way to a modern approach to bachelor and bachelorette parties. They are held in exotic out-of-town locations or as exotic cutting-edge social functions in nightclubs, penthouses, and yachts.

## FINISHING TOUCHES

Design and decorating professionals doing weddings need to become familiar with the religious and cultural traditions and practices they are designing within and get to know the bride and her wishes or the wishes of the decision maker or makers. Wedding professionals also need to understand the different styles of weddings and know in which style category each wedding they are working on falls and where it differs from traditional practice.

Different styles of weddings have different requirements and engender different expectations. The wedding design should focus on the bride and be guided by her personal preferences and personality. The design, style, and theme determine the decorations. Decorations should be stylistically appropriate, thematically consistent, and logistically functional.

Appendix 11 contains a wedding flowers checklist.

## DESIGN VOCABULARY

Terms appear below in the order in which they first occur in this chapter.

Chuppah
Personal flowers
Flower halo
Ark
Torah
Benediction
Unity candle
Liturgy
Narthex
Pew markers
Aisle cloth
Tallit
Bima
Mendhi
Ultraformal
Formal
Semiformal
Informal
Cathedral train
Chapel-length train
Putti
Table cards
Front of the house (FOH)
Snake
Turned
Back bar
Structure
Bobtail van

# STUDIO WORK

1. Research a religious or cultural tradition you did not grow up in and write a two- to three-page essay describing the wedding practices in that tradition. Describe opportunities and requirements for a professional event designer or decorator working in that tradition.
2. Describe the design and decorations for a formal wedding with a nontraditional theme not mentioned in this book. Describe both the ceremony and the reception.
3. A Jewish bride is getting married in the middle of December in a synagogue. She wants a Winter Wonderland reception that does not hint at the Christmas holiday. Describe your design for the chuppah and ceremony and explain how you would decorate the reception, which will be held in the hall of the synagogue after the ceremony. The décor budget is $10,000.
4. What are the situations in which you might be called on to design an Asian theme wedding reception in a country club? Describe the decorations you might do for a buffet reception in this theme.
5. Design a semiformal seated dinner reception in a tent. The décor budget is $12,000.

# RECOMMENDED READINGS AND RESEARCH SITES

Chernak Hefter, Wendy, *The Complete Jewish Wedding Planner,* PSP Press, 1992.

Clark, Beverly, *Planning a Wedding to Remember: The Perfect Wedding Planner,* 6th ed., Wilshire Publications, 2002.

Gerin, Carolyn, and Stephanie Rosenbaum, *Anti-Bride Guide: Tying the Knot Outside of the Box,* Chronicle Books, 2001.

Leviton, Richard, *Weddings by Design: A Guide to the Non-Traditional Ceremony,* HarperSanFrancisco, 1994.

McMahon-Lichte, Shannon, *Irish Wedding Traditions: Using Your Irish Heritage to Create the Perfect Wedding,* Hyperion, 2001.

Pandya, Meenal Atul, *Vivah—Design a Perfect Hindu Wedding,* MeeRa Publications, 2000.

Post, Peggy, *Emily Post's Wedding Etiquette: Cherished Traditions and Contemporary Ideas for a Joyous Celebration,* 4th ed., HarperResource, 2001.

Stewart, Martha, *The Best of Martha Stewart Living Weddings (Best of Martha Stewart Living),* Clarkson Potter, 1999.

Scottish Wedding Information—primarily a site promoting Scotland as a wedding destination; contains information and references helpful to a decorator working on a traditional Scottish-themed wedding
http://www.siliconglen.com/Scotland/12_9.html

The Wedding Gazette—a website edited by Sarah Hartman; offers sage advice, ceremonial information, and lots of options mixed with a plethora of commercial offerings; an interesting site for a bride or a student of wedding planning and design
http://www.weddinggazette.com

Wedding Themes—a United Kingdom–based website that has specific design and décor suggestions for specific themes
http://www.webwedding.co.uk/articles/weddingthemes/content.htm

# Chapter 16

# FESTIVALS, FAIRS, PARADES, AND SPECTACLES

*How do we touch the senses? What will your visitors experience?*

**—Betsy Wiersma, CSEP**

## IN THIS CHAPTER

You will discover what it takes to design and decorate successful fairs, festivals, parades, and spectacles.

**Festivals**
**Fairs**
**Parades**
**Spectacles**

Over 600 community **festivals** are held annually in the United States, according to Festivals.com, a commercial website that has been promoting festivals and community events since 1995. The International Association of Fairs and Expositions (IAFE) represents over 1,400 **fairs** and agricultural expositions, mostly in the United States, Canada, and Mexico. The International Festivals and Events Association (IFEA) has 2,700 members in four regions of the United States, plus Canada, Australia, Europe, and Singapore, and has members and member associations in 41 countries. Using Judeo-Christian scriptures IAFE traces the history of festivals back to Tyre in about 558 B.C.E. It also names two Canadian fairs first held in the late 1700s that are still being produced. IAFE was founded in 1885 and held its 115th annual convention and tradeshow in 2005.

The events discussed in this chapter are part of the universe of events that have a life of their own; each area is an industry unto itself. In my years of professional experience, I have had relatively limited experience in these areas and have called on a number of experts, such as Betsy Wiersma, CSEP who contributed the quote for this chapter. Betsy is an award-winning event and marketing specialist who has served on the president's council of the IFEA, the advisory board of *Special Events* magazine, and the International Special Events Society (ISES). She asks the following questions: "How do we touch the senses? What will your visitors experience? How do we create the wow? . . . If you don't have a wow, you might as well go home."

Fairs, festivals, parades, and spectacles are put on for different reasons, mostly for marketing, celebration, or as commercial endeavors. Fairs and festivals market communities, businesses within communities, or industry. Parades can be held in conjunction with fairs, festivals, or events such as sporting events, or they can be stand-alone events that market their sponsors. Spectacles can be used to promote anything from governments to sporting events to Mickey Mouse. Many of these events are commercial endeavors, and even those which are not depend on the profit motive of vendors and sponsors to drive them. Gregory Pynes is director of meetings for Physicians Education Resource, but in nine years with the town of Addison, he produced events that served between 40,000 and 50,000 citizens. "The city [Addison] views special events as marketing," he says. "It has built a reputation for doing events. They have a special event coordinator. The public is used to going to events there. The public is used to going there to be entertained. They have used events to build a permanent 'buzz' about going to their town to be entertained."

The terms *fair* and *festival* frequently are used interchangeably. It is not unusual to see a fair with *festival* in its name, such as a Renaissance festival that is actually a fair, or a weekend festival referred to as a fair, such as an antiques fair. *Fair* also is used internationally to label expositions and congresses. That usage is an exception to this chapter. Colleen Rickenbacher, CMP, CSEP, explains that festivals last three to four days or run a few weekends, whereas fairs last several weeks. In addition, fairs generally have a location with permanent or semipermanent structures, and festivals take place in parks, streets, and locations that normally serve a different function.

## FESTIVALS

Colleen is an award-winning event planner, author, and speaker and the owner of Colleen Rickenbacher, Inc. As vice president of special events for the Dallas Convention and Visitors Bureau, she was responsible for producing many festivals and community events as well as being involved in a few parades. In regard to festivals, she talks about **accessibility** and the way it drives the design and decoration; in this context, accessibility means the attendees' ease of understanding, of being able to figure out where to go, what there is to see, and what to do next.

"Your customer attendees want it easy," she says. "People want it convenient. They want to understand it easily. Festival décor needs to serve a purpose—show me where it is. Show me where to go. You don't need frivolous décor at a festival; it simply needs to point the way to the next attraction, to the food, to the rest rooms. With festivals and parades you have to keep it simple. It has to be big, it has to be high, and it has to be simple. People look up in crowds." Events need to "make a statement," and décor can help them do that. "If it's an elegant affair, make it very elegant." If it's a sports event, make it all about sports; if it's a music festival, make everything about music and have a lot of music. "Work on the buzz! Work on the wow!"

Designing festivals and fairs is largely a matter of logistics, crowd control, and traffic patterns (Figure 16-1). The layout should allow access to food and entertainment without dead ends that would require a crowd of people to double back on themselves. Rest room access is crucial, as is emergency access. The layout should be reviewed and approved by the fire marshal and/or the local emergency medical provider. Appropriate proximity needs to be considered. For example, it would be inappropriate for the beer tent to be in close proximity to the children's area. Pynes says: "Develop different little places for people to go; it adds interest. Create attractive areas for children. Fairs are family affairs, and families do not want to be in the main tent with the beer." Vendor access is also important. "Design a **back-of-the-house area** into your site layout. This is especially important for heavy food events and food areas in all events so that the vendors can load in, stock, and restock without going through the public areas. You need to plan both how the public is going to be served and how the **F&B** (food and beverage) vendors are going to service themselves."

Décor at festivals is limited and should concentrate on important areas, with a consistent look that establishes the brand identity for the event. Pynes continues: "The decorator's perspective must recognize that this type of event is a marketing opportunity. Establish a consistent look for the event and carry it through the program, schedule of events, directional signage, and all advertising. Use good marketing imagery and carry it throughout the event to reinforce that marketing and enhance the visitor's experience. Décor at festivals is important at entrances because it puts people into the mood and can attract them to the event. Signage throughout the event is critical for crowd control and provides another décor opportunity. Pynes says, "Entrances are so important and chain link fence is so ugly, but you have to control access, especially if alcohol is being served. Do what you can to diminish the negative look. Use fencing for sponsor recognition banners. It is ugly, so use the required sponsor recognition banners to dress it up."

Although you do not need frivolous décor at a festival, you do need to make a statement, and the right selection of décor can help you achieve that. Gregory Pynes calls it **eye candy:** "Eye candy is so important. It needs to look as though something special is going on. Expenditures on eye candy and visuals are hard to justify for publicly funded events. But eye candy is as important as having enough rest rooms, because it makes people excited." That excitement is the buzz, and with it people will come and come back. Without it, they will not, and the event will fizzle after the first year or so.

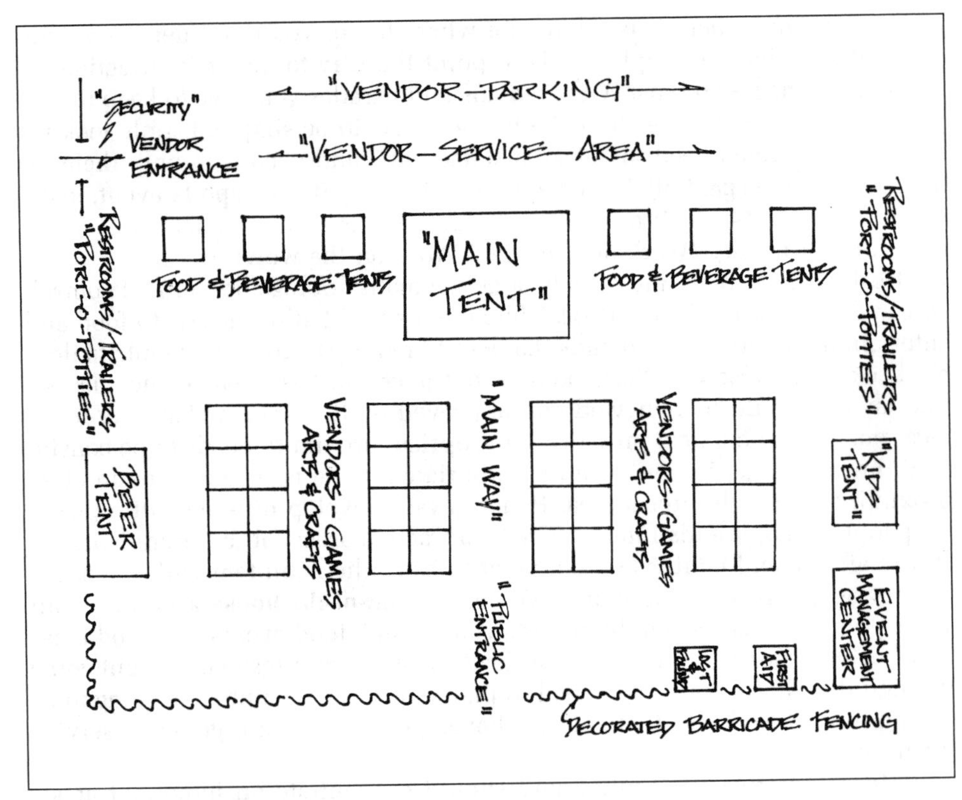


**Figure 16-1**

As Pynes explains, "When Oktoberfest started, it was a one-day event on a Sunday. The city was not sure how it would be received, and the restaurants were unsure what would happen. We had 10,000 people participate. It is now a four-day event that draws over 70,000 people."

Betsy Weirsma has a number of practical design and décor suggestions that have worked for her in doing successful festivals. She reinforces Gregory Pynes's advice about consistency, saying: "Consistency of overall imaging is the most important design factor. Fairs and festivals can look like a hodgepodge. Make the elements that you can control consistent and bold, bold and consistent.

"One way to do that is to choose a color scheme that goes with your logo or uses the colors in your logo and use it everywhere you control. Pick something bold like purple, white, and green and use the logo and those logo colors everywhere."

For creating the wow, she suggests dynamic inflatables and Air Stars (mentioned in Chapters 9 and 13, respectively). She says: "Air Dimensional Design [www.airdd.com] does dynamic inflatables that move and appear to dance. Use the large moving inflatables to mark stages, food, exits, and entrances. The large moving figures become the consistency.

## BIG FOOD EVENT, BIG EYE CANDY

Taste Addison is all about food. It is a weekend festival with food, entertainment, arts and crafts, a carnival, and children's entertainment. In its fourteenth year over 60 of the city's 170-plus restaurants were featured. There was continuous music with a number of popular local bands, both adult and children's activities, and a special upscale dinner Friday night, cooked by internationally known local chefs, that benefited the local regional food bank.

When Taste Addison started, Gregory Pynes wanted to create a statement that would attract visitors and put them in the mood to have a great experience. He contracted with a decorating firm to create a memorable entrance treatment. They built giant forks and knives and faux food. This eye candy became the continuing motif for the marketing, and in 2003 more than 15,000 visitors participated in the event.

Addison has created an event-friendly environment and a city culture. If a city does that and creates events that work, the events will grow.

"Air Stars can create consistency with a wow image. Covered in the daytime with the event logo and lighted at night. Wow!"

Another suggestion involves what she calls **style points:** "Style points are the way people are trained and the way they look. In the way you train, dress, motivate, and inspire your volunteers they become dimensional, dynamic décor."

Idea Portfolio

## WARM AND COZY STYLE POINTS ENHANCE DÉCOR

At an outdoor festival in Indianapolis, a tree-lighting ceremony that took place at Thanksgiving, the weather was always cold. Betsy Wiersma created wonderful warm jackets with the logo of the repeating event embroidered on the back. The festival could not afford to give away hundred-dollar jackets to the volunteers but lent them to the volunteers and gave all of them souvenir T-shirts when they returned the jackets. She also had big Dr. Seuss–inspired hats made that matched the logo colors. Dressed appropriately for the weather, the volunteers went forward into the crowd and about their tasks, serving as living décor at the same time.

Betsy created an imaginative and practical way to add living décor to a festival, using reusable jackets and hats to add color and theme consistency.

**BANNERS AND INFLATABLES: TIPS FROM BETSY WIERSMA**

- Have enough air slits in banners.
- Use proper rigging and weighting in the bottom.
- Partner with professional riggers.
- Have your client pay for an engineering study before using a rigging point that has never been used before.

Betsy goes on to say: "For outdoor summer festivals I like aprons with lots of pockets. Use aprons in your bold logo colors instead of T-shirts, maybe with a gimme cap. The big advantage aprons have over T-shirts is that there is no size problem. When the event is over, the volunteers turn in their aprons for a souvenir T-shirt, or maybe they get to keep the gimme cap." (**Gimme caps** are baseball-style caps with a logo on them, historically given away as a promotional gimmick and now usually sold. "Gimme" comes from "Hey, buddy, gimme a cap!")

Betsy also emphasizes safety and security: "Safety and security issues are huge. Banners are like a sail, and sails move ships. A banner without enough air slits in it once pulled over a lighting rig at a festival I was working on. I had a large 20- by 20-foot inflatable on top of a building. A strange wind occurrence happened, and it was suddenly in traffic."

## FAIRS

Fairs can be seen as annual events rather than special events because of their annual replication of the event experience, but it is impossible to discuss festivals without talking about fairs as well. Fairs are similar to festivals, with the notable exceptions that they seek to attract return visitors and continue for a longer period of time. These two differences affect the design and decoration in one way aesthetically and in another way functionally. To attract return visitors, fairs must offer greater variety and depth of visitor experience. The decorations have to contribute aesthetic details and layers the way they do in a good party, so that the visitors feel that they want to return to discover what they missed the first time. The functional impact on design is the increased exposure to wear and weather. Vast numbers of people will handle the decorative items at ground level. They will touch them, poke and push on them, lean against them, sit on them, and climb them if that is allowed. The wind will blow, the sun will shine on them, or it will rain for the duration of the fair and year-round at permanent fair locations.

Coy Sevier, general manager of Southwest Festivals, Inc., produces Scarborough Faire, a Renaissance festival that is open weekends for two months in the spring, and Scream!, a Halloween theme park that is open during the month of October. These events take place on a permanent fair site in Waxahatchie, Texas. He says that decorations "set the tone from the minute a person walks to the front gate. It is a subliminal thing. It establishes the fantasy. If it is right, they do not consciously notice it. If it is wrong or there is something missing, they notice the shortcomings. What we make is magic. The reward is the looks on faces, the smiles, the laughter."

The details and complex decorations tell a story. This may be a simple story that lets people know what kind of fun to expect in a specific place: "This is where the rides are!" The decorations in this case would feature bright colors replicating people in motion on rides accented with replicas of fireworks, explosions, and other dynamic icons, such as a tornado ("Come ride the Whirlwind!"). Or they may describe a more sophisticated story preparing them for a more complicated experience: "You are entering Pirates' Cove." In this case the guests might enter a cave that emerges facing a lagoon with a fully rigged pirate ship where the entertainment will take place.

Complex decorations add to the visitor's experience, but they pose an operational problem. Against this rich background of décor the signs to the rest rooms and other areas may get lost or at least become less accessible and less easy to read. In fact, Coy Sevier says that one of the biggest challenges to design and decoration in the park is the transition between areas: "One of the trends is to do multiple individual themes within the park. The hardest part about doing that is creating a smooth transition between areas." Fairs offer a richer and more detailed visitor experience than do festivals, and the decoration and design are more complex and less obvious. Getting around a fair is less easy than getting around a festival. A solution to this problem is to follow the suggestions made by Colleen Rickenbacher, CMP, CSEP: "Make it big! Make it easy. And put it high in the air." Large arches in the appropriate style with big easy-to-read signage can be put high in the air, over people's heads.

Another trend that Coy points out is the use on second stories of **faux painting** and **constructed perspective** (Figure 16-2). "Pay attention to what Walt Disney did so many years ago. It was ingenious. The effect, again, is on the subconscious. People want to believe." Faux painting is a method of scenic painting in which a structure or construction method is replicated in paint, such as painting that looks like stone construction. It replicates the color and texture of individual stones and the mortar between them. Shadow and highlights created by sunlight are painted in as well. The painted shadows and highlights do not move with the actual sun, but as Coy suggests, people want to believe the illusion. This is a version of the trompe l'oeil painting discussed in Chapter 6, *Backdrops* and *Props.* Faux painting works best at a distance, as the flat surface can be discerned when seen up close, but once the illusion is established, the public will experience what is called a **suspension of disbelief.** They will subconsciously go along with the illusion.

Constructed perspective frequently is used in conjunction with faux painting and gives a heightened illusion of distance and size. As things appear to get smaller in the distance, items can be constructed that actually get smaller and give the illusion that they are much farther away than they really are; this technique also can be used to make specific items look much larger than they

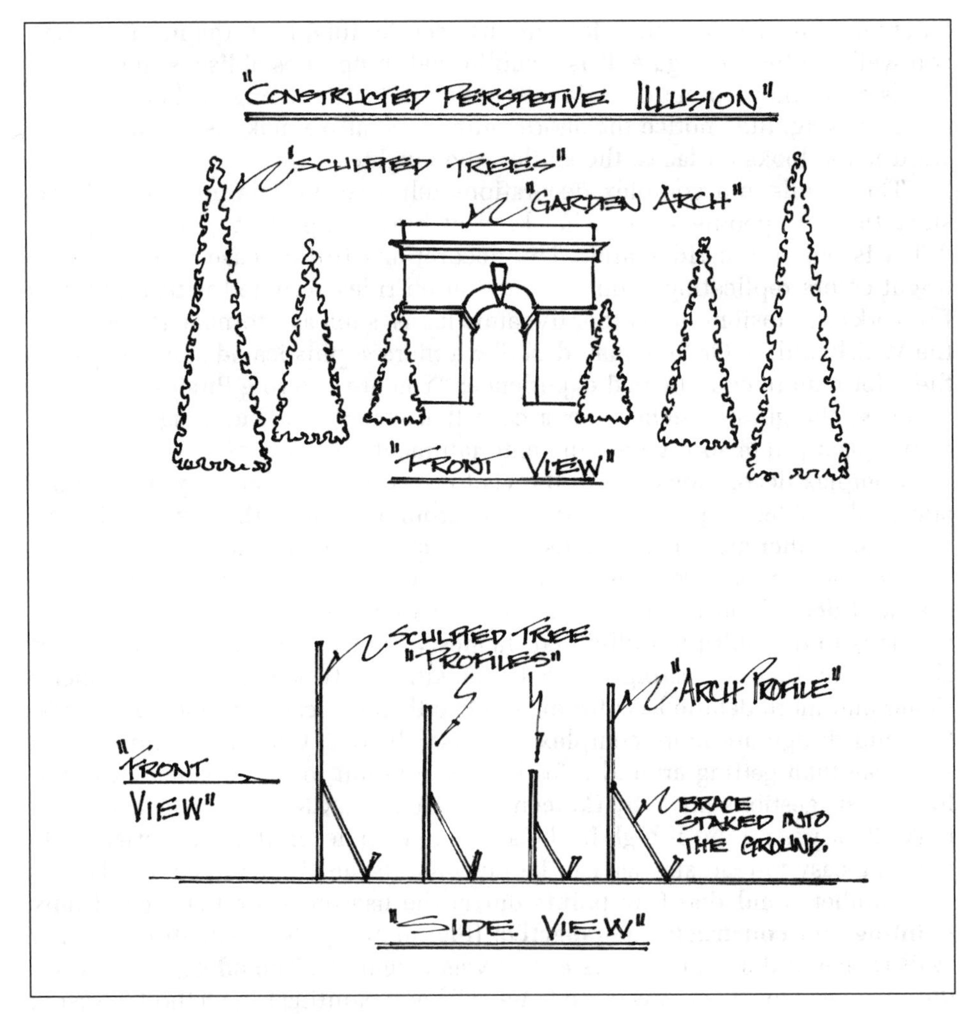


**Figure 16-2**

are in reality. For example, imagine building a picket fence with pickets that were progressively smaller in all dimensions. It would appear to be diminishing in the distance. The suspension of disbelief applies here as well, but for constructed perspective to work, the viewing location of the guests must be controlled. If a decorative element is designed to be seen from one point of view, the illusion will be destroyed if it is seen from a different side.

From a practical viewpoint, one of the biggest problems with decorations at a fair is weather. Coy says: "Ultraviolet rays, wind, and rain can all wreak havoc on the decorations." Paint will fade after exposure to ultraviolet (UV) rays from the sun. Designers of decorations for fairs use paint that has a UV inhibitor in it or add an inhibiting agent to the paint.

Additional resources on fairs and festivals appear in the "Recommended Readings and Research Sites" section at the end of this chapter. Coy Sevier also recommends the books of Paco Underhill, a behavioral marketing research expert and the author of *Why We Buy, The Science of Shopping,* and *The Call of the Mall,* saying that his principles translate readily to fair design.

## PARADES

Parades are held in conjunction with sporting events, fairs, and festivals as well as to celebrate holidays. In New Orleans, they say a parade breaks out at the drop of a hat. There are companies that specialize in designing and decorating floats and companies that direct, produce, and manage parades. Obviously, a parade will reflect its sponsors' goals and objectives. However, the same principles of design and practices regarding decoration apply to all of them. Karen Ranker, parade director for the Neiman Marcus Adolphus Children's Parade and human resources director for The Adolphus Hotel, shares a few ideas with us. All sponsorship dollars from the parade go to Children's Medical Center of Dallas. Karen has worked on the parade for all of its 17 years.

> *When we started producing the parade, we did not theme it. It was for children. It was the holidays. It had to be in good taste, reflecting the images of The Adolphus Hotel and Neiman Marcus. A theme turns out to be very useful. It makes the planning easier, and it makes the aesthetics easier.*
>
> *A parade is a moving pageant. Floats do not make a pageant. A float is 12 feet wide, and it is coming down a street that is 50 feet wide. It is a matter of scale. To become part of a pageant, you need to add music and 100 dancers around it. Then it is a moving pageant. A car with a celebrity in it gets lost in the middle of the street, so we do three to five cars in a pattern, maybe with an inflatable behind them. That has impact and appeal.*
>
> *Our parade is about entertainment, entertaining children. We use a lot of dancers and drill teams and train them to bring the parade out to the people, to within 10 to 12 feet of the people. They do a two- to three-minute dance, and then they work the crowd for several minutes before doing another dance. We tell the dancers in training sessions that we want them to relate to the people. We bring the parade out from the middle of the street to the people. We do a lot of schools: clown schools, bleacher host schools, and inflatable schools. All volunteers must wear the parade volunteer uniform with the year's sweatshirt over red pants.*
>
> *Aesthetically, big blocks of color work. Our costumes are simple but dramatic. We put a lot of look up in the air. We use nine inflatables. We like height, but it has to have texture, height, music,*

*eye-level dancing—visual and auditory . . . lots of music. Every element in the parade is decorated; fire engines, cars—all components sport consistent decorations. We supply all signage and banners so that we control the look, and they are all decorated. We are the masters of felt, glitter garland, and hot glue guns.*

*We use children's celebrity characters. Angelina Ballerina, a HIT Entertainment character, comes down the street in a pretty horse-drawn carriage decorated with live garland, tulle, and puffy bows. Dancers in tutus and music surround her. [HIT Entertainment produces children's television characters in the United States and the United Kingdom. They are the producers of* Barney and Friends.]

*All of our greenery is real: live garland and wreaths. Even Mrs. Claus has elves surrounding her. Fifty kids ride in the parade, all outpatients from Children's Medical Center, and we costume them. We pay attention to small details as is appropriate for The Adolphus and Neiman Marcus corporate images. Neiman Marcus is the title sponsor, and The Adolphus is the founding sponsor, and the parade must communicate our core business values.*

*We maintain complete control over the street picture. No stragglers, no extra personnel, no unattractive equipment is allowed. Controlling the aesthetics is what makes our event special. The audience can expect the best experience possible. The parade being televised actually helps the aesthetics because it raises everybody's performance and presentation level.*

The various decorative elements in the parade are the same elements discussed previously in the material on festivals and fairs. There are a lot of similarities in the design and decorative approaches for a lot of the same reasons. In the case of a fair or festival the people move around, but a parade is very much like a moving festival that comes to the people.

In addition to the design of the parade itself, there is the specialized field of float decorations. The Phoenix Decorating Company says on its website (http://www.phoenixdecoratingco.com) that it uses up to 20 million flowers in the same week when decorating 23 floats for the Rose Parade in Pasadena, California. It uses tons of steel, plastic foam, chicken wire, and aluminum screen in addition to 16 tons of dry organic material such as lentils, dried peas, and cinnamon applied by 16,000 individuals, mostly volunteers who work long swing shifts before and after Christmas.

Elements that come into play in decorating floats include a functional vehicle, usually a truck or auto body, and the chassis structure to support the design. The structure of the design then is sculpted in place, using various wire coverings, and finally it is finished with the chosen materials. Other major considerations are safety concerns such as requiring railings and secure places for riders, using only flame-retardant materials, fire extinguishers, and safety exits for all riders, including the driver. Parades will supply detailed specifications and restrictions to the entrants.

# SPECTACLES

Spectacles are defined by *Merriam-Webster's Unabridged Dictionary* as "something exhibited to view . . . usually something exhibited as unusual and notable . . . an impressive display especially for entertainment . . . a public display appealing or intended to appeal to the eye by its mass, proportions, color, or other dramatic qualities." As with fairs and festivals, spectacles have been around since ancient history, with the Romans having built the Coliseum for their display. Theatrical spectacles were developed and refined during the sixteenth through eighteenth centuries, and those techniques are still in use on Broadway. Today's most visible and popular spectacles are sports-related, specifically the halftime entertainment at major football games such as the Super Bowl and the opening and closing ceremonies of the Olympics.

Spectacles are to other events what festivals are to fairs in that they must be big, have highly visible components, and be easy to understand. Large moving colorful components work for spectacles, which are viewed by large groups of people. Details do not work for spectacles except for television and film purposes. The camera will see small details that a large public group of viewers will not be able to see. It will be noticed while one is watching the Super Bowl halftime show that certain details are put into the show specifically for the cameras. It also will be seen that several times during the broadcast the camera picture will get lost for a moment in the scale of the components around it.

Gregory Pynes, while with the town of Addison, helped develop a pyrotechnical spectacle called Kaboom Town! Kaboom Town! was originally conceived as an Independence Day village that would be created with food,

Idea Portfolio

## LET THE EVENT EVOLVE

Gregory Pynes says: "In subsequent years we encouraged each restaurant in the neighborhood to create its own small village in its parking lot. To enhance the experience we started simulcasting the fireworks with KVIL radio station. The fireworks are actually choreographed to the music played on KVIL. Kaboom Town! evolved into its own spectacle beyond our control. We ended up directing traffic; we had to bring in extra police officers to control traffic from nearby towns and cities. Tens of thousands of people all try to leave at once after the show is over. To lessen that problem we encouraged and gave concerts to keep people from wanting to leave as soon as the fireworks were over."

By recognizing the reality of people's needs and wants, Addison was able to improve the event experience and make it more successful by adding components that encouraged and addressed the natural evolution of the event.

crafts, and entertainment, but people were not coming to the early part of the celebration. They came just for the fireworks.

Gregory's experience illustrates the fact that spectacles need to be kept simple and uncomplicated from the viewers' or participants' point of view. From the producers' point of view they can be anything but simple. The complicated and multilayered closing ceremonies of the 1992 Winter Olympics were an example of how many components can be assembled for a single spectacle.

## FINISHING TOUCHES

Fairs, festivals, parades, and spectacles are put on for marketing, celebration, and commercial purposes. An industry has grown up around each of these types of events, some of which are special events and some of which are annual events.

Décor for these events generally needs to be large, high in the air, and easy to understand, although fairs and spectacles can have more complicated designs. Use people as dynamic three-dimensional live décor. Establish an event logo with bold colors and use those colors throughout. Look for items with impact to enhance the visitors' experience.

Always remember, whether designing or decorating small events or vast spectacles, keep them safe and keep them fun. Good luck and may every day bring a special event your way.

## DESIGN VOCABULARY

Terms appear below in the order in which they first occur in this chapter.

Festivals
Fairs
Accessibility
Back-of-the-house area
F&B
Eye candy
Style points
Gimme cap
Faux painting
Constructed perspective
Suspension of disbelief

## STUDIO WORK

1. You have been asked to design a first-time three-day beach volleyball competition. The operations and logistics are someone else's responsibility; you are in charge of marketing and promotion. What would you do (a) to entertain the spectator visitors and (b) to decorate the event and provide branding?
2. Draw a layout of a food festival expecting 25,000 guests over three days and featuring name entertainment, food tent or tents for 25 restau-

rants, a children's entertainment area, rest room facilities, and emergency access. This can be a rough not-to-scale drawing, but it should be accompanied by a written description and/or an explanation.

3. Describe the design and decorations for a hypothetical fair or parade from your imagination. Use a theme and be specific.

# RECOMMENDED READINGS AND RESEARCH SITES

Grippo, Robert M., and Christopher Hoskins, *Macy's Thanksgiving Day Parade (Images of America)*, Arcadia Publishing, 2004.

Underhill, Paco, *Why We Buy: The Science of Shopping*, Simon and Schuster, 1999.

Underhill, Paco, *The Call of the Mall*, Simon and Schuster, 2004.

Backstage@Festivals.com—a commercial site that promotes festivals nationwide and internationally; has some good information for students of design who may be interested in festival work

http://www.festivals.com

International Association of Fairs and Expositions—the oldest North American association related to fairs and expositions; from the website, "the IAFE represents more than 1,400 fairs in North America and around the world, as well as more than 1,500 members from allied fields"

http://www.fairsandexpos.com

International Festivals & Events Association—apparently the most important international association related to festivals and fairs, with members and associates in 41 countries

http://www.ifea.com

Neiman Marcus Adolphus Children's Christmas Parade—the official site of the parade described and discussed in the text

http://www.childrensparade.com

Rose Parade, the Tournament of Roses—the official site of the Pasadena Rose Parade

http://www.tournamentofroses.com/current/parade.htm

# Part Four

# APPENDIXES


Appendix 1 TYPICAL REQUEST FOR PROPOSAL
Appendix 2 CONTACT SHEET
Appendix 3 EVENT THEMES
Appendix 4 TYPICAL EVENT PROPOSAL
Appendix 5 SPECIAL EVENT SITE INSPECTION CHECKLIST
Appendix 6 ELECTRICAL FORMULA
Appendix 7 BALLOON CHARTS
Appendix 8 LABOR RATE CALCULATION: CHARGE-OUT RATES FOR LABOR
Appendix 9 DISPLAYING THE FLAG
Appendix 10 LIGHTING EQUIPMENT AND VOCABULARY
Appendix 11 WEDDING CHECKLIST

# Appendix 1

# TYPICAL REQUEST FOR PROPOSAL

The following Request For Proposal (RFP) is an actual request for a bid for audiovisual work for an event being designed by the requesting party. It was submitted to three companies, and a supplier selected from those bids.

University of Texas
**M. D. Anderson Cancer Center**
CONVERSATION WITH A LIVING LEGEND
Chantilly Ballroom—October 28, 2004—Luncheon
**Audiovisual Request for Proposal**

Dear Professional Associate,
You are among our preferred associates, and we trust your capability for this job. Please give us your best quote for your best quality work. This is a fund-raising activity, and cost must play a significant part in the decision to award the contract. The bids are due by 5:00 P.M. Friday, August 27, 2004, and we expect to award the contract by Friday, September 3, 2004. Winning bidder(s) will be required to supply certificates of insurance with the University of Texas M.D. Anderson Cancer Center designated as additional insured.

*Please address your bid to:*
Ms. Beth Burroway
Associate Director of Development
University of Texas
M.D. Anderson Cancer Center
1020 Holcomb Blvd #1201
Houston, TX 77030

*Please submit it via e-mail to:*
Jim Monroe, CMP, CSEP
jim@jcmonroe.com

Please bid either section or both sections separately, as we foresee the possibility of awarding lights and sound to one company and visual media to another.

Please let us know in your bid how many rigging points will be required and what size electrical service will be required for sound and lights so that we can get an estimate from Production Associates.

Please bid installation on straight time, being aware that this far out we cannot know when we will get the ballroom and may incur additional overtime charges. Doors are open at 11:00 A.M. on Thursday, October 28.

**LIGHTING AND SOUND**

- Adequate lighting for a 16-foot-deep by 40-foot-wide stage to be placed center on the long wall, opposite the entrance, approximately 10 feet from the wall. There will be a large center stage area requiring separate control and an overall warm and cool wash. There will be a ramp coming upstage right (for a golf cart) that will not have to be lighted and steps downstage left.
- Include a follow spot and operator, UltrArc or equivalent.
- Light a separate 8- by 12-foot podium offstage left.
- Light a ceiling-height 40-foot-wide backdrop from front left and right to wash out wrinkles.
- Lighting needs to be acceptable for image magnification, including backlighting for center area (two park benches), which can be hung from truss supporting backdrop on genii lifts (to be supplied by others).
- Flown sound for up to 1,400 guests giving complete, even coverage throughout room, including delay speakers.
- Two lavalieres for Mr. Jack Nicklaus (our Legend) and the interviewer.
- Two Countryman-style mics on lectern at stage left podium
- All operators, support equipment, installation and dismantle to take place immediately after event, approx. 2:30 P.M., October 28, 2004.
- 9-station, 2-channel ClearCom, 1 wireless.

**VISUAL MEDIA**

- Two 10½-foot by 14-foot rear projection screens for I-mag and possible data projection.
- Adequate projectors.
- Two cameras, one at rear on split risers and one hand-held.
- Tech director, switcher, cameramen, and any and all other equipment or personnel to produce a conference-quality professional production.
- Others will supply masking drape for screens and tech platform.
- VHS or better archival recording, including tape.

It is understood that the bidders are the experts in these areas. We are open to suggestions and hope you will cover any omissions on our part. Feel free to contact Jim Monroe, CMP, CSEP, to discuss this bid, 972-296-3336, or e-mail at jim@jcmonroe.com

Although requesting separate bids for lighting and sound and visual media, we will entertain any combination or inclusive bids submitted *in addition* to our request. Thank you for the time and effort we know you put into this.

Sincerely

Jim Monroe, CMP, CSEP

# Appendix 2

# CONTACT SHEET

EVENT ______________________________ Event Date __________

Principal Client ______________________________

Address ______________________________

______________________________

Telephone Day __________ Night __________ Cell __________

Fax __________ E-mail ______________________________

Referred by ______________________________ Job # __________

Move-in Date and Time ______________________________

Start Time(s) ________ End Time ________ Strike Date and Time ________

Event Location(s) ______________ Event Contact ______________

______________ ______________

______________ ______________

| Player | Role | Company | Phone, Fax, E-mail |
|---|---|---|---|
| | | | |
| | | | |
| | | | |
| | | | |
| | | | |
| | | | |
| | | | |
| | | | |
| | | | |

Contract to ______________ Invoice to ______________

______________ ______________

______________ ______________

______________ ______________

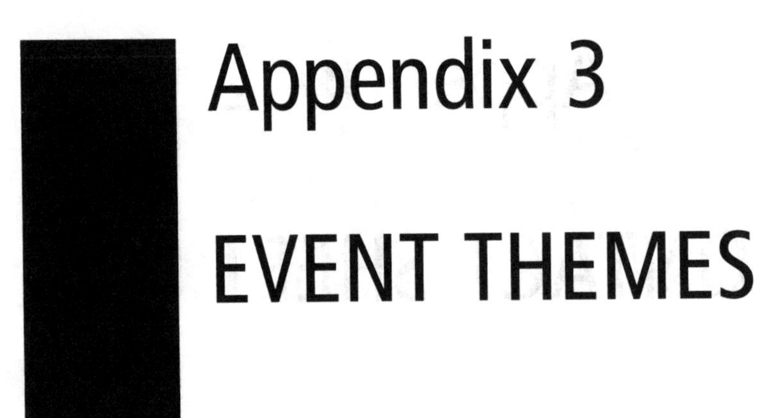

# Appendix 3

# EVENT THEMES

1920s/1930s/1940s
African Safari
Alpine Adventure
America The Beautiful
Art Party
Artist Party (Warhol, Mondrian, etc.)
Asian Fantasy
Atlantis/Undersea
Beach Party
Big Easy
Blue Moon
Caribbean/Tropical Fantasy
Carnival in Rio
Cherry Blossom Festival
Chicago
Cirque
Cities of Europe
City of Lights/Paris
Classical Greece
Coast-to-Coast
Construction Party
Crab Boil/Lobster Boil/Corn Boil
Dance! Dance! Dance!
Derby Party
Dinosaur Dance
Emerald Isle
Exotic Automobiles
Extreme Sports
Fairy Princess
Fais Do Do
Garden Tea
Great Barrier Reef
Hearts and Flowers
Highland Games
Hollywood/Academy Awards

Ice Castle
Jazz
Las Vegas /Monte Carlo Night
Lion King
Luau
Magic
Manhattan Transfer
Mardi Gras
Martini Madness
M.A.S.H.
Matisse's Garden
Medieval Times
Moon over Miami
NASCAR
Nutcracker
Oktoberfest
Old South
Ports of Call/Cruise Ship
Puppy Dog Tales
Renaissance Fair
River Themes (Seine, Thames, the Big Muddy)
Riverboat
Rocky Mountain High
Roman Empire
Rose Garden
Route 66
San Francisco
Sound of Music
South Beach
South of the Border
Speakeasy/Prohibition
Sports Themes
Spring Break
Steeplechase Ball
Surfing Safari
Swamp Thing
Taj Mahal
Temple of Heaven
Top Hat and Tails
Unicorn
Black Tie and Boots
Victorian Valentine
Vienna Waltz
Wild West/Cowboy
Winter Wonderland
Zoo to Do

# Appendix 4

# TYPICAL EVENT PROPOSAL

This is a typical event decoration proposal. It would be typed on company letterhead stationery.

February 24, 2004

Ms. Jean B. Smith, CMP
Meeting Manager
Fredrick TIA, Inc.
2495 Midway Road, Suite 102
Carrollton, TX 75009

**P R O P O S A L**
**CASABLANCA THEME AWARDS PARTY**
**RENAISSANCE NORTH HOTEL**
**MARCH 18, 2004**

JAMES C. MONROE & ASSOCIATES, herein called "Supplier," agrees to supply Fredrick TIA, Inc., herein called "Client," the properties and services described in Exhibit A, for the cost shown below and under the conditions described in Exhibit B. Costs shown are for the use of supplier's properties and include installation and removal unless otherwise noted.

**TOTAL: $5,074.22**

**TERMS:** One-Half **($2,537.11)** due upon acceptance of contract. Balance due on or before completion of installation, March 18, 2004.
All past due invoices carry 1½% interest per month, 18% APR.

**NOTE:** When signed by both parties below, this agreement becomes contractual in nature and shall consist of five (5) pages, including Exhibit B, attached, which contains conditions pertaining to this agreement.

SIGNED, SEALED, AND DELIVERED
At Dallas, TX. on this the ___ day of ________________, 2004

FOR AND ON BEHALF OF
JAMES C. MONROE & ASSOCIATES, by________________________.

SIGNED, SEALED, AND DELIVERED
At Dallas, TX on this the ___ day of ________________, 2004

FOR AND ON BEHALF OF
FREDERICK TIA by ________________________.

## EXHIBIT A

1) **ENTRY:** Mustafa the camel greets guests as they turn the corner into the Garden Terrace entry area. A stuffed faux camel relaxes under a faux palm tree outside our faux tent.

- Camel and palm tree: 250.00
- Colorful draping around entrance: 200.00
- An "Ali Baba" jar 67.50

2) **STAGE:** The stage is backed with a pair of 10-foot palms and four existing plants, with pink uplights.

- Two (2) large (10') empress palms: 225.00
- Uplighting for ambience: 140.00

3) **TABLES:** Twelve (12) tables are clothed in black and gold covers with mixed tall and short centerpieces of crystal, palm leaves, and candles. Six (6) palace vases will have five palm fronds each on a mirror round with five votive candles. Six (6) bubble bowls will sit on a palmetto leaf and hold fire under water candles surrounded by votive candles on a mirror round. 735.00

- Tablecloths and chair ties: By others

4) **ARICA PALMS:** across room to screen casino area from dinner and presentation area.

- Six (6) palms to screen off casino area: 455.00
- Casino: By others

5) **COCKTAIL TABLES:** Six (6) standing cocktail tables are scattered around the cocktail and precasino areas. Tablecloths are the same as the dining tables (supplied by others) and have small "Moroccan" lamps.

- Six (6) 42-inch-high standing cocktail tables: 120.00
- Six (6) black and gold tablecloths: N.I.C.
- Six (6) battery-operated candle lamps with fringed shades: 120.00

**6) CASABLANCA CHARACTERS:** Will be booked from 6 to 7:30 P.M.

- BOGART—An impersonator who does Bogie often and well. He does not so much look like Bogart as sound and act like him. Always a success. 500.00
- SAM—Our African-American piano player will dress and act like Sam. He promises me that he will watch the film before the event. 400.00
- LOUIE—On the other hand, Louis, our French policemen, doesn't have much of a French accent, but he does have the costume. 375.00

**7) DRAYAGE:** 250.00

**8) DESIGN AND COORDINATION FEE:** 750.00

**TOTAL: 4,687.50**
**SALES TAX: 386.72**
**GRAND TOTAL: $5,074.22**

**EXHIBIT B**

**TERMS:** Due when rendered. Service charge of 1½% per month will be added to all unpaid balances after 30 days, annual rate 18%.

CONDITIONS:

**1.** The entity hiring the services is herein called "Client," JAMES C. MONROE & ASSOCIATES is herein called "Supplier."

**2.** DEFAULT: In the event Client fails to pay the agreed cost within ten (10) days after due, or if the equipment is seized or taken by third parties acting against Client, or if an action in bankruptcy, receivership, or insolvency is brought against Client, or if Client enters into any agreement with the creditors, or if Client fails to observe, keep, or perform any of the provisions of this agreement after five (5) days' written notice of default thereof, Supplier has the right of the following remedies:

A. To declare the entire amount immediately due and payable as to any or all items of service, without notice or demand to the Client.

B. To sue for and recover all costs and other payments accrued or accruing with respect to any or all items of service and related properties and equipment.

C. To take possession of any or all related properties and equipment, without demand or notice, wherever they may be located, without any court order or other process of law. The Client hereby waives any and all damages occasioned by such taking of possession.

D. To terminate this agreement as to any or all items of equipment and/or service.

E. To pursue any other remedy or equity.

Notwithstanding any action which the supplier may take, the Client shall be and remain liable for the full performance of all obligations to be performed by the Supplier under this agreement.

3. MANNER OF USE: The Supplier shall supply the service agreed upon in a careful and proper manner. The Client shall be responsible for compliance with all laws, ordinances, and regulations relating to the possession, use, or maintenance of related properties and equipment or service provided.
4. CONCEALED FEATURES: The Supplier shall not be responsible for costs, problems, damages, or additional labor incurred due to concealed, hidden, belowground, or otherwise unknown architectural features, structures, conditions, and anomalies.
5. LOSS OR DAMAGE: The Supplier's responsibility for damage to property or harm to persons shall be limited to such loss or damage resulting solely and directly from Supplier's actions. The Client assumes and shall bear all other risks arising in conjunction with the services provided.
6. PERSONAL PROPERTY: Any properties or equipment delivered in conjunction with the services to be supplied shall at all times remain personal property no matter to what, or how, it is attached, and shall remain Supplier's personal property at all times unless otherwise stated herein.
7. NO WARRANTY: Supplier makes no warranties, either expressed or implied, as to the fitness of services to be supplied for any purpose whatsoever, or the condition of any related properties and equipment. Client acknowledges agreement to receive and accept such equipment and service as is.
8. INDEMNITY: The Client shall indemnify the Supplier against, and shall hold the supplier harmless from, any and all claims, actions, suits, proceedings, costs, expenses, damages, and liabilities, including attorney's fees, arising out of, connected with, or resulting from the equipment and/or services provided, including, without limitation, the manufacture, selection, delivery, possession, use, operation and/or return of equipment, and the installation, removal, or other services provided.
9. GENERAL CONDITIONS:
   A. This agreement shall be binding upon and arising to the benefit of the parties to this agreement and their respective successors, assignees, heirs, devisees, and/or legatees. This agreement contains the entire agreement and understanding of the parties to this agreement.
   B. Each of the parties to this agreement shall do all such acts and such things as shall be necessary to accomplish the intent, purpose, terms, and conditions of this agreement, when necessary, time being expressly of the essence of this agreement. In the event a clause herein is deemed invalid for any reason, the parties hereto agree to reword said clause forthwith upon either's demand, in writing, preserving the agreement consistent with the overall intent herewith.
   C. The original agreement signed, as well as all copies of the original also duly signed, have the same force and effect as the original.

**This agreement shall be controlled and governed by the laws of the State of Texas.**

# Appendix 5

# SPECIAL EVENT SITE INSPECTION CHECKLIST

Cheryl Adams and James C. Monroe authored the following checklist, which you are welcome to use as a basis for your own. I recommend that all event professionals create a checklist that meets their needs and is in a format with which they are comfortable.

### ITEMS TO TAKE ON A SITE INSPECTION:

- Retractable tape measure
- Paper and pencil
- Digital camera
- Site inspection checklist

## EVENT-SPECIFIC CHECKLIST

### PREPARATION

**Demographics of attendees:** age range; gender mix, experience levels, ethnicity and nationality

**Event profile:** purpose of event, duration (start and finish times), format, type of beverage service (if alcohol, full bar or beer and wine, hosted or cash bar), entertainment requirements

### INFORMATION FROM INSPECTION—EVENT-SPECIFIC

1. **Availability**—When is room available? By when must it be cleared?
2. **Condition of room.**
3. **Aesthetics**—What are the colors and patterns in the carpet? Walls? Ceiling?
4. **Chandeliers**—Will they cause projection/rigging problems? Placement and clearance from floor?
5. **Tables and chairs**—What quantity of which sizes? What do banquet chairs look like?
6. **Linens**—What sizes and colors of tablecloths and napkins?

7. **Dimensions and floor plans.**
8. **How will room(s) be set up?**
9. **Catering**—Who? Location of kitchen and service doors.
10. **Lighting**—Type of light fixtures and location of controls. Is there a remote controller? Is there track lighting? Locations?
11. **Sound**—What type of in-house system? Quality? What are the acoustics of the room? Will room require sound? Flown or ground support? Will delay stacks be needed? Front or side fill? Monitors?
12. **Temperature**—Control?
13. **Loading dock**—Height? Restrictions? How many trucks can be accommodated? Can space be reserved?
14. **Access from dock to room**—Distance? Corners in halls? Dimensions of smallest door. Ceiling clearance from dock to room?
15. **Truck parking**—Is there vehicle marshaling space? If not, where is parking? Cost?
16. **Audiovisual**—Who is in house? Capabilities? Competitively priced?
17. **Rigging points**—Where are they? Rigging restrictions?
18. **Projection capability**—Is there a booth? Are there permanent screens? What is a good placement for screens? Will I-mag be needed?
19. **Electrical**—Is there a disconnect? More than one? Where? Capacity: single-phase or three-phase?
20. **Staging**—Sizes, type, and heights? How good is it? What color skirting? Steps: with and without railings? What would be a good placement for the stage?
21. **Air walls**—Locations? Sound buffer?
22. **ADA-compliant?**
23. **Charges**—Are there hidden charges? Electrical? Rigging? Dock?
24. **Hospitality**—Are water/coffee stations available? Deli buffet for crew? Who pays for it and how?
25. **Rest rooms**—Locations and capacity?
26. **Foyer**—Capacity, look, floor plan?
27. **Security**—Procedures? Is there a theft problem with the property? Access to security for equipment? Cost? Will security be needed during event? From whom?
28. **Safety**—What are fire code requirements specific to this room? Who are the first responders on property? Policy regarding vehicles in the building? Policy regarding fog or smoke machines? (Smoke detectors?) Policy regarding live animals?

## OTHER INFORMATION REGARDING SITE

What was your first impression upon arrival?
What are back hallways like? Clean?
Was staff courteous and helpful? Was staff courteous and friendly in the back hallways?
Are rest rooms clean? Do they have amenities? Will they need more? Flowers?
Are there speaker-ready room, green room, or dressing room capabilities near the room?
How is existing directional signage? Will signage be needed? Is signage allowed?
Is there adequate parking? Cost?
Are crowd control stanchions available? Easels? Pipe and drape? Manlift?

# Appendix 6

# ELECTRICAL FORMULA

**Electricity for the Liberal Arts Majors**

The only formula the event designer or decorator is likely to need is the easiest to remember. It is called the West Virginia formula because it looks like the abbreviation for that state. With this formula, you can calculate what power is required for a lighting rig or what size lighting rig you can have installed with the power available.

$W = AV$, which also can be represented as $W = V \times A$
$W$ = watts
$V$ = volts
$A$ = amps (amperes)

Consider *watts* to be the power required by a light source, *volts* to be the type of power supplied, and *amps* to be the measurement of how much current is needed.

For those who are not good at algebra, the variations on this formula are as follows:

$$A = \frac{W}{V}$$

and

$$V = \frac{W}{A}$$

It will be seen that a 60-kw light rig (60,000 watts) will need, at 110 volts, 545.5 amps.

Or, conversely, 600 amps of 110-volt electricity would power up to 66,000 watts of lights.

$$W = V \times A \qquad W = 600 \times 110$$

Stay with me for one more piece of information:

Disconnects, or the power sources in a venue, are rated at what they are fused or protected at: 60 amps, 100 amps, 300 amps, 600 amps, and so on. Except they are either single-phase or three-phase 220-volt services. Single-phase service has two sources of 110-volt current, and at 110 volts it can supply up to twice what it is rated for at 220. Three-phase has three sources of 110-volt current and can supply up to three times what it is rated for at 220.

# Appendix 7

# BALLOON CHARTS

These helium charts are supplied compliments of the Pioneer Balloon Company, manufacturers of Qualatex Balloons.

## MICROFOIL BALLOON HELIUM CHART

*Note:* The listed average inflation sizes and numbers of balloons per helium tank are conservative averages. A properly inflated helium-filled Microfoil balloon will float for at least 3 to 5 days and can be refreshed easily. Actual flying times vary depending on temperature and atmospheric conditions.

| Balloon Description | Inflated Size | Width × Height | Lift Ability | Gas Capacity | Average Number per 242-Cubic-Foot Tank |
|---|---|---|---|---|---|
| 18″ (46 cm) round | 13.5″ × 13.5″ | 34 cm × 34 cm | 0.1 oz. (3 g) | 0.5 cu ft (.015 $m^3$) | 475 |
| 36″ (91 cm) round | 27″ × 27″ | 69 cm × 69 cm | 2.3 oz. (66 g) | 4.4 cu ft (.124 $m^3$) | 50 |
| 18″ (46 cm) heart | 14″ × 13″ | 36 cm × 33 cm | 0.1 oz. (3 g) | 0.5 cu ft (.015 $m^3$) | 475 |
| 36″ (91 cm) heart | 27.5″ × 27″ | 70 cm × 69 cm | 1.2 oz. (34 g) | 4 cu ft (.113 $m^3$) | 55 |
| 20″ (51 cm) star | 18″ × 17.5″ | 46 cm × 45 cm | 0.1 oz. (3 g) | 0.6 cu ft (.016 $m^3$) | 400 |
| 36″ (91 cm) star | 31.5″ × 30″ | 80 cm × 76 cm | 1.1 oz. (32 g) | 2.5 cu ft (.070 $m^3$) | 95 |
| 36″ (91 cm) palm frond (silver)* | 12″ × 32″ | 30 cm × 81 cm | 0.03 oz. (1 g) | 0.6 cu ft (.016 $m^3$) | 390 |
| 45″ (114 cm) shooting star | 18.5″ × 37″ | 47 cm × 94 cm | 0.3 oz. (9 g) | 1.3 cu ft (.036 $m^3$) | 185 |
| 35″ (89 cm) crescent moon | 29″ × 38.5″ | 74 cm × 98 cm | 0.5 oz. (14 g) | 1.3 cu ft (.036 $m^3$) | 185 |

| Balloon Description | Inflated Size | Width × Height | Lift Ability | Gas Capacity | Average Number per 242-Cubic-Foot Tank |
|---|---|---|---|---|---|
| 35″ (89 cm) smilin' sun | 28.5″ × 28.5″ | 72 cm × 72 cm | 0.5 oz. (14 g) | 1.7 cu ft (.048 $m^3$) | 140 |
| 39″ (99 cm) butterfly | 32″ × 19″ | 81 cm × 48 cm | 0.1 oz. (3 g) | 1.3 cu ft (.036 $m^3$) | 185 |
| 20″ (51 cm) daffodil | 17.5″ × 16.5″ | 45 cm × 42 cm | 0.1 oz. (3 g) | 0.7 cu ft (.020 $m^3$) | 340 |
| 23″ (58 cm) gerbera Daisy/ sunflower | 17.5″ × 20″ | 45 cm × 51 cm | 0.2 oz. (6 g) | 0.9 cu ft (.025 $m^3$) | 265 |
| 22″ (56 cm) rose | 17.5″ × 15.5″ | 45 cm × 39 cm | 0.2 oz. (6 g) | 0.8 cu ft (.022 $m^3$) | 300 |
| 22″ (56 cm) tulip | 13″ × 15″ | 33 cm × 38 cm | 0.1 oz. (3 g) | 0.8 cu ft (.022 $m^3$) | 300 |
| 25″ (64 cm) lily | 23″ × 25″ | 58 cm × 64 cm | 0.3 oz. (9 g) | 1.2 cu ft (.034 $m^3$) | 200 |
| 21″ (53 cm) heart | 16″ × 16″ | 41 cm × 41 cm | 0.2 oz. (6 g) | 0.7 cu ft (.020 $m^3$) | 346 |
| 25″ (64 cm) heart & roses | 17″ × 20″ | 43 cm × 51 cm | 0.1 oz. (3 g) | 0.9 cu ft (.025 $m^3$) | 265 |
| 31″ (79 cm) heart & arrow | 23″ × 34″ | 58 cm × 86 cm | 0.7 oz. (20 g) | 1.9 cu ft (.054 $m^3$) | 128 |
| 32″ (81 cm) Hershey's Kisses | 18.5″ × 20.5″ | 47 cm × 52 cm | 0.2 oz. (6 g) | 1 cu ft (.028 $m^3$) | 240 |
| 30″ (76 cm) kisses XOXO | 26″ × 26″ | 66 cm × 66 cm | 0.9 oz. (25 g) | 2.3 cu ft (.065 $m^3$) | 106 |
| 35″ (89 cm) hugs XOXO | 28″ × 28″ | 71 cm × 71 cm | 0.3 oz. (9 g) | 1.7 cu ft (.048 $m^3$) | 141 |
| 45″ (114 cm) Winged heart | 22″ × 35″ | 56 cm × 89 cm | 0.6 oz. (17 g) | 1.7 cu ft (.048 $m^3$) | 141 |
| 27″ (69 cm) ice cream cone | 18″ × 24.5″ | 46 cm × 62 cm | 0.3 oz. (9 g) | 1.2 cu ft (.034 $m^3$) | 195 |
| 27″ (69 cm) cupcake | 16.5″ × 27″ | 42 cm × 69 cm | 0.1 oz. (3 g) | 0.8 cu ft (.022 $m^3$) | 300 |
| 29″ (74 cm) chili pepper | 15″ × 24.5″ | 38 cm × 62 cm | 0.2 oz. (6 g) | 1 cu ft (.028 $m^3$) | 240 |
| 26″ (66 cm) jukebox | 16″ × 19.5″ | 41 cm × 50 cm | 0.3 oz. (9 g) | 1 cu ft (.028 $m^3$) | 240 |
| 21″ (53 cm) blue fish | 18″ × 11.5″ | 46 cm × 29 cm | 0.03 oz. (1 g) | 0.6 cu ft (.016 $m^3$) | 400 |
| 24″ (61 cm) bear | 18″ × 21.5″ | 46 cm × 55 cm | 0.2 oz. (6 g) | 0.9 cu ft (.025 $m^3$) | 265 |

| Balloon Description | Inflated Size | Width × Height | Lift Ability | Gas Capacity | Average Number per 242-Cubic-Foot Tank |
|---|---|---|---|---|---|
| 30″ (76 cm) parrot | 29″ × 33″ | 74 cm × 84 cm | 0.1 oz. (3 g) | 0.7 cu ft (.020 $m^3$) | 340 |
| 35″ (89 cm) pink panther | 26.25″ × 34.5″ | 67 cm × 88 cm | 0.5 oz. (14 g) | 1.5 cu ft (.042 $m^3$) | 160 |
| 32″ (81 cm) tropical fun fish | 24″ × 26″ | 61 cm × 66 cm | 0.3 oz. (9 g) | 1.2 cu ft (.034 $m^3$) | 195 |
| 30″ (76 cm) smilin' black cat | 28″ × 18″ | 71 cm × 46 cm | 1.0 oz. (28 g) | 2.2 cu ft (.062 $m^3$) | 107 |
| 26″ (66 cm) pumpkin | 16.5″ × 25″ | 42 cm × 64 cm | 0.2 oz. (6 g) | 1 cu ft (.028 $m^3$) | 240 |
| 25″ (64 cm) Frankenstein | 21″ × 17″ | 53 cm × 43 cm | 0.3 oz. (9 g) | 1.1 cu ft (.031 $m^3$) | 230 |
| 26″ (66 cm) ghost face mask | 23.5″ × 15″ | 60 cm × 38 cm | 0.2 oz. (6 g) | 0.9 cu ft (.025 $m^3$) | 260 |
| 26″ (66 cm) tombstone | 20″ × 16″ | 51 cm × 41 cm | 0.3 oz. (9 g) | 1.1 cu ft (.031 $m^3$) | 214 |
| 26″ (66 cm) bat | 13″ × 23″ | 33 cm × 58 cm | 0.05 oz. (1.4 g) | 0.7 cu ft (.020 $m^3$) | 372 |
| 24″ (61 cm) football | 21″ × 14.5″ | 53 cm × 37 cm | 0.2 oz. (6 g) | 0.9 cu ft (.025 $m^3$) | 265 |
| 18″ (46 cm) dice | 13″ × 10″ | 33 cm × 25 cm | .05 oz. (1.4 g) | 0.5 cu ft (.015 $m^3$) | 475 |
| 20″ (51 cm) poker chip | 16″ × 16″ | 41 cm × 41 cm | 0.2 oz. (6 g) | 0.8 cu ft (.022 $m^3$) | 300 |
| 30″ (76 cm) playing card/ 30″ rectangle | 16.5″ × 23.5″ | 42 cm × 60 cm | 0.9 oz. (25 g) | 1.5 cu ft (.042 $m^3$) | 160 |
| 29″ (74 cm) slot machine | 23″ × 15″ | 58 cm × 38 cm | 0.4 oz. (11 g) | 1.3 cu ft (.036 $m^3$) | 188 |
| 28″ (71 cm) banner | 10″ × 25″ | 25 cm × 64 cm | 0.9 oz. (25 g) | 0.9 cu ft (.025 $m^3$) | 265 |
| 18″ (46 cm) square | 13″ × 13″ | 33 cm × 33 cm | 0.1 oz. (3 g) | 0.6 cu ft (.016 $m^3$) | 400 |
| 24″ (61 cm) rectangle | 11″ × 20″ | 28 cm × 51 cm | 0.3 oz. (9 g) | 0.9 cu ft (.025 $m^3$) | 265 |
| 23″ (58 cm) thought bubble | 20″ × 20″ | 51 cm × 51 cm | 0.1 oz. (3 g) | 0.9 cu ft (.025 $m^3$) | 265 |
| 19″ (48 cm) Easter egg | 15″ × 12″ | 38 cm × 30 cm | 0.05 oz. (1.4 g) | 0.6 cu ft (.016 $m^3$) | 403 |
| 22″ (56 cm) shamrock | 19″ × 14″ | 48 cm × 36 cm | 0.1 oz. (3 g) | 0.7 cu ft (.020 $m^3$) | 372 |

| Balloon Description | Inflated Size | Width × Height | Lift Ability | Gas Capacity | Average Number per 242-Cubic-Foot Tank |
|---|---|---|---|---|---|
| 27″ (69 cm) gingerbread man | 23″ × 21″ | 58 cm × 53 cm | 0.3 oz. (9 g) | 1.1 cu ft (.031 $m^3$) | 230 |
| 26″ (66 cm) cell phone | 21″ × 12″ | 53 cm × 30 cm | 0.3 oz. (9 g) | 1.1 cu ft (.031 $m^3$) | 226 |
| 24″ (61 cm) shirt | 21″ × 18″ | 53 cm × 46 cm | 0.3 oz. (9 g) | 1 cu ft (.028 $m^3$) | 247 |
| 22″ (56 cm) number one | 12.5″ × 18.5″ | 32 cm × 47 cm | 0.1 oz. (3 g) | 0.7 cu ft (.020 $m^3$) | 367 |

*Gold and emerald green "palm fronds" have less lift than silver and may not float, depending on the altitude.

# LATEX AND CHLOROPRENE BALLOON HELIUM CHART

All 9-inch , 11-inch, and 16-inch pearl and metallic balloons are produced on supersized forms. Although the uninflated balloons look larger than other balloons of the same size, they are designed to inflate to the same size as standard, jewel, and fashion colors.

*Note:* The listed average inflation sizes, lift ability, flying times, and numbers of balloons per helium tank are conservative averages. Actual flying times vary depending on temperature and atmospheric conditions.

| Balloon Type | Inflated Diameter | Lift Ability | Gas Capacity | Average Number per 242-Cubic-Foot Tank | Average Flying Time* |
|---|---|---|---|---|---|
| 5″ (13 cm) round | 5″ (13 cm) | N/A | 0.06 cu ft (.002 $m^3$) | | N/A |
| 7″ (18 cm) round | 7″ (18 cm) | 0.1 oz. (3 g) | 0.12 cu ft (.003 $m^3$) | 2,000 | 6–8 hours |
| 9″ (23 cm) round | 9″ (23 cm) | 0.2 oz. (6 g) | 0.25 cu ft (.007 $m^3$) | 900 | 12–16 hours |
| 11″ (28 cm) standard and special colors | 11″ (28 cm) | 0.35 oz. (10 g) | 0.5 cu ft (.015 $m^3$) | 484 | 18–24 hours |
| 11″ (28 cm) metallic and pearl colors | 11″ (28 cm) | 0.35 oz. (10 g) | 0.5 cu ft (.015 $m^3$) | 484 | 16–18 hours |
| 14″ (36 cm) round | 14″ (36 cm) | 0.8 oz. (22 g) | 1 cu ft (.028 $m^3$) | 242 | 26–30 hours |
| 16″ (41 cm) round | 16″ (41 cm) | 1.2 oz. (34 g) | 1.5 cu ft (.042 $m^3$) | 160 | 30+ hours |

| Balloon Type | Inflated Diameter | Lift Ability | Gas Capacity | Average Number per 242-Cubic-Foot Tank | Average Flying Time* |
|---|---|---|---|---|---|
| 18″ (46 cm) round | 18″ (46 cm) | 1.8 oz. (51 g) | 2 cu ft (.056 m$^3$) | 121 | 36+ hours |
| 24″ (61 cm) round | 24″ (61 cm) | 4 oz. (120 g) | 5 cu ft (.142 m$^3$) | 48 | 2–4 days |
| 6″ (15 cm) heart | 6″ (15 cm) | N/A | .05 cu ft (.002 m$^3$) | | N/A |
| 11″ (28 cm) heart | 11″ (28 cm) | 0.1 oz. (3 g) | 0.3 cu ft (.009 m$^3$) | 806 | 8 hours |
| 17″ (43 cm) heart | 17″ (43 cm) | 0.6 oz. (17 g) | 0.9 cu ft (.025 m$^3$) | 268 | 14 hours |
| 3′ (.9 m) heart | 3′ (91 cm) | 6 oz. (168 g) | 7 cu ft (.198 m$^3$) | 34 | 3–5 days |
| 6″ (15 cm) GEO blossom | 6.5″–7.5″ (16–19 cm) | N/A | 0.1 cu ft (.003 m$^3$) | | N/A |
| 16″ (41 cm) GEO donut | 16″ (41 cm) | 0.5 oz. (14 g) | 0.7 cu ft (.020 m$^3$) | 345 | 22–26 hours |
| 16″ (41 cm) GEO blossom | 16″ (41 cm) | 0.4 oz. (11 g) | 0.6 cu ft (.017 m$^3$) | 403 | 18–24 hours |
| 30″ (76 cm) metallic | 30″ (76 cm) | 6.5 oz. (184 g) | 8 cu ft (.226 m$^3$) | 30 | 3–5 days |
| 3′ (.9 m) giant (inflated to 2.5′) | 2.5′ (76 cm) | 6.5 oz. (184 g) | 8 cu ft (.226 m$^3$) | 30 | 3–5 days |
| 3′ (.9 m) giant (inflated to 3.0′) | 3.0′ (91 cm) | 12 oz. (339 g) | 15 cu ft (.425 m$^3$) | 16 | 3–5 days |
| 646Q giant airship | 6″ (15 cm) | 0.35 oz. (10 g) | 0.61 cu ft (.017 m$^3$) | 390 | 12 hours |
| Cloudbuster Chloroprene Balloons | | | | | |
| 4′ (1.2 m) chloroprene | 4′ (1.2 m) | 1.7 lb. (771 g) | 45 cu ft (1.274 m$^3$) | 5 | 4–5 days |
| 5.5′ (1.7 m) chloroprene | 5.5′ (1.7 m) | 4.7 lb. (2.13 kg) | 87 cu ft (2.464 m$^3$) | 2 | 8 days |
| 8′ (2.4 m) chloroprene | 8′ (2.4 m) | 15.5 lb. (7.03 kg) | 267 cu ft (7.561 m$^3$) | 1 | 18+ days |

*The use of Ultra Hi-Float balloon flight extender is recommended for all helium-filled latex balloons. Ultra Hi-Float can increase the flying times of latex balloons up to 25 times longer than that of untreated balloons. For more information about Ultra Hi-Float, call 800-57FLOAT. Outside the United States, call 502-244-0984.

All Qualatex latex balloons are helium-weight quality and are manufactured in the United States or Canada from 100 percent natural biodegradable latex.

# Appendix 8

# LABOR RATE CALCULATION: CHARGE-OUT RATES FOR LABOR

- Add an average, reasonable markup to the annual total materials costs charged to all projects to determine an annual gross sales (AGS) from materials (AGS,Mat.) figure.
- Total all charges over the year for commissioned sales (such as entertainment and subcontractors), design and delivery fees, and any other items sold that were not labor-related during this period. This can be considered annual gross sales from miscellaneous (AGS,Misc.).
- Add these two sums and subtract them from gross revenues (total sales) to get annual gross sales from labor (AGS,Labor).
- Divide AGS,Labor by the total number of hours charged to revenue-producing projects to achieve the actual charge-out rate realized.

$$\text{AGS,Labor} = \text{AGS} - (\text{AGS,Mat.} + \text{AGS,Misc.})$$
$$\text{Charge-out Rate} = \text{AGS,Labor}/\text{Annual Chargeable Hours}$$

# Appendix 9

# DISPLAYING THE UNITED STATES FLAG

An event professional frequently will be asked to display the flag of the United States in conjunction with events. The United States Flag Code is a federal law that describes the correct use and methods of display for the Stars and Stripes but does not impose penalties for misuse. However, the appropriate and legal display of the flag is a topic that is defended intensely by a large number of citizens. It behooves an event professional to see that the flag is treated with respect and displayed properly at all times.

- On a stage or podium the flag should be placed stage right, that is, to the speaker's right.
- When displayed with the flags of states, cities, localities, or societies, the U.S. flag should be above them all and centered or to the flag's own right of all the others.
- When displayed with the flags of other countries, those flags should be similar-size flags flown on separate staffs at the same height.
- When displayed vertically or horizontally against a wall, the U.S. flag should be uppermost and to the flag's own right.
- When displayed with another flag on crossed staffs, the Stars and Stripes should be on the flag's own right and its staff should be on top of the other.
- If flown across a street, the U.S. flag should be to the north on an east-west street and to the east on a north-south street.
- When displayed across a sidewalk from a building to a pole, the U.S. flag should be away from the building.
- When displayed in a window, the U.S. flag should be on the upper left as viewed from the street.
- A flag displayed on a car should be at the right front fender.
- The flag should never be used as drapery, to cover anything, or for any decoration in general. Red, white, and blue bunting should be used for that purpose, and blue should be at the top.
- The flag should never be used for or as part of advertising.
- The flag should never have anything drawn, marked, or embroidered on it or attached to it.
- The flag should never be part of a costume or worn as apparel, except when worn correctly as a patch that is worn with respect. Rules for wearing a patch

are contained in the Flag Code, but this is a touchy subject and may be subject to state or city laws.

- The federal government assesses no penalty for misuse of the flag; that is left to local jurisdictions. Consult the attorney general's office in the state or the city attorney's office in the city where you have questions regarding this.

# Appendix 10

# LIGHTING EQUIPMENT AND VOCABULARY

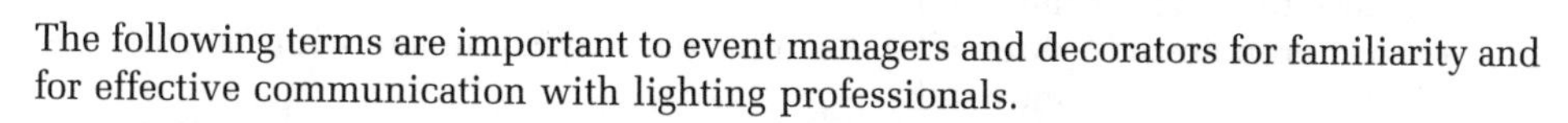

The following terms are important to event managers and decorators for familiarity and for effective communication with lighting professionals.

NONTHEATRICAL LIGHTING EQUIPMENT
THEATRICAL INSTRUMENTS
GENERAL LIGHTING TERMS

## NONTHEATRICAL LIGHTING EQUIPMENT

**Clip-on light.** A spring-loaded temporary lighting fixture designed to hold up to a 150-watt lamp. It allows the lamp to be positioned by clamping it to something secure and swiveling it into the exact position desired.

**Extension swivel socket.** Manufactured by Swivelier, these fixtures are 6-, 8-, 10-, or 12-inch stems between a medium screw (household) base and a medium screw (household) socket on a swivel. They can be screwed into an existing light fixture, such as a recessed can, and a lamp (lightbulb) can be screwed into one and swiveled into the desired position.

**Gooseneck.** Similar to the extension swivel socket described above, except that the stem is flexible so that it can be curved or bent into the desired position.

**MR-16 lamp.** A small (2-inch diameter) intense bright lamp originally designed for low-voltage fixtures but now available to fit household fixtures in several wattages; available in narrow (spot) and wide (flood) beam widths.

**PAR 38 CAN.** A simple can fixture designed to hold a PAR 38 lamp, usually with a yoke and c-clamp or floor base; like a PAR can, described under "Theatrical Instruments," only much smaller.

**PAR-38 lamp.** Thick glass lamp 4¾ inches in diameter, designed for outdoor use; has a parabolic reflector in it to direct and concentrate the light beam. It is available in 100-watt and 150-watt brightness and narrow (spot) and wide (flood) beam widths; also available in limited colors. These lamps are similar to R-40 lamps but are heavier and more durable.

**R-40 lamp.** A thin glass 150-watt lamp 5 inches in diameter, strictly for indoor use; has a spherical reflector to direct the light beam; available in narrow (spot) and wide (flood) beam widths. These lamps are similar to PAR 38 lamps but lighter and more fragile.

## THEATRICAL INSTRUMENTS

**Cyc lights.** Various types of instruments that are designed to wash a large area in up to three colors of light when used to light a cyclorama or backdrop.

**Ellipsoidal spotlight (Leko).** An instrument that puts out a sharp-edged beam of light that can be shaped with shutters or an iris; comes in different sizes and throws, or beam widths; can be used to project gobos onto any surface.

**Follow spot.** A manually operated, long-throw lighting instrument. The operator can raise, lower, and swivel the light as well as change its size with an iris and change the color of the beam.

**Fresnel** (pronounced "phren-ell"). A simple lighting instrument with a slightly adjustable throw or beam width.

**PAR can.** The simplest and most common instrument; it contains a 1-kW (1000-watt) PAR 64 lamp in an aluminum housing, with a yoke and c-clamp and a gel frame for changing colors. To change the beam width (throw), one changes the lamp; 1-kW PAR 64 lamps come in wide, medium, and narrow beam widths.

**Rainlight (pin spot).** Originally designed for discos; a small, heavy low-voltage lighting instrument that is used most frequently in events to pin-spot centerpieces

**Source4.** The commercial trademark for 575-watt instruments that put out the same intensity of light as standard 1-kW lamps. (A 2.4-kW dimmer can control four Source4 instruments and only two 1-kW instruments.)

## GENERAL LIGHTING TERMS

**1K, 24K, 60K.** Lighting jargon used to describe the number of 1,000-watt instruments being used in a lighting job; 1K = 1,000 watts = 1 instrument; 60K = 60,000 watts = 60 instruments.

**Boom.** Refers to any floor-standing tower used to support lights.

**C-clamp.** The clamp that is attached to the yoke of an instrument to attach it to a pipe.

**Chain motors.** Electrical chain hoists that are attached to the ceiling and used to raise and support (fly) truss or flown speakers.

**Color changer.** A device with a scroll of different color gels that can be put on the front of an instrument; the colors can be programmed remotely to change on cue.

**Dimmers.** The electronic devices that supply a controllable source of electric current to the instruments to raise or lower their intensity.

**Disconnect.** A source of electrical power to which **production equipment** is electrically connected; sometimes referred to as **AC,** either **single-phase** or **three-**

**phase** alternating current (AC); the size of the disconnect is referred to by the number of amperes **(AMP)** it can supply, for example, a **three-phase, 100-amp** disconnect.

**Gel.** Heat-resistant plastic film color media that can be put in front of lighting instruments to color the light beam.

**Generator.** A portable self-powered device that can supply a source of power when there is no electrical power, as in a tent or when the existing power is not sufficient to service the event.

**Gobos.** Originally metal silhouette patterns that could be used in ellipsoidal spotlights to project patterns; now available in full-color glass images as well.

**Instrument (lighting instrument).** Refers to any individual lighting fixture.

**Jumpers.** Theatrical jargon for electrical power extension cords.

**Intelligent lighting (robotic lighting** or **moving lights).** Any of a large family of lighting instruments with moving, changing beams of light.

**Light control board.** The remote device that tells the dimmers what to do; also called a **lighting board** or **dimmer board.**

**Patch (patching).** To patch is to assign or plug individual lights into circuits that are assigned to dimmers or directly into the dimmers themselves.

**Production/production equipment.** Lighting, sound, staging, rigging, and any other physical part of a show or production. Companies that supply this equipment and related services generally are referred to as production companies.

**Power source (AC).** See **disconnect,** above.

**Throw.** The distance between the hanging position for a lighting instrument and the stage or object it is lighting. Short-throw instruments have wider beams of light; long-throw instruments have narrow beams.

**Truss.** A welded aluminum structure that is used to fly lighting, scenery, sound, or other production equipment.

**Watts (wattage).** Measures the power of the electricity required and the resultant intensity or brightness of a lamp.

**Yoke.** A U-shaped metal strap that is used to connect the c-clamp to the instrument.

# Appendix 11

# WEDDING CHECKLIST

BRIDE ______________________ GROOM ______________________

ADDRESS ______________________

PHONES ______________________

FAX ______________________

EMAIL ______________________

Referred by ______________________ Event Date ______________________

Move in date & time ______________________

Start time __________ End time __________ Strike day and time __________

Event location ______________________ Event contact ______________________

PLAYERS POSITION CONTACT INFO

**BRIDE***

| Color & Style of Gown (attach picture if available) | FLORAL COST |
| --- | --- |
| Bouquet (style, colors, flowers) | |
| Floral Headpiece | |

**BRIDAL PARTY**

| Color & Style of Gowns (attach picture if possible) | QTY | COST PER EACH | TOTAL COST |
| --- | --- | --- | --- |
| **Honor Attendant Bouquet** - (style, colors, flowers) | | | |
| **Bridesmaids' Bouquets** - (style, colors, flowers) | | | |
| **Flower Girl** - (age, color & style of gown) | | | |
| **Floral Headpiece(s)** | | | |

**BOUTONNIERES***

| | | | | |
|---|---|---|---|---|
| **Groom** | | | | |
| **Best Man** | **Groomsmen** | | | |
| **Fathers** | **Grandfathers** | | | |
| **Ushers** | | | | |
| **Ring Bearer(s)** | | | | |
| **Other** | | | | |

**CORSAGES***

| | | | |
|---|---|---|---|
| **Bride's Mother** | | | |
| **Groom's Mother** | | | |
| **Grandmothers** | | | |
| **Others** | | | |

**CEREMONY**

| | | | |
|---|---|---|---|
| **Alter/Bima** | | | |
| **Aisle/Pew Décor** | | | |
| **Trees & Foliage** | | | |
| **Canopy** | | | |

| | | | |
|---|---|---|---|
| **Candelabra** - (alter)<br><br>**Candelabra** - (aisle) | | | |
| ☐ **Kneeling Bench** ☐ **Unity Candle** | | | |
| **Aisle Cloth** - (material/length) | | | |
| **Entrance/Narthex** | | | |
| **Other Decor** | | | |

**RECEPTION**

| | | | |
|---|---|---|---|
| **ENTRANCE** | | | |
| **STAGE/DANCE FLOOR** | | | |
| **TABLE TREATMENT** | | | |
| **CAKE TABLE** | | | |
| **OTHER** - (buffet, wall décor, lighting, etc.) | | | |

**REHEARSAL DINNER**

| | | | |
|---|---|---|---|
| **Centerpieces** | | | |
| **Other** | | | |

***Bride's Flowers, Boutonnieres, Corsages, and Rehearsal Dinner are traditionally paid for by Groom in some cultures and societies, but this practice varies.**

**BILLING INFO**

**NOTES**

**SKETCH**

# INDEX


AC, *see* Alternating current
Accent lighting, 196
Access doors, 6
Accessibility, 364
Accounting, 96
Accounting software, 77
ADA (Americans with Disabilities Act), 221
Advertising events, 249, 270, 271, 278–280
Aerial displays/shells (pyrotechnics), 237
Aesthetics, 9–10
  and color, 13–15
  and composition, 12–13
  of lighting, 200–206
  and line, 10–12
  practical design, 10–16
  and texture, 15–16
  and venue, 54
Age demographics, 7
Air Dimensional Design, 366
Air-filled balloons, 176
Air Stars, 287
Air tube, 179, 185–186
Aisle cloth, 332
Alberthal, Les, 54, 277
AltaVista, 27
Alternating current (AC), 400–401
Ambience, 54, 204
Ambient light, 204
American Heart Association, 243–244
Americans with Disabilities Act (ADA), 221
Amperes/amperage, 208, 401
Angle of incidence, 201–204
Animals, working with, 219–221
Animated images, 231
Anniversaries, 309–312
Announcement parties, 250
Apparel Mart, 274
*Applied Imagination* (Alex Osborn), 26
Appreciation events, 276, 292–293
Arches, balloon, 177–178, 181
Arch ceilings (balloons), 181
Architect's scale rule, 32, 35
*Architectural Digest,* 27
Architectural floral treatments, 137–140
Architectural renderings, 33
Archives (design development), 29–30
Ark (synagogue), 331
Armatures, 176
Artificial flowers, 135
Artistic drawings, 31, 33
Associates, 71
Asymmetry, 12
ATF (U.S. Department of Alcohol, Tobacco, and Firearms), 236
Attendance history, keeping an, 8
Attendees:
  demographics of, 54
  number of, 8
Auctions, 259–260
  high-visibility displays, 256
  live, 255, 259–260
  silent, 255, 259–260, 264
Audio design, 9
Audioscaping, 5
Authority:
  delegation of, 69
  for purchasing, 94
Awards presentations, 260–262

Bachelor/bachelorette parties, 360–361
Back bar, 355
Backdrops, 101–112
  advanced tips for, 110–111
  alternative, 111–112
  contracting for, 104–106
  decorating with, 107–112
  designing with, 102–107
  dimensional representations, 107
  painted, 104
  rigging of, 108–109
  and risk management, 104, 105, 109
  scenic, 102
Background music, 214, 311
Backlighting, 195, 202
Back-of-the-house area, 365
Balloon(s), 171–189
  arches of, 177–178, 181
  as ceiling treatment, 180–182
  as centerpieces, 177–180
  clusters of, 178
  columns of, 176–178
  decorating with, 172, 176–180
  designing with, 172–176
  effective use of, 173–174
  foil, 173
  helium charts for, 391–394
  helium- vs. air-filled, 176
  and hiring professionals, 175–176
  latex, 171, 173–174, 394–395
  resources on, 189
  and risk management, 174–175
  special effects with, 183–184
  as wall treatment, 182–183
Balloon arches, 177
Balloon Council, 175
Balloon drop, 183
Balloon fill ceilings, 181–182
Balloon House Design Studio, 171
Balloon release, 183
Balloon swags, 176
Balloons To You, 184
Banjo cloth, 148

Banners, 368
Banner-style ceiling treatments, 156–157
Bar/bat mitzvahs, 299, 303–305
Bary, Leo, 172, 184
Batten, 104
BBJ Linen, 161, 328
Beckham, Randy, 235–236
Beeswax candles, 233
Belcher, Charles, 191–192, 209
Benediction, 331
Beverages (as décor), 226–227
Bifulco, Robert, 234–235
Bifulco's Vanishing Sculptures, 235
Bill Reed Decorations, Inc., 10, 106, 274, 291
Bill Tillman Band, 183
Billy Bob's (Fort Worth), 360
Bima, 333–334
Birthday parties, 309–311
Black light, 230
Blaine Kern's Mardi Gras Warehouse, 113–114
Blended colors, 14
Blooming plants, 140, 141
Bobbinets, 146
Bobeche, 232
Bobtail van, 358
Bon vivant, 308
Bookkeeping, 96
Bookmarking, 75
Boom, 400
Bounce (light), 146
Bounce houses, 187
Brainstorming, 26–27, 74
Break-even events, 84
Breakup patterns (lighting), 199
Brocades, 149
Brook Hollow Golf Club, 144, 225
Browsing (as creative technique), 27
Buddhist weddings, 336
Budgets/budgeting, 25, 53, 66–68
Buffet(s):
- decorative, 224–225, 356
- and floral décor, 132–133
- layout of, 355
- lighting for, 357
- living, 216–217
- and weddings, 355–357

Built props, 114–116
Bunting swags, 317
Burris-Meyer, Harold, 107
Bush, George, 226
Butler service, 282
The Buzz, 273

Cable ramps, 208
CAD, *see* Computer aided/assisted drawing/drafting
CADD, *see* Computer aided design and drafting
Cakes, wedding, 351–352
*The Call of the Mall* (Paco Underhill), 371
Cameras, digital, 55
Cancer runs, 245
Candelabrum, 232
Candles, 132, 231–234, 237, 331, 332
Canopies, 156, 158
Carroll, Michael, 224–225
Cash flow, 66, 67
Cathedral train, 337
Catologue library, 75
CBA (Certified Balloon Artist), 175
C-clamp, 400
Ceilings, reflected, 193
Ceiling beams, structural capacity of, 51
Ceiling treatment(s):
- balloons for, 180–182
- fabric for, 155–160
- for weddings, 353

Celtic knotwork, 317
Centerpiece(s), 122–132
- balloon, 178–180
- construct-it yourself, 123
- food, 129–130
- height, 126
- ice, 235
- lights as, 229
- nonfloral, 123–124
- nontraditional, 129–132
- and space allowance, 128
- table, 122–124
- themed, 128, 130
- traditional, 124–129

Certified Balloon Artist (CBA), 175
Certified Meeting Professional (CMP), 63
Chace Candle Company, 232
Chace candles, 232
Chain motors, 400
Chair covers, 163, 165
Chambelane de honor, 309
Chapel-length train, 337–338
Charge-out rate, 87, 396
Charity sponsorships, 285, 287
Charity tie-ins, stand-alone, 288–291
Chatchke, 224
Checklists, event-specific, 54–55
Cherny, Bob, 193–194
Children, working with, 219–221
Children's Medical Center of Dallas, 371, 372
Chloroprene balloons, 394–395
Christian weddings, 331–333
Chuppah, 145, 329, 333–334
CIC (Convention Industry Council), 63
Classic cars (as prop), 115
Clear Com, 197
Client(s):
- contact with, 68–69
- payment history of, 68
- social status/cultural background of, 16, 25

Clip-on lights, 196, 399
Closed composition, 12–13
Close-proximity displays (pyrotechnics), 237
Clusters, balloon, 178
CMP (Certified Meeting Professional), 63
CMP (Complete Meeting Package), 42–43
Coburn, J. W., 291
Cobweb shooters, 319
Cobweb spinners, 319
Cold air inflatables, 185–187
Cole, Edward, 107
Colleen Rickenbacher, Inc., 364
Color(s), 13–15
- blended, 14
- complementary, 14
- contrasting, 14
- cool, 15, 201
- and emotional impact, 15
- neutral, 201
- primary, 14
- pure, 14
- saturated, 201
- secondary, 14
- warm, 15, 201

Color changers (lighting), 199, 400
Colored fans (lasers), 231
Color principles (lighting), 200–201
Color wheel, 14

Columns, balloon, 176–178
Column candles, 232
Comets (pyrotechnics), 237
Coming-out presentations, 304–309
Commando cloth, 146
Commissions, 89, 95
Communication:
design, 31–35, 37
education conference, 246–249
Communications/sales tools, 31
Community buildings/centers (venue), 43
Community events, 287, 288
Compatible floral design, 122
Complementary colors, 14
Complete Meeting Package (CMP), 42–43
Composition, 12–13
Computer aided/assisted drawing/drafting (CAD), 32, 76
Computer aided design and drafting (CADD), 193
Computer-controlled lighting, 205–206
Computer technology, 75–77
Conceptual drawings, 33
Cone effects (lasers), 231
Conferences, 263–265
Confetti drops, 183
Congresses, 150, 263
Constructed perspective, 369
Contact sheet, 22, 381
Contractors, 69
Contract riders, 117, 136, 197
Contrasting colors, 14
Control console, 194
Conventions, 263
Convention and Visitors Bureaus (CVBs), 286
Convention Industry Council (CIC), xxiii, 63, 246–247
Convention vinyl, 148
Cool colors, 15, 201
Coordination (event management), 17–18
Coordination fees, 94
Corporate celebrations/ceremonies, 269–298
advertising events, 278–280
employee parties, 294–296
external events, 270–275
human relations events, 292–296
internal events, 276–278
and promotional goals, 270–272
public relations events, 285–291
and public relations goals, 273–275
receptions, 281–285
resources on, 297–298
Corporate culture, 25
Costs. *See also* Pricing
direct vs. indirect (venue), 53
job, 90–95
labor, 86–87, 401
Cost plus, 87
Cotes de Coeur, 246
Cotton Bowl Association, 187
Courts (malls), 280
Creative design techniques, 26–29, 37
Creative Productions, Inc., 206
Crossbar, 150–151
Cross section, 127
Cues, 193
Cue caller, 197
Cultural background (of client), 16, 25
Cultural demographics, 272
Cultural heritage themes (weddings), 345
Curtains. *See also* Drapes/draping
drop, 283
Kabuki, 283
teaser, 110
traveler, 146
Custom table treatments, 225–226
Custom wall draping, 153–155
Cut flowers, 140, 141
CVBs (Convention and Visitors Bureaus), 286
Cyc lights, 406
Cycloramas, 146

Dallas Convention and Visitors Bureau, 364
Dallas Museum of Art, 153
Daly, John, 121, 126, 133, 292
Damask, 149
Dance floors (lighted), 231
Dance floors (weddings), 353
Dark time, 195
Debutante presentations, 304–309
Decorating contractors, 65
Decorations/decorating:
for advertising events, 278–280
and backdrops, 107–112
with balloons, 176–180
budget for, 66
defined, 4
and design synergy, 4–9
dimensional, 310
for human relations events, 292–296
for nonprofit/charity events, 252–265
with props, 112–117
for public relations events, 285–291
for wedding buffets, 356
Decorative buffets, 224–225, 356
Decorative element(s), 213–239
beverages as, 226–227
candles as, 231–234
children/animals as, 219–221
custom table treatments as, 225–226
food as, 224–227
ice as, 234
lighting effects as, 227–231
living décor as, 216–221
for main vs. incidental entertainment, 214–216
pyrotechnics as, 235–237
resources on, 238–239
and risk management, 221–223
signage as, 221–223
venue as, 103
Decorators, 22
Demographics:
age, 7
attendee, 54
cultural, 272
event, 5
Dermid, Jo, 143, 162, 328
Design/designing, 3–19
aesthetic principles of, 9–16
with backdrops/props, 102–107
with balloons, 172–176
communication of, 31–35
of conference graphics, 264
for conferences and congresses, 263–264
defined, 16
development of, 29–31
of external marketing events, 270–275
fees for, 94
and goals/objectives of event, 5–9
of internal marketing events, 276–278
lighting, 193–194

Design/designing *(Cont)*
of nonprofit events, 244–252
and practicality, 104
resources on, 37
Design director, 22
Designers, 22, 245
*Designing the World's Best Exhibits* (Martin M. Pegler), 262
Designs Behind the Scenes, Inc., 328
Dessert receptions, 357
Diagonal lines, 10
Diagonal movement, 10
Dichroic lens, 205
Digital cameras, 55
Dillon, Sally, 10
Dimensional decorations, 310
Dimmers, 195, 406
Dimmer board, 407
Direct costs, 53
Direct financial control, 65
Direction lighting, 193–194
Disbelief, suspension of, 369
Disc jockey (DJ), 50
Disconnect, 200, 400–401
Discounts, 88, 95
Disney, Walt, 369
Displays:
gift, 359–360
high-visibility, 256
pyrotechnic, 237
of U.S. flag, 397–398
Display fabrics, 148–149
DJ (disc jockey), 50
Dog and pony shows, 24
Dogpile, 27
Dole, Bob, 307
Donated staff, 70–71
Don Ross Nabb Productions, 224
Doors, access, 6
DOT (U.S. Department of Transportation), 236
Downtime, 86–87
Drainage, 51, 53
Drapes/draping, 150–155. *See also* Curtains
custom, 153
pipe and drape, 150–151
semicustom, 151–152
Drawings, artistic, 31
Drayage, 86
Dream World Backdrops, 105
Drinks Fantastic, 227
Drops, *see* Backdrops
Drop curtains, 283
Dry ice foggers, 319
Duffy, Patsy, 125
Duvetyne, 111, 146

Eckhart, Howard, 131, 299–301, 323
Eddie Deen's Ranch, 44
EDS (Electronic Data Systems), 277
Education events, 246–249
Education resources, 73–75
Egress, 105
Eisenstodt, Joan, 246, 266
Elasta-Shield, 117
Electrical disconnects, 41
Electrical formula, 390
Electrical power needs, 51, 53
Electronic Data Systems (EDS), 277
Elevations, scale, 32, 193
Ellipsoidal spotlights, 400
Employee appreciation events, 292–293
Employee parties, 294–296
Employee picnics, 295
Employee resources, 69
Endcap décor, 262
Engineer's scale rule, 32
Entertainment planning, 89, 215–216
Entrance (weddings), 352–353
Entrepreneurs, 308
Estimate sheets, 92
Estimating, 87, 92–93
Ethics, 95
Evaluations, 18
Event(s). *See also specific topics, e.g.:* Nonprofit/charity events
checklists for, 54–55
flow in, 8–9
focus of, 5–6
goals/objectives of, 5–9
history of, 30
space for, 6–8
Event budget, 66
Event design, 4
Event design project profit/loss statement, 83
Event firms, 88
Event management, 16–19
Event managers, 22
Event professionals, 26, 75
Exhibitions, 262
Exhibition fabric, 147–148
Expectations, 5
Expendables, 86
Experience (as resource), 74
Expositions, 262–263
Extension sockets, 196
Extension swivel sockets, 405
External events, 270–275
Eye candy, 365

Fabrics, 143–169
for ceiling treatments, 155–160
exhibition, 147–148
resources on, 168–169
special event specific criteria, 145–149
table linens, 161–167
texture of, 15, 16
for wall treatments, 150–155
Facing, 118
Faille, 149
Fairs, 363–364, 368–371, 375
Fairmont Hotel (Dallas, Texas), 220
Fairy lights, 228
Familiarization trips, 286
Fashion shows, 251
Faux painting, 369
Faux snow, 314, 315
Faux tapers, 232
Faux texturing, 15
F & B (food and beverage) vendors, 365
Fear No Ice, 234
Fees, 94, 95
Feet (wall treatments), 151
Felt, 149
Festivals, 363–368, 375
Festivals.com, 363
Fiber-optic light effects, 228–229
Fight Night, 287
Fill light, 202
Financial records, 96
Financial resources, 65–68
Finder's fee, 95
Fire marshall, 49–50
Fire-resistant fabrics, 145, 167
Firewatch, 133
First contact, 22
First-time events, 251
*Fiscus benjaminus,* 141
Fitting session, 89
Fitzgerald, F. Scott, 123
Five Ws, 23–26
Flags, displaying, 397–398
Flame projectors, 237

Flame-retardant treatments, 114, 145
Flares, 237
Flash and trash, 316
Flash pots, 237
Flats (prop), 112
Flat fell seams, 107
Floating flowers, 138, 139
Floodlights, 196
Floor, structural capacity of, 51
Floor plans, 127
Floral décor, 121–142
  for buffet, 132–133
  centerpieces, 122–132
  garland, 136–137
  hanging baskets/balls, 138
  potted/blooming plants, 140, 141
  pricing of, 88–89
  resources on, 142
  and risk management, 133
  for stage, 133–136
  themed, 129
Floral designers, 88
Floral foam, 136
Floral treatments, architectural, 137–140
Floral wire, 137
Flow, 8–9
Flowers:
  artificial, 135
  for buffets, 132
  cut, 140, 141
  floating, 138–139
  hanging, 138
  personal, 330
  for specific themes, 129
  on stage, 133–136
  wildflowers, 140
Flower halo, 330
Flowering vine illusion, 137–138
Flower theme (weddings), 342
Floyd, Joy Johnson, 161
Fluff, 136
Flying rigging backdrops, 108
Foam, 114
  floral, 136
  low-density, 116–117
Foamcore, 284
Focus:
  of event, 5–6
  of lighting, 195
  natural, 57
Fog, 319
Foggers, 205, 319
FOH (front of the house), 350
Foil balloons, 173
Follow spots (lighting), 197–198, 400
Fonts, 222
Food, 224–227
Food and beverage (F & B) vendors, 365
Food centerpieces, 226
Food stylists, 132
Formal education, 74
Formal weddings, 337–338
Four Seasons Flower Shop, 122
Four Seasons Resort and Conference Center, 327
Frame tents, 47
Free association, 27
Freeman Decorating, 151
Freestyle ceilings, 159–160
Fresnel, 400
Front of the house (FOH), 350
Front truss, 198
Fullness (of drapes), 151
Full-scale models, 34, 35
Fund-raising events, 84, 244–246

Galas, 252–256
Gale Sliger Balloon Reveal, 184
Gale Sliger Productions, 134, 144, 153, 183, 252, 275
Gambling, 255–256
GAP analysis (event review), 78–79
Garden theme (weddings), 342–344
Garlands, 136–137
Garret Creek Ranch and Conference Center, 286, 317
Gather (of drapes), 151
Gel, 195–196, 407
General contractors, 262
General convention contractors, 262
General lighting, 199
General session stage, 283, 284
Generators, 401
*Giant* (film), 275
Gimme caps, 368
Gisler, David, 151
Glitter, iridescent, 314
Glitter garlands, 126
Goals:
  and event objectives, 5–9, 26
  of nonprofit/charity events, 244–252
  nuptial, 328–330
Gobos, 197, 407
Goldblatt, Joe, 16, 271
Google, 27
Goosenecks, 196, 405
Greening, 138
Greening pins, 138
Grommets, 283
Grosh Scenic Rentals, 105
Gross profit, 82
Ground foggers, 319
Ground plan, 127
Ground row (backdrops), 110
Ground-supported stretch fabric, 144
Ground support rigging backdrops, 108
Guests, 8
Guideline for Effective Event Production, 16
Guy tents, 46

Halbreich, Nancy, 144
Hallways, 6
Hanging baskets/balls, 138
Hardman, John, 271
Harley motocycles, 48
Harper, Billy, 106
Haze, 205
Hazers, 205
Head table, 258
Hearn, Leslie, 243–245
Heart walks, 245
Helium charts:
  latex and chloroprene balloons, 394–395
  microfoil balloons, 391–394
Helium-filled balloons, 176
Helium inflatables, 185–187
Henderson, Skitch, 117
Hindu weddings, 335
Historical themes (weddings), 339–340
HIT Entertainment, 372
Holiday parties, 313–321
Holiday themes (weddings), 344–345
Horizontal lines, 10
Hors d'oeuvres receptions, 357
Host, William G., 21, 89
Host Independent Billing Formula, 90
Host Meetings and Event Management, 89

Human relations events, 270, 292–296
Human resources, 68–73
  clients, 68–69
  and employee/contractor relationship, 69
  management of, 69–73
  staff, 69
  strategic partners, 71–72
  suppliers/associates, 71
  volunteers, 69–70
Hummers (pyrotechnics), 237

IAFE (International Association of Fairs and Expositions), 363
Ice, 234
Ice carvings, 234–235
Ice centerpieces, 235
ICW, 40
I&D (installation and dismantle), 46
IFEA, *see* International Festivals and Events Association
Illusions, 110
I-mag, 248, 258
Imitation (as creative technique), 28
Imprinted fabrics, 149
Incentive parties, 295
Incidental entertainment, 89, 214
Incidental theme events, 315
Income/expense projections, 67
In conjunction with (ICW), 40
Independent event designer (pricing), 89–90
Indianapolis festival, 367
Indirect costs, 53
Indirect financial control, 66
Industry knowledge, 74
Inflatables, 185–187, 368. *See also* Balloon(s)
Inflatable slides, 187
Informal weddings, 337, 339
Informational signs, 222
In-kind donations, 70
Inspections, 55–59
Inspiration, 31
Installation and dismantle (I&D), 46
Instrument (light fixture), 201, 407
Intelligent lighting, 185, 197, 205–206, 401
Interaction, encouraging, 7
Interior Design Start website, 302
Internal events, 270, 276–278
International Association of Fairs and Expositions (IAFE), 363
International Festivals and Events Association (IFEA), 363, 364
International Special Events Society (ISES), xxiii, 194, 248, 269, 270, 364
Internet, 25, 30, 104
Interviews, 23–26
Iridescent glitter, 314
ISES, *see* International Special Events Society
Islamic weddings, 335–336
Ito, Jane, 166

Jackson Five, 117
Jaeger, Chris, 328
Jakob, John, 277–278, 294
James C. Monroe & Associates (JCM), 73, 144
Jewish weddings, 332–333
Job cost(s), 90–95
  commissions as, 95
  control of, 90
  design/management fee as, 94
  discounts as, 95
  estimating, 92–93
  and ethics, 95
  and proposal, 90–92
  and purchasing, 93–94
Johnson, Lady Bird, 140
Jumbotron screen, 54, 277
Jumpers, 407
Just, William H., 63
Justice, Robert, 117

Kaboom Town!, 373
Kabuki curtain, 283
Kates, Robert A. (Bobby), xxiv
Kemble, Steve, 269–272, 277, 282, 292, 296
Key light, 202
Key stakeholders, 68
Kickbacks, 95
King, Robin, 206
Knowledge resources, 73–75
Kosher catering, 42–43
KVIL (radio station), 373

Labor costs, 86–87, 396
Lamé, 149
Lamps (lightbulbs), 195
Lanin, Lester, 322
Lasers, 231
Lashley, Edwin III, 225
Latex balloons, 171, 173–174, 394–395
Lecterns, 249
LED (light-emitting diode), 208
Legs (vertical drapes), 110, 146
Lego®, 123
Lego Duplo®, 125
Lekos, 197, 400
Leno cloth, 146
Lenses, 206
Lianne Pereira's Multiple Agenda Outline, 244
Liberal arts, 74
Libraries, 74–75
Life-cycle events, 292, 299, 302–312
Light control board, 407
Light cues, 193
Light-emitting diode (LED), 208
Lighting board, 401
Lighting design, 193
Lighting designers, 193
Lighting directors, 193
Light/lighting, 191–211
  accent, 196
  ambient, 204
  and angle of incidence, 201–204
  backlighting, 195, 202
  black, 230
  and changing technology, 208–209
  clip-on, 196, 399
  and color principles, 200–201
  computer-controlled, 205–206
  creating effects with, 227–231
  cyc, 400
  direction, 193–194
  equipment, 206–207, 399–401
  fairy, 228
  fill, 202
  floodlights, 196
  general, 199
  intelligent, 185, 197, 205–206, 401
  key, 202
  for large events, 199
  levels of, 204–205
  miniature, 227–228
  moving, 401
  neon, 230
  oblique, 15

1K/24K/60K, 400
reflected, 201
resources on, 210–211
and risk management, 208
robotic, 205, 401
rope, 229
for small events, 195–197
stage productions, 197–199
tea, 132
for tented events, 200
terminology for, 400–401
theatrical, 400
for wedding buffets, 357
Light plot, 193
Lines, 10–12, 58
List making (as creative technique), 27
Liturgy, 332
Live auctions, 255, 259–260
Living buffets, 216–217
Living décor, 216–221
Living statues, 216–218
LookSmart, 27
Los Angeles Convention Center, 39
Louver style, 158–159
Low-level displays (pyrotechnics), 237
Luminaire, 228
Luncheons (nonprofit events), 257–259

McCandless system, 201
McGarr, Janie, 144
Maché, 131
Mahler, Henri, 226
Main entertainment, 214
Managing partners, 72–73
Manufacturer's suggested retail price (MSRP), 86
Marfa, Texas, high school marching band, 275
Markets, wholesale, 270, 272
Marketing events (corporate celebrations/ceremonies), 270–275
Marketing Group, 166
Marketing/public relations (nonprofit/charity events), 249–252
Markup, 85
*M.A.S.H.* (TV series), 310
Masks, 110
Masking (by drapes), 110
Materials costs, 86
Material requirements, 5
Media (design development), 29
Meeting Professionals International (MPI), 194
Mendhi, 335
Mental Health Association (MHA), 65
Merchandising, visual, 279
Metallic Design Studio, 225
Meyers, Debbie, 213, 216–218
MHA (Mental Health Association), 65
Microfoil balloons, 391–395
Milestone events, 299–312
bar/bat mitzvahs, 303–305
birthdays, 309–311
debutante/coming-out presentations, 304–309
life-cycle, 302–312
party design for, 300–302
resources on, 324–325
wedding anniversaries, 311–312
Miller, Mike, 227
Miller, Sharon, 227
Mines (pyrotechnics), 237
Miniature lights, 227–228
Moiré, 149
Monochromatic floral design, 122
Monroe, Jayna, xxiv, 192, 246
Monroe, John, 122
Monroe's dance floor rule of thumb, 296
Monroe's four pillar approach, 64
Monroe's guide to flame-retardant/flame resistant fabrics, 145
Monroe's law of venue and design, 57
Monroe's risk management for table linens, 167
Monroe's risk management note, 109
Monroe's rule for off-site events, 49
Monroe's rule of flower ordering, 130
Monroe's rules for lighting events, 196–199
*Monsoon Wedding* (film), 335
Morgue (files), 75
Mortars (pyrotechnics), 237
Movement, diagonal, 10
Moving lights, 401
MPI (Meeting Professionals International), 194
MR-16 lamps, 196, 405
MSRP (manufacturers's suggested retail price), 86
Multidisciplinary craft (decoration), 4
Music, background, 214, 311
Muslin, 146

Napkins, 162–163
Narthex (church vestibule), 332
National Fire Protection Association (NFPA) codes, 50, 114–115, 185
National Wildflower Foundation, 140
Natural lines, 58
Needs assessment, 16
Neiman Marcus, 285, 372
Neiman Marcus Adolphus Children's Parade, 371–372
Neoclassical swags, 151
Neon light, 230
Net drops, 146
Net profit, 82–84
Neutral colors, 201
NFPA codes, *see* National Fire Protection Association codes
Nonevent professionals, 106
Nonprofit (term), 243
Nonprofit/charity events, 243–267
auctions as, 259–260
awards presentations at, 260–262
conferences/conventions/congresses as, 263–265
decorating for, 252–265
and education/content communication, 246–249
fund-raising events, 244–246
galas as, 252–256
goals of, 244–252
luncheons as, 257–259
and marketing/public relations, 249–252
profit events vs., 84–85
receptions as, 256–257
resources on, 267
trade shows/exhibitions/expositions as, 262–263
Nonstandard event venues, 41, 42–46

Nontheatrical lighting equipment, 405–406
Nontraditional theme weddings, 345–346
NorthPark Shopping Center, 271
Nuptial goals and objectives, 328–330
*Nutcracker* ballet, 15

Oasis, 136
Oblique lighting, 15
Occupation Safety and Health Administration (OSHA), 78
O'Connor, Brian, 193, 208
Off-site venues, 41, 48–49
Oldenburg, Claes, 58
Oliphant Studios, 105
1–kilowatt PAR cans, 198
1K lighting, 406
On-site events, 40
Onstage Systems, 191–192
Open composition, 12–13
Operating expenses, 82
Operations events, 270, 276–278
Orthographic projection, 32, 114
Osborn, Alex, 26
OSHA (Occupation Safety and Health Administration), 78
Osmond, Donnie, 275
Overhead, 82–83
Over The Top Design, 73
Ownership, 69

Painted backdrops, 104
Painting:
  faux, 369
  of props, 114
Pantone Matching System (PMS), 59, 278
PAR 38 CAN, 405
PAR-38 lamp, 405
Parabolic curve, 177
Parades, 371–372, 375
Paraffin candles, 233
Parallels, 118
PAR cans, 197, 405, 406
Parking, 51–53
PAR lamps, 196
Party and Event Designers, 131
The Party and Event Designers, 300
Patches/patching, 401
Patios (weddings), 354
PDA (personal digital assistant), 55
Pegged candleholders, 131–132
Pegged votive, 232
Pegler, Martin M., 262
Pei, I. M., 58
Per diem, 73
Pereira, Lianne, 244, 265
Perimeter (weddings), 353–354
Perot, H. Ross, Jr., 291
Personal digital assistant (PDA), 55
Personal flowers, 330
Personal social events, 299, 312–323
Perspective, 107, 369
Petit, George, xxiv
Pew markers, 332
The Phoenix Decorating Company, 372
Photos of props (design communication), 33
Physical impairments, 7
Physical requirements (venue), 49–53
Physical resources, 77–79
Physicians Education Resource, 364
Picks, 126
Picnics, employee, 295
Pillar candles, 232
Pin spots, 406
Pin-spotting (lighting), 205
Pinwheels (pyrotechnics), 237
Pipe and drape, 150–151
Planning (event management), 17
Plan view, 127
Plasma generators, 231
Plates, 193
P&L statement, 82–83
Plywood, 114
PMS, *see* Pantone Matching System
POs, *see* Purchase orders
Podium, 249
Pole tents, 46
Polyester, 161
Poly velour/velvet (polyvel), 148
Postevent inspection, 55
Post-selection site inspection, 55, 57–59
Potted plants, 140, 141
Power requirements, 51, 53, 401
Practices, design/decoration, 21–37
  creative techniques, 26–29
  design communication, 31–35
  design development, 29–31
  research methods, 22–26
  resources on, 37
Preselection site inspection, 55–56
Presentations:
  of awards, 260–262
  of flowers, 134
Presenters, 249
PR events, *see* Public relations events
Pricing, 85–90
  of entertainment, 89
  of independent event designer, 89–90
  of labor, 86–87
  markup, 85
  of materials, 86
  and profit, 85
  as proprietary information, 85
  of props, 106
  of subcontractors, 87–89
Primary colors, 14
"Princess Bride" theme (weddings), 342
Print fabrics, 149
Private special events (PSEs), 299
Pro bono jobs, 94–95
Production (production equipment), 401
Production budget, 66
Production companies, 193
Production equipment, 400, 401
Production manager, 193
Production schedule, 67–68
Production values, 247
Product rollouts, 54, 273, 282–285
Professional balloon artists, 175–176
Profile piece, 112
Profit, 82–85
  gross, 82
  markup vs., 85
  net, 82–84
  overhead, 82–83
  and pricing, 85
  and ROE, 84
  and ROI, 84
Profit and loss (P&L) statement, 82–83
Profit events, nonprofit vs., 84–85
Profit percentage table, 85
Programs, 193
Projection throw, 51
Project partners, 72–73
Promotional goals, 270–272

Props, 101–102, 106, 112–117
built, 114–116
concealing, 112
constructing/painting, 114, 115
contracting for, 104–106
decorating with, 112–117
designing with, 102–107
nonstandard sources for, 105–106
pricing of, 106
resources on, 119–120
and risk management, 104, 105
scenic, 102
sculpting, 116, 117
storage/transportation of, 112
three-dimensional, 113–115
two-dimensional, 112–113
types of, 114–117
Proposal(s):
elements of, 90
example of, 384–387
and job costs, 90–92
for small events, 91
Prototypes, 130–131, 138
PSAs (public service announcements), 274
PSEs (private special events), 299
Public relations (PR) events, 270, 271
decorating for, 285–291
design and goals of, 273–275
nonprofit/charity events, 249
Public service announcements (PSAs), 274
Purchase orders (POs), 88, 93–94
Purchasing, 86, 93–94
Pure colors, 14
Putti, 345
Pynes, Gregory, 364–367, 373–374
Pyrotechnicians, 235
Pyrotechnics, 235–237
Pyrotex, Inc, 235

QBN (Qualatex Balloon Network), 175
Quaker weddings, 336
Qualatex Balloon Network (QBN), 175
Quincineras, 305

R-40 lamp, 400
Rainlights, 400
Ranker, Karen, 371–372
Ratio markup, 88–89
Ray, Cynthia, 153
Real texturing, 15
Rear truss, 198
Receptions:
buffet, 355–357
corporate, 281–285
and nonprofit/charity events, 256–257
wedding, 346–359
Reed, Bill, xxiv, 220, 271, 274
Reference libraries, 74–75
Reflected ceiling, 193
Reflected light, 201
Reflectors, 206
Rehearsal dinners, 360
Religious institutions, 43
Request for Proposal (RFP), 22, 88, 378–380
Research, 16, 22–26
as creative technique, 28
site, 54–55
Residential sites, 44
Resources, 63–79
financial, 65–68
human, 68–73
knowledge/education, 73–75
technical/physical, 75–79
Retail events, 84–85, 270
Return on event (ROE), 84, 246
Return on investment (ROI), 84, 245
Reunions, sports celebrations, 321–323
Reveal, 282–284
RFP, *see* Request for Proposal
Rickenbacher, Colleen, 48, 364–365, 369
Rickles, Don, 217
Riders, contract, 117, 136, 197
Rigging (of backdrops), 108–109
Rigging points, 138
Ripken, Cal, Jr., 226
Risk management:
with backdrops, 104, 105, 109
with balloons, 174–175
with floral décor, 133
with lighting, 208
with props, 104, 105
with signs, 221–222
Roasts, 310–311
Robotic lighting, 205, 401
ROE (return on event), 84, 246
ROI (return on investment), 84, 245
Romantic themes (weddings), 340–342
Rope lights, 229
R-type lamps, 196
Runes, 317
Rural venues, 45–46
Russell Glenn Studios, 137
Ryan, Nolan, 252

Salutes (pyrotechnics), 236
Sample board (design communication), 34
Sandbagging, 108–109
Saturated colors, 201
*Saturday Night Fever* (film), 231
Scale drawings, 31, 32
Scale rules, 32
Scarborough Faire, 368–369
Scatter snow, 314
*Scenery for the Theatre* (Harold Burris-Meyer and Edward Cole), 107
Scenic artists, 107
Scenic backdrops, 102
Scenic props, 102
ScenicSource, LLC, 146
Schwabb, Garrett, 48
Scream!, 368–369
Scrim, sharkstooth, 111–112, 146
Sculpting props, 116, 117
Search engines, 30
Seasonal events, 270
Seasonal greenery, 136
Seasonal themes, 344–345
Seated dinners, 347–355
Secondary colors, 14
Second weddings, 329–330
Sectional views, 127, 193
Secular weddings, 334
Security, 51, 53
Sell More Weddings, 328
Selvedge, 149
Semiformal weddings, 337, 338
Sevier, Coy, 368–371
Sharkstooth scrim, 111–112, 146
Sheer fabrics, 149
Sheet effects (lasers), 231
Sheldon, Arthur F., 81
Shells (pyrotechnics), 236
Shock, Patti, xxiii–xxiv
Shoulder season (off-season discount), 24
Showers (weddings), 359
Shul, 302

Sidelight, 203
Sight acts, 89, 214
Sightlines, 51
Signage, 221–223
Silent auctions, 255, 259–260, 264
Silvers, Julia Rutherford, 101–102, 105, 213
Single-phase AC, 406–407
Site inspection checklist, 49
Site inspections, 49, 55–59
  checklist for, 391–392
  and physical elements, 51
Site research, 54–55
Site selection, 49–53
60K lighting, 406
Skirting, 118
Skiskimas, Jim, 171–173, 184
Skiskimas, Pat, 172
Skolberg, Neils, 146
Sky drops, 147
Slides, inflatable, 187
Sliger, Gale, xxiv, 7, 156, 184, 226, 291, 310, 347, 351
Smith, Tracey, 293
Snake, 350
Snow, faux, 314, 315
Snow Business, 315
Snowmasters, 315
Social directory, 25
Social events, 299–301, 312–323
  holiday parties, 313–321
  party design for, 300–302
  personal, 312–323
  resources on, 324–325
  as reunions, sports celebrations, 321–323
Social fraternities, 305
Social parties, 321–323
Social status (of client), 16, 25
Solenoids, 283
Sound checks, 195
Sound system, 247, 258
Source4 lighting, 406
Southwest Festivals, Inc., 368
Soy wax candles, 233
Space, 6–8, 57
  centerpiece, 128
  as critical element, 79
  as resource, 77
  and storage/transportation, 112
  and tables, 50
Spanish moss, 138
Sparkle fountains (pyrotechnics), 235
Speaker stacks, 134, 136
Specials (lighting), 198
Special event fabrics, 145–149
*Special Events: Event Leadership for a New World* (Joe Goldblatt), 16, 271
*Special Events* magazine, 364
Special use permits (venue), 53
Spectacles, 373–375
The Spirit of Texas, 291
Sponsorship events, 250
Sports celebrations, 321–323
Spots (lighting), 196
Spotlights, ellipsoidal, 406
Squibs, 183
Staff/staffing, 69–71
Stage(s):
  height of, 254
  wedding, 348–350
Stage florals, 133–136
Stage manager, 197
Stage productions (lighting), 197–199
Stage right, 307
Staging, 102, 117–118
Stakeholders, 16, 24, 26, 56, 68
Stanchions, 108–109
Stands, 150
Stand-alone charity tie-ins, 288–291
Stand-alone venues, 40, 44
Standard event venues, 41–42
Steffes, Katy, 327, 328, 339, 347, 348, 351, 356
Storyboards, 34
Strategic partnerships, 71–72
Strategic professional partner relationships, 71
Stretch areas, 280
Stretch fabrics, 149
Striking, 110
String of pearls (balloons), 180
Structural capacity, 51
Structural events, 276
Style points, 367
Styrothane, 117
Subcontractors, 87–89
Subcontracts, 88
Supergraphics, 282
Suppliers, 71
Susan G. Komen Breast Cancer Foundation, 244, 265
Suspension of disbelief, 369
Swags:
  balloon, 176
  bunting, 317
  neoclassical, 151
Swag ceilings (balloons), 181
Swatches, 34
Sweet sixteen parties, 305
SWOT analysis, 78–79
Symmetry, 12
Synergy, 4, 18

Table(s):
  centerpieces (floral décor), 122–132
  head, 258
  layout of, 127
  spacing of, 50
Table cards, 304, 346
Tablecloths, 161–162
Tablehosts, 127
Table linens, 161–167
Table skirting, 165, 167
Table treatments (weddings), 350–351
Tallit, 333
Tapers (candles), 131, 232
Taste Addison, 367
Tea lights, 132
Team building, 276, 293–294
Teasers, 110, 146
Technology:
  and lighting, 208–209
  resources on, 75–77
Temerlin, Liener, 281
Temerlin McClain, 281
Tension, 10–11, 47
Tents, 46–48, 200, 357–359
Tent liner, 160
Terpsichorean Club, 308
Texture, 15–16
Thank-you parties, 250
Thatcher, Margaret, 226
Theatrical lighting equipment, 406
Themes:
  as design approach, 264
  and design development, 30–31
  flowers for, 129
  for traditional wedding, 339
Themed centerpieces, 128, 130
*Themes, Dreams, and Schemes* (Eugene Wigger), 31, 224
Thomson RIA, 293
Three-color wash (lighting), 198
Three-dimensional props, 113–115
Three-phase, 100-amp disconnect, 407

Three-phase AC, 406–407
Three-point system (lighting), 202–203
Throw (lighting), 206, 407
Tie lines, 283
Tiffany, 285
Time resources, 78, 79
Ting ting, 126
Tinker Toy, 123
Toile, 149
*Tonight Show,* 117
Tools/equipment resources, 78, 79
Top rod, 150–151
Torah, 331
Tormentors (vertical drapes), 110, 146
Toxic fumes, 117
Tradeshows, 85, 262, 270, 272
Traditional floral design, 122
Traditional theme weddings, 339–345
Transportation (venues), 51–53
Traveler curtains, 146
Tricolor bunting yardage, 317
Trompe l'oeil, 107
Trusses, 198, 407
Tunnels (lasers), 231
Tuxedo fold, 163–164
24K lighting, 406
Two-dimensional props, 112–113
Tyler Rose Festival, 77
Typestyle, 222

Ultraformal weddings, 337
Ultra Hi-Float, 176
Underhill, Paco, 371
Underwriter reception, 250
Underwritten fund-raisers, 85
Union contracts, 53
Unique venues, 40–41, 45
U.S. Department of Alcohol, Tobbaco, and Firearms (ATF), 236
U.S. Department of Transportation (DOT), 236
U.S. flag, displaying, 397–398
Unity candle, 331, 332
Uplight, 196
Uprights, 151
Urban spaces, 45

Valances, 146, 152, 156, 160
Variation (as creative technique), 28–29
Vari-Lite Company, 205
Velour, 111, 146
Vendors, 71
Venue(s), 39–61
  and aesthetic requirements, 54
  and budgetary requirements, 53
  and decorative element size, 103
  and negative impact, 50
  for nonstandard events, 42–46
  off-site, 48–49
  and physical requirements, 49–53
  post-selection site inspection of, 57–59
  preselection site inspection of, 55–56
  resources on, 60–61
  selection of, 49–53
  site inspections of, 55–59
  site research on, 54–55
  for standard events, 41–42
  and tents, 46–48
  types of, 40–49
Vertical lines, 10, 58
Vertical section, 127
Visual merchandising, 279
Visual pictures, 11–12
Volunteers, 69–70
Votive candles, 132, 232

Wallpaper music, 214, 311
Wall treatments:
  balloons for, 182–183
  and fabric décor, 150–155
Warhol, Andy, 10
Warm colors, 15, 201
Warp, 149
Water (venues), 51–53
Water picks, 136
Watts/wattage, 401
Waxahatchie, Texas, 368–369
Weddings, 327–362
  bachelor/bachelorette parties, 360–361
  Buddhist, 336
  buffet receptions, 355–357
  ceremony, 330–336
  checklist for, 402–406
  Christian, 331–333
  formal, 337–338
  gift displays/teas, 359–360
  Hindu, 335
  hors d'oeuvres/dessert receptions, 357
  informal, 339
  Islam, 335–336
  Jewish, 332–334
  nontraditional themes, 345–346
  nuptial goals and objectives, 328–330
  Quaker, 336
  receptions, 346–359
  rehearsal dinners, 360
  resources on, 362
  seated dinners, 347–355
  secular, 334
  semiformal, 338
  showers, 359
  style of, 337–339
  tented receptions, 357–359
  themes, 339–346
  traditional themes, 339–345
  ultraformal, 337
Wedding anniversaries, 311–312
Wedding cakes, 351–352
Weft/woof, 149
Whistles (pyrotechnics), 237
Wholesale markets, 270, 272
*Why We Buy* (Paco Underhill), 371
Wiersma, Betsy, 363–364, 366–368
WIFM, 70, 94
Wigger, Eugene, 31, 224
Wildflowers, 140
Williams, Deborah K., 328, 329
Win-win situation, 71
World Wide Web, 27, 105
Wrap-up parties, 250
Written descriptions, 31
Wyeth, Andrew, 10
Wyndham Anatole Hotel, 134, 226
WYSIWYG, 209

Yahoo!, 27
Yoke, 407

Zahn, Paula, 226